COMPLETE

BUDGETING

DESKBOOK

JAE K. SHIM

JOEL G. SIEGEL

PRENTICE HALL
Paramus, New Jersey 07652

Printed in the United States of America

10 9 8 7 6 5 4 3 2

This publication is designed to provide accurate and authoritative information in regard to the subject matter covered. It is sold with the understanding that the publisher is not engaged in rendering legal, accounting, or other professional service. If legal advice or other expert assistance is required, the services of a competent professional person should be sought.
—*From the Declaration of Principles jointly adopted by a Committee of the American Bar Association and a Committee of Publishers and Associations*

ISBN 0-13-081436-9

PRENTICE HALL
Paramus, NJ 07652

A Simon & Schuster Company

On the World Wide Web at http://www.phdirect.com

Prentice-Hall International (UK) Limited, *London*
Prentice-Hall of Australia Pty. Limited, *Sydney*
Prentice-Hall Canada Inc., *Toronto*
Prentice-Hall Hispanoamericana, S.A., *Mexico*
Prentice-Hall of India Private Limited, *New Delhi*
Prentice-Hall of Japan, Inc., *Tokyo*
Simon & Schuster Asia Pte. Ltd., *Singapore*
Editora Prentice-Hall do Brasil, Ltda., *Rio de Janeiro*

To

CHUNG SHIM
Dedicated wife

and

ROBERTA M. SIEGEL
Loving wife and colleague

MICHAEL GOLDSTEIN
The most knowledgeable Chief Financial Officer

Contents

About the Authors

JAE K. SHIM is President of the National Business Review Foundation, a financial consultant to several companies, and Professor of Accounting and Finance at California State University, Long Beach. He received his Ph.D. degree from the University of California at Berkeley.

Dr. Shim has 38 books to his credit and has published over 50 articles in accounting and financial journals including *Financial Management, Decision Sciences, Management Science, Long Range Planning, Management Accounting,* and *Advances in Accounting.* Many of his articles have dealt with planning, forecasting, and financial modeling.

Dr. Shim is a recipient of the 1982 Credit Research Foundation Award for his article on financial management.

JOEL G. SIEGEL, Ph.D., CPA, is a self-employed certified public accountant and Professor of Accounting and Finance at Queens College of the City University of New York.

He was previously employed by Coopers and Lybrand, CPAs, and Arthur Andersen, CPAs. Dr. Siegel currently serves and has acted as a consultant in accounting and finance to many organizations, including Citicorp, International Telephone and Telegraph, United Technologies, American Institute of CPAs, and Person-Wolinsky Associates.

Dr. Siegel is the author of 40 books and about 200 articles on accounting and financial topics, including many articles in the area of budgeting. His books have been published by Prentice-Hall, McGraw-Hill, HarperCollins, John Wiley, Macmillan, International Publishing, Barron's, and the American

Institute of CPAs. His articles have been published in many accounting and financial journals, including *Financial Executive, Financial Analysts Journal, The CPA Journal, Practical Accountant,* and the *National Public Accountant.*

In 1972, he was the recipient of the Outstanding Educator of America Award. Dr. Siegel is listed in *Who's Who Among Writers* and *Who's Who in the World.* Dr. Siegel is currently the chairperson of the National Oversight Board.

Acknowledgments

We thank Drew Dreeland for his expert editorial advice and assistance on this book. His efforts are much recognized and appreciated. Thanks also goes to Rodney Eubanks and Rose Kernan for a job well done in developmental editing.

Abraham J. Simon, Ph.D., CPA is acknowledged with appreciation for co-authoring Chapter 2. Thanks goes to Robert Fonfeder, Ph.D., CPA for the co-authoring of Chapter 17. Marc Levine, Ph.D., CPA deserves recognition for co-authoring Chapter 27. Finally, Catherine Carroll, a research assistant at Queens College, deserves credit for her excellent work and intelligence.

What This Book Will Do for You

This book explains what budgets are, how they work, how to prepare and present them, and how to analyze budget figures and results. The practical development and use of budgets at various managerial levels within a business are discussed. The book is intended for business professionals engaged in budgeting, financial planning, profit planning, and control.

A budget is defined as the formal expression of plans, goals, and objectives of management that covers all aspects of operations for a designated time period. The budget is a tool providing targets and direction. Budgets provide control over the immediate environment, help to master the financial aspects of the job and department, and solve problems *before* they occur. Budgets focus on the importance of evaluating alternative actions before decisions are actually implemented.

There is a definite relationship between long-range planning and short-term business plans. The ability to meet near-term budget goals will move the business in the direction of accomplishing long-term objectives. Budgets aid decision making, measurement, and coordination of the efforts of the various groups within the entity. The interaction of each business segment to the whole organization is highlighted. For example, budgets are prepared for units within a department, such as product lines, the department itself, the division which consists of a number of departments, and the company.

This book is written for managers and budgeting persons who are seeking practical approaches and suggestions in handling daily budgeting problems. It is directed toward any business person having any connection with the budgeting process including providing input, preparation of the budget, and analyzing budget results. Budgets are of interest to budget and financial planners, accountants, financial managers and analysts, general business managers, marketing managers, production managers, purchasing managers, personnel managers, industrial engineers, operations research staff, attorneys, economists, and other relevant individuals. The purpose of the book is to enhance the understanding of budgets so as to optimally perform job responsibilities. In particular, managers in *nonfinancial areas* will greatly benefit.

Budgets in both the manufacturing and service environments are discussed. Further, budgeting procedures apply to profit as well as to nonprofit entities. Budgets are used in all size organizations whether they be small, medium, or large.

The book is comprehensive, authoritative, and practical. It is a working guide in budgeting that will pinpoint what to look for, what to watch for, what to do, how to do it, and how to apply it on the job. Emerging trends in budgeting are highlighted so the most up-to-date information is provided.

Attention is given to common budgeting problems and constructive suggestions are offered based on actual experiences. Each unit figure, dollar amount, and percentage change may bring to light an opportunity or challenge. The budgeting process enhances the allocation of personnel, facilities, and other resources in a logical and systematic way. All affected parties should participate in budget preparation.

Profit planning is essential to undertake those activities that will maximize earnings. Budgeting control is effective when it results in maintaining cost per dollar of sales at a minimum and the gross profit of the production mixture at a maximum.

The book includes the traditional tools for planning and control, such as cost-volume-profit (CVP) and contribution analysis, variance analysis, and flexible budgeting. At the same time, there is coverage of computer-based budgeting tools, namely, financial modeling, "what-if" analysis, "goal-seeking" analysis, and practical forecasting techniques.

Throughout the book, we illustrate the use of popular financial planning software such as Interactive Financial Planning System (IFPS) and Simplan. We show how to use for budgeting and "what-if" analysis spreadsheet programs, such as Lotus 1-2-3, Excel, and Quattro Pro, and popular Lotus-based templates such as Business Plan Toolkit and Profit Planner.

Computerized models make it possible to test various options as a basis of the manager's final plan of action. This has the end result of profit improvement and better management performance. Financial models show the relationship between various aspects of the business such as revenues, costs, return on investment, and variability in cost elements with changes in volume.

Budgeting success may be improved by appraising historical budgets as well as by identifying the reasons for variances between budget and actual figures.

The content of the book is clear, concise, and to the point. It is a valuable reference containing "how-to" practice tips in budgeting. The uses of this book are as varied as the topics presented. Keep it handy for easy, quick reference and daily use.

Illustrations and step-by-step instructions are provided. "Real life" examples of budgets are provided and references are made to actual companies and situations. Checklists, summarizing the major areas discussed, are also provided. The book is filled with explanation, commentary, sample budgets and documents, reports, forms, flowcharts, analysis, figures, and practices. Statistical data, charts, exhibits, and diagrams are provided, as needed. You will find formulas and rules of thumb and other "tips" to help in budget preparation and use.

Part 1

INTRODUCTION

Chapter 1

Introduction to Budgeting

Budgeting is done for the company as a whole, as well as for its component segments including divisions, departments, products, projects, services, manpower, and geographic areas. Master (comprehensive) budgeting is a complete expression of the planning operations of the company for a specific period. It is involved with both manufacturing and nonmanufacturing activities. Budgets should set priorities within the organization. It may be in the form of a plan, project, or strategy. Budgets consider external factors such as market trends, economic conditions, etc. The budget should list assumptions, targeted objectives, and agenda before number crunching begins.

A budget is a financial plan to control *future* operations and results. It is expressed in numbers such as dollars, units, pounds, hours, manpower, and so on. It is needed to effectively and efficiently operate. Budgeting, when used effectively, is a technique resulting in systematic, productive management. Budgeting allocates funds to achieve desired outcomes. A budget may span any period of time. It may be short-term (one year or less which is usually the case), intermediate-term (two to three years), or long-term (three years or more). Short-term budgets provide greater detail and specifics. Intermediate budgets examine the projects the company is currently undertaking and start the programs necessary to achieve long-term objectives. Long-term plans are very broad and may be translated into short-term plans. The budget period varies according to its objectives, use, and the dependability of the data used to prepare it. The budget period is contingent upon business risk, sales and operating stability, production methods, and length of the processing cycle.

The first step is to determine the overall or strategic goals and strategies of the business which are then translated into specific long-term goals, annual budgets, and operating plans. Corporate goals include earnings growth, cost minimization, sales, production volume, return on investment and product or service quality. The budget requires the analysis and study of historical information, current trends, and industry norms. Budgets may be prepared of expected revenue, costs, profits, cash flow, production purchases, net worth, and so on. Budgets should be prepared for all major areas of the business.

The techniques and details of preparing, reviewing, and approving budgets varies among companies. The process should be tailored to each entity's individual needs. Five important areas in budgeting are planning, coordinating, directing, analyzing, and controlling. The longer the budgeting period, the less reliable are the estimates.

The purpose of budgets is to furnish the link between nonfinancial plans and controls which constitute daily managerial operations and the corresponding plans and controls designed to accomplish satisfactory earnings and financial position.

Effective budgeting requires the existence of the following:

- Predictive ability
- Clear channels of communication, authority, and responsibility
- Accounting-generated accurate, reliable, and timely information
- Compatability and understandability of information
- Support at all levels of the organization from upper, middle, and lower.

The budget should be reviewed by a group so that there is a broad knowledge base. Budget figures should be honest to assure trust between the parties. At the corporate level, the budget examines sales and production to estimate corporate earnings and cash flow. At the department level, the budget examines the effect of work output on costs. A departmental budget shows resources available, when and how they will be used, and expected accomplishments.

Budgets are useful tools in allocating resources (e.g., machinery, employees), making staff changes, scheduling production, and operating the business. Budgets help keep expenditures within defined limits. Consideration should be given to alternative methods of operations.

Budgets are by departments and responsibility centers. They should reflect the goals and objectives of each department through all levels of the organization. Budgeting aids all departmental areas including management, marketing, personnel, engineering, production, distribution, and facilities.

In budgeting, consideration should be given to the company's manpower and production scheduling, labor relations, pricing, resources, new product introduction and development, raw material cycles, technological trends, inventory levels, turnover rate, product or service obsolescence, reliability of input data, stability of market or industry, seasonality, financing needs, and marketing and advertising. Consideration should also be given to the economy, politics, competition, changing consumer base and taste, and market share.

Budgets should be understandable and attainable. Flexibility and innovation is needed to allow for unexpected contingencies. Flexibility is aided by variable budgets, supplemental budgets, authorized variances, and review and revision. Budgets should be computerized to aid "what-if" analysis. Budgeting enhances flexibility through the planning process because alternative courses of action are considered in advance rather than forcing less-informed decisions to be made on the spot. As one factor changes, other factors within the budget will also change. Internal factors are controllable by the company whereas external factors are usually uncontrollable. Internal factors include risk and product innovation.

Forecasting is *predicting* the outcome of events. It is an essential starting point for budgeting. Budgeting is *planning* for a result and controlling to accomplish that result.

Budgeting is a tool and its success depends upon the effectiveness to which it is used by staff. In a recessionary environment, such as that experienced in the late 1980s and early 1990s, proper budgeting can increase the survival rate. A company may fail from sloppy or incomplete budgeting. Figure 1-1 shows a graphic depiction of budget segments.

We now consider planning, types of budgets, the budgetary process, budget coordination, departmental budgeting, comparing actual to budgeted figures, budget revision and weaknesses, control and audit, participative budgeting, and pros and cons of budgets.

PLANNING

Budgeting is a planning and control system. It communicates to all members of the organization what is expected of them. Planning is determining the activities to be accomplished to achieve objectives and goals. Planning is needed so that a company can operate its departments and segments within it successfully. It looks at what should be done, how it should be done, when it should be done, and by whom. Planning involves the determination of objectives, evaluating alternative courses of action, and authorization to select programs. There should be a good interface of segments within the organization.

Budgets are blueprints for projected action and a formalization of the planning process. Plans are expressed in quantitative and monetary terms.

FIGURE 1–1 Budget Segments

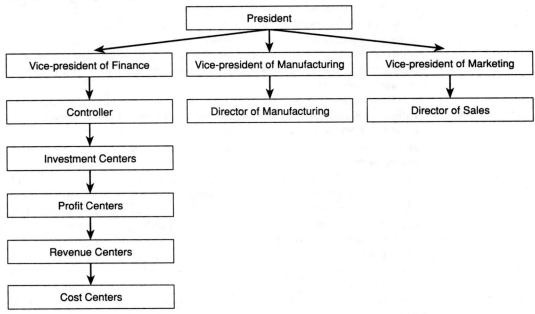

Planning is taking an action based upon investigation, analysis, and research. Potential problems are searched out. Budgeting induces planning in each phase of the company's operation.

A profit plan is what a company expects to follow to attain a profit goal. Managers should be discouraged from spending their entire budget, otherwise, the budgeted funds next period will be cut. Managers should be given credit for their cost savings.

Budget planning meetings should be held routinely to discuss such topics as number of staff needed, objectives, resources, and time schedules. There should be clear communication of how the numbers are established and why, what assumptions were made, and what the objectives are.

TYPES OF BUDGETS

It is necessary to be familiar with the various types of budgets to understand the whole picture and how these budgets interrelate. The types of budgets include master, operating (for income statement items comprised of revenue and expenses), nonoperating, financial (for balance sheet items), cash, sales, production, cost, static (fixed), flexible (variable), direct material, direct labor, overhead, capital expenditure (facilities), and program (appropriations for specific activities such as research and development, and advertising).

Master Budget

A master budget is an overall financial and operating plan for a forthcoming calendar or fiscal year. It is usually prepared annually or quarterly. The master budget is really a number of sub-budgets tied together to summarize the planned activities of the business. The format of the master budget depends upon the size and nature of the business.

Static (Fixed) Budget

The static (fixed) budget is budgeted figures at the expected capacity level. Allowances are set forth for specific purposes with monetary limitations. It is used when a company is relatively stable. Stability usually refers to sales. The problem with a static budget is the absence of flexibility to adjust to unpredictable changes.

In industry, fixed budgets are appropriate for those departments whose work load does not have a direct current relationship to sales, production, or some other volume determinant related to the department's operations. The work of the departments is determined by management decision rather than by sales volume. Most administrative, general marketing, and even manufacturing management departments are in this category. Fixed appropriations for specific projects or programs not necessarily completed in the fiscal period also become fixed budgets to the extent that they will be expended during the year. Examples are appropriations for capital expenditures, major repair projects, and specific advertising or promotional programs.

Flexible (Expense) Budget

The flexible (expense) budget is most commonly used by companies. It allows for variability in the business and for unexpected changes. It is dynamic in nature rather than static. Flexible budgets adjust budget allowances to the actual activity. Flexible budgets are effective when volumes vary within a relative narrow range. They are easy to prepare with computerized spreadsheets such as Lotus 1-2-3.

The basic steps in preparing a flexible (expense) budget are:

1. Determine the relevant range over which activity is expected to fluctuate during the coming period.
2. Analyze costs that will be incurred over the relevant range in terms of determining cost behavior patterns (variable, fixed, or mixed).

3. Separate costs by behavior, determining the formula for variable and mixed costs.

4. Using the formula for the variable portion of the costs, prepare a budget showing what costs will be incurred at various points throughout the relevant range.

Due to uncertainties inherent in planning, three forecasts may be projected: one at an optimistic level, one at a pessimistic or extremely conservative level, and one at a balanced, in-between level.

Operating and Financial Budgets

The operating budget deals with the costs for merchandise or services produced. The financial budget examines the expected assets, liabilities, and stockholders' equity of the business. It is needed to see the company's financial health.

Cash Budget

The cash budget is for cash planning and control. It presents expected cash inflow and outflow for a designated time period. The cash budget helps management keep cash balances in reasonable relationship to its needs and aids in avoiding idle cash and possible cash shortages. The cash budget typically consists of four major sections:

1. receipts section, which is the beginning cash balance, cash collections from customers, and other receipts,

2. disbursement section comprised of all cash payments made by purpose,

3. cash surplus or deficit section showing the difference between cash receipts and cash payments, and

4. financing section providing a detailed account of the borrowings and repayments expected during the period.

Capital Expenditure Budget

The capital expenditure budget is a listing of important long-term projects to be undertaken and capital (fixed assets such as plant and equipment) to be acquired. The estimated cost of the project and the timing of the capital expenditures are enumerated along with how the capital assets are to be financed. The budgeting period is typically for three to ten years. There may be a capital projects committee solely developed for this purpose which is typically separate from the budget committee.

The capital expenditures budget often classifies individual projects by objective such as with the following:

- Expansion and enhancement of existing product lines
- Cost reduction and replacement
- Development of new products
- Health and safety expenditures.

The lack of funds may prevent attractive potential projects from being approved.

An approval of a capital project typically means approval of the project in principle. However, final approval is not automatic. To obtain final approval, a special authorization request is prepared for the project, spelling out the proposal in more detail. The authorization requests may be approved at various managerial levels depending upon their nature and dollar magnitude.

Program Budget

Programming is deciding on the programs to be funded and by how much. A common application of program budgets is to product lines. There is an allocation of resources to accomplish a specific objective with a review of existing and new programs. Some suitable program activities include research and development, marketing, training, preventive maintenance, engineering, and public relations. Funds are usually allocated based on cost effectiveness. In budget negotiations, proposed budgetary figures should be explained and justified. The program budget typically cannot be used for control purposes because the costs shown cannot ordinarily be related to the responsibilities of specific individuals.

Incremental Budget

Incremental budgeting looks at the increase in the budget in terms of dollars or percentages without considering the whole accumulated body of the budget.

There are also self-contained, self-justified increments of projects. Each one specifies resource utilization and expected benefits. A project may be segregated into one or more increments. There are additional increments to complete the project. Manpower and resources are assigned to each increment.

Add-On Budget

An add-on budget is one in which previous years' budgets are examined and adjusted for current information such as inflation and employee raises. Money is added to the budget to satisfy the new requirements. With add-on, there is no incentive for efficiency, but competition forces one to look for new, better ways of doing things. For example, Konica Imaging U.S.A. has combined add-on with zero-based review.

Supplemental Budget

Supplemental budgets provide additional funding for an area not included in the regular budget.

Bracket Budget

A bracket budget is a contingency plan where costs are projected at higher and lower levels than the base amount. Sales are then forecasted for these levels. The purpose of this is that if the base budget and the resulting sales forecast is not achieved, the bracket budget provides management with a sense of earnings impact and a contingency expense plan. A contingency budget may be appropriate when there are downside risks that should be planned for such as a sharp drop in revenue.

Stretch Budget

A stretch budget may be considered a contingency budget on the optimistic side. It is typically only confined to sales and marketing projections that are higher than estimates. It is rarely applied to expenses. Stretch targets may be held informally without making operating units accountable for them. Alternatively, stretch targets may be official estimates for sales/marketing personnel. Expenses may be estimated at the standard budget sales target.

Strategic Budget

Strategic budgeting integrates strategic planning and budgeting control. It is effective under conditions of uncertainty and instability.

Activity-Based Budget

Activity-based budgeting budgets costs for individual activities.

Target Budget

A target budget is a plan in which categories of *major expenditures* are matched to *company goals*. The emphasis is on formulating methods of project funding to move the company forward. There must be strict justification for large dollars and special project requests.

THE BUDGETARY PROCESS

A sound budget process communicates organizational goals, allocates resources, provides feedback, and motivates employees. The budgetary process should be standardized by using budget manuals, budget forms, and formal procedures. Software, Program Evaluation and Review Technique (PERT), and Gantt facilitate the budgeting process and preparation. The timetable for the budget must be kept. If the budget is a "rush job," unrealistic targets may be set.

The budget process used by a company should suit its needs, be consistent with its organizational structure, and take into account human resources. The budgetary process establishes goals and policies, formulates limits, enumerates resource needs, examines specific requirements, provides flexibility, incorporates assumptions, and considers constraints. The budgeting process should take into account a careful analysis of the current status of the company. The process takes longer as the complexity of the operations increase. A budget is based on past experience plus a change in light of the current environment.

The steps in the budgeting process are:

1. Setting objectives.
2. Analyzing available resources.
3. Negotiating to estimate budget components.
4. Coordinating and reviewing components.
5. Obtaining final approval.
6. Distributing the approved budget.

A budget committee should review budget estimates from each segment, make recommendations, revise budgeted figures as needed, and approve or disapprove of the budget. The committee should be available for advice if a problem arises in gathering financial data. The committee can also reconcile diverse interests of budget preparers and users.

The success of the budgeting process requires the cooperation of all levels within the organization. For example, without top management or operating management support, the budget will fail. Those involved in budgeting must be properly trained and guided in the objectives, benefits, steps, and procedures. There should be adequate supervision.

The preparation of a comprehensive budget usually begins with the anticipated volume of sales or services, which is a crucial factor that determines the level of activity for a period. In other cases, factory capacity, the supply of labor, or the availability of raw materials could be the limiting factor to sales. After sales are forecast, production costs and operating expenses can be estimated. The budgeting period varies with the type of business, but it should be long enough to include complete cycles of season, production, inventory turnover, and financial activities. Other considerations are product or service to be rendered and regulatory requirements.

The budget guidelines prepared by top management are passed down through successive levels in the company. Managers at each level may make additions and provide greater detail for subordinates. The managers at each level prepare the plans for items under their control. For example, Philip Morris formulates departmental budgets for each functional area.

The budgeting process will forewarn management of possible problems that may arise. By knowing the problems, solutions may be formulated. For example, at the valleys in cash flow, a shortage of cash may occur. By knowing this in advance, management may arrange for a short-term loan for the financing need rather than face a sudden financing crisis. In a similar vein, planning allows for a smooth manufacturing schedule to result in both lower production costs and lower inventory levels. It avoids a crisis situation requiring overtime or high transportation charges to receive supplies ordered on a "rush basis." Without proper planning cyclical product demand needs may arise straining resources and capacity. Resources include material, labor, and storage.

Bottom-Up vs. Top-Down

A budget plans for future business actions. Managers prefer a participative bottom-up approach to an authoritative top-down approach. The bottom-up method begins at the bottom or operating (departmental) level based on the objectives of the segment. However, operating levels must satisfy the overall company goals. There are estimates of component activities such as product line by department. Each department prepares its own budget before it is incorporated in the master budget. The goals may include growth rates, manpower needs, minimum return on investment, and pricing. In effect, departmental budgets are used to determine the organizational budget. The budget is reviewed, adjusted if necessary, and approved at each higher level. The bottom-up approach would forecast sales by product or other category, then by company sales, and then by market share. The bottom-up method may be used to increase the feeling of unit-level ownership in the budget. Disadvantages are the time-consuming process from participative input, and the fact that some company objectives may be neglected by operating units. Bottom-up does not allow for control of the process, and the resulting budget is likely to be unbalanced with regard to the relationship of expenses to revenue.

Typical questions to answer when preparing a bottom-up budget are: What are the expected promotional and travel expenses for the coming period? What staff requirements will be needed? What are the expected raises for the coming year? How much supplies will be needed?

This approach is particularly necessary when responsibility unit managers are expected to be very innovative. Unit managers know what must be achieved, where the opportunities are, what problem areas must be resolved, and where resources must be allocated.

In the top-down approach, a central corporate staff under the CEO or President determines overall company objectives and strategies, enumerates resource constraints, considers competition, prepares the budget, and makes allocations. Management considers the competitive and economic environment. Top management knows the company's objectives, strategies, resources, strengths, and weaknesses. Departmental objectives follow from the action plans.

Top-down is commonly used in long-range planning. A top-down approach is needed for a company having significant interdependence among operating units to enhance coordination. The top-down approach would forecast first sales based on an examination of the economy, then the company's share of the market and the company's sales, and then would proceed to a forecast of sales by products or other category. A top-down approach may be needed when business unit managers must be given specific performance objectives due to a crisis situation, and when close coordination is required between business units. It is possible that the sum of the unit budgets would not meet corporate expectations. If unit managers develop budgets independently of other units, there are inconsistencies in the assumptions used by different units.

A disadvantage with this approach is that central staff may not have all the knowledge needed to prepare the budget within every segment of the organization. Managers at the operating levels are more knowledgeable and familiar with the segment's operations. Managers will not support or commit to a budget they were not involved in preparing, which will cause a motivational problem. Further, the top-down approach stifles creativity. A budget needs input from affected managers but top management knows the overall picture.

A combination of the bottom-up and top-down approaches may be appropriate in certain cases. Some large companies may use an integration of the methods. For example, Konica Imaging uses a method when it best fits.

The company uses a blend. There is direction supplied from the top and action plans developed by senior management. Each department must then determine how it will actually implement the action, specifically looking at the resources and expenditures required. This is the quantification of the action plans into dollars. It is then reviewed to see if it achieves the desired results. If it does not, it will be kicked back until it is brought in line with the desired outcomes. The what, why, and when is specified from the top, and the how and who is specified from the bottom.

As an example of the budgeting process, Power Cord and Cable Corporation (PCCC) uses a comprehensive or master budget to summarize the objective of all its subunits such as Sales, Production, Marketing, Administrative, Purchasing and Finance. Just as all organizations, PCCC uses a master budget as a blue print for planned operations in a particular time period.

A book solely devoted to budgeting practices by companies is Srinivasan Umapathy, *Current Budgeting Practices in U.S. Industry,* Quorum Books, New York, 1987.

BUDGET COORDINATION

There should be one person responsible for centralized control over the budget who must work closely with general management and department heads. A budget is a quantitative plan of action that aids in coordination and implementation. The budget communicates objectives to all the departments within the company. A budget is a tool of top management to coordinate corporate activities to subordinate departments with each other. The budget presents upper management with coordinated and summarized data as to the financial ramifications of plans and actions of various departments and units within the company.

Budgets are usually established for all departments and major segments in the company. The budget must be comprehensive including all inter-related departments. The budget process should receive input from all departments so there is coordination within the firm. For example, operations will improve when marketing, purchasing, personnel, and finance departments cooperate.

Coordination is obtaining and organizing the needed personnel, equipment, and materials to carry out the business. A budget aids in coordination between separate activity units to ensure that all parts of the company are in balance with each other and know how they fit in. It discloses weaknesses in the organizational structure. The budget communicates to staff what is expected of them. It allows for a consensus of ideas, strategies, and direction.

EXHIBIT 1–1 Statement of Revenue and Expense by Product for the Year 1996

	All Products		A		B		C	
					Product Line			
Itemization	*Amount*	*Percentage Net Sales*	*Amount*	*Percentage Net Sales*	*Amount*	*Percentage Net Sales*	*Amount*	*Percentage Net Sales*
Gross Sales								
Less: Returns and Allowances								
Net Sales								
Less: Variable Cost of Sales								
Manufacturing Contribution Margin								
Direct Distribution Costs								
Variable								
Fixed								
Semi-Direct Distribution								
Expense (Variable)								
Contribution Margin								
Continuing Costs								
Fixed Manufacturing Costs								
Other Indirect Expenses								
Total								
Income before Taxes								
Less: Taxes								
Net Income								

ACTUAL COSTS VS. BUDGET COSTS

A budget provides an "early warning" of impending problems. The effectiveness of a budget depends on how sound and accurate the estimates are. The planning must take all factors into account in a realistic way. The budget figures may be inaccurate because of such factors as economic problems, political unrest, competitive shifts in the industry, introduction of new products, and regulatory changes.

At the beginning of the period, the budget is a plan. At the end of the period, the budget is a control instrument to assist management in measuring its performance against plan so as to improve future performance. Budgeted revenue and costs are compared to actual revenue and costs to determine variances. A determination has to be made whether the variances are controllable or uncontrollable. If controllable, the parties responsible must be identified. Corrective action must be taken to correct any problems.

A comparison should be made between actual costs at actual activity to budgeted costs at actual activity. In this way, there is a common base of comparison. The percentage and dollar difference between the budget and actual figures should be shown. A typical performance report for a division appears in Exhibit 1–2.

Authorized variances in cost budgets allow for an increase in the initial budget for unfavorable variances. This may result from unexpected wage increases, prices of raw materials, and so on. Allowance is given for cost excesses that a manager can justify.

BUDGET REVISION

A budget should be regularly monitored. A budget should be revised to make it accurate during the period because of error, feedback, new data, changing conditions (e.g., economic, political, corporate), or modification of the company's plan. Human error is more likely when the budget is large and complex. A change in conditions will typically affect the sales forecast and re-

EXHIBIT 1–2 XYZ Company Divisional Performance Evaluation December 31, 19XX

Division	Net Sales Actual	Net Sales Expected	Over (Under) Plan	Net Income Actual	Net Income Expected	Over (Under) Plan
A	$1,000	$3,000	($2,000)	$ 500	$ 800	($300)
B	2,000	1,500	500	300	350	(50)
C	4,000	3,600	400	200	100	100
Total	$7,000	$8,100	($1,100)	$1,000	$1,250	($250)

sulting cost estimates. Revisions are more common in volatile industries. The budget revision applies to the remainder of the accounting period.

A company may "roll a budget" which is continuous budgeting for an additional incremental period at the end of the reporting period. The new period is added to the remaining periods to form the new budget. Continuous budgets reinforce constant planning, consider past information, and take into account emerging conditions.

BUDGET WEAKNESSES

The signs of budget weaknesses must be spotted so that corrective action may be taken. Such signs include:

- Managerial goals are off target or unrealistic.
- There is management indecisiveness.
- The budget takes too long to prepare.
- Budget preparers are unfamiliar with the operations being budgeted and do not seek such information. Budget preparers should visit the actual operations first hand.
- Budget preparers do not keep current.
- The budget is prepared using different methods each year.
- There is a lack of raw information going into the budgeting process.
- There is a lack of communication between those involved in budgeting and operating personnel.
- The budget is formulated without input from those affected by it. This will likely result in budgeting errors. Further, budget preparers do not go into the operations field.
- Managers do not know how their budget allowances have been assigned nor what the components of their charges are. If managers do not understand the information, they will not properly perform their functions.
- The budget document is excessively long, confusing, or filled with unnecessary information. There may be inadequate narrative data to explain the numbers.
- Managers are ignoring their budgets because they appear unusable and unrealistic.
- Managers feel they are not getting anything out of the budget process. There are excessively frequent changes in the budget.
- Significant unfavorable variances are not investigated and corrected. These variances may also not be considered in deriving budgeted figures for next

period. Further, a large variance between actual and budgeted figures, either positive or negative, that repeatedly occurs is an indicator of poor budgeting. Perhaps the budgeted figures were unrealistic. Another problem is that after variances are identified, it is too late to correct their causes. Further, variance reporting may be too infrequent.

- There is a mismatching of products or services.

BUDGETARY CONTROL AND AUDIT

As was discussed previously, the budget is a major control device for revenue, costs, and operations. The purpose is to increase profitability and reduce costs, or to meet other corporate objectives as quickly as possible. Budgetary control may also be related to nonfinancial activities such as the life cycle of the product or seasonality. An illustrative budget control report is shown in Exhibit 1–3. Sample electronic budget reports and worksheets appear in Exhibits 1–4 and 1–5.

A budget audit should be undertaken to determine the correctness of the budgeted figures. Was there a proper evaluation of costs? Were all costs included that should have been? What are the cost trends? Are budgeted figures too tight or too loose? Are budgeted figures properly supported by documentation? A budget audit appraises budgeting techniques, procedures, manager attitudes, and effectiveness. The major aspects of the budgeting process have to be examined.

EXHIBIT 1–3 Budget Control Report

I. Budget Savings
   One-year Savings   Amount:
   Two- to Five-Year Savings   Amount:
   More Than Five-Year Savings   Amount:
   Savings Description:
II. Budget Impact
   Reduction in Current Year Budget
     Budget Account
     Budget Amount
   Budget Adjustment Not Needed
III. Budget Participants
   Management: Names: Job Description:
   Employees: Names: Job Description:
IV. Management Incentives:
V. Employee Awards
   Prepared By:
   Reviewed By:
   Approved By:

EXHIBIT 1–4 Departmental Expense Budget

	B	C	D	E	N	O
3	ABC Company Departmental Expense Budget					
4	Department: XYZ			Prepared by: RWB		
5						
6	Item	JAN	FEB	MAR	DEC	TOTAL
7	--------------------	--------	--------	--------	--------	--------
8	People Related (Schedule A1)					
9	Salaries	$11,850	$11,850	$13,050	$13,950	$160,500
10	Benefits	$1,778	$1,778	$1,958	$2,093	$24,750
11	Education	$593	$593	$653	$698	$8,025
12	T&E	$2,000	$2,000	$2,000	$2,000	$30,000
13						
14	Subtotal	$16,220	$16,220	$17,660	$18,740	$222,600
15	--------------------	--------	--------	--------	--------	--------
16	Facility Related					
17	Plant & Equip	$2,000	$2,000	$2,000	$2,000	$24,000
18	Maint & Repairs	$150	$150	$150	$150	$1,800
19	Utilities	$1,000	$1,000	$1,000	$900	$9,100
20	Other	$150	$150	$150	$150	$1,800
21						
22	Subtotal	$3,300	$3,300	$3,300	$3,300	$36,700
23	--------------------	--------	--------	--------	--------	--------
24	Other (Schedule A2)					
25	Supplies	$350	$350	$350	$350	$4,200
26	Outside Svcs	$500	$500	$500	$500	$6,800
27	Postage/Shipping	$550	$110	$110	$110	$2,390
28						
29	Subtotal	$1,400	$960	$960	$960	$13,390
30	--------------------	--------	--------	--------	--------	--------
31	Total Budget	$20,920	$20,480	$21,920	$22,900	$272,690
32	====================	========	========	========	========	========
33	Fixed Assets (Schedule A3)					
34	Furn & Fix	$4,000	$4,000	$5,600	$6,400	$69,600
35	Leasehld Impr	$200	$200	$200	$200	$2,400
36	Capital Equip	$500	$500	$500	$500	$7,200
37						
38	Total Fixed Assets	$4,700	$4,700	$6,300	$7,100	$79,200
39	====================	========	========	========	========	========

The format of this spreadsheet-based budget is a study in simplicity. Grouping expense categories by type, setting off categories with dashed lines, and clearly labeling important totals and subtotals all improve the readability of the finished product. Line items categorized by type, such as people-related items, are keyed to supplemental worksheets that are developed before the final budget is created. Specific cells from supplemental worksheets are then imported directly into the final budget as the budget modules are assembled.

SOURCE: *Lotus*, May 1985, p. 58.

EXHIBIT 1–4 *(Continued)* Departmental Expense Budget

CELL FORMULAS	
Main Budget	**Supplemental Worksheets**
C9: (C0) +D72	C56: (C0) @SUM(C50..C55)
D9: (C0) +E72	D56: (F0) @SUM(D50..D55)
C10: (C0) +D73	C63: (C0) @SUM(C60..C62)
D10: (C0) +E73	D63: (F0) @SUM(D60..D62)
C11: (C0) +D74	D65: +D56+D63
D11: (C0) +E74	D66: +D65-D56
C12: (C0) +D75	E66: +E65-D65
D12: (C0) +E75	D69: (C0) +D50*C50
C14: (C0) @SUM(C9..C13)	+D51*C51+D52
D14: (C0) @SUM(D9..D13)	*C52+D53
C22: (C0) @SUM(C17..C20)	*C53+D54*C54
D22: (C0) @SUM(D17..D20)	D70: (C0) +D60*C60
C25: (C0) +C87	+D61*C61
D25: (C0) +D87	D72: (C0) +@SUM(D69..D70)
C26: (C0) +C88	D73: (C0) +D72*C73
D26: (C0) +D88	D74: (C0) +D72*C74
C27: (C0) +C89	D77: (C0) @SUM(D72..D76)
D27: (C0) +D89	C91: @SUM(C87..C89)
C29: (C0) +@SUM(C25..C27)	D91: @SUM(D87..D89)
D29: (C0) +@SUM(D25..D27)	C101: +D66
C31: (C0) +C14+C22+C29	D101: +E66
D31: (C0) +D14+D22+D29	C106: (C0) +@SUM(C101..C105)
C34: (C0) +C102	D106: (C0) +@SUM(D101..D105)
D34: (C0) +D102	
C35: (C0) +C103	
D35: (C0) +D103	
C36: (C0) +C104	
D36: (C0) +D104	
C38: (C0) +@SUM(C33..C37)	
D38: (C0) +@SUM(D33..D37)	

A listing of the formulas in columns C and D of the main budget and the supplemental worksheets. The formulas shown consist of a plus sign and a cell address from a supplemental worksheet. These formulas tie the main budget to the subtotal in the supplemental worksheet, where most of the calculations are done. When you make changes to these auxillary worksheets, they are automatically reflected in the main budget.

SOURCE: *Lotus*, May 1985, p. 58.

MOTIVATION

Budgets can be used to affect employee attitudes and performance. Budgets should be participative including participation by those to be affected by them. Further, lower level employees are on the operating line every day so they are quite knowledgeable. Their input is needed. Budgets can be used to motivate because participants will internalize the budget goals as their own

EXHIBIT 1–5 Budget Worksheet

	B	C	D	E	F	O	P
41	Supporting Budget Worksheet						
42	Schedule A1: Departmental Personnel						
43	Department: XYZ	Prepared by:RWB					
44	(Insert a 1 in months employee works.)						
45							
46	Employee	Salary/mo	JAN	FEB	MAR	DEC	TOTAL
47	-------------	--------	------	------	------	------	--------
48	Current Staff						
49							
50	Barrett, Robert	$4,000	1	1	1	1	$48,000
51	Caldwell, Mary	$1,800	1	1	1	1	$21,600
52	Carson, Steve	$1,700	1	1	1	1	$20,400
53	Field, Laura	$3,100	1	1	1	1	$37,200
54	Smith, Mary	$1,250	1	1	1	1	$15,000
55							
56	Total/Current	$11,850	5	5	5	5	$142,200
57	-------------	--------	------	------	------	------	--------
58	New Hires						
59							
60	Secretary	$1,200	0	0	1	1	$12,000
61	Clerk	$900	0	0	0	1	$6,300
62							
63	Total/New Hires	$2,100	0	0	1	2	$18,300
64	-------------	--------	------	------	------	------	--------
65	Head Count		5	5	6	7	
66	Net Change		0	0	1	0	
67	-------------	--------	------	------	------	------	--------
68	Worksheet summary						
69	Current Salaries		$11,850	$11,850	$11,850	$11,850	$142,200
70	Add'l Salaries		$0	$0	$1,200	$2,100	$18,300
71							
72	Salaries		$11,850	$11,850	$13,050	$13,950	$160,500
73	Benefits	15%	$1,778	$1,778	$1,958	$2,093	$24,075
74	Education	5%	$593	$593	$653	$698	$8,025
75	T&E		$2,000	$2,000	$2,000	$2,000	$30,000
76							
77	Total Personnel Expense		$16,220	$16,220	$17,660	$18,740	$222,600
78							
79	==============	========	======	======	======	======	========

A supplemental worksheet detailing people-related expenses is valuable in assessing the impact that personnel costs have on the bottom line. Such a worksheet must provide adequate space to accommodate new hiring, as well as on- going head counts. A summary range is also useful since it provides clear updates of changing staffing conditions. The 0 or 1 method of accounting for employee presence makes calculating salary expenses easier, since this notation can be used in worksheet formulas. The net change is the difference between the current and the previous month's head count.

SOURCE: *Lotus,* May 1985, p. 59.

since they participated in their development. Information should be inter-changed among budget participants. An imposed budget will have a *negative* effect upon motivation. Further, there is a correlation between task difficulty and loss of control to negative attitudes.

A budget is a motivational and challenging tool if it is tight, but attainable. It has to be *realistic*. If the budget is too tight, it results in frustration because managers will give up and not try to achieve the unrealistic targets. If it is too loose, complacency will arise and workers may "goof off."

In an article titled "How Challenging Should Profit Budget Targets Be" appearing in the November 1990 issue of *Management Accounting,* Kenneth Merchant states that "the best way to set budget targets is with a probability of achievement by most managers 80 percent-90 percent of the time. Performance above the target level should be supplemented with incentives including bonuses, promotion, and additional responsibility."

ADVANTAGES AND DISADVANTAGES OF BUDGETS

Budgeting involves cost and time to prepare. The benefits of budgeting must outweigh the drawbacks. A budget can be advantageous because it does the following:

- Links objectives and resources.
- Communicates to managers what is expected of them. Any problems in communication and working relationships are identified. Resources and requirements are identified.
- Establishes guidelines in the form of a "road map" to proceed in the right direction.
- Improves managerial decision-making because emphasis is on future events and associated opportunities.
- Encourages delegation of responsibility and enables managers to focus more on the specifics of their plans and how realistic the plans are, and how such plans may be effectively achieved.
- Provides an accurate analytical technique.
- Provides better management of subordinates. For example, a manager can use the budget to encourage salespeople to consider their clientele in long-term strategic terms.
- Fosters careful study before making decisions.
- Helps management become aware of the problems faced by lower levels within the organization. It promotes labor relations.

- Allows for thinking how to make operations and resources more productive, efficient, competitive, and profitable. It leads to cost reduction.

- Allows management to monitor, control, and direct activities within the company. Performance standards act as incentives to perform more effectively.

- Points out deviations between budget and actual resulting in warning signals for changes or alterations.

- Helps identify on a timely basis weaknesses in the organizational structure. There is early notice of dangers or departures from forecasts. The formulation and administration of budgets pinpoints communication weaknesses, assigns responsibility, and improves working relationships.

- Provides management with foresight into potential crisis situations so alternative plans may be instituted.

- Provides early signals of upcoming threats and opportunities.

- Aids coordination between departments to attain efficiency and productivity. There is an interlocking within the business organization. For example, the production department will manufacture based upon the sales department's anticipated sales volume. The purchasing department will buy raw materials based on the production department's expected production volume. The personnel department will hire or lay off workers based on anticipated production levels. Executives are forced to consider relationships among individual operations and the company as a whole.

- Provides a motivational devise setting a standard for employees to achieve.

- Measures of self-evaluation.

- Management can make distasteful decisions and "blame it on the budget."

The disadvantages of a budget are:

- A budget promotes "gamesmanship" in that those managers who significantly inflate requests, knowing they will be reduced, are in effect rewarded by getting what they probably wanted already.

- A budget may reward managers who set modest goals and penalize those who set ambitious goals that are missed.

- There is judgment and subjectivity in the budgeting process.

- Managers may consider budgets as redirecting their flexibility to adjust to changing conditions.

- A budget does not consider quality and customer service.

CONCLUSION

A budget should be based on norms and standards. The budget should be co-ordinated, integrated, organized, systematic, clear, and comprehensive to accomplish optimal results. The budget preparation, review, and evaluation process must be facilitated. An orderly budgeting process will result in less cost, more manhours, and minimization of conflict and turmoil. It will require less revision at a later date. Input-output relationships must also be considered. The budget aids in anticipating problems before they become critical. Short-term budgets should be used for businesses subject to rapid change. It is a tool for planning and for a "what if" analysis. It aids in identifying the best course of action.

As it is in the computer world—garbage in, garbage out—so it is with budgeting. If forecasts are inaccurate so will be the projections, resulting in bad management decisions to the detriment of the firm. A manager must be cautious when analyzing past experience. Unforseen circumstances such as economic downturns and future innovations have direct inputs on present operations. A manager deviating from a budget target must explain why and, of course, is on the defensive. Without proper justification, the manager may be dismissed.

The failure to budget may result in conflicting and contradictory plans as well as in wasting corporate resources. Budget slack should be avoided or minimized. Budget slack is the underestimation of revenues and the overestimation of expenses. Budgets should be revised as circumstances materially change. A manager who has responsibility to meet a budget should also have the authorization to use corporate resources to accomplish that budget. There should be priorities established for the allocation of scarce resources. Budgets may include supplementary information such as break-even analysis by department, by product, and for overall operations.

It is important to avoid the situation in which a manager feels he or she must spend the entire budget or else lose funding in the next period. Managers should not be motivated to spend the entire budget. Rather, cost savings should be realized, and those responsible should be recognized such as through cash bonuses or nonmonetary awards (e.g., trophy, medals). Budget savers should be protected in the funding for future budgets.

Budgets should not be arbitrarily cut across-the-board. This may result in disastrous consequences in certain programs. If budget reductions are necessary, determine exactly where and by how much.

Chapter 2

Planning and Budgeting*

Although planning differs among companies, it is the direction of the company over a period of time to accomplish a desired result. Planning should link short-term, intermediate-term, and long-term goals. The objective is to make the best use of the companies' available resources over the long term. Budgeting is simply one portion of the plan. The annual plan may be based on the long-term plan. The annual budget should be consistent with the long-term goals of the business. There should be a climate conducive to planning and friendly relationships. An objective of planning is to improve profitability. Plans are interrelated.

In planning, management selects long-term and short-term goals and draws up plans to accomplish those goals. Planning is more important in long-run management. The objectives of a plan must be continually appraised in terms of degree of accomplishment and how long it takes to implement. There should be feedback as to the plan's progress. It is best to concentrate on accomplishing fewer targets so proper attention will be given to them. Objectives must be specific and measurable. For example, a target to increase sales by 20 percent is definite and specific. The manager can measure quantitatively the progress toward meeting this target.

The plan is the set of details implementing the strategy. The plan of ex-

* This chapter was coauthored by Abraham J. Simon, Ph.D., CPA, Chairperson of the Department of Accounting and Information Systems at Queens College, and a financial consultant to business.

ecution is typically explained in sequential steps including costs and timing for each step. Deadlines are set.

The planning function includes all managerial activities that ultimately enable an organization to achieve its goals. Because every organization needs to set and achieve goals, planning is often called the first function of management. At the highest levels of business, planning involves establishing company strategies, that is, determining how the resources of the business will be used to reach its objective. Planning also involves the establishment of policies, i.e., the day-to-day guidelines used by managers to accomplish their objectives. The elements of a plan include objectives, performance standards, appraisal of performance, action plan, and financial figures.

All management levels should be involved in preparing budgets. There should be a budget for each responsibility center. Responsibility in particular areas should be assigned for planning to specific personnel. At Adolph Coors Company, planning is ongoing, encouraging managers to assume active roles in the organization.

A plan is a predetermined action course. Planning has to consider the organizational structure, taking into account authority and responsibility. Planning is determining what should be done, how it should be done, and when it should be done. The plan should specify the nature of the problems, reasons for them, constraints, contents, characteristics, category, alternative ways of accomplishing objectives, and listing of information required. Planning objectives include quantity and quality of products and services, as well as growth opportunities.

A plan is a detailed outline of activities to meet desired strategies to accomplish goals. Such goals must be realistic. Planning requires analysis of the situation. The plan should specify the evaluative criteria and measurement methods. The assumptions of a plan must be specified and appraised as to whether they are reasonable. The financial effects of alternative strategies should be noted. Planning should allow for creativity. Planning involves analyzing the strengths and weaknesses of the company and each segment therein. Planning is needed of allocating human resources to organizational units and programs.

Long-term plans should consider new opportunities, competition, resources (equipment, machinery, manpower), diversification, expansion, financial strength, and flexibility. In planning, consideration has to be given to noncyclical occurrences, such as new product or service introduction, modification in manufacturing processes, and discontinuance of a product or service.

Planning is facilitated when the business is stable. For example, a company with a few products or services operating in stable markets can plan better than one with many diverse products operating in volatile markets. Planning should take into account industry and competing company conditions.

A description of products, facilities, resources, and markets should be noted. The emphasis should be on better use of resources including physical facilities and personnel.

In summation, a plan is a detailed outline of activities and strategies to satisfy a long-term objective. An objective is a quantifiable target. The objective is derived from an evaluation of the situation. A diagram of the planning process appears in Figure 2–1.

BUDGETING

Budgeting is a form of planning and policy development considering resource constraints. It is a profit planning mechanism and may look at "what-if" scenarios. Budgets are detailed and communicate to sub-units what is ex-

FIGURE 2–1 Steps in Strategic Planning

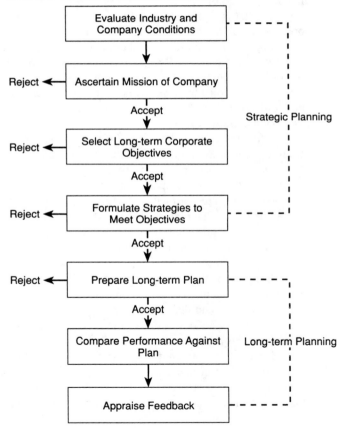

pected of them. Budget information should be provided by those responsible for expenditures and revenue. Planning should be by the smallest practical segment. Budgeting is worthwhile if its use makes the company more profitable than without it.

Budgets are quantitative expressions of the yearly profit plan and measure progress during the period. The shorter the budgeting period, the more reliable. A cumulative budget may drop the prior month and add the next month. A typical department budget appears in Exhibit 2–1. A typical checklist for the budgeting system appears in Exhibit 2–2.

STRATEGIC PLANNING

Strategic plans are long-term, broad plans ranging from 2 to 30 years, with 5 to 10 years being most typical. Strategic planning is continuous and looks

EXHIBIT 2–1 ABC Company Department Budget Report

Department _____   Department Supervisor _____
Period _____

Classification	Dollar Amount Budget	Actual	Over or Under Current Month	Cumulative to Date	Percent Realized Current Month	Moving Average Current	Prior
Direct labor							
1							
2							
3							
4							
Total direct labor							
Indirect labor							
Indirect wages							
Supervisory wages							
Trainees salaries							
Janitors							
Vacations and holidays							
Idle time							
Other salaries							
Sub-total							
Other department costs							
Operating supplies							
Telephone							
Travel							
Consultants							
Memberships							
Tools							
Miscellaneous department expenses							
Sub-total							
Total department expenses							

EXHIBIT 2–2 Checklist for Budgeting System ABC Company

Schedule	Who Is Responsible	Date Needed	Date Received
1. Formulate general goals			
2. Formulate division and department objectives			
3. Estimate:			
a. Sales to customers			
b. Personnel needs			
c. Capital equipment			
d. Financial standing			
4. Prepare budgets for:			
a. Sales			
b. Earnings			
c. Production			
—Direct materials			
—Direct labor			
—Factory overhead			
d. Marketing budget			
—Sales personnel and administration			
—Advertising and promotion			
—Distribution			
—Service and parts			
e. Research and development budget			
f. Capital facilities budget			
g. Cash budget			
h. Budgeted balance sheet			
5. Prepare individual budgets and the master budget			
6. Review budgets and make needed changes			
7. Prepare monthly performance reports			
8. Compare budget to actual figures			
9. Make recommendations for future budgets			

where the company is going. It is done by upper management and divisional managers. Most of the information used is external to the company.

The strategic plan is the mission of the company and looks to existing and prospective products and markets. Strategic plans are designed to direct the company's activities, priorities, and goals. It tries to position the company so as to accomplish opportunities. Strategic goals are for the long-term considering the internal and external environment, strengths, and weaknesses.

Strategy is the means by which the company uses its capital, financial, and human resources to achieve its objectives. It shows the company's future direction and rationale, and looks at expected costs and return. Strategic planning is detailed plans to implement policies and strategies. Risk-taking decisions are made. Strategies may be implemented at different times. Strategic planning should take into account the financial position, economy, political environment, social trends, technology, risks, markets, competition, product line, customer base, research support, manufacturing capabilities, manpower, product life cycle, and major problems.

Strategic planning is a prerequisite to short-term planning. There should be a linkage of the two. There is considerably more subjectivity in a strategic plan than a short-term plan.

The strategic plan is formulated by the chief executive officer and his or her staff. It considers acquisitions and divestitures. Financial policies including debt position are determined. It must consider economic, competitive, and industry factors. It establishes direction, priorities, alternatives, and tasks to be performed. The strategic plan is the guideline for each business segment and is the mechanism of the needed activities to accomplish the common goals.

Strategic planning is irregular. Further, strategic planning problems are unstructured. If a strategy becomes unworkable, abandon it.

The elements of a strategic plan are:

- The company's overall *objectives* such as market position, product leadership, and employee development.
- The *strategies* necessary to achieve the objectives such as engaging in a new promotion plan, enhancing research, product and geographical diversification, and eliminating a division.
- The *goals* to be met under the strategy.
- The *progress-to-date* of accomplishing the goals. Examples of goals are sales, profitability, return on investment, and market price of stock.

In summation, strategic planning is planning for the company as a whole, not just combining the separate plans of the respective parts. There must be a common thread. It looks to the long-term. It is concerned with the few key decisions that determine the company's success or failure. It provides overall direction. It indicates how the long-term goals will be achieved. It is a mission policy statement. Critical issues must be dealt with.

SHORT-TERM PLANS

Short-range plans are typically for one year (although some plans are for two years). The plans examine expected earnings, cash flow, and capital expenditures. Short-term plans may be for a period within one year, such as a month or week. Short-term planning relies primarily on internal information and details tactical objectives. It is structured, fixed, foreseeable, and continually

The interdependencies between departments and activities must be considered. For example, the sales manager depends on sufficient units produced in the production department. Production depends on how many units can be sold. Most budget components are affected by other components. For example, most components are impacted by expected sales volume and inventory levels, while purchases are based on expected production and raw material inventories.

A budget allows for directing and control. Directing is supervising the activities to assure they are carried out in an effective and efficient manner within time and cost constraints. Controlling is measuring the progress of resources and personnel to accomplish a desired objective. A comparison is made between actual results and budgeting estimates to identify problems needing attention.

In summation, the budget must consider the requirements of each department or function, and the relationship that departments or functions have with other departments and functions. Activities and resources have to be coordinated.

DEPARTMENTAL BUDGETING

All department managers within a company must accurately determine their future costs and must plan activities to accomplish corporate objectives. Departmental supervisors must have a significant input into budgeting costs and revenues since they are directly involved with the activity and have the best knowledge of it. Managers must examine whether their budgetary assumptions and estimates are reasonable. Budget targets should match manager responsibilities. At the departmental level, the budget considers the expected work output and translates it into estimated future costs.

Budgets are needed for each department. The sales department must forecast future sales volume of each product or service as well as the selling price. It will probably budget revenue by sales territory and customer. It will also budget costs such as wages, promotion and entertainment, and travel. The production department must estimate future costs to produce the product or service and the cost per unit. The production manager may have to budget work during the manufacturing activity so the work flow continues smoothly. The purchasing department will budget units and dollar purchases. There may be a breakdown by supplier. There will be a cost budget for salaries, supplies, rent, and so on. The stores department will budget its costs for holding inventory. There may be a breakdown of products into categories. The finance department must estimate how much money will be received and where it will be spent to determine cash adequacy. An illustrative budget showing revenue and expense by product line appears in Exhibit 1–1.

determinable. The short-term profit plan is based on the strategic plan. It is concerned with existing products and markets.

There should be a short-term profit plan by area of responsibility (product, service, territory, division, department, project, function, and activity). Short-term plans are usually expressed on a departmental basis. They include the following plans: sales, manufacturing, marketing, management (administration), research, and consolidation (integration).

Short-term planning has more lower-level managers involved in providing input. The line manager is typically involved with short-term rather than long-term plans. In making his short-term plan, the line manager should consider the company's objectives and targets outlined in its long-term plan. The manager's short-term plan must satisfy the long-term objectives of the company.

LONG-TERM PLANS

Long-term planning is usually of a broad, strategic (tactical) nature to accomplish objectives. A long-term plan is typically 5–10 years (or more) and looks at the future direction of the company. It also considers economic, political, and industry conditions. Long-term plans are formulated by upper management. It deals with products, markets, services, and operations. Long-range planning enhances sales, profitability, return on investment, and growth. Long-range plans should be constantly revised as new information becomes available.

Long-range planning covers all major areas of the business including manufacturing, marketing, research, finance, engineering, law, accounting, and personnel. Planning for these areas should be coordinated into a comprehensive plan to attain corporate objectives.

A long-term plan is a combination of the operating and developmental plans. The long-term plan should specify what is needed, by whom, and when. Responsibility should be assigned to segments. Long-term goals include market share, new markets, expansion, new distribution channels, cost reduction, capital maintenance, and reduction of risk. The characteristics of sound long-term objectives include flexibility, motivation, measurability, consistency and compatibility, adequateness, and flexibility. Long-range plans may be used for growth, market share, product development, plant expansion, and financing.

Long-range plans are details of accomplishing the strategic plans. Compared to strategic planning, long-range planning is closer to planning current operations of all units of the business. Long-range planning includes evaluating alternatives, developing financial information, analyzing activities, allocating resources, product planning, market analysis, planning man-

EXHIBIT 2–3 Long-Term Plan

	Amount
Contract acquisitions —Customer	
—Division	
—Company	
Sales backlog —Customer	
—Division	
—Company	
Total sales	
Profit margin	
Return on investment	
Capital expenditures —Assets	
—Leases	

power, analyzing finances, research and development planning, and production planning.

The time period for a long-term plan depends upon the time required for product development, product life cycle, market development, and construction of capital facilities. There are more alternatives available in long-term plans. When there is greater uncertainty in the economic and business environment, long-range plans become more important. However, it is more difficult to plan long-term than short-term because of the greater uncertainties that exist. An illustrative long-term plan appears in Exhibit 2–3.

TIME PERIOD

The budget period depends upon the objective of the budget and the reliability of the data. Most companies budget yearly, month-by-month. For example, a seasonal business should use the natural business year beginning when accounts receivable and inventory are at their lowest level.

The time period for a plan should be as far as is useful. It depends upon the time to develop a market, production period, develop raw material sources, construct capital facilities, product development, and product life cycle. The time period also should take into account the type of industry, reliability of financial data and use to which the data will be put, seasonality, and inventory turnover. Shorter budgeting cycles may be called for when unpredictable and unstable events occur during the year. Short-term budgets have considerably more detail than long-term budgets.

ADMINISTERING THE PLAN

There should be a committee of senior operating and financial executives involved in administering a budget. The administration plan consists of human resource planning for the various functions to be carried out, technological resource planning, and organizational planning.

PROFIT PLAN

A profit plan is the premise upon which management charts an action course for the upcoming year. It is good for planning and control. Alternatives must be evaluated and the profit plan should be flexible to adjust for contingencies. Profit planning includes a study of appraising profits relative to investment. A profit budget may be used to supplement a cost budget. Profit budgets may be by customer, territory, or product.

The profit plan must set forth selling price, sales volume, sales mix, per unit cost, competition, advertising, research, market potential, and economic conditions. Profit may be improved through a closer correlation of manufacturing, selling, and administrative expense budgeting to sales and earnings objectives. Cost reduction programs will lower expenses.

Continuous profit planning is used when planning should be for short time periods and where frequent planning is needed. The yearly or quarterly plan may be revised each month. Exhibit 2–4 presents a sample profit plan schedule.

OPERATIONAL PLAN

The preliminary operational plan is an important part of the strategic plan. It examines the alternative strategies so as to select the best one. The *final* operational plan is much more detailed and is the basis to prepare the annual budgets and to evaluate performance. It also acts as the basis to integrate and communicate business functions. It is concerned with short-term activity or functions of the business. The operational plan typically includes: production, marketing (selling), administration, and finance. It examines properly serving product or service markets.

The operational plan summarizes the major action programs and contains the following information: objective, program description, responsibility assignments, resource needs (e.g., assets, employees), expected costs, time deadlines for each stage, input needed from other business segments, and anticipated results.

DEVELOPMENT PLAN

The development plan typically includes research and development, diversification, and divestment. It relates to developing future products, services, or

EXHIBIT 2–4 Profit Plan Forms
XYZ Bank 1993 Profit Plan Schedule (Preliminary)

		Management Committee	Finance Dept.	Due Date
1.	Begin planning and preparation process for the 1993 Budget cycle.		X	02/03/92 Monday
2.	Complete the 1993 Budget schedule and forward to Executive Management for approval.		X	03/09/92 Monday
3.	Complete Budget Manual Revisions.		X	03/09/92 Monday
4.	Approved budget schedule received from Executive Management.	X		03/20/92 Friday
5.	Meet with Management Committee to review both the Budget manual and schedule.	X		03/20/92 Friday
6.	Approved Mission Statement/Business Strategy received Executive Management.	X		03/25/92 Wednesday
7.	*Distribute Budget/Profit Plan packages to the Segment Managers.*		*X*	*03/26/92 Thursday*
8.	Budget Analysts will call all Segment Managers to assist is or clarify the budget process.		X	03/30/92 Monday
9.	MSA System budget module initialized for the 1993 budget data.		X	03/30/92 Monday
10.	Formal written Business Plan submitted to Executive Management for review and inclusion in 1993 Profit Plan.	X		04/17/92 Friday
11.	*Budget/Profit Plan packages returned to Budget Department for verification and input.*	*X*		*04/17/92 Friday*
12.	Listing of budget packages not received to be referred to Executive Management.		X	04/20/92 Monday
13.	All entry of centrally planned accounts and allocations completed.		X	04/22/92 Wednesday
14.	Preliminary summary of production, capital expenditures and non-earning assets completed and forwarded to the Management Committee.		X	04/27/92 Monday
15.	Preliminary budget results forwarded to Business Segment Managers.		X	05/04/92 Monday
16.	*Preliminary summary of net interest margin forecast completed and submitted to the Management Committee for review. (FIRST SUBMISSION).*		*X*	*05/04/92 Monday*
17.	*Budget/Financial Analysts to meet with Management Committee/Segment Manager to review the 1993 Budget. (WEDNESDAY–FRIDAY).*		*X*	*05/06/92– 05/08/92*
18.	Budget adjustments submitted by Business Segments to the Budget Department for fiscal 1993.		X	05/12/92 Tuesday
19.	Data input of all adjustments complete and distributed to Segment Manager.		X	05/18/92 Monday
20.	Preliminary Profit Plan presented to Management Committee.		X	05/18/92 Monday
21.	*Management Committee Member/Segment Manager meet with CEO and COO for review and approval of 1993 Budget.*	*X*		*05/20/92– 05/27/92*
22.	Final budget revisions submitted to Budget Department.	X		05/29/92 Friday
23.	Adjustments processed and final 1993 Budget and Profit Plan submitted to Executive Management for approval.		X	06/08/92 Monday
24.	*SUBMISSION TO THE BOARD OF DIRECTORS.*		*X*	*06/18/92 Thursday*

markets. The development plan mostly applies to new markets and products. Bonuses should be given for new ideas.

The corporate development plan is concerned with:

- Discovering or creating new products
- Identifying financially lucrative areas and those having growth potential
- Ascertaining what resources are required in terms of assets, manpower, and so on
- Determining the feasibility of expanding operations into new areas.

CONTINGENCY PLANNING

Contingency planning is anticipating in advance unexpected circumstances, occurrences, and situations so that there can be a fast response to a crisis. All possible eventualities should be considered. Contingency planning involves identifying the possible occurrence, ascertaining warning signs and indicators of a problem, and formulating a response.

Contingency planning can be in the form of flexible (bracket) budgets. The plan should be modified if needed to generate the best results. There should be flexibility in the plan to adjust to new information and circumstances and to allow for the resolution of uncertainties.

ACTIVITY BUDGET

An activity budget is a revised analysis of a budget showing expenses at budgeted rates adjusted to actual production volume.

THE BUDGET PROCESS

In one company the author is familiar with, the Financial Planning Department issues guidelines to department managers. The manager then submits his or her plan to Financial Planning. The plan is returned to the manager if guidelines have not been adhered to. Financial Planning coordinates the plan from the bottom up. The budget goes down to the supervisory level. The company also uses program budgeting which involves the allocation of resources.

The budgeting process requires good, timely communication. Upper management must make its budget goals clear to departmental managers. In turn, the managers must explain departmental operating conditions and limitations.

DEPARTMENTAL BUDGETS

The decision units in the plan must be identified, and the manpower and dollar support at each decision unit must be noted. Department managers should plan for specific activities. They should put their budgets and trends in perspective relative to other departments in the company, to competing departments in other companies, and to industry norms. The manager should list the problems needing solution or the opportunities to be further capitalized on.

REPORTS

A typical report for manufacturing cost analysis is presented in Exhibit 2–5. Performance reports are typically issued monthly.

EXHIBIT 2–5 Manufacturing Cost Analysis

Product Line	Units Produced	Material	Labor	Overhead Variable	Overhead Fixed	Total Cost	Average Unit Cost	Average Selling Price	Gross Margin

BUDGET REVISION

A budget should be revised when it no longer acts as a useful planning and control device. Budgets should be revised when a major change in processes or operations occur, or when there are significant changes in salary rates. For example, additional competitors may enter the market with a product that sells at a lower price and is a good substitute for the company's product. This may make meeting the budgeted market share and sales unlikely. If management recognizes that even with increased promotional expenditures, budgeted sales are not realistic, all budgets affected should be revised. These revisions are preferable to using unattainable budgets. Budgets that are repeatedly revised are more informative as a control measure. For a one year budget, budget estimates may be revised quarterly. Budget revisions should be more frequent in unstable businesses.

PERFORMANCE MEASURES

Performance measures should also be directed at the lower levels in terms of each employee. Specific task performance should be measured. Employee performance may be measured by computing revenue per employee, man-hours per employee, and production volume to manhours.

CONTROL AND ANALYSIS

Control is important in budgeting. Budget figures may be checked for reasonableness by looking at relationships. The budgeted costs must be directly tied to planned production output. The manager must be able to strongly defend his initial budget figure and to obtain needed facts. Budget comparisons may be made by current year month to last year month, current year quarter to last year quarter, and cumulative year-to-date. A comparison is therefore made to similar time periods.

Costs should be examined by responsibility. Cost reduction is different from cost control. Cost reduction attempts to lower costs by improving manufacturing methods and procedures, work assignments, and product or service quality. Cost control includes cost reduction. Cost control attempts to obtain cost objectives within the operational setting. Value analysis is an evaluation of cost components in an operation so as to minimize them to achieve higher profits.

Compare the company's segments to similar segments in competing companies. Variations from the plan should be studied and controlled. The integrated (consolidated) plan is usually prepared yearly. A change in one department's plan will likely affect another department's plan.

CASE STUDY I: XYZ RENTAL CAR COMPANY

The Financial Planning department issues guidelines to department managers. The manager then formulates a plan and submits it to Financial Planning. The plan will be returned to the manager if the guidelines have not been adhered to. Financial Planning consolidates the plan from the bottom up. For the field this means from City/District to Zone, then from Zone to Region. For the support locations it means all the departments are consolidated. The "bottom-line" is one budget for the whole company.

The guidelines issued to managers are for such items as wage increases and supplies. Further, for the support department, there is an overhead procedure for such things such as: rent, insurance, benefits, postage, word processing, and computer usage. The guidelines for the field locations (rental locations) are different. They are more strict because a field location deals directly with a sale to a customer. A field location must budget for spending and income whereas a Headquarters department need only to budget its spending. The field also uses other guidelines such as economic conditions to plan for sales.

Salaries are considered one of the greatest expenses at World Headquarters. However, they are also one of the easiest expenses to forecast. A manager knows how much his employees' salaries are. He/she can then budget using the current pay scale plus any increases expected for the upcoming year. However, fringe benefits are difficult to budget. Medical benefits are a running cost; they can be budgeted because the trend is easy to follow. The cost to the company is constantly increasing and that makes it harder for planning managers to predict their future cost.

At the end of each month, a statement is prepared and issued to each department by the Financial Planning department. The statement has the following four columns of information for every line item in the department's budget: actual, budget, prior year's figure, and variance of actual to budget. The manager of the department can determine how well he/she is doing relative to the budget. If the variance is either significantly favorable or unfavorable, then someone from Financial Planning may contact the manager to discuss it. This is more important if the variance is unfavorable. This statement sent to the World Headquarters departments is much different from the statements issued to the field locations in one major way. The field locations have lines for income but the World Headquarters departments' statements have only expenditures.

A unit is a car rental transaction. In forecasting, the company will determine how many transactions it expects to have for the forthcoming year. With that number, the company could then estimate, or budget for, the number of cars it will require to handle the number of expected transactions. This is then taken another step as the next major resource is examined. With the number of transactions and cars forecasted, the company can now budget for the number of people needed to handle the transactions.

To come up with the first number of transactions, the company employs a complex method. Trends are evaluated by first studying previous experience. Trends over the past years could help determine trends for the upcoming years. However, other factors must be taken into account. Many outside issues such as economic and political conditions must also be considered.

A plan is not written in stone. For example, if today is the first day of business, then a twelve-month plan is developed. At the sixth month of the plan, the past six months of actual figures are appraised and there is a reforecast for the next six months.

Each employee submits a detailed report projecting expenses for the new year. The employee includes all items over which he/she has control. Similarly, each employee computes the amount of sales expected. Now the upward process begins. These statements are gathered by the department supervisor who then consolidates them into one budget for that specific department.

The departmental budgets are entered into the computer system where they can be evaluated by upper management. At this time, someone may contact the department supervisor if the budget does not seem right. This process may take a while depending on how much all parties involved agree to the numbers. When this is done, a final version of the overall company budget is established.

Sales people receive weekly statements that compare the budgeted sales with the actual sales. This gives the sales people an idea of how well they are on track with their goals. They also receive quarterly reports that include year-to-date figures. On a monthly basis, every employee receives a statement that details their expenditures in a similar fashion.

CASE STUDY II: A MANUFACTURING COMPANY

The financial policy of ABC Company is to formulate departmental operating budgets annually for each functional area comprising of Fixed Manufacturing, General and Administrative, Research and Development, and Marketing and Sales. Let's use as an example the Sales Information (SI) department within the Sales area. The purpose of the SI department is to understand the business needs of both Headquarter and Field sales personnel and to furnish information assisting them in creating business solutions to obtain a competitive edge. Let us also take a specific project (e.g., a Sales Force Automation project in the SI department). Reference is made to this project to illustrate the financial policies required for justifying and obtaining funding as part of the overall budget.

The Director of each department within the Sales organization presents the annual strategic plan and budget to the Vice President of Sales and President of the company. The elements of the strategic plan and budget describe the present business environment, major issues and objectives, and the funding needed to satisfy these objectives. The departmental operating budgets and strategic plans are then used as a management tool which can provide an overview of annual expenditures and manpower needs to aid in controlling expenses for each functional area of the company. These budgets are then consolidated in preparing the Annual Operating Budget and, as such, serve as a gauge for measuring overall management performance. The Executive Vice President of Marketing and Sales must approve the departmental budgets before incorporation into the Annual Operating Budget. Executive approval is obtained during the presentation of the Annual Operating Budget which is reviewed, modified, and finalized by Senior Management. Final versions must then be approved by the Chairman and Chief Executive Officer before distribution and submission to the Corporate Budget department. Presentations are also made quarterly to Executive Management for revisions.

A Capital Expenditures Forecast is formulated as an estimate of the Company's expected capital spending requirement over the subsequent five year period. It includes all approved projects, whether or not the expenditures have been incurred, and all planned projects having expected expenditures during the period. Projects exceeding one million dollars must be itemized in the forecast and segregated between planned and approved projects. These projects must then be analyzed by type (increased capacity, cost reduction, new venture, administrative requirements, and so on). A commentary detailing the objective and expected benefits from the project is required. The Capital Expenditure Forecast is prepared and reviewed quarterly and distributed to all Executive Management, including the Chairman and Chief Executive Officer. At each review, a detailed package of information is presented that includes a comparison of the actual dollars spent relative to the amount forecasted. An updated Capital Forecast is then prepared.

An illustration of how the original budget and strategic plan was prepared for the Sales Information department is a good example of how the budget process works. The current business environment, key issues and objectives are now explained. During the past year, the Sales Information department, in cooperation with the Information Services Group, began the process of making fundamental changes to the systems infrastructure within the Sales organization. This was needed to bring informational systems into alignment with overall Sales strategies of customized merchandising options, improving product differentiation, and decentralized decision-making authority. The key issues are:

1. to provide tools that all users timely direct access to information, and

2. to develop applications that minimize administrative time in the field sales force so that a greater proportion of effort can be devoted to selling products.

Thus, one major objective for the upcoming year is to improve sales force productivity in information handling. One project that is currently seeking financial approval and, consequently, must also be budgeted for, is a Sales Force Automation project. The scope of this project is very broad, but for our purposes will provide electronic data collection and reporting capabilities, increase accuracy and timeliness of data, reduce the administrative burden and improve the efficiency of communication with electronic mail and fax capabilities. The estimated cost of this project is 30 million dollars for about 2,500 sales representatives and 500 account managers in the company's sales force. These monies must be budgeted in the Original Budget and in the Capital Expenditures Forecast.

The budgeting process for project approval varies depending upon the total cost of the project. It is company policy that for all projects of $100,000 or more, a capital appropriation request form must be prepared. These appropriation requests assist management in appraising each capital investment in terms of its ultimate contribution to the company's growth. These investments are continuously reviewed, approved and controlled through the capital budget, five year plan and/or capital appropriation policies and procedures. According to company financial policy and in reference to this Sales Force Automation project, capital investments are defined as expenditures for computer equipment and product development. This refers to the purchase of handheld computers and the customized software application that will be developed solely for the firm's sales force. Each request requires final approval from different authorization levels of the executive staff based on the dollar amount of the project. The specific approval requirements are:

Project Amount	Final Approval
$3,000,000 or above	Board of Directors
$1,500,000–$2,999,999	Office of the Chairman
$500,000–$1,499,000	Chairman, President, Vice Chairman, or Executive Vice-President
$100,000–$499,999	Functional Director and Vice-President
Less than $100,000	Functional Director

In addition, all capital appropriation requests irrespective of amount, must be approved by the Controller.

Each appropriation request contains a memorandum requesting approval as well as the following data:

- Description and location of project
- Purpose of project
- Capital funds needed
- Economic and financial effect including cash flow and return on investment
- Justification for committing funds.

Once the approvals have been secured, the company can only then make commitments for the project stipulated in the request. No work can be started or monies spent for a project until final approval has been secured. This process usually takes about six to eight weeks and therefore adequate lead time must be allotted in the overall project management process.

The preparation of the capital appropriation form should be completed by the functional area initiating the request as follows:

- Supply technical information such as flow diagrams, simplified layouts, or any type of information which explains the proposed project.

- Provide financial information such as savings and list estimates in enough detail that internal rates of return can be computed and future project performance can be monitored.

- Provide a cover letter explaining project scope, alternatives, and benefits to be obtained from the project.

However, in most instances, before the capital appropriation request form is prepared by the project leaders, the scope and benefits of the project are presented to management to gain a sponsor and receive the necessary "buy-in."

The Sales Force Automation (SFA) project was divided into three phases: prototype, pilot, and national rollout. Separate project funding and capital appropriation forms will be requested and prepared (if needed). At the initial presentations, management must be presented with the total cost of the project in order to determine if it wants to commit to any one phase of the project. Each phase of the project acts as a "kill point" in the event that the project is unsuccessful in meeting the stated objectives. As stated earlier, the total estimated cost of this SFA project, which must be planned for in the Original Budget for 1996, is $30 million. The sponsor of the project is the Sales organization; however, the Sales Information group and the Information Services group are responsible for preparing the capital appropriation request form. The cover letter and memoranda are prepared by the project leader in the SI group to explain from a financial perspective why the technology was selected, as well as the benefits that will potentially be forthcoming. The technical flows and associated spreadsheets detailing costs such as hardware and software, communication costs, maintenance and support are prepared by the Information Services project leader. The prototype phase has only been estimated to cost approximately $25,000 and, therefore, does not require a separate form. The objective of this phase is to test the feasibility of using a handheld computer by the sales representatives. In lieu of a contract between the company and the vendor who will provide the necessary services, a letter of "good faith" will be issued for $25,000. This letter will state how the monies will be utilized and that, if this phase is successful, the $25,000 will be applied to the total cost of the project.

The estimated cost of the pilot phase is $3.0 million. The purpose of this phase is to develop and test the software and hardware with a small group of Sales Reps and Account Managers for approximately nine months. The majority of software development costs are incurred here and are mostly one time setup costs that will not be incurred again in any other phase. In addition, the cost of hardware for the pilot users is included. Very detailed spreadsheets are prepared to identify exactly how the monies will be spent and monitored throughout the pilot. This analysis will later be used as one method of determining the success of the pilot. All of the information from the cost analysis to benefits that have been used to justify the project is required by the Director of the SI group to understand and refer to when explaining the budget and request for project funding. It is crucial that accurate costs are represented in this pilot phase because if there is not enough money in the original budget, justifying and completing the project can be a problem later. The remaining funds for the national rollout primarily represent the cost of hardware for the sales representatives and account managers, as well as the costs for training, supporting and maintaining the SFA system. One stipulation of this project is that each phase of the project is dependent on the success of the prior phase and requires senior management evaluation and approval to continue to provide the necessary funding. Because of the large capital expenditure, management is involved and concerned about the feedback received after each phase.

The company's sales force is one of the largest in the consumer goods industry. However, with regard to sales force automation, the company is behind the times. Major competitors have already been automated for a number of years. Justifying this type of project is a difficult process for the company since many of the benefits gained from an automation project are soft, intangible benefits. Therefore, the results of a return on investment do not look very attractive to upper management in reference to the total dollars required for the project. Consequently, approving a project of this nature and also getting the overall Sales Information departmental budget approved can be difficult. Further, the annual recurring costs of maintaining the SFA system can be relatively high in comparison to the current way of doing business of using a paper system to capture in-store data. Thus, the company's Sales and Executive management must decide if the value gained from obtaining more timely and accurate information to make better strategic business decisions, in addition to reducing the current administrative time incurred by the Sales Reps and Account Managers allowing them to make better quality sales calls, justifies the large capital investment.

This decision involves a significant risk factor, as is typical of any automation project, that makes it crucial that the project be properly "sold in" at all levels, including the President of the company. If the project is not properly "sold in" throughout, this approval process can take an unusually long time and/or could potentially not get approved. In short, the capital appropriation request process should just be a formality in the project approval process.

As each phase of the project is completed and appraised, presentations to management must be made to communicate the status of the project and to review the actual costs spent relative to that budgeted for. If the project is over-budget or if there is a considerable change in scope, a detailed justification process is needed. This is also another "kill point" for the project. If a modification is made to the original scope of the project and a reallocation of funds is necessary, additional approvals are required. At a minimum, the approval of the financial Vice President and the controller is required. It is preferred that this does not occur often.

Overall the financial policies and procedures at the company are a structured method of controlling and monitoring how monies and resources should be allocated. At times, senior management must make some difficult decisions on project approvals to set priorities and the overall strategy for the company. These goals and priorities must be effectively communicated to each departmental Director and his staff to provide the best solution that will continue to make the company a strong competitor.

CASE STUDY III: A SMALL IMAGING MANUFACTURER

This case study analyzes a manufacturer's business planning schedule from a corporate budgetary perspective and analyzes the company's Eastern Sales Region's operating budget.

Historically, the company's budgeting strategy has been participatory. Input is required from all levels of corporate and field management. The budget process is used extensively to communicate the company's goals to all departments and sub-units. Since the manufacturer is still a relatively small company, senior management invites input from all employees on product and market direction.

Overall, the corporate budgeting strategy is fairly standard. The sales forecasts and budgets are created and are then followed by development of the production budget and the cost budgets. Finally all operating budgets and budgeted balance sheets are created. The company implements more of a top down approach to its budgeting process as compared to a more standard bottom up approach.

Another reason to budget revenues in this way is because the market is causing a basic transformation of the company's product mix. Traditionally a hardware based vendor, the company now had to develop and produce more software product lines. The company is unsure as to how its new product mix would be processed by perspective customers.

The company is now moving towards a more traditional bottom up budgeting strategy. As the company's products mature along with the marketplace, it will be easier to implement this strategy.

In July, the company determines its product delivery schedules for the upcoming year. This schedule is very flexible due to the fast growing and changing document image processing marketplace. As new products hit the market from competitors, the company is forced to shift product delivery schedules ahead by as much as nine months. The marketing department, along with domestic and international sales management, is the key contributor in creating the company's product delivery schedule.

In August, several preliminary budget meetings are held. The profit and loss forecast is presented and analyzed. Preliminary facilities and management information systems spending budgets are also created. Only over the last two years has the company begun to stress the Management Information System (MIS) spending budget. As the company has grown from a revenue and employee standpoint, its management information systems department has not kept up. Small departmental databases of information exist and cannot be accessed by outside departments. Availability of personal computer hardware and software to field sales offices has not been adequate. Lack of sufficient telecommunication equipment has also created many operational problems.

Preliminary domestic and international sales planning assumptions are also discussed in August. Final copies of the departmental budget packages and guidelines are sent out to all corporate, regional, and district managers. These guides outline the major planning assumptions, guidelines, and instructions that management will need to complete the planning process. The guide discusses company wide business planning targets, salary and fringe benefit assumptions, capital budget expenditures, and expense budget assumptions. It includes sample forms and electronic spreadsheet models to assist in the planning process. Corporate staff members are assigned to each department to provide assistance.

In September, all departments are required to complete preliminary budgets according to the goals set in the planning guides. Projected domestic and international headcounts are submitted for evaluation. First pass budgets and sales forecasts are due by the end of the month.

The most difficult step in this stage of the company's corporate budgeting process is sales forecasting. The volatile document image processing marketplace causes the company to make quick changes in its forecasts. Every week, the district and regional sales managers report both current sales opportunities and sales pipeline projections. This field input is vital in developing the company's sales forecast for the following year. Through statistical analysis of sales data, the average time to close a sale from the time of initial customer contact is about 16 months. Therefore, sales pipeline analysis and sales success ratios are very instrumental in helping create the sales forecast.

The company's market research and planning departments play a key role in developing the sales forecast. Analysis of competitive product announcements and sales loss reports help identify the direction of the image marketplace. Data from market research groups, consulting firms, trade publications and image industry associations also help shape the sales forecast.

Due to recent changes in the market, it has been forced to plan for more software and services revenue and less hardware revenue. The market is demanding less dependence on hardware and is forcing all image processing companies to provide more software functionality and integration services. This has caused a trickle down effect on all departments within the company. New business units such as the Professional Services Group have been created to address these new market requirements. Research & Development, Marketing, and Customer Services departments have adjusted their budgets in order to properly perform under these new market conditions.

Another difficult component of the master budget is the creation of the production and cost budgets. It designs and builds sophisticated robotic based optical jukeboxes along with microprocessor based image servers. These devices require thousands of components and subassemblies. The company implements a standard cost system to help develop its budgets. Manufacturing management determines the expected production of all its products from the output of the sales forecast. Expected component and subassembly quantities are calculated and standard costs are applied. In addition, factory overhead is applied to each of the company's product lines and is based on various production factors. This budget is continuously monitored through variance analysis.

Many of the components of the company's master budget are due for first pass evaluation in the month of October. The domestic and international sales forecasts are needed for profit and loss projections. First past capital budgets are reviewed in October so that consolidated balance sheets can be created.

In November, all operating budgets, capital budgets, and final balance sheets are due in corporate headquarters. In addition, all departments are required to create a narrative or presentation that will be incorporated into the presentation made to the company's Board of Directors in December. These narratives explain the goals and objectives of each department from both a quantitative and qualitative standpoint.

CASE STUDY IV: DEF CABLE COMPANY

At corporate headquarters a team of executives, consisting of the President of Cable Operations, Vice President of Technology/Engineering, Vice President of Programming, Vice President of Sales and Marketing, Chief Financial Officer and Corporate Controller, prepares the corporation's direction and strategies pertaining to their disciplines. Multiple meetings arrive at the goals, objectives, and strategies of the company.

The executives report their plans and objectives regarding the future to the Chief Executive Officer. The goals and financial targets for short- and long-term planning are then determined by the Chief Operating Officer and the executive staff. The annual targets set for the cable TV company are based on the following two criteria: operating income performance and subscriber growth.

The operating income has traditionally been expected to increase 15 percent over the prior year's actuals for the mature cable systems. However, in the recent depressed markets, the operating income target expectations have been decreased to approximately 11 percent. The targeted increase will vary depending on the status and nature of each individual cable TV system and its maturity.

The subscriber target has historically been a 5 to 6 percent increase over the prior year's base. This target has also been lowered to 3 to 5 percent, depending on the level of the penetration of subscribers at each cable system.

The executives' recommendations to the Chief Operating Officer take into account financial assumptions. When a decision regarding strategic direction of the company is made, a detailed guideline is prepared by the Vice President of Budget and Planning. This guideline details corporate requirements regarding the strategic direction both for a five-year period containing high level financial data and for a one-year financial view containing detailed financial and operational data. The overall strategic direction for cable systems in 1993 was:

- Subscribers growth
- Upgraded services
- New programming
- Revenue stimulation focusing on Pay-Per-View marketing.

In a pre-budget planning meeting the Chief Operating Officer of the Company announces the corporate strategies and targets. A guideline and a corporate assumption package, which includes the budgeting calendar stating the budget submission and review dates, are sent to each entity for the preparation of their short- and long-term budget planning.

Critical assumptions used in creating the plan are identified and explained. These assumptions include economic, political, housing development, new technology, competition, marketing, and pricing.

The entity identifies its business strategies to achieve its objectives. Specific actions to achieve these strategies are clearly identified. Key strategies associated with revenue stimulation initiatives are included. In development of key strategies the system's management considers the following items:

- Subscriber base increase through additional plant construction, rebuilding of the defective plants, extension of existing cable, or aggressive marketing focusing on the existing market

- Strategies to increase revenues through aggressive upgrade campaign, rate increase, subscriber base increase, or increase in Pay-Per-View and other ancillary revenues

- Expense control strategies which may include reduction and control of all discretionary expenses such as Travel and Entertainment, limited compensation increases, or reduction of existing headcount

- Strategies to reduce delinquent subscribers and bad debt loss which may include expansion of collection department or the use of outside agencies or adapting a more aggressive disconnect approach for non-pay subscribers.

CASE STUDY V: A BEVERAGE COMPANY

In its budget, a beverage company predicts its fixed and variable costs. For bills that are fixed, the budgeter does not increase the budget for that bill unless he is given notice in the unlikely case that the fixed cost will increase. For variable costs from the prior year, such as electricity and advertising, the budgeter takes a conservative stance and increases the budget for the expenses by 4 percent due to inflation. Also possible increases in sales will result in a higher cost in the distribution of beverages.

Certain expenses, like advertising, snow removal, cable, car allowance, donations, dues/subscriptions, fire prevention, garbage, insurance, license/permits, postage, promotion, repairs/maintenance, and security monitoring are divided by the eight stores equally. Auto, electric/gas, direct salary, and bank services are divided by the sales percentage. Floor waxing is divided by four stores. With professional fees, one store pays $15,000 while the remaining $5,000 is paid equally by the other seven stores. Rent for the stores are taken from the actual rent from each store with an increase of 7.5 percent. From this information is calculated the total operating expenses needed to run the company. The net profit or loss is derived by the gross profit less the total operating expenses. The interest expense and long-term debt are taken actually from the prior year.

The budgeter is usually off about less than 1 percent in his estimates. Since a beverage company is mostly a stable business, it is easy for the budgeter to predict how the business will do each year. However, long-range forecasts can be problematic, since the economy tends to change yearly and the fickleness of the consumer has a bearing on the budgeted figures.

CASE STUDY VI: A SHOE COMPANY

A shoe company uses the following budgeting procedure. Around June in the year prior to the proposed budgeted year, a meeting is held as to the company's future. Major changes and financial objectives for each segment of the business are addressed. A time schedule is reviewed and agreements are made as to the feasibility of adhering to these time frames.

In July, formal packages are sent to each subsidiary. These packages are sent by the President. They are forms of the various documents which will be used to put together the profit plan or budget.

A calendar is presented which outlines key dates for the planning process. A strategic overview is detailed for each division. The individual segments of the company must determine critical issues to their particular areas.

Based on the corporate strategy, each segment is required to develop a plan that will support the corporate objective. Each division is required to answer primary questions in order to build its strategy. Examples include, but are not limited to, the following:

- Major risks
- Steps to improve productivity
- Options to expand the business.

REFERENCES

1. Patrick Below, George Morrisey, and Betty Acomb, *The Executive Guide to Strategic Planning* (California: Jossey-Bass Publishers, 1987).

2. York Freund, "Critical Success Factors," *Planning Review,* July/August 1988, pp. 20–27.

3. William Guth, *Handbook of Business Strategy* (Mass.: Warren, Gorham and Lamont, 1985).

4. Thomas Lynch, "Business Divisions: A Performance Evaluation," *Financial Executive,* November 1984, pp. 30–43.

5. Kenneth Merchant, "How Challenging Should Profit Budget Targets Be?" *Management Accounting,* November 1990, pp. 46–48.

6. George Steiner, *Strategic Planning—What Every Manager Must Know* (New York: The Free Press, 1979).

Chapter 3

Administering the Budget

A budget should be prepared for each department. Divisional budgets should be consolidated in a binder, and each department should have a separate file folder. The Chief Executive Officer (CEO) should distribute an executive budget memorandum to each department manager detailing the schedule, policies, and benchmarks for next year's budget. Responsibility should be assigned for collection and consolidation of budget information. Budget instructions, forms, and timetables should be provided. Budget forms should be simple and easy to follow.

The budget committee should consider the following items before approving a budget: accuracy of budgetary numbers, reliability of information upon which estimates are based, budget integration, reliability of source data, budgetary assumptions, and achievability of budgetary goals.

TYPES OF REPORTS

Long-term reports may be for the company as a whole or for specific areas. The benefit derived from reports should justify its cost. The three major types of budget reports are for planning, control, and information.

Planning reports may be short term, looking at the company as a whole, each division, each department, and each responsibility center within the department. Short-term planning reports may be of income, cash flow, net assets, and capital expenditures. The reports should be prepared regularly. Special studies may be performed of "problem" segments not performing well. The special studies may be of product or service lines, activities or functions, geographic areas, salesperson performance, and warehousing.

Control reports concentrate on performance effectiveness and areas needing improvement. Budget to actual figures are compared by product, service, territory, and manpower.

Information reports assist in planning and policy formulation. The reports show areas of growth or contraction. They may be in dollars, units, percentages, or ratios. Trends are shown over time. An example of an informative ratio is selling expense to revenue. Informational reports study the trend in earnings, profit by product or service, profit by territory, and profit by customer.

Reports for upper management are comprehensive summaries of overall corporate operations. Top management generally prefers narrative reports. Reports are also prepared for special events of concern to top management. Adequate detail should be provided as needed.

Middle-management reports include summarized information and detailed information on daily operations. A brief report should be presented at budget meetings.

Lower-level management reports typically deal with daily coordination and control operations. The reports usually emphasize production. Exception reports should be prepared indicating problems. Budget reports inform managers of progress made in meeting budgets and what went wrong, if anything.

A critical area should be reported upon more frequently. The frequency of reporting is less as the level of responsibility becomes higher.

Budget reports depend on the requirements of the situation and user. Budget reports should contain the following data:

- Trends over the years
- Comparison to industry norms
- Comparison of actual to budget with explanation and responsible party for variances. Follow-up procedures are needed for control.

Reports should get to the main points. Each report should begin with a summary followed by detailed information and should be comprehendable to those using them. The emphasis should be on clarity rather than complexity. Reports should be logically organized, relevant, and concise. Reports should be updated.

Reports may contain schedules, explanations, graphs, and tables. Reports should contain recommendations and highlight problem areas. The reports should be computerized. An illustrative budget worksheet appears in Exhibit 3–1.

EXHIBIT 3–1 Budget Worksheet

Account:	Date:
For the period:	Time period:
Month	*Components*
Explanation:	
Assumptions:	
Analysis:	

Reports may be of the following types:

Periodic Reports. These are reports prepared at regular intervals. There is a continual comparison between budget and actual figures. They are the usual source of information to maintain control. They may be issued semi-annually, quarterly, monthly, and so on. Monthly reports are most common. Some information may be reported daily (e.g., shipments), while other information may be reported weekly (e.g., sales and production). The timeliness depends on cost/benefit analysis.

Advance Reports. Important partial information may be reported before all information is available for a periodic report. Delay in reporting this information will cause a managerial problem. "Flash reports" should be issued for unusual occurrences that must be reported upon immediately.

Special Studies. Special reports are issued for a specific, nonroutine purpose. Special studies may be required for problem situations or if a negative trend exists such as costs keep rising even though a cost reduction program has been implemented.

Budget reports may contain the following supplementary information depending upon need:

- Percent of capacity utilization
- Changes in marketing and distribution
- Change in selling price
- Average selling price
- Sales volume and units produced
- Distribution cost relative to sales
- Effect on sales of new product introduction, dropping products, and entering new product lines
- Change in the number of employees and manhours.

A performance report should be prepared for each responsibility center going from the lowest level to the highest level. It indicates whether goals

EXHIBIT 3–2 Summary of Department Performance

Item and Description	Actual	Budget	Percent of Budget

have been accomplished. Performance reports evaluate efficiency, and should be repetitive covering a short time period.

The performance-to-budget report should contain the following information by department for year-to-date and for current period:

- Cost accounts
- Budget
- Actual
- Variances and reasons.

An illustrative report summarizing departmental performance is shown in Exhibit 3–2.

A performance-to-budget report (cost and variance statement) should be kept for feedback. It is used by management to evaluate the degree to which operating managers meet their budget. An illustrative performance report is presented in Exhibit 3–3.

Monthly performance reports should contain variances for the month and cumulative variances to date for the year. Variances can be expressed in dollars and as a percentage of budget.

The statistics and graphics in the report should vary depending upon user preference. For example, marketing managers are less inclined to receive statistical data than engineers. However, marketing managers prefer graphs. Graphs may be more informative in presenting relationships and summary comparisons. Graphs include diagrams and charts.

Reports should be timely. If reports are issued periodically, they should be on schedule. If reports must be delayed, a short update should be presented.

THE BUDGET MANUAL

The budget manual communicates throughout the company the policies and procedures for budget preparation. It is the activities and rules to be followed in preparing a budget. It tells how the budget should be used by managers and who is responsible for the different aspects of the budgeting process including preparation, presentation, reporting, evaluation, and approval. It should list positions rather than names to avoid unnecessary updating. A preparation chart would be helpful. It provides the budgeting steps and aids in coopera-

EXHIBIT 3–3 Performance-to-Budget Report

Department Name and Number   *Period*
Operating Manager

	Year-to-Date				Activity	This Period			
---	---	---	---	---	Budget Actual Percent of Budget	---	---	---	---
	Budget	*Actual*	*Variance*	*Account*		*Budget*	*Actual*	*Variance*	*Reason for Variance*	*Extra Budgetary Allowance for Variance*
Totals										

55

tion and coordination. The procedures to be followed to revise the budget based on changing conditions and goals should be specified. For example, revisions may be needed because of changing objectives, new methods, changing economic environment, and errors. The budget manual should be targeted to end-users, and should receive participation from all affected managerial levels.

The budget manual stipulates authority, responsibility, and duties; fosters standardization; documents procedures; simplifies the process; provides communication; answers users questions; enhances supervision; and fosters training. The manual should contain terminology and complicated accounting reports that are unfamiliar to nonaccountants.

The manual includes the following:

- Standardized forms, lists and reports
- Instructions
- Format and coverage of performance reports
- Administrative details
- Follow-up procedures.

Each department should be included in a separate section of the manual with an index tab. Operating department managers and employees should provide input in the preparation of the budget manual. Managers and workers may have different information to impart. There may be operating problems, constraints, and limitations that must receive attention. There should be a standard cost table for different types of expenses used by managers of different departments throughout the organization. This allows for consistency and uniformity.

The manual should be in looseleaf form so pages may be substituted for updates. The budget manual should contain:

- Budget objectives, purposes, procedures, guidelines, and policy
- Desired accomplishments
- Data description
- Personnel duties (who is to prepare, review, approve, and revise the budget).
- Who has authority and responsibility for budget items (There should be a designation of manager or subordinate who will perform the activity.)
- Approval requirements
- Who is to evaluate the difference between budget and actual figures, and who is to take corrective action and when

- Budget timetable
- Illustrative forms, lists, and reports
- Glossary of terminology
- Instructions to complete budget activities
- Uses of budget information
- Policies for budget modification and update calendar
- Communication between upper management and subordinates
- Coordination between departments of the budget
- Explanatory footnotes.

The layout of the manual should enhance its clarity and conciseness. It should be easy to understand for nonaccountants, so it should not contain complex or technical language. It should be arranged logically and orderly with a user friendly index and should be updated as conditions warrant, organized, idea—oriented, and descriptive. It should look professional in design, color, print size, etc., so it is taken seriously by users.

There are many advantages to the budget manual including simplification and standardization of budget procedures. It acts as a reference and provides an organized approach to the budget process. It provides consistency between departments and provides job description guidance to new employees and assists current employees to adjust to new positions when transferred or promoted. The manual helps employee continuity in doing the job.

THE BUDGET SHEET

A budget sheet should be designed to record the information used by the operating manager and budget preparer. The budgeting sheet should include the following information:

- Historical cost records used
- Cost formulas
- Changes in operating conditions
- Forseeable conditions.

A budget data sheet should be prepared for each cost account in each department or cost center. Attached to the data sheet may be graphs, workpaper analysis, mathematical and statistical calculations, and so on. Budget revisions may also be incorporated.

Fixed, variable, and mixed costs are shown on the data sheet. Material,

EXHIBIT 3–4 Budget Data Sheet

	Period Covered
Date prepared	Cost center name and number
Date accepted	Account name and number
Date approved	Activity unit
Date revised	Reason for revision
	Amount of revision
Items	*Costs*
	Total Fixed Variable Semivariable
Total budget	

labor, and overhead should be listed. The sheets should be initialed by those preparing and approving them. The allowances specified in the data sheet should be mutually agreed upon by the preparer and operating manager.

A budget summary sheet should also be prepared summarizing the department's budget by listing each budgeted cost and the budget allowance based on average activity. The summary sheet summarizes the departmental budget data sheets. The operating departmental manager should always be provided with a copy of the budget summary sheet and budget data sheets.

A typical budget data sheet is shown in Exhibit 3–4. A typical budget summary sheet is shown in Exhibit 3–5.

A budget data book should be kept to keep the budgeting information in an orderly manner. The book contains by department the budget data sheets, supporting worksheets and analysis, and budget summary sheets.

BUDGET AUDIT

A budget audit examines whether the budgeting process is effectively operating. It is an evaluation of the budgeting effort. The budget audit examines techniques, procedures, motivation, and budget effectiveness. Effective budgeting should be dynamic.

A budget audit detects problems in the budgeting process. It should be conducted every two to three years by an independent party not a part of the budget staff. The budget auditor should report to upper management, who can

EXHIBIT 3–5 Budget Summary Sheet

Cost center name and number			Prepared date			
			Accepted date			
			Approved date			
		Cost	*Budget Amount*			*Per Unit*
Account Name	*Number*	*Classification*	*Fixed*	*Variable*	*Mixed*	*Cost*

take appropriate action. An outside consultant should be independent and objective, and should provide fresh ideas.

There is an audit plan which assists in arriving at corrective action. The budget audit considers:

- Cost trends and controls
- Budget revisions
- How adequately costs were analyzed
- How costs were identified and classified
- Looseness or tightness of budget allowances
- Completeness of budget documentation, records, and schedules
- Degree of participation by managers and workers
- Quality of supportive data
- The degree of subjectivity involved.

BUDGET CALENDAR

A budget calendar should be prepared for the timing of each aspect or operation of the budget. A timetable must be given to operating managers to submit their proposed budgets so the overall company budget may be prepared on time. The schedule of due dates for documents and reports must be adhered to. Review and approval dates should also be specified. The schedule dates should be realistic and attainable.

A company can begin the process by issuing the Budget Preparation Calendar consisting of an overall review of each sequential step in the budgeting process. Accompanying this is a rough time schedule in which the budgeting process will be implemented identifying deadlines, the personnel responsible, and those to receive this information. The plan furnishes the structure of the budgeting process and the overall objectives. These items are crucial for the budgeting process and must be completed before the process can proceed. An illustrative budget calendar for a company is presented in Exhibit 3–6.

EXHIBIT 3–6 ABC Company Budget Preparation Calendar Fiscal 1994

1. General Guidelines issued to Senior Management Staff by President gives the broad objectives of the company for the ensuing year. These objectives must be specific enough to provide divisions with adequate direction and yet they should be broad enough so as not to prevent creativity. General indication of gross margins, operating profit, net profit and productivity are some of the areas to be addressed.

2. New Products Forecast will provide an indication of new/improved products to be available next year. This will include estimated availability dates and likely segment as applicable.

3. Discussion of Action Plans with particular emphasis on how to achieve objectives (on individual basis) with Senior Management by President. Each Senior Vice President will produce in writing and justify in detail how he will achieve the objectives for next year. For example, Sales and Marketing should give expected sales by Regions supported by level of sales force and related promotional expenses (advertising/conventions and product giveaway).

   (a) Headcount by department/division to support objectives must be justified by each Senior Vice President.

   (b) C.E. Projections outline the major projects to be executed in the budget year as determined by the Department Managers and Facilities Engineering. Projects should be ranked in order of priority with pros and cons of doing and not doing the projects.

   (c) Inventory Projections as furnished by Vice President of respective user department (Film, Chemistry, and Equipment) should indicate the levels of the inventory by major product lines. Where applicable, a minimum, desired and maximum levels to support production and sales should be given.

4. Fringe Benefits Package including payroll increase prepared by the Human Resources Department should outline the basis of the company's contribution of the major programs and fringes. Both quantitative and qualitative factors should be presented. Major areas to be covered are incentives, medical, dental, retirement, life insurance and workmen's compensation. Other expenditures such as FICA and unemployment tax will be computed by Corporate Planning.

5. Budget Package issued to departmental managers by Corporate Planning contains the necessary forms and instructions to prepare the Budget.

6. Preliminary P&L Fiscal 1994 based on sales forecast and assumptions in 2–4 will be prepared by Corporate Planning. This will give an indication of the likely outcome of the actions contemplated. Major directions and proactive measures will then be taken to manage the budget process in line with the President's guidelines.

7. Final Sales Forecast as issued to Senior Management Staff by Sales/Marketing would give sales volume and dollars by major product lines. For example, film and paper (sq.ft. & $), chemistry (quantity & $) and equipment (unit & $). Film and paper should be analyzed by Region, OEM, International, Dealers, National Accounts and Others. New products should be clearly identified. Adequate explanation should be given for any significant changes (over the current year) in volume or price.

8. Departmental Expense Budgets are prepared (monthly basis) by department managers and approved by their respective Senior Management. These include all the operating expenses (excluding payroll, fringes, depreciation and facilities cost) as prepared in the Basic Budget Worksheet.

9. Preliminary Budget incorporate data and payroll, fringes, depreciation and facilities cost as computed by Corporate Planning. The preliminary data is returned to managers for review and any necessary changes.

10. Revisions made by managers to preliminary budget are sent to Corporate Planning on a timely basis.

11–13. Budgets are sent to Senior Vice President and meetings are held to review budgets. Senior

Vice Presidents will present their budgets and negotiate the necessary changes to bring budgets in line with corporate objectives.

14. Preparation of Budgeted Profit and Loss, Cash Flow, Balance Sheet by Corporate Planning and Finance Division. This will provide Management with the financial picture of the budget year.

15–16. Budget Package sent to Senior Management for review and approval prior to presentation to ABC Company.

17. Presentation of Budget Package by Corporate Planning and President to ABC Company for approval.

18. Approved Budgets issued to respective departments. These will form the guide as to the upper limit of expenditures for the coming year.

Part 2

FINANCIAL ANALYSIS

Chapter 4

Analysis of Cost Behavior and Flexible Budgeting

Not all costs behave in the same way. There are certain costs that vary in proportion to changes in volume or activity, such as labor hours and machine hours. There are other costs that do not change even though volume changes. An understanding of cost behavior is helpful to budgeters, cost analysts, and managerial accountants as follows:

- Flexible budgeting
- Break-even and contribution margin analysis
- Appraisal of divisional performance
- Short-term choice decisions.

A LOOK AT COSTS BY BEHAVIOR

Depending on how a cost will react or respond to changes in the level of activity, costs may be viewed as variable, fixed, or mixed (semi-variable). This classification is made within a specified range of activity called the *relevant range*. The relevant range is the volume zone within which the behavior of variable costs, fixed costs, and selling prices can be predicted with reasonable accuracy.

Variable Costs

Variable costs vary in total with changes in volume or level of activity. Examples of variable costs include the costs of direct materials, direct labor, and sales commissions. The following factory overhead items fall into the variable cost category:

- Supplies
- Fuel and power
- Spoilage and defective work
- Receiving costs
- Overtime premium

Fixed Costs

Fixed costs do not change in total regardless of the volume or level of activity. Examples include advertising expense, salaries, and depreciation. The following factory overhead items fall into the fixed cost category:

- Property taxes
- Depreciation
- Insurance
- Rent on factory building
- Indirect labor
- Patent amortization

Mixed (Semi-variable) Costs

Mixed costs contain both a fixed element and a variable one. Salespersons' compensation including salary and commission is an example. The following factory overhead items may be considered mixed costs:

- Supervision
- Inspection
- Service department costs
- Utilities
- Fringe benefits
- Maintenance and repairs
- Compensation insurance

FIGURE 4–1 Cost Behavior Patterns

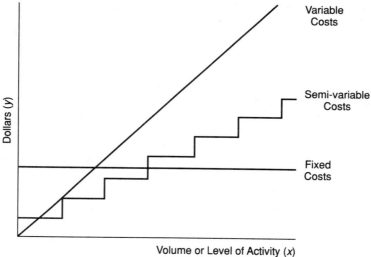

- Employer's payroll taxes
- Rental of delivery truck

Note that factory overhead, taken as a whole, would be a perfect example of mixed costs. Figure 4–1 displays how each of these three types of costs varies with changes in volume.

ANALYSIS OF MIXED (SEMI-VARIABLE) COSTS

For forecasting, planning, control, and decision-making purposes, mixed costs need to be separated into their variable and fixed components. Since the mixed costs contain both fixed and variable elements, the analysis takes the following mathematical form, which is called a *cost-volume formula* (or cost function):

$$Y = a + bX$$

where Y = the mixed cost to be broken up

X = any given measure of activity such as direct labor hours, machine hours, or production volume
a = the fixed cost component
b = the variable rate per unit of X

Separating the mixed cost into its fixed and variable components is the same as estimating the parameter values a and b in the cost function. There are several methods available to be used for this purpose including the high-low method and regression analysis. Both are discussed in the following section.

THE HIGH-LOW METHOD

The high-low method, as the name indicates, uses two extreme data points to determine the values of a (the fixed cost portion) and b (the variable rate) in the equation $Y = a + bX$. The extreme data points are the highest representative X-Y pair and the lowest representative X-Y pair. The activity level X, rather than the mixed cost item Y, governs their selection. The high-low method is explained, step by step, as follows:

Step 1: Select the highest pair and the lowest pair

Step 2: Compute the variable rate, b, using the formula:

$$\text{Variable rate} = \frac{\text{Difference in cost } Y}{\text{Difference in activity } X}$$

Step 3: Compute the fixed cost portion as:

$$\text{Fixed cost portion} = \text{Total mixed cost} - \text{Variable cost}$$

EXAMPLE 4–1 Flexible Manufacturing Company decided to relate total factory overhead costs to direct labor hours (DLH) to develop a cost function in the form of $Y = a + bX$. Twelve monthly observations are collected. They are given in Exhibit 4–1.

EXHIBIT 4–1 Monthly Cost Function

Month	Direct Labor Hours (X)	Factory Overhead (Y)
January	82	2,510
February	101	2,479
March	88	2,080
April	99	2,750
May	93	2,330
June	103	2,690
July	77	2,480
August	102	2,610
September	122	2,910
October	107	2,730
November	101	2,760
December	65	2,109

The high-low points selected from the monthly observations are

	X	Y
High	122 hours	$2,910 (September pair)
Low	88	2,080 (March pair)
Difference	34 hours	$ 830

Thus

$$\text{Variable rate } b = \frac{\text{Difference in } Y}{\text{Difference in } X} = \frac{\$830}{34 \text{ hours}} = \$24.41 \text{ per DLH}$$

The fixed cost portion is computed as

	High	*Low*
Factory overhead (Y)	$2,910	$2,080
Variable expense		
($24.41 per DLH)	($2,978)	($2,148)
	($ 68)	($ 68)

Therefore, the cost function for factory overhead is

− $68 fixed plus $24.41 per DLH.

The high-low method is simple and easy to use. It has the disadvantage, however, of using two extreme data points, which may not be representative of normal conditions. The method may yield unreliable estimates of *a* and *b* in the formula. In this example, the negative value for *a* is questionable. In such a case, it would be wise to drop them and to choose two other points that are more representative of normal situations. Be sure to check the scatter diagram for this possibility.

SIMPLE REGRESSION ANALYSIS

One popular method for estimating the cost function is regression analysis. Simple regression involves one independent variable (e.g., DLH or machine hours alone), whereas multiple regression involves two or more activity variables.

Unlike the high-low method, in an effort to estimate the variable rate and the fixed cost portion, the regression analysis method includes all the observed data and attempts to find a line of best fit.

From the Quattro Pro regression output (Exhibit 4–2), the cost function is

$$Y' = 1,330 + 12.58X$$

$$R^2 = 69.38 \text{ percent}, S_e = 150.78$$

or $1,330 fixed, plus $12.58 per DLH.

EXHIBIT 4-2 Simple Regression (OH vs. DLH)

Simple regression 1: $Y = b_o + b_1 X_1$	
Regression Output	
Constant	1,329.908
Std. Err. of Y Est.	150.7838
R Squared	0.693767
No. of Observations	12
Degrees of Freedom	10
X Coefficient(s)	12.57958
Std. Err. of Coef.	2.642924
T value	4.759720
$Y' = 1{,}330 + 12.58\, X_1$ with $R^2 = 0.6938 = 69.38\%$	

EXAMPLE 4–2 Assume 95 direct labor hours are to be expended next year. The projected factory overhead for next year would be computed as follows:

$$Y' = \$1{,}330 + 12.58\,(95)$$

$$= \$1{,}330 + \$1{,}195 = \$2{,}525$$

If the cost forecaster wants to be 95 percent confident in his/her prediction, the confidence interval would be the estimated cost $(Y') \pm tS_e$. *Note:* As a rule of thumb, we may use $t = 2$.

EXAMPLE 4–3 From Example 4–2, $Y' = \$2{,}525$ and from Exhibit 4–2 you see, $S_e = 150.78$, and $t = 2$.

Therefore, the range for the prediction, given direct labor hours of 95 would be

$$= \$2{,}525 \pm 2(150.78)$$

$$= \$2{,}525 \pm 301.56, \text{ which means}$$

$$= \$2{,}826.56 - \$2{,}223.44$$

MULTIPLE REGRESSION ANALYSIS

Regression analysis provides the opportunity for cost analysts to consider more than one independent variable. In case a simple regression is insufficient to provide a satisfactory cost function (as indicated typically by a low R^2), the budget and cost analysts should use multiple regression. Exhibit 4–4 is an example of multiple regression.

EXAMPLE 4–4   We add the data on machine hours to Exhibit 4–3, as shown below

EXHIBIT 4–3 Extended Data for Cost Prediction

Month	Factory Overhead Cost (Y)	Direct Labor Hours (X_1)	Machine Hours (X_2)
1	2,510	82	88
2	2,479	84	101
3	2,080	74	88
4	2,750	113	99
5	2,330	77	93
6	2,690	91	109
7	2,480	95	77
8	2,610	117	102
9	2,910	116	122
10	2,730	103	107
11	2,760	120	101
12	2,109	76	65

First, two simple regression results (one variable at a time) are presented:

Simple regression 1   *Simple regression 2*

$$Y = b_0 + b_1 X_1$$ $$Y = b_0 + b_2 X_2$$

Then, the following multiple regression results:

Multiple regression

$$Y = b_0 + b_1 X_1 + b_2 X_2$$

Exhibit 4–4 shows simple and multiple regression results that can be used for flexible budgeting.

As can be seen, simple regression 1 (overhead cost versus DLH) yielded

$$Y' = 1,330 + 12.58 X_1$$

$$R^2 = 69.38\%, S_e = 150.78$$

Due to a low R^2, trying the second regression (overhead cost versus MH) yielded

$$Y' = 1,220 + 13.71 X_2$$

$$R^2 = 63.82\%, S_e = 163.88$$

It shows that MH did not fare any better. In fact, R^2 and S_e were worse.

EXHIBIT 4–4

Simple and Multiple Regression Results

Simple regression 2: $Y = b_0 + b_2 X_2$

Regression Output:

Constant	1,220.08
Std. Err. of Y Est.	163.884
R Squared	0.63825
No. of Observations	12
Degrees of Freedom	10
X Coefficient(s)	13.7127
Std. Err. of Coef.	3.26464

$Y' = 1,220 + 13.71 X_2$ with $R^2 = 0.6382 = 63.82\%$

Multiple regression: $Y = b_0 + b_1 X_1 + b_2 X_2$

Regression Output:

Constant	975.155	
Std. Err. of Y Est.	112.717	
R Squared	0.84598	
No. of Observations	12	
Degrees of Freedom	9	
X Coefficient(s)	8.47915	7.8143
Std. Err. of Coef.	2.43363	2.81206

$Y' = 975 + 8.48 X_1 + 7.81 X_2$ with $R^2 = 0.8460 = 84.60\%$

By adding machine-hours (MH) to the simple regression model, you obtain:

$$Y' = 975 + 13.71 X_1 + 7.81 X_2$$

$$R^2 = 84.59\%, S_e = 112.72$$

The explanatory power (R^2) of the regression has increased dramatically to 84.59%, and the standard error of the regression has decreased to 112.72.

FLEXIBLE BUDGETS AND PERFORMANCE REPORTS

A flexible budget is a tool that is extremely useful in cost control. In contrast to a static budget, the flexible budget is characterized as follows:

1. It is geared toward a range of activity rather than a single level of activity.
2. It is dynamic in nature rather than static. By using the cost-volume formula (or flexible budget formula), a series of budgets can be easily developed for various levels of activity.

The static (fixed) budget is geared for only one level of activity and has problems in cost control. Flexible budgeting distinguishes between fixed and variable costs, thus allowing for a budget which can be automatically adjusted (via changes in variable cost totals) to the particular level of activity actually attained. Thus, variances between actual costs and budgeted costs are adjusted for volume ups and downs before differences due to price and quantity factors are computed.

The primary use of the flexible budget is to accurately measure performance by comparing actual costs for a given output with the budgeted costs for the same level of output.

EXAMPLE 4–5   To illustrate the difference between the static budget and the flexible budget, assume that the Assembly Department of Suma Industries, Inc. is budgeted to produce 6,000 units during June. Assume further that the company was able to produce only 5,800 units. The budget for direct labor and variable overhead costs is as follows:

SUMA INDUSTRIES, INC.
The Direct Labor and Variable Overhead Budget
Assembly Department
For the Month of June

Budgeted production	6,000 units
Actual production	5,800 units
Direct labor	$39,000
Variable overhead costs:	
Indirect labor	6,000
Supplies	900
Repairs	300
	$46,200

If a static budget approach is used the performance report will appear as follows:

SUMA INDUSTRIES, INC.
The Direct Labor and Variable Overhead Budget
Assembly Department
For the Month of June

	Budget	Actual	Variance (U or F)*
Production in units	6,000	5,800	200U
Direct labor	$39,000	$38,500	$500F
Variable overhead costs:			
Indirect labor	6,000	5,950	50F
Supplies	900	870	30F
Repairs	300	295	5F
	$46,200	$45,615	$585F

* A variance represents the deviation of actual cost from the standard or budgeted cost. U and F stand for "unfavorable" and "favorable," respectively.

These cost variances are useless, in that they are comparing oranges with apples. The problem is that the budget costs are based on an activity level of 6,000 units, whereas the actual costs were incurred at an activity level below this (5,800 units). From a control standpoint, it makes no sense to try to compare costs at one activity level with costs at a different activity level. Such comparisons would make a production manager look good as long as the actual production is less than the budgeted production. Using the cost-volume formula and generating the budget based on the 5,800 actual units gives the following performance report:

SUMA INDUSTRIES, INC.
Performance Report
Assembly Department
For the Month of June

Budgeted production   6,000 units
Actual production   5,800 units

	Cost-volume formula	Budget 5,800 units	Actual 5,800 units	Variance (U or F)
Direct labor	$6.50 per unit	$37,700	$38,500	$800U
Variable overhead:				
Indirect labor	1.00	5,800	5,950	150U
Supplies	.15	870	870	0
Repairs	.05	290	295	5U
	$7.70	$44,660	$45,615	$955U

Notice that all co.st variances are unfavorable (U), as compared to the favorable cost variables on the performance report based on the static budget approach.

CONCLUSION

Cost analysts and managerial accountants analyze cost behavior

1. for break-even and cost-volume-profit analysis,
2. for appraisal of managerial performance,
3. for flexible budgeting, and
4. for making short-term choice decisions.

This chapter examined three types of cost behavior: variable, fixed, and mixed. It illustrated two popular methods of separating mixed costs into their variable and fixed components: the high-low method and regression analysis. Emphasis was placed on the use of simple and multiple regression. The idea of flexible budgeting was emphasized in an attempt to correctly measure the efficiency of the cost center.

Chapter 5

Cost-Volume-Profit Analysis and Contribution Analysis

Cost-volume-profit (CVP) analysis, together with cost behavior information, helps financial managers perform many useful analyses. CVP analysis deals with how profit and costs change with a change in volume. More specifically, it looks at the effects on profits of changes in such factors as variable costs, fixed costs, selling prices, volume, and mix of products sold. By studying the relationships of costs, sales, and net income, financial management is better able to cope with many planning and budgeting decisions.

Break-even analysis, a branch of CVP analysis, determines the break-even sales. The *break-even point* (the financial crossover point when revenues exactly match costs) does not show up in corporate earnings reports, but financial managers find it an extremely useful measurement in a variety of ways.

QUESTIONS ANSWERED BY CVP ANALYSIS

CVP analysis tries to answer the following questions:

What sales volume is required to break even?

What sales volume is necessary to earn a desired profit?

What profit can be expected on a given sales volume?

How would changes in selling price, variable costs, fixed costs, and output affect profits?

How would a change in the mix of products sold affect the break-even and target income volume and profit potential?

THE CONTRIBUTION MARGIN INCOME STATEMENT

The traditional income statement for external reporting shows the functional classification of costs, i.e., manufacturing costs vs. nonmanufacturing expenses (or operating expenses). An alternative format of income statement, known as the *contribution margin income statement*, organizes the costs by behavior rather than by function. It shows the relationship of variable costs and fixed costs a given cost item is associated with, regardless of the functions.

The contribution approach to income determination provides data that are useful for managerial planning and decision-making, as indicated earlier. The statement highlights the concept of contribution margin, which is the difference between sales and variable costs. The traditional format, on the other hand, emphasizes the concept of gross margin, which is the difference between sales and cost of goods sold.

These two concepts are independent and have nothing to do with each other. Gross margin is available to cover nonmanufacturing expenses, whereas contribution margin is available to cover fixed costs. A comparison is made between the traditional format and the contribution format below.

TRADITIONAL FORMAT		
Sales	$15,000	
Less: Cost of Goods Sold	7,000	
Gross Margin	$8,000	
Less: Operating Expenses		
Selling	$2,100	
Administrative	1,500	3,600
Net Income		$4,400

CONTRIBUTION FORMAT		
Sales		$15,000
Less: Variable Expenses		
Manufacturing	$4,000	
Selling	1,600	
Administrative	500	6,100
Contribution Margin		$8,900
Less: Fixed Expenses		
Manufacturing	$3,000	
Selling	500	
Administrative	1,000	4,500
Net Income		$4,400

Contribution Margin (CM)

For accurate CVP analysis, a distinction must be made between costs as being either variable or fixed. Mixed costs must be separated into their variable and fixed components. In order to compute the break-even point and to perform various CVP analyses, note the following important concepts:

Contribution Margin (CM).   The contribution margin is the excess of sales (S) over the variable costs (VC) of the product or service. It is the amount of money available to cover fixed costs (FC) and to generate profit. Symbolically: CM = S − VC.

Unit CM.   The unit CM is the excess of the unit selling price (p) over the unit variable cost (v). Symbolically: unit CM = p − v.

CM Ratio.   The CM ratio is the contribution margin as a percentage of sales, i.e.,

$$\text{CM ratio} = \frac{CM}{S} = \frac{S - VC}{S} = 1 - \frac{VC}{S}$$

The CM ratio can also be computed using per-unit data as follows:

$$\text{CM ratio} = \frac{CM}{S} = \frac{S - VC}{S} = 1 - \frac{VC}{S}$$

Note that the CM ratio is 1 minus the variable cost ratio. For example, if variable costs account for 70 percent of the price, the CM ratio is 30 percent.

EXAMPLE 5–1   To illustrate the various concepts of CM, consider the following data for Flip Toy Store:

	Total	Per Unit	Percentage
Sales (1,500 units)	$37,500	$25	100%
Less: Variable costs	15,000	10	40
Contribution margin	$22,500	$15	60%
Less: Fixed costs	15,000		
Net income	$ 7,500		

From the data listed above, CM, unit CM, and the CM ratio are computed as:

$$CM = S - VC = \$37{,}500 - \$15{,}000 = \$22{,}500$$

$$\text{Unit CM} = p - v = \$25 - \$10 = \$15$$

$$\text{CM ratio} = \frac{CM}{S} = \frac{\$22{,}500}{\$37{,}500} = 60\% \text{ or } \frac{\text{Unit CM}}{p} = \frac{\$15}{\$25} = 0.6 = 60\%$$

Break-even Analysis

The break-even point represents the level of sales revenue that equals the total of the variable and fixed costs for a given volume of output at a particular capacity use rate. For example, you might want to determine the break-even occupancy rate (or vacancy rate) for a hotel or the break-even load rate for an airliner.

Generally, the lower the break-even point, the higher the profit and the less the operating risk, other things being equal. The break-even point also provides financial managers with insights into profit planning. It can be computed using the following formulas:

$$\text{Break-even point in units} = \frac{\text{Fixed costs}}{\text{Unit CM}}$$

$$\text{Break-even point in dollars} = \frac{\text{Fixed Costs}}{\text{CM ratio}}$$

EXAMPLE 5–2   Using the same data given in Example 5–1, where unit CM = $25 – $10 = $15 and CM ratio = 60%, you get:

$$\text{Break-even point in units} = \$15,000/\$15 = 1,000 \text{ units}$$

$$\text{Break-even point in dollars} = \$15,000/0.6 = \$25,000$$

Or, alternatively,

$$1,000 \text{ units} \times \$25 = \$25,000$$

Graphical Approach in a Spreadsheet Format

The graphical approach to obtaining the break-even point is based on the so-called *break-even (B-E) chart* as shown in Figure 5–1. Sales revenue, variable

FIGURE 5–1 Break-even (B-E) Chart

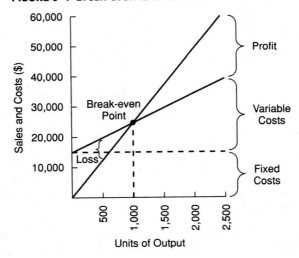

FIGURE 5–2 Profit-Volume (P-V) Chart

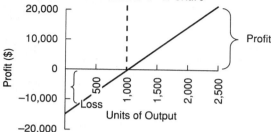

costs, and fixed costs are plotted on the vertical axis while volume, x, is plotted on the horizontal axis. The break-even point is the point at which the total sales revenue line intersects the total cost line. The chart can also effectively report profit potentials over a wide range of activity and therefore can be used as a tool for discussion and presentation.

The profit-volume (P-V) chart as shown in Figure 5–2, focuses directly on how profits vary with changes in volume. Profits are plotted on the vertical axis while units of output are plotted on the horizontal axis. The P-V chart provides a quick condensed comparison of how alternatives on pricing, variable costs, or fixed costs may affect net income as volume changes. The P-V chart can be easily constructed from the B-E chart. Note that the slope of the chart is the unit CM.

Determination of Target Income Volume

Besides determining the break-even point, CVP analysis determines the sales required to attain a particular income level or target net income. The formula is:

$$\text{Target income sales volume} = \frac{\text{Fixed costs plus target income}}{\text{Unit CM}}$$

EXAMPLE 5–3   Using the same data given in Example 5–1, assume that Flip Toy Store wishes to attain a target income of $15,000 before tax.

Then, the target income volume would be:

$$\frac{\$15,000 + \$15,000}{\$25 - \$10} = \frac{\$30,000}{\$15} = 2,000 \text{ units}$$

Impact of Income Taxes

If target income is given on an after-tax basis, the target income volume formula becomes:

$$\text{Target income volume} = \frac{\text{Fixed costs} + [\text{Target after-tax income}/(1\text{-tax rate})]}{\text{Unit CM}}$$

EXAMPLE 5–4 Assume in Example 5–1 that Flip Toy Store wants to achieve an after-tax income of $6,000. The tax rate is 40 percent. Then,

$$\text{Target income volume} = \frac{\$15,000 + [\$6,000/(1-0.4)]}{\$15}$$

$$= \frac{\$15,000 + \$10,000}{\$15} = 1,667 \text{ units}$$

Margin of Safety

The margin of safety is a measure of difference between the actual sales and the break-even sales. It is the amount by which sales revenue may drop before losses begin, and is expressed as a percentage of expected sales:

$$\text{Margin of safety} = \frac{\text{Expected sales} - \text{Break-even sales}}{\text{Expected sales}}$$

The margin of safety is used as a measure of operating risk. The larger the ratio, the safer the situation since there is less risk of reaching the break-even point.

EXAMPLE 5–5 Assume Flip Toy Store projects sales of $35,000 with a break-even sales level of $25,000. The projected margin of safety is

$$\frac{\$35,000 - \$25,000}{\$35,000} = 28.57\%$$

Some Applications of CVP Analysis and What-If Analysis

The concepts of contribution margin and the contribution income statement have many applications in profit planning and short-term decision making. Many "what-if" scenarios can be evaluated using them as planning tools, especially utilizing a spreadsheet program such as Lotus 1-2-3. Some applications are illustrated in Examples 5–6 through 5–10 using the same data as in Example 5–1.

EXAMPLE 5–6 Recall from Example 5–1 that Flip Toy Store has a CM of 60 percent and fixed costs of $15,000 per period. Assume that the company expects sales to go up by $10,000 for the next period. How much will income increase?

Using the CM concepts, you can quickly compute the impact of a change in sales on profits. The formula for computing the impact is:

Change in net income = Dollar change in sales × CM ratio

Thus:

Increase in net income = $10,000 × 60% = $6,000

Therefore, the income will go up by $6,000, assuming there is no change in fixed costs.

If you are given a change in unit sales instead of dollars, then the formula becomes:

Change in net income = Change in unit sales × Unit CM

EXAMPLE 5–7   Assume that the store expects sales to go up by 400 units. How much will income increase? From Example 5–1, the company's unit CM is $15. Again, assuming there is no change in fixed costs, the income will increase by $6,000.

400 units × $15 = $6,000

EXAMPLE 5–8   What net income is expected on sales of $47,500? The answer is the difference between the CM and the fixed costs:

CM: $47,500 × 60%	$28,500
Less: Fixed costs	15,000
Net income	$13,500

EXAMPLE 5–9   Flip Toy Store is considering increasing the advertising budget by $5,000, which would increase sales revenue by $8,000. Should the advertising budget be increased? The answer is no, since the increase in the CM is less than the increased cost:

Increase in CM: $8,000 × 60%	$4,800
Increase in advertising	5,000
Decrease in net income	$(200)

EXAMPLE 5–10   Consider the original data. Assume again that Flip Toy Store is currently selling 1,500 units per period. In an effort to increase sales, management is considering cutting its unit price by $5 and increasing the advertising budget by $1,000.

If these two steps are taken, management feels that unit sales will go up by 60 percent. Should the two steps be taken?

A $5 reduction in the selling price will cause the unit CM to decrease from $15 to $10. Thus,

Proposed CM: 2,400 units × $10	$24,000
Present CM: 1,500 units × $15	22,500
Increase in CM	$ 1,500
Increase in advertising outlay	1,000
Increase in net income	$ 500

The answer, therefore, is yes. Alternatively, the same answer can be obtained by developing comparative income statements in a contribution format:

	(A) *Present* *(1,500 units)*	(B) *Proposed* *(2,400 units)*	(B − A) *Difference*
Sales	$37,500 (@$25)	$48,000 (@$20)	$10,500
Less: Variable cost	15,000	24,000	9,000
CM	$22,500	$24,000	$ 1,500
Less: Fixed costs	15,000	16,000	1,000
Net income	$ 7,500	$ 8,000	$ 500

Sales Mix Analysis

Break-even and cost-volume-profit analyses require some additional computations and assumptions when a company produces and sells more than one product. In multi-product firms, sales mix is an important factor in calculating an overall company break-even point.

Different selling prices and different variable costs result in different unit CM and CM ratios. As a result, the break-even points and cost-volume-profit relationships vary with the relative proportions of the products sold, called the *sales mix*.

In break-even and CVP analyses, it is necessary to predetermine the sales mix and then to compute a weighted average unit CM. It is also necessary to assume that the sales mix does not change for a specified period. The break-even formula for the company as a whole is:

$$\text{Break-even sales in units (or in dollars)} = \frac{\text{Fixed costs}}{\text{Weighted average unit CM}}$$
$$\text{(or CM ratio)}$$

EXAMPLE 5–11   Assume that Knibex, Inc. produces cutlery sets out of high-quality wood and steel. The company makes a deluxe cutlery set and a standard set that have the following unit CM data:

	Deluxe	*Standard*
Selling price	$15	$10
Variable cost per unit	12	5
Unit CM	$ 3	$ 5
Sales mix	60%	40%
Fixed costs	$76,000	

The weighted average unit CM = ($3) (0.6) + ($5) (0.4) = $3.80. Therefore, the company's break-even point in units is

$$\$76,000/\$3.80 = 20,000 \text{ units}$$

which is divided as follows:

Deluxe: 20,000 units $\times$ 60% = 12,000 units

Standard: 20,000 units $\times$ 40% =   8,000

20,000 units

EXAMPLE 5–12   Assume that Panda, Inc. is a producer of recreational equipment. It expects to produce and sell three types of sleeping bags: the Economy, the Regular, and the Backpacker. Information on the bags is given below:

	Budget Mix			
	Economy	*Regular*	*Backpacker*	*Total*
Sales	$30,000	$60,000	$10,000	$100,000
Sales mix	30%	60%	10%	100%
Less: VC	24,000	40,000	5,000	69,000
CM	$ 6,000	$20,000	$ 5,000	$ 31,000
CM ratio	20%	33 1/3%	50%	31%
Fixed costs				$ 18,600
Net income				$ 12,400

The CM ratio for Dante, Inc. is $31,000/$100,000 = 31 percent. Therefore the break-even point in dollars is

$$\$18,600/0.31 = \$60,000$$

which will be split in the mix ratio of 3:6:1 to give us the following break-even points for the individual products:

Economy: $60,000 $\times$ 30% = $18,000

Regular: $60,000 $\times$ 60% = 36,000

Backpacker: $60,000 $\times$ 10% =   6,000

$60,000

One of the most important assumptions underlying CVP analysis in a multi-product firm is that the sales mix will not change during the planning period. But if the sales mix changes, the break-even point will also change.

EXAMPLE 5–13 Assume that total sales from Example 5–12 was achieved at $100,000 but that an actual mix came out differently from the budgeted mix (i.e., for Regular, 60 percent to 30 percent and for Backpacker, 10 percent to 40 percent).

Actual Mix

	Economy	Regular	Backpacker	Total
Sales	$30,000	$30,000	$40,000	$100,000
Sales mix	30%	30%	40%	100%
Less: VC	24,000	20,000*	20,000**	64,000
CM	$–6,000	$10,000	$20,000	$ 36,000
CM ratio	20%	33 1/3%	50%	36%
Fixed costs				$ 18,600
Net income				$ 17,400

     * $20,000 = $30,000 × (100% − 33 1/3%) = $30,000 × 66 2/3%

    ** $20,000 = $40,000 × (100% − 50%) = $40,000 × 50%

Note: The shift in sales mix toward the more profitable backpacker line C has caused the CM ratio for the company as a whole to go up from 31 percent to 36 percent.

    The new break-even point will be

$$\$51,667 = \$18,600/0.36$$

The break-even dollar volume has decreased from $60,000 to $51,667. The improvement in the mix caused net income to increase. It is important to note that generally, the shift of emphasis from low-margin products to high-margin ones will increase the overall profits of the company.

Cost-Volume-Revenue Analysis and Nonprofit Organizations

Cost-volume-profit (CVP) analysis and break-even anlaysis are not limited to profit firms. CVP is appropriately called *cost-volume-revenue (CVR) analysis*, as it pertains to nonprofit organizations. The CVR model not only calculates the break-even service level, but helps answer a variety of "what-if" decision questions.

EXAMPLE 5–14 OCM, Inc., a Los Angeles county agency, has a $1,200,000 lump-sum annual budget appropriation for an agency to help rehabilitate mentally ill patients. On top of this, the agency charges each patient $600 a month for board and care. All of the appropriation and revenue must be spent. The variable costs for rehabilitation activity average $700 per patient per month. The agency's annual fixed costs are $800,000. The agency manager wishes to know how many patients can be served. Let x = number of patients to be served.

Revenue = Total expenses

Lump sum appropriation + $600 (12)$x$ = Variable expenses + Fixed costs

$$\$1,200,000 + \$7,200x = \$8,400\ x + \$800,000$$

$$(\$7,200 - \$8,400)x = \$800,000 - \ \$1,200,000$$

$$- \$1,200x = - 400,000$$

$$x = \$400,000/\$1,200$$

$$x = 333 \text{ patients}$$

Investigate the following two "what-if" scenarios:

1. Suppose the manager of the agency is concerned that the total budget for the coming year will be cut by 10 percent to a new amount of $1,080,000. All other things remain unchanged. The manager wants to know how this budget cut affects the next year's service level.

$$\$1,080,000 + \$7,200x = \$8,400x + \$800,000$$

$$(\$7,200 - \$8,400)x = \$800,000 - \ \$1,080,000$$

$$- \$1,200x = - \$280,000$$

$$x = \$280,000/\$1,200$$

$$x = 233 \text{ patients}$$

2. The manager does not reduce the number of patients served despite a budget cut of 10 percent. All other things remain unchanged. How much more does he/she have to charge his/her patients for board and care? In this case, x = board and care charge per year

$$\$1,080,000 + 333\ x = \$8,400\ (333) + \$800,000$$

$$333x = \$2,797,200 + \$800,000 - \ \$1,080,000$$

$$333x = \$2,517,200$$

$$x = \$2,517,200/333 \text{ patients}$$

$$x = \$7,559$$

Thus, the monthly board and care charge must be increased to $630 ($7,559/12 months).

Assumptions Underlying Break-even and CVP Analyses

The basic break-even and CVP models are subject to a number of limiting assumptions. They are:

- The selling price per unit is constant throughout the entire relevant range of activity.

- All costs are classified as fixed or variable.
- The variable cost per unit is constant.
- There is only one product or a constant sales mix.
- Inventories do not change significantly from period to period.
- Volume is the only factor affecting variable costs.

CONCLUSION

Cost-volume-profit analysis is useful as a frame of reference, as a vehicle for expressing overall managerial performance, and as a planning device via break-even techniques and "what-if" scenarios. The following points highlight the analytical usefulness of CVP analysis as a tool for profit planning and budgeting:

1. A change in either the selling price or the variable cost per unit alters CM or the CM ratio and thus the break-even point.
2. As sales exceeds the break-even point, a higher unit CM or CM ratio will result in greater profits than a small unit CM or CM ratio.
3. The lower the break-even sales, the less risky the business and the safer the investment, other things being equal.
4. A large margin of safety means lower operating risk since a large decrease in sales can occur before losses are experienced.
5. Using the contribution income statement model and a spreadsheet program, such as Lotus 1-2-3™, a variety of "what-if" planning and decision scenarios can be evaluated.
6. In a multi-product firm, sales mix is often more important than overall market share. The emphasis on high-margin products tends to maximize overall profits of the firm.

We discussed how the traditional CVP analysis can be applied to the nonprofit setting. Illustrations were provided. Managerial accountants prepare the income statement in a contribution format which organizes costs by behavior rather than by the functions of manufacturing, sales, and administration. The contribution income statement is widely used as an internal planning and decision-making tool.

Part 3

PREPARATION AND ANALYSIS OF BUDGETS

Chapter 6

Budgeting for Profit Planning

A comprehensive (master) budget is a formal statement of management's expectations regarding sales, expenses, volume, and other financial transactions of an organization for the coming period. Simply put, a budget is a set of pro forma (projected or planned) financial statements. It consists basically of a pro forma income statement, pro forma balance sheet, and cash budget.

A budget is a tool for both planning and control. At the beginning of the period, the budget is a plan or standard; at the end of the period it serves as a control device to help management measure its performance against the plan so that future performance may be improved.

It is important to realize that with the aid of computer technology, budgeting can be used as an effective device for evaluation of "what-if" scenarios. This way, management should be able through simulation to move toward finding the best course of action among various alternatives. If management does not like what they see on the budgeted financial statements in terms of various financial ratios, such as liquidity, activity (turnover), leverage, profit margin, and market value ratios, they can always alter their contemplated decision and planning set.

The budget is classified broadly into two categories:

1. Operating Budget, reflecting the results of operating decisions and
2. Financial Budget, reflecting the financial decisions of the firm.

The operating budget consists of:

- Sales budget
- Production budget
- Direct materials budget
- Direct labor budget
- Factory overhead budget
- Selling and administrative expense budget
- Pro forma income statement.

The financial budget consists of:

- Cash budget
- Pro forma balance sheet.

The major steps in preparing the budget are:

1. Prepare a sales forecast.
2. Determine expected production volume.
3. Estimate manufacturing costs and operating expenses.
4. Determine cash flow and other financial effects.
5. Formulate projected financial statements.

To illustrate how all these budgets are put together, this chapter will focus on a manufacturing company called the Norton Company, which produces and markets a single product. Assume that the company develops the master budget in contribution format for 19B on a quarterly basis. The variable cost-fixed cost breakdown will be highlighted throughout the chapter. Figure 6–1 shows a simplified diagram of the various parts of the comprehensive (master) budget, the master plan of the company.

THE SALES BUDGET

The sales budget is the starting point in preparing the master budget, since estimated sales volume influences nearly all other items appearing throughout the master budget. The sales budget should show total sales in quantity and value. The total sales can be break-even, target income, or projected sales. It may be analyzed further by product, by territory, by customer and, of course, by seasonal pattern of expected sales. Generally, the sales budget includes a computation of expected cash collections from credit sales, which will be used later for cash budgeting.

FIGURE 6–1 Comprehensive (Master) Budget

```
                        ┌─────────────────┐
                        │  Sales Budget   │
                        └─────────────────┘
        ┌──────────────────────┐
        │   Desired Ending     │───▶┌──────────────────┐
        │  Inventory Budget    │    │ Production Budget │
        └──────────────────────┘    └──────────────────┘

        ┌──────────┐   ┌──────────┐   ┌──────────┐
        │  Direct  │   │  Direct  │   │ Factory  │
        │ Material │   │  Labor   │   │ Overhead │
        └──────────┘   └──────────┘   └──────────┘

                     ┌──────────────────┐
                     │ Cost of Goods Sold│
                     │      Budget       │
                     └──────────────────┘

                     ┌──────────────────┐
                     │ Selling Expense   │
                     │      Budget       │
                     └──────────────────┘

                     ┌──────────────────┐
                     │Administrative Expense│
                     │      Budget       │
                     └──────────────────┘

                     ┌──────────────────┐
                     │ Budgeted Income   │
                     │    Statement      │
                     └──────────────────┘

        ┌──────────┐  ┌──────────────────┐  ┌──────────┐
        │ Capital  │─▶│ Budgeted Balance  │◀─│  Cash    │
        │ Budget   │  │      Sheet        │  │ Budget   │
        └──────────┘  └──────────────────┘  └──────────┘
```

EXAMPLE 6–1

THE NORTON COMPANY
Sales Budget
For the Year Ending December 31, 19B

| | *Quarter* | | | | |
	1	*2*	*3*	*4*	*Total*
Expected sales in units	800	700	900	800	3,200
Unit sales price	× $80	× $80	× $80	× $80	× $80
Total sales	$64,000	$56,000	$72,000	$64,000	$256,000

Schedule of Expected Cash Collections

Accounts receivable, 12/31/19A	9,500*				$ 9,500
1st quarter sales ($64,000)	44,800+	$17,920++			62,720
2d quarter sales ($56,000)		39,200	$15,680		54,880
3d quarter sales ($72,000)			50,400	$20,160	70,560
4th quarter sales ($64,000)				44,800	44,800
Total cash collections	$54,300	$57,120	$66,080	$64,960	$242,460

* All $9,500 accounts receivable balance is assumed to be collectible in the first quarter.

+ 70 percent of a quarter's sales are collected in the quarter of sale.

++ 28 percent of a quarter's sales are collected in the quarter following, and the remaining 2 percent are uncollectible.

THE PRODUCTION BUDGET

The production budget is a statement of the output by product and is generally expressed in units. It should take into account the sales budget, plant capacity, whether stocks are to be increased or decreased, and outside purchases. The number of units expected to be manufactured to meet budgeted sales and inventory requirements is set forth in the production budget. The expected volume of production is determined by subtracting the estimated inventory at the beginning of the period from the sum of the units expected to be sold and the desired inventory at the end of the period. The production budget is illustrated as follows:

EXAMPLE 6–2

THE NORTON COMPANY
Production Budget
For the Year Ending December 31, 19B

	Quarter				
	1	*2*	*3*	*4*	*Total*
Planned sales (Example 6–1)	800	700	900	800	3,200
Desired ending inventory*	70	90	80	100+	100
Total needs	870	790	980	900	3,300
Less: Beginning inventory++	80	70	90	80	80
Units to be produced	790	720	890	820	3,220

* 10 percent of the next quarter's sales.

+ Estimated.

++ The same as the previous quarter's ending inventory.

THE DIRECT MATERIAL BUDGET

When the level of production has been computed, a direct material budget should be constructed to show how much material will be required for production and how much material must be purchased to meet this production requirement. The purchase will depend on both expected usage of materials and inventory levels. The formula for computation of the purchase is:

Purchase in units = Usage + Desired ending material inventory units
− Beginning inventory units

The direct material budget is usually accompanied by a computation of expected cash payments for materials.

EXAMPLE 6–3

THE NORTON COMPANY
Direct Material Budget
For the Year Ending December 31, 19B

	Quarter				
	1	*2*	*3*	*4*	*Total*
Units to be produced (Example 6–2)	790	720	890	820	3,220
Material needs per unit (lbs)	× 3	× 3	× 3	× 3	× 3
Material needs for production	2,370	2,160	2,670	2,460	9,660
Desired ending inventory of materials*	216	267	246	250+	250
Total needs	2,586	2,427	2,916	2,710	9,910
Less: Beginning inventory of materials++	237	216	267	246	237
Materials to be purchased	2,349	2,211	2,649	2,464	9,673
Unit price	× $2	× $2	× $2	× $2	× $2
Purchase cost	$4,698	$4,422	$5,298	$4,928	$19,346

* 10 percent of the next quarter's units needed for production.

+ Estimated.

++ The same as the prior quarter's ending inventory.

Schedule of Expected Cash Disbursements

	1	2	3	4	Total
Accounts payable, 12/31/19A	$2,200				$2,200
1st quarter purchases ($4,698)	2,349	2,349**			4,698
2d quarter purchases ($4,422)		2,211	2,211		4,422
3d quarter purchases ($5,298)			2,649	2,649	5,298
4th quarter purchases ($4,928)				2,464	2,464
Total disbursements	$4,549	$4,560	$4,860	$5,113	$19,082

** 50 percent of a quarter's purchases are paid for in the quarter of purchase; the remainder are paid for in the following quarter.

THE DIRECT LABOR BUDGET

The production requirements as set forth in the production budget also provide the starting point for the preparation of the direct labor budget. To compute direct labor requirements, expected production volume for each period is multiplied by the number of direct labor hours required to produce a single unit. The direct labor hours to meet production requirements is then multiplied by the direct labor cost per hour to obtain budgeted total direct labor costs.

EXAMPLE 6–4

THE NORTON COMPANY
Direct Labor Budget
For the Year Ending December 31, 19B

	Quarter				
	1	*2*	*3*	*4*	*Total*
Units to be produced (Example 6–2)	790	720	890	820	3,220
Direct labor hours per unit	× 5	× 5	× 5	× 5	× 5
Total hours	3,950	3,600	4,450	4,100	16,100
Direct labor cost per hour	× $5	× $5	× $5	× $5	× $5
Total direct labor cost	$19,750	$18,000	$22,250	$20,500	$80,500

THE FACTORY OVERHEAD BUDGET

The factory overhead budget should provide a schedule of all manufacturing costs other than direct materials and direct labor. Using the contribution approach to budgeting requires the development of a predetermined overhead rate for the variable portion of the factory overhead. In developing the cash budget, remember that depreciation does not entail a cash outlay and therefore it must be deducted from the total factory overhead in computing cash disbursement for factory overhead.

EXAMPLE 6–5

To illustrate the factory overhead budget, assume that

1. Total factory overhead budgeted = $6,000 fixed (per quarter), plus $2 per hour of direct labor.

2. Depreciation expenses are $3,250 each quarter.

3. All overhead costs involving cash outlays are paid for in the quarter incurred.

THE NORTON COMPANY
Factory Overhead Budget
For the Year Ending December 31, 19B

			Quarter		
	1	2	3	4	Total
Budgeted direct labor hours					
(Example 6–4)	3,950	3,600	4,450	4,100	16,100
Variable overhead rate	× $2	× $2	× $2	× $2	× $2
Variable overhead budgeted	7,900	7,200	8,900	8,200	32,200
Fixed overhead budgeted	6,000	6,000	6,000	6,000	24,000
Total budgeted overhead	13,900	13,200	14,900	14,200	56,200
Less: Depreciation	3,250	3,250	3,250	3,250	13,000
Cash disbursement for overhead	10,650	9,950	11,650	10,950	43,200

THE ENDING INVENTORY BUDGET

The desired ending inventory budget provides us with the information required for the construction of budgeted financial statements. Specifically, it will help compute the cost of goods sold on the budgeted income statement. Secondly, it will give the dollar value of the ending materials and finished goods inventory to appear on the budgeted balance sheet.

EXAMPLE 6–6

THE NORTON COMPANY
Ending Inventory Budget
For the Year Ending December 31, 19B

	Ending Inventory		
	Units	Unit Cost	Total
Direct materials	250 pounds (Example 6–3)	$ 2	$ 500
Finished goods	100 units (Example 6–2)	$41*	$4,100

* The unit variable cost of $41 is computed as follows:

	Unit Cost	Units	Total
Direct materials	$2	3 pounds	$ 6
Direct labor	5	5 hours	25
Variable overhead	2	5 hours	10
Total variable manufacturing cost			$41

THE SELLING AND ADMINISTRATIVE EXPENSE BUDGET

The selling and administrative expense budget lists the operating expenses involved in selling the products and in managing the business. In order to complete the budgeted income statement in contribution format, variable selling and administrative expense per unit must be computed.

EXAMPLE 6–7

THE NORTON COMPANY
Selling and Administrative Expense Budget
For the Year Ending December 31, 19B

	Quarter				
	1	*2*	*3*	*4*	*Total*
Expected sales in units	800	700	900	800	3,200
Variable selling and					
administrative expenses per unit*	× $4	× $4	× $4	× $4	× $4
Budgeted variable expense	$3,200	$2,800	$3,600	$3,200	$12,800
Fixed selling and administrative expenses:					
Advertising	1,100	1,100	1,100	1,100	4,400
Insurance	2,800				2,800
Office salaries	8,500	8,500	8,500	8,500	34,000
Rent	350	350	350	350	1,400
Taxes			1,200		1,200
Total budgeted selling and administrative expenses+	$15,950	$12,750	$14,750	$13,150	$56,600

* Includes sales agents' commissions, shipping, and supplies.

+ Paid for in the quarter incurred.

THE CASH BUDGET

The cash budget is prepared for the purpose of cash planning and control. It presents the expected cash inflow and outflow for a designated time period. The cash budget helps management keep cash balances in reasonable relationship to its needs and aids in avoiding unnecessary idle cash and possible cash shortages. The cash budget consists typically of four major sections:

1. the receipts section, which is the beginning cash balance, cash collections from customers, and other receipts,

2. the disbursements section, which comprises all cash payments made by purpose,

3. the cash surplus or deficit section, which simply shows the difference between the cash receipts section and the cash disbursements section, and

4. the financing section, which provides a detailed account of the borrowings and repayments expected during the budgeting period.

EXAMPLE 6–8   To illustrate, make the following assumptions:

• The company desires to maintain a $5,000 minimum cash balance at the end of each quarter.

- All borrowing and repayment must be in multiples of $500 at an interest rate of 10 percent per annum. Interest is computed and paid as the principal is repaid. Borrowing takes place at the beginning of each quarter and repayment at the end of each quarter.

THE NORTON COMPANY
Cash Budget
For the Year Ending December 31, 19B

		Quarter				
	Example	*1*	*2*	*3*	*4*	*Total*
Cash balance, beginning	Given	10,000	9,401	5,461	9,106	10,000
Add: Receipts:						
Collection from						
customers	1	54,300	57,120	66,080	64,960	242,460
Total cash available		64,300	66,521	71,541	74,066	252,460
Less: Disbursements:						
Direct materials	3	4,549	4,560	4,860	5,113	19,082
Direct labor	4	19,750	18,000	22,250	20,500	80,500
Factory overhead	5	10,650	9,950	11,650	10,950	43,200
Selling and administrative	7	15,950	12,750	14,750	13,150	56,600
Machinery purchase	Given	—	24,300	—	—	24,300
Income tax	Given	4,000	—	—	—	4,000
Total disbursements		54,899	69,560	53,510	49,713	227,682
Cash surplus (deficit)		9,401	(3,039)	18,031	24,353	24,778
Financing:						
Borrowing		—	8,500	—	—	8,500
Repayment		—	—	(8,500)	—	(8,500)
Interest		—	—	(425)	—	(425)
Total financing		—	8,500	(8,925)	—	(425)
Cash balance, ending		9,401	5,461	9,106	24,353	24,353

THE BUDGETED INCOME STATEMENT

The budgeted income statement summarizes the various component projections of revenue and expenses for the budgeting period. However, for control purposes the budget can be divided into quarters or even months depending on the need.

EXAMPLE 6–9

THE NORTON COMPANY
Budgeted Income Statement
For the Year Ending December 31, 19B

	Example No.		
Sales (3,200 units @ $80)	1		$256,000
Less: Variable expenses			
Variable cost of goods sold			
(3,200 units @ $41)	6	$131,200	
Variable selling & administrative	7	12,800	144,000
Contribution margin			112,000
Less: Fixed expenses			
Factory overhead	5	24,000	
Selling and administrative	7	43,800	67,800
Net operating income			44,200
Less: Interest expense	8		425
Income before taxes			43,775
Less: Income taxes	20%		8,755
Net income			35,020

THE BUDGETED BALANCE SHEET

The budgeted balance sheet is developed by beginning with the balance sheet for the year just ended and adjusting it, using all the activities that are expected to take place during the budgeting period. Some of the reasons why the budgeted balance sheet must be prepared are:

- It could disclose some unfavorable financial conditions that management might want to avoid.
- It serves as a final check on the mathematical accuracy of all the other schedules.
- It helps management perform a variety of ratio calculations.
- It highlights future resources and obligations.

EXAMPLE 6–10   To illustrate, use the following balance sheet for the year 19A.

THE NORTON COMPANY
Balance Sheet
December 31, 19A

Assets		Liabilities and Stk. Equity	
Current assets:		Current liabilities:	
Cash	10,000	Accounts payable	2,200
A/R	9,500	Income tax payable	4,000
Material inv.	474	Total cur. liab.	6,200
Finished gd. inv.	3,280		
Total cur. assets	23,254		
Fixed assets:		Stockholders' equity:	
Land	50,000	Common stock, no-par	70,000
Build and eqpt.	100,000	Retained earnings	37,054
Accumtd. depr.	(60,000)		
Total fixed assets	90,000		
Total assets	113,254	Total Liab. and Stk. Eq.	113,254

THE NORTON COMPANY
Budgeted Balance Sheet
December 31, 19B

Assets		Liabilities and Stk. Equity	
Current assets:		Current liabilities:	
Cash	24,353 (a)	Accounts payable	2,464 (h)
Accounts rec.	23,040 (b)	Income tax payable	8,755 (i)
Material inv.	500 (c)	Total cur. liab.	11,219
Finished gd. inv.	4,100 (d)		
Total cur. assets	$51,993		
Fixed assets:		Stockholders' equity:	
Land	50,000 (e)	Common stock, no-par	70,000 (j)
Build and eqpt.	124,300 (f)	Retained earnings	72,074 (k)
Accumtd depr.	(73,000) (g)		
Total fixed assets	101,300		
Total assets	153,293	Total liab. and Stk. Eq.	153,293

Computations:

(a) From Example 6–8 (cash budget).

(b) $9,500 + $256,000 sales − $242,460 receipts = $23,040.

(c) and (d) From Example 6–6 (ending inventory budget).

(e) No change.

(f) $100,000 + $24,300 (from Example 6–8) = $124,300.

(g) $60,000 + $13,000 (from Example 6–5) = $73,000.

(h) $2,200 + $19,346 − $19,082 = $2,464 (all accounts payable relate to material purchases), or 50% of 4th quarter purchase = 50% ($4,928) = 2,464.

(i) From Example 6–9 (budgeted income statement).

(j) No change.

(k) $37,054 + $35,020 net income = $72,074.

Some Financial Calculations

To determine the expected financial condition of the Norton Company for the budgeting year, a sample of financial ratio calculations are in order: (Assume 19xA after-tax net income was $15,000)

	19xA	19xB
Current ratio		
(Current assets/	$23,254/$6,200	$51,993/$11,219
current liabilities)	= 3.75	= 4.63
Return on total assets		
(Net income after taxes/	$15,000/$113,254	$35,020/$153,293
total assets)	= 13.24%	= 22.85%

Sample calculations indicate that the Norton Company is expected to have better liquidity as measured by the current ratio. Overall performance will be improved as measured by return on total assets. This could be an indication that the contemplated plan may work out well.

USING AN ELECTRONIC SPREADSHEET TO DEVELOP A BUDGET PLAN

Examples 6–1 to 6–10 showed a detailed procedure for formulating a master budget. However, in practice a short-cut approach to budgeting is quite common using computer technology. Using a spreadsheet program, financial managers will be able to (1) develop a master budget and (2) evaluate various "what-if" scenarios. Many illustrations will be presented in Chapter 29.

CONCLUSION

Forecasting is an essential element of planning and budgeting. Basically, forecasts of future sales and their related expenses provide the firm with the information needed to plan other activities of the business.

This chapter has emphasized budgets. The process involves developing a sales forecast and, based on its magnitude, generating those budgets needed by a specific firm. Once developed, the budgeting system provides management with a means of controlling their activities and of monitoring actual performance and comparing it to budget goals.

Budgeting can be done with ease with the aid of electronic spreadsheet software, but there are many specialized software for budgeting available in the market.

Chapter 7

Planning and Control for Production

Production applies to all types of inventory including raw materials, work-in-process, and finished goods. In a service business, sales are converted to service capability. In a retail or wholesale business, sales are translated into merchandise purchases. In a manufacturing business, sales are converted into production volume. A customer order ultimately becomes a manufacturing order.

An objective of production is to keep manufacturing facilities in constant operation. Production is the responsibility of the manufacturing manager. The manager wants the best utilization of resources available for efficiency and effectiveness. The production manager can exercise control over volume produced, manufacturing costs, and inventories. A production action plan has to be agreed upon. Production should consider the actual and expected future orders to be received.

An activity level must be set. Production is based on expected units to be sold. Production must take into account having adequate inventory levels to satisfy customer demand, anticipated changes in price, financial health of the business, and sufficiency of storage space.

The budget planning process should consider how much to be produced, when, whether it is sufficient, and what is needed to increase output. There should be proper coordination of activities for all those involved in the production process.

BUDGETARY PROCESS

The budgetary process over production involves the following considerations:

- Update the production budget as needed.
- Ascertain the timing of when product manufacturing should take place.
- Establish material, labor, and overhead needs.
- Determine how much should be manufactured to meet sales targets and inventory requirements.
- Estimate production costs and compare to actual costs. This will help control manufacturing costs.
- Select the location for manufacturing to occur.
- Set guidelines to measure production performance and efficiency.
- Deciding on the budget period for production.

CAPACITY

Capacity is the volume of output expected over a stated time period. Capacity must be adequate to manufacture the planned volume and must be sufficient to handle peak loads. If not, capital budgeting needs to be initiated. Idle capacity and bottlenecks may be minimized through planning and coordination of departments, processes, and machinery. Capacity may be expressed in units, tons, dollars, man-hours, machine hours, direct payroll, or some other suitable surrogate for production. Capacity may be expressed for various time periods including semi-annually, monthly, and yearly. The various types of capacity are:

Ideal capacity.   The maximum output if a facility maintained continuous operation at optimum efficiency, allowing for no losses of any kind, even those considered normal or unavoidable. This capacity concept will always result in an unfavorable variance because it is impossible to achieve.

Practical (effective) capacity.   The output volume possible if a facility is operated continuously allowing for normal and unavoidable losses such as vacations, holidays, and repairs. This level is the practical upper limit.

Expected (planned, budgeted) capacity.   The average annual volume projected to meet anticipated marketing needs for a single year. It is similar to practical capacity but allows for idleness of facilities due to absence of sufficient product demand.

Normal capacity. The same as expected capacity, but projected for a longer time span (e.g., five years).

Operating (current) capacity. The same as expected capacity, but projected for a time period within one year (e.g., quarter, month, week, or day).

Idle or unused capacity. The output potential not being used.

BUDGET TIME PERIOD

The production time period should typically match the sales budget period. There may be, however, extenuating circumstances dictating a slightly different period. A shorter budgetary period allows for greater accuracy and control. The time period will depend upon the availability of adequate or specialized equipment, availability of labor, training period, raw material availability, overall stability, stability of product line models and styles, customization to special customer orders, sales budget period, production length and cycle, desired modifications in product, order time for replenishment of materials and supplies, technological factors, inventory obsolescence problems, and economic climate. Typically, the budget period is one year broken down into quarters.

PRODUCTION CONSIDERATIONS

Sales people must be attuned to production problems and, similarly, production people must monitor sales developments. For example, sales emphasis may need to be placed on those products that may efficiently be produced. Sales people should report trends in products, customers, emerging needs, quality problems, competitive reaction, and so on. Production standards may be expressed in terms of labor hours, pieces or feet of material, machine hours, and repair hours. These standards are developed by engineers. Standards of production are needed. The manufacturing operations to be performed are specified.

PRODUCTION BUDGET

The production budget must be coordinated with sales, marketing, and the financial standing of the company. The production budget is typically prepared by the manufacturing executives and foreman and should take into account standards, historical experience, and anticipated future conditions. The production budget should be in terms of units by individual product or categories and should be broken down by each major product line considering sizes, styles, and so on. It is crucial that there be efficient production with cost control.

The production budget aids in planning, coordination, and control. It is interrelated with other budgets such as sales, financing, capital facilities, and costs.

Figure 7–1 charts how a production plan is derived and broken down. Figure 7–2 is a graphic depiction of sales, production, and inventory budgets. A manufacturing department budget may take the form as indicated in Exhibit 7–1.

The production budget takes into account the following:

- A balancing of inventory levels to working capital levels.
- The distribution time and outlets to get the product to the customer such as type of delivery and time required.
- Marketing needs for the product.
- The "get ready" time for the product including setup time, testing, and marketing.
- Manufacturing requirements and capacity to produce the products in terms of human resources and equipment.
- Direct labor needs.

FIGURE 7–1 Planning Production

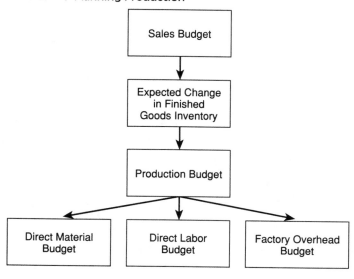

FIGURE 7-2 Chart of Sales, Production, and Inventory Budgets

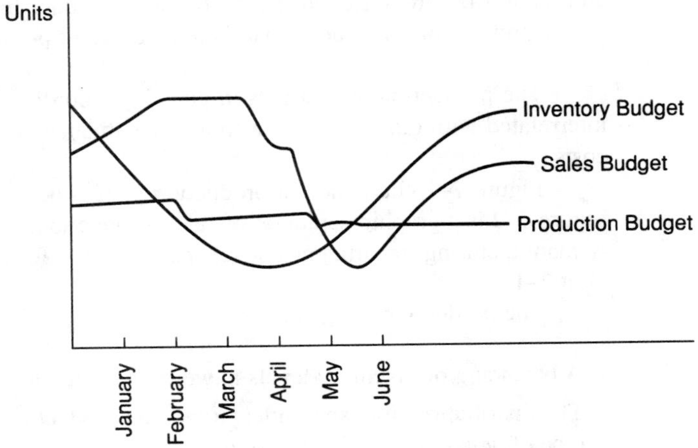

- Inventory balances.
- Inventory policy for work-in-process and finished goods.
- Availability of raw materials.
- Plant capacity.
- Stability of labor force.
- Economic order quantity and economic order point.
- Company size.
- Type of product.
- Internal controls.
- Product obsolescence.

EXHIBIT 7-1 Manufacturing Department Budget

Materials
  Direct
  Indirect
Labor
  Direct
  Indirect
Fringe Benefits
Factory Overhead
  Rent
  Utilities
  Insurance
  Property Taxes
  Depreciation
  Factory Supplies

The budgeting of production differs between companies producing standard orders vs. those manufacturing customized orders. In the former situation, the merchandise should be available at the time orders are received. If merchandise is customized to an order, production quantities are only certainly known as orders are received. While an estimate may be possible based on historical experience, the expected business environment, and current sales data, you still need to know how many orders have been actually received. In budgeting production quantities, you must consider the orders received and expected orders.

The unit production budget involves the following steps:

1. Determine the level of production after a time period has been chosen considering inventory balances, reorder time, safety stock level, inventory carrying and ordering costs, product obsolescence and perishability, inventory price trends, and the financial health of the business.

2. Decide upon when and where production will occur considering adequacy of manufacturing facilities, availability of storage, ability to meet peak production periods, coordination of production to purchasing, and financial ability to support higher inventory balances.

3. Decide upon which production operations are required.

4. Establish manufacturing standards and measure manufacturing efficiency.

5. Determine material, labor, and overhead requirements for production.

6. Decide upon which machinery is needed for manufacturing.

7. Update estimates based on new experience.

The production volume budget is prepared after the formulation of the sales budget. It estimates how many units are to be produced to meet sales expectations. The production volume budget is the basis for budgeting the manufacturing costs of direct material, direct labor, and factory overhead.

A production budget is prepared after sales have been budgeted. The total number of units to be manufactured depends upon expected sales, the anticipated change in inventory, and expected spoilage and waste. An illustrative production budget follows:

Unit Production Budget
For the Month Ended December 31, 19XX

Budgeted Sales
Add: Desired Ending Inventory
   Total Needed
Less: Beginning Inventory
Units to be Produced

EXHIBIT 7–2

XYZ COMPANY
Manufacturing Plan by Product
For the Year Ended December 31, 19XX

Product A	Expected Sales	Add Ending Inventory	Needed	Less Beginning Inventory	Expected Units to be Completed
Jan.	100,000	20,000	120,000	10,000	110,000
Feb.	150,000	30,000	180,000	25,000	155,000
March	120,000	40,000	160,000	55,000	105,000
1st Quarter etc.					

An illustrative production plan by product for a company appears in Exhibit 7–2.

EXAMPLE 7–1   Beginning inventory is 10,000 units with desired ending inventory being 15,000 units. Expected sales are 100,000 units. Each unit requires 3 pieces of material. Beginning pieces and ending pieces are 30,000 and 35,000, respectively. The production and purchases are computed below.

Expected sales	100,000
+ Desired ending inventory	15,000
Needed	115,000
− Beginning inventory	10,000
Production	105,000
Needed for production 105,000 × 3	315,000
+ Desired ending inventory	35,000
Need	350,000
− Beginning inventory	30,000
Purchases	320,000

EXAMPLE 7–2   Product X has historically constituted 10 percent of sales volume. If the current sales budget is $2 million, the output needed for product X is $200,000 ($2 million × 10 percent). If the price per unit is $40, this translates to 5,000 units.

EXAMPLE 7–3   Expected sales are $500,000 and production is estimated at 20 percent of sales. This translates to $100,000 of production.

An illustrative dollar production budget follows:

Variable costs (10,000 units × $10)	$100,000
Fixed costs (10,000 units × $3)	30,000
Production costs	$130,000
Costs of idle capacity	15,000
Total budgeted costs	$145,000

EXHIBIT 7–3 Total Cost of a Finished Product

Parts	Days to Manufacture	Number of Parts in Finished Product	Cost per Part	Total Cost
A	20	2	$10	$ 20
B	15	3	20	60
C	6	4	8	32
Assembly	1			15
Total cost of finished product				$127

An illustration of the computation of the total cost of a finished product is shown in Exhibit 7–3.

CAPACITY AND PRODUCTION PLANNING

It is necessary to examine the where, how, what, and when of manufacturing. Manufacturing executives are responsible for the production plan. The production department plans and schedules production and assigns responsibilities in the manufacturing area.

A long-term production plan (5 years) is needed to estimate project plant capacity requirements involving capital additions, the structure of the factory, cash flow, and manpower. In long-term planning, only a significant change in inventory needs to be considered. Once it is clear that the company has enough capacity to carry out the production requirement, the production plan begins. The production plan will typically be expressed in quarters or months. It should be consistent with short-term profit goals.

Production planning by major product line should be coordinated with profit planning and control. Higher production levels result in greater efficiency and lower unit costs. Production planning spots weaknesses and trouble areas beforehand that must be addressed.

All production factors must be used in a coordinated fashion to achieve maximum utilization of available resources. There needs to be a balance between sales, production volume, and inventory balances; they are all interrelated.

Production must meet customer needs and must be informed as to the status of sales and any problems. The manager should consider alternative combinations of capacity and operations. To produce the desired units, estimates are needed of materials, labor hours, machine hours, service hours, and machine availability.

The production method should generate the quantity needed at the appropriate quality at minimum cost. Production methods may change to meet changing times in terms of, for example, new manufacturing processes.

The production plan should constitute the best balance between sales, inventory levels, and stable production. There should be planning of physical volume of production for each product at its unit cost. Production should take place in adequate quantities without causing inventory buildups, excessive production costs, and waste in machinery and manpower.

Again, the production budget is tied into the company's expected sales and financial status. There should be coordination between production and sales. For example, manufacturing may be easier for standardization of products so there are fewer styles and sizes, but this may adversely affect total sales. The production department may want to smooth out production to constantly use manufacturing facilities and to regularly employ labor. However, the drawbacks would be redistributed sales emphasis, larger inventory balances, and an increased financial commitment.

Inventory levels are important to know in production planning, both work-in-process and finished goods. If inventory levels are low and sales demand is high, more will need to be produced. Study the following example:

Units required for sales	50,000
Add: Ending finished goods	10,000
Total	60,000
Less: Beginning finished goods	7,500
Units to be completed	52,500
Add: Equivalent units in final work-in-process	2,500
Total	55,000
Less: Equivalent units in beginning work-in-process	3,000
Equivalent units to be manufactured	58,000

A report should be prepared comparing expected production to actual production and the variance should be computed along with the reasons for it. There should be a record of the machinery to be used, the number of machines, manufacturing operations to be performed, and hourly production.

If the product consists of many parts to be manufactured, a parts production budget should be prepared. This budget shows when parts are to be started and completed.

Production planning should also indicate when production is to begin and end. The starting dates are important in deciding on when raw materials should be ordered and worker availability required.

Production planning involves product engineering, materials requirements planning, production control, industrial planning, quality control, shipping, and distribution. Some production planning tips are to identify process changes to increase capability, and rearrange facilities to lower costs and improve productivity when warranted.

Production Planning Tips

- Avoid unusual activities or expensive overtime hours to meet projected levels through sound planning.
- Avoid "rush orders" for supplies because of higher prices to be paid.
- Identify any bottlenecks in manufacturing.
- Make changes in capacity levels when warranted.
- Determine and evaluate productivity measures including production per factory worker, production per direct labor hour, and production relative to factory salaries.
- Identify capacity constraints and limitations.
- Identify special plant and manufacturing requirements before problems arise such as low ceilings, inadequate storage space, poor ventilation, and dusty surroundings.
- Update manufacturing processes to reflect technological changes.
- Subcontract work when economically and qualitatively expedient.

Production Planning Considerations

- Characteristics of the manufacturing process.
- Product development.
- Product perishability.
- Selling price stability.
- Plant capacity.
- Ordering costs.
- Factory costs.
- Storage capacity and costs.
- Stability of production.
- Demand elasticity.
- Time period for production.
- Service capability.
- Financial ability of the company to finance inventory.
- Availability and cost of raw materials.
- Susceptibility to loss from fire or water damage.
- Labor relationships, needs, and availability.
- Factory repairs and servicing.
- Protection against price increases.

- Engineering and research and development aspects.
- Availability of capital facilities (e.g., machinery).
- Regularity of employment.
- Economical production runs.
- Economical purchase quantities.

The production manager should determine what effect a change in product design will have on schedules, output, and revenue. The timing of the new product and its effect on production should be determined.

Merchandise should be available when orders are received. However, in special (customized) order situations the goal is to produce the items shortly after the order is received.

The assembly of a product in the different stages has to be considered. It must be determined what products will be made from what materials. Labor availability and competency must be determined in production planning.

Manufacturing work should be well distributed during production. It should be determined when and at what rate goods should be produced. When, if at all, should the plant be closed? Which products should be produced in which months?

Production must be properly planned and distributed in terms of work load. It must be determined when the goods should be produced and at what rate. For example, one product line may be manufactured in one month and another product line in another month. This may be necessary because of retooling machines, weather conditions, and so on.

A stable level of production is better for morale because it avoids periodic layoffs. To avoid employee layoffs and its undesirable effects on the company and workers, production should be planned continuously. In this regard, inventory may be increased during slow seasons. The sales manager must be notified of production difficulties, costs, and capacity constraints.

Production planning is tied to the capital budget through:

1. extraordinary repairs,
2. rearrangement and reinstallation, and
3. needed plant additions.

In the event that plant equipment is insufficient, management may take steps to obtain additional capacity or to modify production and sales requirements. In production planning, consideration must be given on the time it will take to make machinery operational.

Inventory models and linear programming may be helpful in inventory and production planning. These statistical techniques are discussed in Chapters 26–28.

MANUFACTURING

In budgeting production, it should be determined which activities are important and why. These activities should be properly scheduled in time and cost estimates should be made. Review and control points should be established in the manufacturing operation to assure that everything is proceeding properly. The product should be manufactured as economically as possible. Control points should be established during processing. The production rate should take into account anticipated revenue, capacity constraints, availability of raw materials, inventory balances, and working capital position.

The manufacturing schedule must be monitored to see if it is proceeding as planned. The deviation between scheduled production and actual production must be examined. The reports may be prepared quarterly, monthly, or daily as the need arises.

Continuous processing involves the automatic and repeating processing of goods. Batch processing occurs when a large processing unit takes place in periodic stages.

In special order situations, the product should be manufactured as soon as possible after the orders are received. In the customized situation, preplanning is more difficult and more modifications will be needed.

Value engineering identifies, values, and tests a function of a part or product to assure it results in the lowest total costs. Alternative ways are identified until the lowest cost is reached. It attempts to assure that each cost element, including material, labor, supplies, and repairs, contributes in a positive sense to the product. By improving value while controlling costs, the company's competitive situation will be improved. Value engineering does involve tradeoffs in improving a product at a specified cost. An objective is to improve performance and quality at less cost.

Financial executives may adjust manufacturing cost bases to conform to modifications made in the production process so as to satisfy cost considerations and merchandise valuation. The production reporting system must be flexible. The location and time for manufacturing goods may be based on the relative cost, availability of skilled labor, community and local considerations, union considerations, and employment distribution targets.

Just-in-time (JIT) inventory systems integrate five functions of the production process (sourcing, storage, transportation, operations, and quality control) into one controlled manufacturing process. In manufacturing, JIT means that a company produces only the quantity needed for delivery to dealers or customers. In purchasing, it means suppliers deliver subassemblies just in time to be assembled into finished goods. In delivery, it requires selecting a transportation mode that will deliver purchased components and materials in small-lot sizes at the loading dock of the manufacturing facilities just in time to support the manufacturing process. JIT systems will be thoroughly discussed in the next chapter.

INVENTORY BUDGET

The budget for inventory investment should be prepared after manufacturing costs have been determined. A sample unit cost budget follows:

		Unit Cost		
Product	*Material*	*Labor*	*Overhead*	*Total*
X	$1	$1.50	$1.25	$3.75

The finished goods inventory may be computed as follows:

XYZ Company
Finished Goods Budget
For the Year Ended December 31, 19X1

Product	*Quantity*	*Unit Price*	*Total*
B	10,000	$2.50	$25,000

A summary of the expected inventory investment may take the following form:

XYZ Company
Planned Inventories
For the Year Ended December 31, 19X1

Item	*Amount*
Raw materials and supplies	$115,000
Work-in-process	80,000
Finished goods	65,000
Total	$360,000

INVENTORY CONSIDERATIONS

Inventory budgets should consider raw materials, work-in-process, and finished goods. An objective is to have the optimum inventory balance. Inventory balances to be maintained depend upon many factors including:

- Expected sales. Higher inventory balances are needed if huge sales demand is projected.
- How long it takes a product to be produced. For example, if it takes 15 days for manufacturing, the minimum inventory level should be at least one month. The longer the period, the greater should be the inventory balance.
- Flexibility in inventory policy is needed to support stable production levels.

- Durability of the merchandise in terms of fad changes, technology, perishability, obsolescence, and product demand.

- How the product is distributed and how long it takes for that distribution.

- Larger raw material inventory balances are needed to support higher production levels. The raw material inventory also depends on how long it takes to receive materials from suppliers. What is the length of time from order to delivery?

- If higher amounts of raw materials are ordered, the per unit ordering cost is lower because it is spread over more units.

- A lower inventory balance reduces carrying costs and the cash tied up in inventory. There is also less danger of inventory risks such as obsolescence, perishability, and theft. However, an inadequate inventory level may lead to lost business and customers may switch to other suppliers.

The inventory reporting system should clearly indicate how much is on hand. Inventory policies should take into account quality standards and desired inventory turnover rates.

If production is stable for the year, inventory will change based on seasonal fluctuations. Inventory levels should be adequate to satisfy sales demands. There should be reasonable and adequate stocking to meet interim sales needs at the high and low points of the season.

Production should not result in inventory buildups because the merchandise cannot be sold. Further, higher inventory balances may force selling price reductions to move the inventory. On the other hand, insufficient inventory quantities may cause production disruptions and extra costs to expedite, setup costs, and overtime. Profit will be foregone on lost sales from having insufficient inventory on hand. There will also be lost customer goodwill if sales delivery dates are missed.

While an increase in inventory provides a hedge in case of production forecasting errors, higher inventory balances increase carrying costs and reduce cash flow. Carrying costs include insurance, property taxes, storage, and handling.

Minimum-maximum inventory levels should be established. A minimum level is needed to have sufficient stocking for customer needs. A maximum level is required to put a cap on storage costs, minimize inventory theft, and prevent product obsolescence. The minimum-maximum range may take into account inventory turnover rates.

Inventory planning and control should be specifically assigned so responsibility is known. The inventory policy will vary with company characteristics and the nature of the inventory problems. Inventory policies should be kept current.

There should be an analysis of inventory levels and turnover so as to minimize inventory costs where practical. Some businesses use a standard inventory turnover in setting inventory levels.

$$\text{Inventory Turnover} = \frac{\text{Units Withdrawn}}{\text{Units in Inventory}}$$

EXAMPLE 7–4 160,000 units of product X are budgeted to be sold for the year. The budgeted average inventory balance during the year is 40,000.

$$\text{Inventory Turnover} = \frac{160,000}{40,000} = 4 \text{ times}$$

Management believes a turnover of 6 (a 2-month supply) is an appropriate standard for the year for product X. Management should take appropriate steps to bring the supply down from 3 months (12/4) to 2 months.

An illustration of deriving an inventory balance based on production and shipments follows:

Month	Production Schedule	Budgeted Shipments	Balance
Beginning balance			100
January	50	20	130
February	60	40	150
March	40	50	140

If the budget is prepared before the beginning of the year, the beginning inventory will have to be budgeted.

The value of the finished inventory would be computed as shown below:

Product	Quantity	Unit Price	Amount
X	3,000	$2	$ 6,000
Y	2,000	5	10,000
Z	4,000	3	12,000
Total			$28,000

A similar approach would be used for raw materials, supplies, and work-in-process.

Inventory is typically viewed as the level of goods on hand while *replenishment* is the way to maintain that level.

Inventory models may be used to solve the following problems, among others:

• Reducing production costs

• Computing economic production runs

• Achieving the best balance in production between sales and inventories

• Allocating manufacturing capacity to products.

Inventory management policies must be considered, such as economic order quantity and economic order point (see Chapter 8).

COST OF GOODS SOLD

An estimated cost of goods sold schedule follows:

XYZ Company
Schedule of Estimated Cost of Sales
For the Year Ended December 31, 19XX

Raw Materials	
Inventory, January 1, 19XX	$40,000
Add: Purchases	400,000
Total available	$440,000
Less: Inventory, December 31, 19XX	25,000
Transfer to work-in-process	$415,000
Direct labor	500,000
Manufacturing overhead	600,000
Total manufacturing costs	$1,515,000
Add: Work-in-process, January 1, 19XX	30,000
Total	$1,545,000
Less: Work-in-process, December 31, 19XX	45,000
Transfer to finished goods	$1,500,000
Add: Finished goods, January 1, 19XX	300,000
Total	$1,800,000
Less: Finished goods, December 31, 19XX	200,000
Estimated cost of goods sold	$1,600,000

INVENTORY MANAGEMENT

The purpose of inventory management is to develop policies that will achieve an optimal inventory investment. The optimal level of inventory varies among industries and among companies in a particular industry. Successful inventory management minimizes inventory at all stages of manufacturing while retaining cost-effective production volume. This improves profitability and cash flow. By operating with minimum inventory levels and with short production lead times, the company increases its flexibility. This flexibility is needed to immediately respond to changing market conditions.

Inventory files should contain inventory location, quantity on hand, and quantity committed. Adequate inventory must be maintained to meet customer orders, properly utilize machines, keep production schedules, and assure smooth production activity. By maintaining a functional inventory supply, a company will be able to protect itself against unplanned changes in supply. Some inventory must be held at the different manufacturing stages as hedges against the variabilities of supply and demand as well hedging in the event problems surface in the manufacturing process itself. A sales forecast is the starting point for effective inventory management since expected sales determines how much inventory is needed.

Inventory records should provide needed information to satisfy the needs of the financial, sales, purchasing, and production managers. Inventory information may include the following by major type: unit cost, historical usage, quantity on order, minimum-maximum quantities, quantities in transit, delivery times, scheduling dates, and quantities set aside for specific contracts, production orders and customers. With regard to minimum-maximum quantities, such a procedure is practical when *stability* exists in the rate of sale or the use of the product and where the order time is short. The minimum is a "cushion" to be used only in an emergency. The maximum is the "ceiling" of the desirable inventory. The reorder point is between the minimum and maximum.

There should be a master item file containing identification, description, and specifications of the item's raw material, component parts, and assembly relationship. An item specification should include up-to-date data about the part, the production process, the uses of the item, possible substitutions, demand information, competitive factors, and the overall supply. Information may also be furnished about suppliers and relevant information that may affect the availability and price of the item.

The goal is to maximize sales with minimum inventory. Thus, inventory levels should be closely correlated to the selling cycle. A poor inventory management system may be revealed by failure to meet production plans, expediting of parts, slow-moving or obsolete goods, poor customer service, "rush" jobs in the factory, production bottlenecks, downtime, poor forecasts and deficient performance reporting, and internal conflicts between members of the organization such as production and marketing.

An advantage of a "bloated" inventory is the resulting reduction in production costs from larger production runs. It also provides a safety buffer if there is a nondelivery of raw materials or the prior department's manufacturing process breaks down.

Sales forecasting is crucial because an inaccurately high sales forecast can result in high inventory levels, markdowns, obsolescence, and inventory write-offs. An inaccurately low forecast will result in low inventory and lost sales. See Chapter 18 which covers sales forecasting.

Suppliers should be evaluated in terms of fairness in pricing, meeting delivery times, quality of goods shipped (e.g., in accordance with product specifications), and ability to meet "rush" jobs.

There are many benefits to be obtained from proper inventory management including:

- Reduces waste and cost arising from excess storage, handling, and obsolescence.
- Reduces the risk of inventory theft.
- Reduces production delays because needed raw materials are maintained. This results in lower production costs and longer runs.
- Improves customer service because needed materials are available.

Inventory Management Policies

- Appraise the adequacy of the raw materials level, which depends on expected production, condition of equipment, supplier reliability, and seasonal considerations. Raw material requirements may be forecast using such techniques as statistical analysis of historical trends and cycles, econometric models, and Delphi methods. Recommendation: Have sound material management guidelines to specify what and how much should be stored. Manufacturing requires an appropriate balance of parts to produce an end item. What to Watch Out For: A situation in which you have four of five needed components, because this results in having four excess inventories when a stockout of the fifth occurs.
- Forecast future movements in raw materials prices, so that if prices are expected to increase, additional materials are bought at lower prices.
- Discard slow-moving products to reduce inventory carrying costs and improve cash flow.
- Stock higher profit margin items for quick sale.
- Guard against inventory buildup, since it is associated with substantial carrying and opportunity costs.
- Minimize inventory levels when liquidity and/or inventory financing problems exist.
- Plan for a stock balance that will guard against and cushion the possible loss of business from a shortage in materials. The timing of an order also depends on seasonability factors.
- Ensure that inventory is received when needed so that production runs smoothly. What To Do: Compare vendor and production receipts to promised delivery due dates.
- A long sales order entry process requires the stocking of additional inventory.
- Try to convince customers to keep higher stock levels to reduce the company's inventory of finished goods.
- Examine the quality of merchandise received. The ratio of purchase returns

to purchases should be enlightening. A sharp increase in the ratio indicates that a new supplier may be warranted. A performance measurement and evaluation system should exist to appraise vendor quality and reliability (e.g., meeting promised delivery dates). If there is a problem with the vendor, problems will arise in production scheduling, imbalances in work-in-process, and "rush" purchase orders.

- Keep a careful record of back orders. A high back order level indicates that less inventory balances are needed. This is because back orders may be used as indicators of the production required, resulting in improved production planning and procurement. The trend in the ratio of the dollar amount of back orders to the average per-day sales will prove useful.

- Appraise the acquisition and inventory control functions. Any problems must be identified and rectified. In areas where control is weak, inventory balances should be restricted.

- Accuracy is needed for the bills of materials to indicate the parts and quantities received to produce an end product. What To Do: Conduct audits on the production floor when the parts are assembled.

- Have accurate inventory records and assign inventory responsibilities to managers. For example, assign to the engineering manager responsibility for the bills of material. Do you have the necessary inventory measurement tools (e.g., scales)?

- Closely supervise warehouse and materials handling staff to guard against theft and to maximize efficiency.

- Frequently review stock lines for poor earnings.

- Minimize the lead time in the acquisition, manufacturing, and distribution functions. The lead time is how long it takes to receive merchandise from suppliers after an order is placed. Depending upon lead times, an increase in inventory stocking may be required or the purchasing pattern may have to be altered. What To Do: Calculate the ratio of the value of outstanding orders to average daily purchases to indicate the lead time for receiving orders from suppliers. The ratio indicates whether you should increase the inventory balance or change your buying pattern. Are vendors keeping their delivery date promises?

- Examine the time between raw materials input and the completion of production to see if production and engineering techniques can be implemented to hasten the production operation.

- Examine the degree of spoilage and take steps to reduce it.

- Prepare an inventory analysis report presenting the number of months of insurance coverage. The report should highlight items with excess inventory coverage resulting from such causes as changes in customer demand or poor inventory practices.

- Maintain proper inventory control, such as through the application of computer techniques. For example, a point-of-sale computerized electronic register may be used by a retail business. The register continually updates inventory for sales and purchases. This data facilitates the computation of reorder points and quantity per order.

- Look at the trend in the unit cost of manufactured items. Reasons for variations should be analyzed to see if they are due to factors within or beyond company control (i.e., increase in oil prices, managerial inefficiencies).

- Have economies in production run size to reduce setup costs and idle time.

- Have vendors consign inventory to you and invoice as used.

- Utilize computer techniques and operations research to properly control inventory. For example, statistical forecasting methods can be used to determine inventory levels related to a pre-set acceptability level of outage probability.

The purchasing department can assist in inventory management in the following ways:

- Have blanket orders for operating supplies

- Have tight control over subcontracted operations

- Determine a price for raw materials that will protect the company in volatile markets

- Gradually increase purchase size as you get to know the supplier better

- Schedule delivery of raw materials using statistical and just-in-time techniques

Symptoms of Problems in Inventory Management

- Periodic extension of back orders
- Material shortages
- Material inventory writedowns at the end of the accounting period
- Uneven production and downtime
- Order cancellations
- Periodic lack of storage space
- Frequent layoffs and rehirings
- Differing rates of turnover among inventory items within the same inventory category
- Significant differences between book inventory and physical inventory

Good internal control over inventory is necessary to guard against theft or other irregularities. A surprise inventory count should periodically occur to assure agreement between the book inventory and physical inventory. Have controlled audit groups of work-in-process moving through the manufacturing process to see the accuracy with which work-in-process is documented.

Major shortages may take place and be unnoticed for a long time if satisfactory control is lacking. Inventory is vulnerable to theft. Good control is needed in the acquisition and handling phases. Segregation should exist in purchasing, receiving, storing, and shipping of inventories.

INVENTORY ANALYSIS

Inventory analysis should include consideration of the following:

- Customer order backlog as a percent of the inventory balance
- Inventory carrying cost by month and by year
- Inventory months' supply on hand by period for the major product lines
- Customer order backlog in weeks as a percent of the production process cycle (lead time)
- Safety stock and slow-moving (obsolete) inventory as a percent of cost of sales and of the inventory balance

Try to have work-in-process processed into finished goods as soon as possible. Work-in-process should arise only from manageable variability in the production process.

In inflationary and tight money periods, flexibility in inventory management is needed. For example, the quantity to be ordered may have to be adjusted to reflect increased costs.

The financial manager must consider the obsolescence and spoilage risk of inventory. For example, technological, perishable, fashionable, flammable, and specialized goods usually have high salability risk. The nature of the risks should be taken into account in computing desired inventory levels. The marketing department should be held accountable for obsolete and slow-moving items that they originally recommended. Before a product design is changed at the insistence of marketing, it should be carefully reviewed.

Different inventory items vary in profitability and the amount of space they occupy. Inventory management involves a tradeoff between the costs of keeping inventory versus the benefits of holding it. Higher inventory levels result in increased costs from storage, casualty and theft insurance, spoilage, higher property taxes for larger facilities, increased manpower requirements, and interest on borrowed funds to finance inventory acquisition. However, an increase in inventory lowers the possibility of lost sales from stockouts and the incidence of production slowdowns from inadequate inventory. Additionally, large volume purchases will result in greater purchase discounts. Inventory levels are also affected by short-term interest rates. For instance, as short-term interest rates increase, the optimum level of holding inventory will be reduced.

To reduce costs of handling inventory:

- Use several assembly lines and move crews to the next line which has already been setup.
- Hasten routing reproduction by using standardized forms.
- Keep materials at subassemblies, not final assemblies.
- Minimize seasonal stocking of material.
- Consolidate the number of inventory storage locations and/or warehouses.
- Simplify and standardize the product.
- Avoid shutting down the plant, such as having varying vacations.
- Decrease the time between filling an order and replacing the stock sold.
- Stop supplying "old" service parts but rather give customers the blueprint so they may internally manufacture them.

The inventory balance to be held depends upon:

- Vertical integration of the product line as indicated by manufactured versus purchased parts.
- Accuracy of manufacturing documents (e.g., route sheets, bill of materials).
- Accuracy of inventory records considering the deviation between the books and physical amounts.
- Reliability in estimating customer needs. Here, consideration should be given to the forecasting error.

Inventory of raw materials depends upon:

- Expected level and seasonability of production
- Reliability of supply sources

Inventory of work-in-process typically varies the most. Inventory of work-in-process depends upon:

- Length and time of the production run
- Number of stages in the production cycle, lot-sizing, quality problems, lead time, line balancing, and manufacturing scheduling

Work-in-process inventory may be viewed as a "liability" to inventory managers. Work-in-process takes away essential production capacity and cash while increasing the risk of obsolescence and shrinkage. While high machine utilization is good, an associated buildup of work-in-process is bad.

Inventory should be counted at regular, cyclic intervals because this provides the ability to check inventory on an ongoing basis as well as to reconcile the book and physical amounts. Recommendation: To lessen the time needed for counting, use standardized labeling procedures and quantity markings as well as orderly warehouse stocking. Tip: Take the count during nonworking hours to guard against duplicate counting. Alternatively, warehouse pickers could carefully enter daily movement when the cycle count takes place. Cyclic counting has the following advantages.

- Permits the efficient use of a few full-time experienced counters throughout the year
- Enables the timely detection and correction of the causes of inventory error
- Does not require a plant shutdown, as does a year-end count
- Facilitates the modifications of computer inventory programs, if needed

MATERIALS REQUIREMENTS PLANNING

The manager can use materials requirements planning, which is a technique using bills of material, inventory information, and the production schedule to compute material requirements. It indicates when material should be replenished and how much to order. Tip: Determine raw materials needed per item at each level. Note: A particular component may be needed for a number of assemblies at different levels. It is a good approach to formulate and maintain appropriate due dates on orders. If the production schedule changes, the timing and amount of materials needed will also change. The production quantities (how much) are based on specific identifiable customer orders. Note: Consider replacement (service) parts needs of customers. The amount ordered is based on periodic forecasts. There must be immediate feedback of changes in the production schedule (e.g., due to changes in priority) in order to adjust and control the planning and scheduling system. There should exist a master assembly schedule.

There is a linkage of production planning, business planning, materials requirements planning, capacity requirements planning, and the support systems for material and capacity. The output generated by these systems should be linked with the financial reports. Financial reports include inventory forecasts, shipping budget, purchase commitment analysis, and the overall business plan. Materials requirement planning will aid in planning manufacturing resources.

Materials requirements planning requires information about bills of material, routing of parts through the production stages, lead times, and availability of material information and status.

In materials requirements planning, ascertain material requirements at what level and when to order to produce the needed finished goods. Materials requirements planning is involved with having sufficient materials when needed to manufacture quality products in a timely and efficient manner.

A production and inventory management system involves:

- A product structure, such as the materials needed and when to produce
- The necessary sequence of production steps
- The work centers involved in production and their functions
- Managing product configuration and available parts

The production schedule depends on the organization of the work centers, time-phased material requirements, production constraints (e.g., bottlenecks), and routing sequences.

In scheduling production, all constraints should be looked at simultaneously. Of course, the production schedule will influence the lead time needed. Note: High machine utilization does not necessarily mean good production performance.

CONTROLS

Production planning must allow for controls of quantities, quality, and costs. Production control involves materials control, manufacturing processing flow, routing and scheduling, dispatching, and follow-up. Improved utilization of manufacturing facilities will help to avoid idle capacity, reduce the capacity needed during peak times, and reduce manufacturing costs. Units should be manufactured in economical lots. Machinery and labor should be optimally used. There are extra costs associated with uneconomic production runs. There should be a comparison of lower per unit manufacturing cost for larger production runs against the cost of higher storage costs. Volume discounts will reduce the purchase cost of raw materials.

CONCLUSION

A production budget determines how much is to be produced. After production has been estimated, the costs of direct material, direct labor, and factory overhead may be budgeted. Production may be expressed in units, dollars, hours, and so on.

REFERENCES

Thomas Gunn, *Manufacturing for Competitive Advantage* (Mass.: Ballinger Publishing, 1987).

Elizabeth Haas, "Breakthrough Manufacturing," *Harvard Business Review,* March-April 1987, pp. 75–81.

Robert Hayes and Kim Clark, "Why Some Factories Are More Productive Than Others," *Harvard Business Review,* Sept.-Oct. 1986, pp. 66–73.

Jeremy Main, "Manufacturing the Right Way," *Fortune,* May 21, 1990, pp. 54–64.

Otis Port, "A Smarter Way to Manufacture," *Business Week,* April 30, 1990, pp. 110–117.

Dale Sauers, "Analyzing Inventory Systems," *Management Accounting,* May 1986, pp. 30–36.

Chapter 8.

Planning and Control of Material Purchases and Usage

After determining the number of units to be produced, the company prepares the materials requirement budget and the materials purchase budget. Purchase of materials depends on production requirements and inventories. The direct materials budget involves a balancing of raw material needed for production, the raw material inventory balances, and the purchase of raw materials. The direct materials budget may provide for allowances for waste and spoilage. This chapter discusses the procedures for developing these budgets and inventory policies.

MATERIALS BUDGETS

The materials and inventory budgets in a typical manufacturing firm involves a determination of:

1. The quantities and cost of raw materials to be used.
2. The quantities and value of materials to be carried in the inventory. The inventory balance depends upon how long it takes to receive raw materials from suppliers after the order is placed.
3. The quantities and cost of materials to be purchased. The amount to purchase considers expected production and raw material levels. The units of

raw material needed equals the raw material usage multiplied by the units of production. In budgeting purchases, consideration should be given to expected price changes, interest cost to finance inventory, volume and cash discounts, desired delivery date, warehousing availability and cost, and obsolescence risk.

4. The quantity and value of finished goods to be carried in the inventory.

There are basically two methods of developing the inventory budget of raw materials:

1. Budget each important item separately based upon the production budget.
2. Budget materials as a whole or classes of materials based upon selected production factors.

Practically all companies must use both methods to some extent.

Budgeting Individual Items of Material

The following steps should be taken in budgeting the major individual items of materials:

1. Determine the physical units of material required for each item of goods which is to be produced during the budget period.
2. Accumulate these into total physical units of each material item required for the production plan.
3. Determine for each item of material the quantity which should be on hand periodically to provide for the production budget with a reasonable degree of safety.
4. Deduct material inventories, which it is expected will be on hand at the beginning of the budget period, to ascertain the total quantities to be purchased. The formula for computation of the purchase is:

Purchase in units = Usage + Desired ending material inventory units
− Beginning inventory units

5. Develop a purchase policy which will insure that quantities will be on hand at the time they are needed. The purchase policy must consider such factors as economic order quantities (EOQ), economy of transportation, quantity discounts, and possible stockouts.
6. Translate the inventory and purchase requirements into dollars by applying the expected prices of materials to the budgeted quantities. *Note:* The dollar amount of purchases is one of the major cash disbursement items in the cash budget.

Budget Based on Production Factors

For those items of materials which cannot be budgeted individually, the budget must be based on production factors such as total budgeted labor hours, productive hours, standard allowed hours, cost of materials consumed, or cost of goods manufactured.

EXAMPLE 8–1   Assume that cost of materials consumed (other than basic materials which are budgeted individually) is budgeted at $2,000,000 and that past experience demonstrates that these materials and supplies should be held to a rate of 4 times per year; then an average inventory of $500,000 should be budgeted. This would mean that individual items of material could be held in stock about 60 days (360 days/4).

SAMPLE MATERIALS PURCHASE BUDGET

The following example illustrates a typical method of budgeting the quantities and cost of raw materials to be purchased. Assume that there are three classes of materials: X, Y, and Z.

Class X. Materials for which a definite quantity and monthly distribution is established in advance.

Class Y. Material items for which definite quantities are established for the entire budget period but for which no definite monthly distribution program is established.

Here the distribution to months of the total cost of $4,031 must be made on the basis of past experience of budgeted production factors such as machine hours. The figures in Exhibit 8–3 may be assumed, based on past experience.

Class Z. Miscellaneous material items which are grouped together and budgeted only in terms of total dollar purchases for the total budget period.

EXHIBIT 8–1 Class X Materials

	Item A			Item B			
	Units	Standard Unit Cost	Amount	Units	Standard Unit Cost	Amount	Total
July	300	$1.10	$330	650	$2.00	$1,300	$1,630
August	200	1.00	200	700	2.00	1,400	1,600
September	500	1.00	500	400	2.10	840	1,340
October	250	1.00	250	250	2.25	563	813
November	300	1.00	300	350	2.25	788	1088
December	400	1.00	400	250	2.25	563	963
Total	1,950		$1,980	2,600		$5,453	$7,433

EXHIBIT 8–2 Class Y Materials

	Total Units Required to be Purchased	Estimated Price per Unit	Total Cost
Item H	2,500	0.25	625
I	3,400	0.34	1,156
J	4,500	0.23	1,035
K	2,700	0.45	1,215
Total	13,100		$4,031

EXHIBIT 8–3 Distribution Based on Past Experience

	Percentage Distribution Based on Past Experience	Material Items				
		H	I	J	K	Total
July	30%	$188	$ 347	$ 311	$ 365	$1,209
August	20%	125	231	207	243	806
September	10%	63	116	104	122	403
October	20%	125	231	207	243	806
November	10%	63	116	104	122	403
December	10%	63	116	104	122	403
Total	100.00%	$625	$1,156	$1,035	$1,215	$4,031

The distribution to months is again made on the basis of past experience or production factors. The following figures may be assumed, based on budgeted machine hours (cost of Class Z materials is assumed to be $5 per hour):

EXHIBIT 8–4 Class Z Materials

	Budgeted Productive Hours	Distribution to Months
July	150	$ 750
August	240	1,200
September	175	875
October	80	400
November	95	475
December	100	500
Total	840	$4,200

Note that total purchases required for Class Z materials amount to $4,200.

The total purchase budget may then be summarized as follows:

EXHIBIT 8–5 Total Purchase Budget

	Class X Materials	Class Y Materials	Class Z Materials	Total
July	$1,630	$1,209	$ 750	$3,589
August	1,600	806	1,200	3,606
September	1,340	403	875	2,618
October	813	806	400	2,019
November	1,088	403	475	1,966
December	963	403	500	1,866
Total	$7,433	$4,031	$4,200	$15,664

The estimated days material is to be held may be computed. Assume direct material used is budgeted at $500,000 with an expected turnover rate of 4 times. Thus, the average inventory is budgeted at $125,000. Material will be stored about 90 days (360/4). Material price and usage variances are discussed in Chapter 16. An illustrative budget is presented in Exhibit 8–6.

EXHIBIT 8–6 XYZ Company Purchases Budget
For the Year Ended December 31, 19X1

Type of Raw Material	Production	Ending + Inventory	Beginning − Inventory	Budgeted Price	Budgeted Purchases
A	200,000 etc.	40,000	20,000	$1.50	$330,000

INVENTORY PLANNING AND PURCHASING POLICIES

The purpose of inventory planning is to develop policies which will achieve an optimal investment in inventory. This objective is achieved by determining the optimal level of inventory necessary to minimize inventory related costs.

Inventory related costs fall into three categories:

1. Ordering costs, which includes all costs associated with preparing a purchase order.

2. Carrying (holding) costs, which include storage costs for inventory items plus the cost of money tied up in inventory.

3. Shortage (stockout) costs, which include those costs incurred when an item is out of stock. These include the lost contribution margin on sales plus lost customer goodwill.

There are many inventory planning models available which try to answer basically the following two questions: How much to order? When to order? They include the so-called economic order quantity (EOQ) model, the reorder point, and the determination of safety stock.

Economic Order Quantity

The economic order quantity (EOQ) determines the order quantity that results in the lowest sum of carrying and ordering costs. The EOQ is computed as:

$$EOQ = \sqrt{\frac{2\,OD}{C}}$$

where C = carrying cost per unit, O = ordering cost per order, and D = annual demand (requirements) in units.

If the carrying cost is expressed as a percentage of average inventory value (e.g., 12 percent per year to hold inventory), then the denominator value in the EOQ formula would be 12 percent times the price of an item.

EXAMPLE 8–2   Assume the Cypress Store buys sets of steel at $40 per set from an outside vendor. It will sell 6,400 sets evenly throughout the year. The store desires a 16 percent return on its inventory investment since the 16 percent represents the interest charge on borrowed money. In addition, rent, taxes, etc. for each set in inventory is $1.60 per year. The ordering cost is $100 per order. Then the carrying cost per dozen is 16%($40) + $1.60 = $8.00 per year. Therefore,

$$EOQ = \sqrt{\frac{2(6,400)\,(\$100)}{\$8.00}} = \sqrt{160,000} = 400 \text{ sets}$$

Total number of orders per year = D/EOQ = 6,400/400 = 16 orders

Total inventory costs = Carrying cost + Ordering cost

$$= C \times (\text{EOQ}/2) + O\,(D/\text{EOQ})$$

$$= (\$8.00)\,(400/2) + (\$100)\,(6,400/400)$$

$$= \$1,600 + \$1,600 = \$3,200$$

Based on these calculations, the Cypress Store's inventory policy should be the following:

1. The store should order 400 sets of steel each time it places an order and order 16 times during a year.

2. This policy will be most economical and cost the store $3,200 per year.

Reorder Point

Reorder point (ROP), which determines when to place a new order, requires a knowledge about the lead time, which is the time interval between placing an order and receiving delivery. Reorder point (ROP) can be calculated as follows:

Reorder point = (average usage per unit of lead time × lead time)
+ safety stock

First, multiply average daily (or weekly) usage by the lead time in days (or weeks) yielding the lead time demand. Then add safety stock to this to provide for the variation in lead time demand to determine the reorder point. If average usage and lead time are both certain, no safety stock is necessary and it should be dropped from the formula.

EXAMPLE 8–3   Assume in Example 8–2, lead time is constant at one week, and that there are 50 working weeks in a year. Then the reorder point is

128 sets = (6,400 sets/50 weeks) × 1 week.

Therefore, when the inventory level drops to 128 sets, the new order should be placed. Suppose, however, that the store is faced with variable usage for its steel and requires a safety stock of 150 additional sets to carry. Then the reorder point will be 128 sets plus 150 sets, or 278 sets.

Figure 8–1 shows this inventory system when the order quantity is 400 sets and the reorder point is 128 sets.

FIGURE 8–1 Basic Inventory System with EOQ and Reorder Point

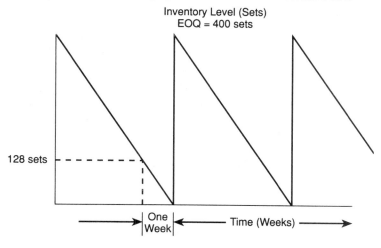

Inventory Level (Sets)
EOQ = 400 sets

128 sets

One Week

Time (Weeks)

EOQ with Quantity Discounts

The economic order quantity (EOQ) model does not take into account quantity discounts, which is unrealistic in many cases. Usually, the more you order, the lower the unit price you pay. Quantity discounts are price reductions for large orders offered to buyers to induce them to buy in large quantities. If quantity discounts are offered, the buyer must weigh the potential benefits of reduced purchase price and fewer orders that will result from buying in large quantities against the increase in carrying costs caused by higher average inventories. Hence, the buyer's goal in this case is to select the order quantity which will minimize total costs, where total cost is the sum of carrying cost, ordering cost, and product cost:

$$\text{Total cost} = \text{Carrying cost} + \text{Ordering cost} + \text{Product cost}$$

$$= C \times (Q/2) + O \times (D/Q) + PD$$

where P = unit price and Q = order quantity.

A step-by-step approach in computing economic order quantity with quantity discounts is summarized below.

1. Compute the economic order quantity (EOQ) when price discounts are ignored and the corresponding costs using the new cost formula given above. *Note*: EOQ = $\sqrt{2OD/C}$.
2. Compute the costs for those quantities greater than the EOQ at which price reductions occur.
3. Select the value of Q which will result in the lowest total cost.

Advantages and Disadvantages of Quantity Discounts

Buying in large quantities has some favorable and some unfavorable features. The advantages are lower unit costs, lower ordering costs, fewer stockouts, and lower transportation costs. On the other hand, there are disadvantages such as higher inventory carrying costs, greater capital requirement, and higher probability of obsolescence and deterioration.

Determination of Safety Stock

When lead time and demand (or usage) are not certain (or variable), the firm must carry extra units of inventory, called safety stock as protection against possible stockouts. To determine the appropriate level of safety stock size, you must consider the service level or stockout costs. Safety stock must be added to the reorder point (ROP), which tells you when to place an order.

FIGURE 8–2 Service Level of 90 Percent

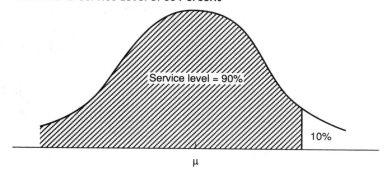

Service level can be defined as the probability that demand will not exceed supply during the lead time. Thus, a service level of 90 percent implies a probability of 90 percent that usage will not exceed supply during lead time. Figure 8–2 shows a service level of 90 percent.

To determine the optimal level of safety stock size, you might also want to measure costs of not having enough inventory, or stockout costs. Below are three cases for computing the safety stock. The first two do not recognize stockout costs; the third case does. In the case of uncertain usage and/or lead time, the reorder point (ROP) is computed as follows:

ROP = Expected usage during lead time + safety stock

= lead time × average usage per unit of time + safety stock

CASE 1: VARIABLE USAGE RATE, CONSTANT LEAD TIME

ROP = Expected usage during lead time + safety stock

$$= \bar{u}\, LT + z\, \sqrt{LT}\, (\sigma u)$$

where

$\bar{u}$ = average usage rate
LT = lead time
σu = standard deviation of usage rate
z = standard normal variate (see Normal Distribution—
        Table 1 in Appendix B)

EXAMPLE 8–4   Norman's Pizza uses large cases of tomatoes at an average rate of 50 cans per day. Usage can be approximated by a normal distribution with a standard deviation of 5 cans per day. Lead time is 4 days. Thus,

FIGURE 8–3 Service Level of 99 Percent

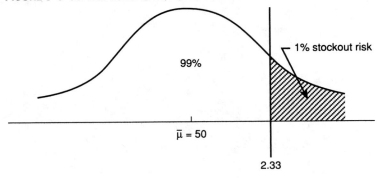

$$\bar{u} = 50 \text{ cans per day}$$

$$LT = 4 \text{ days}$$

$$\sigma u = 5 \text{ cans}$$

How much safety stock is necessary for a service level of 99 percent? And what is the ROP?

For a service level of 99 percent, $z = 2.33$ (from Table 1 in Appendix B). Thus,

$$\text{Safety stock} = 2.33 \ 4 \ (5) = 23.3 \text{ cans}$$

$$\text{ROP} = 50(4) + 23.3 = 223.3 \text{ cans}$$

A diagram appears in Figure 8–3 depicting the service level.

CASE 2: CONSTANT USAGE RATE, VARIABLE LEAD TIME

$$\text{ROP} = \text{Expected usage during lead time} + \text{safety stock}$$

$$= u \, \overline{LT} + z \, u \, (\sigma LT)$$

where

$$u = \text{constant usage rate}$$
$$\overline{LT} = \text{average lead time}$$
$$\sigma LT = \text{standard deviation of lead time}$$

EXAMPLE 8–5 Norton's hamburger shop uses 10 gallons of cola per day. Lead time is normally distributed with a mean of 6 days and a standard deviation of 2 days. Thus,

$$u = 10 \text{ gallons per day}$$

$$\overline{LT} = 6 \text{ days}$$

$$\sigma LT = 2 \text{ days}$$

How much safety stock is necessary for a service level of 99 percent? And what is the ROP?

For a service level of 99 percent, $z = 2.33$ (from Normal Distribution Table 1 in Appendix B). Thus,

$$\text{Safety stock} = 2.33 \,(10)\,(2) = 46.6 \text{ gallons}$$

$$\text{ROP} = 10(6) + 46.6 = 106.6 \text{ gallons}$$

CASE 3: INCORPORATION OF STOCKOUT COSTS

This case specifically recognizes the cost of stockouts or shortages, which can be quite expensive. Lost sales and disgruntled customers are examples of external costs. Idle machine and disrupted production scheduling are examples of internal costs.

Example 8–6 illustrates the probability approach to show how the optimal safety stock can be determined in the presence of stockout costs.

EXAMPLE 8–6   Assume ABC Store buys sets of steel at $40 per set from an outside vendor. ABC will sell 6,400 sets evenly throughout the year. The carrying cost per set is $8.00. If the lead time and demand are certain, then reorder point is:

$$\text{Reorder point} = 1 \text{ week} \times \frac{6,400}{50 \text{ weeks}} = 1 \times 128$$

$$= 128 \text{ sets}$$

Assume that the total usage over a one-week period is uncertain and expected to be:

Total usage	Probability
78	.2
128	.4
178	.2
228	.1
278	.1
	1.00

The stockout cost is estimated at $12.00 per set. Exhibit 8–6 shows the computation of safety stock.

The computation shows that the total costs are minimized at $1,200, when a safety stock of 150 sets is maintained. Therefore, the reorder point is:

$$128 \text{ sets} + 150 \text{ sets} = 278 \text{ sets.}$$

EXHIBIT 8–6 Computation of Safety Stock

Safety Stock Levels in Units	Stockout and Probability	Average Stockout in Units	Average Stockout Costs	No. of Orders	Total Annual Stockout Costs	Carrying Costs	Total
0	50 with .2 100 with .1 150 with .1	35*	$420**	16	$6,720***	0	$7,140
50	50 with .1 100 with .1	15	180	16	2,880	400****	3,280
100	50 with .1	5	60	16	960	800	1,760
150	0	0	0	16	0	1,200	1,200

  * $50(.2) + 100(.1) + 150(.1) = 10 + 10 + 15 = 35$ units
  ** 35 units $\times$ \$12.00 = \$420
  *** \$420 $\times$ 16 times = \$6,720
  **** 50 units $\times$ \$8.00 = \$400

JUST-IN-TIME (JIT) MANUFACTURING

The inventory control problem occurs in almost every type of organization. It exists whenever products are held to meet some expected future demand. In most industries, cost of inventory represents the largest liquid asset under the control of management. Therefore, it is very important to develop a production and inventory planning system that will minimize both purchasing and carrying costs.

Effective purchasing and management of materials is a high priority in most manufacturing firms. Material cost, as a proportion of total product cost, has continued to rise significantly during the last few years and, hence, is a primary concern of top management.

In recent years, the Japanese have demonstrated the ability to manage their production systems effectively. Much of their success has been attributed to what is known as the Just-In-Time (JIT) approach to production and inventory control, which has generated a great deal of interest among practitioners. The "Kanban" system—as they call it—has been a focal point of interest, with its dramatic impact on the inventory performance and productivity of the Japanese auto industry. An overview of the Just-In-Time (JIT) approach follows.

What is Just-in-Time (JIT)?

JIT is a demand-pull system. Demand for customer output (not plans for using input resources) triggers production. Production activities are "pulled," not "pushed" into action. JIT production, in its purest sense, is buying and producing in very small quantities just in time for use. The basic idea has its roots in Japan's densely populated industrial areas and its lack of resources, both of which have produced frugal personal habits among the Japanese people. The idea was developed into a formal management system by Toyota in order to meet the precise demands of customers for various vehicle models and colors with minimum delivery delays.

As a philosophy, JIT targets inventory as an evil presence that obscures problems that should be solved, and that by contributing significantly to costs, large inventories keep a company from being as competitive or profitable as it otherwise might be. Practically speaking, JIT has as its principal goal the elimination of waste, and the principal measure of success is how much or how little inventory is on hand. Virtually anything that achieves this end can be considered a JIT innovation.

Furthermore, the little inventory that exists in a JIT system must be of good quality. This requirement has led to JIT purchasing practices uniquely able to deliver high-quality materials.

JIT Compared With Traditional Manufacturing

JIT manufacturing is a demand-pull, rather than the traditional "push" approach. The philosophy underlying JIT manufacturing is to produce a product when it is needed and only in the quantities demanded by customers. Demand pulls products through the manufacturing process. Each operation produces only what is necessary to satisfy the demand of the succeeding operation. No production takes place until a signal from a succeeding process indicates a need to produce. Parts and materials arrive just in time to be used in production.

Reduced Inventories.   The primary goal of JIT is to reduce inventories to insignificant or zero levels. In traditional manufacturing, inventories result whenever production exceeds demand. Inventories are needed as a buffer when production does not meet expected demand.

Manufacturing Cells and Multifunction Labor.   In traditional manufacturing, products are moved from one group of identical machines to another. Typically, machines with identical functions are located together in an area referred to as a department or process. Workers who specialize in the operation of a specific machine are located in each department. JIT replaces this traditional pattern with a pattern of manufacturing cells or work centers. Each cell is set up to produce a particular product or product family. Workers are assigned to cells and are trained to operate all machines within the cell. Thus, labor in a JIT environment is multifunction labor, not specialized labor. Each manufacturing cell is basically a minifactory or a factory within a factory.

Total Quality Control. JIT carries with it a stronger emphasis on quality control. A defective part brings production to a grinding halt. Poor quality simply cannot be tolerated in a stockless manufacturing environment. In other words, JIT cannot be implemented without a commitment to total quality control (TQC). TQC is essentially an endless quest for perfect quality. This approach to quality is opposed to the traditional belief, called acceptable quality level (AQL). AQL allows defects to occur provided they are within a predetermined level.

Decentralization of Services. JIT requires easy and quick access to support services, which means that centralized service departments must be scaled down and their personnel assigned to work directly to support production. For example, with respect to raw materials, JIT calls for multiple stock points, each one near where the material will be used. There is no need for a central warehouse location.

Suppliers as Outside Partners. The most important aspects of the JIT purchasing concept focus on (1) new ways of dealing with suppliers, and (2) a clear-cut recognition of the appropriate purchasing role in developing corporate strategy. Suppliers should be viewed as "outside partners" who can contribute to the long-run welfare of the buying firm rather than as outside adversaries.

Better Cost Management. JIT recognizes that with simplification comes better management, better quality, better service, and better cost. Traditional cost accounting systems have a tendency to be very complex, with many transactions and reporting of data. Simplification of this process will transform a cost "accounting" system into a cost "management" system that can be used (1) to support management's needs for better decisions about product design, pricing, marketing, and mix and (2) to encourage continual operating improvements.

Benefits of JIT

The potential benefits of JIT are numerous. First, JIT practice reduces inventory levels, which means lower investments in inventories. Since the system requires only the smallest quantity of materials needed immediately, it reduces the overall inventory level substantially. In many Japanese companies that use the JIT concept, inventory levels have been reduced to the point that makes the annual working capital turnover ratio much higher than that experienced by U.S. counterparts. For instance, Toyota reported inventory turnover ratios of 41 to 63, while comparable U.S. companies reported inventory turnover ratios of 5 to 8.

Second, since purchasing under JIT requires a significantly shorter delivery lead time, lead time reliability is greatly improved. Reduced lead time and increased reliability also contribute to a significant reduction in the safety stock requirements.

Third, reduced lead times and set-up times increase scheduling flexibility. The cumulative lead time, which includes both purchasing and production lead times, is reduced. Thus, the firm schedule within the production planning horizon is reduced. This results in a longer "look-ahead" time that can be used to meet shifts in market demand. The smaller lot size production made possible by reduced set-up time, also adds flexibility.

Fourth, improved quality levels have been reported by many companies. When the order quantity is small, sources of quality problems are quickly identifiable and can be corrected immediately. In many cases, employee quality consciousness also tends to improve, producing an improvement in quality at the production source.

Fifth, the costs of purchased materials may be reduced through more extensive value analysis and cooperative supplier development activities.

Sixth, other financial benefits reported include:

1. Lower investments in factory space for inventories and production
2. Less obsolescence risk in inventories
3. Reduction in scrap and rework
4. Decline in paperwork
5. Reduction in direct material costs through quantity purchases.

Examples of JIT Implementation in the U.S.

The following are some of the many implementation experiences of JIT in the U.S.:

- The Oldsmobile division of General Motors (GM) has implemented a JIT project which permits immediate electronic communication between Oldsmobile and 70 of its principal suppliers who provide 700 to 800 parts representing around 85 percent of the parts needed for the new GM-20 cars.

- PTC Components, a supplier to GM, has assisted GM in its use of stockless production by sending one truck a week to deliver timing chains to several GM's engine plants rather than to accumulate a truckload to ship to each plant.

- Ford introduced JIT production at its heavy-duty truck plant in Kentucky, which forced Firestone to switch the tire searching point from Mansfield to Dayton, Ohio. By combining computerized ordering and halving inventory, Firestone has been able to reduce its own finished goods inventory. In addition, its production planning is no longer guesswork.

- Each day a truck from Harley-Davidson Motor Co. transports 160 motorcycle seats and assorted accessories 800 miles overnight to Harley's assembly plant in York, PA, as a part of their advanced "Materials as Needed" (MAN) program—its version of JIT.

- The Hoover Company has used JIT techniques in its two plants at North Canton, Ohio for a number of years for production scheduling and material flow control of 360 different models and 29,000 part numbers.

- Some plants of Du Pont used JIT and had an inventory savings of 30 cents on the dollar for the first year.

- The Vancouver division of Hewlett-Packard reported the following benefits two years after the adoption of the JIT method:

Work-in-process inventory dollars	down 82%
Space used	down 40%
Scrap/rework	down 30%
Production time:	
Impact printers	down 7 days to 2 days
Thermal printers	down 7 days to 3 hours
Labor efficiency	up 50%
Shipments	up 20%

Note: The implementation experiences listed above do not suggest a quick or across-the-board adaption of this concept. In many companies (particularly U.S. firms), the JIT purchasing concept simply may not be practical or feasible. In others, it may not be applicable to all product lines. However, many progressive companies currently are either investigating or implementing some form of the system.

CONCLUSION

A comprehensive profit planning and control program involves budgeting the materials and parts used in the production process. The budgetary process includes the material usage and purchase budgets and requires a development of policies which will achieve an optimal investment in inventory. This chapter discussed the procedures for materials usage and purchases and traditional issues surrounding inventory planning and control, such as the EOQ model, reorder point, and determination of safety stock. In addition, it discussed the basic concepts underlying the Just-in-Time (JIT) system. JIT was compared with the traditional system.

Chapter **9**

Planning and Control of Direct Labor

For many businesses, labor costs are the highest cost. Therefore, labor cost must be estimated, controlled, and analyzed. The direct labor budget is for the entire plant and for each department. The direct labor budget will have an effect upon employees and the company's relationship with them.

The direct labor budget reveals the labor hours expected, the total cost, manpower requirements, and type of workers needed. The direct labor budget should consider the wages paid and hours expended in production activities. A work study of the operations involved would be helpful in setting standards. It applies to factory workers. Direct labor should be budgeted by time, cost, product, and service. Indirect labor is not directly associated with producing the product such as supervisory salaries, custodian wages, and repairman compensation. Overtime should be listed separately.

Labor planning includes manpower requirements, salary structure, contract agreements, job appraisal, training, and hiring. Direct labor planning aids in recruitment, training, and worker utilization.

This chapter will consider the preparation of the direct labor budget and labor reports, fringe benefits, and the control and analysis of labor.

DIRECT LABOR BUDGET

The labor budget is designed to provide a labor force that will meet production needs. The labor budget estimates labor hours and worker skills required.

143

It determines total labor cost for production. The timing of cash payments for worker salaries are projected. Desired labor performance is specified.

The direct labor budget shows the wages paid to employees for producing a product during the manufacturing stages (e.g., assembling, finishing). The total direct labor cost considers each product and all departments in the manufacturing process.

Direct labor budgets vary by industry and company. Supervisors should provide their labor needs by type, quantity, and quality. Labor requirements are based on sales and production plans. The labor budget helps in planning and controlling labor. The budget should identify each major labor cost including fringe benefits and payroll taxes.

The objectives of the labor budget are to:

- Determine how many and type of employees are needed.
- Estimate labor hours needed to perform the necessary tasks.
- Ascertain the labor hour schedule.
- Measure employee performance.
- Control labor costs.

The labor budget procedures consider the production process, performance standards, organizational structure, dispersion of physical facilities (e.g., location, distances), and environment.

Direct labor is directly charged to a product or process. Direct labor for a service is the direct labor cost to provide that service. The direct labor budget indicates the expected cost of direct labor to produce products in the quantities needed as per the production budget. Therefore, the direct labor budget is prepared after the production budget. The direct labor budget establishes the direct labor hourly needs, employees required, per unit labor cost, cash flow requirements, and cost control. The estimation of direct labor cost depends on the standard cost per hour and the estimated production hours.

Budgeting for labor hours and cost depends to a large measure on the standardization of labor operations and on the sufficiency of labor records applying to historical labor performance and costs. The direct labor budget must be flexible and adjusted as orders are received. There is a continual updating of the direct labor budget. The labor budget may be revised because of a modification to a contract, change in facilities, lack of product demand, and changing economic conditions.

Many companies have three or four employees in nonproductive jobs (indirect labor) for each direct worker manufacturing a product. For a project, direct labor is the labor identifiable to that project. Normal nonproductive time may be considered part of total labor time. A portion should be allocated to direct labor time, e.g., coffee breaks and personal time.

The company should strive for regularity of employment in budget-

EXHIBIT 9–1 ABC Manufacturing Company
Direct Labor Budget
For the Year Ending December 31, 1995

Date and Department	Units to Manufacture	Unit Standard Hours	Total Standard Hours	Hourly Rate	Total Cost
January					
Dept. A	30,000	.2	6,000	$1.50	$9,000
Dept. B					
Dept. C					
etc.					

ing for sales, production, and labor. An illustrative direct labor budget appears in Exhibit 9–1.

EXAMPLE 9–1 A production budget provides for 2,000 completed units of a product. The product requires four operations involving direct labor time. The standard times for these operations are:

$\frac{1-}{1.50}$	$\frac{2}{.50}$	$\frac{3}{1.25}$	$\frac{4}{2}$

The planned direct labor hours are computed below:

Operation		Direct Labor Hours
1	$2,000 \times 1.50$	3,000
2	$2,000 \times .50$	1,000
3	$2,000 \times 1.25$	2,500
4	$2,000 \times 2.00$	4,000
		10,500

A schedule showing the computation of the average wage rate follows:

Operation No. 1	Planned Wage Rate	Number of Direct Labor Employees	Weighted Amount	Average Wage Rate
Group X	$ 8	5	$ 40	
Group Y	10	6	60	
		11	$100	$9.10

LABOR REPORTS

Labor reports should be prepared showing labor problems, reasons, responsibility, and proposed corrections. It should examine labor turnover and discuss the causes. Labor reports should be prepared for the entire company for

EXHIBIT 9–2 Illustrative Labor Report

Operator Number	Operator Name	Labor Hours			Labor Cost			
		Actual	Standard	Variance	Actual	Standard	Variance	Reason

each department, and for each responsibility center within each manufacturing department. There should be exception reporting. An illustrative labor report is presented in Exhibit 9–2. An illustrative direct labor report showing variance analysis appears in Exhibit 9–3.

EXHIBIT 9–3 Direct Labor Report Showing Variance Analysis

Date ————————
Department ————————
Supervisor ————————

Employee Number	Employee Operator Name	Direct Labor Cost			Reasons for Variance
		Actual	Standard	Variance	
13	Blake	$ 15	$ 12	$ 3U	Insufficient training
15	Hartman	19	18	1U	Machine breakdown
20	Simon	25	20	5U	Lack of materials
23	Frier	40	36	4U	Operator inefficiency
27	Whitman	50	40	10U	Fatigue
Total		$149	$126	$23U	

Variance as a percent of standard=$23/$126=18.3%

FRINGE BENEFITS

Human Resources must prepare the fringe benefits package which includes the overall payroll increase and the improvements in fringe benefits. It considers what the company can afford. For example, an unprofitable company must control costs. The package is also based on data obtained from nationwide personnel studies, local business surveys, surveys of the industry organizations, union information, and so on. Each department is allocated a portion of this increase which is assigned to individual employees based on performance and their position in their pay range.

LABOR COST CONTROL AND ANALYSIS

Labor analysis involves comparing actual labor performance to standard labor performance, computing output per labor hour, comparing indirect hours to direct hours, determining revenue per worker, and studying the turnover rate. A listing of employees should be approved. There should be adequate staff to perform activities. However, overstaffing may require layoffs. The number of employees should be consistent with the company's goals. Excessive pay should be avoided by controlling raises, putting the right worker on the right job (e.g., a low-priced worker for a low-priced job not a high-priced one, restricting overtime, and using part-time workers so as to cut salaries and fringe benefits.

Labor requirements should be studied, reviewed, and approved. Labor costs should be held to a minimum but employee attitudes must be considered. Labor may be minimized through product redesign and selecting efficient methods. Overtime must be authorized.

Excessive labor time must be avoided by improving worker training and efficiency, better scheduling, improving supervision, improving the quality of machinery and tools, and improving working conditions. Examine previous trends in labor hours to units produced by department and product. If there is a problem, workers may be shifted between departments. The relationship between indirect labor and direct labor should be considered. If indirect labor is excessive, it should be reduced. An evaluation should be made whether worker time is spent effectively. Employee productivity may be measured by examining the trend in the ratios of sales to wages, sales to labor hours, and sales to units produced.

Chapter **10**

Factory Overhead

The production executive should prepare the factory overhead budget. Overhead is based on the work load or volume the department is expected to handle. Factory overhead is not identifiable directly to a specific product, process, or job. Factory overhead includes factory rent, insurance, salaries, fringe benefits, power and supplies. Factory overhead may be allocated to products based on direct labor cost, direct labor hours, machine hours, or any other surrogate for production. The factory overhead budget should consider inventory position, production mix, and length of production run. Because factory overhead consists of many diverse expenses there exist cost control and cost allocation problems.

TYPES OF OVERHEAD COSTS

Costs must be properly classified and accounted for. There must be accurate classification of overhead costs into fixed and variable categories to properly forecast overhead for the year.

Fixed costs are expenses that remain constant in total regardless of changes in activity within a relevant range. Examples are rent, insurance, and taxes. Fixed cost per unit changes as volume changes. Fixed costs must be properly allocated.

Variable costs are expenses that vary in total in direct proportion to changes in activities, such as machine hours and labor hours within a relevant range. Examples are direct materials and gasoline expense based on mileage driven. Variable cost per unit is constant.

Variable overhead is typically expressed as standard unit allowances. Variable costs are typically harder to predict than fixed costs. For example, it is harder to predict fuel costs and health care costs than monthly rent and straight-line depreciation on a fixed asset.

Semi-variable (mixed) cost is one that varies with changes in volume but, unlike a variable cost, does not vary in direct proportion. In other words, this cost contains both a variable and fixed component. Examples are the rental of a delivery truck, where a fixed rental fee plus a variable charge based on mileage is made; and power costs, where the expense consists of a fixed amount plus a variable charge based on consumption.

Indirect materials may be budgeted based on indirect materials consumed previously. Indirect labor should be budgeted based on the nature of the jobs. Indirect labor can be computed by measuring past costs relative to factory manhours. Indirect labor may range from 15 percent–80 percent of direct labor depending upon the type of business.

Power, heat, and light often vary in direct proportion to production volume. Power allowance should be given to new equipment and for variation in expected machine hours and employee work hours. Power should take into account the factory square footage and layout.

Repairs and maintenance are significant and may aggregate 5 percent–10 percent in many companies. Repair budget estimates should consider the condition of the machinery and equipment. Additional repair should be budgeted for new additional equipment that might be needed.

The purpose of repairs and maintenance cost control is to obtain the lowest possible cost in the long-term, consistent with efficient plant operation. There is a joint responsibility between the maintenance and production departments. Repairs and maintenance should be segregated between (1) routine and repetitive (e.g., preventive maintenance, oil change) and (2) nonroutine and irregular (e.g., replacing roof, installing new motor for machine). There should be a separate budget for each of these two major classifications.

Maintenance expense reports should be kept by item of machinery, type of maintenance, and category of repair. A typical maintenance expense exception report appears in Exhibit 10–1.

By keeping track of the maintenance costs by machine category you can determine where the problems lie and what corrective action may be needed. Cost savings in repairs and maintenance may be very substantial. A control problem is the divided responsibility between production and maintenance staffs.

One purpose of controlling maintenance costs is to obtain the lowest possible cost consistent with effective plant and equipment operation. Cost

EXHIBIT 10–1 Maintenance Expense—Exception Report

Repair Order Number	Explanation	Actual	Budget	Variance	Percent
1	Repair machine B	$10,500	$10,000	$500	5%
2	Reinforce machine C flooring	6,600	6,000	600	10
Total					

control may be achieved through better quality maintenance efforts, better installation of machinery, preventive maintenance, and more frequent inspections. Factory office expense considers production and record keeping that may affect the office routine.

Illustrative factory overhead budgets appear in Exhibits 10–2 and 10–3.

EXHIBIT 10–2 ABC Company
Factory Overhead Budget I
For the Year Ending December 31, 19XX

Itemization	Amount
Indirect labor	$100,000
Indirect materials	40,000
Insurance	20,000
Repairs and maintenance	50,000
Payroll taxes	30,000
Heat and light	10,000
Property taxes	15,000
Depreciation	5,000
Total	$270,000

EXHIBIT 10–3 Factory Overhead Budget II

	Plant X	Plant Y	Plant Z	Total
Direct Costs				
Taxes				
Royalties				
Oil				
Total Direct Costs				
Indirect Costs				
Labor				
Maintenance				
Insurance				
Supplies				
Travel				
Power				
Total Indirect Costs				
Total Costs				

ALLOCATION

Variable overhead can be assigned to periods fairly accurately, while fixed overhead allocation is more arbitrary. The responsibility for variable overhead is primarily with operating managers while the responsibility for fixed overhead is primarily with general managers.

TOTAL COST MANAGEMENT

Total cost management (TCM) is the management of all the company's resources and activities that use resources. There is a focus on operations, activities, functions, circumstances, events, and conditions that "drive" resource consumption costs. An objective of total cost management is to eliminate those activities not having value.

STATIC VERSUS FLEXIBLE BUDGET

A static budget has two characteristics:

1. It is geared toward only one level of activity, and
2. Actual results are always compared against budgeted costs at the original budget activity level.

A production manager has two responsibilities to discharge in the performance of his duties: production control and cost control. Production control is involved with assuring that production goals in terms of output are met. Cost control is involved with assuring that output is produced at the least possible cost, consistent with quality standards. These are different responsibilities and they must be kept separate in attempting to assess how well the production manager is performing. This points out that the main difficulty with the static budget is its complete failure to distinguish between the production control and the cost control dimensions of a manager's performance.

There are four problems involved in overhead cost control. First, manufacturing overhead is usually comprised of many separate costs. Second, these separate costs are often very small in dollar amount, making it highly impractical to control them in the same way that direct materials and direct labor costs are controlled. Third, these small, separate costs are often the responsibility of different managers. And fourth, manufacturing overhead costs vary in behavior, some fixed, some variable, and some mixed in nature. Most of these problems can be overcome by the use of a flexible budget. Flexible budgets always outperform static budgets from a managerial cost control point of view.

A flexible budget differs from a static budget on two points. First, it does not confine itself to only one level of activity, but rather is geared toward a range of activity. Second, actual results need not be compared against budgeted costs at the original budget activity level. Since the flexible budget covers a range of activity, if actual costs are incurred at a different activity level from that originally planned, then the manager is able to construct a new budget, as needed, to compare with actual results. Hence, the term flexible budget. In sum, the characteristics of a flexible budget are:

1. It is geared toward all levels of activity within the relevant range, rather than toward only one level of activity.

2. It is dynamic rather than static. It can be tailored for any level of activity within the relevant range, even after the period is over. That is, a manager can look at what activity level is attained during a period and then turn to the flexible budget to determine what costs should have been at that activity level.

Once the flexible budget has been prepared, the manager is ready to compare actual results for a period with the comparable budget level within the relevant range. The manager is not limited to a single budget level as with the static budget.

The basic idea of the flexible budget approach is that through a study of cost behavior patterns, a budget can be prepared that is geared to a range of activity, rather than to a single level. The basic steps in preparing a flexible budget are:

1. Determine the relevant range over which activity is expected to fluctuate during the coming period.

2. Analyze costs that will be incurred over the relevant range in terms of determining cost behavior patterns (variable, fixed, or mixed).

3. Separate costs by behavior, determining the formula for variable and mixed costs.

4. Using the formula for the variable portion of the costs, prepare a budget showing what costs will be incurred at various points throughout the relevant range.

It is important to select an appropriate activity base for preparing a flexible budget. For example, choose to use units of production as the activity base for developing a flexible budget. Rather than units of production, you could have used some other base such as direct labor-hours or machine-hours.

What is "the best" in terms of an activity base will vary from firm to firm. There are at least three factors to be considered in the activity base decision:

1. The existence of a causal relationship between the activity base and the overhead costs.
2. The avoidance of dollars in the activity base itself.
3. The selection of an activity base that is simple and can be easily understood.

There should be a direct causal relationship between the activity base and a company's variable overhead costs. That is, the variable overhead costs should vary as a result of changes in the activity base. In a machine shop, for example, one would expect power usage and other variable overhead costs to vary in relationship to the number of machine-hours worked. Machine-hours would therefore be the proper base to use in the flexible budget. Other common activity bases include direct labor-hours, mileage driven by salespersons, contacts made by salespersons, number of invoices processed, and so on. Any one of these could be used as the base for preparing a flexible budget in the proper situation.

Whenever possible, the activity base should be expressed in units rather than in dollars. If dollars are used, they should be standard dollars rather than actual dollars. The problem with dollars is that they are subject to price-level changes which can cause a distortion in the activity base if it is expressed in dollar terms.

The activity level should be simple and easily understood. A base that is not easily understood by the manager will probably result in confusion and misunderstanding rather than serve as a positive means of cost control.

Flexible (variable) budgets may be used in manufacturing, selling, and administrative activities of the business. Flexible budgeting is used for cost control, cost estimation, and profit planning. Variable budgets are more suitable if there are recurring operations, heterogeneous expenses, and if output may be appropriately measured. A variable budget is not needed if there are only fixed costs. The purpose of the variable budget is to identify how much an expense item in a responsibility center is affected by the amount of work conducted in that center.

It is rare that planned volume will be the same as actual volume. Thus, expected costs will differ from actual costs solely because of the difference between projected and actual activity. A flexible budget acts as a tool for cost control because it reveals what costs should be at various production levels. The more unstable the industry, the greater the need for flexible budgets. The activity base should be minimally impacted by variable factors except for output. The activity base to apply factory overhead may be based on units, direct labor hours, machine hours, pounds, and so on.

In today's production industry, a successful manager must preserve, conserve, qualify, and truly manage the resources available. The flexible budget is recognized both as a plan for allocating resources and as a process through which the plan is controlled. Besides, flexible budgeting can result in information that can help in understanding and controlling the causes of variances; it also can indicate which cost overruns result from factors beyond your control and which are manageable.

Budgeting forces managers to think about a firm's strengths and weaknesses and provides a way of measuring a firm's performance within a specified fiscal framework. For many firms, flexible budgeting is a more effective approach than static budgeting. A flexible budget allows firms to adjust capital requirements to business demands; therefore, flexible budgets are more useful, especially to firms that are growing rapidly. A typical factory overhead report appears in Exhibit 10–4.

EXHIBIT 10–4 Factory Overhead Report

Type of Expenditure	Explanation	Man-hours	Rate per Hour	Fixed		Variable		Variance	
				Man-hours	Amount	Man-hours	Amount	Man-hours	Amount

CONTROL AND ANALYSIS

Budgetary control must be simple and comprehensible to operating managers. However, budgeting overhead is more difficult than direct material and direct labor because the responsibility for control of overhead is widely disbursed within the company. Overhead cost items behave differently with changing volume and involve long-term commitments. There are many nominal items of cost making up overhead and many different sources and methods of overhead items.

A determination should be made as to which factory overhead is controllable or uncontrollable to operating managers. Flexible budgeting is an effective control tool. Cost control is effective *before* costs are incurred, not after cost incurrence. Cost controls should be implemented over cost drivers. Costs must be assigned based on responsibility for control purposes and should be segregated by department.

Stringent control may be kept over fixed overhead, but variable overhead costs are more flexible. Many factory overhead costs are the responsibility of general upper management such as costs for plant and equipment, leases, pensions, and salaries of production executives. A company may adopt a policy that a factory overhead cost will not be incurred that exceeds the budget limit, unless it is approved. There should be a running balance of overhead expenditures for control purposes. There should be a timetable set for each project, and an examination of the relationship between maintenance and production workers.

Chapter 11

Budgeting General and Administrative Expenses

General and administrative (G&A) expenses may be identified with a particular activity, function, segment, unit, or product line. The general and administrative budget is primarily the expense for top management functions. It is typically the responsibility of office management who should thus be charged with the responsibility of proposing a budget for these items. Administrative expenses relate to the supervision of all major activities of the business rather than any one specifically. Responsibility should be assigned to specific managers for administrative expenses.

Some G&A expenses are unique and unpredictable. This makes the budgeting process more difficult and results in variances. Examples of administrative expenses are executive salaries and travel expenses, legal and accounting costs, office salaries, office rent, office expenses, office insurance, office postage, dues, depreciation expense on administrative assets, training, and contributions. An illustrative general and administrative expense budget appears in Exhibit 11–1.

This chapter will discuss administrative department budgets, budgetary process, and cost control and analysis.

ADMINISTRATIVE DEPARTMENTS

Administrative departments include general administration, personnel, accounting, legal, insurance, computer services, and treasury. Administration

EXHIBIT 11–1 General and Administrative Expense Budget 1994

Item of Expense	Prior Year				Proposed Budget		
	Budget	Actual	Over (Under) Budget		Request	Increase (Decrease) from Previous Year Budget	
			Amount	Percent		Amount	Percent
Public relations							
Industrial relations							
Finance							
Corporate planning							
Executive office							
Legal							
Office salaries							
Fringe benefits							
Insurance							
Payroll taxes							
Business conferences							
Patent expense							
Postage							
Rent							
Repairs							
Supplies							
Travel							
Employee relations							
Dues and memberships							
Computer							
Depreciation							
Entertainment							
Licenses							
Subscriptions							
Communications							
Total							

is personnel existing because of the organization structure. Examples are office managers and staff. A typical administrative department budget appears in Exhibit 11–2.

BUDGETARY PROCESS

Many administrative expenses depend on management policies, inflationary effects, and so on. However, some depend on budgeted sales volume. Administrative budgets are developed considering the organizational chart showing the number of employees in each department, the functions they perform, and the objectives to be accomplished.

Engineering budgets may be segregated into appropriate categories

EXHIBIT 11–2 Administrative Department Budget

	Amount
Headcount	
Professional	
Clerical	
Miscellaneous	
Total	
Payroll	
Professional	
Clerical	
Overtime	
Miscellaneous	
Total	
Employee Benefits	
Payroll taxes	
Insurance	
Miscellaneous	
Total	
Office supplies	
Rent	
Telephone	
Taxes	
Advertising	
Utilities	
Bad debts	
Office expense	
Insurance	
Travel	
Promotion and entertainment	
Total	

such as product improvement, manufacturing problems, and cost reduction. The completion dates for each major work stage should be specified.

Office expense budgets should take into account proposed changes in office procedure, new forms, or records. Office postage should take into account expected changes in postal rates and volume of mail.

Credit and collection costs should consider economic conditions. Legal and accounting, and other professional costs, should take into account the cost of retainers and special services.

COST CLASSIFICATION

General and administrative expenses may be fixed or variable. Although administrative expenses are usually constant, some relate to changes in activity. Bonuses to administrative personnel based on profits are considered a variable cost.

COMPENSATION ARRANGEMENTS

The staffing of the general and administrative group should be realistic. Work should be performed at reasonable cost. There should be a balance in work-load among personnel.

Executive expenses may be fixed by the Board of Directors. Compensation of officers and directors is typically known in advance at the beginning of the year, and is therefore easy to budget. Bonuses and incentives are often based on earnings which can be estimated.

General and administrative salaries can be reliably estimated because the names of employees and their salaries are known. The percentage of salary increases is stated in the contract or union agreement. Merit pay may be budgeted based on a percentage of payroll. Salaries should take into account cost of living increases. New hires can be listed with their salary rates. Special arrangements should be noted. Fringe benefits may be budgeted based on salaries. Actuaries can estimate pension expense.

CONTRIBUTIONS

Contributions to recognized charities should be approved by the Board of Directors. An executive should be held responsible. The contribution may be stated per employee or as a percentage of net income.

FINANCIAL EXPENSES

Financial income and expenses may be based on the related financial instrument. Interest expense can be determined from the financial budget. The financial budget reveals the amount of debt which is the basis to compute interest expense. Interest expense may be budgeted based on the anticipated interest rate and the amount of the borrowing. Tax expense is based on the budgeted net income, and is estimated by the tax accountant.

OTHER EXPENSES

An estimate must be made of budgeted professional fees for attorneys, accountants, auditors, engineers, and consultants. The budgeted general and administrative costs will be determined by expected activities in other areas. For example, salaries may vary with production. Research will vary with sales and production. G&A expenses should include the cost of keeping excess or idle facilities.

CONTROL AND ANALYSIS

Administrative costs must be correctly classified as to source. There should be controls on costs and performance. Administrative expenses are controlled by top management decisions; they do not relate to production but rather are period costs. Administrative expenses must be kept within authorized limits. An illustrative departmental budget may take the following form:

Department Budget

Department Name:
Department Manager:
Period:

Classification	Budgeted Cost	Actual Cost	Variance	Percent of Variance to Budget

General and administrative costs should be grouped by responsibility center before being distributed or allocated. Responsibility to individuals or executives should be assigned for G&A costs to accomplish control over them. Each G&A group must know their responsibility, limitations, and to whom they report. The output expected for a G&A group should be specified. Budgeted expenses must be substantiated with documentation. Proper supervision is needed for control. Productivity must be maintained at the required level. Control is less with administrative costs than production costs because many administrative positions are not subject to specific measurement, standardization, or prediction.

Cost reduction may arise from consolidation of duplicate or unnecessary activities. Control of G&A includes controlling overtime and "hidden" areas.

G&A costs should be analyzed by type. Past administrative expenses should be reviewed for propriety or necessity. If administrative costs are increasing significantly in disproportion to sales or production, the reasons should be identified. There should be a balance between G&A expenses and other corporate variables including total costs and sales. There may be a policy that G&A costs cannot exceed a specified percentage of sales (e.g., 10 percent of sales). Comparisons should be made of G&A expenses to sales over the years, to competing companies, and to industry norms. Some administration expenses may be related to revenue, direct labor hours, number of transactions, or operating income.

Chapter 12

Marketing Expenses

Direct costs are specifically identifiable to the segment while indirect costs are general charges that must be allocated in some manner to each segment. There should be a promotion and advertising plan, a selling expense plan, and a marketing plan. Further, there should be optimal coordination between the sales plan and the marketing plan. Marketing expenses are discretionary, and supplementary authorization may be needed for additional expenditures.

Selling expenses may be related to sales. They include sales salaries, commissions, and training. Selling expenses may be budgeted and reported by department, day, transaction, and source of sale. Sales promotion expenses should be budgeted by product, media, activity, territory, and salesperson category.

The unit cost of an operation equals total expenditures divided by units of measure.

DISTRIBUTION COSTS

The main groupings of distribution costs are project (appropriation), general (administrative), standardized, and competitive. Distribution costs are costs expended to sell varying products in different territories. They encompass the costs for activities after goods are manufactured until they are received by customers. Distribution costs are the costs to sell or market and are under the responsibility of sales or marketing executives. Distribution costs include

EXHIBIT 12–1 Distribution Cost Budget

Direct selling		$500,000
Transportation costs		
Air	$100,000	
Rail	40,000	
Truck	60,000	
Ship	50,000	
Total		250,000
Storage and warehousing		50,000
Market research		40,000
Other		25,000
Total distribution costs		$865,000

salesperson salaries and commissions, advertising, packaging, promotion, market research, transportation, credit and collection, storage, warehousing, accounting for distribution efforts, and applicable home office expenses. These costs constitute a high percentage of total costs. A distribution cost budget may take the form as shown in Exhibit 12–1.

It must be decided how much to spend in distribution, types of expenditures, when they should be made, and where the expenditures belong. The objective is to obtain the best sales results.

Distribution costs for planning and control should be identified by responsibility, type of expense, program, business segment, territory, distribution channel, product, order size, pricing, financing, and method of sale.

Distribution efforts should be concentrated based on market potential. Distribution effort may be improved by revising territorial boundaries to lower selling cost and obtain greater coverage, by changing the distribution channel, by reassigning salespeople, by changing the product mix, by altering customer mix, and by changing the method of sale. Distribution efforts must be coordinated in the overall plan including advertising, sales promotion, transportation, direct selling, storage, and warehousing. The best combination of distribution factors should be selected to maximize profits. Distribution costs are an important element in determining selling price.

There is an interrelationship between the sales and distribution cost budgets. The purpose is to have the best selling effort to generate the highest earnings. There is also a need for a coordination with production and finance.

Competitive service distribution costs are actual service costs of an activity, function, or operation that are compared with competitive prices. These competitive prices may be from competing companies or industry norms. Examples are maintenance, warehousing, and pricing. To measure these costs appropriately, operations must be segregated and identifiable. Service require-

EXHIBIT 12–2 Project Budget Report

Number	Name	Hours	Professional Salaries	Clerical Salaries	Consultant Salaries	Other Expenses	Total	Commit- ments	Estimated Cost to Complete	Total Cost	Project Budget	Under or Over Budget

ments must be determined. The services are charged based on the competitive prices.

Project (appropriation) distribution costs do not directly relate to volume but rather to a project. Examples are advertising, promotion, market research, and sales engineering. This involves specific projects to accomplish long-term sales. A comparison is made between budget and actual distribution costs for the project.

The budget offers control over distribution activities and costs. Distribution costs should be budgeted in absolute dollars and as a percentage of net sales. Distribution costs should be budgeted by territory, salesperson, project or program, product, and call. An illustrative project budget appears in Exhibit 12–2.

The distribution budget helps to coordinate distribution procedures among the sales plan, manufacturing plan, and financial plan. It helps to select the best combination of distribution resources including sales volume, selling prices, and selling effort. It helps foster cost control.

SELLING EXPENSES

The initial responsibility for the selling expense budget belongs with the vice-president of marketing or the equivalent sales manager. The selling expense budget depends on the forecasted sales.

The proper amount of sales effort needed must be determined. Sales effort must be evaluated by product, territory, and customer. Selling effort is subject to diminishing returns in that after a point the additional sales volume generated from selling efforts do not justify the additional cost and time.

Some selling expenses are constant and set by administrative policy. Examples are the periodic appropriation of advertising, rent, and salaries. Some selling expenses vary with sales. Examples are sales commissions, freight out, and packaging. Sales personnel requirements may be set by number and grade. An illustrative budget for field selling expenses appears in Exhibit 12–3. An illustrative budget report for a sales manager appears in Exhibit 12–4.

EXHIBIT 12–3 Field Selling Expenses
Budget Report for Month of May 1993

Salesperson Name _____
Sales Territory _____

		May 1994			Cumulative		Over or Under Budget	
Explanation	Allowance	Actual	Budget	Over or (Under) Budget	Actual	Budget	Amount	Percent
Days traveled								
Field selling expenses:								
Lodging	$85 per diem							
Food	25 per diem							
Telephone	10 per diem							
Valet	8 per diem							
Subtotal								
Travel:								
Auto	$.25 per mile							
Airplane								
Railroad								
Total travel								
Conventions								
Promotion & Entertainment	$30 per diem							
Miscellaneous	$6 per diem							
Total expense								
Selling-related Ratios:								
Cost per travel day								
Cost per telephone call								
Sales generated per call								
Comments:								

EXHIBIT 12–4

XYZ Company
Budget Report
General Sales Manager

	Current Month		Cumulative	
	Over (Under)		Over (Under)	
	Actual	Budget	Actual	Budget
Number of staff				
Expenses				
Salaries				
Fringe benefits				
Dues				
Rent				
Insurance				
Depreciation				
Supplies				
Promotion and entertainment				
Travel				
Total expenses				
Percentage of net sales				

ADVERTISING

Advertising may be regional, local, national, or international. Advertising is an element of distribution costs. It must be coordinated with other distribution costs, sales, and production. A determination must be made of how much, when, where, and how advertising should be used to obtain the most benefit. Advertising expenditures must be timed appropriately to accomplish maximum results. Advertising depends on the effectiveness of competition, economic conditions, market situation, and product leadership. The company's financial position also determines how much can be spent. The amount of advertising should be critically studied and responsibility assigned. A comparison should be made with the size and use of competitor's advertising budgets.

Advertising funding should be based upon expected sales results. Compare the trend in the ratio of advertising with sales. Determine advertising effectiveness including media measures.

Advertising objectives may be to:

1. increase sales,

2. increase or maintain selling prices,

3. reduce selling efforts and cost,

4. maintain or expand market share,

5. develop new markets,

6. counteract competition,

7. establish brand loyalty,

8. educate customers on how to use the product,

9. stimulate new products,

10. improve public relations,

11. counteract governmental regulation, and

12. improve public image about the company and its products.

Advertising for a product line should be reviewed annually to ensure that the company is not promoting obsolete merchandise. Advertising should only be incurred for viable products. Advertising and sales promotion are significant elements in marketing and are directly related. In retail, they are essential. A manufacturer may contribute to the advertising budget of retailers.

Advertising is a discretionary expense and may be tied to a percentage of sales. It considers management policy, competitive advantage, plans for new products or entering new markets, and planned modification to existing products.

Advertising departments must justify their expenditures before funds are appropriated. Advertising managers must specifically enumerate their goals, outline methods to achieve objectives, and estimate the cost of each component of the program. The advertising department must be held accountable for its commitments.

Advertising should be appropriated by type of media (e.g., radio, television, newspapers, periodicals, trade publications, direct mail, and door-to-door solicitation). Advertising effectiveness should be determined.

Advertising costs should be broken down by media, territory, customer, product, service, and project. They should be segregated into direct and indirect for the cost objective at hand.

The advertising budget considers the company's image, product line, and brand. Advertising may be increased as competition warrants it.

The advertising and sales promotion budget may be prepared separately from the marketing budget but coordinated thereto. Further, the advertising budget should be coordinated with selling, manufacturing, and finance costs.

Advertising cost standards should be formulated to control costs. Advertising standards may be based on cost per sales transaction, cost per dollar sales, cost per request for information, cost per unit of space, and cost per account.

The budget considerations include the following:

- The projected marginal advertising expense per unit.
- The profit per product.
- The projected additional units to be sold with incremental advertising outlays.

The advertising budget figures may be based upon:

- Percentage of previous years' sales.
- Percent of budgeted sales.
- Fixed amount per unit of product.
- Keeping pace with what competition is spending.
- Percent of previous year's net income.
- Percent of previous year's gross profit.
- An arbitrary change to last year's actual advertising expenditures.
- A percentage of average sales for a multiyear period (e.g., 3 years, 5 years).
- Amount based on how much competitors are spending. Reference may be made to industry averages.

The advertising budget is designed to improve sales, maintain selling prices, establish new markets, meet competition, foster an image, counteract proposed governmental legislation, build consumer confidence, and counteract bad publicity.

Advertising budgets for consumers are broken down into programs or projects. Advertising expenditures are summarized by media and may show space (time) cost, product cost, and talent cost.

The advertising budget may be based on a lump-sum appropriation in general and by area. This amount may be based on a percentage of historical, current, or projected sales. Percentages assigned should also consider industry averages. The total appropriation is then broken down by each project.

It is preferred to budget advertising based on a percent of budgeted sales rather than on actual sales for the previous year, because budgeted sales is the best estimate of what's anticipated considering the current environment and economic conditions. Advertising based on budgeted sales controls the expenditure since it's tied to expected sales volume. This approach is more suitable if many diverse products or services are involved, and if the advertising is joint for all these products or services. In this case, it may not be practical to assign advertising to specific products or services. The lump-sum approach is more appropriate with established products, stable business environment, and a track record of experience. However, a major flaw with lump-sum appropriation is that there is no careful appraisal of specific goals and the cost to achieve them. Specific products must be addressed when the sales strategy is constantly changing and new products are being introduced. A lump-sum appropriation may be putting more advertising money in the wrong products and less advertising money in the right products. A solution may be to vary the percentage of advertising to sales by product or service category. This approach may be more suitable for retail businesses.

Budgeting advertising per unit may be appropriate for manufacturers involved with either uniform or few products. Examples are specialty goods. Advertising will be tied to budgeted unit sales. This plan is simply applied.

The advertising budget may also be based on another method, which is preferred. The advertising program objectives are reviewed and the estimated cost of meeting those objectives is determined. A total amount of advertising needed is determined from this detailed analysis.

If advertising is for immediate results, sales should serve as the benchmark for determining how much advertising should be budgeted. Estimate how much advertising is needed to attain the desired sales volume. Historical ratios of advertising to sales are studied to approximate which advertising cost generates sales results. Advertising may be directed toward immediate results. If an advertising agency is used, that agency may provide input as to how much advertising is needed.

EXHIBIT 12–5 Advertising Budget

Classification	Product Budget	Actual Expenditures	Commitments	Total	Estimated Cost to Complete	Balance Available

A typical advertising budget format appears in Exhibit 12–5. An advertising and promotion expense budget appears in Exhibit 12–6.

A comparison should be made between successive budgeted advertising cost and expected additional profit by program. Advertising graphs and charts may also be useful. The following schedule in Exhibit 12–7 shows the effect of successive advertising outlays on profitability.

A variance analysis report for advertising and sales promotion appears in Exhibit 12–8.

Another way to formulate advertising is based on appraising the objectives and to accomplish those objectives at the needed advertising expenditures. The individual cost elements are then combined to obtain the total appropriation. Considerations include the timing of expenditures, advertising media to be used, products, territories, and market research.

Advertising may be aimed at less immediate results. Examples are establishing brand loyalty, developing new markets, and creating goodwill. In

EXHIBIT 12–6 Advertising and Promotion Expense Budget

	Amount
Personal demonstrations	
Newspaper ads	
Journal and magazine ads	
Shopper ads	
Direct mail	
Telephone ads and directories	
Radio ads	
Catalogues	
Samples	
Exhibits	
House-to-house solicitation	
Total advertising and promotion expense	

EXHIBIT 12–7 Increase in Advertising and Profitability

(1) Additional Advertising Outlay	(2) Additional Volume in Units	(3) Additional Profit per Unit	(4) = (1) ÷ (2) Incremental Advertising Cost per Unit	(5) Unit Incremental Profit	(6) = (2) × (5) Profit
$5,000	20,000	$.60	$.25	$.35	$7,000
5,000	15,000	.50	.33	.17	2,550

EXHIBIT 12–8 Budget and Actual Advertising and Sales Promotion

Media Category	Budget	Actual	Committed Funds	Total	Estimated Cost to Complete	Total Cost	Balance Available
Television	$ 400	$ 135	$ 145	$ 280	$ 60	$ 340	$ 60
Radio	500	200	100	300	90	390	110
Newspapers	700	300	200	500	125	625	75
Magazines	600	100	300	400	100	500	100
Catalogs	900	500	100	600	175	775	125
Displays	300	50	100	150	60	210	90
Direct mail	600	400	150	550	20	570	30
Total	$4,000	$1,685	$1,095	$2,780	$630	$3,410	$590

this case, advertising appropriations may be based on the company's financial health and cash flow, the amount required to accomplish objectives (e.g., a small advertising budget may have no discernible benefit), and the expected growth rate. The following costs should be determined:

- Costs by product, territory, and media
- Trend in advertising expense and sales
- Advertising cost per dollar sales
- Advertising cost per unit sold
- Advertising cost per customer
- Advertising cost per transaction.

Advertising may reduce direct selling costs and may increase sales volume so as to improve overall profitability. Advertising for necessities should be expanded in poor economic times and advertising for luxuries should be concentrated on in good times.

PACKAGING

Product development may consider packaging changes and new types of packaging. Repackaging may be designed to save costs.

SALES PROMOTION

Sales promotion may involve consideration of programs, trade shows, and store fixtures. Sales promotion costs for dealers should be broken down by campaign, program, meeting, contest, and special event. Each cost should be explained as to objective and justification.

TRAVEL AND ENTERTAINMENT

Each salesperson may be asked to prepare his/her own budget for travel and entertainment.

MARKETING BUDGETS

Budgets help direct sales efforts. Sales should be budgeted by salesperson, product, customer, and territory. In fact, budgets should be comprised of sales volume and sales dollars by salesperson broken down by territory. There may be lump-sum appropriations representing maximum limits of expenditure. Selling expense budgets should identify controllable expenses. A budget may be based on the following:

Item	Basis
Lodging, food, and telephone	Daily allowance
Automobile	Planned miles
Other	Special authorization

Though no formal guidelines are imposed for the marketing department's budget, in order to meet specific percentage of sales numbers, there is informal pressure to conform to industry standards. The marketing budget depends upon expected sales calls, promotion efforts, market share, order size and frequency, costs to obtain and maintain an account, market share, competition, territory, and distribution.

The distribution cost budget should be correlated with the production and financial budgets. The distribution cost budget is directly tied to the sales plan. Distribution costs should be budgeted in total and for each distribution activity to obtain sales results. Distribution cost budgets should be by home office subunits and "field" subunits and based on those markets providing the greatest profitability. Budgeted costs should depend upon the following for each territory: potential customers, sales effort required per dollar of cost, population density, size of geographic area, buying power, and competition.

Advertising budgets depend upon the product line, territories, and classification of customers. Travel expenses may be tied to sales. Warranty expenses are budgeted based on a percentage of sales. Billing rates to departments may be based on competing companies' rates.

An illustrative budget for a marketing division appears in Exhibit 12–9.

EXHIBIT 12–9 XYZ Company Marketing Division Budget

Department	Type of Budget	Current Year Quarter					Previous Year	Increase (Decrease)
		1	*2*	*3*	*4*	*Total*		
Direct selling	Administrative							
East								
North								
South								
West								
Total								
Advertising and promotion	project							
New York								
California								
Texas								
Storage and warehousing	standard							
Oregon								
Mass.								
Florida								
Wisconsin								
Administrative								
General and administrative	administrative							
Customer relations	administrative							
Market research	project							
Branch offices	administrative							
Total								

ANALYSIS AND EVALUATION

A comparison of actual to budgeted costs can be used for distribution efforts of a repetitive, routine nature. Distribution cost analysis is to obtain the best distribution policy or method. Distribution costs should be analyzed by activity and functional area to aid in planning and control. Consideration must be given to territories, products, distribution channels, selling prices, customers, and type of selling effort.

Compare each individual distribution cost to sales, such as advertising to sales, travel to sales, and so on. A low ratio is favorable because a smaller distribution expense is needed to generate sales. Lower ratios reveal better productivity of efforts. Distribution cost analysis may be made by sales terms, by order size, by segment (e.g., department, store, branch), by distribution channel (wholesaler, retailer, manufacturer, direct to customer), by product or service, by territory (city, state, district, county), by salesperson, by type of customer, by method of sale (salesperson, mail order, house solicitation, company store), by method of delivery (over-the-counter, store delivery), and by terms of sale (cash, installment, short-term financing).

The productivity of distribution efforts is important. Examine the trend in distribution expenses relative to sales for reasonableness and weakness. The company's distribution costs and activities should be compared to those being used by the competition.

Distribution expenses are usually tied to sales. If sales are increasing because of higher sales prices but sales volume is about the same, then only a few of the distribution expenses will increase. The work volume to process orders and the delivery costs will be the same. However, advertising and promotion costs will increase to overcome sales resistance to the higher prices. When sales volume increases, most of the distribution expenses increase. However, advertising and sales promotion may not increase in the same proportion to sales volume. If there is increased sales volume from larger orders only from existing customers, then the delivery, credit, and collection costs will not increase in proportion to sales. If additional salespersons are to be hired, increased training costs should be budgeted.

Selling expense should be related to net sales for effectiveness. Fixed appropriations of selling expenses may be considered irreducible since a minimum is needed to operate.

The number of calls and sales per call should be budgeted and then compared to actual calls and sales per call. Variances should be determined.

The company's advertising expenditures can be compared to other competing companies by product. Reference should be made to *Advertising Age*.

CONTROL

Distribution cost control involves functional responsibility and cost objectives. Costs should be assigned to responsibility centers.

Distribution costs by territory may be controlled by reorganizing the territory so that effort is more consistent with benefits (e.g., selling expenses may be reduced with better coverage), by altering warehouse facilities in the territory, by identifying neglected customers who may buy, by altering method of sale, by changing distribution channel, by reassigning salespeople, by eliminating unprofitable territories, and by modifying advertising policy by territory.

General (administrative) functions are not suitable for quantitative measurement. However, there are some continuing, routine functions. Payroll is particularly significant. Examples are general sales office expenses and sales executive expenses. Perhaps some duplicate or unimportant functions can be eliminated to save money.

Standardized activities are repetitive and subject to quantitative measurement. Examples are the handling of merchandise in the storage facility

EXHIBIT 12–10 Sales Engineering Project Budget Report

Project Number	Project Name	Hours	Actual Costs by Type	Budgeted Costs by Type	Variance	Estimated Costs to Complete	Commitments

and field selling expense. The costs must be segregated by function. A comparison is made between budget and actual. The field selling expense may be based on a per diem standard allowance. For example, entertainment may be at a per diem rate, telephone may be at a monthly allowance, auto may be at a standard mileage rate, and other direct selling costs may require special authorization.

A sample sales engineering project budget report appears in Exhibit 12–10.

REFERENCE

Louis Stern and Frederick Sturdivant, "Customer-driven distribution systems," *Harvard Business Review*, July-August 1987, pp. 34–41.

Chapter 13

Budgeting for Research and Development

Research and development (R&D) may be internal or external (acquired from outside). R&D should be in conformity with the long-term goals of the company. Short-term objectives must be met along the way. An up-to-date company should spend more on new technology. A company with older technology usually spends less on R&D and more on engineering to sustain current products and processes.

Projects should be ranked in priority order. The best R&D projects should be undertaken given the constraints of financial resources, manpower, and facilities. R&D objectives must be realistic, and sufficient in quantity and quality. Proposed R&D projects should be carefully screened. On average, about 1 of 3 ideas will be successful. Technological objectives should be based on where the company wants to be in 3 to 10 years.

R&D should result in either a new product, or a better existing product, or a reduction in manufacturing costs. R&D should, however, be primarily directed toward the future rather than current product maintenance. Corporate funds may be spent for the following major areas: research and exploration, development, and sustainment. The product life cycle is depicted in Figure 13–1.

The R&D budget depends on a company's financial capability and technological progress. R&D expenditures are needed to remain competitive. Funds may be used by engineering to prevent current products from becoming out-of-date. Attention is given to product and productivity improvement.

The R&D budget should consider expected benefits, marketing uncertainty, risk of developing a successful product, product life cycle, type of

FIGURE 13-1 Product Life Cycle

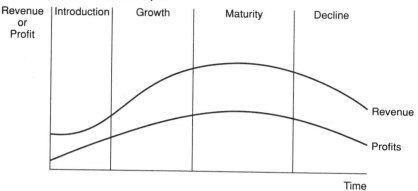

manpower, technological orientation and advances, market share, competition, desired growth rate, availability of facilities, diversification, type of industry, financial resources, availability of raw materials, changes in consumer taste, staff capability, previous research efforts and results, time needed, and importance of the project to the company.

CHARACTERISTICS OF R&D PLANNING

R&D involves the planning and appraisal of individual projects. In the pre-planning phase, there is a continual appraisal and review of projects, considering limitations. R&D planning should consider:

- New or improved products developed over the past five years.
- The percentage of new product sales to total sales.
- Research progress.
- Cost/benefit of research.
- Relationship between the research department and sales department for new products.
- How long it takes to go from the laboratory to commercial production.
- R&D expenditures to sales for the company relative to competition and industry norms.

R&D projects have direct and indirect costs associated with them. R&D costs include:

- Personnel costs including outside consulting fees. Personnel costs typically represent 60–65 percent of R&D costs.

- Cost of materials and supplies.
- Cost of intangibles bought from other companies.
- Outside contractor costs.
- Travel for research.
- Periodicals.
- Membership dues and attendance at technical meetings.
- Rentals.
- Depreciation on R&D laboratory and equipment.
- Property taxes.

In the budget preparation phase, there is a reconciliation of budget costs of various research activities with the total estimated cost of maintaining R&D laboratories. R&D effort should be taken only if the return provided from the research efforts justify its costs and risk and if the new product can be introduced before it is out of date or out of favor.

R&D BUDGET

The R&D budget allotment may depend upon the expected return on investment (ROI) and the stability of the research staff. The research must provide an acceptable return. The return on an R&D project may be determined via net present value, internal rate of return, payback period, discounted payback period, accounting rate of return, and residual income.

When research staffers request more dollars or time, a new ROI should be computed. A decision must then be made either to spend more money or to drop the projects. Actual ROI of a research project should be compared to its estimated ROI. Variances should be noted and investigated as to cause. Corrective actions should be taken.

$$\begin{array}{c} \text{Money for R\&D without} \\ \text{affecting ROI} \end{array} = \begin{array}{c} \text{Expected ROI before} \\ \text{R\&D expenditure} \end{array} - \frac{\text{Expected ROI}}{100} \times \begin{array}{c} \text{Invest-} \\ \text{ment} \end{array}$$

The R&D budget should equal or be less than the amount derived from the above formula. The figure should be compared to what is required to maintain the research staff.

The R&D budget may be based on a percentage of retained earnings. This approach is used by some companies having a basic consumer product line. The desired percentage varies with company size and maturity. R&D may also be based on a model tied to financial information such as stock price, desired maximum earnings, return on sales, obsolescence rate, and engineering personnel. Correlation coefficients are computed between R&D funding and the financial information.

Because R&D has high risk, there should be a reserve established in the event of slowdowns or termination in funding levels. R&D risk by product line and market must be appraised. There is greater risk when a company moves from established products and markets to new products and markets. There is greater risk the longer the period between the R&D activity and the start of cash flow generated by the project.

R&D conducted for specified departments (e.g., marketing, manufacturing) should be charged to them. After the total R&D budget is prepared, the amounts have to be allocated to specific projects (programs) including supporting services.

If a proposal involving R&D cannot be scheduled, no budget should be prepared for the entire project. Rather, there should be a step-by-step budget allocating a specific amount for research work. After the first step is completed, a budget allotment may be made for the second step. R&D may be tied into sales, production, and expected market factors as product line diversification, expansion of product lines, and entering new markets.

The president evaluates the present technical programs. The R&D vice-president then appraises the technical limitation of research personnel considering its ability to perform the work relative to existing and future projects. Also considered is the research needed to maintain market share. Input is received from the marketing and planning staff. The company's overall financial condition is considered along with outside data and statistics. The R&D vice-president prepares a transfer budget which is a portion of R&D costs to be charged to marketing.

There may be unallocated research funds reserved for a special project the president desires aside from existing projects. Research programming studies research fields to be investigated and the depth of such coverage.

The company must decide how much money to assign to R&D, and how much to each R&D activity or segment. The amount funded for research depends upon the amount required to achieve satisfactory results, desired growth, number of programs, project priorities, competition, trade and industry statistics, manpower, economic conditions, and political factors. A maximum limit should be placed on R&D funding.

In some companies, R&D budgeting is done by those preparing the operating budget. In other companies, R&D budgeting is performed by a separate group reporting to the R&D director. It is more difficult to predict in the R&D area than in operating budgets.

R&D budgets should be by division, department, and responsibility center within the department. The budget for technical departments is the sum of the total budget for all R&D activities and sustaining engineering activities. Projects often involve operations of several departments. The project manager coordinates the budget for several departments. The format of an R&D division budget appears in Exhibit 13–1.

EXHIBIT 13–1 R&D Division Budget for the Year Ended December 31, 19XX

| | Quarter | | | | |
Item	1	2	3	4	Total
Controllable					
Payroll					
Materials and supplies					
Travel					
Professional dues					
Laundry					
Heat, light, and power					
Total					
Noncontrollable					
Depreciation					
Taxes					
Insurance					
Total					
Total					

Performance standards for research should be developed and compared to actual performance. Performance standards include cost per hour, cost per operation, cost per patent, number of patents approved, research hours by activity, number of tests, number of formulas, and number of requisitions. Actual costs incurred by program and discipline may be compared against the funds apportioned or budgeted for each R&D program and discipline.

Program budgeting is research-related or applies to technical jobs applicable to programs.

The budget for R&D may be based upon:

- A percentage of net income
- A percentage of operating earnings before R&D expense
- A percentage of budgeted sales
- A percentage of cash flow
- R&D cost per hour (total R&D project costs/chargeable hours)
- R&D per unit
- Cost of particular projects
- Product life cycle
- A percentage of investment in capital assets.

A project budget usually follows a study of work performed. R&D may be classified as follows: new products, existing product enhancement, factory (projects asked for by the factory), sales service (projects requested by the sales department) and fundamental (having no immediate commercial use).

EXHIBIT 13-2 R&D Budget

Salaries
  Administration
  Nonadministrative
  Technical staff
    Total salaries
Materials and supplies
  Equipment
  Laboratory
  Repairs
    Total materials and supplies
Other direct expenses
  Taxes
  Insurance
  Utilities
  Membership dues
  Travel and entertainment
  Depreciation
    Total other direct expenses
Total R&D

A high priority in funding should be given to developmental projects. Developmental projects should be ranked in terms of expenses, capital investment, expected profitability, financing available, and expected royalty earnings.

Typical R&D budgets are shown in Exhibits 13–2 and 13–3.

EXHIBIT 13-3 XYZ Company

Research and Development Budget for the Year Ended December 31, 19XX

Project	Needed New Staff	Total Manhours	Cost
Research			
Hydro 2			
Laser 4			
Electronic 3			
Completed projects			
Total research			
Development			
Gauges			
Modes			
Tubes			
Tester			
Total development			
Total project budgets			
Administrative			
General			
Library			
Research			
Patent			
Total administrative			
Grand Total			

An illustrative budget report is presented in Exhibit 13–4.

EXHIBIT 13–4 Budget Report

Department name:
Department manager:
Period:

Project	Current Month			Year-to-Date		
	Budget	Actual	Variance	Budget	Actual	Variance

An illustrative R&D expense budget is shown in Exhibit 13–5.

EXHIBIT 13–5 R&D Expense Budget

Expense	Category	Actual	Latest	Estimate	Budget	Variance

Illustrative project budgets appear in Exhibits 13–6 and 13–7.

EXHIBIT 13–6 R&D Budget

Project	Budget Manhours	Actual Manhours	Variance	Budgeted Cost	Actual Cost	Variance

EXHIBIT 13–7 R&D Budget

Project	Project Number	Manhours	Costs	Commitments	Estimated Cost and Hours to Complete	Budget Variance

EXHIBIT 13–8 Proposed R&D Budget

Budget	Employees	Manhours	Cost for Period	Cumulative Cost

There should be a periodic R&D project status report of dollar expenditures, technical accomplishments, objectives, schedule of conformance, potential, and current priority classification.

A proposed R&D budget is presented in Exhibit 13–8. Illustrative R&D status reports are presented in Exhibits 13–9, 13–10 and 13–11.

EXHIBIT 13–9 Project Status Report

| Project | | Month | | Cumulative to Date | | | Estimated Cost to Complete | | | | |
Project Identifier	Manhours	Salaries	Other Expense	Total Manhours	Amount	Purchase Commitments	Manhours	Amount	Total Cost	Project Budget	Cost (Over) or Under
New product research											
Project A											
Project B											
Project C											
Total											
Product improvements											
Project E											
Project F											
Project G											
Project H											
Total											
Sales service											
Project X											
Project Y											
Total											
Fundamental research											
Project S											
Project T											
Total											
Total R&D											

EXHIBIT 13–10 R&D Project Status Report

	Month		Cumulative				
Project Number	Manhours	Expenditures	Manhours	Expenditures	Commitments	Budget	Cost Overrun

EXHIBIT 13–11 Project Status Report

Project name:
Account number:
Date began:
Estimated completion date:
Priority code:
Total estimated cost:
Review date:
Budget:
Actual:
Status:
Accomplishments and progress:
Remarks:
Recommendation:

R&D PLANNING

R&D is needed for growth and as a minimum to maintain competitive position. R&D should be accumulated by type of expenditure and by department or cost center. R&D success is never certain, but must be stated in terms of possibility. R&D does *not* relate to sales but rather to new products being developed. R&D personnel and facilities must be evaluated.

R&D projects should be appraised periodically, e.g., quarterly, to gauge performance. A project screening sheet should be prepared examining the proposed R&D in terms of financial, technical, manufacturing, marketing, strategic, legal, and safety aspects. There should be progress points to evaluate R&D efforts. The program evaluation and review technique (PERT) may be used to track R&D.

Because a high percentage of R&D consists of labor cost, research scientists and engineers should prepare time sheets of hours spent on specific projects. There must be a determination of:

- Salaries to manhours
- Research commitments
- R&D to net sales
- Average R&D projects per period
- R&D by product

- Estimated project costs
- Estimated rates of return.

There should be an ongoing appraisal of how well R&D programs are using their funds. Are R&D project time estimates and costs reasonable? Budget and actual costs for the R&D projects should be compared and variances determined. If excessive research time and cost is being used for a particular project, a study should be made as to that project's feasibility.

R&D costs may be related to sales, production, labor hours, number of employees, profit, and number of segments. You must examine where the funds are being used, how successful the R&D efforts are being funded by type, where additional funds should be placed, and where less funding should go to.

Expenditures must be kept within budget constraints. Project controls should exist. Control reports are needed by commitment and expenditure. In the control phase, a comparison is made between the technical and financial aspects of projects. There is a review of the feasibility of current research projects. Projects may need to be dropped or deferred. Such projects should be noted and recorded for control purposes of the dollar amounts involved. R&D costs should be allocated by responsibility segment and then to each project or program within that segment.

CONCLUSION

The R&D budget depends upon the product life cycle and the degree of competition. A significant amount of cost control should be placed over high-risk R&D projects.

REFERENCES

John Chambers, Robert Emerald, and Albert Rubenstein, "Coupling Corporate Strategy and R&D Planning," *Managerial Planning,* May-June 1985, pp. 35–39, 42–49.

Naomi Freundlich, "Spreading the Risks of R&D," *Business Week,* 1989, pp. 60–64.

William Kimmerly, "R&D Strategic Planning in Turbulent Environments," *Managerial Planning,* March-April 1983, pp. 8–13.

Philip Roussel, "Cutting Down the Guesswork in R&D," *Harvard Business Review,* September-October 1983, pp. 154–160.

Roland Schmitt, "Successful Corporate R&D," *Harvard Business Review,* May-June 1985, pp. 124–128.

Chapter 14

Budgeting for Capital Expenditures

The capital expenditure budget is typically compiled by senior management in conjunction with engineering and technical services. The capital expenditure budget is of a *long-term* nature. Capital assets include buildings, land, equipment, machines, and computers. The assets involve a large cash outlay. The future of the business hinges on the selection of the right capital investment projects, the decision to replace existing capital assets, and the decision to abandon or sell existing assets.

The capital budget depends upon a company's financial position, working capital, liquidity, cash status, sales, profitability, return on investment, tax position, governmental incentives, payback period, risk, future prospects, productivity, new product development, technical obsolescence, capacity utilization, market share, desired diversification, time span, maintenance priorities, replacement options, economic conditions, political factors, nature of industry, timing of needed capital expenditures, problem areas, safety standards, laws and regulations, and pollution requirements. Capital expenditures involve large cash outlays and high risk. They significantly affect a company's long-term profitability. They involve uncertain benefits because of the long time period involved. The stopping of a capital expenditure project can result in huge financial losses. Capital expenditures must be justified and approved.

A desired return on investment (ROI) for capital expenditures may be specified, such as 15 percent. Capital expenditures may be targeted as a percentage of annual depreciation charges, such as 200 percent.

Capital expenditures are projects or proposals that involve significant expenditure and benefit more than one year. However, capital projects may be 20 or more years. There is planning and control of capital projects. Projects should be prioritized based on profitability or strategic importance. The planning period depends on the industry. Capital expenditures may be made for new acquisitions, improvements, and replacements. A capital asset cannot be bought unless it is included in the capital budget. Retirements are also considered. Examples of capital investments are new equipment, purchase and distribution facilities, land, building, furniture, machinery, plant, and computerization.

The capital expenditures budget lists capital assets to be bought, sold, or discarded. The company's cash and debt position should be evaluated to determine if sufficient funds exist to buy capital assets.

Plant and equipment must be properly controlled, insured, and used. Capital expenditures must be within approved limits and must be appropriately accounted for. Reliable figures are needed to support capital expenditure requests. Duplication of effort must be avoided. The actual expenditures should be compared to the budgeted expenditures on a continuous basis to aid in control.

The timing of capital expenditures depends on available funds, start-up time, and alternatives. A determination must be made of which capital expenditures are urgent, which can be delayed for a reasonable time period, and which are not essential. The capital budget should consider present and needed facilities. The capital budget must consider commitments. Capital expenditures must conform to the long-term plan and must provide a satisfactory return. The capital budget should be consistent with the company's strategic plan.

Capital expenditures may be made for one or more of the following reasons: growth, expense reduction, increased sales volume and/or production, preventive maintenance, normal replacement, new business, modification in production methods, efficiency, effectiveness, improve product quality, change in style, and competitive standing.

Fixed assets are basically acquired to either increase revenue or to lower expenses. New fixed assets may result in increased volume and improved quality. Costs may be reduced from more efficient machinery and equipment and less maintenance expenditures.

Capital expenditures may be made for replacement of obsolete equipment or expansion, such as that needed for new product lines. Capital expenditures should be examined in terms of need and reasons. Fixed assets must be used efficiently and productivity must be improved. The financial attractiveness of alternative proposals should be evaluated.

An example of a capital budget appears in Exhibit 14–1.

EXHIBIT 14–1 Capital Expenditures Budget for the Year Ending December 31, 19XX

Buildings	$2,000,000
Machinery	500,000
Equipment	$600,000
Total	$3,100,000

TYPES OF CAPITAL EXPENDITURES

Capital projects are proposed by operating managers and must be approved by top management. Capital expenditures should be classified by feasibility, need, consequence, class, and category. They may be required or optional. Capital expenditures may be for profit generation by providing either additional revenue or cost reduction. These include the marketing of a new product, expanding production, manufacturing under proposed contracts, improving the quality of products or services, and replacing machinery to economize on costs.

Capital expenditures should be classified for budgeting purposes as (1) normal or (2) special. Normal capital expenditures are routine, less costly, and made to maintain the current operational level. Typically, each project does not involve a significant outflow. The expenditure should be adequate to satisfy the need. An example is a minor replacement of machinery.

Some capital expenditures are minor and not subject to detailed planning. Examples are minor building renovatings and low-cost machinery. These minor expenditures may be lumped together with a blanket appropriation.

Special capital expenditures involve nonroutine, significant cash outlay for major specific projects. An example is the construction of a new plant to meet customer demand. Optional projects include plant expansion, new ventures, modified techniques, and replacement of operating equipment. The expenditure should be consistent with the desired ROI.

Some capital expenditures result in profit reductions such as capital outlays required by law, enhancing staff morale, and improving R&D. Other capital expenditures are required by government, such as for employee safety and for building codes.

THE BUDGETING PROCESS

The capital budget passes through different managerial levels. Top management must approve *major* capital expenditures. Divisional and departmental managers suggest the capital expenditures needed. Department managers typically suggest all *minor* capital expenditures.

A current capital budget typically covers 3–5 years in annual segments of planned capital expenditures. Engineering studies may support capital expenditure requests. The capital budget committee evaluates requests and approves or rejects them.

The four steps in the capital expenditure budgetary process are:

1. approving the project,
2. approving the estimate,
3. authorizing the project, and
4. follow-up.

The capital expenditure proposal should contain a description, recommendations, source data, pros and cons of the proposal, starting date, and completion date.

Capital expenditures should be prioritized in terms of operating necessities and non-necessities. Dates to be considered include:

- Delivery dates when items are needed
- Dates manpower will be available
- Marketing schedules for products to be manufactured.

Capital expenditure policy should consider:

- Life of the asset
- Expected capacity of the item
- Legal liability exposure
- Availability of financing
- Effect upon costs
- Regulatory requirements
- Availability of personnel
- Nature of industry
- Stage of the business cycle
- Growth potential
- Desired rate of return
- Age of assets
- Competition.

In the fixed-asset budget are included beginning fixed-asset balance, additions, deletions, expected capital expenditures, construction-in-process adjustments, explanatory comments, depreciation, and ending fixed—asset balance. The budget format should include class, category, project number, project title, project life, ROI, and capital costs.

Illustrative capital expenditure budgets appear in Exhibits 14–2 through 14–6. A typical budget for plant and equipment is shown in Exhibit 14–7.

Capital budgets should be modified when errors are discovered or circumstances change. Revisions would be needed for design changes, changes in cost estimates, unusual developments in the economy, or market place. The production budget may require capital additions. Extraordinary repairs are typically included in the capital expenditure budget, but ordinary repairs are included in the expense budget.

AUTHORIZATION OF CAPITAL BUDGET

Capital expenditures should be kept within authorized limits for major projects. Projects in excess of the budget limitation may be reviewed by upper management for special approval. The authorization to cancel a project should come from management who approved it. If a project is a succession of individual projects, a partial authorization may be given. An illustrative capital budget request schedule form is presented in Exhibit 14–8.

Capital expenditures for specific plant and equipment must be approved. An authorization form must be completed. The reason and purpose of the expenditure is typically given. Illustrative authorization forms appear in Exhibits 14–9 and 14–10.

The amount authorized should be compared to actual costs incurred at periodic intervals. Further, commitments must be recorded and monitored since the total appropriated amount may eventually be exceeded. The estimated cost to complete should also be noted along with any anticipated overruns or underruns.

EXHIBIT 14–2 Capital Expenditure Budget

Item	To Maintain Current Operations	To Expand	Total
L	$100,000	$150,000	$250,000
B	75,000	80,000	155,000
Machinery	200,000	250,000	450,000
Total	$375,000	$480,000	$855,000

EXHIBIT 14-3 Preliminary Capital Budget

Item No.	Work Order No.	Appropriation No.	Description of Job by Department	Unit Projected Total Cost Classified by Date of Expenditure				Estimated Expenditures, 1993–4–5 Classified by Accounting Disposition				
				Before 1993	1993	1994	1995	After 1995	Additional Facilities	Replacements	Rehabilitation	Expense
												Repairs	Other

EXHIBIT 14–4 Capital Expenditure Budget

Project	Budgeted Amount	Amount Authorized	Unexpended Balance	Actual Expenditures	Amount Subject to Authorization	Amount Spent

EXHIBIT 14–5 Capital Expenditure Budget

	Amount to Be Expended by Quarter					
	1	2	3	4	Total	In Later Periods
Approved Projects:						
Proposed New Projects:						
Proposed Replacements:						

EXHIBIT 14–6 Capital Asset Budget

		Division X					
		Commitments		Expenditures			
Type of Project	Carryforward Amount	New Commitments	Total Amount Available	On Previous Years' Commitments	Current Year Authorization	Total for Year	Carryforward to Future Years
Capital Expenditures							
Capital Leases							

EXHIBIT 14–7 Budget for Plant and Equipment

Classification	Amount at Beginning of Year	Additions	Subtractions	Depreciation	Amount at End of Year

ANALYSIS OF CAPITAL PROJECTS

The actual versus expected profit for each project should be compared. Further, an analysis should be made comparing the difference between actual and budgeted capital expenditures along with justification. Some analytical questions to be answered include: Are specialized fixed assets required? If capacity is expanded, what effect will it have on storage space?

CONTROL OVER CAPITAL EXPENDITURES

There should be financial control of individual projects during their activity. Capital expenditure outlays should be documented by vendor. Contractor price quotations should be audited. A capital expenditures budget manual should be prepared.

EXHIBIT 14–8 XYZ Company Annual Capital Budget Request 19X3

	Appropriations				Expected Capital Expenditures				
	19X0	19X1		Total					
	Prior	This		Committed					
Description	Year	Year	ROI	Amount	19X2	19X3	19X4	19X5 and later	Total
Growth & Expansion									
XYZ Plant									
ABC Recovery System									
Etc.									
Total Expansion									
Replacements									
Absolutely Needed									
Grinder									
Conveyor									
Crusher									
Air pollution									
Needed to Maintain									
Competitive Position									
Color Retention									
Quality Control Facility									
Optimal but Recommended									
Roofing-T Plant									
Landscaping									
Lift Trucks									
Contingency Funding									
Total									

EXHIBIT 14–9 Capital Expenditure Authorization

Division name: Date:

Location:

Reason for authorization:

Estimated total cost:

Item requested:

Description:

Cost estimate breakdown:

Comments and recommendations:

	Approved	Rejected	Date	Reason

Requested by:

Approved by:

CAPITAL BUDGET FORMS

Request forms should be completed and approved for capital expenditures. A commitment record contains the purchase orders issued. There is an appropriation form for capital expenditures. The form provides information on the benefits to be derived from the proposed project and on the expected cost savings. The authorization sets forth the type and scope of the project. A typical annual capital budget request form is shown in Exhibit 14–11.

EXHIBIT 14–10 Capital Expenditure Authorization

Division _____

Plant _____

Date _____

        The capital expenditure is required because of:

- Cost reduction
- Normal replacement
- Alteration in manufacturing process
- New quality control guidelines
- Improved sales volume
- Style change
- New product

        Description and justification _____

Estimated cost

   Material

   Labor

   Overhead

   Contingency

   Total cost

Expected return on investment

   Payback period

   Life

   Construction period

   Disposal value

Manager's comments and recommendations

Requested by_____

Approved by_____

EXHIBIT 14–11 Annual Capital Budget Request Form

Description	Appropriations	Capital Expenditures Made	Future Commitments

    A preliminary budget request form may contain the information shown in Exhibit 14–12.

EXHIBIT 14–12 Preliminary Budget Request Information

Division name and number

Department name and number

Date

Responsible individuals

Classification of project

Original request or supplementary request

Funds requested

Description of proposal

Time schedule

   Beginning date

   Expected ending date

Benefits expected

Priority level

Expected return

Approvals

EXHIBIT 14–13 Appropriation Request Form

Division
Department
Responsibility center
Project description
Project location
Expected expenditures
  Original request amount
  Already approved
  Future request
  Total project cost
Return on investment
Payback period
Net present value
Internal rate of return
Background information
Recommendations
Classifications
Nature of capital project proposal

An appropriation request form is used by the responsibility unit to detail supporting information for the capital proposal. This is used to appraise the soundness of the proposed capital project. A request form for capital expenditures may involve the following information: title of project, description of project, project goals, proposed budget, analysis and appraisal, justifica-

EXHIBIT 14–14 Preliminary Budget Request Form

Division   Department name and number
                            Date

Type of capital expenditure
  New
  Expansion
  Replacement
  Cost reduction
  Other (Describe)
Request
  Initial
  Supplementary
Priority level
Description of proposal
Funds requested
Identification of capital expenditure
Anticipated net cash flows
Time schedule
Expected return rate
Approvals
  Department manager
  Division manager
  Vice-president

EXHIBIT 14–15 An Alternative Capital Expenditures Request Form

Responsibility center name:
Responsibility center number:
Period covered:

Description	Quantity	Justification	Budgeted Cost	Date of Acquisition

Prepared by: Date:
Approved by: Date:

tion, supporting calculations, and time estimates. Exhibit 14-13 presents an appropriation request form. An illustrative request form appears in Exhibit 14–14. An alternative request form is shown in Exhibit 14–15.

A capital budget form summarizes proposed capital projects for the budget period by responsibility unit. An illustrative capital budget form is shown in Exhibit 14–16.

EXHIBIT 14–16 Capital Budget Form

Department	Description of Item	Item Number	Status	Total Expenditure	Expected ROI	Priority	Classification

CAPITAL EXPENDITURE REPORTS

The capital expenditure report should include information of the authorized amount, actual costs, committed funds, unencumbered balance, estimated cost to complete, and overrun (underrun). A capital expenditures process report form appears in Exhibit 14–17.

Typical reports showing the comparison of actual expenditures to budgeted expenditures are shown in Exhibits 14–18 and 14–19. A capital expenditure status report may be prepared periodically and may contain the information presented in Exhibit 14–20.

A progress report should be prepared to determine if everything is proceeding as planned and what corrective steps are needed. A detailed analysis of capital expenditures may not be possible when an urgent development occurs. An example is a machine breakdown causing a delay on the assembly line. A capital expenditures progress report monitors each project's progress and indicates any underruns or overruns. Sample progress reports are presented in Exhibits 14–21 through 14–26.

EXHIBIT 14-17 Capital Expenditures in Process Report ABC Corporation

Item Number	Description	Approval Amount	Initial Expected Project Completion Date	Incurred to Date	Balance for Completion	Total	Expected Variation	Favorable or Unfavorable	Expected Completion Date	Comments

EXHIBIT 14–18 Year-to-Date Comparisons of Actual to Budget Capital Expenditures

Type	Budgeted Projects	Projects Not Budgeted	Total	Amount Budgeted	Actual Expenditures	Over (Under) Budget

EXHIBIT 14–19 Capital Expenditure Performance Report (Actual vs. Estimated)

Department name
Department number
Authorization number
Description
Date today
Date activity started

Item	Authorized Amount	Actual Amount to Date	Variance	Percent	Analysis
1	$10,000	$10,200	$200	.02	Higher prices for component parts
2	6,000	6,300	300	.05	Delay due to strike

EXHIBIT 14–20 Capital Expenditure Status Report Information

Cost data
    Budgeted figure
    Cumulative actual expenditures
    Committed amounts
    Unexpended amount
    Expected cost to complete
    Variance between actual and budget
Dates
    Date started
    Anticipated completion date
    Days delayed
Degree of Completion
Percent of time completed to date
Percent of cost completed to date
Explanatory Remarks
Quality
Abnormal occurrences and reasons

EXHIBIT 14–21 Capital Expenditure Progress Report

Item Number	Description	Amount Approved	Expected Date of Completion	Expend- itures to Date	Amount Needed for Completion	Total	Budget	Variance	Remark

EXHIBIT 14–22 XYZ Manufacturing Company Project Number

Department and Cost	Authorized Amount	Actual Expenditures to Date	Purchase Commitments	Total Expenditures & Commitments	Balance Remaining
Research					
Wages	$5,000	$3,000	$500	$3,500	$1,500
Supplies	4,000	2,500	600	3,100	900
Power	etc.				
Total					
Development					
Wages					
Traveling					
Other					
Total					
Patent					
Lawyers' Fees					
Patent Applications					
Total					
Administrative					
Wages					
Depreciation					
Total					

EXHIBIT 14–23 Capital Expenditure Projects

Project Number	Description	Initial Starting Date	Actual Expenditures Current Month	Cumulative	Commitments and Expenditures to Date	Estimated Amount to Complete	Current Estimated Total Cost	Appropriated Amount	Over (Under) Appropriation

EXHIBIT 14–24 Capital Expenditure Project Status Report

Division   Period
Location
Project number
Title
Category
Return on investment
Payback period
Discounted payback period
Present value
Internal rate of return
Project appropriation and investment
Capital expenditure items

Total Actual Amount Approved	Actual Amount Spent to Date	Original Budgeted Amount	Revised Budgeted Amount	Variance	Reason

Analysis and comments
Preparer
Reviewer

EXHIBIT 14–25 Capital Expenditure Appropriation Status Report

Number	Classification	Description	Order Number	Amount Appropriated	Completion Date	Estimate	Commitments	Actual Expenditures	Variance

EXHBIIT 14–26 Status of Capital Expenditures Appropriated

Appropri- ation Number	Description	Work Order Number	Appropri- ation	Com- pletion Date	Initial Estimate	Outstanding Commitments	Actual Expendi- tures to Date	Estimated Cost to Complete	Total Cost	Over (Under) Initial Estimate

CONCLUSION

The capital expenditure budget projects how much is needed to invest in capital assets to satisfy the company's requirements. The types of assets in which funds should be placed are revealed. The timing and nature of these expenditures directly affects the long-term viability of the business.

Chapter 15

Decision Making Through Capital Budgeting

Capital budgeting relates to planning for the best selection and financing of long-term investment proposals. Capital budgeting decisions are not equally essential to all companies; the relative importance of this essential function varies with company size, the nature of the industry, and the growth rate of the firm. As a business expands, problems regarding long-range investment proposals become more important. Strategic capital budgeting decisions can turn the tide for a company.

The types of scarce resources that may be committed to a project include cash, time of key personnel, machine hours, and floor space in a factory. When estimating costs for a proposed project, the allocation of the company's scarce resources must be converted in terms of money.

There are two broad categories of capital budgeting decisions, namely, *screening decisions* and *preference decisions*. Screening decisions relate to whether a proposed project satisfies some present acceptance standard. For instance, your company may have a policy of accepting cost reduction projects only if they provide a return of, say, 15 percent. On the other hand, preference decisions apply to selecting from *competing* courses of action. For example, your company may be evaluating four different machines to replace an existing one in the manufacture of a product. The selection of the best machine is referred to as a preference decision.

The basic types of investment decisions are selecting between proposed projects and replacement decisions. Selection requires judgments concerning future events of which you have no direct knowledge. You must consider timing and risk. Your task is to minimize your chances of error. To help you deal with uncertainty, you may use the risk-return trade-off method. Discounted cash flow methods are more realistic than are methods not taking into account the time value of money in appraising investments. Consideration of the time value of money becomes more essential in inflationary periods. Capital budgeting can be used in profit and nonprofit settings.

Planning for capital expenditures requires you to determine the "optimal" proposal, the number of dollars to be spent, and the amount of time required for completion. An appraisal is needed of current programs, evaluating new proposals, and coordinating interrelated proposals within the company. In planning a project, consideration should be given to time, cost, and quality, which interreact. For control, budgeted cost and time should be compared to actual cost and time.

Capital budgeting decisions must conform to your cash position, financing strategy, and growth rate. Will the project provide a return exceeding the long-range expected return of the business? Projects must be tied into the company's long-range planning, taking into account corporate strengths and weaknesses. The objectives of the business and the degree to which they depend on economic variables (e.g., interest rate, inflation), production (e.g., technological changes), and market factors must be established. Also, the capital budget may need to be adjusted after considering financial, economic, and political concerns. But consideration should be given to "sunk" and "fixed" costs that are difficult to revise once the initial decision is made.

Recommendation: Use cost-benefit analysis. Is there excessive effort for the proposal? Can it be performed internally or must it be done externally (e.g., make or buy)? Is there a more efficient means and less costly way of accomplishing the end result? Further, problem areas must be identified. An example is when long-term borrowed funds are used to finance a project where sufficient cash inflows will not be able to meet debt at maturity.

Suggestion: Measure cash flows of a project using different possible assumed variations (e.g., change in selling price of a new product). By modifying the assumptions and appraising the results you can see the sensitivity of cash flows to applicable variables. An advantage is the appraisal of risk in proposals based on varying assumptions. An increase in risk should result in a higher return rate.

Taxes must be considered in making capital budgeting decisions because a project that is acceptable on a before-tax basis may not be acceptable on an after-tax basis. Taxes have an effect on the amount and timing of cash flows.

What-if questions are often the most crucial and difficult with regard to the capital expenditure budget; informed estimates are needed of the major assumptions. Spreadsheets can be used to analyze the cash flow implications of acquiring fixed assets.

Once an investment proposal is approved, there must be an implementation of controls over expenditures and a reporting system regarding the project's status. Expenditures should be traced to the project and controls in place assuring the expenditures are in conformity with the approved investment proposal. There should be continuous monitoring of the project's progress relative to the original plan.

Factors to Consider in Determining Capital Expenditures:

- Rate of return
- Budget ceiling
- Probability of success
- Competition
- Tax rate
- Dollar amounts
- Time value of money
- Risk
- Liquidity
- Long-term business strategy
- Forecasting errors.

Types of Capital Budgeting Decisions to Be Made:

- Cost reduction program
- Undertaking an advertising campaign
- Replacement of assets
- Obtaining new facilities or expanding existing ones
- Merger analysis
- Refinancing an outstanding debt issue
- New and existing product evaluation
- Nonprofit investments (e.g., health and safety).

Exhibit 15–1 shows a typical project application form, while Exhibit 15–2 presents an advice of project change. In Exhibit 15–3 an appropriation request is presented.

This chapter discusses the various capital budgeting methods including accounting rate of return, payback, discounted payback, net present value, profitability index, and internal rate of return. Consideration is also given to

EXHIBIT 15–1
Project Application

DEPARTMENT NAME					APPLICATION NO.
DEPARTMENT CODE _____					OFFENSIVE ☐
FUNCTION CODE _____					DEFENSIVE ☐
PROJECT TITLE					
DESCRIPTION/OBJECTIVES					

EXPENDITURE AMOUNTS

FISCAL YEAR	1st Qtr.	2nd Qtr.	3rd Qtr.	4th Qtr.	TOTAL
19					
19					
19					
19					
19					
TOTAL					

DATE	SUBMITTED BY

COMMENTS

_____
For The Division

contingent proposals, capital rationing, and nondiscretionary projects. The incorporation of risk into the analysis is also considered.

Net present value, internal rate of return, and profitability index are equally effective in selecting economically sound, independent investment proposals. But the payback method is inadequate since it does not consider the time value of money. For mutually exclusive projects, net present value, internal rate of return, and profitability index methods are not always able to rank projects in the same order; it is possible to come up with different rankings under each method. Risk should be taken into account in the capital budgeting process using probabilities, simulation, and decision trees.

EXHIBIT 15–2
Advice of Project Change

DEPARTMENT NAME		DATE	
DEPARTMENT CODE		APPROPRIATION REQUEST NO.	
PROJECT TITLE			

EXPENDITURE AMOUNTS

	ORIGINAL AUTHORIZED	LATEST ESTIMATE	INCREASE (DECREASE)
CAPITAL			
EXPENSE			
TOTAL			

AMOUNT SPENT TO DATE $ _____ AMOUNT COMMITTED TO DATE $ _____

WHY IS THIS NEW AMOUNT BEING REQUESTED?

_____   _____
PROJECT SPONSOR   DEPARTMENT/AREA SUPERVISOR

PROJECT TO BE CONTINUED ☐
REVISED REQUEST REQUIRED ☐
SEE COMMENT ON REVERSE   FINAL APPROVER _____
SIDE ☐   DATE _____

ACCOUNTING (SIMPLE) RATE OF RETURN

Accounting rate of return (ARR) measures profitability from the conventional accounting standpoint by comparing the required investment (sometimes average investment) to future annual earnings.

Rule of Thumb: Select the proposal with the highest ARR.

EXHIBIT 15–3
Appropriation Request

ORIG. DEPT. NAME		DEPT. CODE	APPROPRIATION NO.
BUDGET CAPITALIZED ☐ EXPENSED ☐		PROJECT APPLIC. NO.	
ACCOUNTING CODE		PROJECT APPL. TOT. EXP. $	APPROPRIATION TOTAL $
DESCRIPTION			
PURPOSE			
CURRENT FACILITIES			
PROPOSED FACILITIES			
COST JUSTIFICATION (SAVINGS/BENEFITS)			

PROPOSED EXPENDITURES		APPROVALS		DATE
Equipment Cost	_____	Originator	_____	___
Material Cost	_____		_____	___
Installation Costs:	_____		_____	___
External Services	_____	Dept/Area Suprv.	_____	___
Internal Services	_____	V. President	_____	___
Miscellaneous Costs	_____	Controller	_____	___
Freight	_____	Division Head	_____	___
Taxes	_____	C.E.O.	_____	___
Total	_____	Bd. of Dir.	_____	___

EXAMPLE 15–1

Initial investment	$8,000
Life	15 years
Cash inflows per year	$1,300

$$\text{Depreciation} = \frac{\text{Cost} - \text{Salvage value}}{\text{Life}} = \frac{\$8,000 - 0}{15} = \$533$$

$$\text{ARR} = \frac{\text{Cash inflows per year} - \text{Depreciation}}{\text{Initial investment}}$$

$$\frac{\$1,300 - \$533}{\$8,000} = \frac{\$767}{\$8,000} = 9.6\%$$

If you use average investment, ARR is

$$\text{ARR} = \frac{\$767}{\$8.000/2} = \frac{\$767}{\$4,000} = 19.2\%$$

Note: When average investment is used rather than the initial investment, Accounting Rate of Return is doubled.

Advantages of ARR:

- Easy to comprehend and calculate
- Considers profitability
- Numbers relate to financial statement presentation
- Considers full useful life

Disadvantages of ARR:

- Ignores time value of money
- Uses income data rather than cash flow data

Note: In an automated environment, the cost of the investment would include engineering, software development, and implementation.

PAYBACK PERIOD

Payback is the number of years required to recover your initial investment. Payback assists in evaluating a project's risk and liquidity, faster rate of return, and earlier recoupment of funds. A benefit of payback is that it permits companies with a cash problem to evaluate the turnover of scarce resources in order to recover earlier those funds invested. In addition, there is likely to be less possibility of loss from changes in economic conditions, obsolescence, and other unavoidable risks when the commitment is short—term.

Supporters of the payback period point to its use where preliminary screening is more essential than precise figures, in situations where a poor credit position is a major factor, and when investment funds are exceptionally scarce. Some believe that payback should be used in unstable, uncertain industries subject to rapid technological change because the future is so unpredictable that it is futile to predict cash flows more than two years in advance. As reported in the July/August 1988 issue of *Financial Executive,* a majority of executives want payback in three years or less.

A company may establish a limit on the payback period beyond which an investment will not be made. Another business may use payback to choose one of several investments, selecting the one with the shortest payback period.

Advantages of Payback:

- Easy to use and understand
- Effectively handles investment risk
- Good approach when a weak cash-and-credit position influences the selection of a proposal
- Can be used as a supplement to other more sophisticated techniques since it does indicate risk.

Disadvantages of Payback:

- Ignores the time value of money
- Does not consider cash flows received after the payback period
- Does not measure profitability
- Does not indicate how long the maximum payback period should be
- Penalizes projects that result in small cash flows in their early years and heavy cash flows in their later years.

Warning: Do not select a proposal simply because the payback method indicates acceptance. You still must use the discounting methods such as present value and internal rate of return.

EXAMPLE 15–2   You are considering a new product. It will initially cost $250,000. Expected cash inflows are $80,000 for the next five years. You want your money back in four years.

$$\text{Payback period} = \frac{\text{Initial investment}}{\text{Annual cash inflow}} = \frac{\$250,000}{\$80,000} = 3.125$$

Because the payback period (3.125) is less than the cutoff payback period (4), you should accept the proposal.

EXAMPLE 15–3   You invest $40,000 and receive the following cash inflows:

Year 1	$15,000
Year 2	20,000
Year 3	28,000

$$\text{Payback period} = \frac{\$40,000}{\underset{\text{Year 1}}{} \quad \underset{\text{Year 2}}{} \quad \underset{\text{Year 3}}{}} = 2.18 \text{ years}$$

$$\underbrace{\frac{\$15,000 + \$20,000}{\$35,000}}_{\text{2 years}} + \underbrace{\frac{\$5,000}{\$28,000}}_{+ \quad .18}$$

If there are unequal cash inflows each year, to determine the payback period just add up the annual cash inflows to come up with the amount of the cash outlay. The answer is how long it takes to recover your investment.

Note: As reported in the November 1987 issue of *Management Accounting* published by the National Association of Accountants, it was found that the majority of manufacturers use an unadjusted payback period of between two and four years when appraising advanced manufacturing equipment.

PAYBACK RECIPROCAL

Payback reciprocal is the reciprocal of the payback time. This often gives a quick, accurate estimate of the *internal rate of return (IRR)* on an investment when the project life is more than twice the payback period and the cash inflows are uniform every period.

EXAMPLE 15–4 ABC Company is contemplating three projects, each of which would require an initial investment of $10,000, and each of which is expected to generate a cash inflow of $2,000 per year. The payback period is five years ($10,000/$2,000), and the payback reciprocal is 1/5, or 20 percent. The table of the present value of an annuity of $1 shows that the factor of 5.00 applies to the following useful lives and internal rates of return:

Useful Life	IRR
10 years	15%
15	18
20	19

It can be observed that the payback reciprocal is 20 percent as compared with the IRR of 18 percent when the life is 15 years, and 20 percent as compared with the IRR of 19 percent when the life is 20 years. This shows that the payback reciprocal gives a reasonable approximation of the IRR if the useful life of the project is at least twice the payback period.

DISCOUNTED PAYBACK PERIOD

Before looking at discounted cash flow methods, it should be pointed out that less reliability exists with discounted cash flow analysis if there is future uncertainty, the environment is changing, and cash flows themselves are difficult to predict.

Take into account the time value of money by using the discounted payback method. The payback period will be longer using the discounted method because money is worth less over time.

How to Do it: Discounted payback is computed by adding the present value of each year's cash inflows until they equal the investment.

EXAMPLE 15–5   Assume the same facts as in Example 15–3 and a cost of capital of 10 percent.

$$\text{Discounted payback} = \frac{\text{Initial cash outlay}}{\text{Discounted annual cash inflows}}$$

	$40,000	
Year 1	Year 2	Year 3
$15,000 +	$20,000 +	$28,000
×.9091 ×	.8264 ×	.7513
$13,637 +	$16,528 +	$21,036

$$\$30,165 \quad + \quad \frac{\$\ 9,835}{\$21,036}$$

$$2 \text{ years} \quad + \quad .47 \quad = 2.47 \text{ years}$$

NET PRESENT VALUE

The present value method compares the present value of future cash flows expected from an investment project to the initial cash outlay for the investment. Net cash flow is the difference between forecasted cash inflow received because of the investment and the expected cash outflow of the investment. You should use as a discount rate the minimum rate of return earned by the company on its money. As reported in the November 1987 issue of *Management Accounting* (p. 29), 36 percent of manufacturers used discount rates of between 13 percent and 17 percent and more than 30 percent used discount rates of over 19 percent. A company should use as the discount rate its cost of capital.

Rule of Thumb: Considering inflation, the cost of debt, and so on, the anticipated return should be about 10–13 percent.

Note: The net present value method discounts all cash flows at the cost of capital, thus implicitly assuming that these cash flows can be reinvested at this rate.

An advantage of net present value is that it considers the time value of money. A disadvantage is the subjectivity in determining expected annual cash inflows and expected period of benefit.

Recommendation: If a proposal is to provide a return, invest in it only if it provides a positive net present value. If two proposals are mutually exclusive (acceptance of one precludes the acceptance of another), then accept the proposal with the highest present value.

Note: In an advanced automated environment, the terminal value requires managerial accountants to forecast technological, economic, operational, strategic, and market developments over the investment's life so that a reasonable estimate of potential value may be made.

Caution: Using the return rate earned by the company as the discount rate may be misleading in certain cases. It may be a good idea to examine also the return rate investors earn on similar projects. If the hurdle rates selected are based upon the company's return on average projects, an internal company decision will occur that helps to increase the corporate return. Yet if the company is earning a very high rate of return, you will accept many good projects but also reject some good ones. What if the project rejected would really enhance value?

If the corporate return rate is below what investors can earn elsewhere, you delude yourself in believing it's an attractive investment. The project may involve below-normal profitability, lower per share value, and result in lower creditor and investor ratings of the firm.

The net present value method typically provides more reliable signals than other methods. By employing net present value and using best estimates of reinvestment rates, you can select the most advantageous project.

EXAMPLE 15–6   You are considering replacing Executive 1 with Executive 2. Executive 2 requires a payment upon contract signing of $200,000. He will receive an annual salary of $330,000. Executive 1's current annual salary is $140,000. Because Executive 2 is superior in talent, you expect an increase in annual cash flows from operations (ignoring salary) of $350,000 for each of the next ten years. The cost of capital is 12 percent.

As indicated in the following calculations, since there is a positive net present value, Executive 1 should be replaced with Executive 2.

Year	Explanation	Amount	×	Factor	=	Present Value
0	Contract signing bonus	$–200,000	×	1		$–200,000
1–10	Increased salary ($300,000 – $140,000)	–160,000	×	5.6502[a]		– 904,032
1–10	Increase in annual cash flow from operations	+350,000	×	5.6502[a]		1,977,570
	Net present value					$873,538

[a] Present value of an ordinary annuity factor for 10 years and an interest rate of 12 percent.

EXAMPLE 15–7   You own a business for which you have received a $1,000,000 offer. If you do not sell, you will remain in business for eight years and will invest another

$50,000 in your firm. If you stay, you will sell your business in the eighth year for $60,000.

You expect yearly sales to increase by 50 percent from its present level of $500,000. Direct material is proportional to sales. Direct labor is proportional to sales, but will increase by 30 percent for all labor. Variable overhead varies with sales, and annual fixed overhead will total $70,000, including depreciation. Straight-line depreciation will increase from $7,000 to $10,000. At the end of eight years, all fixed assets will be fully depreciated. Selling and administrative expenses are assumed to remain constant. The cost of capital is 14 percent.

Your current year's income statement is

Sales		$500,000
Less: Cost of sales		
Direct material	$100,000	
Direct labor	120,000	
Variable overhead	50,000	
Fixed overhead	65,000	335,000
Gross margin		$165,000
Less: Selling and administrative expenses[a]		40,000
Net income		$125,000

[a] Includes your salary of $20,000.

Your forecasted income statement for each of the next eight years follows:

Sales $500,000 × 1.5		$750,000
Less: Cost of sales		
Direct material $100,000 × 1.5	$150,000	
Direct labor $120,000 × 1.5 × 1.3	234,000	
Variable overhead $50,000 × 1.5	75,000	
Fixed overhead	70,000	529,000
Gross margin		$221,000
Less: Selling and administrative expenses		40,000
Net income		$181,000

Your annual cash flow from operations is

Net income	$181,000
Add: Depreciation	10,000
Salary	20,000
Annual cash flow from operations	$211,000

A comparison of your alternatives follows:

Sell business	+$1,000,000

Stay in business

Year	Explanation	Amount	×	Factor	=	Present Value
0	Investment in assets	$– 50,000	×	1		$–50,000
1–8	Annual cash inflow	+211,000	×	4.6389		+978,808
8	Sales price of business	+ 60,000	×	0.3506		+ 21,036
	Net present value					$+949,844

Since the net present value is higher to sell the business ($1,000,000) than staying in business ($949,844), you should sell now.

EXAMPLE 15–8 You are considering replacing an old machine with a new one. The old machine has a book value of $800,000 and a remaining life of ten years. The expected salvage value of the old machine is $50,000, but if you sold it now, you would obtain $700,000. The new machine costs $2,000,000 and has a salvage value of $250,000. The new machine will result in annual savings of $400,000. The tax rate is 50 percent, and the cost of capital is 14 percent. Use straight-line depreciation. You must determine whether to replace the machine.

The net increase in annual cash flow is

	Net Income	Cash Flow
Annual savings	$400,000	$400,000
Less: Incremental depreciation		

New machine $\dfrac{\$2,000,000-\$250,000}{10} = \$175,000$

Old machine $\dfrac{\$800,000-\$50,000}{10} = \$75,000$

	Net Income	Cash Flow
Incremental depreciation	100,000	
Income before tax	$300,000	
Tax, 50%	150,000	150,000
Income after tax	$150,000	
Net cash inflow		$250,000

The net present value follows:

Year	Explanation	Amount	×	Factor	Present Value
0	Cost of new machine	$–2,000,000	×	1.000	$– 2,000,000
0	Sale of old machine	700,000	×	1.000	700,000
1	Investment tax credit	200,000	×	.877	175,400
1	Tax benefit from loss on sale of old machine	50,000	×	.877	43,850
1–10	Yearly increase in cash flows	250,000	×	5.216	1,304,000
10	Incremental salvage value	200,000	×	.270	54,000
					$ 102,100

The replacement of the old machine with a new machine should be made because of the resulting positive net present value.

Deciding whether to lease or purchase involves comparing the leasing and purchasing alternatives.

EXAMPLE 15–9   You have decided to acquire an asset costing $100,000 with a life of five years and no salvage value. The asset can be purchased with a loan or it can be leased. If leased, the lessor wants a 12 percent return. Lease payments are made in advance at the end of the year prior to each of the 10 years. The tax rate is 50 percent, and the cost of capital is 8 percent.

$$\text{Annual lease payment} = \frac{\$100,000}{1+3.3073} = \frac{\$100,000}{4.3073}$$
$$= \$23,216 \text{ (rounded)}$$

Year	Lease Payment	Tax Savings	After-Tax Cash Outflow	Factor	Present Value
0	$23,216		$23,216	1.0000	$23,216
1–4	23,216	$11,608[a]	11,608	3.3121	38,447
5		11,608	(11,608)	.6806	(7,900)
					$53,763

[a] 23,216 × 50% = $11,608.

If you buy the asset, you will take out a 10 percent loan. Straight-line depreciation is used with no salvage value.

$$\text{Depreciation} = \frac{\$100,000}{5} = \$20,000$$

$$\text{Annual loan payment} = \frac{\$100,000}{3.7906} = \$26,381$$

The loan amortization schedule follows:

Year	Loan Payment	Beginning-of-Year Principal	Interest[a]	Principal[b]	End-of-Year Principal
1	$26,381	$100,000	$10,000	$16,381	$83,619
2	26,381	83,619	8,362	18,019	65,600
3	26,381	65,600	6,560	19,821	45,779
4	26,381	45,779	4,578	21,803	23,976
5	26,381	23,976[c]	2,398	23,983[c]	

[a] 10% × Beginning-of-year principal.

[b] Loan payment − interest.

[c] Slight difference due to rounding.

The computation of the present value of borrowing follows

	(1)	(2)	(3)	(4)	(5)	(6)	(7)	(8)
							PV	PV of
	Loan		Depre-	Total	Tax	Cash	Factor	Cash
Year	Payment	Interest	ciation	Deduction	Savings	Outflow	at 8%	Outflow
1	$26,381	$10,000	$20,000	$30,000	$15,000	$11,38 1	.9259	$10,538
2	26,381	8,362	20,000	28,362	14,181	12,200	.8573	10,459
3	26,381	6,560	20,000	26,560	13,280	13,101	.7938	10,400
4	26,381	4,578	20,000	24,578	12,289	14,092	.7350	10,358
5	26,381	2,398	20,000	22,398	11,199	15,182	.6806	10,333
								$52,088

(4) = (2) + (3)
(5) = (4) × 50%
(6) = (1) − (5)
(8) = (6) × (7)

The present value of borrowing ($52,088) is less than the present value of leasing ($53,763). Thus, the asset should be bought.

PROFITABILITY INDEX

The *profitability (ranking) index* (also called excess present value index, cost-benefit ratio) is a net rather than an aggregate index and is employed to differentiate the initial cash investment from later cash inflows. If you have budget constraints, proposals of different dollar magnitude can be ranked on a comparative basis. Use the index as a means of ranking projects in descending order of attractiveness.

$$\text{Profitability index} = \frac{\text{Present value of cash inflows}}{\text{Present value of cash outflows}}$$

Rule of Thumb: Accept a proposal with a profitability index equal to or greater than 1.

Caution: A higher profitability index does not always coincide with the project with the highest net present value.

Key Point: The internal rate of return and the net present value approaches may give conflicting signals when competing projects have unequal times. The profitability index gives the correct decision, however, and is superior under these circumstances.

Capital rationing occurs when a business is unable to invest in projects with a net present value greater than or equal to zero. Typically, the firm establishes an upper limit to its capital budget based on budgetary constraints.

Note: With capital rationing, the project with the highest ranking index rather than net present value should be selected for investment.

Exhibit 15–4 shows the capital rationing decision process.

EXHIBIT 15–4 Capital Rationing Decision Process

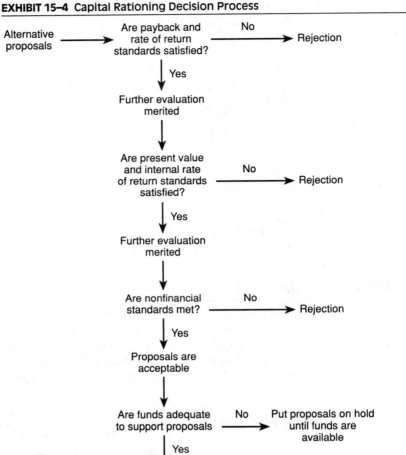

EXAMPLE 15–10 Assume the following information regarding two proposals:

	Proposal A	*Proposal B*
Initial investment	$100,000	$10,000
Present value of cash inflows	500,000	90,000

The net present value of proposal A is $400,000 and that of proposal B is $80,000. Based on net present value, proposal A is better. However, this is very misleading when a budget constraint exists. In this case, proposal B's profitability index of 9 far surpasses proposal A's index of 5. Thus, profitabil-

CHAP. 15: DECISION MAKING THROUGH CAPITAL BUDGETING **215**

ity index should be used in evaluating proposals when budget constraints exist. The net result is that proposal B should be selected over proposal A.

EXAMPLE 15–11

Projects	Investment	Present Value	Profitability Index	Ranking
A	$ 70,000	$112,000	1.6	1
B	100,000	145,000	1.45	2
C	110,000	126,500	1.15	5
D	60,000	79,000	1.32	3
E	40,000	38,000	.95	6
F	80,000	95,000	1.19	4

The budget constraint is $250,000. You should select projects A, B, and D as indicated by the following calculations.

Project	Investment	Present Value
A	$ 70,000	$112,000
B	100,000	145,000
D	60,000	79,000
	$230,000	$336,000

where

Net present value = $336,000 − $230,000 = $106,000

Unfortunately, the profitability index method has some limitations. One of the more serious is that it breaks down whenever more than one resource is rationed.

A more general approach to solving capital rationing problems is the use of *mathematical* (or zero-one) programming. Here the objective is to select the mix of projects that maximizes the net present value subject to a budget constraint.

EXAMPLE 15–12 Using the data given in Example 15–11, we can set up the problem as a mathematical programming one. First, we label project A as X_1, B as X_2, and so on; the problem can be stated as follows:

Maximize NPV = $42,000X_1 + $45,000X_2 + $16,500X_3$
$$+ $19,000X_4 − $2,000X_5 + $15,000X_6$$

subject to

$$$70,000X_1 + $100,000X_2 + $110,000X_3 + $60,000X_4 + $40,000X_5$$

$$+ $80,000X_6 \leq $250,000$$

$$X_1 = 0, 1, (i = 1, 2, \ldots 6)$$

Using the mathematical program solution routine, the solution to this problem is

$$X_1 = 1, X_2 = 1, X_4 = 1$$

and the net present value is $106,000. Thus, projects A, B, and D should be accepted.

Contingent Proposals

A contingent proposal is one that requires acceptance of another related one. Hence, the proposals must be looked at together. You compute a profitability index for the group.

EXAMPLE 15–13

Proposal	Present Value of Cash Outflow	Present Value of Cash Inflow
A	$160,000	$210,000
B	60,000	40,000
Total	$220,000	$250,000

$$\text{Profitability index} = \frac{\$250,000}{\$220,000} = 1.14$$

INTERNAL RATE OF RETURN (TIME-ADJUSTED RATE OF RETURN)

The internal rate of return is the return earned on a given proposal. It is the discount rate equating the net present value of cash inflows to the net present value of cash outflows to zero. The internal rate of return assumes cash inflows are reinvested at the internal rate. This method involves trial-and-error computations. However, the use of a computer or programmable calculator simplifies the internal rate-of-return process. The internal rate of return can be compared with the required rate of return (cutoff or hurdle rate).

Rule of Thumb: If the internal rate of return equals or exceeds the required rate, the project is accepted. The required rate of return is typically a company's cost of capital, sometimes adjusted for risk.

Advantages of IRR:

- Considers the time value of money
- More realistic and accurate than the accounting rate of return method.

Disadvantages of IRR:

- Difficult and time consuming to compute, particularly when there are uneven cash flows
- Does not consider the varying size of investment in competing projects and their respective dollar profitabilities
- When there are multiple reversals in the cash flow stream, the project could yield more than one IRR.

To solve for internal rate of return where unequal cash inflows exist, use the trial-and-error method while working through the present value tables.

Guidelines:

1. Compute net present value at the cost of capital, denoted here as r_1.
2. See if net present value is positive or negative.
3. If net present value is positive, use a higher rate (r_2) than r_1. If net present value is negative, use a lower rate (r_2) than r_1. The exact internal rate of return at which net present value equals zero is somewhere between the two rates.
4. Compute net present value using r_2.
5. Perform interpolation for exact rate.

EXAMPLE 15–14 A project costing $100,000 is expected to produce the following cash inflows:

YEAR	
1	$50,000
2	30,000
3	20,000
4	40,000

Using trial and error, you can calculate the internal rate as follows:

Year	10%	Present Value	16%	Present Value	18%	Present Value
1	.909	$45,450	.862	$43,100	.847	$42,350
2	.826	24,780	.743	22,290	.718	21,540
3	.751	15,020	.641	12,820	.609	12,180
4	.683	27,320	.552	22,080	.516	20,640
		$+112,570		$+100,290		$ +96,710
Investment		−100,000		−100,000		−100,000
Net present value		$ +12,570		$ +290		$ − 3,290

The internal rate of return on the project is a little more than 16 percent because at that rate the net present value of the investment is approximately zero.

If the return on the investment is expected to be in one lump sum after a period of two years, you can use the Present Value of $1 table to find the internal rate.

EXAMPLE 15–15 You are considering two mutually exclusive investment proposals. The cost of capital is 10 percent. Expected cash flows are as follows:

Project	Investment	Year 1	Year 6
A	$10,000	$12,000	
B	10,000		$20,000

Internal rates of return are

$$\text{Project A}: \frac{\$10,000}{\$12,000} = .8333$$

Looking across one year on the table, .8333 corresponds to an internal rate of 20 percent.

$$\text{Project B}: \frac{\$10,000}{\$20,000} = .5000$$

Looking across six years on the table, .5000 corresponds to an internal rate of 12 percent. Project A should be selected because it has a higher internal rate of return than project B.

If the cash inflows each year are equal, the internal rate of return is computed first by determining a factor (which happens to be the same as the payback period) and then looking up the rate of return on the Present Value of an Annuity of $1 table.

EXAMPLE 15–16 You invest $100,000 in a proposal that will produce annual cash inflows of $15,000 a year for the next 20 years.

$$\text{Factor} = \frac{\$100,000}{\$15,000} = 6.6667$$

Refer to the Present Value of an Annuity of $1 table. Looking across 20 years, the factor closest to 6.6667 is 6.6231 in the 14 percent column. Hence the internal rate is about 14 percent.

EXAMPLE 15–17

Initial investment	$12,950
Estimated life	10 years
Annual cash inflows	$3,000
Cost of capital	12%

The internal rate of return calculation follows, including interpolation to get the exact rate.

$$\text{PV of annuity factor} = \frac{\$12,950}{\$3,000} = 4.317$$

The value 4.317 is somewhere between 18 percent and 20 percent in the 10-year line of the Present Value of annuity table. Using interpolation you get

	Present Value of Annuity Factor	
18%	4.494	4.494
IRR		4.317
20%	4.192	
Difference	.302	.177

Therefore,

$$IRR = 18\% + \frac{.177}{.302}(20\% - 18\%)$$
$$= 18\% + .586(2\%) = 18\% + 1.17\% = 19.17\%$$

Because the internal rate of return (19.17 percent) exceeds the cost of capital (12 percent), the project should be accepted.

NONDISCRETIONARY PROJECTS

Some investments are made out of necessity rather than profitability (e.g., pollution control equipment, safety equipment). Here you will have solely a negative cash flow. Hence, your discretionary projects must earn a return rate in excess of the cost of capital to compensate for the losses on nondiscretionary projects.

EXAMPLE 15–18 A company's cost of capital is 14 percent and $30 million of capital projects, 25 percent of which are nondiscretionary projects. It thus must earn $4.2 million per year (14% × $30 million). The $22.5 million of discretionary projects ($30 million − 25%) must earn 18.7 percent ($4.2 million/$22.5 million) rather than 14 percent to achieve the overall corporate earnings goal of $4.2 million.

COMPARISON OF METHODS

In general, the discounting cash flow methods (net present value, internal rate of return, and profitability index) reach the same conclusions for competing proposals. But these methods can give different rankings to mutually exclusive proposals in certain cases. Any one of the following conditions can cause contradictory rankings:

- Project lives of different duration.
- A higher cost for one project relative to another.
- The trend in cash flow of one project that is the reverse of that of another.

One of the following characteristics of the company may also produce conflicting rankings:

- Future investment opportunities are expected to be different than at present, and the investor knows whether they will be better or worse.
- There is capital rationing, a maximum level of funding for capital investments.

The major cause for different rankings of alternative projects under present value and internal rate of return methods relates to the varying assumptions regarding the reinvestment rate employed for discounting cash flows. The net present value method assumes cash flows are reinvested at the cost of capital rate. The internal rate of return method assumes cash flows are reinvested at the internal rate.

Key Point: The net present value method typically provides a correct ranking because the cost of capital is a more realistic reinvestment rate.

Recommendation: Which method is best for a business really depends upon which reinvestment rate is nearest the rate the business can earn on future cash flows from a project.

Note: The board of directors typically reviews the company's required rate of return each year and may increase or decrease it, depending on the company's current rate of return and cost of capital.

The minimum rate of return required for a proposal may be waived in a situation where the proposal has significant future benefit (example: research and development), applies to a necessity program (example: safety requirement), and has qualitative benefit (example: product quality).

EXAMPLE 15–19 Assume the following:

| Project | \multicolumn{6}{c}{Cash Flows} |
	0	1	2	3	4	5
A	$(100)	$120				
B	(100)					$201.14

Computing Internal Rate of Return and Net Present Value at 10 percent gives the different rankings as follows:

	Internal Rate of Return	Net Present Value
A	20%[a]	9.09
B	15%	24.90

[a] From present value of $1 table, the IRR for a factor of .8333 $\left(\frac{\$100}{\$120}\right)$ is 20 percent.

The general rule is to follow Net Present Value ranking. Thus, project B would be chosen over project A.

CAPITAL BUDGETING PROCESS

Questions to be asked in the capital budgeting process:

- How is risk incorporated into the analysis?
- Is risk versus return considered in choosing projects?
- Prior to making a final decision, are all the results of the capital budgeting techniques considered and integrated?
- In evaluating a proposal, are both dollars and time considered?
- Is the proposal consistent with long-term goals?
- Does each project have a cost-benefit analysis?
- Do you know which proposals and products are most profitable? How much business is in each?
- Are there projects of an unusual nature?
- Do you periodically track the performance of current programs in terms of original expectations?
- In the capital budgeting process, are qualitative factors also considered, such as marketing, production, and economic and political variables?
- Has the proposal been considered incorporating the company's financial health?
- What is the quality of the project?

- Given the current environment, are your capital investments adequate?
- Are you risk prone or risk averse?
- Is the discounted payback method being used?
- How are probable cash flows computed?
- How do you compute the expected life?

To look at the entire picture of the capital budgeting process, a comprehensive example is provided.

EXAMPLE 15–20 You are deciding whether to buy a business. The initial cash outlay is $35,000. You will receive annual net cash inflows (excluding depreciation) of $5,000 per year for 10 years. The cost of capital is 10 percent. The tax rate is 50 percent. Should you buy this business?

The annual cash inflow follows:

Years 1–10

	Net Income	Cash Flow
Annual cash savings	$5,000	$+5,000
Depreciation ($35,000/10)	3,500	
Income before tax	$1,500	
Tax, 50%	750	−750
Net income	$ 750	
Net cash flow		$+4,250

Average rate of return on investment:

$$\frac{\text{Net income}}{\text{Average investment}} = \frac{\$750}{\$35,000/2} = \frac{\$750}{\$17,500} = 4\%$$

Payback period:

$$\frac{\text{Initial investment}}{\text{Annual net cash inflow}} = \frac{\$35,000}{\$4,250} = 8.2 \text{ years}$$

Net present value:

Year	Explanation	Amount	¥	Factor	=	Present Value
0	Initial investment	$−35,000	×	1		$− 35,000
1–10	Annual net cash inflow	+ 4,250	×	6.1446		26,095
	Net present value					$ −8,905

Profitability index:

$$\frac{\text{Present value of cash inflow}}{\text{Present value of cash outflow}} = \frac{\$26,095}{\$35,000} = .74$$

Internal rate of return:

$$\text{Factor} = \frac{\text{Initial outlay}}{\text{Annual net cash flow}} = \frac{\$35,000}{\$4.250} = 8.2$$

Referring to the Present Value of Annuity table, look for the intersection of 10 years and a factor of 8.2. Looking up the column you find 4 percent, which is the internal rate.

Conclusion: The business should not be bought for the following reasons:

1. An average rate of return of 4 percent is low.
2. The payback period is long.
3. The net present value is negative.
4. The internal rate of return of 4 percent is less than the cost of capital of 10 percent.

CAPITAL BUDGETING AND INFLATION

The accuracy of capital budgeting decisions depends upon the accuracy of the data regarding cash inflows and outflows. Example: failure to incorporate price-level changes due to inflation in capital budgeting situations can result in errors in the prediction of cash flows and thus in incorrect decisions.

Typically, the managerial accountant has two options dealing with a capital budgeting situation with inflation: Either (1) restate the cash flows in nominal terms and discount them at a nominal *cost of capital* (*minimum required rate of return*) or (2) restate both the cash flows and cost of capital in *constant* terms and discount the constant cash flows at a constant cost of capital. The two methods are basically equivalent.

EXAMPLE 15–21 A company has the following projected cash flows estimated in real terms:

Real Cash Flows (000s)

Period	0	1	2	3
	−100	35	50	30

The nominal cost of capital is 15 percent. Assume that inflation is projected at 10 percent a year. Then the first cash flow for year 1, which is $35,000 in current dollars, will be $35,000 \times 1.10 = \$38,500$ in year 1 dollars. Similarly the cash flow for year 2 will be $50,000 \times (1.10)^2 = \$60,500$ in year 2 dollars, and so on. By discounting these nominal cash flows at the 15 percent nominal cost of capital, you come up with the following net present value:

Period	Cash Flows	Present Value Factors	Present Values
0	−100	1.000	−100
1	38.5	.870	33.50
2	60.5	.756	45.74
3	39.9	.658	26.25
		Net present value =	5.49 or $5,490

Instead of converting the cash flow forecasts into nominal terms, we could convert the cost of capital into real terms by using the following formula:

$$\text{Real cost of capital} = \frac{1 + \text{nominal cost of capital}}{1 + \text{inflation rate}} - 1$$

In the example, this gives

$$\text{Real cost of capital} = \frac{(1 + .15)}{(1 + .10)}$$

$$= \frac{1.15}{1.10} = 0.045 \text{ or } 4.5 \text{ percent.}$$

You will obtain the same answer except for rounding errors ($5,490 versus $5,580).

Period	Cash Flows	Present Value Factor = $1/(1 + .045)n$	Present Values
0	−100	1.000	−100
1	35	$\frac{1}{1(1 + .045)} = .957$	33.50
2	50	$\frac{1}{1(1.045)^2} = .916$	45.80
3	30	$\frac{1}{1(1.045)^3} = .876$	26.28
		Net present value =	5.58 or $5,580

POSTAUDIT PROJECT REVIEW

The postaudit (postcompletion) project review is a second aspect of reviewing the performance of the project. A comparison is made of the actual cash flow from operations of the project with the estimated cash flow used to justify the project. There are several reasons why the postaudit project review is helpful. First, managers proposing projects will be more careful before recommending a project. Second, it will identify those managers who are repeatedly optimistic or pessimistic regarding cash flow estimates. How reliable are the proposals submitted and approved (perhaps additional investments can be made to result in even greater returns)? Top management will be better able to appraise the bias that may be expected when a certain manager proposed a project.

The postaudit review also provides an opportunity to:

- Reinforce successful projects
- Strengthen or salvage "problem" projects
- Stop unsuccessful projects before excessive losses occur
- Enhance the overall quality of future investment proposals.

In conducting a postaudit, employ the same technique used in the initial approval process to maintain consistency in evaluation. For example, if a project were approved using present value analysis, implement the identical procedures in the postaudit review.

According to the "management-by-exception" principle, the managers responsible for the original estimates should be asked to furnish a complete explanation of any significant differences between estimates and actual results.

Recommendation: For control, project performance appraisal should not be conducted by the group that proposed the project. Rather, internal auditors should be given this responsibility to maintain independence. A review report should be issued. Typically, only projects above a specified dollar amount require postaudit, periodic evaluation, or both.

CAPITAL BUDGETING AND NONPROFIT ORGANIZATIONS

With regard to nonprofit institutions, the only real problem in using capital budgeting is the selection of an appropriate discount rate. Some nonprofit entities employ the interest rate on special bond issues (e.g., building a school) as the discount rate. Other nonprofit organizations employ the interest rate that could be earned by depositing money in an endowment fund instead of spending it on capital improvements. Other nonprofit institutions use discount rates that are arbitrarily established by governing boards.

Caution: Guard against using an excessively low discount rate. This may result in accepting projects that will be unprofitable. To guard against this problem, the Office of Management and Budget promulgates a discount rate of at least 10 percent on all projects to be considered by federal government units (Office of Management and Budget Circular No. A-94, March 1972).

Recommendation: In the case of nonprofit units such as schools and hospitals, the discount rate should be the average rate of return on private sector investments. The average discount rate will provide more meaningful results than using a specific interest rate on a special bond issue or the interest return on an endowment fund.

RISK AND UNCERTAINTY

Risk analysis is important in making capital investment decisions because of the significant amount of capital involved and the long-term nature of the investments being considered. The higher the risk associated with a proposed project, the greater the return rate that must be earned on the project to compensate for that risk. You must consider the interrelation of risk among all investments. By properly diversifying, you can obtain the best combination of expected net present value and risk.

Note: Do not automatically reject a high-risk project. For example, a new product with much risk may be accepted if there is a chance of a major breakthrough in the market. The business may be able to afford a few unsuccessful new products if one is developed for extraordinary return.

Probabilities can be assigned to expected cash flows based on risk. The probabilities are multiplied by the monetary values to derive the expected monetary value of the investment. A probability distribution function can be generated by computer.

Rule of Thumb: The tighter the probability distribution of expected future returns, the lower is the risk associated with a project.

Several methods to incorporate risk into capital budgeting are

- Risk-adjusted discount rate
- Standard deviation and coefficient of variation
- Certainty equivalent
- Semivariance
- Simulation
- Sensitivity analysis
- Decision (probability) trees.

Other means of adjusting for uncertainty include

- Decreasing the expected life of an investment
- Use of pessimistic estimates of cash flow
- Comparison of the results of optimistic, pessimistic, and best-guess estimates of cash flows.

Risk-Adjusted Discount Rate

Risk can be included in capital budgeting by computing probable cash flows on the basis of probabilities and assigning a discount rate based on the riskiness of alternative proposals.

Using this approach, an investment's value is determined by discounting the expected cash flow at a rate allowing for the time value of money and for the risk associated with the cash flow. The cost of capital (discount rate) is adjusted for a project's risk. A profitable investment is indicated by a positive net present value. Using the method, you judge the risk class of the proposed capital investment and the risk-adjusted discount rate appropriate for that class.

Suggestion: If doubtful of your results, check them by estimating the cost of capital of other companies specializing in the type of investment under consideration.

EXAMPLE 15–22 You are evaluating whether to accept proposal A or B. Each proposal mandates an initial cash outlay of $12,000 and has a three-year life. Annual net cash flows along with expected probabilities are as follows.

Proposal A:

Expected Annual Cash Inflow	*Probability*
$5,800	.4
6,400	.5
7,000	.1

Proposal B:

Expected Annual Cash Inflow	*Probability*
$3,400	.3
8,000	.5
11,000	.2

The inflation rate and interest rate are estimated at 10 percent. Proposal A has a lower risk since its cash flows show greater stability than those of proposal B. Since proposal A has less risk, it is assigned a discount rate of 8 percent, while proposal B is assigned a 10 percent discount rate because of the greater risk.

Proposal A:

Cash Flow	*Probability*	*Probable Cash Flow*
$5,800	.4	$2,320
6,400	.5	3,200
7,000	.1	700
Expected annual cash inflow		$6,220

Proposal B:

Cash Flow	Probability	Probable Cash Flow
$3,400	.3	$1,020
8,000	.5	4,000
11,000	.2	2,200
Expected annual cash inflow		$7,220

Proposal A:

Year	Explanation	Amount	×	Factor	=	Present Value
0	Initial investment	$-12,000	×	1		$-12,000
1-3	Annual cash flow	+6,220	×	2.5771[a]		+16,030
	Net present value					$+4,030

Proposal B:

Year	Explanation	Amount	×	Factor	=	Present Val
0	Initial investment	$-12,000	×	1		$-12,000
1-3	Annual cash flow	+7,220	×	2.4869[b]		+17,955
	Net present value					$+5,955

[a] Using an 8 percent discount rate.

[b] Using a 10 percent discount rate.

Even though project B has more risk, it has a higher risk-adjusted net present value. Project B should thus be selected.

Standard Deviation and Coefficient of Variation

Risk is a measure of dispersion around a probability distribution. It is the variability of cash flow around the expected value. Risk can be measured in either absolute or relative terms. First, the expected value, $\bar{A}$, is

$$\bar{A} = \sum_{n=1}^{n} A_i p_i$$

where A_i = the value of the ith possible outcome
p_i = the probability that the ith outcome will take place
n = the number of possible outcomes

Then, the absolute risk is determined by the standard deviation

$$\sigma = \sqrt{\sum_{t=1}^{n} (A_i - \bar{A})^2 p_i}$$

The relative risk is expressed by the coefficient of variation:

$$\frac{\sigma}{\overline{A}}$$

EXAMPLE 15–23 You are considering investing in one of two projects. Depending on the state of the economy, the projects would provide the following cash inflows in each of the next five years:

Economic Condition	Probability	Proposal A	Proposal B
Recession	.3	$1,000	$ 500
Normal	.4	2,000	2,000
Boom	.3	3,000	5,000

We now compute the expected value ($\overline{A}$), the standard deviation (σ) and the coefficient of variation ($\sigma/\overline{A}$).

Proposal A:

A_i	p_i	$A_i p_i$	$(A_i - \overline{A})$	$(A_i - \overline{A})^2$
$1,000	.3	$300	−$1,000	$1,000,000
2,000	.4	800	0	0
3,000	.3	900	1,000	1,000,000
		$\overline{A}$ = $2,000		σ^2 = $2,000,000

Because $\sigma^2 = \$2,000,000$, $\sigma = \$1,414$. Thus,

$$\frac{\sigma}{\overline{A}} = \frac{\$1,414}{\$2,000} = .71$$

Proposal B:

A_i	p_i	$A_i p_i$	$(A_i - \overline{A})$	$(A_i - \overline{A})^2$
$ 500	.3	$ 150	$−1,950	$ 3,802,500
2,000	.4	800	450	202,500
5,000	.3	1,500	2,550	6,502,500
		$\overline{A}$ = $2,450		σ^2 = $10,507,500

Since, $\sigma^2 = \$10,507,500$, $\sigma = \$3,242$. Thus,

$$\frac{\sigma}{\overline{A}} = \frac{\$3,242}{\$2,450} = 1.32$$

Therefore, proposal A is relatively less risky than is proposal B, as measured by the coefficient of variation.

Certainty Equivalent

The certainty equivalent approach relates to utility theory. You specify at what point the company is indifferent to the choice between a certain sum of dollars and the expected value of a risky sum. The certainty equivalent is multiplied by the original cash flow to obtain the equivalent certain cash flow. You then use normal capital budgeting. The risk-free rate of return is employed as the discount rate under the net present value method and as the cutoff rate under the internal rate of return method.

EXAMPLE 15–24   A company's cost of capital is 14 percent after taxes. Under consideration is a four-year project that will require an initial investment of $50,000. The following data also exists:

Year	After-Tax Cash Flow	Certainty Equivalent Coefficient
1	$10,000	.95
2	15,000	.80
3	20,000	.70
4	25,000	.60

The risk-free rate of return is 5 percent.
Equivalent certain cash inflows are

Year	After-Tax Cash Inflow	Certainty Equivalent Coefficient	Equivalent Certain Cash Inflow	×	Present Value Factor At 5%	=	Present Value
1	$10,000	.95	$9,500		.9524		$9,048
2	15,000	.80	12,000		.9070		10,884
3	20,000	.70	14,000		.8638		12,093
4	25,000	.60	15,000		.8227		12,341
							$44,366

Net Present Value:

Initial investment	$–50,000
Present value of cash inflows	+44,366
Net present value	$– 5,634

Using trial and error, you arrive at an internal rate of 4 percent.

The proposal should be rejected because of the negative net present value and an internal rate (4 percent) less than the risk-free rate (5 percent).

Semivariance

Semivariance is the expected value of the squared negative deviations of the possible outcomes from an arbitrarily chosen point of reference. Semivariance appraises risks applicable to different distributions by referring to a fixed point designated by you. In computing semivariance, positive and negative deviations contribute differently to risk, whereas in computing variance, a positive and negative deviation of the same magnitude contributes equally to risk.

Key Point: Since there is an opportunity cost of tying up capital, the risk of an investment is measured principally by the prospect of failure to earn the return.

Simulation

You obtain probability distributions for a number of variables (e.g., investment outlays or unit sales) when doing a simulation. Selecting these variables from the distributions at random results in an estimated net present value. Since a computer is used to generate many results using random numbers, project simulation is expensive.

Sensitivity Analysis

Forecasts of many calculated net present values and internal rates of return under various alternatives are compared to identify how sensitive net present value or internal rate of return is to changing conditions. You determine whether one or more than one variable significantly affects net present value once that variable is changed. If net present value is materially changed, you are dealing with a much riskier asset than was originally forecast. Sensitivity analysis provides an immediate financial measure of possible errors in forecasts. It focuses on decisions that may be sensitive.

Sensitivity analysis can take various forms. (Example: A managerial accountant may want to know how far annual sales must decline to break even on the investment. Sensitivity analysis can also be used to test the sensitivity of a decision to estimates of selling price and per unit variable cost.)

Key Point: Sensitivity analysis provides managers with an idea of the degree to which unfavorable occurrences such as lower volumes, shorter useful lives, or higher costs are likely to impact the profitability of a project. It is employed due to the uncertainty in dealing with real-life situations.

Decision Trees

A decision (probability) tree graphically shows the sequence of possible outcomes. The capital budgeting tree shows cash flows and net present value of the project under different possible circumstances.

Advantages:

- Shows possible outcomes of the contemplated project
- Makes you more cognizant of adverse possibilities
- Depicts the conditional nature of later years' cash flows.

Disadvantage:

- Many problems are too complex to allow for a year-by-year depiction. (Example: A three-year project with three possible outcomes following each year has 27 paths).

EXAMPLE 15–25   You want to introduce one of two products. The probabilities and present values of expected cash inflows are

Product	Investment	Present Value of Cash Inflows	Probability
A	$225,000		
		$450,000	.4
		200,000	.5
		−100,000	.1
B	80,000		
		320,000	.2
		100,000	.6
		−150,000	.2

	Initial Investment (1)	Probability (2)	P/V of Cash Inflows (3)	P/V of Cash Inflows (2) × (3) = (4)
Product A	$225,000	.40	$450,000	$180,000
		.50	200,000	100,000
		.10	−100,000	−10,000
				$270,000
or				
Product B		.20	$320,000	$64,000
		.60	100,000	60,000
	$80,000	.20	−150,000	−30,000
				$94,000

Net present value:

Product A: $270,000 − $225,000 = $45,000
Product B: $ 94,000 − $ 80,000 = $14,000

Product A should be selected.

Correlation of Cash Flows over Time

When cash inflows are independent from period to period, it is fairly easy to measure the overall risk of an investment proposal. In some cases, however, especially with the introduction of a new product, the cash flows experienced in early years affect the size of the cash flows in later years. This is called the *time dependence of cash flows,* and it has the effect of increasing the risk of the project over time.

EXAMPLE 15–26 Janday Corporation's after-tax cash inflows (ATCI) are time dependent, so that year 1 results ($ATCI_1$) affect the cash flows in year 2 ($ATCI_2$) as follows:

If $ATCI_1$ is $8,000 with a 40 percent probability, the distribution for $ATCI_2$ is

0.3	$5,000
0.5	10,000
0.2	15,000

If $ATCI_1$ is $15,000 with a 50 percent probability, the distribution for $ATCI_2$ is

0.3	$10,000
0.6	20,000
0.1	30,000

If $ATCI_1$ is $20,000 with a 10 percent chance, the distribution for $ATCI_2$ is

0.1	$15,000
0.8	40,000
0.1	50,000

The project requires an initial investment of $20,000, and the risk-free rate of capital is 10 percent.

The company uses the expected net present value from decision tree analysis to determine whether the project should be accepted. The analysis is as follows:

Time 0	Time 1	Time 2	NPV at 10%	Joint Probability	Expected NPV
		.3 $5,000	$–8,595[a]	.12[b]	$ –1,031
	$8,000 .5	10,000	–4,463	.20	–893
	.4	.2 15,000	–331	.08	–26
		.3 $10,000	$1,901	.15	285
$–20,000	.5 $15,000 .6	20,000	10,165	.30	3,050
	.1	.1 30,000	18,429	.05	921
		.1 $15,000	$10,576	.01	106
	$20,000 .8	40,000	21,238	.08	2,499
		.1 50,000	39,502	.01	395
				1.00	$5,306

[a] $NPV = PV - I = \$8{,}000 \, PVIF_{10.1} + \$5{,}000 \, PVIF_{10.2} - \$20{,}000$
$= \$8{,}000(.9091) + \$5{,}000(.8264) - \$20{,}000$
$= \${-}8{,}595$
[b] Joint probability of the first path $= (.4)(.3) = .12$

Since the NPV is positive ($5,306), Janday Corporation should accept the project.

Normal Distribution and NPV Analysis: Standardizing the Dispersion

With the assumption of *independence* of cash flows over time, the expected NPV would be

$$NPV = PV - I$$

$$= \sum_{t=1}^{n} \frac{\overline{A}_t}{(1+r)^t} - I$$

The standard deviation of NPVs is

$$\sigma = \sqrt{\sum_{t=1}^{n} \frac{\sigma_t^2}{(1+r)^{2t}}}$$

The expected value ($\overline{A}$) and the standard deviation σ give a considerable amount of information by which to assess the risk of an investment project. If the probability distribution is *normal*, some probability statement regarding the project's NPV can be made.

Example. The probability of a project's NPV providing an NPV of less than or greater than zero can be computed by standardizing the normal variate x as follows:

$$z = \frac{x - NPV}{\sigma}$$

where x = the outcome to be found
   NPV = the expected NPV
   z = the standardized normal variate whose probability value can be found in Exhibit 15–5.

EXAMPLE 15–27   Assume an investment with the following data:

	Period 1	Period 2	Period 3
Expected cash inflow ($\overline{A}$)	$5,000	$4,000	$3,000
Standard deviation (σ)	1,140	1,140	1,140

Assume that the firm's cost of capital is 8 percent and the initial investment is $9,000. Then the expected NPV is

$$NPV = PV - I$$
$$= \frac{\$5,000}{(1+.08)} + \frac{\$4,000}{(1+.08)^2} + \frac{\$3,000}{(1+.08)^3} - \$9,000$$
$$= \$5,000(PVIF_{8,1}) + \$4,000(PVIF_{8,2}) + \$3,000(PVIF_{8,3}) - \$9,000$$
$$= \$5,000(.9259) + \$4,000(.8573) + \$3,000(.7938) - \$9,000$$
$$= \$4,630 + \$3,429 + \$2,381 - \$9,000 = \$1,440$$

The standard deviation about the expected NPV is

$$\sigma = \sqrt{\sum_{t=1}^{n} \frac{\sigma_t^2}{(1+r)^{2t}}}$$

$$= \sqrt{\frac{\$1,140^2}{(1+.08)^2} + \frac{\$1,140^2}{(1+.08)^4} + \frac{\$1,140^2}{(1+.08)^6}}$$

$$= \sqrt{\$2,888,411} = \$1,670$$

The probability that the NPV is less than zero is then

$$z = \frac{x - \text{NPV}}{\sigma} = \frac{0 - \$1,440}{\$1,670} = -.862$$

The area of normal distribution that is z standard deviations to the left or right of the mean may be found in Exhibit 15–5. A value of z equal to −.862 falls in the area between 0.1949 and 0.1922. Therefore, there is approximately a 19 percent chance that the project's NPV will be zero or less. Putting it another way, there is a 19 percent chance that the internal rate of return of the project will be less than the risk-free rate.

EXHIBIT 15–5 Normal Probability Distribution Table

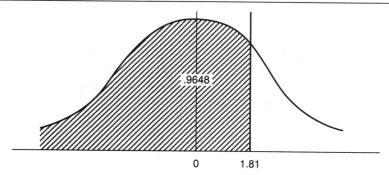

Areas Under the Normal Curve

Z	0	1	2	3	4	5	6	7	8	9
.0	.5000	.5040	.5080	.5120	.5160	.5199	.5239	.5279	.5319	.5359
.1	.5398	.5438	.5478	.5517	.5557	.5596	.5636	.5675	.5714	.5753
.2	.5793	.5832	.5871	.5910	.5948	.5987	.6026	.6064	.6103	.6141
.3	.6179	.6217	.6255	.6293	.6331	.6368	.6406	.6443	.6480	.6517
.4	.6554	.6591	.6628	.6664	.6700	.6736	.6772	.6808	.6844	.6879
.5	.6915	.6950	.6985	.7019	.7054	.7088	.7123	.7157	.7190	.7224
.6	.7257	.7291	.7324	.7357	.7389	.7422	.7454	.7486	.7517	.7549
.7	.7580	.7611	.7642	.7673	.7703	.7734	.7764	.7794	.7823	.7852
.8	.7881	.7910	.7939	.7967	.7995	.8023	.8051	.8078	.8106	.8133

EXHIBIT 15–5 Continued

Z	0	1	2	3	4	5	6	7	8	9
.9	.8159	.8186	.8212	.8238	.8264	.8289	.8315	.8340	.8365	.8389
1.0	.8413	.8438	.8461	.8485	.8508	.8531	.8554	.857 7	.8599	.8621
1.1	.8643	.8665	.8686	.8708	.8729	.8749	.8770	.879 0	.8810	.8830
1.2	.8849	.8869	.8888	.8907	.8925	.8944	.8962	.898 0	.8997	.9015
1.3	.9032	.9049	.9066	.9082	.9099	.9115	.9131	.914 7	.9162	.9177
1.4	.9192	.9207	.9222	.9236	.9251	.9265	.9278	.929 2	.9306	.9319
1.5	.9332	.9345	.9357	.9370	.9382	.9394	.9406	.941 8	.9430	.9441
1.6	.9452	.9463	.9474	.9484	.9495	.9505	.9515	.952 5	.9535	.9545
1.7	.9554	.9564	.9573	.9582	.9591	.9599	.9608	.961 6	.9625	.9633
1.8	.9641	.9648	.9656	.9664	.9671	.9678	.9686	.969 3	.9700	.9706
1.9	.9713	.9719	.9726	.9732	.9738	.9744	.9750	.975 6	.9762	.9767
2.0	.9772	.9778	.9783	.9788	.9793	.9798	.9803	.980 8	.9812	.9817
2.1	.9821	.9826	.9830	.9834	.9838	.9842	.9846	.985 0	.9854	.9857
2.2	.9861	.9864	.9868	.9871	.9874	.9878	.9881	.988 4	.9887	.9890
2.3	.9893	.9896	.9898	.9901	.9904	.9906	.9909	.991 1	.9913	.9916
2.4	.9918	.9920	.9922	.9925	.9927	.9929	.9931	.993 2	.9934	.9936
2.5	.9938	.9940	.9941	.9943	.9945	.9946	.9948	.994 9	.9951	.9952
2.6	.9953	.9955	.9956	.9957	.9959	.9960	.9961	.996 2	.9963	.9964
2.7	.9965	.9966	.9967	.9968	.9969	.9970	.9971	.997 2	.9973	.9974
2.8	.9974	.9975	.9976	.9977	.9977	.9978	.9979	.997 9	.9980	.9981
2.9	.9981	.9982	.9982	.9983	.9984	.9984	.9985	.998 5	.9986	.9986
3.0	.9987	.9990	.9993	.9995	.9997	.9998	.9998	.999 9	.9999	1.000

CONCLUSION

Capital budgeting is the selection of the optimum alternative long-term investment opportunity. It indicates the best alternatives for corporate resources. It involves the calculation of the number of years required to earn your money back, the return earned on a proposal, and the net present value of cash flows to be derived.

Chapter 16

Using Variance Analysis as a Financial Tool

A standard cost is a predetermined cost of manufacturing, servicing, or marketing an item during a given future period. It is based on current and projected future conditions. The norm is also dependent upon quantitative and qualitative measurements. Standards may be based on engineering studies looking at time and motion. While the development of standards is primarily the responsibility of the industrial engineer, the budget preparer should work closely with the engineer to assure that the formulated standard is accurate and useful for control purposes.

Standards are set at the beginning of the period. They may be in physical and dollar terms. Standards assist in the measurement of both effectiveness and efficiency. Examples are sales quotas, standard costs (e.g., material price, wage rate), and standard volume. Variances are not independent, so a favorable variance in one responsibility area may result in an unfavorable one in other segments of the business.

Variance analysis compares standard to actual performance. It may be done by department, program, or cost center. When more than one department is used in a production process, individual standards should be developed for each department in order to assign accountability to department managers. Variances may be as detailed as necessary considering the cost-benefit relationship. Evaluation of variances may be done yearly, quarterly,

This chapter is, for the most part, taken from Joel Siegel, Jae Shim, and Nicky Dauber, *Corporate Controller's Handbook of Financial Management,* Chapter 18. (N.J.: Prentice-Hall, 1991).

monthly, daily, or hourly, depending upon the importance of identifying a problem quickly. Since you do not know actual figures (e.g., hours spent) until the end of the period, variances can only be calculated then. A significant variance requires highlighting who is responsible and taking corrective action. Insignificant variances need not be looked into further unless they recur repeatedly and/or reflect potential difficulty. Generally, a variance should be investigated when the inquiry is anticipated to result in corrective action that will reduce costs by an amount exceeding the cost of the inquiry.

When the production cycle is long, variances that are computed at the time of product completion may be too late for prompt corrective action to be taken. In such a case, inspection may be undertaken at "key" points during the processing stage. This allows for spoilage, labor inefficiency, and other costs associated with problems to be recognized before product completion.

One measure to materiality is to divide the variance by the standard cost. A variance of less than 5 percent may be deemed immaterial. A 10 percent variation may be more acceptable to a company using tight standards compared to a 5 percent variation to a company employing loose standards. In some cases, materiality is looked at in terms of dollar amount or volume level. For example, you may set a policy looking into any variance that exceeds $10,000 or 20,000 units, whichever is less. Guidelines for materiality also depend upon the nature of the particular element as it affects performance and decision-making. For example, where the item is critical to the future functioning of the business (e.g., critical part, promotion, repairs), limits for materiality should be such that reporting is encouraged. Further, statistical techniques can be used to ascertain the significance of cost and revenue variances. The budget preparer must establish an acceptable range of tolerance for management (e.g., percent). Even if a variance never exceeds a minimum allowable percentage or minimum dollar amount, the budget preparer may want to bring it to management's attention if the variance is consistently close to the prescribed limit each year. Perhaps this may indicate the standard is out-of-date and proper adjustment to current levels is mandated so as to improve overall profit planning. It could also indicate lax cost control requiring a check by the supervisor as to operations.

Because of the critical nature of costs, such as advertising and maintenance, materiality guidelines are more stringent. Often the reason for the variance is out-of-date standards or a poor budgetary process. Thus, it may not be due to actual performance. By questioning the variances and trying to find answers, the manager can make the operation more efficient and less costly. It must be understood, however, that quality should be maintained. If a variance is out of management's control, follow-up action by management is not called for. For instance, utility rates are not controllable internally.

Standards may change at different operational volume levels. Further, standards should be periodically appraised, and when they no longer realistically reflect conditions they should be modified. Standards may become unrealistic because of internal events (e.g., product design) or external conditions such as management and competitive changes. For instance, standards should be revised when prices, material specifications, product designs, labor rates, labor efficiency, and production methods change to such a degree that present standards no longer provide a useful measure of performance. Changes in the methods or channels of distribution, or basic organizational or functional changes, would require changes in selling and administrative activities.

Note: Significant favorable variances should also be investigated and should be further taken advantage of. Those responsible for good performance should be rewarded.

For variable and semi-variable costs, the accuracy of standards developed depends on the ability of the method to measure the correlation between cost incurrence and output bases. Regression analysis may provide reliable association.

Variances are interrelated and hence the net effect must be examined. For example, a favorable price variance may arise when lower quality materials are bought at a cheaper price but the quantity variance will be unfavorable because of increased production time to manufacture the goods due to poor material quality.

In the case of automated manufacturing facilities, standard cost information can be integrated with the computer that directs operations. Variances can then be identified and reported by the computer system and necessary adjustments made as the operation proceeds.

In appraising variances, consideration should be given to information that may have been omitted, for whatever reason, from the reports. Have there been changes in the production processes which have not been reflected in the reports? Have new product lines increased set-up times that necessitate changes in the standards?

USEFULNESS OF VARIANCE ANALYSIS

Standards and variance analyses resulting therefrom are essential in financial analysis and decision-making.

Advantages of Standards and Variances

- Aid in inventory costing
- Assist in decision-making
- Sell price formulation based on what costs should be

- Aid in coordinating by having all departments focus on common goals
- Set and evaluate corporate objectives
- Cost control and performance evaluation by comparing actual to budgeted figures. The objective of cost control is to produce an item at the lowest possible cost according to predetermined quality standards.
- Highlight problem areas through the "management by exception" principle
- Pinpoint responsibility for undesirable performance so that corrective action may be taken. Variances in product activity (cost, quality, quantity) are typically the foreman's responsibility. Variances in sales orders and market share are often the responsibility of the marketing manager. Variances in prices and methods of deliveries are the responsibility of purchasing personnel. Variances in profit usually relate to overall operations. Variances in return on investment relate to asset utilization.
- Act in motivating employees to accomplish predetermined goals
- Facilitate communication within the organization such as between top management and supervisors
- Assist in planning by forecasting needs (e.g., cash requirements)
- Establish bid prices on contracts
- Simplify bookkeeping procedures by keeping the records at standard cost.

Standard costing is not without some drawbacks. Examples: The possible biases in deriving standards and the dysfunctional effects of establishing improper norms and standards.

When a variance has multiple causes, each cause should be cited.

STANDARD SETTING

Standards may be set by engineers, production managers, purchasing managers, personnel administrators, managerial accountants, and so on. Depending upon the nature of the cost item, computerized models can be used to corroborate what the standard costs should be. Standards may be established through test runs or mathematical and technological analysis.

Standards are based on the particular situation being appraised. Some examples follow:

Situation	Standard
Cost reduction	Tight
Pricing policy	Realistic
High-quality goods	Perfection

Capacity may be expressed in units, weight, size, dollars, selling price, direct labor hours, and so on. It may be expressed in different time periods (e.g., weekly, monthly, yearly).

Types of Standards

- *Basic.* These are not changed from period to period and are used in the same way as an index number. They form the basis to which later period performance is compared. What is unrealistic about it is that no consideration is given to a change in the environment.

- *Maximum efficiency.* These are perfect standards assuming ideal, optimal conditions, allowing for no losses of any kind even those considered unavoidable. They will always result in unfavorable variances. Realistically, certain inefficiencies will occur such as materials will not always arrive at work stations on time and tools will break. Ideal standards cannot be used in forecasting and planning because they do not provide for normal inefficiencies.

- *Currently attainable* (*practical*). These refer to the volume of output possible if a facility operated continuously, but after allowing for normal and unavoidable losses such as vacations, holidays, and repairs. Currently attainable standards are based on efficient activity. They are possible but difficult to achieve. Considered are normal occurrences such as anticipated machinery failure and normal materials shortage. Practical standards should be set high enough to motivate employees and low enough to permit normal interruptions. Besides pointing to abnormal deviations in costs, practical standards may be used in forecasting cash flows and in planning inventory. Attainable standards are typically used in practice.

- *Expected.* These are expected figures based on foreseeable operating conditions and costs. They come very close to actual figures.

Standards should be set at a level that is realistic to accomplish. Those affected by the standards should participate in formalizing them so there will be internalization of goals. When reasonable standards exist employees typically become cost conscious and try to accomplish the best results at the least cost. If standards are too tight, they will discourage employee performance. If they are too loose, they will result in inefficient operations. If employees receive bonuses for exceeding normal standards, the standards may be even more effective as motivation tools.

A standard is not an absolute and precise figure. Realistically, a standard constitutes a range of possible acceptable results. Thus, variances can and do occur within a normal upper-lower limit. In determining tolerance limits, relative magnitudes are more important than absolute values. For instance, if the standard cost for an activity is $100,000 a plus or minus range of $4,000 may be tolerable.

Variance analysis is usually complicated by the problem of computing the number equivalent units of production.

Variances may be controllable, partly controllable, or uncontrollable. It is not always easy to assign responsibility even in the case of controllable variances. The extent to which a variance is controllable depends on the nature of the standard, the cost involved, and the particular factors causing the variance.

PLANNING VARIANCE

The planning variance arises when expected industry or other environmental factors do not materialize. For example, at the beginning of the period, the sales projection may be based on reviewing supply and demand. However, because of actual conditions in the industry, the actual sales may be much lower. This sales unit variance may then be deemed a planning error, and not a performance problem. Industry sales are typically considered beyond management control.

SALES VARIANCES

Sales standards may be established to control and measure the effectiveness of the marketing operations, as well as for other relevant purposes such as stimulating sales, reallocating sales resources, and providing incentive awards. The usual standard set for a salesperson, branch, or territory is a sales quota. While the sales quota is typically expressed in dollars it may also be expressed in volume. Other types of standards that may be set to evaluate sales efforts are number of calls, order size, gross profit obtained, new customers obtained, and number of regular customers retained. Sales variances are computed to gauge the performance of the marketing function.

EXAMPLE 16-1   Western Corporation's budgeted sales for 19X1 were

Product A 10,000 units at $6.00 per unit	$60,000
Product B 30,000 units at $8.00 per unit	240,000
Expected sales revenue	$300,000
Actual sales for the year were	
Product A 8,000 units at $6.20 per unit	$49,600
Product B 33,000 units at $7.70 per unit	254,100
Actual sales revenue	$303,700

There is a favorable sales variance of $3,700, consisting of the sales price variance and the sales volume variance.

The sales price variance equals

(Actual Selling Price versus Budgeted Selling Price) × Actual Units Sold

Product A ($6.20 versus $6.00 × 8,000)	$1,600 Favorable
Product B ($7.70 versus $8.00 × 33,000)	9,900 Unfavorable
Sales price variance	$8,300 Unfavorable

The sales volume variance equals

(Actual Quantity versus Budgeted Quantity) × Budgeted Selling Price

Product A (8,000 versus 10,000 × $6.00)	$12,000 Unfavorable
Product B (33,000 versus 30,000 × $8.00)	24,000 Favorable
Sales volume variance	$12,000 Favorable

The sales price variance indicates if the product is being sold at a discount or premium. Sales price variances may be due to uncontrollable market conditions or managerial decisions. However, a sales price variance is not recorded in the books.

The analysis of sales volume includes consideration of budgets, standards, sales plans, industry comparisons, and manufacturing costs. Note that high sales volume does not automatically mean high profits. There may be high costs associated with the products.

An unfavorable sales volume variance may arise from poor marketing or to price cuts by competing companies. If the unfavorable volume variance is coupled with a favorable price variance, your company may have lost sales by raising its prices.

The sales volume variance reflects the effect on the total budgeted contribution margin that is caused by changes in the total number of units sold. The variance can be caused by unpredictable product demand, lack of product demand, or from poor sales forecasting.

An unfavorable total sales variance may signal a problem with the marketing manager because he or she has control over sales, advertising, and often pricing. Another possible cause of the unfavorable sales situation may be due to a lack in quality control, substitution of poorer quality components due to deficient purchasing, or deficient product design emanating from poor engineering.

The sales variances (price and volume) are prepared only for the product sales report and the sales district report.

The sales vice-president is responsible for sales variances and must explain deviations to the president.

An electronic worksheet can be used to compute sales variances (refer to the July, 1985 issue of LOTUS, pp. 46–48).

COST VARIANCES

When a product is made or a service is performed, you must determine these five measures:

1. Actual cost equals actual price times actual quantity, where actual quantity equals actual quantity per unit of work times actual units of work produced

2. Standard cost equals standard price times standard quantity, where standard quantity equals standard quantity per unit of work times actual units of work produced.

3. Total (control) variance equals actual cost less standard cost

   Total (control) variance has the following elements:

4. Price (rate, cost) variance:

   (Standard Price versus Actual Price) × Actual Quantity

5. Quantity (usage, efficiency) variance:

   (Standard Quantity versus Actual Quantity) × Standard Price

   These are computed for both material and labor.

A variance is unfavorable when actual cost is higher than standard cost.

MATERIAL VARIANCES

Quantity and delivery standards must be established before a standard price per unit can be determined. Material price standards are set by the cost accounting department and/or purchasing department because they have knowledge of price data and market conditions. The company should increase the initial standard price per unit to a standard weighted-average price per unit to incorporate expected price increases for the period. The standard price should reflect the total cost of buying the material which includes the basic price less discounts plus freight, receiving, and handling. The standard price must coincide with the specific quality material. In setting the material price standard, the price should be in accord with the firm's inventory policies regarding the most economical order size and/or frequency of ordering. It is further assumed that buying, shipping, and warehousing will occur on favorable terms. Special bargain prices are ignored unless they are readily available. The material price standard should include normal or unavoidable spoilage allocations.

You can use the material price variance to evaluate the activity of the purchasing department and to determine the impact of raw material cost changes on profitability. A material price variance may be isolated at the time of purchase or usage.

The material quantity variance is the responsibility of the production supervisor. Material quantity standards should not only include the raw materials but also purchased parts, cartons, and packing materials which are visible in, or can be directly related to, the product. Material quantity standards are basically determined from material specifications prepared by engineers based on product design and production flow. The standard quantity should be based on the most economical size and quality of product. It should be increased to take into account normal waste, rejections, and spoilage. The standard should consider prior experience for the same or similar operation. Test runs may be made under controlled conditions. Material standards may be aided by analyzing previous experiences using descriptive statistics and/or test runs under controlled conditions. Physical standards for materials are based on determinations of kind and quality specifications, quantity specifications, and assembly specifications. When many different types of raw materials are needed for a product, the types and standard quantities of each raw material is itemized on the *standard bill of materials.*

EXAMPLE 16-2   The standard cost of one unit of output (product or service) was $15: three pieces at $5 per piece. During the period, 8,000 units were made. Actual cost was $14 per unit; two pieces at $7 per piece.

Total Material Variance		
Standard quantity times standard price (24,000 × $5)	$120,000	
Actual quantity times actual price (16,000 × $7)	112,000	
	$ 8,000	F
Material Price Variance		
(Standard price versus actual price) times actual quantity		
($5 versus $7 × 16,000)	$ 32,000	U
Material Quantity Variance		
(Standard quantity versus actual quantity) times standard		
price (24,000 versus 16,000 × $5)	$ 40,000	F

When the amount of material purchased is different from the amount issued to production, the stores account should be carried at standard cost and a price variance determined at the time of purchase. When material is issued, a quantity (usage) variance is determined. In this case, the variances are determined as follows:

Material Price Variance
(Actual price versus standard price) times actual quantity bought
Material Quantity Variance
(Actual quantity issued versus standard quantity issued) times standard price

EXAMPLE 16-3   Material purchased was 20,000 pounds. Material issued to production was 15,000 pounds. Material budgeted per unit is one pound. Budgeted price is $2.50 per pound while actual price is $3.00 per pound. Production was 10,000 units.

Material Price Variance	
(Actual price versus standard price) times quantity purchased	
($3.00 versus $2.50) × 20,000	$10,000 U
Material Quantity Variance	
(Actual quantity issued versus standard quantity) × standard price	
(15,000 versus 10,000) × $2.50	$12,500 U

You cannot control material price variances when higher prices are due to inflation or shortage situations, or when rush orders are required by the customer who will bear the ultimate cost increase.

If the material price variance is favorable, one would expect higher quality material being acquired. Thus, a favorable usage variance should be forthcoming. If it is not, there is an inconsistency. A favorable material price variance may occur from other causes such as when actual price is less than expected because of excess supply of the raw material in the industry.

The controllable portion of a price variance should be segregated from the uncontrollable in management reports. Exhibit 16-1 presents a Daily Material Price Variance Report. Generally, the material quantity variance is the responsibility of the production department. However, the purchasing department will be responsible for inferior goods to economize on cost.

The reason and responsible party for an unfavorable material variance follows:

Exhibit 16-1 Detail of Material Price Variance

Date _____ Prepared by _____ Approved by _____

Voucher No.	Item No.	Item Name	Vendor No.	Quantity Purchased	Standard Cost Per Unit	Total	Actual Cost Per Unit	Total	Variance Per Unit	Total	Percent from Standard	Explanation

Reason	Responsible Party
Overstated price paid, failure to take discounts, improper specifications, insufficient quantities, use of a lower grade material purchased to economize on price, uneconomical size of purchase orders, failure to obtain an adequate supply of a needed variety, purchase at an irregular time, or sudden and unexpected purchase required	Responsible Party Purchasing

Poor mix of materials, poorly trained workers, improperly adjusted machines, substitution of nonstandard materials, poor production scheduling, poor product design or production technique, lack of proper tools or machines, carelessness in not returning excess materials to storeroom, or unexpected volume changes	Production Manager
Failure to detect defective goods	Receiving Foreman
Inefficient labor, poor supervision, or waste on the production line	
Inaccurate standard price	Budgeting
Excessive transportation charges or too small a quantity purchased	Traffic management
Insufficient quantity bought because of a lack of funds	Financial

To correct an unfavorable material price variance, you can increase selling price, substitute cheaper materials, change a production method or specification, or engage in a cost-reduction program. An unfavorable price variance does not automatically mean the purchasing department is not performing well. It may point to a need for new pricing, product, or buying decisions. For these purposes, price variances may be broken down by product, vendor class, or other appropriate distinction. When several types of raw materials are used, it might be better to break down the price variance by major category of material used (e.g., steel, paint).

Tip: You should examine the variability in raw material costs. Look at price instability in trade publications. Emphasize vertical integration to reduce the price and supply risk of raw materials.

To aid in identifying material usage variances, if additional material is required to complete the job, additional materials requisitions could be issued in a different color with a distinctive code number to show that the quantity of material is above standard. This approach brings attention to the excessive usage of materials while production is in process and allows for the early control of a developing problem. When material usage is recorded by flow meters, such as in chemical operations, usage variances can be identified on materials usage forms in a similar manner as excess labor hours identified on labor time tickets.

Managers should have the option to acquire cheaper raw materials or to combine available resources so that overall corporate costs are minimized. For instance, slightly inferior raw materials (i.e., lower grade of metals) may intentionally be purchased at bargain price. The material price variance may thus be quite favorable. However, such raw material component may cause above average defective finished items and/or excessive productive labor hours resulting in an unfavorable efficiency variance. The manager may have permission to engage in this tradeoff if it results in a significant net reduction in total manufacturing costs. A standard cost system should not be rigid in the sense that an unfavorable variance is regarded as always being bad. One should look to see if overall corporate objectives have been accomplished. Since many interdependencies exist, one should look at the entire picture rather than at just the fact that a given variance is unfavorable.

When computing material price variances, it may be good to eliminate increasing costs due to inflation, which are not controllable by management.

Illustration of How Inflationary Cost Increases May Be Isolated from the Material Price Variance

Assume the following data for Charles Company for 19X1.	
Standard price of material per foot	$3.00
Actual price of material per foot	3.80
Actual material used	10,000 ft.
The inflation rate for the year is 16%.	

The direct material price variance can be broken down into the inflation aspect and the controllable element.

Price variance due to inflation	
(Standard price versus Inflation adjusted price) × actual quantity	
$3.00 versus $3.48 × 10,000 ft	$4,800
Controllable price variance	
(Inflation adjusted price versus actual price) × actual quantity	
$3.48 versus $3.80 × 10,000 ft	$3,200
Proof—Material Price Variance	
(Standard price versus actual price) × actual quantity	
$3.00 versus $3.80 × 10,000 ft	$8,000

It is important to have prompt reporting to lower managerial levels. Production managers should immediately be informed of variances so problems are identified and corrections made at the production level.

Exhibit 16-2 presents a daily material usage report. Exhibit 16-3 presents a monthly material variance report.

EXHIBIT 16-2 Daily Material Usage Report

	Cost Center Material Type			Unit Date	Month		Year	
Date	*Variance*	*Daily Variance Percent*	*Explanation*	*Variance*	*Variance Percent*	*Variance*	*Variance Percent*

EXHIBIT 16-3 Monthly Material Variance Report

Department	Month		Year to Date	
	Variance	*Percent*	*Variance*	*Percent*

LABOR VARIANCES

Standard labor rates may be computed based on the current rates adjusted for future changes in such variables as:

- Union contracts
- Changes in operating conditions
- Changes in the mix of skilled versus unskilled labor
- The average experience of workers.

The wage system affects the standard cost rates. The basic rates are (1) day or hourly, (2) straight piece rate, and (3) multiple piece rates or bonus systems. Wage incentive systems can be tied to a standard cost system once standards have been formulated.

While direct labor quantities may be obtained from engineering estimates, line supervisors can corroborate the estimates by observing and timing employees. When salary rates are set by union contract, the labor rate variance will usually be minimal. For planning purposes, the rate standard should be the average rate expected to prevail during the planning period. **Note:** Labor rates for the same operation may vary due to seniority or union agreement.

Labor time standards should include only the elements controllable by the worker or work center. If the major purpose of a cost system is control, there should be a tight labor time standard. If costing or pricing is the major purpose of the cost system, looser labor standards are needed. Labor efficiency standards are typically estimated by engineers on the basis of an analysis of the production operation. The standard time may include allowances for normal breaks, personal needs, and machine downtime.

Labor variances are determined in a manner similar to that in which material variances are determined. Labor variances are isolated when labor is used for production.

EXAMPLE 16-4   The standard cost of labor is four hours times $9 per hour, or $36 per unit. During the period, 7,000 units were produced. The actual cost is six hours times $8 per hour, or $48 per unit.

Total Labor Variance	
Standard quantity times standard price (28,000 × $9)	$252,000
Actual quantity times actual price (42,000 × $8)	336,000
	$84,000 U
Labor Price Variance	
(Standard price versus actual price) times actual quantity	
($9 versus $8 × 42,000)	$42,000 F
Labor Quantity Variance	
(Standard quantity versus actual quantity) × standard price	
(28,000 versus 42,000 × $9)	$126,000 U

Possible causes of *unfavorable* labor variances are:
For a labor price (rate) variance:

- Increase in wages
- Poor scheduling of production resulting in overtime work
- Use of workers commanding higher hourly rates than expected.

For a labor efficiency variance:

- Poor supervision
- Use of unskilled workers paid lower rates or the wrong mixture of labor for a given job
- Use of poor quality machinery
- Improperly trained workers
- Poor quality of materials requiring more labor time in processing
- Machine breakdowns
- Employee unrest
- Production delays due to power failure.

Possible reasons for a labor price variance and the one responsible follow.

Reason	*Responsible Party*
Use of overpaid or excessive number of workers	Production manager or union contract
Poor job descriptions or excessive wages	Personnel
Overtime and poor scheduling of production	Production Planning

In the case of a shortage of skilled workers, it may be impossible to avoid an unfavorable labor price variance.

Price variances due to external factors are beyond management control (e.g., a new minimum wage established by the government).

The cause and responsible party for an unfavorable labor efficiency variance follows:

Cause	Responsible Entity
Poor quality workers or poor training	Personnel or Training
Inadequate supervision, inefficient flow of materials, wrong mixture of labor for a given job, inferior tools or idle time from production delays	Foreman
Employee unrest	Personnel or Foreman
Improper functioning of equipment	Maintenance
Insufficient material supply or poor quality	Purchasing

To control against an unfavorable labor efficiency variance due to inadequate materials or sales orders, a daily direct labor report should be prepared.

An unfavorable labor efficiency variance may indicate that better machinery is needed, plant layout should be revised, improved operating methods are needed, and better employee training and development are required.

If a permanent change occurs in the amount of labor required or the labor wage rate for the various types of employee help, the production manager may wish to switch to more capital assets than labor.

Variances Interrelate.

A favorable labor efficiency variance coupled with an unfavorable labor rate variance may mean that more higher skilled labor was employed than was necessary. However, the supervisor would be justified in doing this if a rush order arose in which the selling price was going to be upwardly adjusted.

Exhibit 16-4 presents a daily labor mix report. Exhibit 16-5 presents a labor performance report. Studying this report aids in evaluating labor effectiveness and in proposing a revision in labor policies. A graph of weekly labor efficiency is presented in Figure 16-1.

EXHIBIT 16–4 Daily Labor Mix Report

Department Skill Level	Actual Hours	Actual Hours in Standard Proportions	Output Variance
I			
II			
III			

EXHIBIT 16-5 Labor Performance Report

Department

Machine Operator	*Achieved in Percent*	*Explanation*	*Month to Date in Percent*	*Year to Date in Percent*

Day   *Date*

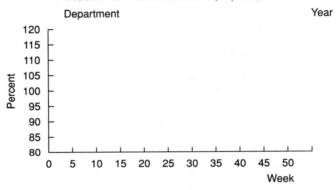

FIGURE 16-1 Labor Efficiency by Week

Department   Year

OVERHEAD VARIANCES

Management is concerned with the tradeoff between fixed and variable costs. As the output level increases, the capital intensive business will be more efficient. The cost associated with a wrong decision is the variance between the total costs of operating the given plant and the total costs of operating the most efficient one based on the actual output level.

Overhead variances may be determined by department and by cost center. Fixed and variable overhead variances should be analyzed independently. In many firms, variances are expressed in both dollars and physical measures.

Variable Overhead Variances

The two variances associated with variable overhead are price (spending) and efficiency.

Variable Overhead Price (Spending) Variance
Actual variable overhead versus Budget adjusted to actual hours (actual hours × standard variable overhead rate)
Variable Overhead Efficiency Variance
Budget adjusted to actual hours versus budget adjusted to standard hours (standard hours × standard variable overhead rate)

Variable overhead variance information is helpful in arriving at the output level and output mix decisions. The production department is usually responsible for any variable overhead variance that might occur. It also assists in appraising decisions regarding variable inputs.

EXAMPLE 16-5   The standard hours is three hours per unit. The standard variable overhead rate is $12 per hour. Actual variable overhead is $13,000. There are 2,500 actual hours. Production is 1,000 units. The variable overhead variances are:

Variable Overhead Price Variance	
Actual variable overhead	$13,000
Budget adjusted to actual hours (2,500 × $4)	10,000
Price Variance	$3,000 U
Variable Overhead Efficiency Variance	
Budget adjusted to actual hours	$10,000
Budget adjusted to standard hours (3,000 × $4)	12,000
Efficiency Variance	$2,000 F

Fixed Overhead Variances

Fixed overhead may be analyzed in terms of the budget (flexible-budget, spending) variance and volume (production volume) variances. The volume variance may be further broken down into the efficiency and pure volume variances.

Fixed Overhead Budget Variance
Actual fixed overhead versus budgeted fixed overhead (denominator or budget hours × standard fixed overhead rate).

Note: Budgeted fixed overhead may also be referred to as lump-sum amount.

Fixed Overhead Volume Variance
Budgeted fixed overhead versus standard overhead (standard hours × standard fixed overhead rate)

The breakdown of the volume variance follows:

Fixed Overhead Efficiency Variance
(Actual hours versus standard hours) × standard fixed overhead rate
Fixed Overhead Pure Volume Variance
(Actual hours versus budgeted hours) × standard fixed overhead rate

Fixed overhead variance data provide information about decision-making astuteness when buying some combination of fixed plant size variable production inputs. However, variances for fixed overhead are of questionable usefulness for control purposes, since these variances are usually beyond the control of the production department.

The volume variance is a measure of the cost of deviating from denominator (budgeted) volume used to set the fixed overhead rate. When actual volume is less than budgeted volume, the volume variance will be unfavorable. In the opposite case, the volume variance is favorable because it is considered as a benefit of better than anticipated utilization of facilities.

EXAMPLE 16-6   Standard hours are two hours per unit. Standard fixed overhead rate is $20 per hour. Actual hours per unit are two. Total production is 9,500 units. Actual hours are 20,200. Actual fixed overhead is $420,000. The denominator activity is 10,000 units. The fixed overhead variances are:

Fixed Overhead Budget Variance	
Actual fixed overhead	$420,000
Budgeted fixed overhead ($10,000 \times 2 = 20,000 \times \$20$)	400,000
Budget Variance	$20,000 U
Volume Variance	
Budgeted fixed overhead	$400,000
Standard fixed overhead ($9,500 \times 2 = 19,000 \times \$20$)	380,000
Volume Variance	$20,000 U

The production volume variance of $20,000 is now broken down into the efficiency and pure volume variances.

Fixed Overhead Efficiency Variance	
(Actual hours versus standard hours) × standard fixed overhead rate	
(20,200 versus 19,000) × $20	$24,000 U
Fixed Overhead Pure Volume Variance	
(Actual hours versus budget hours) × standard fixed overhead rate	
(20,200 versus 20,000) × $20	$4,000 F

Variances for Total Overhead

One way, two-way, and three-way analysis may be used for total overhead.

One-Way Method
The total (control, net) variance is:
Total Overhead Variance
Actual overhead
Standard overhead (standard hours × standard overhead rate)

Two-Way Method
Under the two-variance method, the overhead variance comprises the controllable (budget, flexible budget, spending) and volume (capacity, idle capacity, activity, denominator) variances.
Controllable Variance
Actual overhead
Budget adjusted to standard hours
  Fixed overhead (denominator hours × standard fixed overhead rate)
  Variable overhead (standard hours × standard variable overhead rate)
Volume (Production) Variance
Standard overhead
Budget adjusted to standard hours

The controllable (budget) variance may indicate changes in the amount charged for overhead services or in the correlation between overhead items and the variable used to measure output. If such changes are of a permanent nature, output levels may have to be revised. Management uses the overhead budget variance as a basis for determining the extent to which the cost centers were within their budgeted cost levels. Such variances are useful in formulating decisions regarding cost center operations.

The controllable variance is the responsibility of the foreman, since he influences actual overhead incurred. An unfavorable variance may be due to price increases, a lack of control over costs, and to waste. The volume variance is the responsibility of management executives and production managers, since they are involved with plant utilization. **Note:** A consistently unfavorable volume variance may be due to having purchased the incorrect size plant. An unfavorable volume variance may arise from controllable factors such as poor scheduling, lack of orders, shortages or defectiveness in raw materials, inadequate tooling, lack of employees, machine breakdowns, long operating times, and incompetent workers. Uncontrollable factors for the overhead volume variance are decrease in customer demand, excess plant capacity, and calendar fluctuations (e.g., differences in number of working days in a month).

Overhead capacity variances can bring to a manager's attention the existence of slack resources. Idle capacity may imply long-run operating planning deficiencies. The volume of activity is often determined outside the factory based on customer orders. If this is the case, volume variances may not be controllable by the department head or even by the plant manager. They should still be reported to plant managers to help in explaining the total overhead variance to higher management. Responsibility for the factory overhead volume variance rests with those responsible in generating volume. In some cases, marketing managers, rather than manufacturing managers, bear this responsibility.

Possible Reasons for a Recurring Unfavorable Overhead Volume Variance

- Buying the wrong size plant
- Improper scheduling
- Insufficient orders
- Shortages in material
- Machinery failure
- Long operating time
- Inadequately trained workers.

When idle capacity exists, this may indicate long-term operating planning problems.

A deficiency of controllable overhead variance analysis is the failure to segregate the responsibility for increased costs due to inflation from those due to inefficient spending. This deficiency can be corrected through a revised method of overhead analysis taking into account inflation [see A. Adelberg and R. Polimeni, "The Analysis of Factory Overhead Variances (Under Conditions of General and Specific Price-Level Changes)," *Cost and Management,* December 1987, pp. 28–31].

Note: A favorable variance may be causing an unfavorable one. For example, lower maintenance expenditures for equipment may lower the overhead budget variance, but lead to machinery breakdowns causing an unfavorable volume variance.

Three-Way Method

The three-variance method involves further analysis of the two-variance method. The three-way approach consists of the spending, efficiency, and volume variances. **Note:** The volume variance is identical under the three-way and two-way approaches. The controllable variance under the two-way method is broken down into the spending and efficiency variances under the three-way method.

Spending Variance
Actual overhead
Budget adjusted to actual hours
   Fixed overhead (denominator hours × standard fixed overhead rate)
   Variable overhead (Actual hours × standard variable overhead rate)
Efficiency Variance
Budget adjusted to actual hours
Budget adjusted to standard hours
Volume (Production) Variance
Budget adjusted to standard hours
Standard overhead

The efficiency variance is the responsibility of the foreman and arises from inefficiencies or efficiencies in the production process. The variance is unfavorable when actual hours exceed standard hours charged to production. Inefficiencies may arise from such factors as unskilled labor, modification of operations, deficient machinery, and inferior quality materials.

Spending and efficiency variances are under the responsibility of the department supervisor. The volume variance is attributable to executive management since the decision as to the degree of plant utilization rests with them. Idle capacity may be due to the lack of a proper balance between production facilities and sales. It may also arise from a favorable selling price that recover fixed overhead at an exceptionally low production level.

EXAMPLE 16-7   The standards for total overhead are:

Variable overhead 2 hrs. @ $6 = $12 per unit
Fixed overhead 2 hrs. @ $20 = $40 per unit

The actual figures are:

Production 9,500 units
Donominator activity 10,000 units
Variable overhead $115,000
Fixed overhead $420,000
Actual hours 20,200

Part 1: *One-Way Analysis*
Control Variance

Actual overhead ($115,000 + $420,000)		$535,000
Standard overhead (9,500 × 2 = 19,000 × $26)		494,000
Control Variance		$ 41,000 U

Part 2: *Two-Way Analysis*
Controllable Variance

Actual overhead		$535,000
Budget adjusted to standard hours		
Fixed overhead (10,000 × 2 = 20,000 × $20)	$400,000	
Variable overhead (19,000 × $6)	114,000	
		514,000
Controllable Variance		$ 21,000 U

Volume (*Production*) *Variance*

Budget adjusted to standard hours		$514,000
Standard overhead		494,000
Volume Variance		$ 20,000 U

OR

Budgeted hours	20,000
Standard hours	19,000
Difference in hours	1,000
× Fixed overhead rate	× $20
Volume Variance	$ 20,000 U

Part 3: *Three-Way Analysis*
Spending Variance

Actual overhead		$535,000
Budget adjusted to actual hours		
Fixed overhead (10,000 × 2 = 20,000 × $20)	$400,000	
Variable overhead (20,200 × $6)	121,200	
		521,200
Spending Variance		$ 13,800 U

Efficiency Variance

Budget adjusted to actual hours		$521,200
Budget adjusted to standard hours		514,000
Efficiency Variance		$ 7,200 U

OR

Actual hours	20,200
Standard hours	19,000
Difference in hours	1,200
× Standard variable overhead rate	× $6
Efficiency Variance	$ 7,200 U

Volume Variance

Budget adjusted to standard hours		$514,000
Standard overhead		494,000
Volume Variance		$ 20,000 U

A comprehensive illustration showing *all* the variances for material, labor, and overhead follows in Example 16-8.

EXAMPLE 16-8   The following standards are given:

		Per Unit
Direct Material	5 lbs. @ $ 4 per lb.	$ 20
Direct Labor	3 hrs. @ $12 per hr.	36
Variable overhead	3 hrs. @ $ 7 per hr.	21
Fixed overhead	3 hrs. @ $20 per hr.	60
		$137

Actual data follow:

Production 9,800 units
Denominator (budget) activity 11,000 units
Purchases 50,000 lbs. @ $150,000
Direct material used 44,000 lbs.
Direct labor 22,000 hrs. @ $220,000
Variable overhead $125,000
Fixed overhead $450,000

Part 1: *Material*
Material Price Variance
(Actual price versus standard price) × actual quantity bought
($3 versus $4) × 50,000 $ 50,000 F
Material Quantity Variance
(Actual quantity issued versus standard quantity) × standard price
(44,000 versus 49,000) × $4 $ 20,000 F
Part 2: *Labor*
Control Variance
Standard quantity × standard price (29,400 × $12) $352,800
Actual quantity × actual price (22,000 × $10)   220,000
Control Variance $132,800 F
Labor Price Variance
(Actual price versus standard price) × actual quantity
    ($10 versus $12) × 22,000 $ 44,000 F
Labor Quantity Variance
(Actual quantity versus standard quantity) × standard price
(22,000 versus 29,400*) × $12 $ 88,800 F
*9,800 × 3 = 29,400
Part 3: *Variable Overhead*
Variable Overhead Price Variance
Actual variable overhead $125,000
Budget adjusted to actual hours (22,000 × $7)   154,000
Price Variance $ 29,000 F
Variable Overhead Efficiency Variance
Budget adjusted to actual hours $154,000
Budget adjusted to standard hours (9,800 × 3 =
    29,400 × $7) $205,800
Efficiency Variance $ 51,800 F

Part 4: *Fixed Overhead*
Fixed Overhead Budget Variance

Actual fixed overhead	$450,000	
Budgeted fixed overhead (11,000 × 3 = 33,000 × $20)	660,000	
Budget Variance	$210,000	F

Fixed Overhead Volume Variance

Budgeted fixed overhead	$660,000	
Standard overhead (9,800 × 3 = 29,400 × $20)	588,000	
Volume Variance	$ 72,000	U

The fixed overhead volume variance is broken down into the fixed overhead efficiency variance and fixed overhead pure volume variance.

Fixed Overhead Efficiency Variance
(Actual hours versus standard hours) × standard fixed overhead rate

(22,000 versus 29,400) × $20	$148,000	F

Fixed Overhead Pure Volume Variance
(Actual hours versus budgeted hours) × standard fixed overhead rate

(22,000 versus 33,000) × $20	$220,000	U

Part 5: *One-Way Analysis*
Total Overhead Variance

Actual overhead	$575,000	
Standard overhead (29,400 × $27)	793,800	
Total Overhead Variance	$218,800	F

Part 6: *Two-Way Analysis*
Controllable Variance

Actual overhead		$575,000	
Budget adjusted to standard hours			
Fixed overhead (11,000 × 3 = 33,000 × $20)	$660,000		
Variable overhead (9,800 × 3 = 29,400 × $7)	205,800	865,800	
Controllable Variance		$290,800	F

Volume Variance

Budget adjusted to standard hours	$865,800	
Standard overhead	793,800	
Volume Variance	72,000	U

Part 7: *Three-Way Analysis*
Spending Variance

Actual overhead		$575,000	
Budget adjusted to actual hours			
Fixed overhead (11,000 × 3			
= 33,000 × $20)	$660,000		
Variable overhead (22,000 × $7)	154,000	814,000	
Spending Variance		$239,000	F

Efficiency Variance

Budget adjusted to actual hours	$814,000	
Budget adjusted to standard hours	865,800	
Efficiency Variance	$ 51,800	F

Volume Variance

Budget adjusted to standard hours	$865,800	
Standard overhead	793,800	
Volume Variance	$ 72,000	U

INTERRELATIONSHIP OF VARIANCES

With regard to variance analysis for all production costs (direct material, direct labor, and overhead), it is important to note that each variance does *not* represent a separate and distinct problem to be handled in isolation. All variances in one way or another are interdependent. For example, the labor rate variance may be favorable because lower paid workers are being used. This could lead to: (1) an unfavorable material usage variance because of a higher incidence of waste, (2) an unfavorable labor efficiency variance because it takes longer hours to make the equivalent number of products, (3) an unfavorable overhead efficiency variance because the substandard work causes more hours to be spent for a specified output, and (4) an unfavorable overhead volume variance arising from abnormally high machine break downs because of lower-skilled operators.

A tradeoff between variances may be a managerial objective. For example, a material price variance may be favorable because of a bargain purchase opportunity or because of a combination of available resources designed to save overall corporate costs. However, the raw material acquired may be somewhat inferior in quality to that which is usually purchased. In processing, use of this material may lead to greater waste or more labor hours in producing a finished item that will satisfy product quality guidelines. The company goal here may be to minimize total production costs through the tradeoff of a favorable price variance and an unfavorable quantity variance. The net effect of the variances, in this case, is what counts.

MIX AND YIELD VARIANCES FOR MATERIAL AND LABOR

Mix refers to the relative proportion of various ingredients of input factors such as materials and labor. Yield is a measure to productivity.

Material and Labor Mix Variances

The material mix variance indicates the impact on material costs of the deviation from the standard mix. The labor mix variance measures the impact of changes in the labor mix on labor costs.

Formulas

$$\text{Material Mix Variance} = \left(\begin{array}{c} \text{Actual Units} \\ \text{Used at} \\ \text{Standard Mix} \end{array} - \begin{array}{c} \text{Actual Units} \\ \text{Used at} \\ \text{Actual Mix} \end{array} \right) \times \begin{array}{c} \text{Standard} \\ \text{Unit} \\ \text{Price} \end{array}$$

$$\text{Labor Mix Variance} = \left(\begin{array}{c} \text{Actual Hrs.} \\ \text{Used at} \\ \text{Standard Mix} \end{array} - \begin{array}{c} \text{Actual Hrs.} \\ \text{Used at} \\ \text{Actual Mix} \end{array} \right) \times \begin{array}{c} \text{Standard} \\ \text{Hourly} \\ \text{Rate} \end{array}$$

Mix and Yield Variances

The material quantity variance is divided into a material mix variance and a material yield variance. The material mix variance measures the impact of the deviation from the standard mix on material costs, while the material yield variance reflects the impact on material costs of the deviation from the standard input material allowed for actual production. We compute the material mix variance by holding the total input units constant at their actual amount.

We compute the material yield variance by holding the mix constant at the standard amount. The computations for labor mix and yield variances are the same as those for materials. If there is no mix, the yield variance is the same as the quantity (or usage) variance.

Formulas

$$\text{Material Yield Variance} = \left(\begin{array}{c} \text{Actual Units} \\ \text{Used at} \\ \text{Standard Mix} \end{array} - \begin{array}{c} \text{Actual} \\ \text{Output at} \\ \text{Standard Mix} \end{array} \right) \times \begin{array}{c} \text{Standard} \\ \text{Unit} \\ \text{Price} \end{array}$$

$$\text{Labor Yield Variance} = \left(\begin{array}{c} \text{Actual Hrs.} \\ \text{Used at} \\ \text{Standard Mix} \end{array} - \begin{array}{c} \text{Actual Output} \\ \text{Hrs. at} \\ \text{Standard Mix} \end{array} \right) \times \begin{array}{c} \text{Standard} \\ \text{Hourly} \\ \text{Rate} \end{array}$$

Probable Causes of Unfavorable Mix Variances

(a) When capacity restraints force substitution

(b) Poor production scheduling

(c) Lack of certain types of labor

(d) Certain materials are in short supply

Probable Causes of Unfavorable Yield Variances

(a) The use of low quality materials and/or labor

(b) The existence of faulty equipment

(c) The use of improper production methods

(d) An improper or costly mix of materials and/or labor

EXAMPLE 16-9   **(Mix Variances)** J Company produces a compound composed of Materials Alpha and Beta which is marketed in 20 lb. bags. Material Alpha can be substituted for Material Beta. Standard cost and mix data have been determined as follows:

	Unit Price	Standard Unit	Standard Mix Proportions
Material Alpha	$3	5 lbs.	25%
Material Beta	4	15	75
		20 lbs.	100%

Processing each 20 lbs. of material requires 10 hrs. of labor. The company employs two types of labor, "skilled" and "unskilled," working on two processes, assembly and finishing. The following standard labor cost has been set for a 20 lb. bag.

	Standard Hrs.	Standard Wage Rate	Total	Standard Mix Proportions
Unskilled	4 hrs.	$2	$8	40%
Skilled	6	3	18	60
	10	2.60	26	100%

At standard cost, labor averages $2.60 per unit. During the month of December, 100 20-lb. bags were produced with the following labor costs:

	Actual Hrs.	Actual Rate	Actual Wages
Unskilled	380 hrs.	$2.50	$950
Skilled	600	3.25	1,950
	980		$2,900

Material records show:

	Beginning Inventory	Purchase	Ending Inventory
Material Alpha	100 lbs.	800 @ $3.10	200 lbs.
Material Beta	225	1,350 @ $3.90	175

We now want to determine the following variances from standard costs.

(a) Material purchase price

(b) Material mix

(c) Material quantity

(d) Labor rate

(e) Labor mix

(f) Labor efficiency

We will show how to compute these variances in a tabular form as follows:

(a) *Material Purchase Price Variance*

	Material Price per Unit			Actual Quantity Purchased	Variance ($)
	Standard	Actual	Difference		
Material Alpha	$3	$3.10	$.10 U	800 lbs.	$80 U
Material Beta	4	3.90	.10 F	1,350	135 F
					$55 F

(b) *Material Mix Variance*

	Units Which Should Have Been Used at Standard Mix*	Actual Units at Actual Mix**	Diff.	Standard Unit Price	Variance ($)
Material Alpha	525 lbs.	700 lbs.	175 U	$3	$525 U
Material Beta	1,575	1,400	175 F	4	700 F
	2,100	2,100			$175 F

     * This is the standard mix proportions of 25% and 75% applied to the actual material units used of 2,100 lbs.

       ** Actual units used = Beginning inventory + purchases − Ending inventory. Therefore,

         Material Alpha: 700 lbs. = 100 +   800 − 200

         Material Beta: 1,400 lbs. = 225 + 1,350 − 175

The material mix variance measures the impact on material costs of the deviation from the standard mix. Therefore, it is computed holding the total quantity used constant at its actual amount and allowing the material mix to vary between actual and standard. As shown above, due to a favorable change in mix, we ended up with a favorable material mix variance of $175.

(c) *Material Quantity Variance*

	Units Which Should Have Been Used at Standard Mix	Standard Units at Standard Mix	Diff.	Standard Unit Price	Variance ($)
Material Alpha	525 lbs.	500 lbs.	25 U	$3	$75 U
Material Beta	1,575	1,500	75 U	4	300 U
	2,100	2,000			$375 U

The total material variance is the sum of the three variances:

Purchase price variance	$55 F
Mix variance	175 F
Quantity variance	375 U
	$145 U

The increase of $145 in material costs was due solely to an unfavorable quantity variance of 100 pounds of material Alpha and Beta. The unfavorable quantity variance, however, was compensated largely by favorable mix and price variances. J Company must look for ways to cut down waste and spoilage.

The labor cost increase of $300 ($2,900–$2,600) is attributable to three causes:

1. An increase of $.50 per hour in the rate paid to skilled labor and $.25 per hour in the rate paid to unskilled labor
2. An unfavorable mix of skilled and unskilled labor
3. A favorable labor efficiency variance of 20 hours

Three labor variances are computed below.

(d) *Labor Rate Variance*

	Labor Rate per Hr. Standard	Labor Rate per Hr. Actual	Diff.	Actual Hrs. Used	Variance ($)
Unskilled	$2	$2.50	$ .5 U	380 hrs.	$190 U
Skilled	3	3.25	.25 U	600	150 U
					$340 U

(e) *Labor Mix Variance*

	Actual Hrs. at Standard Mix*	Actual Hrs. at Actual Mix	Diff.	Standard Rate	Variance ($)
Unskilled	392 hrs.	380 hrs.	12 F	$2	$24 F
Skilled	588	600	12 U	3	36 U
	980	980			$12 U

* This is the standard proportions of 40% and 60% applied to the actual total labor hrs. used of 980.

(f) *Labor Efficiency Variance*

	Actual Hrs. at Standard Mix	Standard Hrs. at Standard Mix	Diff.	Standard Rate	Variance ($)
Unskilled	392 hrs.	400 hrs.	8 F	$2	$16 F
Skilled	588	600	12 F	3	36 F
	980	1,000			$52 F

The total labor variance is the sum of these three variances:

Rate variance	$340 U
Mix variance	12 U
Efficiency variance	52 F
	$300 U

which is proved to be:

Total Labor Variance

	Actual Hrs. Used	*Actual Rate*	*Total Actual Cost*	*Standard Hrs. Allowed*	*Standard Rate*	*Total Standard Cost*	*Variance ($)*
Unskilled	380 hrs.	$2.50	$ 950	400	$2	$ 800	$150 U
Skilled	600	3.25	1,950	600	3	1,800	150 U
			$2,900			$2,600	$300 U

The unfavorable labor variance, as evidenced by the cost increase of $300, may be due to:

1. Overtime necessary because of poor production scheduling resulting in a higher average labor cost per hour; and/or

2. Unnecessary use of more expensive skilled labor. J Company should put more effort into better production scheduling.

EXAMPLE 16-10   **(Yield Variances)** The Giffen Manufacturing Company uses a standard cost system for its production of a chemical product. This chemical is produced by mixing three major raw materials, A, B, and C. The company has the following standards.

36 lbs. of Material A	@	$1.00	=	$ 36.00
48 lbs. of Material B	@	2.00	=	96.00
36 lbs. of Material C	@	1.75	=	63.00
120 lbs. of standard mix	@	$1.625	=	$195.00

The company should produce 100 lbs. of finished product at a standard cost of $1.625 per lb. ($195.00/120 lbs.) To convert 120 pounds of materials into 100 pounds of finished chemical requires 400 DLH at $3.50 per DLH, or $14.00 per pound. During the month of December, the company produced 4,250 pounds of output with the following direct labor: 15,250 hrs. @ $3.50

	Materials Purchased During the month	*Materials used During the month*
Material A	1,200 @ $1.10	1,160 lbs.
Material B	1,800 @ 1.95	1,820
Material C	1,500 @ 1.80	1,480

The material *price variance is isolated at the time of purchase.* We want to compute the material purchase price, quantity, mix, and yield variances.

We will show the computations of variances in a tabular form as follows:

(a) *Material Variances*

Material Purchase Price Variance

	Material Price per unit		Diff.	Actual Quantity Purchased	Variance ($)
	Standard	Actual			
Material A	$1.00	$1.10	$.10 U	1,200 lbs.	$120 U
Material B	2.00	1.95	.05 F	1,800	90 F
Material C	1.75	1.80	.05 U	1,500	75 U
					$105 U

The material quantity variance computed below results from changes in the mix of materials as well as from changes in the total quantity of materials. The standard input allowed for actual production consists of 1,275 pounds of Material A, 1,700 pounds of Material B and 1,275 pounds of Material C, a total of 4,250 pounds. The actual input consisted of 1,160 pounds of Material A, 1,820 pounds of Material B and 1,480 pounds of Material C, a total of 4,460 pounds. To separate these two changes, the material quantity variance is subdivided into a material mix variance and a material yield variance, as shown below.

Material Quantity Variance

	Actual Units Used at Actual Mix	"Should have been" inputs based upon actual output	Diff.	Standard Unit Price	Variance ($)
Material A	1,160 lbs.	1,275 lbs.	115 F	$1.00	$115 F
Material B	1,820	1,700	120 U	2.00	240 U
Material C	1,480	1,275	205 U	1.75	358.75 U
	4,460	4,250			$483.75 U

The computation of the material mix variance and the material yield variance for the Giffen Manufacturing Company is given below.

Material Mix Variance

	"Should have been" individual inputs based upon total actual throughput*	Actual Units Used at Actual Mix	Diff.	Standard Unit Price	Variance ($)
Material A	1,338 lbs.	1,160 lbs.	178 F	$1.00	$178 F
Material B	1,784	1,820	36 U	2.00	72 U
Material C	1,338	1,480	142 U	1.75	248.5 U
	4,460	4,460			$142.5 U

* This is the standard mix proportions of 30%, 40%, and 30% applied to the actual material units used of 4,460 pounds.

Material Yield Variance

	Expected Input Units at Standard Mix	"Should have been" inputs based upon actual output*	Diff.	Standard Unit Price	Variance ($)
Material A	1,338 lbs.	1,275 lbs.	63 U	$1.00	$ 63 U
Material B	1,784	1,700	84 U	2.00	168 U
Material C	1,338	1,275	63 U	1.75	110.25 U
	4,460	4,250			$341.25 U**

* This is the standard mix proportions of 30%, 40%, and 30% applied to the actual throughput of 4,460 pounds or *output* of 4,250 pounds.

** The material yield variance of $341.25 U can be computed alternatively as follows.

Actual input quantity at standard prices
Material A 1,338 lbs. @ $1.00 = $1,338
Material B 1,784 lbs. @ 2.00 = 3,568
Material C 1,338 lbs. @   1.75 = 2,341.5 $7,247.50

Actual output quantity at standard price
4,250 lbs. @   1.625 $6,906.25
Hence, $7,247.5 − $6,906.25 = $341.25 U

The material mix and material yield variances are unfavorable indicating that a shift was made to a more expensive (at standard) input mix and that an excessive quantity of material was used. Poor production scheduling requiring an unnecessarily excessive use of input materials and an undesirable mix of Materials A, B, and C was responsible for this result. To remedy the situation, the company must ensure that:

(a) The material mix is adhered to in terms of the least cost combination without affecting product quality;

(b) The proper production methods are being implemented;

(c) Inefficiencies, waste, and spoilage are within the standard allowance; and

(d) Quality materials, consistent with established standards are being used.

Employees seldom complete their operations according to standard times. Two factors should be brought out in computing labor variances if the analysis and computation will be used to fix responsibility:

1. The change in labor cost resulting from the efficiency of the workers, measured by a labor efficiency variance. (In finding the change, allowed hours are determined through the material input.)

2. The change in labor cost due to a difference in the yield, measured by a labor yield variance. (In computing the change, actual output is converted to allowed input hours.)

For the Giffen Manufacturing Company, more efficient workers resulted in a savings of 383.33 hours (15,250 hrs. − 14,866.67 hrs.). Priced at the standard rate per hour, this produced an unfavorable labor efficiency variance of $1,341.66 as shown below:

Labor Efficiency Variance	
Actual hrs. at standard rate	$53,375
Actual hrs. at expected output	
(4,460 hrs. × 400/120 = 14,866.67 hrs. @ $3.5)	52,033.34
	$ 1,341.66 U

With a standard yield of 83 1/3% (=100/120), 4,250 pounds of finished material should have required 17,000 hours of direct labor (4,250 lbs. × 400 DLH/100). Comparing the hours allowed for the actual input, 14,866.67 hours with the hours allowed for actual output, 17,000 hours, we find a favorable labor yield variance of $7,466.66, as shown below.

Labor Yield Variance	
Actual hrs. at expected output	$52,033.34
Actual output (4,250 lbs. × 400/100 =	
17,000 hrs. @ $3.5 or 4,250 lbs. @ $14.00)	59,500
	$ 7,466.66 F

The labor efficiency variance can be combined with the yield variance to give us the *traditional* labor efficiency variance, which turns out to be favorable as follows.

Labor efficiency variance	$ 1,341.66 U
Labor yield variance	7,466.66 F
	$ 6,125 F

This division is necessary when there is a difference between the actual yield and standard yield, if responsibility is to be fixed. The producing department can not be rightfully credited with a favorable efficiency variance of $6,125. Note, however, that a favorable yield variance, which is a factor most likely outside the control of the producing department, more than offsets the *unfavorable* labor efficiency variance of $1,341.66, for which the producing department rightfully should have been responsible.

PROFIT VARIANCE ANALYSIS

Gross profit analysis is determining the causes for the change in gross profit. Any variances that impact upon gross profit are reported to management so corrective steps may be taken.

Causes of Profit Variance:

- Changes in unit sales price and cost
- Changes in the volume of products sold
- Changes in sales mix.

Analysis of the changes furnishes data needed to bring actual operations in line with budgeted expectations. Comparisons should be made between budgeted and actual operations for the current year or between actual operations for the previous year and those for the current year. Changes in gross profit may be looked at in terms of the entire company or by product line.

In an effort to improve profitability, the change in character of sales or mix of sales is just as important as the increase in total volume. For example, if the total volume in the budget is constant, but a larger proportion of high-margin products are sold than were budgeted, then higher profits will result. For instance, in the furniture business, there is an increasing trend toward more expensive and durable pieces carrying a higher margin per unit, although volume may not be all that great. Computations and analysis of sales mix variances are a very important part of profit analysis. It provides an additional insight into (a) what caused the increase or decrease in profit over the previous year and (b) why the actual profit differed from the original expectation.

Gross profit (or contribution margin) is usually the joint responsibility of the managers of the sales department and the production department; the sales department manager is responsible for the sales revenue component, and the production department manager is accountable for the cost-of-goods-sold component. However, it is the task of top management to ensure that the target profit is met. The sales department manager must hold fast to prices, volume and mix; the production department supervisor must control the costs of materials, labor and factory overhead, and quantities; the purchasing manager must purchase materials at budgeted prices; and the personnel manager must employ the right people at the right wage rates. The internal audit department must ensure that the budgetary figures for sales and costs are being adhered to by all the departments which are, directly or indirectly, involved in contributing to making profit.

The computation of the production mix variance is very similar to that of the sales mix variance. While the sales mix variance is part of profit analysis, the production mix variance for materials and labor is an important part of cost variance analysis. You must realize, however, that the analysis of standard cost variances should be understood as part of what is broadly known as profit analysis. In industries where each cost element is substituted for each other and production is at or near full capacity, how you combine different types of materials and different classes of labor will affect the extent to which the costs are controlled and gross profit is maximized. The production volume variance must be further analyzed to separate the effect on costs of a change in mix of the production inputs such as materials and labor.

The yield variances for materials, labor, and overhead are useful in managerial control of material consumption. In some cases, the newly found mix is accompanied by either a favorable or unfavorable yield of the finished product. Usually, the favorable mix variance may be offset by an unfavorable yield variance, or vice versa. It is the responsibility of the laboratory or the engineering department to ensure that no apparent advantage created by one type of variance is canceled out by another.

Taken as a whole, the analysis of profit involves careful evaluation of all facets of variance analysis, that is, sales variances and cost variances. Especially, the effect of changes in mix, volume, and yield on profits must be separated and analyzed. The analysis of these variances provide management with added dimensions to responsibility accounting since it provides additional insight into what caused the increase or decrease in profits or why the actual profit deviated from the target profit. Analyzing the change in gross profit via an effective responsibility accounting system based on the control of costs and sales variances is a step toward maximization of profits.

Following is a discussion of the computation of the profit variances.

Profit Variance Analysis for a Single Product:

(a) Sales price variance
= (Actual price − Budget or standard price) × Actual sales
(b) Cost price variance
= (Actual cost − Budget or standard cost) × Actual sales
(c) Sales volume variance
= (Actual sales − Budget or standard sales) × Budget or standard price
(d) Cost volume variance
= (Actual sales − Budget or standard sales) × Budget or standard cost per unit
(e) Total volume variance
= Sales volume variance − Cost volume variance

Profit Variance Analysis for Multiple Products:

The total volume variance in a single product situation is comprised of (a) sales mix variance and (b) sales quantity variance.

(a) Sales mix variance
= (Actual sales at budget or standard mix − Budget or standard sales at budget or standard mix) × Budget or standard CM (or GM) per unit

CM = contribution margin and GM = gross margin.

higher for 19X2 than for 19X1 yet the gross profit achieved actually declined. Given below are the store's unaudited operating results for 19X1 and 19X2. No fixed costs were included in the cost of goods sold per unit.

		Model X				Model Y		
		Cost of				Cost of		
		Goods	Sales			Goods	Sales	
	Selling	Sold per	(in	Sales	Selling	Sold	(in	Sales
Year	Price	Unit	units)	Revenue	Price	per Unit	units)	Revenue
1	$150	$110	2,800	$420,000	$172	$121	2,640	$454,080
2	160	125	2,650	424,000	176	135	2,900	510,400

We explain why the gross profit declined by $34,990. We include a detailed variance analysis of price changes and changes in volume both for sales and cost. Also we subdivide the total volume variance into changes in price and changes in quantity.

Sales price and sales volume variances measure the impact on the firm's CM (or GM) of changes in the unit selling price and sales volume. In computing these variances, all costs are held constant in order to stress changes in price and volume. Cost price and cost volume variances are computed in the same manner, holding price and volume constant. All these variances for the Lake Tahoe Ski Store are computed below.

Sales Price Variance

Actual Sales for 19X2:
  Model X 2,650 × $160 = $424,000
  Model Y 2,900 × 176 = 510,400 $934,400
Actual 19X2 sales at 19X1 prices:
  Model X 2,650 × $150 = $397,500
  Model Y 2,900 × 172 = 498,800   896,300
                                                     $ 38,100 F

Sales Volume Variance

Actual 19X2 sales at 19X1 prices: $896,300
Actual 19X1 sales (at 19X1 prices):
  Model X 2,800 × $150 = $420,000
  Model Y 2,640 × 172 = 454,080   874,080
                                                     $ 22,220 F

Cost Price Variance

Actual cost of goods sold for 19X2:
  Model X 2,650 × $125 = $331,250
  Model Y 2,900 × 135 = 391,500 $722,750
Actual 19X2 sales at 19X1 costs:
  Model X 2,650 × $110 = $291,500
  Model Y 2,900 × 121 = 350,900   642,400
                                                     $ 80,350 U

Cost Volume Variance

Actual 19X2 sales at 19X1 costs:	$642,400
Actual 19X1 sales (at 19X1 costs):	
Model X 2,800 × $110 = $308,000	
Model Y 2,640 × 121 = 319,440	627,440
	$ 14,960 U

Total volume variance = sales volume variance − cost volume variance
$$= \$22{,}250 \text{ F} - \$14{,}960 \text{ U} = \underline{\$7{,}260 \text{ F}}$$

The total volume variance is computed as the sum of a sales mix variance and a sales quantity variance as follows:

Sales Mix Variance

	19X2 Actual Sales at 19X1 Mix*	19X2 Actual Sales at 19X2 Mix	Diff.	19X1 Gross Profit per Unit	Variance ($)
Model X	2,857	2,650	207 U	$40	$8,280 U
Model Y	2,693	2,900	207 F	51	10,557 F
	5,550	5,550			$2,277 F

    * This is the 19X1 mix (used as standard or budget) proportions of 51.47% (or 2,800/5,440 = 51.47%) and 48.53% (or 2,640/5,440 = 48.53%) applied to the actual 19X2 sales figure of 5,550 units.

Sales Quantity Variance

	19X2 Actual Sales at 19X1 Mix*	19X1 Actual Sales at 19X1 Mix	Diff.	19X1 Gross Profit per Unit	Variance ($)
Model X	2,857	2,800	57 F	$40	$2,280 F
Model Y	2,693	2,640	53 F	51	2,703 F
	5,550	5,440			$4,983 F

A favorable total volume variance is due to a favorable shift in the sales mix (that is, from Model X to Model Y) and also to a favorable increase in sales volume (by 110 units) which is shown as follows.

Sales mix variance	$2,277 F
Sales quantity variance	4,983 F
	$7,260 F

However, there remains the decrease in gross profit. The decrease in gross profit of $34,990 can be explained as follows.

	Gains	Losses
Gain due to increased sales price	$38,100 F	
Loss due to increased cost		80,350 U
Gain due to increase in units sold	4,983 F	
Gain due to shift in sales mix	2,277 F	
	$45,360 F	$80,350 U
Hence, net decrease in gross profit = $80,350 − $45,360 =		$34,990 U

Despite the increase in sales price and volume and the favorable shift in sales mix, the Lake Tahoe Ski Store ultimately lost $34,990 compared to 19X1. The major reason for this comparative loss was the tremendous increase in cost of goods sold, as indicated by an unfavorable cost price variance of $80,350. The costs for both Model X and Model Y increased quite significantly over 19X1. The Store must take a close look at the cost picture. Even though only variable costs were included in cost of goods sold per unit, both variable and fixed costs should be analyzed in an effort to reduce controllable costs. In doing that, it is essential that responsibility be clearly fixed to given individuals. In a retail business like the Lake Tahoe Ski Store, operating expenses such as advertising and payroll of store employees must also be closely scrutinized.

EXAMPLE 16-12   **(Sales Mix and Quantity Variances)** Shim and Siegel, Inc. sells two products, C and D. Product C has a budgeted unit CM (contribution margin) of $3 and Product D has a budgeted unit CM of $6. The budget for a recent month called for sales of 3,000 units of C and 9,000 units of D, for a total of 12,000 units. Actual sales totaled 12,200 units, 4,700 of C, and 7,500 of D. We compute the sales volume variance and break this variance down into the (a) sales quantity variance and (b) sales mix variance.

Shim and Siegel's sales volume variance is computed below. As you can see, while total unit sales increased by 200 units, the shift in sales mix resulted in a $3,900 unfavorable sales volume variance.

	Actual Sales at Actual Mix	Standard Sales at Budget Mix	Difference	Budgeted CM per Unit	Variance ($)
Product C	4,700	3,000	1,700 F	$3	$5,100 F
Product D	7,500	9,000	1,500 U	6	9,000 U
	12,200	12,000			$3,900 U

In multiproduct firms, the sales volume variance is further divided into a sales quantity variance and a sales mix variance. The computations of these variances are shown below.

	Sales Quantity Variance				
	Actual Sales at Budgeted Mix	Standard Sales at Budgeted Mix	Difference	Standard CM per Unit	Variance ($)
Product C	3,050	3,000	50 F	$3	$150 F
Product D	9,150	9,000	150 F	6	900 F
	12,200	12,000			$1,050 F

	Sales Mix Variance				
	Actual Sales at Budgeted Mix	Actual Sales at Actual Mix	Difference	Standard CM per Unit	Variance ($)
Product C	3,050	4,700	1,650 F	$3	$4,950 F
Product D	9,150	7,500	1,650 U	6	9,900 U
	12,200	12,200			$4,950 U

The sales quantity variance reflects the impact on the CM or GM (gross margin) of deviations from the standard sales volume, whereas the sales mix variance measures the impact on the CM of deviations from the budgeted mix. In the case of Shim and Siegel, Inc., the sales quantity variance was favorable, i.e., $1,050 F and the sales mix variance was unfavorable, i.e., $4,950 U. These variances indicate that while there was favorable increase in sales volume by 200 units, it was obtained by an unfavorable shift in the sales mix, that is, a shift from Product D, with a high margin, to product C, with a low margin.

Note that the sales volume variance of $3,900 U is the algebraic sum of the following two variances.

Sales quantity variance	$1,050 F
Sales mix variance	4,950 U
	$3,900 U

In conclusion, the product emphasis on high margin sales is often a key to success for multiproduct firms. Increasing sales volume is one side of the story; selling the more profitable products is another.

In view of the fact that Shim and Siegel, Inc. experienced an unfavorable sales volume variance of $3,900 due to an unfavorable (or less profitable) mix in the sales volume, the company is advised to put more emphasis on increasing the sale of Product D.

In doing that the company might wish to:

(a) Increase the advertising budget for succeeding periods to boost Product D sales;

(b) Set up a bonus plan in such a way that the commission is based on quantities sold rather than higher rates for higher margin items such as Product D or revise the bonus plan to consider the sale of Product D;

(c) Offer a more lenient credit term for Product D to encourage its sale;

(d) Reduce the price of Product D enough to maintain the present profitable mix while increasing the sale of product. This strategy must take into account the price elasticity of demand for Product D.

NONMANUFACTURING ACTIVITIES

When nonmanufacturing activities repeat and result in a homogeneous product, standards may be used. The manner of estimating and employing standards can be similar to that applicable with a manufactured product. For instance, standards may be used for office personnel involved in processing sales orders, and a standard unit expense for processing a sales order may be derived. The variance between the actual cost of processing a sales order with the standard cost can be appraised by management and corrective steps taken. The number of payroll checks prepared should be a reliable measure of the activity of the payroll department. The number of invoices or vouchers prepared apply to billing and accounts payable. In these two cases, a standard cost per unit could be based on the variable expenses involved.

Variance analysis is used in nonproduction-oriented companies such as service businesses. Since you are not dealing with a product, a measure of volume other than units is necessary, for example, time spent. The measure of revenue is fee income.

The cost variances are still the same as in a manufacturing concern, namely budgeted costs versus actual costs. You also can derive the gross margin or contribution margin variance as the difference between that budgeted and that actually obtained. The profitability measures are expressed as a percent of sales rather than as dollars per unit. The relationship between costs and sales is often highlighted.

Service firms typically have numerous variances expressed in physical, rather than dollar, measures. Examples of physical measures are number of customers serviced and turnover rate in customers.

AN ILLUSTRATIVE VARIANCE ANALYSIS REPORT
FOR A SERVICE BUSINESS

For a service business, cost variances may be reported to management in special reports. For example, the variance in time and cost spent for processing payments to creditors may be analyzed. Exhibit 16-6 provides an illustrative format for a variance analysis report for a service business.

EXHIBIT 16-6 Variance Analysis Report for a Service Business

Function	Variance in Time	Variance in Cost
Processing purchase orders		
Processing receiving reports		
Processing vendors' invoices		
Preparing checks		
Filing paid vouchers and supporting documents		

Variances for these functions are useful only for large companies where the volume of activity allows for the arrangement and analysis of such repetitive tasks.

VARIANCES TO EVALUATE MARKETING EFFORT

Prior to setting a marketing standard in a given trade territory, you should examine prior, current, and forecasted conditions for the company itself and that given geographical area. Standards will vary depending upon geographical location. In formulating standard costs for the transportation function, minimum cost traffic routes should be selected on the basis of the given distribution pattern.

Standards for advertising cost in particular territories will vary depending upon the types of advertising media needed, which are in turn based on the type of customers the advertising is intended to reach, as well as the nature of the competition.

Some direct selling costs can be standardized, such as product presentations for which a standard time per sales call can be established. Direct selling expenses should be related to distance traveled, frequency of calls made, and so on. If sales commissions are based on sales generated, standards can be based on a percentage of net sales.

Time and motion studies are usually a better way of establishing standards than prior performance, since the past may include inefficiencies.

Cost variances for the selling function may pertain to the territory, product, or personnel.

Variances in Selling Expenses

The control of selling expenses is not as significant for a company manufacturing a standard line of products with a limited number of established customers as for a manufacturer of custom products in a very competitive market. For the latter, significant advertising and salesmen costs are mandated. The variance in selling costs is equal to the actual cost versus the flexible budgeted cost.

Assume actual cost is $88,000 and the flexible budget is:

$$\$40,000 + (5\% \times \text{sales revenue}) + (\$.03 \text{ per unit shipped})$$

If sales revenue is $500,000 and 100,000 units are shipped, the flexible budgeted cost is:

$$\$40,000 + (5\% \times \$500,000) + (\$.03 \times 100,000 \text{ units}) = \underline{\$68,000}$$

The variance is unfavorable by $20,000. Perhaps advertising and travel should be further investigated. These costs are highly discretionary in that they may easily be altered by management.

Further refinement of the selling expense variance is possible. Each element of selling expense (i.e., advertising, travel, commissions, shipping costs) could be looked at in terms of the difference between budgeted cost and actual cost.

Sales Personnel Performance

Actual sales may not be the best measure of sales personnel performance. They do not take into account differing territory potentials. Also, a high volume salesperson may have to absorb a high selling cost, making the profit generated by him low. Profit is what counts, not sales! The evaluation of sales personnel based on the trend in their sales generated over the years shows signs of improvement. However, not considered here are customer's market demand, potential markets as defined by the company, product mix, and cost incurrence.

Travel expense standards are often formulated based on distance traveled and the frequency of customer calls. Standards for salesperson automobile expense may be in terms of cost per mile traveled and cost per day. Entertainment and gift expenditures can be based on the amount, size, and potential for customers. The standard might relate to cost per customer or cost per dollar of net sales. Selling expense standards are frowned upon by sales managers because they may create ill-will among sales personnel. The standards also do not take into account sales volume or product mix.

Profitability per salesperson may be a good measurement yardstick. Sales, less variable product costs, less selling expenses, per salesperson will give the relevant profitability. Not considered here, however, are territory expectations or territory demand.

Standard costing procedures and performance measures should be used to control sales personnel costs and to compute earnings generated by salesperson category. Further, revenue, cost, and profit by type of sales solicitation (i.e., personal visit, telephone call, mail) should be determined. A break-even analysis for individual salesmen may also be performed. Sales commissions should be higher for higher profit merchandise. Any quotas established should be based on a desired sales mix.

Consideration of fixed versus variable costs for a function is critical in marketing cost control and in deciding whether to add or drop sales regions and product lines. Fixed marketing costs include administrative salaries, wages of warehousing and shipping personnel, rent, and insurance. Variable marketing costs are comprised of processing, storing, and shipping goods, which tend to fluctuate with sales volume. Also of a variable nature, are sales personnel salaries and commissions as well as travel and entertainment.

It is difficult to project marketing costs because they may materially change as market conditions are altered. An example is a modification in the channels of distribution. Also, customer brand loyalty is difficult to predict. The point here is that it is more difficult to forecast and analyze marketing costs than manufacturing costs. Thus, standards established in this area are quite tentative and very difficult to manage.

ILLUSTRATIVE MARKETING PERFORMANCE REPORTS

Exhibit 16-7 presents an illustrative format for a marketing performance report designed for the vice-president of marketing.

EXHIBIT 16-7 A Marketing Performance Report Designed for the Vice-President of Marketing

	Budget	Percent	Actual	Percent	Variance
Sales					
Less: Standard variable cost of sales					
Manufacturing margin					
Less: Variable distribution costs					
Contribution margin					
Less: Regional fixed charges					
Controllable regional contribution margin					
Less: Marketing fixed charges (i.e., central marketing administration costs, national advertising)					
Marketing contribution margin					

Exhibit 16-8 presents an illustrative format for a marketing performance report designed for the regional sales manager.

The marketing manager should be responsible for standard variable cost of sales, distribution costs (i.e., packing, freight out, marketing administration), and sales. The reason standard variable cost of sales is used is not to

(b) Sales quantity variance

$$= \left(\begin{array}{l} \text{Actual sales at} \\ \text{budget or standard} \\ \text{mix} \end{array} - \begin{array}{l} \text{Actual sales at budgeted or} \\ \text{standard mix} \end{array} \right) \times \begin{array}{l} \text{Budget or} \\ \text{standard CM} \\ \text{(or GM) per} \\ \text{unit} \end{array}$$

(c) Total volume variance

= Sales mix variance + sales quantity variance

$$\text{or} = \left(\begin{array}{l} \text{Actual sales} \\ \text{at actual mix} \end{array} - \begin{array}{l} \text{Budgeted or standard sales} \\ \text{at budgeted or standard} \\ \text{mix} \end{array} \right) \times \begin{array}{l} \text{Budget or} \\ \text{standard CM} \\ \text{(or GM) per} \\ \text{unit} \end{array}$$

The sales price variance and the cost price variance are calculated the same way as for a single product.

Frequently, a contribution margin approach is superior to the gross profit approach. That is because "gross profit" has as a deduction for fixed costs which may be beyond the control of a particular level of management. A simple example follows:

	Budget (00) omitted		Actual (00) omitted		Variance	
	Unit A	Unit B	Unit A	Unit B	Unit A	Unit B
Sales Price	$10	$5	$11	$6	$1 F	$1
Units	10	8	10	8	–0–	–0–
Variable Manufacturing Costs	$4	$3	$6	$4	$2 U	$1
Fixed Manufacturing Costs	$3	$1	$4	$2	$1 U	$1
Manufacturing Contribution Margin per Unit	$6	$2	$5	$2	$1 U	$–0–
Gross Profit per Unit	$3	$1	$1	$0	$2 U	$1

Using the above data, an unfavorable manufacturing contribution margin variance of $10 for Unit A and $0 for Unit B is more meaningful than the $20 and $8 unfavorable gross profit variance if local management had no control over fixed costs.

EXAMPLE 16-11 (Profit Variance Analysis)
The Lake Tahoe Ski Store sells two ski models, Model X and Model Y. For the years 19X1 and 19X2, the store realized a gross profit of $246,640 and only $211,650, respectively. The owner of the store was astounded since the total sales volume in dollars and in units was

EXHIBIT 16-8 A Marketing Performance Report Designed for the Regional Sales Manager

	Budget	Percent	Actual	Percent	Variance
Sales					
Less: Standard variable cost of sales					
Manufacturing margin					
Less: Variable distribution costs (i.e., sales personnel commissions, freight out)					
Contribution margin					
Less: Regional fixed charges (i.e., salesmen salaries, travel and entertainment, local advertising)					
Controllable regional contribution margin					

have the marketing area absorb manufacturing efficiencies and inefficiencies. An illustrative format follows.

Sales
Less: Standard variable cost of sales
Less: Distribution costs
Profitability

The profit figure constitutes the marketing efforts contribution to fixed manufacturing costs and administration costs.

How to Analyze Salesperson Variances

You should appraise sales force effectiveness within a territory, including time spent and expenses incurred.

EXAMPLE 16-13 Sales data for your company follow.

Standard cost	$240,000
Standard salesperson days	2,000
Standard rate per salesperson day	$ 120
Actual cost	$238,000
Actual salesperson days	1,700
Actual rate per salesperson day	$ 140

Total Cost Variance

Actual cost	$238,000
Standard cost	240,000
	$ 2,000 F

The control variance is broken down into salesperson days and salesperson costs.

Variance in Salesperson Days	
Actual days versus standard days times standard rate per day	
(1,700 versus 2,000 × $120)	$36,000 F

The variance is favorable because the territory was handled in fewer days than expected.

Variance in Salesperson Costs	
Actual rate versus standard rate times actual days	
($140 versus $120 × 1,700)	$34,000 U

An unfavorable variance results because the actual rate per day is greater than the expected rate per day.

EXAMPLE 16-14 A salesperson called on 55 customers and sold each an average of $2,800 worth of merchandise. The standard number of calls is 50, and the standard sales is $2,400. Variance analysis looking at calls and sales follows.

Total Variance	
Actual calls × actual sale 55 × $2,800	$154,000
Standard calls × standard sale 50 × $2,400	120,000
	$ 34,000

The elements of the $34,000 variance are

Variance in Calls	
Actual calls versus standard calls × standard sale	
(55 versus 50 × $2,400)	$ 12,000
Variance in Sales	
Actual sale versus standard sale × standard calls	
($2,800 versus $2,400 × 50)	$ 20,000
Joint Variance	
(Actual calls versus standard calls) × (Actual sale versus standard sale)	
(55 versus 50) × ($2,800 versus $2,400)	$ 2,000

Additional performance measures of sales force effectiveness include meeting sales quotas, number of orders from existing and new customers, profitability per order, and the relationship between salesperson costs and revenue obtained.

The trend in the ratios of (1) selling expense to sales, (2) selling expense to sales volume, and (3) selling expense to net income should be computed. Are selling expenses realistic in light of revenue generated? Are selling expenses beyond limitations pointing to possible mismanagement and violation of controls?

Variances in Warehousing Costs

In warehousing, standards for direct labor may be in terms of cost per item handled, cost per pound handled, cost per order filled, and cost per shipment. Variances in warehousing costs can be calculated by looking at the cost per unit to store the merchandise and the number of orders anticipated.

EXAMPLE 16-15   The following information applies to a product:

Standard cost	$12,100
Standard orders	5,500
Standard unit cost	$ 2.20
Actual cost	$14,030
Actual orders	6,100
Actual unit cost	$ 2.30
Total Warehousing Cost Variance	
Actual cost	$14,030
Standard cost	12,100
	$ 1,930 U

The total variance is segregated into the variance in orders and variance in cost.

Variance in Orders	
Actual orders versus standard orders × standard unit cost	
6,100 versus 5,500 × $2.20	$ 1,320 U
Variance in Cost	
Actual cost per unit versus standard cost per unit × actual orders	
$2.30 versus $2.20 × 6,100	$ 610 U

VARIANCES IN ADMINISTRATIVE EXPENSES

As business expands, there is a tendency for administrative expenses to increase proportionately and to get out of line. However, central general and administrative expenses typically are of a fixed cost nature and hence there is less need to monitor these types of costs. Here, comparison of budgeted to actual costs can be made quarterly or even yearly! These comparisons should be done by department or unit of responsibility. Suggested standards for administrative expenses appear below.

Administrative Function	Unit of Standard Measurement
Handling orders	Number of orders handled
Billing	Number of invoices
Check writing	Number of checks written
Clerical	Number of items handled
Customer statements	Number of statements
Order writing	Number of orders
Personnel	Number of employees hired
Payroll	Number of employees

Selling and administrative variances for nonoperating items are the responsibility of top management and staff. Such items include taxes and insurance. Performance reports may be prepared for the administrative function, such as the salaries of top executives, and for general department service costs, such as data processing. Performance measures may also be of a nonmonetary nature, such as the number of files processed, the number of phone calls taken, and the number of invoices written. Variances between the dollar and nondollar factors can be determined and analyzed.

CAPITAL EXPENDITURES

Variance reports are useful in controlling capital expenditures by studying the actual versus budgeted costs, as well as actual versus budgeted times for proposals at each stage of activity. Such reports enable management to take corrective cost-saving action such as changing the construction schedule. The director of the project is held accountable for the construction cost and time budget. Component elements within the project should also be analyzed. You can also compare the expected payback period and actual payback period. This assists in measuring operational results and budgeting efficiency. Also, estimated cash flows of the project can be compared with actual cash flows.

VARIANCE ANALYSIS REPORTS

Performance reports may be prepared looking at the difference between budgeted and actual figures for (1) production in terms of cost, quantity, and quality; (2) sales; (3) profit; (4) return on investment; (5) turnover of assets; (6) income per sales dollar; (7) market share; and (8) growth rate. Variance reports raise questions rather than answer them. For example, is sales volume down because of deficiencies in sales effort or the manufacturer's inability to produce? Variance analysis reports may be expressed not only in dollars, but also in percentages, ratios, graphs, and narrative.

Performance reports are designed to motivate managers and employees to change their activities and plans when variances exist. They should be terse and should concentrate on potential difficulties and opportunities. A section for comments should be provided so that explanations may be given for variances.

The timeliness of performance reports and detail supplied depends upon the management level the report is addressed to and the nature of the costs whose performance is being measured. A production supervisor may need daily information on the manufacturing operations, the plant superintendent may need only weekly data from his supervisor, and the vice-president for manufacturing may be satisfied with monthly performance figures for each plant. As you become more distant from the actual operation, the time interval for performance evaluation lengthens. Also, as you climb the ladder in the organization, performance reports contain data in increasingly summarized form.

Since performance reports depend upon the organizational structure, they should be designed based on the company's organization chart. Performance reports designed for a senior vice-president might deal with the entire business operations of the firm and the earnings derived from it; the vice-president of manufacturing would look at the efficiency of the production activity; the vice-president of marketing would evaluate the selling and distribution function; a plant head would be concerned with the output and earnings generated from his plant; a department head within the plant would be concerned with cost control.

Performance reports should contain analytical information. To obtain it we should evaluate source data such as work orders, material requisitions, and labor cards. Reasons for inefficiency and excessive costs should be noted such as those due to equipment malfunction and low quality raw materials.

For labor, the productivity measurement ratio of volume output per direct labor hour should be computed. Further, the output of the individual or machine should be compared to the "normal" output established at the beginning of the reporting period. Operating efficiency can thus be measured. A labor efficiency ratio can also be computed which is the variation between actual hours incurred and standard hours.

With regard to the evaluation of the divisional manager, fixed costs are generally not controllable by him, but variable costs are. There are instances, however, where variable costs are controllable by those above the division manager's level. An example is fringe benefits. These items should be evaluated independently since the division manager has no responsibility for them. The opposite may also be true, that is, the department manager may have control over certain fixed expenses such as lease costs. In such cases he should similarly be assigned responsibility, although a successor not involved in the lease negotiation may not be assigned responsibility.

Appraisal of Marketing Department

Revenue, cost, and profitability information should be provided by product line, customer, industry segment, geographic area, channel of distribution, type of marketing effort, and average order size. New product evaluations should also be undertaken balancing risk with profitability. Analysis of competition in terms of strengths and weaknesses should be made. Sales force effectiveness measures should also be employed for income generated by salesmen, call frequency, sales incentives, sales personnel costs and dollar value of orders generated per hours spent. Promotional effectiveness measures should be employed for revenue, marketing costs, and profits prior to, during, and subsequent to promotional efforts, including a discussion of competitive reactions. Advertising effectiveness measures, such as sales generated based on dollar expenditure per media and media measures (i.e., audience share), are also useful. Reports discussing product warranty complaints and disposition should also be provided.

Marketing costs may be broken down into the following areas: selling, promotion, credit evaluation, accounting, and administration (i.e., product development, market research). Another element is physical distribution—inventory management, order processing, packaging, warehousing, shipping outbound transportation, field warehousing, and customer services.

Control of marketing costs is initiated when such costs are assigned to functional groups such as geographic area, product line, and industry segment. Budgeted costs and rates should be provided and comparisons made between standard costs and actual costs at the end of the reporting period.

CONCLUSION

Variance analysis is essential in the organization for the appraisal of all aspects of the business, including manufacturing, marketing, and service. Variances should be investigated if the benefits outweigh the costs of analyzing and correcting the source of the variance. Variance analysis reports should be in dollars and percentages.

Significant unfavorable variances must be examined to ascertain whether they are controllable by management or uncontrollable because they relate solely to external factors. When controllable, immediate corrective action must be undertaken to handle the problem. The manager should provide his recommendations. If a variance is favorable, an examination should be made of the reasons for it so that corporate policy may include the positive aspects found. Further, the responsible entity for a favorable variance should be recognized and rewarded.

Different degrees of significance of variances may be present including:

- The variance is within tolerable and normal range and thus no remedial steps are necessary.
- The variance is intolerable and thus either performance must be improved or new standards formulated in light of the current environment.
- The decision model was inappropriate considering the goal to be achieved and thus a more relevant model should be developed.

Reports on operating performance should show where performance varies from standard, the trend of performance, and the reasons for the variances, including the manager's explanation.

Reporting systems differ among companies regarding the frequency and timeliness of reports, details presented, arrangement of data, employee distribution, and size of variances necessitating follow-up. Variances can be evaluated by divisions, subdivisions, departments, and cost centers. Variance analysis should be made to the point that additional savings from cost control justify the additional cost of appraisal and reporting.

If responsibility for a variance is joint, corrective action should also be joint. If correction of an unfavorable variance involves a conflict with a corporate policy, the policy should be reevaluated and perhaps changed. If the policy is not changed, the variance should be considered uncontrollable.

Even if a variance is below a cut-off percent or dollar figure, management may still want to investigate it if the variance is consistently unfavorable because it may reveal a problem (e.g., poor supervision, wasteful practice). The cumulative impact of a repeated small unfavorable variance may be just as damaging as an occasional one.

Common reasons why budget and actual figures differ are the failure to take into account organizational changes, expense classification, consolidation, new accounting policies, and different revenue or expense recognition methods being used for budget versus accounting purposes.

Chapter 17

Zero-Base Budgeting and Project Budgeting*

This chapter discusses both zero-base budgeting and project (program) budgeting.

ZERO-BASE BUDGETING

In recession, companies face decreasing earnings, spiraling costs, and increasing pressure to hold down prices. Zero-base budgeting (ZBB), also called priority-based budgeting, involves a review of programs, activities, or functions with a view toward improving cost efficiency. It involves evaluating competing alternative programs, deciding on discretionary funding levels, appraising effectiveness, and examining managers' priorities. Management should do nothing that cannot be cost justified. Unit objectives should be linked to corporate targets.

Under ZBB, budgeted figures for product lines, functions, or activities are stated at *minimum* funding levels. The survival level is the service level and funding below which the decision unit might as well be eliminated. Anything in excess of the minimum level must be justified. Under ZBB, the manager must justify *all* activities as if they were being considered for the first time. For example, if a manager wishes to produce product X or render ser-

* This chapter was coauthored by Robert Fonfeder, Ph.D., CPA, a budgeting consultant to companies and Professor of Accounting at Hofstra University, School of Business.

287

vice Y, he or she must be able to justify its value. If he or she is unable to do so, that product or service will *not* be funded. In essence, ZBB starts fresh each year, basically ignoring what occurred previously. The focus is on the present and future practicality of the item. It is sort of like "cleaning house." A purpose of ZBB is to prevent previously approved, but presently unnecessary or inefficient, activities to continue.

ZBB is useful for estimating both manufacturing and service costs. It is particularly suitable over operations and programs under management discretion. For example, ZBB can be used in manufacturing, marketing, administration, engineering, research, and capital budgets.

ZBB results in the logical, efficient allocation of corporate resources. An important element in ZBB is examining the input-output relationship. However, do not spend too much time with projects unlikely to be funded. ZBB asks the following questions:

- What are the objectives of the activity?
- Are these objectives being achieved and measured?
- What are the consequences of not funding an activity?
- How will an alternative effect the quality of the product or service?
- How will the alternative effect other costs and activities?

The usual budgeting approach involves adding or subtracting a percentage increase or decrease to the prior period's budget to obtain a new budget. The previous period's costs are deemed basic and the focus is typically on what revisions are needed for the coming year. Adjustments may be made for losses, inflation, and so on. Have there been any changes in the economic and political environments that will have an effect on the activity to be performed? The traditional method emphasizes inputs instead of outputs applicable to goal accomplishment and thus does not call for the appraisal of the company's activities from a cost/benefit viewpoint. Exhibit 17-1 presents the differences between traditional and zero-base budgeting.

EXHIBIT 17-1 Traditional vs. Zero-Base Budgeting

Traditional	*Zero-Base Budgeting*
1. Starts from existing base.	1. Starts with zero base.
2. Appraises cost/benefit for new activities.	2. Analyzes cost/benefit for all activities.
3. Starts with dollars.	3. Starts with objectives and activities.
4. Does not consider new approaches of operating as integral elements of the process.	4. Explicitly looks to new approaches.
5. Results in a nonalternative budget.	5. Results in selecting several levels of service and cost.

Texas Instruments in 1969 was the first company to use ZBB because of volatile sales and changing business mix. After that, other companies have used it successfully including Gerber Products, Westinghouse Electric, New York Telephone, Ohio Bell Telephone, Florida Power and Light, Combustion Engineering, Owens-Illinois, and Xerox. Also see Carol Fischer's article on the favorable experiences of Merchants Insurance Group in *Controllers Quarterly* (volume 6, number 3, 1990, pp. 11–14).

This chapter now examines the ZBB process, decision packages, determining and analyzing activity units, ranking proposals, and the benefits and shortcomings of ZBB.

THE ZBB PROCESS

The ZBB process starts with the formulation of corporate objectives and assumptions. Financial managers must make certain assumptions with regard to increases in salary and fringe benefits, inflation rates, and so on. It may be advisable to test ZBB in one division or segment before adopting it throughout the organization. ZBB should be "phased in" gradually. Some companies initially only apply ZBB to about 25 percent of their budgets until they gather sufficient experience with it. There should be flexibility to modify the levels at which packages are developed, the review and ranking process, the planning assumptions, and time constraints.

ZBB requires each manager to justify his or her budget request in detail from a zero base, and thus mandates an appraisal of the output from each activity or function of a given cost/responsibility center. The consequences of rejecting a proposed project on the company must also be considered.

The activities of the segment or center are expressed as decision packages that are to be evaluated and ranked in priority order at various levels. A body of structured information is ultimately gathered that facilitates the allocation of funds by management to those activities which will accomplish the greatest company good. Exhibit 17-2 presents the process in formulating and implementing ZBB.

EXHIBIT 17-2 ZBB Process

Planning assumptions
Ranking
Evaluation and control
Budget preparation
Identify decision units
Analyze decision units

EXHIBIT 17-3 Children's Playhouse
Sample Zero-Base Budget
For the Year Ending December 31, 19XX

	Carnival	*Candy Drive*	*Cake and Dessert Auction*	*Recycling Program*	*Yearly Skit Program*	*Total*
Revenues:						
Sales	$8,000.00	$3,500.00	$2,000.00	$1,000.00	$1,000.00	$15,500.00
Expenditures:						
Equipment rental	2,000.00	0.00	0.00	0.00	0.00	2,000.00
Facilities rental	1,000.00	0.00	450.00	0.00	350.00	1,800.00
Security	100.00	0.00	100.00	0.00	100.00	300.00
Total expenses	3,100.00	0.00	550.00	0.00	450.00	4,100.00
Excess Revenue						
Over Expenditures	$4,900.00	$3,500.00	$1,450.00	$1,000.00	$ 550.00	$11,400.00

The following decision packages arise as a result of the formulation stage:

- A decision package in which an activity is maintained "as is." In other words, there is status quo in that the current level and method of activity is presented in decision package format.
- A decision package comprised of a base level plus incremental levels of activity for ongoing programs. Alternatives are stated.
- A decision package for new activities or programs.

Clear and realistic goals must be established for each decision package. A computer should be used to keep track of decision packages so that financial information may easily be obtained and proper comparisons can be made. An internal audit should be conducted to determine whether the company has selected the "right" decision packages. Actual results should be compared to what was expected, and the reasons for any variances should be determined.

An illustrative zero-base budget is presented in Exhibit 17-3.

DECISION PACKAGES

In the initial step of ZBB, decision packages are formulated. The decision package includes a description, specific measures, and responsible parties. Each decision package indicates the manager's recommended way of accomplishing a given product or service in terms of cost and time. Also indicated are alternative means of providing the product or rendering the service in dollars and time. For example, lowering the quality will lower the cost. Shortening the time may increase the cost due to overtime. Consideration should be given to the track records of the decision packages. Have any shown poor results in prior periods? The information should be arranged in a standardized format sheet. Management will review these decision packages for approval or disapproval. The decision package contains the following information:

- Description of the activity and reasons to perform it.
- Statement of objectives and benefits of the program.
- The agenda for accomplishing the objective.
- The priority of the program.
- The costs to be incurred and time required, along with analysis.
- The anticipated benefits from the program. The manager should ask "what am I getting from this expenditure?"
- Alternative methods of accomplishing the activity in terms of time and cost.
- Outcome measures.
- Resources required.
- Support needed by other decision units.
- The implications of rejecting a program on the company as a whole and segments within.
- The staff and support needed to conduct the activity.
- Relevant data such as legal ramifications, technical and operational feasibility, and risks.
- Consequences of not performing an activity.

Decision packages can be either *mutually exclusive* or *incremental.* The former are alternative packages meaning that the acceptance of one precludes the acceptance of another. Incremental packages apply to different effort levels. For example, one package may require 1,000 labor hours per month while another may need 1,200 hours for that same time period.

Some packages may apply to the long-term while others to the short term. Will there be immediate and tangible results? There is a matching of resources with objectives. Resources are directed to higher payout areas.

Be careful that decision packages are complete and not lumped together. A problem may arise when decision packages cross functional and organizational lines.

ACTIVITY UNITS

The activity unit is the basic cost element of ZBB. It is the lowest unit within the company for which the budget is prepared. It may be a program, function, organizational unit, or line item. A manager is responsible for this unit's performance. The unit is appraised to assure it is accomplishing corporate objectives. Examples of decision units are research and development, computer services, legal services, and quality control. Activities fixed by statute, industry practice, or other constraints are given priority. In some cases, an activity may be needed to boost morale.

Decision units need to be at a high organizational level so that the responsible manager has effective control over the activities. Decision units should generally be selected to parallel the flow of responsibility for budgetary decision making. Comparisons may be made for decision units that are similar in size in terms of personnel and dollars. The definition of the activity units should be specific enough to avoid complications arising from a multiplicity of activities in a decision unit.

ANALYZING DECISION UNITS

Once the activity goals have been identified, the decision manager describes how his or her department presently operates and how the resources may be employed (personnel and dollars). The description of operations cannot be excessively detailed, but should include the essential activities, and is typically organized to define the work flow.

Measurements of productivity and effectiveness are needed. In making decisions, financial data, work load, and performance standards must be considered for the activity. Examples of measurement performances include:

1. Quality control—number of rejects or other problems.
2. Production control—number of production bottlenecks and lack of productivity.
3. Internal audit—audits should be made of information provided by each reporting unit.
4. Regional sales manager—number of customers lost.

ZBB requires that alternative operating methods be considered. After studying both the present and alternative operating methods, the manager and supervisors select the best operating method. Alternative operating modes include centralizing the function, decentralizing the activity, combining the functions, contracting the activity, and eliminating the function.

ZBB must be controlled such as by utilizing the following control measures:

- Quarterly output appraisal using pre-established performance norms.
- Quarterly plan and budget modifications for the company and decision units based on changing circumstances and new information.
- Monthly financial review of each decision unit based on a comparison of actual costs to budgeted costs.

RANKING PROPOSALS

Ranking is based on input from decision unit managers and top management. Consideration should be given to quantitative and qualitative factors. Cost/benefit analysis is undertaken for each decision unit.

In the ranking process, decision packages are ranked in the order of decreasing benefit to the company. Further, ranking determines the advantages to be gained at each expenditure level and identifies the ramifications of rejecting those decision packages ranked below that given expenditure level.

In ranking, the manager ascertains what is the most crucial service of his or her unit. The highest priority is assigned to the minimum increment of service, which is the amount of service the company must engage in to provide meaningful service. Additional increments of service are then provided in priority order.

Top management should perform the *final* ranking of decision packages prepared by managers in the various divisions, departments, and segments within the company. The initial rankings should be done at the lower management levels (e.g., cost centers) where the packages are first developed. The intermediate rankings should be done at the middle management levels after the packages are reviewed, giving consideration to lower management level recommendations. When the lower level manager's recommendation is rejected, he or she should be informed as to the reasons why. To avoid overwhelming higher management levels with too much detail, the ranked decision packages may be combined into the major candidates for review and ranking.

A cutoff must be established by management for programs and activities at each of the approval levels. For example, a 70 percent cutoff line may be set for middle management while a 90 percent cutoff line may be established for upper management. The 70 percent middle management cutoff line would require the manager to remove the highest ranked packages until the expenditures represented for the removed packages equal 70 percent of last year's budget. These packages are then reviewed for reasonableness. Those remaining decision packages would then be carefully studied and researched as appropriate.

A ranking table is prepared for the decision packages of each responsibility center. This table aids in deciding which proposals will or will not be financed. However, also rank nonfunded packages so that they may be added to the budget if additional dollars become available. Further, lower priority items now may later become higher priority items. Adjustments should be made to the priority listing during the period depending upon changing circumstances.

Various ranking techniques can be used including single standard, voting, and major category. Single standard is an approach that is most suitable for similar packages. All packages are appraised based on only one aspect such as cost/benefit ratio, profit, return on investment, net present value, or dollar savings. This method is *not* good for dissimilar packages because it may omit a vital program such as health and safety.

In the voting approach, a voting committee is established. Each committee member evaluates the decision packages. The packages are then discussed at the committee meeting. A committee vote determines the ranking. In any event, the committee does approve legally required programs. Further, it gives special attention to projects involving minimum requirements to the organization.

The major category system classifies decision packages into categories. A ranking is then made of decision packages by category. Some categories are more important than others. Therefore, budgets may vary depending on the category. For example, a category having significant growth potential may be funded five times more than one having questionable prospects. Thus, the former category will likely have a greater percentage of its decision packages funded. This approach is good because greater emphasis is given to important categories.

After allocation decisions have been made, detailed budgets are prepared. These budgets are typically prepared on the basis of incremental activities reflected on the ranking table.

EXAMPLE 17-1 A company prepares a decision package for each product that department managers want to manufacture. Assume 250 possible products (old and new), there will be 250 decision packages.

An illustrative decision package for product X to be produced in Department A follows:

Product X—Decision Package

	Cost	Time Required
Alternative A	$100,000	6 months
Recommended Way	$125,000	5 months
Alternative B	$140,000	5 1/2 months

Each of the decision packages for all 250 products is then submitted to upper management. Upper management then appraises the decision packages from all the departments of the company, including that of Department A. A budget ceiling will place a dollar cutoff on how many products may be supported. A priority ranking is given to all the packages. Those above the budget cutoff will be funded in some fashion. In this example, the decision package for product X may be rejected because it does not pass the cutoff. If it is accepted, upper management will give permission to the department manager to manufacture the product either in the recommended way or in an alternative fashion. An alternative approach may be selected because it is cheaper or takes less time.

ADVANTAGES AND DISADVANTAGES OF ZBB

The advantages of ZBB include:

- ZBB makes the budgeting process more logical and less political.
- ZBB assists in formulating priorities and standards to be accomplished.
- It is good for planning, and identifies and controls resources. Further, the specification of alternatives may lead to innovate and better ways to perform.
- ZBB allows for consideration of alternative courses of action.
- ZBB aids in cost control.
- ZBB improves effectiveness and efficiency.
- ZBB encourages the reorganization of activities to accomplish overall objectives and improve performance.
- ZBB matches service levels to available resources. Resources should be used to accomplish the maximum benefit.
- ZBB allows senior management to define service levels needed for each responsibility or activity unit.
- ZBB improves planning and communication throughout the company such as between upper, middle, and lower management. All levels of the organization are involved in the process. Subordinates should participate since they have on-the-job working knowledge that can be of benefit to supervisors. Creativity is fostered by participants.

The disadvantages of ZBB include:

- ZBB may be considered by some a threat to their jobs and activities. Therefore, competition rather than cooperation may exist.

- Resistance will occur because staff are reluctant to change their ways. For example, lower management may view ZBB as a waste of time, and are being forced by upper management to do it. Lower-level managers may feel enormous stress.
- Upper management may not support the process and disregard ZBB information and implications.
- Political pressures will still be asserted to receive proper funding and as a result internal conflicts and resentment may arise.
- ZBB is expensive and the benefits may not justify such significant cost outlays.
- ZBB takes a lot of time to implement since line managers are starting at a minimal funding level. Line managers may not have so much time to spend.
- Paperwork is voluminous.
- It is difficult to determine performance levels.
- Some decision packages are interrelated making ranking difficult.

Because of the problems of time and cost, it may be best to use ZBB over multi-year periods (e.g., two years) rather than in a single year. To do it annually may not be cost-effective.

CONCLUSION

ZBB is used to describe the activities or functions of the business. It accomplishes many benefits at different funding levels through priority ranking. It specifies alternative service options to be achieved that best meets the budgetary requirements of the business. ZBB enables managers to take into account the value of the units relative to the company as a whole. However, unforseen events may require immediate revision to decision packages. It is a continual process.

PROGRAM (PROJECT) BUDGETS

Program or project budgeting should be integrated into the financial and managerial accounting systems. Programs may be by division, department, or segment within the department. The program budget is the estimated cost of performing the activities or functions. Programming is structuring the methods to accomplish an outcome. For example, a program budget may assign financial resources to a specific organizational function such as marketing research or quality control.

Goals are identified and the program to accomplish that goal is formulated. There is an appraisal of alternatives to determine the most efficient and least costly way to accomplish the objectives of the program. The steps necessary to accomplish the goal should be specified. Scarce resources are optimally allocated to projects and programs. Program budgeting requires a detailed schedule to accomplish steps.

Program budgeting is planning, programming, and budgeting. It accumulates and studies the detailed plans. It contains a combination of resources (facilities, machinery, manpower, raw materials, labor, and capital) to accomplish a goal within a planning period. Alternatives are evaluated. The budget implements the long-term plan, and decision making moves progressively downward. The emphasis is on output goals of products and services rather than input goals. Program budgeting is future-oriented looking at the impact on the future of current decisions and choices. It involves allocating resources and concentrating operations to accomplish program objectives.

In comparison to operating budgets for one year, program budgets are formulated for projects or programs of a one-time, long-term nature involving significant cash outlays. Problems should be anticipated beforehand. Responsibility should be assigned for specific activities. Project costs should be evaluated for reasonableness. Adjustments to the plan may have to be made.

There should be a cost/benefit analysis for programs. Programs should be ranked in priority order. The interrelationship between programs must be provided for.

Costs may be traced to individual projects or products, as well as to individuals generating those costs. This is accomplished by giving each project a number and requiring employees to key in code numbers when requisitioning supplies, preparing expense reimbursement forms, and for salaries directly attributable to the project.

A goal may be to maximize the program's output subject to budget constraints. A budget ceiling may be established based on prior year sales, competition, desired growth rate, and future expectations. Program activities include engineering, maintenance, research and development, public relations, marketing, and training.

Project benefits are used for capital assets and research and development programs. Examples are planning and budgeting for capital facilities, a new product line, an R&D undertaking, and a government contract.

The project should be broken down into major activities or tasks, which should then be subdivided further into specific sub-activities. Program budgeting looks at the tasks necessary to complete the program, the manpower required, and how long each function takes.

Work packages will have to be authorized by cost centers. A typical work-authorization form appears in Exhibit 17-4.

EXHIBIT 17-4 Work Authorization Form

Project:
Work-package number:
Issue date:
Revision date:
Revision number:

Work Description	Cost Center	Labor Materials	Beginning Hours	Ending Date	Date

A time sheet should be prepared for project activities. The progress in meeting time deadlines should be noted. A time schedule should be set for each stage of the project. The time schedule should be separately stated for the phases of planning, programming, and budgeting. A Gantt (bar) chart may be used to chart the time of activities. Activities may also be scheduled using the Program Evaluation and Review Technique (PERT). Quality of work should be inspected at key points.

Part 4

FINANCIAL FORECASTING AND QUANTITATIVE METHODS

Chapter 18

Forecasting, Budgeting and Planning

Management in both private and public organizations typically operates under conditions of uncertainty or risk. Probably the most important function of business management is forecasting. A forecast is a starting point for planning. The objective of forecasting is to reduce risk in decision making. In business, forecasts are the basis for capacity planning, production and inventory planning, manpower planning, planning for sales and market share, financial planning and budgeting, planning for research and development and top management's strategic planning. Sales forecasts are especially crucial aspects of many financial management activities, including budgets, profit planning, capital expenditure analysis, and acquisition and merger analysis. Figure 18-1 illustrates how sales forecasts relate to various managerial functions of business.

WHO USES FORECASTS?

Forecasts are needed for marketing, production, purchasing, manpower, and financial planning. Further, top management needs forecasts for planning and implementing long-term strategic objectives and for planning capital expenditures. More specifically, marketing managers use sales forecasts:

1. to determine optimal sales force allocations,

2. to set sales goals, and

3. to plan promotions and advertising.

FIGURE 18-1 Sales Forecasts and Managerial Functions

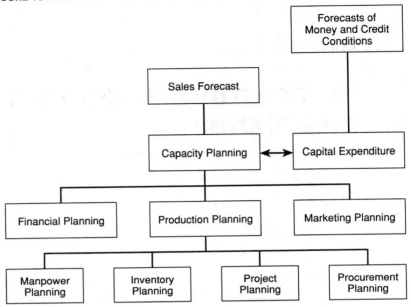

Other things such as market share, prices, and trends in new product development are required. Production planners need forecasts in order to:

- Schedule production activities
- Order materials
- Establish inventory levels
- Plan shipments.

Some other areas which need forecasts include material requirements (purchasing and procurement), labor scheduling, equipment purchases, maintenance requirements, and plant capacity planning.

As shown in Figure 18-1, as soon as the company is confident that it has sufficient capacity, the production plan is developed. If the company does not have sufficient capacity, it will require planning and budgeting decisions for capital spending for capacity expansion.

On this basis, the financial manager must estimate the future cash inflow and outflow. He must plan cash and borrowing needs for the company's future operations. Forecasts of cash flows and the rates of expenses and revenues are needed to maintain corporate liquidity and operating efficiency. In planning for capital investments, predictions about future economic activity are required so that returns or cash inflows accruing from the investment may be estimated.

Forecasts must also be made of money and credit conditions and interest rates so that the cash needs of the firm may be met at the lowest possible cost. The finance and accounting functions must also forecast interest rates to support:

1. the acquisition of new capital,

2. the collection of accounts receivable to help in planning working capital needs, and

3. capital equipment expenditure rates to help balance the flow of funds in the organization.

Sound predictions of foreign exchange rates are increasingly important to financial managers of multinational companies (MNCs).

Long-term forecasts are needed for the planning of changes in the company's capital structure. Decisions as to whether to issue stock or debt in order to maintain the desired financial structure of the firm require forecasts of money and credit conditions.

The personnel department requires a number of forecasts in planning for human resources. Workers must be hired and trained, and for these personnel there must be benefits provided that are competitive with those available in the firm's labor market. Also, trends that affect such variables as labor turnover, retirement age, absenteeism, and tardiness need to be forecast as input for planning and decision making.

Managers of nonprofit institutions and public administrators must also make forecasts. Hospital administrators face the problem of forecasting the health care needs of the community. In order to do this efficiently, a projection has to be made of:

• The growth in absolute size of population

• The changes in the number of people in various age groupings

• The varying medical needs these different age groups will have.

Universities forecast student enrollments, cost of operations, and in many cases, what level of funds will be provided by tuition and by government appropriations.

The service sector which today accounts for two-thirds of the U.S. gross domestic product (GDP), including banks, insurance companies, restaurants, and cruiseships, need various projections for their operational and long-term strategic planning. Take a bank, for example. The bank must forecast:

- Demands of various loans and deposits
- Money and credit conditions so that it can determine the cost of money it lends.

TYPES OF FORECASTS

The types of forecasts used by businesses and other organizations may be classified in several categories, depending on the objective and the situation for which a forecast is to be used. Two types are discussed below: sales forecasts and financial forecasts.

Sales Forecasts

As discussed in the previous section, the sales forecast gives the expected level of sales for the company's goods or services throughout some future period and is instrumental in the company's planning and budgeting functions. It is the key to other forecasts and plans.

Financial Forecasts

Although the sales forecast is the primary input to many financial decisions, some financial forecasts need to be made independently of sales forecasts. These include forecasts of financial variables such as the amount of external financing needed, earnings, cash flows, and the prediction of corporate bankruptcy.

FORECASTING METHODS

There is a wide range of forecasting techniques which the company may choose from. There are basically two approaches to forecasting: qualitative and quantitative. They are as follows:

Qualitative Approach: forecasts based on judgment and opinion.

- Executive opinions
- Delphi technique

- Sales force polling
- Consumer surveys
- Techniques for eliciting experts' opinions—PERT derived

Quantitative Approach:

(1) Historical forecasts

- Naive methods
- Moving averages
- Exponential smoothing
- Trend analysis
- Decomposition of time series

(2) Associative (Causal) forecasts

- Simple regression
- Multiple regression
- Econometric modeling

FIGURE 18-2 Forecasting Methods

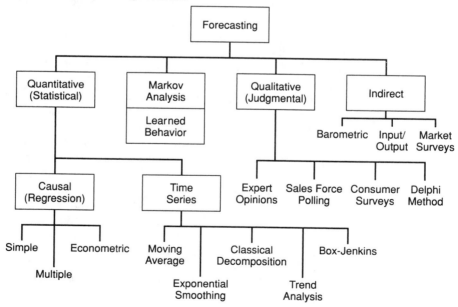

Figure 18-2 summarizes the forecasting methods. The list presented is neither comprehensive nor exhaustive. Sophisticated time series methods such as Box-Jenkins are reserved for an advanced forecasting text. Quantitative models work superbly as long as little or no systematic change in the environment occurs. When patterns or relationships do change, by themselves, the objective models are of little use. It is here where the qualitative approach based on human judgment is indispensable. Because judgmental forecasting also bases forecasts on observation of existing trends, they, too, are subject to a number of shortcomings. The advantage, however, is that they can identify systematic change more quickly and interpret better the effect of such change on the future.

The qualitative method is discussed in this chapter, while various quantitative methods along with their illustrations will be discussed in Chapters 21 through 25.

SELECTION OF FORECASTING METHOD

The choice of a forecasting technique is significantly influenced by the stage of the product life cycle, and sometimes by the firm or industry for which a decision is being made.

In the beginning of the product life cycle, relatively small expenditures are made for research and market investigation. During the first phase of product introduction, these expenditures start to increase. In the rapid growth stage, considerable amounts of money are involved in the decisions; therefore a high level of accuracy is desirable. After the product has entered the maturity stage, the decisions are more routine, involving marketing and manufacturing. These are important considerations when determining the appropriate sales forecast technique.

After evaluating the particular stages of the product, and firm and industry life cycles, a further probe is necessary. Instead of selecting a forecasting technique by using whatever seems applicable, decision—makers should determine what is appropriate. Some of the techniques are quite simple and rather inexpensive to develop and use, whereas others are extremely complex, require significant amounts of time to develop, and may be quite expensive. Some are best suited for short-term projections, whereas others are better prepared for intermediate- or long-term forecasts.

What technique or techniques to select depends on the following criteria:

1. What is the cost associated with developing the forecasting model compared with potential gains resulting from its use? The choice is one of benefit-cost trade-off.

2. How complicated are the relationships that are being forecasted?

3. Is it for short-run or long-run purposes?

4. How much accuracy is desired?

5. Is there a minimum tolerance level of errors?

6. How much data are available? Techniques vary in the amount of data they require.

THE QUALITATIVE APPROACH

The qualitative (or judgmental) approach can be useful in formulating short-term forecasts and also can supplement the projections based on the use of any of the qualitative methods. Four of the better known qualitative forecasting methods are Executive Opinions, the Delphi Method, Sales Force Polling, and Consumer Surveys.

Executive Opinions

The subjective views of executives or experts from sales, production, finance, purchasing and administration are averaged to generate a forecast about future sales. Usually this method is used in conjunction with some quantitative method such as trend extrapolation. The management team modifies the resulting forecast based on its expectations.

The advantage of this approach is that the forecasting is done quickly and easily, without need of elaborate statistics. Also, the jury of executive opinions may be the only feasible means of forecasting in the absence of adequate data. The disadvantage, however, is that of "group think." This is a set of problems inherent to those who meet as a group. Foremost among these problems are high cohesiveness, strong leadership, and insulation of the group. With high cohesiveness, the group becomes increasingly conforming through group pressure which helps stifle dissension and critical thought. Strong leadership fosters group pressure for unanimous opinion. Insulation of the group tends to separate the group from outside opinions, if given.

The Delphi Method

The Delphi Method is a group technique in which a panel of experts is individually questioned about its perceptions of future events. The experts do not meet as a group in order to reduce the possibility that consensus is reached because of dominant personality factors. Instead, the forecasts and accompanying arguments are summarized by an outside party and returned to the experts along with further questions. This continues until a consensus is reached

EXHIBIT 18-1 An Example of the Use of the Delphi Method

1 *Population* *(in Millions)*	*2* *Midpoint*	*3* *Number of* *Panelists*	*4* *Probability Distribution* *of Panelists*	*5* *Weighted* *Average* *(2 × 4)*
30 and above	—	0	.00	0
20–30	25	1	.05	1.25
15–19	17	2	.10	1.70
10–14	12	2	.10	1.20
5–9	7	7	.35	2.45
2–4	3	8	.40	1.20
Less than 2	1	0	.00	0
Total		20	1.00	7.80

Case example: "In 1982, a panel of 20 representatives, with college educations, from different parts of the U.S.A., were asked to estimate the population of Bombay, India. None of the panelists had been to India since World War I.
"The population was estimated to be 7.8 million, which is very close to the actual population."
Source: Singhvi, Surendra. "Financial Forecast: Why and How?" *Managerial Planning.* March/April, 1984.

by the group, especially after only a few rounds. This type of method is useful and quite effective for long-range forecasting. The technique is done by "questionnaire" format and thus it eliminates the disadvantages of group think. There is no committee or debate. The experts are not influenced by peer pressure to forecast a certain way, as the answer is not intended to be reached by consensus or unanimity. Low reliability is cited as the main disadvantage of the Delphi Method, as well as lack of consensus from the returns.

Sales Force Polling

Some companies use as a forecast source salespeople who have continual contacts with customers. They believe that the sales force who are closest to the ultimate customers may have significant insights regarding the state of the future market. Forecasts based on sales force polling may be averaged to develop a future forecast, or they may be used to modify other quantitative and/or qualitative forecasts that have been generated internally in the company.

The advantages to this method of forecasting are that:

1. it is simple to use and understand,

2. it uses the specialized knowledge of those closest to the action,

3. it can place responsibility for attaining the forecast in the hands of those who most affect the actual results, and

4. the information can be easily broken down by territory, product, customer or salesperson. The disadvantages include salespeople being overly optimistic or pessimistic regarding their predictions, and inaccuracies due to broader economic events that are largely beyond their control.

Consumer Surveys.

Some companies conduct their own market surveys regarding specific consumer purchases. Surveys may consist of telephone contacts, personal interviews, or questionnaires as a means of obtaining data. Extensive statistical analysis is usually applied to survey results in order to test hypotheses regarding consumer behavior.

PERT-Derived Forecasts

A technique known as PERT (Program Evaluation and Review Technique) has been useful in producing estimates based on subjective opinions such as executive opinions or sales force polling. The PERT methodology requires that the expert provide three estimates:

1. pessimistic (a),
2. the most likely (m), and
3. optimistic (b).

The theory suggests that these estimates combine to form an expected value, or forecast, as follows:

$$EV = (a + 4m + b)/6$$

with a standard deviation of

$$\sigma = (b - a)/6$$

where EV = expected value (mean) of the forecast

σ = standard deviation of the forecast

For example, suppose that management of a company believes that if the economy is in recession, the next year's sales will be $300,000 and if the economy is in prosperity $330,000. Their most likely estimate is $310,000. The PERT method generates an expected value of sales as follows:

$$EV = (\$300,000 + 4 (\$310,000) + \$330,000)/6 = \$311,667$$

with a standard deviation of

$$\sigma = (\$330,000 - \$300,000)/6 = \$5,000$$

Advantages: (1) It is often easier and more realistic to ask the expert to give optimistic, pessimistic and most likely estimates than a specific forecast value. (2) The PERT method includes a measure of dispersion (the standard deviation), which makes it possible to develop probabilistic statements regarding the forecast. For example, in the above example the forecaster is 95 percent confident that the true value of the forecasted sales lies between plus or minus two standard deviations from the mean ($311,667). That is the true value can be expected between $211,667 and $411,667.

COMMON FEATURES AND ASSUMPTIONS INHERENT IN FORECASTING

As pointed out, forecasting techniques are quite different from each other. But there are certain features and assumptions that underlie the business of forecasting. They are:

1. Forecasting techniques generally assume that the same underlying causal relationship that existed in the past will continue to prevail in the future. In other words, most of our techniques are based on historical data.
2. Forecasts are very rarely perfect. Therefore, for planning purposes, allowances should be made for inaccuracies. For example, the company should always maintain a safety stock in anticipation of stockouts.
3. Forecast accuracy decreases as the time period covered by the forecast (that is, the time horizon) increases. Generally speaking, a long-term forecast tends to be more inaccurate than a short-term forecast because of the greater uncertainty.
4. Forecasts for groups of items tend to be more accurate than forecasts for individual items, since forecasting errors among items in a group tend to cancel each other out. For example, industry forecasting is more accurate than individual firm forecasting.

STEPS IN THE FORECASTING PROCESS

There are five basic steps in the forecasting process. They are:

1. Determine the what and why of the forecast and what will be needed. This will indicate the level of detail required in the forecast (for example, forecast by region, forecast by product, etc.), the amount of resources (for example, computer hardware and software, manpower, etc.) that can be justified, and the level of accuracy desired.

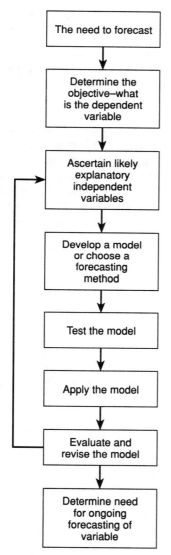

FIGURE 18-3 The Forecasting Process

2. Establish a time horizon, short term or long term. More specifically, project for the next year or next five years, etc.

3. Select a forecasting technique. Refer to the criteria discussed before.

4. Gather the data and develop a forecast.

5. Identify any assumptions that had to be made in preparing the forecast and using it.

6. Monitor the forecast to see if it is performing in a manner desired. Develop an evaluation system for this purpose. If not, go to Step 1.

CONCLUSION

Financial management uses forecasts for budgeting purposes. A forecast aids in determining volume of production, inventory needs, labor hours required, cash requirements, and financing needs. There is a variety of forecasting methods available. However, consideration has to be given to cost, preparation time, accuracy, and time period involved. The assumptions that a particular forecast method is based on must be clearly understood by the budget analyst to obtain maximum benefit.

Chapter 19

Evaluation of Forecasts Used for Budgeting

The cost of a prediction error can be substantial. The forecaster must always find ways to improve his forecasts. That means that he might want to examine some objective evaluations of alternative forecasting techniques. This section presents the guidelines he or she needs. Two evaluation techniques are presented here. The first is in the form of a checklist. A forecaster could use it to evaluate either a new model he or she is in the process of developing or an existing model. The second is a statistical technique for evaluating a model.

COST OF PREDICTION ERRORS

There is always a cost involved with a failure to predict a certain variable accurately. It is important to determine the cost of the prediction error in order to minimize the potentially detrimental effect on the future profitability of the company. The cost of the prediction error can be substantial, depending upon the circumstances. For example, failure to make an accurate projection on sales could result in poor production planning, too much or too little purchase of labor, and so on, thereby causing potentially huge financial losses.

The cost of the prediction error is basically the contribution or profit lost on an inaccurate prediction. It can be measured in terms of lost sales, disgruntled customers, and idle machines.

EXAMPLE 19-1   Assume that a company has been selling a toy doll costing $.60 for a price of $1.00 each. The fixed cost is $300. The company has no privilege of returning any unsold dolls. It has predicted sales of 2,000 units. However, unforeseen competition has reduced sales to 1,500 units. Then the cost of its prediction error—that is, its failure to predict demand accurately—would be calculated as follows:

1. Initial predicted sales = 2,000 units.

   Optimal decision: purchase 2,000 units.

   Expected net income = $500 [(2,000 units × $.40 contribution) − $300 fixed costs]

2. Alternative parameter value = 1,500 units.

   Optimal decision: purchase 1,500 units.

   Expected net income = $300 [(1,500 units × $.40 contribution) − $300 fixed costs]

3. Results of original decision under alternative parameter value.

   Expected net income:

   Revenue (1,500 units × $1.00) − Cost of dolls (2,000 units × $.60) − $300 fixed costs = $1,500 − $1,200 − $300 = $0.

4. Cost of prediction error, (2) − (3) = $300.

FORECAST EVALUATION CHECKLIST

Two main items to be checked are the data and the model with its accompanying assumptions. The questions to be raised are the following:

1. Is the source reliable and accurate?
2. If using more than one source that is reliable and accurate, is the source used the best?
3. Are the data the most recent available?
4. If the answer to question 3 is yes, are the data subject to subsequent revision?
5. Is there any known systematic bias in the data which may be dealt with?

The model and its accompanying assumptions should be similarly examined. Among other things, the model must make sense from a theoretical standpoint. The assumptions should be clearly stated and tested, as well.

MEASURING ACCURACY OF FORECASTS

The performance of a forecast should be checked against its own record or against that of other forecasts. There are various statistical measures that can be used to measure performance of the model. Of course, the performance is measured in terms of forecasting error, where error is defined as the difference between a predicted value and the actual result.

$$\text{Error } (e) = \text{Actual } (A) - \text{Forecast } (F)$$

MAD, MSE, RMSE, and MAPE

The commonly used measures for summarizing historical errors include the *mean absolute deviation* (MAD), the *mean squared error* (MSE), the *root mean squared error* (RMSE), and the *mean absolute percentage error* (MAPE). The formulas used to calculate MAD, MSE, and RMSE are:

$$\text{MAD} = \Sigma \mid e \mid /n$$

$$\text{MSE} = \Sigma \, e^2/n - 1$$

$$\text{RMSE} = \sqrt{\Sigma e^2/n}$$

Sometimes it is more useful to compute the forecasting errors in percentages rather than in amounts. The MAPE is calculated by finding the absolute error in each period, dividing this by the actual value of that period, and then averaging these absolute percentage errors, as shown below.

$$\text{MAPE} = \Sigma \mid e \mid /A /n$$

The following example illustrates the computation of MAD, MSE, RMSE, and MAPE.

EXAMPLE 19-2   Sales data of a microwave oven manufacturer are given below:

Period	Actual (A)	Forecast (F)	e(A–F)	|e|	e^2	Absolute Percent Error |e|/A
1	217	215	2	2	4	.0092
2	213	216	−3	3	9	.0014
3	216	215	1	1	1	.0046
4	210	214	−4	4	16	.0190
5	213	211	2	2	4	.0094
6	219	214	5	5	25	.0023
7	216	217	−1	1	1	.0046
8	212	216	−4	4	16	.0019
			−2	22	76	.0524

Using the figures,

$$\text{MAD} = \Sigma \mid e \mid /n \quad 22/8 = 2.75$$

$$\text{MSE} = \Sigma \, e^2/(n-1) = 76/7 = 10.86$$

$$\text{RMSE} = \sqrt{\Sigma \, e^2/n} = 76/8 = \text{SQRT } 9.5 = 3.08$$

$$\text{MAPE} = \Sigma \mid e \mid /A \, /n = .0524/8 = .0066$$

One way these measures are used is to evaluate the forecasting ability of alternative forecasting methods. For example, using either MAD or MSE, a forecaster could compare the results of exponential smoothing with alphas and elect the one that performed best in terms of the lowest MAD or MSE for a given set of data. Also, it can help select the best initial forecast value for exponential smoothing.

The *U* Statistic and Turning Point Errors

There are still several statistical measures for measuring accuracy of the forecast. Two standards may be identified. First, one could compare the forecast being evaluated with a naive forecast to see if there are vast differences. The naive forecast can be anything like the same as last year, moving average, or the output of an exponential smoothing technique. In the second case, the forecast may be compared with the outcome when there is enough to do so. The comparison may be with the actual level of the variable forecasted, or the change observed may be compared with the change forecast.

The Theil *U* Statistic is based upon a comparison of the predicted change with the observed change. It is calculated as:

$$U = (1/n) \, \Sigma \, (F - A)^2/(1/n) \, \Sigma \, F^2 + (1/n) \, \Sigma \, A^2$$

As can be seen, $U = 0$ is a perfect forecast, since the forecast would equal actual and $F - A = 0$ for all observations. At the other extreme, $U = 1$ would be a case of all incorrect forecasts. The smaller the value of U, the more accurate are the forecasts. If U is greater than or equal to 1, the predictive ability of the model is lower than a naive no-change extrapolation. *Note:* Many computer software packages routinely compute the *U* Statistic.

Still other evaluation techniques consider the number of turning point errors which is based on the total number of reversals of trends. The turning point error is also known as "error in the direction of prediction." In a certain case, such as interest rate forecasts, the turning point error is more serious than the accuracy of the forecast.

Figure 19-1 Monitoring Forecast Errors

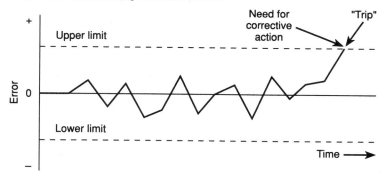

CONTROL OF FORECASTS

It is important to monitor forecast errors to ensure that the forecast is performing well. If the model is performing poorly based on some criteria, the forecaster might reconsider the use of the existing model or might switch to another forecasting model or technique. The forecasting control can be accomplished by comparing forecasting errors to predetermined values or limits. Errors that fall within the limits would be judged acceptable while errors outside of the limits would signal that corrective action is desirable (see Figure 19-1).

Tracking Signals

Forecasts can be monitored using either tracking signals or control charts. A tracking signal is based on the ratio of cumulative forecast error to the corresponding value of MAD.

$$\text{Tracking signal} = \Sigma \, (A - F)/\text{MAD}$$

The resulting tracking signal values are compared to predetermined limits. These are based on experience and judgment and often range from plus or minus 3 to plus or minus 8. Values within the limits suggest that the forecast is performing adequately. By the same token, when the signal goes beyond this range, corrective action is appropriate.

EXAMPLE 19-3   Referring to Example 19-1, the deviation and cumulative deviation have already been computed:

$$\text{MAD} = \Sigma \mid A - F \mid /n = 22/8 = 2.75$$

$$\text{Tracking signal} = \Sigma \, (A - F)/\text{MAD} = -2/2.75 = -0.73$$

A tracking signal is as low as −0.73, which is substantially below the limit (−3 to −8). It would not suggest any action at this time.

Note: After an initial value of MAD has been computed, the estimate of the MAD can be continually updated using exponential smoothing.

$$\text{MAD}_t = \alpha \, (A - F) + (1 - \alpha) \, \text{MAD}_{t-1}$$

Control Charts

The control chart approach involves setting upper and lower limits for individual forecasting errors instead of for cumulative errors. The limits are multiples of the estimated standard deviation of forecast, S_f, which is the square root of MSE. Frequently, control limits are set at 2 or 3 standard deviations.

$$\pm 2 \, (\text{or } 3) \, S_f$$

Note: Plot the errors and determine if all errors are within the limits, so that the forecaster can visualize the process and can determine if the method being used is in control.

EXAMPLE 19-4 For the sales data below, using the naive forecast, you can determine if the forecast is in control. For illustrative purposes, 2 sigma control limits are used.

Year	Sales	Forecasts	Error	Error^2
1	320			
2	326	320	6	36
3	310	326	−16	256
4	317	310	7	49
5	315	317	−2	4
6	318	315	3	9
7	310	318	−8	64
8	316	310	6	36
9	314	316	−2	4
10	317	314	3	9
			−3	467

First, compute the standard deviation of forecast errors as follows:

$$S_f = \sqrt{e^2 / (n - 1)} = \sqrt{467/(9 - 1)} = 7.64$$

Two sigma limits are then plus or minus 2(7.64) = − 15.28 to + 15.28

Figure 19-2 Control Chart for Forecasting Errors

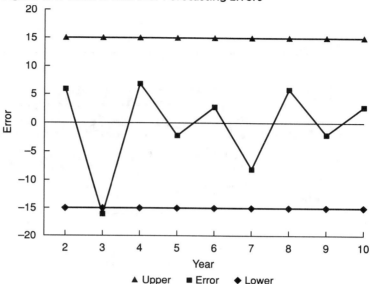

Note: The forecast error for year 3 is below the lower bound, so the forecast is not in control (see Figure 19-2). The use of other methods such as moving average, exponential smoothing, or regression would possibly achieve a better forecast.

Note: A system of monitoring forecasts needs to be developed. The computer may be programmed to print a report showing the past history when the tracking signal "trips" a limit. For example, when a type of exponential smoothing is used, the system may try a different value of α (so the forecast will be more responsive) and continue forecasting.

Chapter 20

Financial Forecasting and a CPA's Involvement in Prospective Financial Statements

Financial forecasting, an essential element of planning, is the basis for budgeting activities. It is also needed when estimating future financing requirements. The company may look either internally or externally for financing. Internal financing refers to cash flow generated by the company's normal operating activities. External financing refers to capital provided by parties external to the company. You need to analyze how to estimate *external* financing requirements. Basically, forecasts of future sales and related expenses provide the firm with the information to project future external financing needs. This chapter discusses:

1. the percent-of-sales method to forecast the amount of external financing needed,

2. the CPA's involvement in prospective financial statements, and

3. earnings forecast.

THE PERCENT-OF-SALES METHOD FOR FINANCIAL FORECASTING

Percent of sales is the most widely used method for projecting the company's financing needs. This method involves estimating the various expenses, assets, and liabilities for a future period as a percent of the sales forecast and then using these percentages, together with the projected sales, to construct pro forma balance sheets.

Basically, forecasts of future sales and their related expenses provide the firm with the information needed to project its future needs for financing. The basic steps in projecting financing needs are:

1. Project the firm's sales. The sales forecast is the most important initial step. Most other forecasts (budgets) follow the sales forecast.

2. Project additional variables such as expenses.

3. Estimate the level of investment in current and fixed assets required to support the projected sales.

4. Calculate the firm's financing needs.

The following example illustrates how to develop a pro forma balance sheet and how to determine the amount of external financing needed.

EXAMPLE 20-1 Assume that sales for 19X1 = $20, projected sales for 19X2 = $24, net income = 5 percent of sales, and the dividend payout ratio = 40 percent. Exhibit 20-1 illustrates the method, step by step. All dollar amounts are in millions.

EXHIBIT 20-1 Pro Forma Balance Sheet (in Millions of Dollars)

	Present (19X1)	% of Sales (19X1 Sales =$20)	Projected (19X2 Sales =$24)	
Assets				
Current assets	2	10	2.4	
Fixed assets	4	20	4.8	
Total assets	6		7.2	
Liabilities and Stockholders' Equity				
Current liabilities	2	10	2.4	
Long-term debt	2.5	n.a.	2.5	
Total liabilities	4.5		4.9	
Common stock	0.1	n.a.	0.1	
Paid-in capital	0.2	n.a.	0.2	
Retained earnings	1.2		1.92 (a)	
Total equity	1.5		2.22	
Total liabilities and stockholders' equity	6		7.12	Total financing provided
			0.08 (b)	External financing needed
			7.2	Total

(a) 19X2 retained earnings = 19X1 retained earnings + projected net income
        − cash dividends paid
        =$1.2 + 5% ($24) − 40%[5%($24)]
        =$1.2 + $1.2 − $0.48 = $2.4 − 0.48 = $1.92
(b) External financing needed = projected total assets − (projected total
        liabilities + projected equity)
        =$7.2 − ($4.9 + $2.22) = $7.2 − $7.12 = $0.08

The steps for the computations are outlined as follows:

Step 1. Express those balance sheet items that vary directly with sales as a percentage of sales. Any item such as long-term debt that does not vary directly with sales is designated "n.a.," or "not applicable."

Step 2. Multiply these percentages by the 19X2 projected sales = $24 to obtain the projected amounts as shown in the last column.

Step 3. Simply insert figures for long-term debt, common stock and paid-in-capital from the 19X1 balance sheet.

Step 4. Compute 19X2 retained earnings as shown in (b).

Step 5. Sum the asset accounts, obtaining a total projected assets of $7.2, and also add the projected liabilities and equity to obtain $7.12, the total financing provided. Since liabilities and equity must total $7.2, but only $7.12 is projected, we have a shortfall of $0.08 "external financing needed."

Thus, the amount of external financing needed is $800,000, which can be raised by issuing notes payable, bonds, stocks, or any combination of these financing sources.

The major advantage of the percent-of-sales method of financial forecasting is that it is simple and inexpensive to use. One important assumption behind the use of the method is that the firm is operating at full capacity. This means that the company has no sufficient productive capacity to absorb a projected increase in sales and thus requires additional investment in assets. Therefore, the method must be used with extreme caution if excess capacity exists in certain asset accounts. To obtain a more precise projection of the firm's future financing needs, however, the preparation of a cash budget may be required.

THE CERTIFIED PUBLIC ACCOUNTANT'S INVOLVEMENT AND RESPONSIBILITY WITH PROSPECTIVE FINANCIAL STATEMENTS

The American Institute of Certified Public Accountants (AICPA) in Statement of Position 45-4 provides guidelines for business enterprises which publish financial forecasts. Improved financial forecasting should be of concern to the AICPA and the Securities and Exchange Commission as a basis for financial decision making, for security analysis, and in affecting the future market value of securities through investor expectations. Exhibit 20-2 presents an excerpt from the 1983 Annual Report of Masco Corporation which contains:

1. a five-year cash flow forecast,
2. forecasts of a five-year growth rate for sales, and
3. key assumptions used in the forecasts.

EXHIBIT 20-2 Management Forecast Disclosure by Masco Corporation
FIVE-YEAR FORECAST

We have included in this annual report a sales forecast for each of our major product lines and operating groups for 1988.

While we recognize that long-term forecasts are subject to many variables and uncertainties, our experience has been that our success is determined more by our own activities than by the performance of any industry or the economy in general. In addition, the balance and diversity of our products and markets have been such that a shortfall in expected performance in one area has been largely offset by higher than anticipated growth in another.

Although variations may occur in the forecast for any individual product line, we have a relatively high level of confidence that our overall five-year growth forecast is achievable.

ASSUMPTIONS USED IN FORECAST

1. Average 2–3 percent annual real growth in GNP.
2. Average inflation 5–7 percent.
3. Present tax structure to continue.
4. No change in currency exchange rates.
5. No acquisitions.
6. No additional financing.
7. Dividend payout ratio 20 percent.
8. Four percent after-tax return on investment of excess cash.
9. No exercise of stock options.

FIVE-YEAR CASH FLOW FORECAST

(in Thousands)	*1984–1988*
Net Income	$850,000
Depreciation	280,000
	1,130,000
Working Capital	(230,000)
Note Payments	(280,000)
Capital Expenditures	(260,000)
Dividends	(170,000)
Net Cash Change	190,000
Beginning Cash, 1-1-84	210,000
Cash, 12-31-88	$400,000

SALES GROWTH BY PRODUCTS

	Sales Forecast		Actual Sales *(in Thousands)*		
	5-Year Growth Rate 1984–1988	1988	5-Year Growth Rate 1979–1983	1983	1978
Products for the Home and Family	14%	$1,225,000	16%	$638,000	$308,000
Products for Industry	16%	875,000	9%	421,000	278,000
Total Sales	15%	$2,100,000	13%	$1,059,000	$586,000

SALES GROWTH BY SPECIFIC MARKETS AND PRODUCTS[1][2]

	Forecast		Actual *(in Thousands)*		
	5-Year Growth Rate 1984–1988	*1988*	*5-Year Growth Rate 1979–1983*	*1983*	*1978*
Masco Faucet Sales[3]	15%	$490,000	9%	$243,000	$155,000
Faucet Industry Sales-Units	7%	35,000	(5)%	25,000	32,000
Masco Market Share-Units	2%	38%	5%	34%	27%
Housing Completions	4%	1,700	(4)%	1,400	1,700
Independent Cold Extrusion Industry Sales	13%	$580,000	1%	$310,000	$290,000
Masco Cold Extrusion Sales[3]	14%	$170,000	5%	$88,000	$70,000
Truck Production	7%	3,400	(8)%	2,400	3,700
Auto Production	4%	8,200	(6)%	6,800	9,200
Masco Auto Parts Sales	13%	$210,000	8%	$113,000	$76,000

(1) Excludes foreign sales. (2) Industry data Masco estimates. (3) Includes foreign sales.
Source: 1983 Annual Report of Masco Corporation, p. 42.

There are three types of functions that CPAs can perform with respect to prospective financial statements that will be relied upon by third parties: examination, compilation, and application of agreed-upon procedures. CPAs must prepare prospective financial statements according to AICPA standards. There must be disclosure of the underlying assumptions.

Prospective financial statements may be for general use or limited use. General use is for those not directly dealing with the client. The general user may take the deal or leave it. Limited use is for those having a direct relationship with the client.

Prospective financial statements may be presented as a complete set of financial statements (balance sheet, income statement, and statement of cash flows). However, in most cases, it is more practical to present them in summarized or condensed form. At a minimum, the financial statement items to be presented are:

- Sales
- Gross margin
- Nonrecurring items
- Taxes
- Income from continuing operations
- Income from discontinued operations
- Net income
- Primary and fully diluted earnings per share
- Material changes in financial position.

Pro-forma financial statements and partial presentations are not considered prospective financial statements.

The American Institute of CPA's Code of Professional Ethics includes the following guidelines regarding prospective financial statements:

- Cannot vouch for the achievability of prospective results
- Must disclose assumptions
- Accountant's report must state the nature of the work performed and the degree of responsibility assumed.

CPAs are not permitted to furnish services on prospective financial statements if the statements are solely appropriate for limited use but are distributed to parties not involved directly with the issuing company. They are not allowed to use plain-paper services on prospective financial statements for third-party use.

FINANCIAL FORECAST

A prospective financial statement may be classified as either a forecast or a projection. A financial forecast presents management's expectations, and there is an expectation that all assumptions will take place. *Note:* A financial forecast encompasses a presentation that management expects to occur but that is not necessarily most probable. A financial forecast may be most useful to general users, since it presents the client's expectations. A financial forecast and not a financial projection may be issued to passive users, or those not negotiating directly with the client.

A financial forecast may be given a single monetary amount based on the best estimate, or as a reasonable range. *Caution:* This range must not be chosen in a misleading manner.

Irrespective of the accountant's involvement, management is the only one who has responsibility for the presentation because only management knows how it plans to run the business and accomplish its plans.

FINANCIAL PROJECTION

A financial projection presents a "what-if" scenario that management does not necessarily expect to occur. However, a given assumption may actually occur if management moves in that direction. A financial projection may be most beneficial for limited users, since they may seek answers to hypothetical questions based on varying assumptions. These users may wish to alter their scenarios based on anticipated changing situations. A financial projection, like a forecast, may contain a range.

A financial projection may be presented to general users only if it supplements a financial forecast. Financial projections are not permitted in tax shelter offerings and other general-use documents.

TYPES OF ENGAGEMENTS

The following five types of engagements may be performed by the CPA in connection with prospective financial statements:

Plain paper: The CPA's name is not associated with the prospective statements. This service can only be conducted if all of the following conditions are satisfied:

- The CPA is not reporting on the presentation.
- The prospective statements are on paper not identifying the accountant.
- The prospective financial statements are not shown with historical financial statements that have been audited, reviewed, or compiled by the CPA.

Internal use: The prospective financial statements are only assembled, meaning mathematical and clerical functions are performed. Assembling financial data is permitted if the following two criteria exist:

- Third parties will not use the statements.
- The CPA's name is associated with the statement.

Note that assembling prospective financial statements is limited only to internal use. Appropriate language on the statements might be "For Internal Use Only."

Compilation: This is the lowest level of service performed for prospective financial statements directed for third parties. The compilation engagement involves:

- Assembling prospective data.
- The conduct of procedures to ascertain whether the presentation and assumptions are appropriate.
- Preparation of a compilation report.

With a compilation, no assurance is given regarding the presentation or assumptions, but rather it serves to identify obvious matters to be investigated further. Working papers must be prepared to show that there was proper planning and supervision of the work, as well as compliance with required compilation procedures. The CPA must also obtain a management letter from the client regarding representations given to him.

Warning: A compilation should not be made when the forecasted financial statements exclude disclosure of the significant assumptions or when the financial projections exclude the hypothetical assumptions.

Agreed-upon procedures: This relates to applying procedures agreed to or requested by specific users, and to issuing a report. The report identifies the procedures undertaken, gives the accountant's findings, and restricts distribution of the report to the particular parties. The specified users have to participate in establishing the nature and procedures. Also, the procedures undertaken must be more than just reading the prospective data.

Examination: The CPA appraises the preparation underlying the supporting assumptions and the presentation of prospective financial information in accordance with AICPA standards. A report is then issued on whether AICPA guidelines have been adhered to and whether the assumptions are reasonable. It is the highest level of assurance. An adverse opinion must be given if there is a failure to disclose a material assumption or if disclosed assumptions are unreasonable. For example, there may not be reasonable expectation that the actual figure will fall within the range of assumptions presented in a forecast having a range. A disclaimer opinion is necessary in the event of a scope limitation, such as when a required examination procedure cannot be performed because of client restrictions or inappropriate circumstances.

EARNINGS FORECAST

For many years financial analysts have predicted earnings per share and stock price performance. Considerable emphasis has been placed on such forecasts in order to provide guidance to investors. Recently, management forecast disclosures in financial statements have placed greater emphasis on the development of forecasting methodology in this area. The accuracy of these earnings forecasts has been given much attention recently primarily due to the SEC's position on financial forecasts and issuance of a Statement of Position by the AICPA.

EXHIBIT 20-3

A. Description of Data

Price—Price as of the day prior to date of report; shown in eighths.

Actual—Fiscal Year and EPS Earnings per share for the most recently reported fiscal year end. Industry and Sector aggregates are computed by share-weighting the EPS of each constituent company.

Estimates—Fiscal Year One and Fiscal Year Two Mean—Average of all available estimates. Aggregates are share weighted.

Percent Change—Actual—Percent change of mean estimate from last year's actual EPS.

Relative—Percent change of mean estimate from last year's actual EPS relative to the average change for all I/B/E/S Summary Data companies (unweighted).

6 mo.—Percent change of mean estimate from its level 6 months ago.

Revisions—% up—Percent of estimates revised up since last month.

% down—Percent of estimates revised down since last month.

Coefficient of Variation—Coefficient of variation—Industry and sector aggregates are net income weighted, i.e., individual company coefficients of variation are weighted by their shares times their mean estimate.

Estimated 5 Yr. Growth Rate—The median or mid-point in the series of reported estimates. Aggregates are net income weighted.

S.D.—Standard deviation of the estimates for long term growth; indicates the range in percentage points within which 2/3rds of the estimated growth rates fall. Aggregates are net income weighted.

B. Data for International Oils (Industry and Firm Level), March 1985

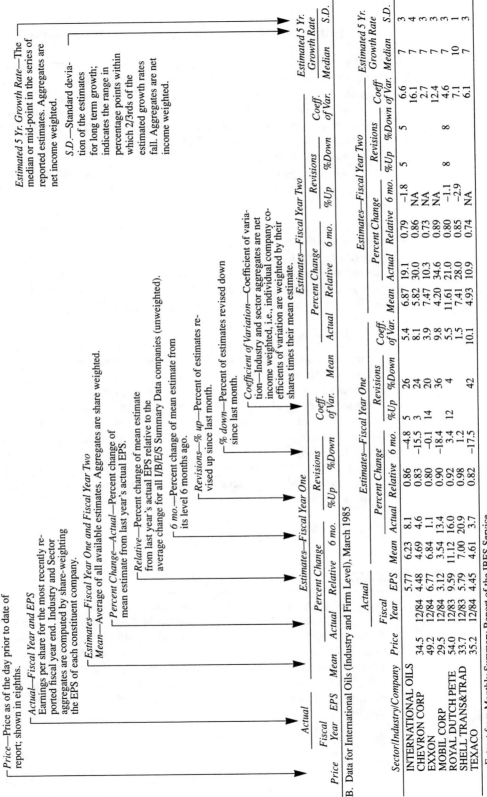

Sector/Industry/Company	Price	Actual Fiscal Year	Actual EPS	FY1 Mean	FY1 %Chg Actual	FY1 %Chg Relative	FY1 %Chg 6 mo.	FY1 Rev %Up	FY1 Rev %Down	FY1 Coeff. of Var.	FY2 Mean	FY2 %Chg Actual	FY2 %Chg Relative	FY2 %Chg 6 mo.	FY2 Rev %Up	FY2 Rev %Down	FY2 Coeff. of Var.	5 Yr. Growth Median	5 Yr. Growth S.D.
INTERNATIONAL OILS			5.77	6.23	8.1	0.86	-4.8	5	26	5.4	6.87	19.1	0.79	-1.8	5	5	6.6	7	3
CHEVRON CORP	34.5	12/84	4.48	4.69	4.6	0.83	-15.5	3	24	8.1	5.82	30.0	0.86	NA			16.1	7	4
EXXON	49.2	12/84	6.77	6.84	1.1	0.80	-0.1	14	20	3.9	7.47	10.3	0.73	NA			2.7	7	3
MOBIL CORP	29.5	12/84	3.12	3.54	13.4	0.90	-18.4		36	9.8	4.20	34.6	0.89	NA			12.4	7	3
ROYAL DUTCH PETE	54.0	12/83	9.59	11.12	16.0	0.92	3.4	12	4	5.5	11.61	21.0	0.80	-1.1	8	8	4.6	7	3
SHELL TRANS&TRAD	33.7	12/83	5.79	7.00	20.9	0.98	1.2			1.5	7.41	28.0	0.85	-2.9			7.1	10	1
TEXACO	35.2	12/84	4.45	4.61	3.7	0.82	-17.5		42	10.1	4.93	10.9	0.74	NA			6.1	7	3

Extract from Monthly Summary Report of the IBES Service

Source: Lynch, Jones, and Ryan, *IBES Monthly Summary Data* (New York, NY).

EXHIBIT 20-4*

Pros and Cons of Security Analyst and Univariate Time-Series Model Approaches to Forecasting

SECURITY ANALYST APPROACH TO FORECASTING

Pros

1. Ability to incorporate information from many sources.
2. Ability to adjust to structural change immediately.
3. Ability to update continually as new information becomes available.

Cons

1. High initial setup cost and high ongoing cost to monitor numerous variables, make company visits, and so on.
2. Heavy dependence on the skills of a single individual.
3. Analyst may have an incentive not to provide an unbiased forecast (e.g., due to pressure to conform to consensus forecasts).
4. Analyst may be manipulated by company officials (at least in the short run).

UNIVARIATE TIME-SERIES MODEL APPROACH TO FORECASTING

Pros

1. Ability to detect and exploit systematic patterns in the past series.
2. Relatively low degree of subjectivity in the forecasting (especially given the availability of computer algorithms to identify and estimate models).
3. Low cost and ease of updating.
4. Ability to compute confidence intervals around the forecasts.

Cons

1. Limited number of observations available for newly formed firms, firms with structural change, and so on.
2. Financial statement data may not satisfy distributional assumptions of time-series model used.
3. Inability to update forecasts between successive interim or annual earnings releases.
4. Difficulty of communicating approach to clients (especially the statistical methodology used in identifying and estimating univariate models).

* Source: Foster, George, *Financial Statement Analysis,* 2nd ed., Prentice-Hall, Englewood Cliffs, N.J., 1986, p. 278.

Security Analysts vs. Time-Series Models

Forecasts of earnings per share (EPS) for business firms are published by both management and security analysts. Unfortunately, however, the accuracy of EPS forecasts by security analysts has been shown to be little if any better than that produced by some "naive" models such as extrapolating the past trend of earnings. Indeed, it increasingly appears that the change in EPS may be a random variable.

Projections of EPS are frequently made by independent security analysts. Examples of forecast sources include:

1. Value Line Investment Survey,
2. Lynch, Jones and Ryan's Institutional Brokers Estimate System (IBES),
3. Standard & Poor's The Earnings Forecaster, and
4. Zacks Investment Research's Icarus Service.

Exhibit 20-3 presents an excerpt from the monthly report from Lynch, Jones, and Ryan's IBES Service which contains various earnings forecasts by individual security analysts. Exhibit 20-4 summarizes the pros and cons of both approaches.

Exhibit 20-5 shows sources of earnings forecasting data preferred by financial analysts.

EXHIBIT 20-5 What Are Your Present Sources of Earnings Forecasting Data?

Rank	1	2	3	4	5
Company contacts	56	28	24	8	9
Own research	55	15	5	1	
Industry statistics	19	14	14	7	
Other analysis	12	17	2	8	11
Historical financial data	8	12	8	5	4
Economic forecasts	7	7	10	3	
Competition	1	7	2	6	1
Computer simulation					2
Field trips		1			
Government agencies			2		
Industry & trade sources	1	7	17	3	5
Public relations of a promotional nature					1
Retired directors					1
Rumor					2
Wall Street sources	1	4	9	3	4

Rank   1 = most preferred
              5 = least preferred

Source: Carper, Brent W., Barton Jr., Frank M., Wunder Haroldene F. "The Future of Forecasting." *Management Accounting*. August, 1979. pp. 27–31.

CONCLUSION

Financial forecasting, an essential element of planning, is a vital function of financial managers. It is needed where the future financing needs are being estimated. Basically, forecasts of future sales and their related expenses provide the firm with the information needed to project its financing requirements. Furthermore, financial forecasting involves earnings forecasts which provide useful information concerning the expectations of a firm's future total market return. This is of interest to budget analysts. Also presented was a CPA's involvement with prospective financial statements.

Chapter 21

Moving Averages and Smoothing Methods

This chapter discusses several forecasting methods that fall in the quantitative approach category. The discussion includes naive models, moving averages, and exponential smoothing. Trend analysis and regressions are covered in future chapters. The qualitative methods were described in the previous chapter.

NAIVE MODELS

Naive forecasting models are based exclusively on historical observation of sales or other variables such as earnings and cash flows. They do not attempt to explain the underlying causal relationships which produce the variable being forecast.

Naive models may be classified into two groups. One group consists of simple projection models. These models require inputs of data from recent observations, but no statistical analysis is performed. The second group is composed of models, while naive, are nevertheless complex enough to require a computer. Traditional methods such as classical decomposition, moving average, and exponential smoothing models are some examples.

Advantages: It is inexpensive to develop, store data, and operate.

Disadvantages: It does not consider any possible causal relationships that underly the forecasted variable.

1. A simple example of a naive model type would be to use the actual sales of the current period as the forecast for the next period. Let us use the symbol Y'_{t+1} as the forecast value and the symbol Y_t as the actual value. Then,

$$Y'_{t+1} = Y_t$$

2. If you consider trends, then

$$Y'_{t+1} = Y_t + (Y_t - Y_{t-1})$$

This model adds the latest observed absolute period-to-period change to the most recent observed level of the variable.

3. If you want to incorporate the rate of change rather than the absolute amount, then

$$Y'_{t+1} = Y_t \frac{Y_t}{Y_{t-1}}$$

EXAMPLE 21-1 Consider the following sales data:

Month	19X1 Monthly Sales of Product
1	$3,050
2	2,980
3	3,670
4	2,910
5	3,340
6	4,060
7	4,750
8	5,510
9	5,280
10	5,504
11	5,810
12	6,100

We will develop forecasts for January 19X2 based on the aforementioned three models:

1. $Y'_{t+1} = Y_t = \$6,100$

2. $Y'_{t+1} = Y_t + (Y_t - Y_{t-1}) = \$6,100 + (\$5,810 - \$5,504)$
$$= \$6,100 + \$306 = \$6,406$$

3.
$$Y'_{t+1} = Y_t \frac{Y_t}{Y_{t-1}}$$

$$= \$6,100 \times \frac{\$6,100}{5,810} = \$6,100 \,(1.05)$$

$$= \$6,405$$

The naive models can be applied, with very little need of a computer, to develop forecasts for sales, earnings, and cash flows. They must be compared with more sophisticated models such as the regression and Box-Jenkins methods for forecasting efficiency.

SMOOTHING TECHNIQUES

Smoothing techniques are a higher form of naive models. There are two typical forms: moving average and exponential smoothing. Moving average is the simpler of the two forms.

Moving Averages

Moving averages are averages that are updated as new information is received. With the moving average, a manager simply employs the most recent observations to calculate an average, which is used as the forecast for the next period.

EXAMPLE 21-2   Assume that the marketing manager has the following sales data.

Date	Actual Sales (Y_t)
Jan. 1	46
2	54
3	53
4	46
5	58
6	49
7	54

In order to predict the sales for the seventh and eighth days of January, the manager must pick the number of observations for averaging purposes. Consider two cases: one is a six-day moving average and the other is a three-day average.

Case 1

$$Y'_7 = \frac{46 + 54 + 53 + 46 + 58 + 49}{6} = 51$$

$$Y'_8 = \frac{54 + 53 + 46 + 58 + 49 + 54}{6} = 52.3$$

where Y' = predicted

Case 2

$$Y'_7 = \frac{46 + 58 + 49}{3} = 51$$

$$Y'_8 = \frac{58 + 49 + 54}{3} = 53.6$$

Date	Actual Sales	Predicted Sales (Y'_t) Case 1	Case 2
Jan. 1	46		
2	54		
3	53		
4	46		
5	58		51
6	49		53.6
7	54	51	
8		52.3	

In terms of weights given to observations, in Case 1, the old data received a weight of 5/6, and the current observation got a weight of 1/6. In Case 2, the old data received a weight of only 2/3 while the current observation received a weight of 1/3.

Thus, the marketing manager's choice of the number of periods to use in a moving average is a measure of the relative importance attached to old versus current data.

The moving average is simple to use and easy to understand. However, there are two shortcomings.

1. It requires you to retain a great deal of data and carry it along with you from forecast period to forecast period.
2. All data in the sample are weighted equally. If more recent data are more valid than older data, why not give it greater weight?

The forecasting method known as exponential smoothing discussed below overcomes these disadvantages.

Exponential Smoothing

Exponential smoothing is a popular technique for short-run forecasting by financial managers. It uses a weighted average of past data as the basis for a forecast. The procedure gives heaviest weight to more recent information and smaller weight to observations in the more distant past. The reason for this is that the future is more dependent upon the recent past than on the distant past.

The method is known to be effective when there is randomness and no seasonal fluctuations in the data. One disadvantage of the method, however, is that it does not include industrial or economic factors such as market conditions, prices, or the effects of competitors' actions.

The Model

The formula for exponential smoothing is:

$$Y'_{t+1} = \alpha\, Y_t + (1 - \alpha)\, Y'_t$$

or in words,

$$Y'_{new} = \alpha Y_{old} + (1 - \alpha) Y'_{old}$$

where Y'_{new} = Exponentially smoothed average to be used as the forecast.
Y_{old} = Most recent actual data.
Y'_{old} = Most recent smoothed forecast.
α = Smoothing constant.
The higher the α, the higher the weight given to the more recent information.

EXAMPLE 21-3 The following data on sales are given below.

Time period (t)	Actual sales (1,000) (Y_t)
1	$60.0
2	64.0
3	58.0
4	66.0
5	70.0
6	60.0
7	70.0
8	74.0
9	62.0
10	74.0
11	68.0
12	66.0
13	60.0
14	66.0
15	62.0

To initialize the exponential smoothing process, you must have the initial forecast. The first smoothed forecast to be used can be:

1. First actual observations.

2. An average of the actual data for a few periods.

For illustrative purposes, use a six-period average as the initial forecast Y'_7 with a smoothing constant of $\alpha = 0.40$.

$$\text{Then } Y'_7 = (Y_1 + Y_2 + Y_3 + Y_4 + Y_5 + Y_6)/6$$
$$= (60 + 64 + 58 + 66 + 70 + 60)/6 = 63$$

Note that $Y_7 = 70$. Then Y'_8 is computed as follows:

$$Y'_8 = \alpha Y_7 + (1 - \alpha) Y'_7$$
$$= (0.40)(70) + (0.60)(63)$$
$$= 28.0 + 37.80 = 65.80$$

Similarly:

$$Y'_9 = \alpha Y_8 + (1 - \alpha) Y'_8$$
$$= (0.40)(74) + (0.60)(65.80)$$
$$= 29.60 + 39.48 = 69.08$$

and

$$Y'_{10} = \alpha Y_9 + (1 - \alpha) Y'_9$$
$$= (0.40)(62) + (0.60)(69.08)$$
$$= 24.80 + 41.45 = 66.25$$

By using the same procedure, the values of Y'_{11}, Y'_{12}, Y'_{13}, Y'_{14}, and Y'_{15} can be calculated. The following table shows a comparison between the actual sales and predicted sales by the exponential smoothing method.

Due to the negative and positive differences between actual sales and predicted sales, the forecaster can use a higher or lower smoothing constant α, in order to adjust his/her prediction as quickly as possible to large fluctuations in the data series. For example, if the forecast is slow in reacting to increased sales, (that is to say, if the difference is negative), he/she might want to try a higher value. For practical purposes, the optimal may be picked by minimizing what is known as the mean squared error (MSE), which will be discussed in more detail in a later chapter.

$$\text{MSE} = \sum_{t=1}^{n}(Y_t - Y'_t)^2/(n - i)$$

where i = the number of observations used to determine the initial forecast (in our example, $i = 6$).

Exhibit 21-1 presents a comparison of actual sales with predicted sales. In Exhibit 21-1:

$$\text{MSE} = 307.27/(15 - 6) = 307.27/9 = 34.14$$

The idea is to select the α that minimizes MSE, which is the average sum of the variations between the historical sales data and the forecast values for the corresponding periods.

EXHIBIT 21-1 Comparison of Actual Sales and Predicted Sales

Time period (t)	Actual sales (Y_t)	Predicted sales (Y'_t)	Difference ($Y_t - Y'_t$)	Difference^2 ($Y_t - Y'_t)^2$
1	$60.0			
2	64.0			
3	58.0			
4	66.0			
5	70.0			
6	60.0			
7	70.0	63.00	7.00	49.00
8	74.0	65.80	8.20	67.24
9	62.0	69.08	−7.08	50.13
10	74.0	66.25	7.75	60.06
11	68.0	69.35	−1.35	1.82
12	66.0	68.81	−2.81	7.90
13	60.0	67.69	−7.69	59.14
14	66.0	64.61	1.39	1.93
15	62.0	65.17	−3.17	10.05
				307.27

THE COMPUTER AND EXPONENTIAL SMOOTHING

As a financial manager, you will be confronted with complex problems requiring large sample data. You will also need to try different values of α for exponential smoothing. Virtually all forecasting software has an exponential smoothing routine. Figure 21-1 is a sample output from a computer program for exponential smoothing. Notice that the best α for this particular example is .9, because it gives the least MSE.

CONCLUSION

Various quantitative forecasting methods exist. Naive techniques are based solely on previous experience. Smoothing approaches include moving average and exponential smoothing. Moving averages and exponential smoothing employ a weighted average of past data as the means of deriving the forecast.

Figure 21-1 Sample Computer Printout for Exponential Smoothing

```
        PLEASE ENTER THE NUMBER OF OBSERVATIONS.
?10
        ENTER YOUR DATA NOW.
        THE DATA SHOULD BE SEPARATED BY COMMAS.

?117,120,132,141,140,156,169,171,174,182
        ENTER THE NUMBER OF PERIODS OVER WHICH
YOU COMPUTE THE AVERAGE TO BE USED AS THE FIRST
FORECAST VALUE.

?1
        **********EXPONENTIAL SMOOTHING PROGRAM -SINGLE SMOOTHING****
******
                        JAE K. SHIM
```

PERIOD	ACTUAL VALUE	ESTIMATED VALUE	ERROR
1	117.00	.00	
2	120.00	117.00	

THE VALUE OF THE EXPONENTIAL SMOOTHER IS .1

3	132.00	117.30	14.70
4	141.00	118.77	22.23
5	140.00	120.99	19.01
6	156.00	122.89	33.11
7	169.00	126.20	42.80
8	171.00	130.48	40.52
9	174.00	134.54	39.46
10	182.00	138.48	43.52

THE TOTAL ABSOLUTE ERROR IN ESTIMATE IS   255.34
THE MEAN SQUARED ERROR IS   1136.48

THE VALUE OF THE EXPONENTIAL SMOOTHER IS .2

3	132.00	117.60	14.40
4	141.00	120.48	20.52
5	140.00	124.58	15.42
6	156.00	127.67	28.33
7	169.00	133.33	35.67
8	171.00	140.47	30.53
9	174.00	146.57	27.43
10	182.00	152.06	29.94

THE TOTAL ABSOLUTE ERROR IN ESTIMATE IS   202.24
THE MEAN SQUARED ERROR IS   690.23

THE VALUE OF THE EXPONENTIAL SMOOTHER IS .3

3	132.00	117.90	14.10
4	141.00	122.13	18.87
5	140.00	127.79	12.21
6	156.00	131.45	24.55
7	169.00	138.82	30.18
8	171.00	147.87	23.13
9	174.00	154.81	19.19
10	182.00	160.57	21.43

THE TOTAL ABSOLUTE ERROR IN ESTIMATE IS   163.66

```
THE VALUE OF THE EXPONENTIAL SMOOTHER IS .4
     3            132.00            118.20          13.80
     4            141.00            123.72          17.28
     5            140.00            130.63           9.37
     6            156.00            134.38          21.62
     7            169.00            143.03          25.97
     8            171.00            153.42          17.58
     9            174.00            160.45          13.55
    10            182.00            165.87          16.13
THE TOTAL ABSOLUTE ERROR IN ESTIMATE IS   135.31
THE MEAN SQUARED ERROR IS    308.97

THE VALUE OF THE EXPONENTIAL SMOOTHER IS .5
     3            132.00            118.50          13.50
     4            141.00            125.25          15.75
     5            140.00            133.12           6.88
     6            156.00            136.56          19.44
     7            169.00            146.28          22.72
     8            171.00            157.64          13.36
     9            174.00            164.32           9.68
    10            182.00            169.16          12.84
THE TOTAL ABSOLUTE ERROR IN ESTIMATE IS   114.16
THE MEAN SQUARED ERROR IS    226.07

THE VALUE OF THE EXPONENTIAL SMOOTHER IS .6
     3            132.00            118.80          13.20
     4            141.00            126.72          14.28
     5            140.00            135.29           4.71
     6            156.00            138.12          17.88
     7            169.00            148.85          20.15
     8            171.00            160.94          10.06
     9            174.00            166.98           7.02
    10            182.00            171.19          10.81
THE TOTAL ABSOLUTE ERROR IN ESTIMATE IS   98.13
THE MEAN SQUARED ERROR IS    174.23

THE VALUE OF THE EXPONENTIAL SMOOTHER IS .7
     3            132.00            119.10          12.90
     4            141.00            128.13          12.87
     5            140.00            137.14           2.86
     6            156.00            139.14          16.86
     7            169.00            150.94          18.06
     8            171.00            163.58           7.42
     9            174.00            168.77           5.23
    10            182.00            172.43           9.57
THE TOTAL ABSOLUTE ERROR IN ESTIMATE IS   85.76
THE MEAN SQUARED ERROR IS    140.55

THE VALUE OF THE EXPONENTIAL SMOOTHER IS .8
     3            132.00            119.40          12.60
     4            141.00            129.48          11.52
     5            140.00            138.70           1.30
     6            156.00            139.74          16.26
     7            169.00            152.75          16.25
     8            171.00            165.75           5.25
     9            174.00            169.95           4.05
    10            182.00            173.19           8.81
THE TOTAL ABSOLUTE ERROR IN ESTIMATE IS   76.05
THE MEAN SQUARED ERROR IS    117.91

THE VALUE OF THE EXPONENTIAL SMOOTHER IS .9
     3            132.00            119.70          12.30
     4            141.00            133.77          10.23
     5            ???.??            ???.??          ??.??
```

```
        6          156.00          140.00          16.00
        7          169.00          154.40          14.60
        8          171.00          167.54           3.46
        9          174.00          170.65           3.35
       10          182.00          173.67           8.33
THE TOTAL ABSOLUTE ERROR IN ESTIMATE IS    68.30
THE MEAN SQUARED ERROR IS    102.23
        SUMMARY RESULTS



THE EXPONENTIAL SMOOTHER  .1   WITH A MEAN SQUARED ERROR OF   1136.48
THE EXPONENTIAL SMOOTHER  .2   WITH A MEAN SQUARED ERROR OF    690.23
THE EXPONENTIAL SMOOTHER  .3   WITH A MEAN SQUARED ERROR OF    447.49
THE EXPONENTIAL SMOOTHER  .4   WITH A MEAN SQUARED ERROR OF    308.97
THE EXPONENTIAL SMOOTHER  .5   WITH A MEAN SQUARED ERROR OF    226.07
THE EXPONENTIAL SMOOTHER  .6   WITH A MEAN SQUARED ERROR OF    174.23
THE EXPONENTIAL SMOOTHER  .7   WITH A MEAN SQUARED ERROR OF    140.55
THE EXPONENTIAL SMOOTHER  .8   WITH A MEAN SQUARED ERROR OF    117.91
THE EXPONENTIAL SMOOTHER  .9   WITH A MEAN SQUARED ERROR OF    102.23
```

Chapter 22

Time Series Analysis and Classical Decomposition

A time series is a sequence of data points at constant time intervals such as a week, month, quarter, and year. Time series analysis breaks data into components and projects them into the future. The four commonly recognized components are trend, seasonal, cycle, and irregular variation:

1. The *trend component* (*T*) is the general upward or downward movement of the average over time. These movements may require many years of data to determine or describe them. The basic forces underlying the trend include technological advances, productivity changes, inflation, and population change.

2. The *seasonal component* (*S*) is a recurring fluctuation of data points above or below the trend value that repeats with a usual frequency of one year, e.g., Christmas sales.

3. *Cyclical components* (*C*) are recurrent upward and downward movements that repeat with a frequency that is longer than a year. This movement is attributed to business cycles (such as recession, inflation, unemployment, and prosperity), so the periodicity (recurrent rate) of such cycles does not have to be constant.

4. The *irregular* (or *random*) *component* is a series of short, erratic movements that follow no discernible pattern. It is caused by unpredictable or nonrecurring events such as floods, wars, strikes, elections, environmental changes, and the passage of legislation.

TREND ANALYSIS

Trends are the general upward or downward movements of the average over time. These movements may require many years of data to determine or describe them. They can be described by a straight line or a curve. The basic forces underlying the trend include technological advances, productivity changes, inflation, and population change. Trend analysis is a special type of simple regression. This method involves a regression whereby a trend line is fitted to a time series of data. In practice, however, one typically finds linear and nonlinear curves used for business forecasting.

Linear Trend

The *linear* trend line equation can be shown as

$$Y = a + bt$$

where t = time.

The formula for the coefficients a and b are essentially the same as the cases for simple regression. However, for regression purposes, a time period can be given a number so that $\Sigma t = 0$. When there is an odd number of periods, the period in the middle is assigned a zero value. If there is an even number, then -1 and $+1$ are assigned the two periods in the middle, so that again $\Sigma t = 0$.

With $\Sigma t = 0$, the formula for b and a reduces to the following:

$$b = \frac{n\Sigma tY}{n\Sigma t^2}$$

$$a = \frac{\Sigma Y}{n}$$

EXAMPLE 22-1 Case 1 (odd number)

	19X1	19X2	19X3	19X4	19X5
$t =$	−2	−1	0	+1	+2

Case 2 (even number)

	19X1	19X2	19X3	19X4	19X5	19X6
$t =$	−3	−2	−1	+1	+ 2	+3

In each case $\Sigma t = 0$.

EXAMPLE 22-2 Consider ABC Company, whose historical sales are:

Year	Sales (in millions)
19X1	$10
19X2	12
19X3	13
19X4	16
19X5	17

Since the company has five years' data, which is an odd number, the year in the middle is assigned a zero value.

Year	t	Sales (in millions) (Y)	tY	t^2	Y^2
19X1	−2	$10	−20	4	100
19X2	−1	12	−12	1	144
19X3	0	13	0	0	169
19X4	+1	16	16	1	256
19X5	±2	17	34	4	289
	0	68	18	10	958

$$b = \frac{(5)\,(18)}{(5)\,(10)} = \frac{90}{50} = 1.8$$

$$a = \frac{68}{5} = 13.6$$

Therefore, the estimated trend equation is

$$Y' = \$13.6 + \$1.8t$$

To project 19X6 sales, we assign +3 to the t value for the year 19X6.

$$Y' = \$13.6 + \$1.8(3)$$
$$= \$19$$

FORECASTING USING DECOMPOSITION OF TIME SERIES

When sales exhibit seasonal or cyclical fluctuation, use a method called classical decomposition for dealing with seasonal, trend, and cyclical components together. Note that the classical decomposition model is a time series model. This means that the method can only be used to fit the time series data, whether it is monthly, quarterly, or annually. The types of time series data the company deals with include sales, earnings, cash flows, market share, and costs.

Assume that a time series is combined into a model that consists of the four components: trend (T), cyclical (C), seasonal (S), and random (R). Assume the model is of a multiplicative type, i.e.,

$$Y_t = T \times C \times S \times R$$

This section illustrates step by step the classical decomposition method by working with the quarterly sales data. The approach basically involves the following four steps:

1. Determine seasonal indices, using a four-quarter moving average.
2. Deseasonalize the data.
3. Develop the linear least squares equation in order to identify the trend component of the forecast.
4. Forecast the sales for each of the four quarters of the coming year.

The data used here are the quarterly sales data for the video set over the past four years. (See Exhibit 22-1.) The analysis begins by showing how to identify the seasonal component of the time series.

EXHIBIT 22-1 Sales Data for Video Set

Year	Quarter	Sales
1	1	4.8
	2	4.1
	3	6
	4	6.5
2	1	5.8
	2	5.2
	3	6.8
	4	7.4
3	1	6
	2	5.6
	3	7.5
	4	7.8
4	1	6.3
	2	5.9
	3	8
	4	8.4

EXHIBIT 22-2 Moving Average Calculations for the Video Set Sales Time Series

Year	Quarter	Sales	4-Qtr Moving Average	Centered Moving Average
1	1	5.8		
	2	5.1		
			6.35	
	3	7		6.475
			6.6	
	4	7.5		6.7375
			6.875	
2	1	6.8		6.975
			7.075	
	2	6.2		7.1875
			7.3	
	3	7.8		7.325
			7.35	
	4	8.4		7.4
			7.45	
3	1	7		7.5375
			7.625	
	2	6.6		7.675
			7.725	
	3	8.5		7.7625
			7.8	
	4	8.8		7.8375
			7.875	
4	1	7.3		7.9375
			8	
	2	6.9		8.075
			8.15	
	3	9	0	
	4	9.4		

Step 1: Use moving average to measure the combined trend-cyclical (*TC*) components of the time series. This way we eliminate the seasonal and random components, *S* and *R*.

More specifically, Step 1 involves the following sequences of steps:

(a) Calculate the four-quarter moving average for the time series, discussed in the above. However, the moving average values computed do not correspond directly to the original quarters of the time series.

(b) Resolve this difficulty by using the midpoints between successive moving-average values. For example, since 6.35 corresponds to the first half of quarter 3 and 6.6 corresponds to the last half of quarter 3, you use (6.35 + 6.6)/2 = 6.475 as the moving average value of quarter 3. Similarly, you associate (6.6 + 6.875)/2 = 6.7375 with quarter 4. A complete summary of the moving-average calculation is shown in Exhibit 22-2.

EXHIBIT 22-3 Seasonal Random Factors for the Series

Year	Quarter	Sales	4-Qtr Moving Average	Centered Moving Average TC	Seasonal-Random SR = Y/TC
1	1	4.8			
	2	4.1			
			5.35		
	3	6		5.475	1.096
			5.6		
	4	6.5		5.738	1.133
			5.875		
2	1	5.8		5.975	0.971
			6.075		
	2	5.2		6.188	0.840
			6.3		
	3	6.8		6.325	1.075
			6.35		
	4	7.4		6.400	1.156
			6.45		
3	1	6		6.538	0.918
			6.625		
	2	5.6		6.675	0.839
			6.725		
	3	7.5		6.763	1.109
			6.8		
	4	7.8		6.838	1.141
			6.875		
4	1	6.3		6.938	0.908
			7		
	2	5.9		7.075	0.834
			7.15		
	3	8			
	4	8.4			

EXHIBIT 22-4 Seasonal Component Calculations

Quarter	Seasonal-Random Component SR	Seasonal Factor S	Adjusted S
1	0.971		
	0.918		
	0.908	0.932	0.931
2	0.840		
	0.839		
	0.834	0.838	0.836
3	1.096		
	1.075		
	1.109	1.093	1.092
4	1.133		
	1.156		
	1.141	1.143	1.141
		4.007	4.000

FIGURE 22-1 Actual versus Deseasonalized Data

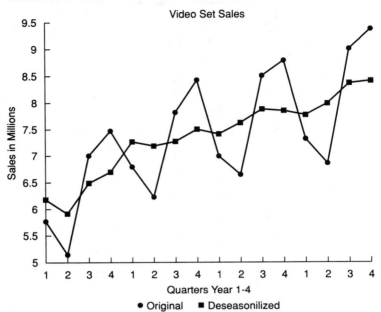

(c) Next, calculate the ratio of the actual value to the moving average value for each quarter in the time series having a four-quarter moving average entry. This ratio in effect represents the seasonal-random component, $SR = Y/TC$. The ratios calculated this way appear in Exhibit 22-3.

(d) Arrange the ratios by quarter and then calculate the average ratio by quarter in order to eliminate the random influence.

For example, for quarter 1

$$(0.975 + 0.929 + 0.920)/3 = 0.941$$

(e) The final step, shown below, adjusts the average ratio slightly (for example, for quarter 1, 0.941 becomes 0.939), which will be the *seasonal index*.

Step 2: After obtaining the seasonal index, you must first remove the effect of season from the original time series. This process is referred to as deseasonalizing the time series.

For this, divide the original series by the seasonal index for that quarter. This is shown in Exhibit 22-4.

EXHIBIT 22-5 Deseasonalized Data

Year	Quarter	Sales	Seasonal S	Des. Data	t	tY	t^2
1	1	4.8	0.931	5.16	1	5.16	1
	2	4.1	0.836	4.90	2	9.80	4
	3	6	1.092	5.50	3	16.49	9
	4	6.5	1.141	5.69	4	22.78	16
2	1	5.8	0.931	6.23	5	31.16	25
	2	5.2	0.836	6.22	6	37.30	36
	3	6.8	1.092	6.23	7	43.61	49
	4	7.4	1.141	6.48	8	51.87	64
3	1	6	0.931	6.45	9	58.02	81
	2	5.6	0.836	6.70	10	66.96	100
	3	7.5	1.092	6.87	11	75.58	121
	4	7.8	1.141	6.83	12	82.00	144
4	1	6.3	0.931	6.77	13	88.00	169
	2	5.9	0.836	7.05	14	98.76	196
	3	8	1.092	7.33	15	109.94	225
	4	8.4	1.141	7.36	16	117.75	256
				101.77	136	915.18	1,496

t–bar = 8.5 y–bar = 6.3608

$b_1 = 0.1474$

$b_0 = 5.1080$

$Y = 5.1080 + 0.1474\,C$

$t = 17$
18
19
20

Step 3: Looking at the graph in Exhibit 22-2, you see the time series seem to have an upward linear trend. To identify this trend, develop the least squares trend equation. This procedure is shown in Exhibit 22-5, which will be discussed in Chapter 23.

Step 4: Develop the forecast using the trend equation and adjust these forecasts to account for the effect of season. The quarterly forecast, as shown in Exhibit 22-6 can be obtained by multiplying the forecast based on trend times the seasonal factor.

EXHIBIT 22-6 Quarter-to-Quarter Forecasts

Year	Quarter	Trend Forecast	Seasonal Factor	Quarterly Forecast
5	1	7.6135	0.931	7.0856
	2	7.7609	0.836	6.4910
	3	7.9083	1.092	8.6323
	4	8.0557	1.141	9.1949

CONCLUSION

A time-series is a chronologically arranged sequence of data on a particular variable. Several methods are available to analyze the time-series data. Trend analysis and decomposition of time series are such models. Trend analysis—linear and curvilinear—can be used effectively when the company has no data. The classical decomposition method is used for seasonal and cyclical situations.

Chapter 23

Regression Analysis

Regression analysis is a statistical procedure for estimating mathematically the average relationship between the dependent variable and the independent variable(s). *Simple regression* involves one independent variable, price or advertising in a demand function, whereas *multiple regression* involves two or more variables, that is price and advertising together. This chapter will discuss *simple (linear) regression* to illustrate the *least-squares method,* which means to assume the $Y = a + bX$ relationship.

THE LEAST-SQUARES METHOD

The least-squares method is widely used in regression analysis for estimating the parameter values in a regression equation. The regression method includes all the observed data and attempts to find a line of best fit. To find this line, a technique called the least-squares method is used.

To explain the least-squares method, we define the error as the difference between the observed value and the estimated one and denote it with u.

Symbolically,

$$u = Y - Y'$$

where Y = observed value of the dependent variable
Y' = estimated value based on $Y' = a + bX$

Figure 23-1 Y and Y′

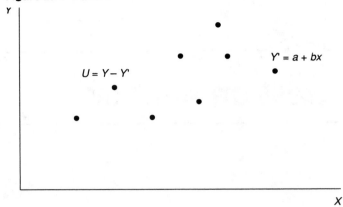

The least-squares criterion requires that the line of best fit be such that the sum of the squares of the errors (or the vertical distance in Figure 23-1 from the observed data points to the line) is a minimum, i.e.,

$$\text{Minimum: } \Sigma u^2 = \Sigma(Y - a - bX)^2$$

Using differential calculus you obtain the following equations, called normal equations:

$$\Sigma Y = na + b\Sigma X$$

$$\Sigma XY = a\Sigma X + b\Sigma X^2$$

Solving the equations for b and a yields

$$b = \frac{n\Sigma XY - (\Sigma X)(\Sigma Y)}{n\Sigma X^2 - (\Sigma X)^2}$$

$$a = \overline{Y} - b\overline{X}$$

where $\overline{Y} = \Sigma Y / n$ and $\overline{X} = \Sigma X / n$.

EXAMPLE 23-1 To illustrate the computations of b and a, refer to the data in Exhibit 23-1. All the sums required are computed and shown below.

EXHIBIT 23-1

Advertising X (OOO)	Sales Y (000)	XY	X²	Y²
$ 9	$ 15	135	81	225
19	20	380	361	400
11	14	154	121	196
14	16	224	196	256
23	25	575	529	625
12	20	240	144	400
12	20	240	144	400
22	23	506	484	529
7	14	98	49	196
13	22	286	169	484
15	18	270	225	324
17	18	306	289	324
$174	$225	3,414	2,792	4,359

From EXHIBIT 23-1 above:

$$\Sigma X = 174; \ \Sigma Y = 225; \ \Sigma XY = 3,414; \ \Sigma X^2 = 2,792.$$

$$\overline{X}M = \Sigma X/n = 174/12 = 14.5; \ \overline{Y}X = \Sigma Y/n = 225/12 = 18.75.$$

Substituting these values into the formula for b first:

$$b = \frac{n\Sigma XY - (\Sigma X)(\Sigma Y)}{n\Sigma X^2 - (\Sigma X)^2} = \frac{(12)(3,414) - (174)(225)}{(12)(2,792) - (174)^2} = \frac{1,818}{3,228} = 0.5632$$

$$a = \overline{Y} - b\overline{X} = 18.75 - (0.5632)(14.5) = 18.75 - 8.1664 = 10.5836$$

Thus, $Y' = 10.5836 + 0.5632 X$

EXAMPLE 23-2   Assume that the advertising of $10 is to be expended for next year; the projected sales for the next year would be computed as follows:

$$Y' = 10.5836 + 0.5632X$$

$$= 10.5836 + 0.5632 (10)$$

$$= \$16.2156$$

Note that ΣY^2 is not used here but rather is computed for R-squared (R^2).

USE OF LOTUS 1–2–3™ FOR REGRESSION

Spreadsheet programs such as *Lotus 1–2–3*™ have a regression routine which you can use without any difficulty. As a matter of fact, in reality, you do not compute the parameter values a and b manually. Exhibit 23-2 shows, step by step, how to use the Lotus regression command.

At this juncture of the discussion, note from the output

$$a = 10.58364$$

$$b = 0.563197$$

That is, $Y' = 10.58364 + 0.563197X$

Other statistics shown on the printout are discussed later in the chapter.

EXHIBIT 23-2 Using Lotus 1-2-3™ Regression Command

Step 1. Enter the data on X and Y as shown below:

(X) Adv. (000)	(Y) Sales (000)
9	15
19	20
11	14
14	16
23	25
12	20
12	20
22	23
7	14
13	22
15	18
17	18

Step 2. Press "/Data Regression"

Step 3. Define X and Y range

Step 4. Define output range

Step 5. Hit Go

This will produce the following regression output:

Regression Output	
Constant	10.58364 ($a = 10.58364$)
Std. Err. of Y Est.	2.343622
R Squared	0.608373
No. of Observations	12
Degrees of Freedom	10
X Coefficient(s)	0.563197 ($b = 0.563197$)
Std. Err. of Coef.	0.142893

The result shows:

$$Y' = 10.58364 + 0.563197$$

A word of caution: Before attempting a least-squares regression approach, it is extremely important to plot the observed data on a diagram,

Figure 23-2 Scatter Diagram

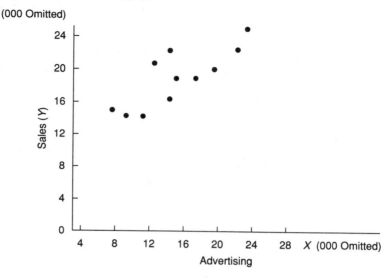

called the scattergraph (See Figure 23-2.). The reason is that you might want to be sure that a linear (straight-line) relationship existed between Y and X in the past sample.

If for any reason there was a nonlinear relationship detected in the sample, the linear relationship you assumed ($Y = a + bX$) would not provide a good fit. In order to obtain a good fit and achieve a high degree of accuracy, you should be familiar with statistics relating to regression such as R-squared (R^2) and t-value, which are discussed later.

REGRESSION STATISTICS

Regression analysis is a statistical method. Hence, it uses a variety of statistics to confirm the accuracy and reliability of the regression results. They include:

1. Correlation coefficient (r) and coefficient of determination (R^2)
2. Standard error of the estimate (S_e) and prediction confidence interval
3. Standard error of the regression coefficient (S_b) and t statistic

Each of these statistics is explained below.

1. Correlation coefficient (r) and coefficient of determination (R^2): The correlation coefficient r measures the degree of correlation between Y and X. The range of values it takes on is between −1 and +1. More widely used, however, is the coefficient of determination, designated R^2 (read as R-squared). Simply put, R^2 tells you how good the estimated regression equation is. In other words, it is a measure of "goodness of fit" in the regression. Therefore, the higher the R^2, the more confidence you can have in your estimated equation. More specifically, the coefficient of determination represents the proportion of the total variation in Y that is explained by the regression equation. It has the range of values between 0 and 1.

EXAMPLE 23-3   The statement "Sales is a function of advertising expenditure with $R^2 = 70$ percent," can be interpreted as "70 percent of the total variation of sales is explained by the regression equation or the change in advertising and the remaining 30 percent is accounted for by something other than advertising, such as price and income."

The coefficient of determination is computed as

$$R^2 = 1 - \frac{\sum (Y - Y')^2}{\sum (Y - \bar{Y})^2}$$

In a simple regression situation, however, there is a short-cut method available:

$$R^2 = \frac{[n\sum XY - (\sum X)(\sum Y)]^2}{[n\sum X^2 - (\sum X)^2][n\sum Y^2 - (\sum Y)^2]}$$

Comparing this formula with the one for b, you can see that the only additional information needed to compute R^2 is $\sum Y^2$.

EXAMPLE 23-4   To illustrate the computations of various regression statistics, refer to the data in Exhibit 23-1. Using the shortcut method for R^2,

$$R^2 = \frac{(1,818)^2}{(3,228)[(12)(4,359) - (225)^2]} = \frac{3,305,124}{(3,228)(52,308 - 50,625)}$$

$$= \frac{3,305,124}{(3,228)(1,683)} = \frac{3,305,124}{5,432,724} = 0.6084 = 60.84\%$$

This means that about 60.84 percent of the total variation in sales is explained by advertising and the remaining 39.16 percent is still unexplained. A relatively low R^2 indicates that there is a lot of room for improvement in our estimated forecasting formula ($Y' = \$10.5836 + \$0.5632X$). Price or a combination of advertising and price might improve R^2.

EXAMPLE 23-5   In the example of trend analysis (Example 23-4),

$$R^2 = \frac{(90)^2}{(50)[(5)(958)-(68)^2]} = \frac{8,100}{(50)(4,790-4,624)}$$

$$= \frac{8,100}{(50)(166)} = \frac{8,100}{8,300} = 0.9759 = 97.59\%$$

The very high R^2 (97.59 percent) indicates that trend line is an excellent fit and there is a growing trend of sales over time.

2. Standard Error of the Estimate (S_e) and Prediction Confidence Interval: The standard error of the estimate, designated S_e, is defined as the standard deviation of the regression. It is computed as:

$$S_e = \sqrt{\frac{\sum(Y-Y')^2}{n-2}} = \sqrt{\frac{\sum Y^2 - a\sum Y - b\sum XY}{n-2}}$$

This statistic can be used to gain some idea of the accuracy of your predictions.

EXAMPLE 23-6   Returning to the example data, S_e is calculated as:

$$S_e = \sqrt{\frac{4,359 - (10.5836)(225) - (0.5632)(3,414)}{12-2}}$$

$$= \sqrt{\frac{54.9252}{10}} = 2.3436$$

Suppose you wish to make a prediction regarding an individual Y value, such as a prediction about the sales when an advertising expense = $10. Usually, you would like to have some objective measure of the confidence you can place in your prediction, and one such measure is a *confidence* (*or prediction*) *interval* constructed for Y.

A confidence interval for a predicted Y, *given a value for X,* can be constructed in the following manner.

$$Y' \pm tS_e \sqrt{1 + \frac{1}{n} + \frac{(X_p - \overline{X})^2}{\sum X^2 - \frac{(\sum x)^2}{n}}}$$

where Y' = the predicted value of Y given a value for X;

   X_p = the value of an independent variable used as the basis for prediction.

Note: t is the critical value for the level of significance employed. For example, for a significant level of 0.025 (which is equivalent to a 95 percent confidence level in a two-tailed test), the critical value of t for 10 degrees of freedom is 2.228 (see Table 2 in Appendix B). As can be seen, the confidence interval is the linear distance bounded by limits on either side of the prediction.

EXAMPLE 23-7

If you want to have a 95 percent confidence interval of your prediction, the range for the prediction, given an advertising expense of $10 would be between $10,595.10 and $21,836.10, as determined as follows: Note that from Example 23-2, $Y' = \$16.2156$

The confidence interval is therefore established as follows:

$$\$16.2156 \pm (2.228)(2.3436)\sqrt{1+\frac{1}{12}+\frac{(10-14.5)^2}{2792-(174)^2/12}}$$

$$= \$16.2156 \pm (2.228)(2.3436)(1.0764)$$

$$= \$16.2156 \pm 5.6205$$

which means the range for the prediction, given an advertising expense of $10 would be between $10.5951 and $21.8361. Note that $10.5951 = $16.2156 − 5.6205 and $21.8361 = $16.2156 + 5.6205.

3. Standard Error of the Regression Coefficient (S_b) and t *Statistic*

The standard error of the regression coefficient, designated S_b, and the t statistic are closely related. S_b is calculated as:

$$S_b = \frac{S_e}{\sqrt{\sum (X - \overline{X})^2}}$$

or in short-cut form

$$S_b = \frac{S_e}{\sqrt{\sum X^2 - \overline{X} \sum X}}$$

S_b gives an estimate of the range where the true coefficient will "actually" fall.

Note: t statistics (or t value) is a measure of the statistical significance of an independent variable X in explaining the dependent variable Y. It is determined by dividing the estimated regression coefficient b by its standard error S_b. It is then compared with the table t value (See Table 2 in Appendix B). Thus, the t statistic measures how many standard errors the coefficient is away from zero. Rule of thumb: Any t value greater than +2 or less than −2 is acceptable. The higher the t value, the greater the confidence we have in the coefficient as a predictor. Low t values are indications of low reliability of the predictive power of that coefficient.

EXAMPLE 23-8   The S_b for our example is:

$$S_b = \frac{2.3436}{\sqrt{2,792 - (14.5)(174)}}$$

$$= \frac{2.3436}{\sqrt{2,792 - 2,523}} = \frac{2.3436}{\sqrt{269}} = .143$$

$$\text{Thus, } t \text{ statistic} = \frac{b}{S_b} = \frac{.5632}{.143} = 3.94$$

Since, $t = 3.94 > 2$, you conclude that the b coefficient is statistically significant. As was indicated previously, the table's critical value (cut-off value) for 10 degrees of freedom is 2.228 (from Table 2 in Appendix B).

Note: (1) t statistic is more relevant to multiple regressions which have more than one b's.

(2) R^2 tells you how good the forest (overall fit) is while t statistic tells you how good an individual tree (an independent variable) is.

Note: In summary, the table t value, based on a degree of freedom and a level of significance, is used:

1. To set the prediction range—upper and lower limits—for the predicted value of the dependent variable.
2. To set the confidence range for regression coefficients.
3. As a cutoff value for the t-test.

Exhibit 23-3 shows a Lotus 1–2–3™ output that contains the statistics discussed so far.

EXHIBIT 23-3 Lotus 1–2–3™ Regression Result

Constant	10.58364
Std. Err. of Y Est.	2.343622 (S_e)
R Squared	0.608373 (R^2)
No. of Observations	12
Degree of Freedom	10
X Coefficient(s)	0.563197
Std. Err. of Coef.	0.142893 (S_b)
t value	0.394138 (Calculated Independently)

The result shows:

$$Y' = 10.58364 + 0.563197\,X$$

with:

1. R squared ($R^2 = .608373 = 60.84\%$)
2. Standard Error of the Estimate ($S_e = 2.343622$)
3. Standard Error of the Coefficient ($S_b = 0.142893$)
4. t value $= 3.94$

All of the above are the same as the ones manually obtained.

CONCLUSION

Regression analysis is the examination of the effect of a change in independent variables on the dependent variable. It is a popularly used method to forecast sales. This chapter discussed the well-known estimation technique, called the least-squares method.

To illustrate the method, assume a simple regression, which involves one independent variable in the form of $Y = a + bX$. In an attempt to obtain a good fit, various regression statistics were discussed. These statistics tell you how good and reliable your estimated equation is and help you to set the confidence interval for your prediction.

Most importantly, how to use spreadsheet programs such as Lotus 1–2–3™ to perform regressions, step by step, was discussed. The program calculates not only the regression equation, but also all the regression statistics discussed in this chapter.

Chapter 24

Multiple Regression

Multiple regression analysis is a powerful statistical technique that is perhaps the most widely used by forecasters. Multiple regression attempts to estimate statistically the average relationship between the dependent variable (e.g., sales) and two or more independent variables (e.g., price, advertising, income, etc.).

In reality, financial managers will face more multiple regression situations than simple regression. In order to obtain a good fit and to achieve a high degree of accuracy, they should be familiar with statistics relating to regression such as R squared (R^2) and t value. *Note:* Look beyond the statistics discussed here. Furthermore, forecasters will have to perform additional tests unique to multiple regression.

APPLICATIONS

Applications of multiple regression are numerous. Multiple regression analysis is used to do the following:

1. To find the overall association between the dependent variable and a host of explanatory variables. For example, overhead costs are explained by volume, productivity, and technology.

2. To attempt to identify the factors that influence the dependent variable. For example,

(a) Factors critical in affecting sales include price and competition.

(b) Financial analysts might seek causes of a change in stock prices or price-earnings (P-E) ratios by analyzing growth in earnings, variability of earnings, stock splits, inflation rates, beta, and dividend yields.

(c) Advertising directors wish to study the impact on consumer buying of advertising budgets, advertising frequency, media selection, and the like.

3. To use it as a basis for providing sound forecasts of the dependent variable. For example, sometimes cash collections from customers are forecasted from credit sales of prior months since cash collections lag behind sales.

The Model

The multiple regression model takes the following form:

$$Y = b_o + b_1 X_1 + b_2 X_2 \ldots + b_k X_k + u$$

where Y = dependent variable, X's = independent (explanatory) variables, b's = regression coefficients, u = error term.

Two examples are in order. A Lotus 1-2-3™ regression printout is shown in Exhibit 24-1.

EXAMPLE 24-1 When a simple regression is insufficient to provide a satisfactory fit (as indicated typically by a low R squared), the manager should use multiple regression. Presented below is an example of both simple and multiple regressions and of their Lotus 1-2-3™ spreadsheet printout. The sales manager is trying to develop a model for forecasting annual sales for toothpaste using advertising budgets for the current year and for two previous years.

Assume the following data:

EXHIBIT 24-1 Annual Data for Toothpaste Sales with Current and Previous Advertising Budgets (in $Millions)

Year	Sales (Y_t)	Advertising Budget (X_t)	$X_t - 1$	$X_t - 2$
1983	113.750	15.000		
1984	124.150	14.000	15.000	
1985	133.000	15.400	14.000	15.000
1986	126.000	18.250	15.400	14.000
1987	162.000	17.300	18.250	15.400
1988	191.625	23.000	17.300	18.250
1989	189.000	19.250	23.000	17.300
1990	210.000	23.056	19.250	23.000
1991	224.250	26.000	23.056	19.250
1992	245.000	28.000	26.000	23.056

Exhibit 24-2 presents two Lotus 1–2–3™ regression results:

EXHIBIT 24-2 Lotus 1–2–3™ Multiple Regressions

Regression Output:		
Constant		−9.59129
Std. Err. of Y Est.		16.06997
R Squared		0.894576
No. of Observations		10
Degrees of Freedom		8
X Coefficient(s)	9.107319	
Std. Err. of Coef.	1.105363	
t statistic	8.239210	

Regression Output:		
Constant		−37.8770
Std. Err. of Y Est.		12.16478
R Squared		0.940992
No. of Observations		8
Degrees of Freedom		5
X Coefficient(s)	4.970408	6.934206
Std. Err. of Coef.	1.522161	1.821730
t statistics	3.265362	3.806383

The simple regression model shows:

$$Y_t = -9.59 + 9.11\, X_t \qquad\qquad R^2 = 89.45\%$$
$$(1.11)*$$

The multiple regression model with advertising budgets for two previous years is:

$$Y_t = -37.88 + 4.97\, X_{t-1} + 6.93 X_{t-2}$$
$$(1.52) \qquad (1.82)$$

with $R^2 = 94.1\%$

This model has two advantages:

1. The explanatory power has increased from 89.45 percent to 94.1 percent
2. From the forecaster's point of view, using only lagged variables does not require any assumptions about actual future budgets.

EXAMPLE 24-2   The Los Alamitos Equipment Company wants to identify trends in demand for its heavy equipment so that funds available for investment, and related ex-

---

* Standard error of regression coefficient S_b.

penditures, can be efficiently allocated. The company collected data on real GNP and the Treasury bill rate, as given in Exhibit 24-3.

EXHIBIT 24-3 Los Alamitos Equipment Company
Real GNP and Treasury Bill Rate

Year	Sales (Y)	Time (X_1)	GNP (X_2)	T Bill (X_3)
1993	921.58	30	1,489.3	12.42
1992	913.01	29	1,485.8	12.81
1991	934.99	28	1,506.9	11.75
1990	913.17	27	1,525.8	15.05
1989	903.33	26	1,512.5	14.90
1988	906.66	25	1,510.1	14.39
1987	891.65	24	1,477.9	13.61
1986	922.27	23	1,464.2	9.15
1985	915.71	22	1,461.4	9.62
1984	897.52	21	1,496.2	13.35
1983	904.71	20	1,489.3	11.84
1982	922.57	19	1,486.6	9.67
1981	912.60	18	1,469.2	9.38
1980	913.99	17	1,472.6	9.38
1979	916.93	16	1,468.4	8.57
1978	916.26	15	1,448.8	7.31
1977	918.31	14	1,437.0	6.48
1976	809.61	13	1,400.0	6.39
1975	977.15	12	1,388.4	6.11
1974	892.60	11	1,385.8	5.50
1973	886.17	10	1,363.3	4.84
1972	875.18	9	1,341.3	4.63
1971	858.59	8	1,315.4	4.67
1970	847.57	7	1,303.3	5.15
1969	840.74	6	1,295.8	5.16
1968	837.22	5	1,287.2	4.92
1967	814.76	4	1,259.7	5.63
1966	799.99	3	1,248.4	6.33
1965	791.62	2	1,221.0	5.39
1964	777.73	1	1,206.3	5.75

Simple (trend) regression:

Regression Output:		
Constant		821.3202
Std. Err. of Y Est.		33.27495
R Squared		0.546165
No. of Observations		30
Degrees of Freedom		28
X Coefficient(s)	4.074369	
Std. Err. of Coef.	0.701887	
t value	5.804873	

Thus, $Y = 821.32 + 4.07 X_1$ with R squared (R^2) = 54.62%

EXHIBIT 24-3 (Continued)

Multiple regression:

Regression output			
Constant		221.6548	
Std. Err. of Y Est.		24.01704	
R Squared		0.780458	
No. of Observations		30	
Degrees of Freedom		26	
X Coefficient(s)	1.989438	0.504100	−8.92803
Std. Err. of Coef.	1.854864	0.130802	2.821173
t value	1.072551	3.853918	−3.16465

Thus, $Y = 221.65 + 1.99 X_1 + 0.50 X_2 - 8.92 X_3$

$$R_2 = 78.05\%$$

The company tried one simple (trend) equation and one multiple regression model:

1. a trend equation, and

2. a multiple regression model which incorporates explanatory factors besides trend.

The results are as follows:

Simple regression (trend) equation

$$Y = 821.32 + 4.07 X_1 \qquad R^2 = 54.62\%$$
$$(0.70)$$

Multiple regression equation

$$Y = 221.65 + 1.99 X_1 + 0.50 X_2 - 8.92 X_3 \qquad R^2 = 78.05\%$$
$$(1.85) \quad (0.13) \quad (2.82)$$

where X_1 = time, X_2 = real GNP, and X_3 = 90-day T bill rate

NONLINEAR REGRESSION

Thus far, a linear relationship has been assumed. In some cases, however, a nonlinear form may be more appropriate. For example, in Example 24-1, it is sometimes difficult to assume that a linear relationship exists between lagged advertising budgets and sales, because of the diminishing returns effect of accumulated advertising.

In addition to the nonlinearity which might be associated with the decay it is frequently postulated that the sales-advertising relationship is *S-shaped*. That is, at lower levels of advertising the ability of the ads to reach the audience is at best limited. At moderate spending levels, the audience reach expands and sales grow at a relatively more rapid pace. At a higher and higher level, the sale response slows and eventually is oversaturated.

A popular formulation to account for this phenomenon is as follows:

$$Y_t = b_0 + b_1 \, 1/X_{t-1} + b_2 \, 1/X_{t-2} \qquad\qquad b_1, b_2 < 0$$

This specification represents a hyperbola, and describes an S-shaped relationship. The following example illustrates this, using the data in Exhibit 24-4.

EXAMPLE 24-3

EXHIBIT 24-4 Annual Data for Toothpaste Sales With Current and Previous Advertising Budgets (in $Millions)

Year	Sales (Y_t)	Advertising Budget (X_t)	X_{t-1}	X_{t-2}	$1/X_{t-1}$	$1/X_{t-2}$
1983	113.750	15.000				
1984	124.150	14.000	15.000		0.067	
1985	133.000	15.400	14.000	15.000	0.071	0.067
1986	126.000	18.250	15.400	14.000	0.065	0.071
1987	162.000	17.300	18.250	15.400	0.055	0.065
1988	191.625	23.000	17.300	18.250	0.058	0.055
1989	189.000	19.250	23.000	17.300	0.043	0.058
1990	210.000	23.056	19.250	23.000	0.052	0.043
1991	224.250	26.000	23.056	19.250	0.043	0.052
1992	245.000	28.000	26.000	23.056	0.038	0.043

Regression Output:		
Constant		413.9353
Std. Err. of Y Est.		9.190343
R Squared		0.966321
No. of Observations		8
Degrees of Freedom		5
X Coefficient(s)	−1614.35	−2514.22
Std. Err. of Coef.	448.4473	487.7338
t statistics	−3.59987	−5.15491

Using the nonlinear form specified above yields

$$Y_t = 413.94 - 1614.35 \, 1/X_{t-1} - 2514.22 \, 1/X_{t-2} \qquad R^2 = 96.63\%$$
$$\qquad\quad (448.45) \qquad\qquad (487.73)$$

STATISTICS TO LOOK FOR IN MULTIPLE REGRESSIONS

In multiple regressions that involve more than one independent (explanatory) variable, managers must look for the following statistics:

- t statistics
- R bar squared ($\bar{R}^2$) and F statistic
- Multicollinearity
- Autocorrelation (or serial correlation)

t statistics

The t statistic was discussed earlier, but is discussed again here since it is more valid in multiple regressions than in simple regressions. The t statistic shows the significance of each explanatory variable in predicting the dependent variable. It is desirable to have as large (either positive or negative) a t statistic as possible for each independent variable. Generally, a t statistic greater than +2.0 or less than −2.0 is acceptable. Explanatory variables with low t value can usually be eliminated from the regression without substantially decreasing R^2 or increasing the standard error of the regression. In a multiple regression situation, the t statistic is defined as

$$t \text{ statistic} = \frac{b_i}{S_{bi}}$$

where $i = i$th independent variable

R bar squared ($\bar{R}^2$) and F statistic

A more appropriate test for goodness of fit for multiple regressions is R bar squared ($\bar{R}^2$):

$$\bar{R}^2 = 1 - (1 - R^2)\frac{n-1}{n-k}$$

where n = the number of observations
k = the number of coefficients to be estimated

An alternative test of the overall significance of a regression equation is the F test. Virtually all computer programs for regression analysis show an F statistic.

The F statistic is defined as

$$F = \frac{(Y' - \bar{Y})^2 / k}{(Y - Y')^2 / k - k - 1} = \frac{\text{Explained variation}/k}{\text{Unexplained variation}/n - k - 1}$$

If the F statistic is greater than the table value, it is concluded that the regression equation is statistically significant in overall terms.

Multicollinearity

When using more than one independent variable in a regression equation, there is sometimes a high correlation between the independent variables themselves. Multicollinearity occurs when these variables interfere with each other. It is a pitfall because the equations with multicollinearity may produce spurious forecasts. Multicollinearity can be recognized when:

- The t statistics of two seemingly important independent variables are low.
- The estimated coefficients on explanatory variables have the opposite sign from that which would logically be expected.

There are two ways to resolve the problem of multicollinearity:

1. One of the highly correlated variables may be dropped from the regression.
2. The structure of the equation may be changed using one of the following methods:

(a) Divide both the left- and right-hand side variables by some series that will leave the basic economic logic but remove multicollinearity,

(b) Estimate the equation on a first-difference basis,

(c) Combine the collinear variables into a new variable, which is their weighted sum.

Autocorrelation (Serial Correlation)

Autocorrelation is another major pitfall often encountered in regression analysis. It occurs if there is a correlation between successive errors. The Durbin-Watson statistic provides the standard test for autocorrelation. Table 4 in Appendix B provides the values of the Durbin-Watson statistic for specified sample sizes and explanatory variables. The table gives the significance points for d_L and d_U for tests on the autocorrelation of residuals (when no explanatory variable is a lagged endogenous variable). The number of explanatory variables, K_J excludes the constant term. Generally speaking:

Durbin-Watson Statistic	*Autocorrelation*
Between 1.5 and 2.5	No autocorrelation
Below 1.5	Positive autocorrelation
Above 2.5	Negative autocorrelation

Autocorrelation usually indicates that an important part of the variation of the dependent variable has not been explained. *Recommendation:* The best solution to this problem is to search for other explanatory variables to include in the regression equation.

CHECKLISTS: HOW TO CHOOSE THE BEST FORECASTING EQUATION

Choosing among alternative forecasting equations basically involves two steps. The first step is to eliminate the obvious losers. The second is to select the winner among the remaining contenders.

How to Eliminate Losers

- Does the equation make sense? Equations that do not make sense intuitively or from a theoretical standpoint must be eliminated.
- Does the equation have explanatory variables with low t statistics? These equations should be reestimated or dropped in favor of equations in which all independent variables are significant. This test will eliminate equations where multicollinearity is a problem.
- How about a low $\bar{R}^2$? The $\bar{R}^2$ can be used to rank the remaining equations in order to select the best candidates. A low $\bar{R}^2$ could mean:

1. A wrong functional was fitted.
2. An important explanatory variable is missing.
3. Other combinations of explanatory variables might be more desirable.

How to Choose the Best Equation

- Best Durbin-Watson statistic. Given equations that survive all previous tests, the equation with the Durbin-Watson statistic closest to 2.0 can be a basis for selection.
- Best forecasting accuracy. Examining the forecasting performance of the equations is essential for selecting one equation from those that have not been eliminated. The equation whose prediction accuracy is best in terms of measures of forecasting errors, such as MAD, MSE, RMSE, or MPE (discussed in detail in Chapter 19) generally provides the best basis for forecasting.

It is important to note that Lotus 1–2–3™ does not calculate many statistics such as R bar squared ($\bar{R}^2$), F statistic, and Durbin-Watson statistic.

You must use regression packages such as *Statistical Analysis System (SAS)*, *STATPACK*, and *Statistical Packages for Social Scientists (SPSS)*, to name a few. These packages all have PC versions.

USE OF A COMPUTER STATISTICAL PACKAGE FOR MULTIPLE REGRESSION

EXAMPLE 24-4   Stanton Consumer Products Corporation wishes to develop a forecasting model for its dryer sale by using multiple regression analysis. The marketing department has prepared the following sample data:

Month	Sales of Washers (X_1)	Disposable Income (X_2)	Savings (X_3)	Sales of Dryers (Y)
January	$45,000	$16,000	$71,000	$29,000
February	42,000	14,000	70,000	24,000
March	44,000	15,000	72,000	27,000
April	45,000	13,000	71,000	25,000
May	43,000	13,000	75,000	26,000
June	46,000	14,000	74,000	28,000
July	44,000	16,000	76,000	30,000
August	45,000	16,000	69,000	28,000
September	44,000	15,000	74,000	28,000
October	43,000	15,000	73,000	27,000

The computer statistical package called STATPACK was employed to develop the regression model. Exhibit 24-5 contains the input data and output that results using three explanatory variables. To help you understand the listing, illustrative comments are added whenever applicable.

1. *The forecasting equation.* From the STATPACK output we see that

$$Y' = -45.796 + 0.597X_1 + 1.177X_2 + 0.405X_3$$

Suppose that in November the company expects

X_1 = sales of washers = $43.00
X_2 = disposable income $15,000
X_3 = savings = $75,000

Then the forecast sales for the month of November would be

$$Y' = -45.796 + 0.597(43) + 1.177(15) + 0.405(75)$$
$$= -45.796 + 25.671 + 17.655 + 30.375$$
$$= 27.905 \text{ or } \$27,905$$

EXHIBIT 24-5 STATPACK Computer Statistical Package

```
RUN ***STATPACK

STATPACK


ARE YOU A STATPACK EXPERT
?* NO

THE RESPONSE 'SOS' MAY BE ENTERED IN ORDER TO GAIN ADDITIONAL
INFORMATION ABOUT THE RESPONSE NEEDED BY STATPACK. SOS MAY BE
ENTERED ONLY IF THE QUESTION IS FOLLOWED BY THE CHARACTERS ?*

SPECIFY THE NAMES OF THE INPUT AND OUTPUT FILES(FORM:IN,OUT)
?***  ◀────── Indicates that all input and output will be on the screen or printer.

WHAT ANALYSIS DO YOU WISH TO PERFORM
?* MULTIPLE REGRESSION

HOW MANY ROWS IN YOUR DATA MATRIX ◀────── How many observations?
?* 10

HOW MANY COLUMNS ◀────── How many variables?
?* 4

NOW, ENTER EACH ROW
?45,16,71,29
?42,14,70,24
?44,15,72,27
?45,13,71,25
?43,13,75,26
?46,14,74,28
?44,16,76,(28) ◀──────Entered incorrectly
?45,16,69,28
?44,15,74,28
?43,15,73,27

DO YOU WISH TO PRINT THE DATA JUST READ IN
?* NO

DO YOU WISH TO CHANGE SOME VALUES
?* YES
```

EXHIBIT 24-5 (Continued)

```
TYPE EDIT CODE
?* SOS

THE FOLLOWING CODES SIGNIFY TYPES OF EDIT FEATURES.
   0  -  NO MORE EDIT
   1  -  REPLACE AN INDIVIDUAL VALUE
   2  -  REPLACE AN ENTIRE ROW
   3  -  ADD A ROW
   4  -  DELETE A ROW
   5  -  SORT DATA (DESCENDING)
   6  -  SORT DATA (ASCENDING)
?* 1

TYPE ROW NUMBER, COLUMN NUMBER, AND NEW VALUE
?7,4,(30) ◄────── Corrected input value for July

TYPE EDIT CODE
?* 0

DO YOU WISH TO PRINT THE DATA MATRIX
?* YES
     45.000    16.000    71.000    29.000
     42.000    14.000    70.000    24.000
     44.000    15.000    72.000    27.000
     45.000    13.000    71.000    25.000
     43.000    13.000    75.000    26.000
     46.000    14.000    74.000    28.000
     44.000    16.000    76.000    30.000
     45.000    16.000    69.000    28.000
     44.000    15.000    74.000    28.000
     43.000    15.000    73.000    27.000

SPECIFY THE DEPENDENT VARIABLE
?* 4

HOW MANY INDEPENDENT VARIABLES
?* 3

SPECIFY THESE VARIABLES
?1,2,3
```

EXHIBIT 24-5 (Continued)

```
VARIABLE    REG.COEF.   STD.ERROR COEF.   COMPUTED T
   1         0.59697        0.08113         7.35866
   2         1.17684        0.08 07        13.99748
   3         0.40511        0.04223         9.59200

INTERCEPT                  -45.79634
MULTIPLE CORRELATION         0.99167
STD. ERROR OF ESTIMATE       0.28613

                    ANALYSIS OF VARIANCE FOR THE REGRESSION
        SOURCE OF VARIATION      D.F.   SUM OF SQ.    MEAN SQ.    F VALUE
ATTRIBUTABLE TO REGRESSION        3      29.109        9.703     118.515
DEVIATION FROM REGRESSION         6       0.491        0.082
            TOTAL                 9      29.600
```

2. *The coefficient of determination.* Note that the STATPACK output gives the value of R, not R^2 (and not $\bar{R}^2$, for that matter). In this example, $R = 0.99167$, so

$$R^2 = (0.99167)^2 = 0.983$$

In the case of multiple regression, $\bar{R}^2$ is more appropriate, as was discussed previously.

$$\bar{R}^2 = 1 - (1 - R^2)\frac{(n-1)}{(n-k)}$$
$$= 1 - (1 - 0.983)\frac{10-1}{10-3} = 1 - 0.017(9/7)$$
$$= 1 - 0.0219 = 0.978$$

This tells you that 97.8 percent of total variation in sales of dryers is explained by the three explanatory variables. The remaining 2.2 percent was unexplained by the estimated equation.

3. *The standard error of the estimate* (S_e). This is a measure of dispersion of actual sales around the estimated equation. The output shows $S_e = 0.28613$.

4. *Computed* t. You read from the output

	t Statistic
X_1	7.35866
X_2	13.99748
X_3	9.59200

All t values are greater than a rule-of-thumb table t value of 2.0. (Strictly speaking, with $n - k - 1 = 10 - 3 - 1 = 6$ degrees of freedom and a level of significance of, say, 0.01, you see from Table 2 in Appendix B that the table t value is 3.707.) For a two-sided test, the level of significance to look up was .005. In any case, we conclude that all three explanatory variables we have selected were statistically significant.

5. F *test*. From the output, you see that

$$F = \frac{\text{Explained variance}/k = 29.109/3}{\text{Unexplained variance}/(n - k - 1) = 0.491/6}$$

$$= 9.703/0.082 = 118.515. \text{ (which is given in the printout)}$$

At a significance level of 0.01, our F value is far above the value of 9.78 (which is from Table 3 in the Appendix), so you conclude that the regression as a whole is highly significant.

6. *Conclusion.* Based on statistical considerations, you see that:

- The estimated equation had a good fit.
- All three variables are significant explanatory variables.
- The regression as a whole is highly significant.
- The model can be used as a forecasting equation with a great degree of confidence.

Chapter 25

Cash Flow Forecasting For Budgeting

A forecast of cash collections and potential writeoffs of accounts receivable is essential in cash budgeting and in judging the appropriateness of current credit and discount policies. The critical step in making such a forecast is estimating the cash collection and bad debt percentages to be applied to sales or accounts receivable balances. This chapter discusses several methods of estimating cash collection rates (or payment proportions) and illustrates how these rates are used for cash budgeting purposes.

The first approach, which is based on the Markov model, involves the use of a probability matrix based on the estimates of what is referred to as transition probabilities. This method is described on a step-by-step basis using an illustrative example. The second approach involves a simple average. The third approach, empirically tested and improved by the author, offers a more pragmatic method of estimating collection and bad debt percentages by relating credit sales and collection data. This method employs regression analysis. By using these approaches, a financial planner should be able to:

• Estimate future cash collections from accounts receivable.

• Establish an allowance for doubtful accounts.

• Provide a valuable insight into better methods of managing accounts receivable.

MARKOV APPROACH

The Markov (probability matrix) approach has been around for a long time. This approach has been successfully applied by Cyert and others to accounts receivable analysis, specifically to the estimation of that portion of the accounts receivable that will eventually become uncollectible. The method requires classification of outstanding accounts receivable according to age categories that reflect the stage of account delinquency (e.g., current accounts, accounts one month past due, accounts two months past due, and so forth). Consider the following example.

EXAMPLE 25-1

XYZ department store divides its accounts receivable into two classifications: 0 to 60 days old and 61 to 120 days old. Accounts that are more than 120 days old are declared uncollectible by XYZ. XYZ currently has $10,000 in accounts receivable: $7,000 from the 0-60-day-old category and $3,000 from the 61–120-day-old category. Based on an analysis of its past records, it provides us with what is known as the matrix of transition probabilities. The matrix is given as shown in Exhibit 25-1.

EXHIBIT 25-1 Probability Matrix

From To	Collected	Uncollectible	0–60-Days Old	61–120-Days Old
Collected	1	0	0	0
Uncollectible	0	1	0	0
0–60-days old	.3	0	.5	.2
61–120-days old	.5	.1	.3	.1

Transition probabilities are nothing more than the probability that an account receivable moves from one age stage category to another. We noted three basic features of this matrix. First, notice the squared element, 0 in the matrix. This indicates that $1 in the 0–6-day-old category cannot become a bad debt in one month's time. Now look at the two circled elements. Each of these is 1, indicating that, in time, all the accounts receivable dollars will either be paid or become uncollectible. Eventually, all the dollars do wind up either as collected or uncollectible, but XYZ would be interested in knowing the probability that a dollar of a 0–60-day-old or a 61–120-day-old receivable would eventually find its way into either paid bills or bad debts. It is convenient to partition the matrix of transition probabilities into four submatrices, as follows.

$$\begin{bmatrix} I & O \\ R & Q \end{bmatrix}$$

so that

$$I = \begin{bmatrix} 1 & 0 \\ 0 & 1 \end{bmatrix} \quad O = \begin{bmatrix} 0 & 0 \\ 0 & 0 \end{bmatrix}$$

$$R = \begin{bmatrix} .3 & 0 \\ .5 & .1 \end{bmatrix} \quad Q = \begin{bmatrix} .5 & .2 \\ .3 & .1 \end{bmatrix}$$

Now we are in a position to illustrate the procedure used to determine:

- Estimated collection and bad debt percentages by age category.
- Estimated allowance for doubtful accounts.

Step-by-step, the procedure is as follows:

Step 1. Set up the matrix $[I - Q]$.

$$[I - Q] = \begin{bmatrix} 1 & 0 \\ 0 & 1 \end{bmatrix} - \begin{bmatrix} .5 & .2 \\ .3 & .1 \end{bmatrix} = \begin{bmatrix} .5 & -.2 \\ -.3 & .9 \end{bmatrix}$$

Step 2. Find the inverse of this matrix, denoted by **N.**

$$N = [I - Q]^{-1} = \begin{bmatrix} 2.31 & .51 \\ .77 & 1.28 \end{bmatrix}$$

Note: The inverse of a matrix can be readily performed by spreadsheet programs such as Lotus 1–2–3™, Microsoft's Excel™, or Quattro Pro™. For example, Lotus 1–2–3 selects \Data Matrix Invert.

Step 3. Multiply this inverse by matrix **R.**

$$NR = \begin{bmatrix} 2.31 & .51 \\ .77 & 1.28 \end{bmatrix} \begin{bmatrix} .3 & 0 \\ .5 & .1 \end{bmatrix} = \begin{bmatrix} .95 & .05 \\ .87 & .13 \end{bmatrix}$$

Note: For example, in Lotus 1–2–3™, you will select "\Data Matrix Multiply."

NR gives us the probability that an account will eventually be collected or become a bad debt. Specifically, the top row in the answer is the probability that $1 of XYZ's accounts receivable in the 0–60-day-old category will be placed in the collected and bad debt categories. There is a .95 probability that $1 currently in the 0–60-day-old will be paid, and a .05 probability that it will eventually become a bad debt. Turning to the second row, the two entries represent the probability that $1 now in the 61–120-day-old category will be placed in the collected and bad debt categories. You can see from this row that there is a .87 probability that 41 currently in the 61–120-day-category will be collected and a .13 probability that it will eventually become uncollectible.

If XYZ wants to estimate the future of its $10,000 accounts receivable ($7,000 in the 0–60-day category and $3,000 in the 61–120-day category), it must set up the following matrix multiplication:

$$[7,000 \quad 3,000]\begin{bmatrix} .95 & .05 \\ .87 & .13 \end{bmatrix} = [9,260 \quad 740]$$

Hence, of its $10,000 in accounts receivable, XYZ expects to collect $9,260 and to lose $740 to bad debts. Therefore, the estimated allowances for the collectible accounts is $740.

The variance of each component is equal to

$$A = be(cNR - (cNR)_{sq})$$

where $c_i = b_i / \sum_{i=1}^{2} b_i$ and e is the unit vector.

In our example, $b = (7,000 \quad 3,000)$, $c = (.7 \quad .3)$. Therefore,

$$A = [7,000 \quad 3,000]\begin{bmatrix} 1 \\ 1 \end{bmatrix}[.7 \quad .3]\begin{bmatrix} .95 & .05 \\ .87 & .13 \end{bmatrix}$$

$$\left[-[.7 \quad .3]\begin{bmatrix} .95 & .05 \\ .87 & .13 \end{bmatrix}^{sq}\right] = 10,000 \quad [.926 \quad .074]$$

$$-[.857476 \quad .005476] = [685.24 \quad 685.24]$$

which makes the standard deviation equal to $26.18 ($\sqrt{\$685.24}$). If you want to be 95 percent confident about your estimate of collections, set the interval estimate at $9,260 + 2(26.18)$, or $9,207.64 –$9,312.36, assuming $t = 2$ as a rule of thumb. You would also be able to set the allowance to cover the bad debts at $740 + 2(26.18)$, or $792.36.

ACCOUNT ANALYSIS

The most straightforward way to estimate collection percentages is to compute the percentages of collections realized from past months. Once the experience has been analyzed, the results can be adjusted for trends and applied to the credit sales portrayed in the sales forecast. An example illustrates the technique.

EXAMPLE 25-2 Assume that an analysis of collection experience for August sales revealed the following collection data:

Description	% of Total Credit Sales
Collected in August	2.3
September	80.2
October	9.9
November	5.1
December	.5
Cash discounts	1.0
Bad debt losses	1.0
Total	100.0

If next year's sales in August could be expected to fall into the same pattern, then application of the percentages to estimated August credit sales would determine the probable monthly distribution of collections. The same analysis applied to each month of the year would result in a reasonably reliable basis for collection forecasting. The worksheet (August column) for cash collections might look as follows:

	Description		
Month of Sale	% Total	Sales Net	August Collection
April	.5	$168,000	$ 840
May	4.2	192,000	8,064
June	8.9	311,100	2,768
July	82.1	325,600	267,318
August	2.3	340,000	7,820
Total Collections			286,810
Cash Discounts (July)	1.0	325,600	(3,250)
Losses	1.0		(3,400)
Total			$280,160

REGRESSION APPROACH

A more scientific approach to estimating cash collection percentages (or payment proportions) is to use multiple regression. There is typically a time lag between the point of a credit sale and realization of cash. More specifically, the lagged effect of credit sales and cash inflows is distributed over a number of periods, as follows:

$$C_t = b_1 S_{t-1} + b_2 S_{t-2} + \ldots b_i S_{t-i}$$

where C_t = cash collection in month t

S_t = credit sales made in period t

$b_1, b_2, \ldots b_i$ = collection percentages (the same as P'_i, and

i = number of periods lagged

By using the regression method discussed previously, you will be able to estimate these collection rates. We can utilize /Data Regression of Lotus 1-2-3™ or special packages such as SAS, Systat, or Statgraphics.

It should be noted that the cash collection percentages, $(b_1, b_2, \ldots, b_i)$ may not add up to 100 percent because of the possibility of bad debts. Once you estimate these percentages by using the regression method, you should be able to compute the bad debt percentage with no difficulty.

Exhibit 25-2 shows the regression results using actual monthly data on credit sales and cash inflows for a real company. Equation I can be written as follows:

$$C_t = 60.6\%(S_{t-1}) + 24.3\%(S_{t-2}) + 8.8\%(S_{t-3})$$

This result indicates that the receivables generated by the credit sales are collected at the following rates: first month after sale, 60.6 percent; second month after sale, 24.3 percent; and third month after sale, 8.8 percent. The bad debt percentage is computed as 6.3 percent $(100 - 93.7 \text{ percent})$.

It is important to note, however, that these collection and bad debt percentages are probabilistic variables; that is, variables whose values cannot be known with precision. However, the standard error of the regression coefficient and the 5-value permit us to assess the probability that the true percentage is between specified limits. The confidence interval takes the following form:

$$b \pm t\, S_b$$

where S_b = standard error of the coefficient.

EXHIBIT 25-2 Regression Results for Cash Collection (C_t)

Independent Variables	Equation I	Equation II
S_{t-1}	0.606[a]	0.596[a]
	(0.062)[b]	(0.097)
S_{t-2}	0.243[a]	0.142
	(0.085)	(0.120)
S_{t-3}	0.088	0.043
	(0.157)	(0.191)
S_{t-4}		0.136
		(0.800)
R^2	0.754	0.753
Durbin-Watson	2.52[c]	2.48[c]
Standard error of the estimate (S_e)	11.63	16.05
Number of monthly observations	21	20
Bad debt percentages	0.063	0.083

[a] Statistically significant at the 5 percent significance level.

[b] This figure in the parentheses is the standard error of the e estimate for the coefficient (S_b).

[c] No autocorrelation present at the 5 percent significance level.

EXAMPLE 25-3   To illustrate, assuming $t = 2$ as rule of thumb at the 95 percent confidence level, the true collection percentage from the prior month's sales will be

$$60.6\% \pm 2(6.2\%) = 60.6\% \pm 12.4\%$$

Turning to the estimation of cash collections and allowance for doubtful accounts, the following values are used for illustrative purposes:

$S_{t-1} = \$77.6$, $S_{t-2} = \$58.5$, $S_{t-3} = \$76.4$, and forecast average monthly net credit sales = \$75.2

Then,

(a) the forecast cash collection for period t would be

$$C_t = 60.6\%(77.6) + 19.3\%(58.5) + 8.8\%(76.4) = \$65.04$$

If the financial manager wants to be 95 percent confident about this forecast value, then the interval would be set as follows:

$$C_t \pm t \, S_e$$

where S_e = standard error of the estimate.

To illustrate, using $t = 2$ as a rule of thumb at the 95 percent confidence level, the true value for cash collections in period t will be

$$\$65.04 \pm 2(11.63) = \$65.04 \pm 23.26$$

(b) the estimated allowance for uncollectible accounts for period t will be

$$6.3\% \, (\$75.2) = \$4.74$$

By using the limits discussed so far, financial planners can develop flexible (or probabilistic) cash budgets, where the lower and upper limits can be interpreted as pessimistic and optimistic outcomes, respectively. They can also simulate a cash budget in an attempt to determine both the expected change in cash collections for each period and the variation in this value.

In preparing a conventional cash inflow budget, the financial manager considers the various sources of cash, including cash on account, sale of assets, incurrence of debt, and so on. Cash collections from customers are emphasized, since that is the greatest problem in this type of budget.

EXAMPLE 25-4   The following data are given for Erich Stores:

	September Actual	October Actual	November Estimated	December Estimated
Cash sales	$ 7,000	$ 6,000	$ 8,000	$ 6,000
Credit sales	50,000	48,000	62,000	80,000
Total sales	$57,000	$54,000	$70,000	$86,000

Past experience indicates net collections normally occur in the following pattern:

- No collections are made in the month of sale.
- 80 percent of the sales of any month are collected in the following month.
- 19 percent of sales are collected in the second following month.
- 1 percent of sales are uncollectible.

You can project total cash receipts for November and December as follows:

	November	December
Cash receipts		
Cash sales	$ 8,000	$ 6,000
Cash collections		
September sales		
50,000 (19%)	9,500	
October sales		
48,000 (80%)	38,400	
48,000 (19%)		9,120
November sales		
62,000 (80%)		49,600
Total cash receipts	$55,900	$64,720

EXAMPLE 25-5   *Cash Collections and Discount Policy*

The treasurer of John Loyde Co. plans for the company to have a cash balance of $91,000 on March 1. Sales during March are estimated at $900,000. February sales amounted to $600,000, and January sales amounted to $500,000. Cash payments for March have been budgeted at $580,000. Cash collections have been estimated as follows:

- 60 percent of the sales for the month are to be collected during the month.
- 30 percent of the sales for the preceding month are to be collected during the month.

• 8 percent of the sales for the second preceding month are to be collected during the month.

The treasurer plans to accelerate collections by allowing a 2 percent discount for prompt payment. With the discount policy, he expects to collect 70 percent of the current sales and will permit the discount reduction on these collections. Sales of the preceding month will be collected to the extent of 15 percent with no discount allowed, and 10 percent of the sales of the second preceding month will be collected with no discount allowed. This pattern of collection can be expected in subsequent months. During the transitional month of March, collections may run somewhat higher. However, the treasurer prefers to estimate collections on the basis of the new pattern so that the estimates will be somewhat conservative.

1. Estimate cash collections for March and the cash balance at March 31 under the present policy.
2. Estimate cash collections for March and the cash balance at March 31 according to the new policy of allowing discounts.
3. Is the discount policy desirable?

The solutions for (1) and (2) are:

	Under the Present Policy	Under the Discount Policy
Balance, March 1	$ 91,000	$ 91,000
Collections		
From March sales	540,000 ($900,000 × 60%)	617,400[a]
From February sales	180,000 ($600,000 × 30%)	90,000 ($600,000 × 15%)
From January sales	40,000 ($500,000 × 8%)	50,000 ($500,000 × 10%)
Total cash available	$851,000	$848,400
Less disbursements	580,000	580,000
Balance, March 31	$271,000	$268,400

[a] $900,000 × 70% × 98% = $617,400

The answers to (3) is:

No, because under the discount policy, the March 31 cash balance will be smaller as indicated above ($268,400 as compared to $271,000 under the present policy).

EXAMPLE 25-6 The following is a sample printout of a cash collection budget generated from Up Your Cash Flow.

EXHIBIT 25-3

Your Company, Inc.
Cash Collection Budget
on the Year

Sales	Jan.	Feb.	Mar.	Apr.	May	Jun.	Jul.	Aug.	Sep.	Oct.	Nov.	Dec.	Total
	129,030	129,030	129,030	129,030	192,610	192,610	162,690	129,030	192,610	129,030	162,690	192,610	1,870,000
Previous months													
December previous years	20,000	10,000											30,000
Collection current year													
Jan. 129,030 × 45;40;15	58,063	51,612	19,355										129,030
Feb. 129,030 × 45;40;15		58,063	51,612	19,355									129,030
Mar. 129,030 × 45;40;15			58,063	51,612	19,355								129,030
Apr. 129,030 × 45;40;15				58,063	51,612	19,355							129,030
May 192,610 × 45;40;15					86,675	77,044	28,891						192,610
Jun. 192,610 × 45;40;15						86,675	77,044	28,891					192,610
Jul. 162,690 × 45;40;15							73,210	65,076	24,404				162,690
Aug. 129,030 × 45;40;15								58,063	51,612	19,355			129,030
Sep. 192,610 × 45;40;15									86,675	77,044	28,891		192,610
Oct. 129,610 × 45;40;15										58,063	51,612	19,355	129,030
Nov. 162,690 × 45;40;15											73,210	65,076	138,286
Dec. 192,610 × 45;40;15												86,674	86,674
Total Collections	78,063	119,675	129,030	129,030	157,642	183,074	179,145	152,030	162,691	154,462	153,713	171,105	1,769,680

The assumption used for cash collections is that:
45% of the months sales are collected in the month the sale is made.
40% of the sale is collected in the 1st month following the sale.
15% is collected in the 2nd month following the sale.
in other words 45;40;15

384

IS CASH FLOW SOFTWARE AVAILABLE?

Computer software allows for day-to-day cash management, forecasting and budgeting cash flows, determining cash balances, planning and analyzing cash flows, finding cash shortages, investing cash surpluses, accounting for cash transactions, automating accounts receivable and payable, and dial-up banking. Computerization improves availability, accuracy, timeliness, and monitoring of cash information at minimal cost. Daily cash information aids in planning how to use cash balances. It enables the integration of different kinds of related cash information such as collections on customer accounts and cash balances, and the effect of cash payments on cash balances.

Spreadsheet program software such as Lotus 1–2–3™, Microsoft's Excel™, and Quattro Pro™ can assist you in developing cash budgets and answering a variety of "what-if" questions. For example, you can see the effect on cash flow from different scenarios (e.g., the purchase and sale of different product lines). There are computer software packages specially designed for cash budgeting and management. Three popular ones are briefly described below.

1. *Up Your Cash Flow:* This program contains automatically prepared spreadsheets for profit/loss forecasts, cash flow budgets, projected balance sheet, payroll analysis, term loan amortization schedule, sales/cost of sales by product, ratio analysis, and graphs. It is a menu-driven system and you can customize it to your forecasting needs. The system requirements are:

- PC compatibles, DOS version 2.0 or later
- 512K RAM and a hard drive
- Prints on 132 column, 80-column or HP Laser Jet.

It is available from:

Granville Publications Software
10960 Wilshire Blvd., Suite 826
Los Angeles, CA 90024
(800) 873-7789

2. *Cash Flow Analysis:* This software provides projections of cash inflow and cash outflow. You input data into eight categories: sales, cost of sales, general and administrative expense, long-term debt, other cash receipts, inventory build-up/reduction, capital expenditures (acquisition of long-term assets such as store furniture), and income tax. The program allows changes in assumptions and scenarios and provides a complete array of reports. The system requirements are:

- PC compatibles, DOS version 2.0 or later
- 512K RAM and a hard drive.

It is available from:

Superior Software
16055 Ventura Blvd., Suite 725
Encino, CA 91436
(800) 421-3264
(818) 990-1135

3. *Quicken:* This program is a fast, easy to use, inexpensive accounting program that can help you manage your personal finances or small business. It can help you manage your cash flow. You record bills as postdated transactions when they arrive; the program's Billminder feature automatically reminds you when bills are due. Then, you can print checks for due bills with a few keystrokes. Similarly, you can record invoices and track aged receivables. Together, these features help you to maximize cash on hand. The system requirements are:

- PC compatibles, DOS version 2.0 or later
- At least 320K RAM. Two floppy disks or a hard disk are highly recommended
- Prints on almost any printer.

It is available from:

Intuit, Inc.
P.O. Box 3014
Menlo Park, CA 94026
(800) 624-8742

CONCLUSION

Two methods of estimating the expected collectible and uncollectible patterns were presented. One advantage of the Markov model is that the expected value and standard deviation of these percentages can be determined, thereby making it possible to specify probabilistic statements about these figures. You must be careful about these results, however, since the model makes some strong assumptions. A serious assumption is that the matrix of transition probabilities is constant over time. Do not expect this to be perfectly true.

Updating of the matrix may have to be done, perhaps through the use of such techniques as exponential smoothing and time series analysis.

The regression approach is relatively inexpensive to use in the sense that it does not require a lot of data. All it requires is data on cash collections, and credit sales. Furthermore, credit sales values are all predetermined; use previous months' credit sales to forecast cash collections, that is, there is no need to forecast credit sales. The model also allows you to make numerous statistical inferences about the cash collection percentages and forecast values.

Extensions of these models can be made toward setting credit and discount policies. Corresponding to a given set of policies, there are

- An associated transition matrix in the Markov model
- Associated collection percentages in the regression model.

By computing long-term collections and bad debts for each policy, an optimal policy can be chosen that maximizes expected long-run profits per period.

Part **5**

FINANCIAL MODELS

Chapter 26

Practical Business Aspects to Planning Models

Today more and more companies are using, developing, or experimenting with some form of corporate planning model. This is primarily due to the development of planning and modeling software packages that make it possible to develop the model without much knowledge of computer coding and programming. The attractive features of corporate modeling are the formulation of budgets, budgetary planning and control, and financial analyses that can be used to support management decision making. However, corporate modeling involves much more than the generation of financial statements and budgets. Depending on the structure and breadth of the modeling activity, a variety of capabilities, uses, and analyses are available.

Exhibit 26-1 presents a chart showing several modeling tools that can be used at various levels of the planning process. The organizational levels are divided into Corporate, Business, and Functional, with the processed divided into objectives setting, specific multi-year planning, and budgeting.

A corporate planning model is an integrated business planning model in which marketing and production models are linked to the financial model. More specifically, a corporate model is a description, explanation, and interrelation of the functional areas of a firm (accounting, finance, marketing, production, and others) expressed in terms of a set of mathematical and logical relationships so as to produce a variety of reports including financial statements. The ultimate goals of a corporate planning model are to improve quality of planning and decision making, to reduce the decision risk, and, more importantly, to influence or even to shape the future environment.

FIGURE 26–1. Modeling Tools to Be Used at Various Stages/Levels of the Planning Process

Stage in Planning Process / Organizational Level	Cycle 1 Objectives Setting	Cycle 2 Specific Multiyear Planning	Cycle 3 Budgeting
Corporate	national econometric models (DRI, Wharton)	pro forma portfolio funds flows (multiple years), capital investment models (multiple years)	budgeting models
Divisional (Business)	industry econometric models (DRI, Wharton)	(DRI, PIMS) pro forma business funds flows (multiple years), capital investments (businesses).	
Functional		mktg models, R&D models, warehouse/plant location, capital investment (function).	operations management, models scheduling

Source: Lorange, pg. 269.

Generally speaking, a corporate model can be used to:

1. Simulate an alternative strategy by evaluating its impact on profits.
2. Help establish corporate and divisional goals.
3. Measure the interactive effect of parts with the firm.
4. Help management better understand the business and its functional relationships and help improve decision making ability.
5. Link the firm's goals and strategies to its master budgets.
6. Assess critically the assumptions underlying environmental constraints.

TYPES OF ANALYSIS

The type of the corporate model that management is seeking would depend upon what types of analysis it wishes to perform. There are typically three types of model investigations.

The first type of questions to be raised is "What is" or "what has been" questions, such as the relationship between variables of the firm and external macroeconomic variables such as GNP or inflation. The goal of this type of model investigation is to obtain a specific answer based on the stipulated relationship. For example, what is or has been the firm's profit when the price of raw material was $12.50?

The second type of investigation focuses on "what-if" questions. This is done through simulation or sensitivity analysis. This analysis often takes the following form: "What happens under a given set of assumptions if the decision variable(s) is changed in a prescribed manner?" For example, "What will happen to the company's cash flow and net income if it is contemplating a reduction of the price by 10 percent and an increase in the advertising budget by 25 percent?"

The third type of question that can be addressed by way of corporate planning modeling takes the following form: "What must be done in order to achieve a particular objective?" This type of analysis is often called *goal seeking*. It usually requires the use of optimization models such as linear programming and goal programming.

TYPICAL QUESTIONS ADDRESSED VIA CORPORATE MODELING

The following is a list of questions management addresses itself using corporate modeling.

- What are the effects of different pricing policies?
- What is the effect of different interest rates and current exchange rates on the income statement and balance sheet of the firm?
- What will be the demand for the end products of the firm at various locations and different times?
- What is and will be the unit contribution margin for certain production, transportation, and sales allocations?
- What will the absence and turnover rates of the employees of the firm be and what effect will they have?
- What is the effect of advertising and distribution expenditures on sales?
- What marketing strategy can and should the firm follow?
- What do price-demand or supply relations on the output or input side of the firm look like? What are the effects of price/cost changes on sales?
- How do certain states of the national or world economy influence sales of the firm on the one side and purchase price of the production factors on the other?
- What is the nature of the conditions that must be fulfilled if the total sales of the firm at a certain time are supposed to be higher than a certain budget value?

- Should the firm produce and sell a certain product, purchase and sell the product, or not get involved at all?
- In what range will the return on investment on various projects and units lie?
- How will the income statement, the balance sheet, and the cash flow statement develop for several operating divisions? What will their contributions be?
- What effects with respect to the financial position of the firm could an acquisition or merger with another firm have?

Benefits derived from the corporate planning models include:

1. The ability to explore more alternatives
2. Better quality decision making
3. More effective planning
4. A better understanding of the business
5. Faster decision making
6. More timely information
7. More accurate forecasts
8. Cost savings.

TYPES OF MODELS

Corporate planning models can be categorized according to two approaches: simulation and optimization. Simulation models are attempts to mathematically represent the operations of the company or of the conditions in the external economic environment. By adjusting the values of controllable variables and assumed external conditions, the future implications of present decision making can be estimated. Probabilistic simulation models incorporate probability estimates into the forecast sequence, while deterministic models do not. Optimization models are intended to identify the best decision, given specific constraints.

HISTORY OF MODELS

The rudiments of corporate modeling can be placed in the early 1960s with the large, cumbersome simulation models developed by major corporations such as AT&T, Wells Fargo Bank, Dow Chemical, IBM, Sun Oil, and Boise

Cascade. Most of the models were written in one of the general programming languages (GPLs), such as FORTRAN, and were used for generating pro forma financial statements. The models typically required several man-years to develop and, in some cases, never provided benefits sufficient to outweigh the costs of development. Planning models were considered an untested concept, suitable only for those corporations large enough to absorb the costs and risks of development.

Important advancements in computer technology in the early 1970s provided the means for greater diversity and affordability in corporate modeling. Interactive computing facilities allowed for faster and more meaningful input/output sequences for modelers; trial-and-error adjustments of inputs and analyses were possible while on-line to the central computer or to an outside timesharing service. The advent of corporate simulation languages enabled financial managers with little experience with GLPs to write modeling programs in an English-like programming language; for example, to name a few, IFPS™, Compete™, Encore Plus™, and SIMPLAN™. In addition, a number of spreadsheet programs such as Lotus 1–2–3™ became available for use by corporate planning modelers. By 1979, nearly every Fortune 1,000 company was using a corporate simulation model. This statistic will definitely increase to cover small and medium size firms.

As companies gained experience in developing basic, deterministic simulations, renewed effort was directed toward consolidating and integrating smaller models into the larger corporate models first attempted in the 1960s. Furthermore, certain companies were attempting the more difficult optimization models and were increasing predictive power by using econometric models to link their simulations with product markets and the external economy. Early successes with the simpler models led to a boom in modeling, but an increasing number of failures in more ambitious projects soon moderated the general enthusiasm. As the economy entered a recession and became more unstable (less predictable), the weaknesses in the rationale underlying many corporate models were revealed. Managers realized that the purpose of a model must be well defined and that the end users should be involved in its development. Although the bad experiences of the mid 1970s have prejudiced some executives against models to the present day, most veterans of the period have developed a realistic attitude toward the capabilities of models and are employing recent advancements in techniques to construct more serviceable models.

CURRENT TRENDS IN MODELING

Several surveys of financial model-making in the United States and the United Kingdom firms have been conducted over the past 15 years. The firms

EXHIBIT 26-2 Results of Surveys for the Use of Corporate Models

Author	Sample Size (Responses)	Corporate Use of or Development of Models
Gershefski [7]	323	63 (20%)
Naylor and Schauland [17]	346	253 (73%)
McLean and Neale [14]	410	245 (60%)
Brightman and Harris [5]	237	126 (53%)
Klein [12]	204	175 (86%)

represented a broad cross-section of industries and services, with sales ranging from $1 million to over $1 billion annually. The specific purposes of the surveys varied somewhat among researchers, but each was designed to estimate the general acceptance and development of corporate modeling. While different sample sizes and populations prevent pooling the results, it is instructive to discuss important issues and common findings.

The earliest survey results, reported by Gershefski [7], revealed that 63 (20 percent) of 323 firms sampled in 1968 were working with corporate planning models. Naylor and Schauland [17] found that 253 (73 percent) of 346 firms were using or developing corporate planning models in 1975. Recent surveys by McLean and Neale [14] and by Klein [12] indicated that 60 and 80 percent of companies surveyed, respectively (410 and 204, respectively), were using some type of financial model. The results indicate that corporate modeling has become a common tool in U.S. business firms. See Exhibit 26-2.

Among the reasons cited by corporations for using planning models were

- Economic uncertainty
- Shortages of resources
- Diminishing increase in productivity
- International competition
- Tight money and inflation
- Political upheavals (affecting foreign operations)
- Environmental problems
- New business opportunities [15].

There was general agreement that models enabled managers to run alternative analyses and to adjust decision variables, while reducing the time needed for report writing. The many possible applications of corporate planning models are listed in Exhibit 26-3. Financial forecasting and pro-forma balance sheet statements were the most common applications of most companies. The models proved to be useful tools in "what-if" analysis, sensitivity analysis, simulations, best/worst case scenarios, goal seeking, optimization, and report preparation.

EXHIBIT 26-3 Applications of Corporate Planning Models

Financial forecasting	Construction scheduling
Pro-forma financial statements	Tax planning
Capital budgeting	Energy requirements
Market decision making	Labor contract negotiation fees
Merger and acquisition analysis	Foreign currency analysis
Lease versus purchase decisions	Utilities
Production scheduling	Load forecasting
New venture evaluation	Rate cases
Manpower planning	Generation planning
Profit planning	
Sales forecasting	
Investment analysis	

A consistent finding among the surveys was the involvement of top management in successful modeling efforts. Naylor [14] and Klein [12] found that in 50 to 90 percent of the companies using models, upper managers (e.g., president or vice-president, finance; controller; treasurer; executive vice president) participated in the definition and implementation of the model. The background of the participants in Klein's survey was predominantly in finance, followed by computer science and accounting. The end users of the models were usually strategic planning groups, the treasurer's department, and the controller's department.

The only detailed figures on actual developmental costs of modeling were supplied by Naylor [16]. The average cost (labor, computer time, materials) in 1975 for developing a model in house with no outside assistance was $82,752. The average cost to firms that received help from outside consultants was $29,225, with markedly shorter development schedules. Ironically, most executives believed that outside consultants were too expensive and avoided hiring them [5], [12]. Furthermore, Ang and Chua [2] reported survey results showing that only three of 31 companies hired outside consultants on subsequent efforts.

Despite the growing diversity of modeling techniques available, the vast majority of corporate models encountered in the surveys were basic, deterministic simulations. Probabilistic considerations were seldom incorporated into the models by any but the largest corporations. As recently as 1983, Naylor [15] found that no firms were using optimization models as a planning tool. Evidently, the accuracy of optimization models, as well as their clarity to upper management, must improve before they receive significant use.

Attitudes and Problems

The reluctance of many firms to experiment with corporate planning models derives chiefly from a fear of the unknown. Confusion over what models are and how they are used precludes serious investigation of their potential benefits. Myths that discourage managers from considering models include the following:

- Models are complicated. On the contrary, most effective models are fairly simple structures, incorporating only the essential processes of the problem under investigation. The math involved is often basic algebra, and modeling languages reduce complex terminology.

- The company is not large enough. Models do not consist solely of comprehensive simulations. Some of the most frequently used models center on a limited number of key relationships.

- The company does not own a computer. Models are being designed for use on inexpensive personal computers, and outside time-sharing services are available.

- The company does not have any modelers. Modern planning languages have so simplified the modeling process that even a novice quickly becomes competent. Outside consultants are also available for assistance.

Attitudes toward modeling have progressed from the rather deteriorated outlook of the mid-1970s to today's more optimistic viewpoint. The past trend probably explains the general negativity of earlier results reported by Higgins and Finn [9] in their literature review of top management attitudes toward modeling in the United Kingdom. In summarizing the activities comprising the senior executive's role, the authors concluded that most of the manager's duties involved behavioral, interpersonal communication problems requiring his direct ministering. The majority view of managers emphasized that models could not capture the essential complexity of the organization and ignored the political and behavioral issues. In the few areas where a model could prove useful, the executive had insufficient time to learn how to apply it. At that time, the picture of an executive seated at a computer and engaged in problem analysis was unrealistic. The ultimate finding, however, was not a wholesale abandonment of corporate planning models among managers, but rather the delegation of modeling analysis to lower managers. Thus, models seemed destined to become strictly a middle management tool.

At about the same time, many surveys showed the importance of obtaining top management's support to ensure success in any model-making project. However, top managers in over 50 percent of the companies sampled believed their models had improved forecasts; 31 percent were undecided. More encouraging results followed. Wagner [22] reported that upper management in his survey not only requested that models be built but participated in their development. The finished products received a high average utility rating of 3.9 out of a total of 5. A similar evaluation in 1980 by top management at 410 U.S. firms (annual sales exceeding $100 million) yielded a 4.95 rating out of 7 for their computer-based planning models. None of the CEOs considered the models useless. Klein [12] found evidence of significant cost savings through modeling, with one vice president of finance reporting a $600,000 savings through use of a financial planning model.

The growing acceptance of planning models has enabled managers and technicians to identify areas requiring improvement and to formulate criteria for success. Optimization models are one technique in need of refinement.

Note: Optimization models are inscrutable "black boxes" to those managers who have had no part in the modeling effort [18]. Naturally, top management has little confidence in forecasts produced by a model they cannot understand. The need to monitor several financial and nonfinancial variables precludes the construction of simple optimization models.

No serious limitations in modeling were noted by respondents in Naylor's 1976 survey. The criticisms were directed at the inflexibility of some models, poor documentation by the model builder, and excessive input data requirement. Aggarwal and Khera [1] identified several points of inflexibility in most models. Models usually simulate only one cause-and-effect relationship, whereas multiple effects are often present. Similarly, the intended results of a control action may be accompanied by unintended results. In that instance, the desirability of the two consequences must be compared on a common utility scale. When several consequences of a decision are separated in time, a means for making comparisons among them is required, similar to a discount rate in capital budgeting. Such techniques are rarely available in practice.

The reasons for discontinuation of corporate planning models in 31 of the largest U.S. corporations were reported by Ag and Chua [2]. The majority of firms sampled were industries, followed by retailers, transporters, utilities, banks, and finance and insurance institutions. The 31 firms having discontinued models comprised only 27 percent of the total sample of 113 corporations. Twenty-nine of the 31 models were designed for producing pro-forma financial statements, and were discontinued within three years of construction. The various reasons for the rejections are listed in Exhibit 26-4.

EXHIBIT 26-4 Reasons for Discontinued Models

Lack of sufficient flexibility
Lack of adequate management support
Excessive amounts of input data required
Replaced by a better model
The need no longer existed
The model did not perform as expected
New management de-emphasized planning
Poor documentation
Lack of user interest
Excessive development costs
Excessive operating costs
Excessive development time required

The common justifications were model deficiencies and human problems in implementation. Three of the prevalent reasons (inflexibility, lack of management support, excessive input data requirements) are familiar shortcomings, as discussed earlier. The need for management's support for successful model making cannot be overemphasized; its role as champion of the effort is essential for companywide acceptance of the final product. It is interesting to note that excessive development time and costs were not often a basis for rejection.

A novel insight on success factors in modeling was provided by Simon, et al. [21]. The authors asserted that the modeler must be specious; the modeler must understand that management's expressed need for a particular model may perceive from the manager's behavior, rather than from his or her verbal request, the type of model needed. If an incorrect determination is made, the model may never be implemented. Two of the five categories of uses for models outlined in the study were legitimate and straightforward: Type I models are simulation/optimization techniques, and Type II models condition data for easier utilization. When the modeler perceives that management's objectives are not consistent with those of Type I or II models, one of three alternative choices is implied:

- Type III: Merely a subterfuge for establishing a data link, forcing one part of the organization to channel information to another.
- Type IV: A means of supplying a formal rationale for decisions reached in the past.
- Type V: A means of establishing a manager's reputation—simply a remake of a previously successful model.

A table of management behavior was provided by the authors as a guide for modelers in determining the type of model implied in the original request and in subsequent feedback.

STATE-OF-THE-ART AND RECOMMENDED PRACTICE

The acceptance of corporate planning models has resulted in many firms' establishing planning departments responsible for developing and implementing planning models. The structure of the typical corporate financial model is an integration of smaller modules used by each department or business unit for planning purposes. Figure 26-1 shows that marketing, production, and financial models from each business unit can be consolidated to drive a comprehensive model used by upper management.

Optimal procedures for assembling effective models are still largely at

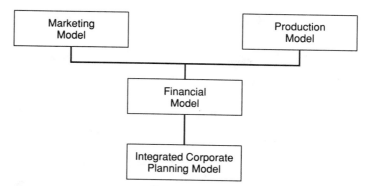

Figure 26-1 Typical Structure of an Integrated Planning

the discretion of the individual planning department, but useful guidelines have been published. Suggestions offered by Hammond [8] serve as practical considerations in evaluating the timeliness of a proposed modeling project and in guiding the project. The modeling effort could be divided into ten stages of activities:

1. Determine which process(es) can be modeled effectively.
2. Decide whether to use a model.
3. Formalize the specifications of the model (e.g., inputs and outputs, structure, etc.).
4. Prepare a proposal.
5. Conduct modeling and data gathering concurrently.
6. Debug the model.
7. Educate the prospective users.
8. Have users validate the model.
9. Put model to use.
10. Update and modify the model as needed.

Hammond cautioned that several iterations between certain stages may be necessary and that there may be several failures before a valid model is obtained. See Exhibit 26-5 for a list of prerequisites for modeling and control factors for success.

The anatomy of the contemporary financial model is composed of five parts: the documentation supporting the calculations; input assumptions regarding future periods; the projections and decision points leading to the forecasted values; managerial (financial) ratios; and graphics displaying information from decision points. The forecasting systems used depend upon the breadth and planning horizon of the model; typical methods include market research and Delphi method, time series analysis such as moving averages,

EXHIBIT 26-5 Success Factors in Modeling

Uncontrollable Prerequisites

Operations understood, data plentiful

Relevant data accessible

Budgets, plans, and control systems are well defined,
  understood

Modelers have management's support

Management scientists accept responsibility for implementation

Similar innovative techniques used in the past

Manager and modeler share status and background

Controllable Factors

Involve potential users in development process

Define model's goals explicitly

Input and output are in familiar formats

Company procedures are modified little at first

Look for common management problems to model

Start simple and keep it simple

Allow for ample judgmental inputs

Be realistic about planning time and expected results

Put a manager (not a modeler) in charge

Define roles clearly

Demonstrate part of model early on

Build model within users' organization

Develop expertise to manage and update mode

Provide ample documentation

exponential smoothing, Box-Jenkins, and various casual methods, such as life cycle analysis and regression.

Forecasting methods should be reviewed periodically by an independent party to ensure that the techniques have not become outdated. This can be determined only by maintaining a current management information system (MIS), which provides data to econometric models of the external environment. *Note:* The critical importance of external data in determining company strategy is the central theorem of MIS. Thus, planners make assumptions about the business environment for a particular planning horizon, based upon the output from the MIS. The information is combined with internal data to prepare demand forecasts, and the results can be input to a planning model or used to check the validity of forecasts produced by current techniques.

Planning and modeling languages (PMLs) have been a major incentive in involving higher management in modeling. General programming languages, such as FORTRAN, are seldom used in current models; oddly, COBOL, the "business language," has never been used extensively in modeling. The advantages of PMLs are steadily edging out GPLs: with PMLs, models are built more easily with shorter development and data processing, are more easily understood by upper management, and are periodically updated with enhancement from the vendor.

Today more than 70 PMLs are available at reasonable cost, including IFPS™, SIMPLAN™, Encore Plus™, and Venture™. A further convenience offered to companies looking into modeling is premade planning packages sold by software vendors. The packages have often been criticized for their inflexibility, but the newer models allow for more user specificity. Analytical portfolio models are commercial packages that tell a conglomerate how to distribute resources across the portfolio of profit centers. Boston Consulting Group, Arthur D. Little, and McKinsey have developed models that categorize investments into a matrix of profit potentials and recommended strategies.

A model for Profit Impact of Market Strategy (PIMS) is offered by the Strategic Planning Institute. The package is a large multiple regression model used to identify the optimal strategy in a given business environment. Similar packages will likely proliferate in the future as more companies are forced to use decision models to remain competitive. Furthermore, more and more spreadsheet-based add-ins and templates for budgeting are being developed for Lotus 1–2–3™, Microsoft Excel™, and Quattro Pro™.

MIS AND PERSONAL COMPUTERS

The analytic and predictive capabilities of corporate planning models depend in large part upon the supporting data base. Information technology has advanced to the point that data bases consist of logic-mathematical models and highly integrated collections of data, derived from both inside and outside the firm. The data bases are now called management information systems (MISs) or decision support systems (DSSs) because they store the data and decision tools used by management.

A primary value of the MIS's large storage capacity for data is the potential to more accurately model the external economy and to forecast business trends. Managers are finding that effective long-range planning depends primarily upon a thorough understanding of their competitors and the forces at work in the marketplace. A considerable body of data is required to develop insight into the competitive environment.

Note: Information derived from within the company has little strategic value for those purposes, thus the collection of external data should be emphasized. As a result, the relevance of information to future conditions is the standard by which input of data to the MIS is controlled.

Once the strategic data have been stored in the mainframe computer system, managers need quick access to the data base and a means for inputing alternative data sets and/or scenarios into the econometric models. Only recently have such activities been made possible by the development of communication links between mainframe systems and PCs. Many of the applications of the mainframe-PC connection involve rather basic analyses, such as accounts payable, receivables, general ledger, and the like. However, internal financial planning packages (e.g., IFPS) are currently available, as are external time-sharing services, such as Dow Jones, Lockheed's Dialog, and The Source.

The outlook for the next few years indicates increasing integration of the microcomputer with the mainframe. A recent survey of more than 1,000 organizations showed that 67 percent of middle management and 22 percent of top management of non-data-processing departments were using personal computers. The results indicate significant momentum at the top of corporate management for the use of PCs which should intensify the need for mainframe connections.

Corporate planning software packages for PCs are already proliferating. Applications now available range from cash flow analysis and budget projections to regressions, time series analysis, and probabilistic analysis.

PC World listed 116 software packages for financial and business analysis on the IBM PC; many were suitable as corporate planning models. The trend in PC technology is aimed toward incorporating as many mainframe, analytical capabilities into the microcomputer as the market will support.

THE FUTURE OF CORPORATE PLANNING MODELS

The interest in obtaining corporate models is likely to continue. The concept of the strategic business unit (SBU) as an object of analysis may prove to be unviable. There has been no consistent definition of SBU, and most models treat them as independent of one another, even though this may not be accurate. The SBU is typically forced into short-term profit making (rather than long-term development), eventually sapping its vitality. Consequently, an improved rationale may cause modes to be built around a different grouping of profit centers.

Expect to see an increased linking of portfolio models with corporate simulation and optimization models. Modeling software will become more modular in order to perform limited analyses or comprehensive projections. More software will be written for microcomputers, graphics will improve, and modeling languages will become more user friendly. The future of modeling is somewhat assured because it is intimately linked with the continued expansion of the computer market. Though shakeouts may frequently occur among hardware manufacturers, planning models will always have a market, as software writers improve their understanding of the planner's needs and produce more efficient decision-making tools.

CONCLUSION

Financial planning models comprise a functional branch of a general corporate model. In the face of uncertainty about the future, management is particularly interested in following the best possible course of action under a given circumstance. The model is used as a tool to help minimize risk and uncertainty and to develop the best course of action for the company. For example, management is able to examine the effects of proposed mergers and acquisitions with much less uncertainty and to estimate with more confidence the potential profits from new markets.

REFERENCES

1. Aggarwal, R. and I. Khera. "Using management science models: A critique for planners." *Managerial Planning* 28(4):12–15, 1980.

2. Ang, J. and J. Chua. "Corporate planning models that failed." *Managerial Planning* 29(4):34–38, 1980.

3. Baxendale, Sidney J. "Integrated Operational and Financial Modeling at a Public Utility," *Public Utilities Fortnightly,* February 1987, 39–45.

4. Kador, John, "The Software That Changed Decision Making at Xerox," *Business Software Review,* January 1987, 20–22.

5. Brightman, H. J. and S. E. Harris. "The planning and modeling language revolution: A managerial perspective." *Business* 32(4):15–21, 1982.

6. Ferris, D. "The micro-mainframe connection." *Datamation* 29(11):126–141, 1983.

7. Gershefski, G. W. "Computer models for corporate planning." *Long Range Planning* 8(1):14–25, 1975.

8. Hammond, J. S. "Dos and don'ts of computer models for planning." *Harvard Business Review* 52:110–123, 1974.

9. Higgins, J. C. and R. Finn. "Managerial attitudes toward computer models for planning and control." *Long Range Planning* 9:107–112, 1976.

10. Kennedy, J. "Financial applications." *PC World—Annual Software Review,* pp. 324–340, 1983.

11. Kingston, P. L. "Anatomy of a financial model." *Managerial Planning* 26:1–7, 1977.

12. Klein, R. "Computer-based financial modeling." *Journal of Systems Management* 33(5):6–13, 1982.

13. Lorange, Peter and Richard Vancil, *Strategic Planning Systems,* Prentice-Hall Inc., Englewood Cliffs, New Jersey, 1977.

14. McLean, E. R. and G. L. Neale. "Computer-based planning models come of age." *Harvard Business Review* 58:46–54, 1980.

15. Naylor, T. H. "Strategic Planning Models," *Managerial Planning* 30(1):3–11, 1983.

16. ———. (ed.) *Simulation in Business Planning and Decision Making,* The Society for Computer Simulation (Simulation Councils, Inc.), La Jolla, CA 1981.

17. Naylor, T. H. and H. Schauland. "A survey of users of corporate planning models." *Management Science* 22(9):927–937, 1976.

18. Naylor, T. H. and M. J. Mansfield. "The design of computer based planning and modeling systems." *Long Range Planning* 10:16–25, 1977.

19. Powers, P. D. "Computers and financial planning." *Long Range Planning* 8(6):53–59, 1975.

20. Shim, Jae K. and R. McGlade. "Current trends in the use of corporate planning models." *Journal of Systems Management,* September 34(9), 1984.

21. Simon, L. S., C. Lamar, and G. H. Haines, Jr. "Managers' use of models." *Omega* 4(3):253–263, 1976.

22. Wagner, G. R. "Enhancing creativity in strategic planning through computer systems." *Managerial Planning* 28:10–17, 1979.

Chapter 27

Budgeting Through Financial Modeling*

Many companies are increasingly using financial modeling to develop their budgets. This chapter discusses:

- What is a financial model?
- What are some typical uses of financial models?
- What are the types of financial modeling?
- How widespread is the use of financial modeling in practice?
- How do you build a financial model?

The use of spreadsheets and financial modeling languages for financial modeling is discussed in Chapter 28.

A FINANCIAL MODEL

A financial model, narrowly called a budgeting model, is a system of mathematical equations, logic and data which describes the relationships among financial and operating variables. A financial model can be viewed as a subset of broadly defined corporate planning models or a stand-alone functional sys-

---

* This chapter was coauthored by Marc Levine, Ph.D., CPA, a consultant and Professor of Accounting and Information Systems at Queens College.

tem that attempts to answer a certain financial planning problem. A financial model is one in which:

1. one or more financial variables appear (expenses, revenues, investment, cash flow, taxes, earnings, etc.);
2. the model user can manipulate (set and alter) the value of one or more financial variables; and
3. the purpose of the model is to influence strategic decisions by revealing to the decision maker the implications of alternative values of these financial variables. Figure 27-1 shows a flowchart of a simplified financial planning model.

Financial models fall into two types: simulation models, better known as what-if models and optimization models. What-if models attempt to simulate the effects of alternative management policies and assumptions about the firm's external environment. They are basically a tool for management's laboratory. Optimization models are the ones in which the goal is to maximize or minimize an objective, such as present value of profit or cost. Multi-objective techniques such as goal programming are being experimented. Models can be deterministic or probabilistic. Deterministic models do not include any random or probabilistic variables, whereas probabilistic models incorporate random numbers and/or one or more probability distributions for variables such as sales, costs, etc. Financial models can be solved and manipulated computationally to derive from it the current and projected future implications and consequences. Due to technological advances in computers (such as spreadsheets, financial modeling languages, graphics, data base management systems, and networking), more companies are using modeling.

BUDGETING AND FINANCIAL MODELING

Basically, a financial model is used to build a comprehensive budget (that is, projected financial statements such as the income statement, balance sheet, and cash flow statement). Such a model can be called a budgeting model, since you are essentially developing a master budget with such a model. Applications and uses of the model, however, go beyond developing a budget. They include:

- Financial forecasting and analysis
- Capital expenditure analysis
- Tax planning
- Exchange rate analysis

FIGURE 27-1 Flowchart of a Simplified Financial Planning Model

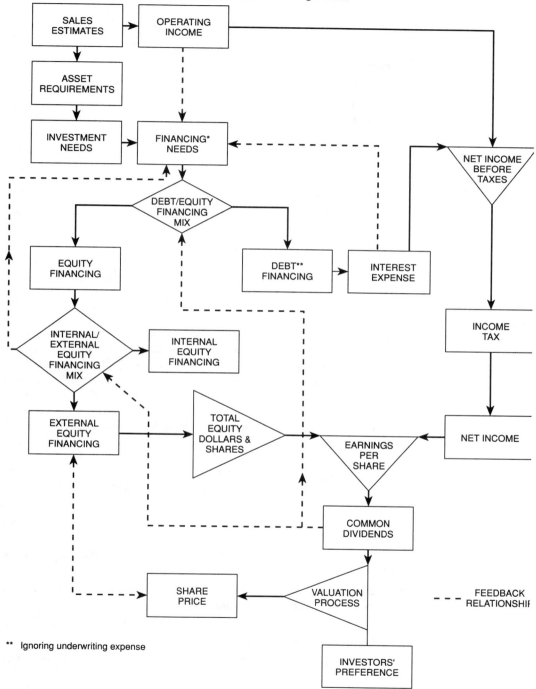

Source: Naylor, Thomas (ed.), *Simulation in Business Planning and Decision Making,* The Society for Computer Simulation, La Jolla, CA 1981.

- Analysis for mergers and acquisitions
- Labor contract negotiations
- Capacity planning
- Cost-volume-profit analysis
- New venture analysis
- Lease/purchase evaluation
- Appraisal of performance by segments
- Market analysis
- New product analysis
- Development of long-term strategy
- Planning financial requirements
- Risk analysis
- Cash flow analysis
- Cost and price projections.

USE OF FINANCIAL MODELING IN PRACTICE

The use of financial modeling, especially a computer-based financial modeling system is rapidly growing. The reason is quite simple: the growing need for improved and quicker support for management decisions as a decision support system (DSS) and the wide and easy availability of computer hardware and software.

Some of the functions currently served by financial models, as described by the users, are:

- Projecting financial results under any given set of assumptions; to evaluate the financial impact of various assumptions and alternative strategies; and to prepare long range financial forecasts.
- Computing income, cash flow, and ratios for five years by months; also energy sales, revenue, power generation requirements, operating and manufacturing expenses, manual or automatic financing, and rate structure analysis.
- Providing answers and insights into financial "what-if" questions, and to produce financial scheduling information.
- Forecast the balance sheet and income statement with emphasis on alternatives for the investment securities portfolio.
- Projecting operating results and various financing needs, such as plant and property levels and financing requirements.

- Computing manufacturing profit, given sales forecasts, and any desired processing sequence through the manufacturing facilities; simulate effect on profits of inventory policies.
- Generating profitability reports of various cost centers.
- Projecting financial implications of capital investment programs.
- Showing the effect of various volume and activity levels on budget and cash flow.
- Forecasting corporate sales, costs, and income by division, by month.
- Providing:

  1. sales revenue for budget;
  2. a basis for evaluating actual sales department performance; and
  3. other statistical comparisons.

- Determine pro forma cash flow for alternative development plans for real estate projects.
- Analyzing the impact of an acquisition on company earnings.
- Determining economic attractiveness of new ventures, i.e., products, facilities, acquisitions, etc.
- Evaluate alternatives of leasing or buying computer equipment.
- Determining corporate taxes as a function of changes in price.
- Evaluate investments in additional capacity at each major refinery.
- Generating income statements, cash flow, present value, and discounted rate of return for potential mining ventures, based on production and sales forecasts.

Supported by the expanded capabilities provided by models, many companies are increasingly successful in including long-term strategic considerations in their business plans, thus enabling them to investigate the possible impact of their current decisions on the long term welfare of the organization.

QUANTITATIVE METHODS USED IN FINANCIAL MODELS

In view of the development of sophisticated quantitative models for analysis in business planning and decision making, there is a rapid growing trend for their use, certainly with the aid of computer technology. Here is a list of these techniques used by the model builders:

Econometric and statistical methods

- Simple and multiple regressions
- Econometric modeling
- Time series models
- Exponential smoothing
- Risk analysis
- Simulation

Optimization models

- Linear programming
- Goal programming
- Integer programming
- Dynamic programming

DEVELOPING FINANCIAL MODELS

Development of financial models essentially involves three steps:

1. definition of variables,
2. input parameter values, and
3. model specification.

As far as model specification goes, this chapter will concentrate only on the simulation-type model in this section. Generally speaking, the model consists of three important ingredients:

1. Variables
2. Input parameter values
3. Definitional and/or functional relationships.

Definition of Variables

Fundamental to the specification of a financial model is the definition of the variables to be included in it. There are basically three types of variables: policy variables (Z), external variables (X), and performance variables (Y).

Policy variables. The policy variables (often called control variables) are those that management can exert some degree of control over. Examples of financial variables are cash management, working capital, debt management,

FIGURE 27-2 Financial Model Variables

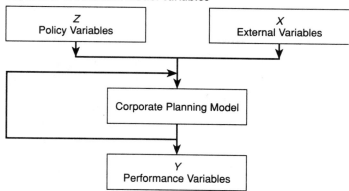

depreciation, tax, merger-acquisition decisions, the rate and direction of the firm's capital investment programs, the extent of its equity and external debt financing and the financial leverage represented thereby, and the size of its cash balances and liquid asset position. Policy variables are denoted by the symbol Z in Figure 27-2.

External variables. The external variables are the environmental variables that are external to the company and which influence the firm's decisions from outside of the firm, generally exogenous in nature. Generally speaking, the firm is embedded in an industry environment. This industry environment, in turn, is influenced by overall general business conditions. General business conditions exert influences upon particular industries in several ways. Total volume of demand, product prices, labor costs, material costs, money rates, and general expectations are among the industry variables affected by the general business conditions. The symbol X represents the external variables in Figure 27-2.

Performance variables. The performance variables measure the firm's economic and financial performance, which are usually endogenous. They are represented by the symbol Y in Figure 27-2. The Y's are often called output variables. The output variables of a financial model would be the line items of the balance sheet, cash budget, income statement, or statement of changes in cash flow. How to define the output variables of the firm will depend upon the goals and objectives of management. They basically indicate how management measures the performance of the organization or some segments of it. Management is likely to be concerned with:

1. the firm's level of earnings;
2. growth in earnings;

3. projected earnings;

4. growth in sales; and

5. cash flow.

Frequently when you attempt to set up a financial model you face risk or uncertainty associated with particular projections. In a case such as this, treat some of these variables, such as sales, as random variables with given probability distributions. The inclusion of random variables in the model transforms it from a deterministic model to a risk analysis model. However, the use of the risk analysis model in practice is rare because of the difficulty involved in modeling and computation.

Input Parameter Values

The model includes various input parameter values. For example, in order to generate the balance sheet, the model needs to input beginning balances of various asset, liability, and equity accounts. These input and parameter values are supplied by management. The ratio between accounts receivable and financial decision variables such as the maximum desired debt-equity ratio would be good examples of parameters.

Model Specification

Once you define various variables and input parameters for your financial model, you must then specify a set of mathematical and logical relationships linking the input variables to the performance variables. The relationships usually fall into two types of equations: definition equations and behavioral equations. Definitional equations take the form of accounting identities. Behavioral equations involve theories or hypotheses about the behavior of certain economic and financial events. They must be empirically tested and validated before they are incorporated into the financial model.

Definitional Equations. Definitional equations are exactly what the term refers to—mathematical or accounting definitions. For example,

$$\text{Assets} = \text{Liabilities} + \text{Equity}$$
$$\text{Net Income} = \text{Revenues} - \text{Expenses}$$

These definitional equations are fundamental definitions in accounting for the balance sheet and income statement, respectively. Two more examples are given below:

$$\text{CASH} = \text{CASH}(-1) + \text{CC} + \text{OCR} + \text{DEBT} - \text{CD} - \text{LP}$$

This equation is a typical cash equation in a financial model. It states that ending cash balance (CASH) is equal to the beginning cash balance (CASH(−1)) plus cash collections from customers (CC) plus other cash receipts (OCR) plus borrowings (DEBT) minus cash disbursements (CD) minus loan payments (LP).

$$INV = INV(-1) + MAT + DL + MO - CGS$$

This equation states that ending inventory (INV) is equal to the beginning inventory (INV(-1)) plus cost of materials used (MAT) plus cost of direct labor (DL) plus manufacturing overhead (MO) minus the cost of goods sold (CGS).

Behavioral Equations. Behavioral equations describe the behavior of the firm regarding the specific activities that are subject to empirical testing and validation. The classical demand function in economics is:

$$Q = f(P) \text{ or more specifically } Q = a - bP$$

It simply states that the quantity demanded is negatively related to the price, i.e., the higher the price the lower is the demand. However, the firm's sales is more realistically described as follows:

$$SALES = f(P, ADV, I, GNP, Pc, \text{etc.}) \text{ or}$$

assuming linear relationship among these variables, you can specify the model as follows:

$$SALES = a + bP + cADV + dI + eGNP + fPc$$

which states that the sales are affected by such factors as price (P), advertising expenditures (ADV), consumer income (I), gross national product (GNP), prices of competitive goods (Pc), etc.

With the data on SALES, P, ADV, I, GNP, and Pc, you will be able to estimate parameter values $a, b, c, d, e,$ and f, using linear regression. You can test the statistical significance of each of the parameter estimates and can evaluate the overall explanatory power of the model, measured by the t statistic and R squared, respectively. This way you will be able to identify the most influential factors that affect the sales of a particular product. With the best model chosen, management can simulate the effects on sales of alternative pricing and advertising strategies. You can also experiment with alternative assumptions regarding the external economic factors such as GNP, consumer income, and prices of competitive goods.

Model Structure. A majority of financial models that have been in use are recursive and/or simultaneous models. Recursive models are the ones in which each equation can be solved one at a time by substituting the solution values of the preceding equations into the right hand side of each equation. An example of a financial model of the recursive type is given below:

1. SALES   = A − B*PRICE + C*ADV
2. REVENUE = SALES*PRICE
3. CGS   = .70*REVENUE
4. GM   = SALES − CGS
5. OE   = $10,000 + .2*SALES
6. EBT   = GM − OE
7. TAX   = .46*EBT
8. EAT   = EBT − TAX

In this example, the selling price (PRICE) and advertising expenses (ADV) are given. A, B, and C are parameters to be estimated and

SALES   = sales volume in units
REVENUE = sales revenue
CGS   = cost of goods sold
GM   = gross margin
OE   = operating expenses
EBT   = earnings before taxes
TAX   = taxes
EAT   = earnings after taxes

Simultaneous models are frequently found in econometric models which require a higher level of computational methods such as matrix inversion. An example of a financial model of this type is presented below:

(1) INT   = .10*DEBT
(2) EARN = REVENUE − CGS − OE − INT − TAX − DIV
(3) DEBT = DEBT(−1) + BOW
(4) CASH = CASH(−1) + CC + BOW + EARN − CD − LP
(5) BOW = MBAL − CASH

Note that earnings (EARN) in equation (2) is defined as sales revenue minus CGS, OE, interest expense (INT), TAX, and dividend payment (DIV). But INT is a percentage interest rate on total debt in equation (1). Total debt in equation (3) is equal to the previous period's debt (DEBT(−1)) plus new borrowings (BOW). New debt is the difference between a minimum cash balance (MBAL) minus cash. Finally, the ending cash balance in equation (5) is defined as the sum of the beginning balance (CASH(−1)), cash collection, new borrowings and earnings minus cash disbursements and loan payments of the existing debt (LP). Even though the model presented here is a simple variety, it is still simultaneous in nature, which requires the use of a method capable of solving simultaneous equations. Very few of the financial modeling languages have the capability to solve this kind of system.

Decision Rules. The financial model may, in addition to the ones previously discussed, that is definitional equations and behavioral equations, include basic decision rules specified in a very general form. The decision rules are not written in the form of conventional equations. They are described algebraically using conditional operators, consisting of statements of the type: "IF . . . THEN . . . ELSE." For example, suppose that you wish to express the following decision rule: "If X is greater than 0, then Y is set equal to X multiplied by 5. Otherwise, Y is set equal to 0." Then you can express the rule as follows:

$$Y = \text{IF } X \text{ GT } 0 \text{ THEN } X*5 \text{ ELSE } 0$$

Suppose the company wishes to develop a financing decision problem based upon alternative sales scenarios. To determine an optimal financing alternative, managers might want to incorporate some decision rules into the model for a "what-if" or sensitivity analysis.

Some examples of these decision rules are as follows:

- The amount of dividends paid are determined on the basis of targeted earnings available to common stockholders and a maximum dividend payout ratio specified by management.

- After calculating the external funds needed to meet changes in assets as a result of increased sales, dividends, and maturing debt, the amount of long-term debt to be floated is selected on the basis of a prespecified leverage ratio.

- The amount of equity financing to be raised is chosen on the basis of funds needed which are not financed by new long-term debt, but is constrained by the responsibility to meet minimum dividend payments.

In the model just described, simultaneity is quite evident. A sales figure is used to generate earnings and this in turn lead to, among other items, the level of long-term debt required. Yet the level of debt affects the interest expense incurred within the current period and therefore earnings. Furthermore, as earnings are affected, so are the price at which new shares are issued, the number of shares to be sold, and thus earnings per share. Earnings per share then "feed back" into the stock price calculation.

Lagged Model Structure. Lagged model structure is common in financial modeling. Virtually all balance sheet equations or identities are of this type. For example,

$$\text{Capital} = \text{capital} (-1) + \text{net income} + \text{contributions} - \text{cash dividends}$$

More interestingly,

$$CC = a*\text{SALES} + b*\text{SALES}(-1) + c*\text{SALES}(-2)$$

where CC = cash collections from customers
   a = percent received in the month of sale.
   b = percent received in the month following sale.
   c = percent received in the second month following sale.

This indicates that the realization of cash lags behind credit sales.
Figure 27-3 illustrates a sample financial (budgeting) model.

FIGURE 27-3 Sample Comprehensive Financial (Budgeting) Model

A Corporate Financial Model

Balance Sheet Equations

$$\text{Cash}_t = \text{Cash}_{t-1} + \text{Cash receipts}_t - \text{Cash disbursements}_t$$

$$\text{Accounts receivable}_t = (1 - a)\,\text{Sales} + (1 - b - a)\,\text{Sales}_{t-1}$$
$$+ (1 - c - b - a)\,\text{Sales}_{t-2}$$

$$\text{Inventory}_t = \text{Inventory}_{t-1} + \text{Inventory purchase}_t$$
$$- \text{Variable cost per unit} \left(\frac{\text{Sales}_t}{\text{Selling price per unit}} \right)$$

$$\text{Plant} = \text{Initial value}$$

$$\text{Accounts payable}_t = (m)\,\text{Variable selling/administrative expenses}_{t-1}$$
$$+ (n)\,\text{Variable selling/administrative expenses}_t$$
$$+ \text{Inventory purchase}_t + \text{Fixed expenses}_t$$

$$\text{Bank loan}_t = \text{Bank loan}_{t-1} + \text{Loan}_t - \text{Loan repayment}_t$$

$$\text{Common stock} = \text{Initial value}$$

$$\text{Retained earnings}_t = \text{Retained earnings}_{t-1} + \text{Net income}_t$$

Income Statement and Cash Flow Equations

$$\text{Cash receipts}_t = (a)\,\text{Sales}_t + (b)\,\text{Sales}_{t-1}$$
$$+ (c)\,\text{Sales}_{t-2} + \text{Loan}_t$$

FIGURE 27-3 (Continued)

$$\text{Cash disbursements}_t = \text{Accounts payable}_{t-1} + \text{Interest}_t$$
$$+ \text{Loan repayments}_t$$

$$\text{Inventory purchase}_t \ [\geq 0] = \text{Variable cost per unit}$$

$$\left(\frac{\text{Sales}_t + \text{Sales}_{t-1} + \text{Sales}_{t-2} + \text{Sales}_t}{\text{Selling price per unit}} \right)^3 - \text{Inventory}_{t-1}$$

$$\text{Interest}_t = (i) \ \text{Bank loan}_t$$

$$\text{Variable cost of sales}_t = \left(\frac{\text{Variable cost per unit}}{\text{Selling price per unit}} \right)$$

$$\text{Variable selling/}$$
$$\text{administrative expenses}_t = (x) \ \text{Sales}_t$$

$$\text{Net income before taxes}_t = \text{Sales}_t - \text{Interest}_t$$
$$+ \text{Variable cost of sales}_t$$
$$+ \text{Variable selling/administrative expenses}_t$$
$$- \text{Fixed expenses}_t - \text{Depreciation}_t$$

$$\text{Tax expense}_t \ (\geq 0) = (r) \ \text{Net income before taxes}_t$$
$$\text{Net income}_t = \text{Net income before taxes}_t - \text{Tax expense}_t$$

Input Variables (Dollars)
$\text{Sales}_{t-1,t-2,t-3}$
Loan_t
Loan repayment$_t$
Fixed expense$_t$
Depreciation$_t$
Selling price per unit
Variable cost per unit

Input Parameters
Accounts receivable collection patterns
a—Percent received within current period
b—Percent received with one-period lag
c—Percent received with two-period lag
$a + b + c < 1$

FIGURE 27-3 (Continued)

Lag in accounts payable cash flow

m—Percent paid from previous period

n—Percent paid from current period

$m + n = 1$

r = Tax rate

i = Interest rate

x = Ratio of variable selling/administrative expense to sales

Initial Values (*Dollars*)

Plant

Common stock

Cash_{t-1}

$\text{Sales}_{t-1, t-2}$

Inventory_{t-1}

$\text{Retained earnings}_{t-1}$

Bank loan_{t-1}

$\text{Variable selling/administrative expenses}_{t-1}$

$\text{Accounts payable}_{t-1}$

Assumptions: time interval equals one month; accounts payable paid in full in next period; no lag between inventory purchase and receipt of goods; and no dividends paid.

Chapter 28

Development of Optimal Budgets

This chapter illustrates how optimization techniques such as linear programming or goal programming can help to develop an optimal budget. For this purpose, the material will be illustrated with a simple example.

OPTIMAL BUDGET AND LINEAR PROGRAMMING

Linear programming (LP) is a mathematical technique designed to determine an optimal decision (or an optimal plan) chosen from a large number of possible decisions. The optimal decision is the one that meets the specified objective of the company, subject to various restrictions or constraints. It concerns itself with the problem of allocating scarce resources among competing activities in an optimal manner. The optimal decision yields the highest profit, contribution margin (CM), or revenue, or the lowest cost. A linear programming model consists of two important ingredients:

1. Objective function. The company must define the specific objective to be achieved.

2. Constraints. Constraints are in the form of restrictions on availability of resources or meeting minimum requirements. As the name linear programming indicates, both the objective function and constraints must be in linear form.

EXAMPLE 28-1   A firm wishes to find an optimal product mix. The optimal mix would be the one that maximizes its total CM within the allowed budget and production capacity. Or the firm may want to determine a least cost combination of input materials while meeting production requirements, employing production capacities, and using available employees.

Applications of LP are numerous. They include:

1. Developing an optimal budget
2. Determining an optimal investment portfolio
3. Scheduling jobs to machines
4. Determining a least-cost shipping pattern
5. Scheduling flights
6. Gasoline blending.

Formulation of LP.   To formulate an LP problem, certain steps are followed. They are:

1. Define what are called decision variables that you are trying to solve for.
2. Express the objective function and constraints in terms of these decision variables. All the expressions must be in linear form.

LP will be used first to find the optimal product mix and then to develop the budget for the optimal program.

EXAMPLE 28-2   The Sigma Company produces and sells two products: snowmobiles (A) and outboard motors (B). The sales price of A is $900 per unit and that of B $800 per unit. The production department estimates on the basis of standard cost data that the capacity required for manufacturing one unit of A is 10 hours while one unit of product B requires 20 hours. The total available capacity for the company is 160 hours. The variable manufacturing costs of A are $300 per unit and they are all paid in cash at the same rate at which the production proceeds. The variable manufacturing costs of B are $600 per unit. These costs are also paid in cash. For simplicity, assume no variable selling costs. Demand forecasts have been developed: the maximum amount of product A that can be sold is 8 units whereas that of B is 12 units. Product A is sold with one period credit while one half of the sales of product B is received in the same period in which the sales are realized.

Additional information:

- The company has existing loans which require $2,100 in payment.
- The company plans to maintain a minimum balance of $500.
- The accounts payable balance of $900 must be paid in cash in this period.

EXHIBIT 28-1 Sample Balance Sheet

Assets			Liabilities		
Current assets			Current liabilities		
Cash	$1,000		Accounts payable	900	
			Short-term loan	10,000	
Accounts Receivable	6,800				10,900
Inventory	6,000	13,800	Equity		7,400
Fixed assets		4,500		Total liabilities &	$18,300
Total assets		$18,300		equity	

- The balance sheet and the fixed overhead budget are given in Exhibit 28-1 and Exhibit 28-2.

Formulation of the LP Model.

Begin formulation of the model by setting up the objective function which is to maximize the company's total contribution margin (CM). By definition, CM per unit is the difference between the unit sales price and the variable cost per unit:

	Product	
	A	*B*
Sales price	$900	$800
Variable cost	300	600
CM per unit	$600	$200

Define A = the number of units of product A to be produced
B = the number of units of product B to be produced.

Then the total CM is:

$$TCM = 600A + 200B$$

Remember that demand forecasts indicated that there were upper limits of the demand of each product as follows:

$$A \leq 6, B \leq 10$$

The planned use of capacity must not exceed the available capacity. Specifically, you need the restriction:

$$10A + 20B \leq 160$$

EXHIBIT 28-2 Sample Fixed Overhead Budget

Expenses involving cash	$1,900
Accruals	800
Depreciation	500
	$3,200

You also need the cash constraint. It is required that the funds tied up in the planned operations not exceed the available funds. The initial cash balance plus the cash collections of accounts receivable are available for the financing of operations. On the other hand, you need some cash to pay for expenses and maintain a minimum balance. The cash constraint you are developing involves two stages. In the first stage, observe that the cash receipts and disbursements can be considered fixed regardless of the planned production and sales:

Funds initially available		
Beginning cash balance	$1,000	
Accounts receivable	6,800	7,800
Funds to be disbursed		
Accounts payable	$ 900	
Repayment of loans	2,100	
Fixed cash expenses	1,900	4,900
Difference		2,900
Minus: Minimum cash balance required		500
Funds available for the financing of operations		$2,400

In the second stage, observe the cash receipts and disbursements caused by the planned operations.

First, the total sales revenues:

Product A	900A
B	800B

The cash collections from:

Product A	(0) 900A = 0
B	(.5) 800B = 400B

Secondly, the variable manufacturing costs are:

Product A	300A
B	600B

Therefore, the cash disbursements for:

Product A	(1) 300A = 300A
B	(1) 600B = 600B

Then, the cash constraint is formulated by requiring that the cash disbursements for planned operations must not exceed the cash available plus the cash collections resulting from the operations:

$$300A + 600B \leq 2400 + 0 + 400B$$

EXHIBIT 28-3 LINDO LP Program Output

```
:MAX 600A+200B
>ST
>A<6
>B<10
>10A+20B<160
>300A+200B<2400
>END
:LOOK ALL

MAX     600A + 200B
SUBJECT TO
  2)    A<=6
  3)    B<=10
  4)    10A+20B<=160
  5)    300A+200B<=2400
:GO
 LP OPTIMUM FOUND  AT STEP  2

OBJECTIVE FUNCTION VALUE

1)    4200.00000

VARIABLE      VALUE                 REDUCED COST
        A     6.000000                  .000000
        B     3.000000                  .000000

ROW           SLACK OR SURPLUS    DUAL PRICES
  2)                   .000000     300.000000
  3)                  7.000000        .000000
  4)                 40.000000        .000000
  5)                   .000000       1.000000

NO. ITERATIONS=     2

DO RANGE  (SENSITIVITY) ANALYSIS? >
  4)                 40.000000        .000000
  5)                   .000000       1.000000

NO. ITERATIONS=     2

 DO RANGE (SENSITIVITY) ANALYSIS? > YES

  RANGES IN WHICH THE BASIS IS UNCHANGED

                   OBJ COEFFICIENT RANGES
VARIABLE     CURRENT       ALLOWABLE      ALLOWABLE
             COEF          INCREASE       DECREASE
        A    600.000000    INFINITY       300.000000
        B    200.000000    200.000000     200.000000

                   RIGHTHAND SIDE RANGES
ROW          CURRENT       ALLOWABLE      ALLOWABLE
             RHS           INCREASE       DECREASE
  2            6.000000      2.000000       2.000000
  3           10.000000    INFINITY         7.000000
  4          160.000000    INFINITY        40.000000
  5         2400.000000   400.000000     600.000000
```

This can be simplified to form the following:

$$300A + 200B \leq 2400$$

Using a widely used LP program known as LINDO (Linear Interactive Discrete Optimization) program, shown in Exhibit 28-3, you obtain the following optimal solution:

$$A = 6, B = 3, \text{ and } CM = \$4,200$$

Exhibit 28-3 Generation of Budgets on the Basis of Optimal Mix

The sales budget would look like:

Product	Price	Quantity	Revenues
A	$900	6	$5,400
B	800	3	$2,400
			$7,800

Similarly, production and cost budgets can be easily developed. We will skip directly to show the cash budget (Exhibit 28-4), budgeted balance sheet (Exhibit 28-5), and budgeted income statement (Exhibit 28-6).

EXHIBIT 28-4 Cash Budget

Beginning cash balance			$1,000
Accounts receivable		6,800	
Cash collections from credit sales			
A: (0) 900A = (0) (900) (6)	0		
B: (.5)800B = 400B = 400(3)	1,200	1,200	8,000
Total cash available			9,000
Cash disbursements:			
Production:			
A: 300A = 300(6)	1,800		
B: 600B = 600(3)	1,800	3,600	
Fixed cash expenses:			
Accounts payable balance	900		
Repayment of loan	2,100		
Fixed expenses	1,900	4,900	$8,500
Ending cash balance			$ 500

EXHIBIT 28-5 Budgeted Income Statement

Sales		$7,800 (1)
Less: Variable costs		3,600 (2)
Contribution margin (CM)		4,200
Less: Fixed expenses		
Depreciation	500	
Payables in cash	1,900	
Accruals	800	3,200
Operating income		$1,000

EXHIBIT 28-6 Budgeted Balance Sheet

Assets:		
Current assets:		
Cash	$500 (1)	
Accounts receivable	6,600 (2)	
Inventories	6,000 (3)	
Total current assets		13,100
Fixed assets:		
Beg. balance	4,500	
Less: Accumulated		
Depreciation	(500)	4,000
Total assets		$17,100
Liabilities:		
Current liabilities:		
Accounts payable	800 (4)	
Short-term debt	7,900 (5)	8,700
Equity		8,400 (6)
Total liabilities & equity		$17,100

Supporting calculations:

(1)	A	B	Total
	$900(6) = 5,400$	$800(3) = 2,400$	7,800
(2)	$300(6) = 1,800$	$600(3) = 1,800$	3,600

Supporting calculations:

1. from the cash budget
2. A: $900(6) = 5,400$
   B: $400(3) = \underline{1,200}$
   $6,600$
3. Production and sales were assumed to be equal. This implies there is no change in inventories.
4. Accrual of fixed costs
5. Beginning balance – repayment = $\$10,000 - 2,100 = 7,900$
6. Beginning balance + net income = $\$7,400 + 1,000 = 8,400$

GOAL PROGRAMMING AND MULTIPLE CONFLICTING GOALS

In the previous section, you learned how to develop an optimal program (or product mix), using LP. LP, however, has one important drawback in that it is limited primarily to solving problems in which the objectives of management can be stated in a single goal, such as profit maximization or cost minimization. But management must now deal with multiple goals which are often incompatible and in conflict with each other. Goal programming (GP) circumvents this difficulty. In GP, unlike LP, the objective function may consist of multiple, incommensurable, and conflicting goals. Rather than maximizing or minimizing the objective criterion, the deviations from these set goals are minimized, often based on the priority factors assigned to each goal. The fact management will have multiple goals which are in conflict means that instead of maximizing or minimizing those goals, management will attempt merely to *satisfice*. In other words, they will look for a satisfactory solution rather than an optimal one.

Examples of Multiple Conflicting Goals

For example, consider a corporate investor who desires investments that will have a maximum return and minimum risk. These goals are generally incompatible and therefore unachievable. Other examples of multiple conflicting goals can be found in businesses that want to:

1. Maximize profits and increase wages paid to employees;
2. Upgrade product quality and reduce product costs;
3. Pay larger dividends to shareholders and retain earnings for growth;
4. Increase control of channels of distribution and reduce working-capital requirements; and
5. Reduce credit losses and increase sales.

In order to illustrate how to use a GP model in order to develop an optimal more exactly satisfactory budget, Example 28-3 will use the same data.

EXAMPLE 28-3   Further assume that:

- Fixed cash receipts include:
  (a) new short-term loan amount of $1,200,
  (b) a dividend payment of $700, and
  (c) a capital expenditure of $500.

Now the company has two goals: income and working capital. In other words, instead of maximizing net income or contribution margin, the company has a realistic, satisfactory level of income to achieve. On the other hand, the company wants a healthy balance sheet with working capital at least at a given level. (For example, a lending institution might want to see that before approving any kind of line of credit.)

For illustrative purposes, make the following specific assumptions:

- The company wants to achieve a return of 20 percent on equity. That means 15 percent of $7,400 = $1,110, which translates into a CM of $1,110 + 3,200 (fixed expenses) = $4,310.
- The company wants a working capital balance to be at least $3,000. Currently, it is $2,900 (current assets of $13,800 − current liabilities of $10,900 = $2,900).

These two goals are clearly in conflict. The reason is: you can increase the working capital by increasing cash funds or the inventory. However, the funds in the form of idle cash and the goods in the form of unsold inventories will not increase profits.

The first goal can be set up as follows:

$$600A + 200B + d\text{-} - d\text{+} = \$4,310$$

Note that working capital balance = beginning balance + net income + depreciation − dividends − capital expenditures = beginning balance + (sales − variable costs − fixed costs) − dividend − capital expenditure. Using this definition, the second goal can be set up as follows:

$$2{,}900 + \overbrace{900A + 800B}^{\text{Sales}} - \overbrace{300A - 600B}^{\text{Variable costs}} - \overbrace{2{,}700 - 700 - 500}^{\text{Fixed expenses}} \geq 3{,}000$$

This can be simplified to form an inequality:

$$600A + 200B \geq 4{,}000$$

Then your GP model is as follows:

$$\text{Min } d = d\text{-} + d\text{+}$$

$$
\begin{array}{lll}
\text{subject to} & A & \leq 6 \\
& B & \leq 10 \\
& 10A + 20B & \leq 160 \\
& 300A + 200B & \leq 2{,}400 \\
& 600A + 200B & \geq 4{,}000 \\
& 600A + 200B + d\text{-} - d\text{+} = 4{,}310 \\
& \text{all variables} \geq 0 &
\end{array}
$$

This particular problem can be easily solved by LINDO, as shown in Exhibit 28-7.

The GP solution is:

$$A = 6, B = 2, d- = 310, d+ = 0,$$

which means that the income target was underachieved by $310. Just as in the case of LP, financial executives will be able to develop the budget using this optimal solution in exactly the same manner as presented in the previous section. More sophisticated GP models can be developed with "preemptive" priority factors assigned to multiple goals. For example, the goal can be ranked according to "preemptive" priority factors. Also, the deviational variables at the same priority level may be given different weights in the objective function so that the deviational variables within the same priority have the different cardinal weights. (This topic is not treated here and should be referred to in an advanced operations research text.)

EXHIBIT 28-7 LINDO GP Model Output

MAX	D1 + D2			*Note:* D1 = D⁻
				D2 = D⁺

SUBJECT TO

    2) A ≤ 6
    3) B ≤ 10
    4) 10 A + 20 B ≤ 160
    5) 300 A + 200 B ≤ 2400
    6) 600 A + 200 B ≥ 4000
    7) D1 − D2 + 600 A + 200 B = 4310

END
:GO

OBJECTIVE FUNCTION VALUE

1)   310.000000

VARIABLE	VALUE	REDUCED COST	*Note:*
D1	310.000000	.000000	D⁻ = 310
D2	.000000	−2.000000	D+ = 0
A	6.000000	.000000	A = 6
B	2.000000	.000000	B = 2
ROW	SLACK OR SURPLUS	DUAL PRICES	
2)	.000000	.000000	
3)	8.000000	.000000	
4)	60.000000	.000000	
5)	200.000000	.000000	
6)	.000000	−1.000000	
7)	.000000	1.000000	

NO. ITERATIONS = 3

CONCLUSION

This chapter presented how optimization techniques such as LP and GP can help to develop an overall optimal plan for the company. However, in the Naylor study it was found that only 4 percent of the users of corporate planning models employed an optimization type model. The disadvantage with using optimization models to develop optimal plans for a firm as a whole is that problems are difficult to define and the firm has multiple objectives.

It is not easy, however, to develop an optimization model that incorporates performance variables such as ROI, profits, market share and cash flow, as well as the line items of the income statement, balance sheet and cash flow statement. Despite the availability of goal programming that handles multiple objectives, the possibility of achieving global optimization is very rare at the corporate level. The usage tends to be limited to submodels and suboptimization within the overall corporate level. Thus, the use of these models in corporate modeling will probably continue to be focused at the operational level. Production planning and scheduling, advertising, resource allocation, and many other problem areas will continue to be solved with huge success by these techniques.

Chapter 29

Use of Spreadsheets, Add-Ins, Templates, and Financial Modeling Languages

Financial forecasting and planning can be done using a microcomputer with a powerful spreadsheet program such as Lotus 1–2–3™, templates, or add-ins. Besides using spreadsheet programs, more and more companies are developing computer-based models for financial planning and budgeting, using powerful, yet easy-to-use, financial modeling languages such as Comshare's *Interactive Financial Planning System* (to be discussed later). The models help not only to build a budget for profit planning but also to answer a variety of "what-if" scenarios. The resultant calculations provide a basis for choice among alternatives under conditions of uncertainty.

This chapter will illustrate how to use the more popular ones such as Lotus 1–2–3™, IFPS™, and SIMPLAN™. Spreadsheet add-ins and templates are briefly described in Chapter 23.

USE OF A SPREADSHEET PROGRAM (LOTUS 1–2–3™) FOR FINANCIAL MODELING

This section discusses how to use spreadsheet programs such as Lotus 1–2–3™ and a stand-alone package such as Up Your Cash Flow to develop a financial model. For illustrative purposes, the material will cover: 1. three examples of projecting an income statement, and 2. forecasting financial distress with Z score.

Projecting an Income Statement

The following sample Cases will show how to develop a projected contribution income statement (in Case 1) and a projected traditional income statement (in Case 2) for two hypothetical firms:

Case 1

Sales for 1st month = $60,000

Cost of sales = 42 percent of sales, all variable

Operating expenses = $10,000 fixed plus 5 percent of sales

Taxes = 46 percent of net income

Sales increase by 5 percent each month

1. Based on this information, Case 1 will create a spreadsheet for the contribution income statement for the next 12 months and in total.

2. It will then do the same by assuming that sales increase by 10 percent and operating expenses = $10,000 plus 10 percent of sales. This is an example of "what-if" scenarios.

Case 2

Delta Gamma Company wishes to prepare a three-year projection of net income using the following information:

1. 1993 base year amounts are as follows:

Sales revenues	$4,500,000
Cost of sales	2,900,000
Selling and administrative expenses	800,000
Net income before taxes	800,000

2. Use the following assumptions:

- Sales revenues increase by 6 percent in 1994, 7 percent in 1995, and 8 percent in 1996.

- Cost of sales increase by 5 percent each year.

- Selling and administrative expenses increase only 1 percent in 1994 and will remain at the 1994 level thereafter.

- The income tax rate = 46 percent

Case 2 will develop a spreadsheet for the income statement for the next three years.

EXHIBIT 29-1 Spreadsheet for Contribution Income Statement

	1	2	3	4	5	6	7	8	9	10	11	12	TOTAL
Sales	$60,000	$63,000	$66,150	$69,458	$72,930	$76,577	$80,406	$84,426	$88,647	$93,080	$97,734	$102,620	$955,028
Less: VC													
Cost of sales	$25,200	$26,460	$27,783	$29,172	$30,631	$32,162	$33,770	$35,459	$37,232	$39,093	$41,048	$43,101	$401,112
Operating ex.	$3,000	$3,150	$3,308	$3,473	$3,647	$3,829	$4,020	$4,221	$4,432	$4,654	$4,887	$5,131	$47,751
CM	$31,800	$36,540	$38,367	$40,285	$42,300	$44,415	$46,635	$48,967	$51,415	$53,986	$56,686	$59,520	$550,916
Less: FC													
Op. expenses	$10,000	$10,000	$10,000	$10,000	$10,000	$10,000	$10,000	$10,000	$10,000	$10,000	$10,000	$10,000	$120,000
Net income	$21,800	$26,540	$28,367	$30,285	$32,300	$34,415	$36,635	$38,967	$41,415	$43,986	$46,686	$49,520	$430,916
Less: tax	$10,028	$12,208	$13,049	$13,931	$14,858	$15,831	$16,852	$17,925	$19,051	$20,234	$21,475	$22,779	$198,221
NI after tax	$11,772	$14,332	$15,318	$16,354	$17,442	$18,584	$19,783	$21,042	$22,364	$23,753	$25,210	$26,741	$232,695

EXHIBIT 29-2 "What If" Spreadsheet for Contribution Income Statement

	1	2	3	4	5	6	7	8	9	10	11	12
Sales	$60,000	$66,000	$72,600	$79,860	$87,846	$96,631	$106,294	$116,923	$128,615	$141,477	$155,625	$171,187
Less: VC												
Cost of sales	$25,200	$27,720	$30,492	$33,541	$36,895	$40,585	$44,643	$49,108	$54,018	$59,420	$65,362	$71,899
Operating ex.	$6,000	$6,600	$7,260	$7,986	$8,785	$9,663	$10,629	$11,692	$12,862	$14,148	$15,562	$17,119
CM	$28,800	$38,280	$42,108	$46,319	$50,951	$56,046	$61,650	$67,815	$74,597	$82,057	$90,262	$99,288
Less: FC												
Op. expenses	$10,000	$10,000	$10,000	$10,000	$10,000	$10,000	$10,000	$10,000	$10,000	$10,000	$10,000	$10,000
Net income	$18,800	$28,280	$32,108	$36,319	$40,951	$46,046	$51,650	$57,815	$64,597	$72,057	$80,262	$89,288
Less: tax	$8,648	$13,009	$14,770	$16,707	$18,837	$21,181	$23,759	$26,595	$29,715	$33,146	$36,921	$41,073
NI after tax	$10,152	$15,271	$17,338	$19,612	$22,113	$24,865	$27,891	$31,220	$34,882	$38,911	$43,342	$48,216

EXHIBIT 29-3 Delta Gamma Company
Three-Year Income Projections (1993–1996)

	1993	1994	1995	1996
Sales	$4,500,000	$4,770,000	$5,103,900	$5,512,212
Cost of sales	$2,900,000	$3,045,000	$3,197,250	$3,357,113
Gross profit	$1,600,000	$1,725,000	$1,906,650	$2,155,100
Selling & adm. exp.	$800,000	$808,000	$816,080	$824,241
Earnings before tax	$800,000	$917,000	$1,090,570	$1,330,859
tax	$368,000	$421,820	$501,662	$612,195
Earnings after tax	$432,000	$495,180	$588,908	$718,664

EXHIBIT 29-4 Delta Gamma Company Budget Assumptions

Category	Assumptions

Sales: *alternative 1 from book up you cash flow*

Cost of goods sold: *use 45% of sales*

Advertising: *5% of sales*

Automobile: *company has 4 autos @ 1500 ea. 4 x 1500 = 6000 ÷ 12 = 500 per month*

Bad debts: *maintain @ 2% of sales — I hope!*

Business promotion: *Prev year was $65,000. 10% increase equals $71,500 ÷ 12*

Collection costs: *use 1000 per month*

Continuing education: *$1000 per month*

Depreciation: *$84,000 for year — use 7000 per month*

Donations: *$10,000 for year = ÷ 12*

Insurance—general: *agent said $24,000; use 2000 per month*

Insurance—group: *15 employees @ 1500 ea = 22500 ÷ 12 = monthly #.*

Insurance—life: *600 per month*

Interest: *expect to borrow 250m @ 15% = 37,500 ÷ 12 = 3125 per month + other borrowings*

Office Supplies: *2% of sales — and keep it there please!*

Rent: *4000 per month*

Repairs and maintenance: *use 400 per month*

Salaries: *schedule the payroll per month*

Taxes and license: *Prior years was 1.5% of sales use same this year.*

Taxes, payroll: *20% of monthly payroll*

Telephone—utilities: *$29000 last year. Use 33000 ÷ 12. Travel — use $1000 per*

EXHIBIT 29-5 Delta Gamma Company Budget for Period January to December

	Jan.	Feb.	Mar.	Apr.	May	Jun.	Jul.	Aug.	Sep.	Oct.	Nov.	Dec.	Total
Sales	$129,030	$129,030	$129,030	$129,030	$192,610	$192,610	$162,690	$129,030	$192,610	$129,030	$162,690	$192,610	$1,870,000
Cost of Sales @ 45%	58,063	58,063	58,063	58,063	86,675	86,675	73,211	58,063	86,675	58,063	73,211	86,675	841,500
Gross profit	70,967	70,967	70,967	70,967	105,935	105,935	89,479	70,967	105,935	70,967	89,479	105,935	1,028,500
Advertising @ 5%	6,450	6,450	6,450	6,450	9,600	9,600	8,100	6,450	9,600	6,450	8,100	10,050	93,750
Automobile	500	500	500	500	500	500	500	500	500	500	500	500	6,000
Bad debts @ 2%	2,580	2,580	2,580	2,580	3,840	3,840	3,240	2,580	3,840	2,580	3,240	3,920	37,400
Business promotions	5,958	5,958	5,958	5,958	5,958	5,958	5,958	5,958	5,958	5,958	5,958	5,962	71,500
Collection costs	1,000	1,000	1,000	1,000	1,000	1,000	1,000	1,000	1,000	1,000	1,000	1,000	12,000
Continuing education	1,000	1,000	1,000	1,000	1,000	1,000	1,000	1,000	1,000	1,000	1,000	1,000	12,000
Depreciation	7,000	7,000	7,000	7,000	7,000	7,000	7,000	7,000	7,000	7,000	7,000	7,000	84,000
Donations	833	833	833	833	833	833	833	833	833	833	833	837	10,000
Dues & subscriptions	833	833	833	833	833	833	833	833	833	833	833	837	10,000
Insurance—general	2,000	2,000	2,000	2,000	2,000	2,000	2,000	2,000	2,000	2,000	2,000	2,000	24,000
Insurance—group	1,875	1,875	1,875	1,875	1,875	1,875	1,875	1,875	1,875	1,875	1,875	1,875	22,500
Insurance—life	600	600	600	600	600	600	600	600	600	600	600	600	7,200
Interest	3,125	3,125	3,125	3,125	4,375	4,375	4,375	4,450	4,450	4,450	4,450	4,450	47,875
Legal & accounting	1,000	1,000	1,000	1,000	1,000	1,000	1,000	1,000	1,000	1,000	1,000	1,000	12,000
Office supplies @ 2%	2,580	2,580	2,580	2,580	3,840	3,840	3,240	2,580	3,840	2,580	3,240	3,920	37,400
Rent	4,000	4,000	4,000	4,000	4,000	4,000	4,000	4,000	4,000	4,000	4,000	4,000	48,000
Repairs	400	400	400	400	400	400	400	400	400	400	400	400	4,800
Salaries	21,000	21,000	21,000	21,000	21,000	21,000	24,833	24,833	24,833	24,833	24,833	24,835	275,000
Taxes & license @ 1.5%	1,935	1,935	1,935	1,935	2,880	2,880	2,430	1,935	2,880	1,935	2,430	2,890	28,000
Taxes, payroll	4,200	4,200	4,200	4,200	4,200	4,200	4,966	4,966	4,966	4,966	4,966	4,970	55,000
Telephone—utilities	2,750	2,750	2,750	2,750	2,750	2,750	2,750	2,750	2,750	2,750	2,750	2,750	33,000
Travel	1,000	1,000	1,000	1,000	1,000	1,000	1,000	1,000	1,000	1,000	1,000	1,000	12,000
Profit	$(1,652)	$(1,652)	$(1,652)	$(1,652)	$25,451	$25,451	$7,546	$(7,576)	$20,777	$(7,576)	$7,471	$20,139	$85,075

Case 3

Case 3 will make specific assumptions as shown in Exhibit 29-4 and will develop a budget using Up Your Cash Flow.

FORECASTING FINANCIAL DISTRESS WITH Z SCORE

There has recently been an increasing number of bankruptcies. Will the company of the stock you own be among them? Who will go bankrupt? Will your major customers or suppliers go bankrupt? What warning signs exist and what can be done to avoid corporate failure?

How to Use Prediction Models

Prediction models can help in a number of ways. In merger analysis, it can help to identify potential problems with a merger candidate. Bankers and other business concerns can use it to determine whether or not to approve a new loan (credit) or to extend the old one. Investors can use it to screen out stocks of companies which are potentially risky. Internal auditors can use such a model to assess the financial health of the company. Those investing in or extending credit to a company may sue for losses incurred. The model can help as evidence in a lawsuit.

Financial managers, investment bankers, financial analysts, security analysts and auditors have been using early warning systems to detect the likelihood of bankruptcy. But their system is primarily based on financial strength of a company. Each ratio (or set of ratios) is examined independent of others. Plus, it is the professional judgment of a financial analyst which decides what the ratios are really telling.

To overcome the shortcomings of financial ratio analysis, it is necessary to combine mutually exclusive ratios into a group to develop a meaningful predictive model. Regression analysis and multiple discriminant analysis (MDA) are two statistical techniques that have been used thus far.

Z Score Model

This section describes the Z score predictive model which uses a combination of several financial ratios to predict the likelihood of future bankruptcy. Altman developed a bankruptcy prediction model that produces a Z score as follows:

$$Z = 1.2*X_1 + 1.4*X_2 + 3.3*X_3 + 0.6*X_4 + 0.999*X_5$$

where X_1 = Working capital/total assets
X_2 = Retained earnings/total assets
X_3 = Earnings before interest and taxes (EBIT)/total assets
X_4 = Market value of equity/book value of debt (Net worth for privately held firms)
X_5 = Sales/total assets

Altman also established the following guideline for classifying firms:

Z score	Probability of failure
1.8 or less	Very high
3.0 or higher	Unlikely
1.81–2.99	Not sure

The Z score is known to be about 90 percent accurate in forecasting business failure one year in the future and about 80 percent accurate in forecasting it two years in the future. They are more updated versions of Altman's model.

Exhibit 29-6 shows the 11-year financial history and the Z scores of Navistar International (formerly, International Harvester). Figure 29-1 presents the corresponding graph. The data of Navistar International was obtained from Moody's and Standard & Poor's for the period 1979 to 1990.

The graph in Figure 29-1 shows that Navistar International performed at the edge of the ignorance zone ("unsure area"), for the year 1979. Since 1980, though, the company started signalling a sign of failure. However, by selling stock and assets, the firm managed to survive. Since 1983, the company showed an improvement in its Z scores, but it still has a long way to go.

More Applications of the Z Score

Various groups of business people can take advantage of this tool for their own purposes. For example,

1. *Merger analysis.* The Z score can help to identify potential problems with a merger candidate.
2. *Loan credit analysis.* Bankers and lenders can use it to determine if they should extend a loan. Other creditors, such as vendors, have used it to determine whether to extend credit.
3. *Investment analysis.* The Z score model can help an investor in selecting stocks of potentialy troubled companies.

**EXHIBIT 29-6 Navistar International
Z Score Data**

	Balance Sheet							Income $		Stk Data	Calculations						Misc Graph Values		
Year	Cur Asts CA	Total Asts TA	Current Liab CL	Total Liab TL	Retained Erngs RE	Net Worth NW	Wrkng Captl WC	SALES	EBIT	Market Val MKT	WC/ TA	RE/ TA	EBIT/ TA	MKT/ TL	SALES/ TA	Z Score A	TOP GRAY B	BOTTOM GRAY C	Year X
	Graph																		
1979	3266	5247	1873	3048	1505	2199	1393	8426	719	1122	0.2655	0.2868	0.1370	0.3681	1.6059	3.00	2.99	1.81	1979
1980	3427	5843	2433	3947	1024	1896	994	6000	-402	1147	0.1701	0.1753	-0.0688	0.2960	1.0269	1.42	2.99	1.81	1980
1981	2672	5346	1808	3864	600	1482	864	7018	-16	376	0.1616	0.1122	-0.0030	0.0973	1.3128	1.71	2.99	1.81	1981
1982	1656	3699	1135	3665	-1078	34	521	4322	-1274	151	0.1408	-0.2914	-0.3444	0.0412	1.1684	-0.18	2.99	1.81	1982
1983	1388	3362	1367	3119	-1487	234	21	3600	-231	835	0.0062	-0.4423	-0.0687	0.2677	1.0708	0.39	2.99	1.81	1983
1984	1412	3249	1257	2947	-1537	302	155	4861	120	575	0.0477	-0.4731	0.0369	0.1951	1.4962	1.13	2.99	1.81	1984
1985	1101	2406	988	2364	-1894	42	113	3508	247.1	570	0.0470	-0.7872	0.1027	0.2411	1.4580	0.89	2.99	1.81	1985
1986	698	1925	797	1809	-1889	53	-100	3357	163	441	-0.0517	-0.9813	0.0846	0.2436	1.7436	0.73	2.99	1.81	1986
1987	785	1902	836	1259	-1743	643	-51	3530	219	1011	-0.0267	-0.9162	0.1153	0.8026	1.8558	1.40	2.99	1.81	1987
1988	1280	4037	1126	1580	150	866	154	4082	451	1016	0.0381	0.0372	0.1117	0.6430	1.0111	1.86	2.99	1.81	1988
1989	986	3609	761	1257	175	914	225	4241	303	1269	0.0623	0.0485	0.0840	1.0095	1.1751	2.20	2.99	1.81	1989
1990	2663	3795	1579	2980	81	815	1084	3854	111	563	0.2856	0.0213	0.0292	0.1888	1.0155	1.60	2.99	1.81	1990

Figure 29-1 Navistar International
Altman's Z Score

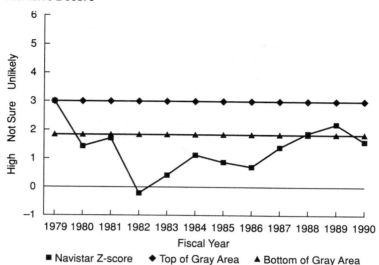

4. *Auditing analysis.* Internal auditors are able to use this technique to assess whether the company will continue as a going concern.

5. *Legal analysis.* Those investing or giving credit to your company may sue for losses incurred. The Z score can help in your company's defense.

Words of Caution

The Z score offers an excellent measure for predicting a firm's insolvency. But, like any other tool, one must use it with care and skill. The Z score of a firm should be looked upon not for just one or two years but for a number of years. Also, it should not be used as a sole basis of evaluation.

The Z score can also be used to compare the economic health of different firms. Here again extreme care should be exercised. Firms to be compared must belong to the same market. Also, Z scores of the same period are to be compared. (A copy of Lotus based template of a Z Score Predictive Model is provided in this book.) For further reference, see Kyd, Charles W., "Forecasting Bankruptcy with Z Scores." *Lotus,* September 1985, pp. 43–47 and Shim, Jae K. "Bankruptcy Prediction: Do It Yourself," *Journal of Business Forecasting,* Winter 1992.

FINANCIAL MODELING LANGUAGES

Remember that financial models are essentially used to generate pro forma financial statements and financial ratios. These are the basic tools for budgeting and profit planning. Also, the financial model is a technique for risk analysis and "what-if" experiments. The financial model is also needed for day-to-day operational and tactical decisions for immediate planning problems. For these purposes, the use of computers are essential.

In recent years, spreadsheet software and computer-based financial modeling software have been developed and utilized for budgeting and planning in an effort to speed up the budgeting process and to allow CFOs to investigate the effects of changes in budget assumptions and scenarios. These languages do not require any knowledge of computer programming on the part of the financial officers. They are all English-like languages. Among the well-known system packages are:

1. IFPS (Interactive Financial Planning System)
2. SIMPLAN
3. Venture
4. EXPRESS
5. Encore! Plus, Ferox Microsystems (Alexandria, Virginia)
6. MicroFCS, Pilot Executive Software (Boston, Massachusetts)

In what follows, each of the first two more widely used (IFPS and SIMPLAN), are discussed with illustrations. Then the section covers each of the next two (EXPRESS and Encore Plus) briefly.

IFPS (Interactive Financial Planning System)

IFPS is a multipurpose, interactive financial modeling system, often called a decision support system (DSS), which supports and facilitates the building, solving, and asking of "what-if" questions of financial models. The output from an IFPS model is in the format of a spreadsheet, that is a matrix or table in which:

- The rows representing user-specified variables such as market share, sales, growth in sales, unit price, gross margin, variable cost, contribution margin, fixed cost, net income, net present value, internal rate of return, and earnings per share.

- The column designates a sequence of user-specified time periods such as month, quarter, year, total, percentages, or divisions.
- The entries in the body of the table display the values taken by the model variable over time or by segments of the firm such as divisions, product lines, sales territories, and departments.

IFPS offers the following key features:

- Like other special purpose modeling languages, IFPS provides an English-like modeling language. That means without an extensive knowledge of computer programming, the budget analyst can build financial models of his/her own, and use them for "what-if" scenarios and managerial decisions.
- IFPS has a collection of built-in financial functions that perform calculations such as net present value (NPV), internal rate of return (IRR), loan amortization schedules, and depreciation alternatives.
- IFPS also has a collection of built-in mathematical and statistical functions such as linear regression, linear interpolation, polynomial autocorrelation, and moving average functions.
- IFPS supports use of leading and/or lagged variables which are commonly used in financial modeling. For example, cash collections lag behind credit sales of prior periods.
- IFPS also supports deterministic and probabilistic modeling. It offers a variety of functions for sampling from probability distributions such as uniform, normal, bivariate normal, and user-described empirical distributions.
- IFPS is non-procedural in nature. This means that the relationships, logic, and data used to calculate the various values in the output do not have to be arranged in any particular top-to-bottom order in an IFPS model. IFPS automatically detects and solves a system of two or more linear or nonlinear equations.
- IFPS has extensive editing capabilities that include adding statements to and deleting statements from a model, making changes in existing statements, and making copies of parts or all of a model.
- IFPS supports sensitivity analysis by providing the following solution options:
  (a) WHAT-IF: The IFPS lets you specify one or more changes in the relationships, logic, data, and/or parameter values, in the existing model and recalculates the model to show the impact of these changes on the performance measures.
  (b) GOAL-SEEKING: In the GOAL SEEKING mode, IFPS can determine what change would have to take place in the value of a specified

variable in a particular time period to achieve a specified value for another variable. For example, a financial manager can ask the system to answer the question "What would the unit sales price have to be for the project to achieve a target return on investment of 20 percent?"

(c) SENSITIVITY: This particular command is employed to determine the effect of a specified variable on one or more other variables. The SENSITIVITY command is similar to the WHAT-IF command but it produces a convenient, model-produced tabular summary for each new alternative value of the specified variable.

(d) ANALYZE: The ANALYZE command examines in detail those variables and their values that have contributed to the value of a specified variable.

(e) IMPACT: The IMPACT command is used to determine the effect on a specified variable of a series of percentage changes in one or more variables.

(f) IFPS/OPTIMUM: The IFPS/OPTIMUM routine is employed to answer questions of "What is the best?" type rather than "What-if."

(g) Other features of IFPS include:
  —routine graphic output
  —interactive color graphics
  —data files that contain both data and relationships
  —a consolidation capability that lets the financial officer produce composite reports from two or more models.
  —Extraction of data from existing non-IFPS data files and placing them in IFPS-compatible data files.
  —Operating on all major computer mainframes and microcomputers.

The following section presents, step by step, how to build a model using IFPS. (The following example was adapted from Comshare's *IFPS Fundamental Seminar Book,* 1987, pp. 6–20, with permission).

EXAMPLE 29-1 This example illustrates how to use IFPS.

The MCL Corporation is considering diversifying and wishes to evaluate the profitability of the new venture over the next two years. A quarterly profit picture is desired. Marketing research has provided the following information: (1) The total market for the product will be 7,000 units at the start of production and will grow at the rate of 1 percent per quarter; (2) MCL's initial share of the market is 11 percent, and this is expected to grow at the rate of one-half percent per quarter if intense marketing efforts are maintained; (3) the selling price is expected to be $2.50 per unit the first year and $2.65 the following year; (4) the standard cost system has produced the following estimates: (a) selling expenses, $.233 per unit; (b) labor cost $.61 per unit; and (c) raw materials, $.42 per unit; (5) general and administrative expenses are estimated to be $450 in the first quarter with a quarterly growth rate of 1 percent; and (6) setup costs for the line are $3,500.

First log in to your computer and access IFPS.

1. *Establishing the Model*

INTERACTIVE FINANCIAL PLANNING SYSTEM

ENTER NAME OF FILE CONTAINING MODELS AND REPORTS
? PROFIT

FILE PROFIT NOT FOUND—NEW FILE WILL BE CREATED
READY FOR EXECUTIVE COMMAND
? MODEL EXAMPLE

BEGIN ENTERING NEW MODEL
? AUTO 10, 5

10? (Model is entered as shown in Exhibit 29-7)

2. *Displaying the Model*

Once the model is complete, the solution can be displayed by using a sequence of commands like those that follow. A brief discussion of each command follows the illustration.

180? SOLVE

MODEL NEWPROD VERSION OF 12/20/93 16:38—11 COLUMNS 17 VARIABLES

ENTER SOLVE OPTIONS

? COLUMNS 1994,5-8,1995,GROWTH

? WIDTH 72, 16, 8

? ALL

ALL instructs IFPS to print the values of all variables as shown in Exhibit 29-8.

3. *"What-if" Analysis*

Instead of merely solving a model, as it is, the WHAT IF command can be used to determine the effect of changes in the definitions of variables in the model. The examples that follow show how these questions can be answered:

EXHIBIT 29-7 Entering the IFPS Model

10 COLUMNS 1-8, 1994, 1995, GROWTH
15 *EXAMPLE OF IFPS
20 *
25 **
30 PERIODS 4
35 * SALES DATA AND PROJECTIONS
40 PRICE = 2.5 FOR 4, 2.65
45 MARKET SHARE = .11, PREVIOUS MARKET SHARE + .005
50 TOTAL MARKET = 7000, PREVIOUS TOTAL MARKET*1.01
55 SALES VOLUME = L45*L50
60 * PREVIOUS CALCULATIONS
65 SALES REVENUE = SALES VOLUME*PRICE
70 NET INCOME = SALES REVENUE – TOTAL EXPENSES
75 * COSTS
80 UNIT SELLING COST = .233
85 UNIT LABOR COST = .61
90 UNIT MATERIAL COST = .42
95 UNIT COST = SUM(UNIT SELLING COST THRU UNIT MATERIAL COST)
100
65 SALES REVENUE = SALES VOLUME*PRICE
70 NET INCOME = SALES REVENUE – TOTAL EXPENSES
75 * COSTS
80 UNIT SELLING COST = .233
85 UNIT LABOR COST = .61
90 UNIT MATERIAL COST = .42
95 UNIT COST = SUM(UNIT SELLING COST THRU UNIT MATERIAL COST)
100 VARIABLE COST = UNIT COST*SALES VOLUME
105 ADMIN EXPENSES = 450, PREVIOUS ADMIN EXPENSES*1.01
110 TOTAL EXPENSES = VARIABLE COST + ADMIN EXPENSES
115 *PERFORMANCE MEASURES
120 INITIAL INVESTMENT = 3500.0
125 DISCOUNT RATE = .12
130 PRESENT VALUE = NPVC(NET INCOME, DISCOUNT RATE, INITIAL
     INVESTMENT)
140 RATE OF RETURN = IRR(NET INCOME, INITIAL INVESTMENT)
145 *
150 COLUMN 1989 FOR L55,L65,L70,L100,L105, L110,L120 = '
155   SUM(C1 THRU C4)
160 COLUMN 1990 FOR L55,L65,L70,L100,L105, L110,L120 = '
165   SUM(C5 THRU C8)
170 COLUMN GROWTH FOR L55,L65,L70,L100,L105,L110,L120 =
175   100*(C10-C9)/C9
END OF MODEL
?

EXHIBIT 29-8 IFPS Output

Example of IFPS	1994	5	6	7	8	1995	Growth
*Sales data and projections							
Price		2.650	2.650	2.650	2.650		
Market share		.1300	.1350	.1400	.1450		
Total market		7284	7357	7431	7505		
Sales volume	3341	946.9	993.2	1040	1088	4069	21.76
Previous calculations							
Sales revenue	8354	2509	2632	2757	2884	10782	29.07
Net income	2306	845.1	904.6	965.2	1027	3742	62.25
Costs							
Unit selling cost		.2330	.2330	.2330	.2330		
Unit labor cost		.6100	.6100	.6100	.6100		
Unit material cost		.4200	.4200	.4200	.4200		
Unit cost		1.263	1.263	1.263	1.263		
Variable cost	4220	1196	1254	1314	1374	5139	21.76
Admin. expenses	1827	468.3	473.0	477.7	482.5	1901	4.060
Total expenses	6047	1664	1727	1792	1857	7040	16.41
Performance measures							
Initial investment	3500	0	0	0	0	0	−100
Discount rate		.1200	.1200	.1200	.1200		
Present value		−623.5	139.7	931.3	1750		
Rate of return			.1676	.3988	.5812		

Case	Question
1	What if the total market size starts out at 6,000 units instead of 7,000, but grows by 5 percent per quarter, instead of 1 percent?
2	What if the selling price is $2.70 in the second year instead of $2.65 (and total market follows the original assumptions)?
3	What if, in addition to the price being $2.70 in 1994, unit material cost is three cents higher than expected in both years?

Note that Cases 1 and 2 are independent, while Case 3 builds on the changes made in Case 2. To handle both kinds of situations, two different WHAT IF commands are available:

WHAT IF   Enables the user to modify temporarily as many individual model statements as desired to determine the effect on the solution. Each WHAT IF erases the assumptions made by the previous one.

WHAT IF CONTINUE   Since each WHAT IF normally starts from the base case, this command makes possible, successive, cumulative, WHAT IF statements.

In the printout shown in Exhibit 29-9, the user has asked to see only selected variables. In Case 1, individual variable names, separated by commas, are used. In Case 2, model line numbers have been used instead. Case 3 illustrates the use of THRU to print an inclusive list of variables.

The SOLVE OPTIONS entered earlier to specify columns and page layout remain in effect through the modeling session.

Summary of "What-if" Analysis

Case 1   If the total market size starts out at 6,000 units and grows by 5 percent per quarter, then net income will go up by 111.5 percent.

Case 2   If the selling price is $2.70 in the second year, then the net income will go up by 71.07 percent.

Case 3   If, in addition to price being $2.70 in 1994, unit material cost is three cents higher than expected in both years, then the variable cost will go up by 21.76 percent.

4. "Goal-Seeking" Analysis

The GOAL SEEKING command allows the user to work backward. That is, the user tells IFPS what assumption can be adjusted and what objective is to be sought. IFPS then solves the model repetitively until it finds the value that yields the desired objective. To illustrate the use of this command, consider the following two situations:

Case	Question
1	Market share estimates could be less than originally expected. How low could it be and still provide first quarter net income of $700 and 3 percent more in each subsequent quarter?
2	The required initial investment might be larger than originally expected. How much larger could it be and still permit a 25 percent return over the eight-quarter horizon?

The first question is really asking what market share would have to be in each column to achieve a certain net income in the same column. The second question asks what investment has to be in column 1 to produce a certain rate of return in column 8.

As shown in Exhibit 29-10, the second question is handled by enclosing the column number in parentheses after the variable name. The variable is then said to be "subscripted."

The command BASE MODEL is issued before GOAL SEEKING. Without this command, modifications made by the last WHAT IF command would still be in effect.

EXHIBIT 29-9 What-if Analysis Output

? WHAT IF
WHAT IF CASE 1
ENTER STATEMENTS
? TOTAL MARKET = 6000, PREVIOUS TOTAL MARKET * 1.05
? SOLVE
ENTER SOLVE OPTIONS
? NET INCOME, PRESENT WORTH, RATE OF RETURN
***** WHAT IF CASE 1 *****
1 WHAT IF STATEMENT PROCESSED

	1994	5	6	7	8	1995	GROWTH
NET INCOME	1941	846.7	960.9	1084	1215	4107	111.5
PRESENT WORTH		−966.3	−155.6	733.1	1702		
RATE OF RETURN			.0703	.3240	.5318		

ENTER SOLVE OPTIONS
? WHAT IF
WHAT IF CASE 2
ENTER STATEMENTS
? PRICE = 2.5 FOR 4, 2.70
? SOLVE
ENTER SOLVE OPTIONS
? L70, L130, L140
***** WHAT IF CASE 2 *****
1 WHAT IF STATEMENT PROCESSED

	1994	5	6	7	8	1995	GROWTH
NET INCOME	2306	892.5	954.3	1017	1081	3945	71.07
PRESENT WORTH		−582.4	222.7	1057	1919		
RATE OF RETURN			.1952	.4333	.6198		

ENTER SOLVE OPTIONS
? WHAT IF CONTINUE
WHAT IF CASE 3
ENTER STATEMENTS
? UNIT MATERIAL COST = UNIT MATERIAL COST + .03
? SOLVE
ENTER SOLVE OPTIONS
? UNIT MATERIAL COST THRU VARIABLE COST
***** WHAT IF CASE 3 *****
2 WHAT IF STATEMENTS PROCESSED

	1994	5	6	7	8	1995	GROWTH
UNIT MATERIAL CO		.4500	.4500	.4500	.4500		
UNIT COST		1.293	1.293	1.293	1.293		
VARIABLE COST	4320	1224	1284	1345	1407	5261	21.76

EXHIBIT 29-10   Goal Seeking Analysis: Investment/Rate of Return

ENTER SOLVE OPTIONS
? BASE MODEL
? GOAL SEEKING
GOAL SEEKING CASE 1
ENTER NAME OF VARIABLE TO BE ADJUSTED TO ACHIEVE
PERFORMANCE
? MARKET SHARE
ENTER COMPUTATIONAL STATEMENT FOR PERFORMANCE
? NET INCOME = 700, PREVIOUS NET INCOME * 1.03
***** GOAL SEEKING CASE 1 *****

	1994	5	6	7	8	1995	GROWTH
MARKET SHARE		.1243	.1259	.1274	.1291		

ENTER SOLVE OPTIONS
? NET INCOME, PRESENT WORTH, RATE OF RETURN

	1994	5	6	7	8	1995	GROWTH
NET INCOME	2929	787.9	811.5	835.8	860.9	3296	12.55
PRESENT WORTH		−89.41	595.2	1281	1967		
RATE OF RETURN		.0822	.3446	.5494	.7073		

ENTER SOLVE OPTIONS
? GOAL SEEKING
GOAL SEEKING CASE 2
ENTER NAME OF VARIABLE TO BE ADJUSTED TO ACHIEVE
PERFORMANCE
? INITIAL INVESTMENT(1)
ENTER COMPUTATIONAL STATEMENT FOR PERFORMANCE
? RATE OF RETURN(8) = 25%
***** GOAL SEEKING CASE 2 *****

	1994	5	6	7	8	1995	GROWTH
INITIAL INVESTMENT	4595	0	0	0	0	0	−100

ENTER SOLVE OPTIONS
? RATE OF RETURN

	1994	5	6	7	8	1995	GROWTH
RATE OF RETURN				.0835	.2500		

ENTER SOLVE OPTIONS
?

Summary of "Goal-Seeking" Analysis

Case 1   The market share could be as low as .1243 in the first quarter and still provide first quarter net income of $700 and 3 percent more in each subsequent quarter.

Case 2   The initial investment would have to be $4,595 in order to permit a 25 percent return over the eight-quarter horizon.

Prospective users of IFPS are encouraged to refer to the following sources from Comshare, 3001 S. State St., P.O. Box 1588, Ann Arbor, Michigan 48106:

- IFPS Cases and Models, 1979.
- IFPS Tutorial, 1980.
- IFPS User's Manual, 1984.
- IFPS/Personal User's Manual, 1984.
- IFPS University Seminar, 1984.
- Comprehensive Fundamentals of IFPS, 1984.
- Papers Available from the Comshare University Support Programs.

SIMPLAN: A Planning and Modeling System

SIMPLAN is more than a financial modeling package. In fact, it is an integrated, multipurpose planning, budgeting, and modeling system. A diagram of SIMPLAN's mode organization is provided in Figure 29-2.

As can be seen from Figure 29-2, in addition to the general financial modeling function, the system has the capability to perform:

1. sales forecasting and time series analysis; and
2. economic modeling.

Thus, sophisticated users can really take advantage of the package. For forecasting sales, interest rates, material supplies, factor input prices, and other key variables, SIMPLAN offers a variety of time series forecasting models. These include time trends, exponential smoothing, and adaptive forecasting. Forecasts developed by any of these methods may be incorporated directly into SIMPLAN models and reports.

As for econometric modeling capability, SIMPLAN offers models for sales, market share and industry which can, with SIMPLAN, be specified, estimated, validated, simulated, and linked directly to division financial and production models or corporate financial models. SIMPLAN can be used to estimate single-equation and simultaneous-equation linear and nonlinear models to simulate the effects of alternative marketing strategies and economic conditions on market share and industry demand. Direct access from SIMPLAN to all series of the NBER (National Business and Economic Research) macroeconomic database is available on several time-sharing networks.

FIGURE 29-2 SIMPLAN Mode Organization

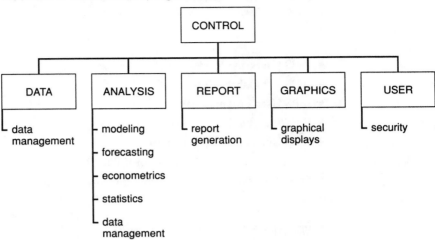

With SIMPLAN, 16 major functions are integrated into a single planning and modeling system. These functions include:

- Database creation
- Database manipulation
- Consolidation
- Model specification
- Model changes
- Report formulation
- Report changes
- Statistical analysis
- Forecasting
- Econometrics
- Model solution
- Validation
- Policy simulation
- Report generation
- Security
- Graphical display

SIMPLAN contains a number of commands to facilitate logical operations. Suppose, for example, if the cash balances (CASH) fall below some minimum level (MBAL), the company's line of credit may be automatically increased by the amount of cash shortfall. The SIMPLAN commands to accomplish this task would be as follows:

$$\text{IF CASH} < \text{MBAL}$$

$$\text{DEBT} = \text{DEBT} (-1) + \text{MBAL} - \text{CASH}$$

$$\text{CASH} = \text{MBAL}$$

SIMPLAN uses a set of logical comparison operations, as well as an IF and GO TO command.

For a complete instruction about the system, refer to R. Britton Mayo and Social Systems, Inc., *Corporate Planning and Modeling with SIMPLAN,* Addison-Wesley Publishing Company, 1979.

EXAMPLE 29-2 The sample model developed using SIMPLAN is designed to calculate the current asset portion of a typical balance sheet. First, Exhibit 29-11 shows a list of data records or variables to be used. Exhibit 29-12 presents a sample model on SIMPLAN. The definitional equations, behavioral equations, and decision rules (using, for example, IF ELSE statements) constructed here are basically self-explanatory. The first simulation for the period 1994–97 is given Exhibit 29-13. To give the reader an idea of policy simulation, suppose that you want to determine the effects of an increase in the sales growth rate from 7 percent to 8.5 percent. Basically, all you need to do is to replace statement 3 with

$$3 \text{ GROWTHRATE} = 8.5$$

With this new policy assumption, Exhibit 29-14 shows the simulated results.

EXHIBIT 29-11 SIMPLAN Data Records and Variables

Name	Abbreviation	Units
Accounts payable	AP	$000
Accounts receivable (net)	AR	$000
Cash	CASH	$000
Cost of goods sold	COGS	$000
Accounts receivable collected	COLLECTION	$000
Total current assets	CURASSETS	$000
Dollar value of sale	DOLLARSALE	$000
Fixed costs	FIXEDCOST	$000
Sales growth rate	GROWTHRATE	%
Cost of labor	LABOR	$/unit
Raw material cost	MATCOST	$/unit
Raw material inventory	MATERIALS	000 lbs.
Current value of inventory	MATVALUE	$000
Reduction of accounts payable	PAYMENTS	$000
Selling price	PRICE	$/units
Production volume	PRODUCTION	000 units
Additions to inventory	PURCHASES	000 lbs.
Inventory reorder point	REORDER	000 lbs.
Sales	SALES	000 units
Production cost per unit	UNITCOST	$/unit
Variable costs	VARCOST	$000
Production payroll	WAGES	$000

EXHIBIT 29-12 The Complete SIMPLAN Model

3	GROWTHRATE = 7
5	PRICE = 1.2
10	MATCOST = .6
15	REORDER = 3000
20	LABOR = .285
30	UNITCOST = LABOR+MATCOST
40	PRODUCTION = SALES(−1)
50	MATERIALS = MATERIALS(−1)-PRODUCTION
60	WAGES = LABOR*PRODUCTION
70	SALES = SALES(−1)*(1 + GROWTHRATE/100)
80	FIXEDCOST = 50
90	VARCOST = UNITCOST*SALES
100	COGS = FIXEDCOST + VARCOST
110	DOLLARSALE = SALES*PRICE
120	IF MATERIALS<REORDER
130	PURCHASES = REORDER + 2*PRODUCTION-MATERIALS
140	MATERIALS = MATERIALS + PURCHASES
145	ELSE
146	PURCHASES = 0
150	END
160	COLLECTION = 3/4*AR(−1)
170	AR = AR(−1) − COLLECTION + DOLLARSALE
180	PAYMENTS = .6*AP(−1)
190	AP = AP(−1) − PAYMENTS + (PURCHASES*MATCOST)
200	CASH = CASH(−1) + COLLECTION-PAYMENTS − WAGES
210	MATVALUE = MATERIALS*MATCOST
220	CURASSETS = CASH + AR + MATVALUE

Note that total current assets grow at an annual rate of 13.44 percent as opposed to 12.61 percent. The result indicates that a change in the assumed growth rate does not produce as large a change in the company's assets. In this case, a 1.5 percent increase in the growth rate causes cash and accounts receivable to rise by .67 percent and 1.4 percent, respectively; thus, the company's financial position in terms of liquidity and working capital appears to be relatively inelastic with respect to the assumed growth rate in sales.

EXPRESS

EXPRESS, developed by Management Decision Systems, provides the standard set of financial planning and analysis features including the generation of pro forma financial statements, budgeting, analysis, projections, target analysis, and consolidations. One of the special modeling features of the system is risk analysis (including Monte Carlo simulation). EXPRESS contains a variety of analytical and statistical features. Besides the standard mathematical capabilities, the system has the following automatic built-in calculations:

EXHIBIT 29-13 The Initial SIMPLAN Result

Policy Assumptions					
	1994	1995	1996	1997	Average
Sales growth rate (%)	7.00	7.00	7.00	7.00	7.00
Selling price ($/unit)	1.20	1.20	1.20	1.20	1.20
Raw material price ($/unit)	0.60	0.60	0.60	0.60	0.60
Cost of labor ($/unit)	0.28	0.28	0.28	0.28	0.28
Inventory reorder point (000 lbs.)	3,000	3,000	3,000	3,000	3,000

Results (all in $000 unless otherwise noted)					
	1994	1995	1996	1997	Percent Growth
Cash	1,432	1,997	1,860	2,346	17.88
Accounts receivable (net)	1,527	1,481	1,546	1,645	2.51
Current value of inventory	1,920	2,827	2,278	2,976	15.73
Total current assets	4,879	6,306	5,684	6.967	12.61
Sales (000 units)	856	916	980	1,049	7.00
Variable costs	758	811	867	928	7.00
Fixed costs	50	50	50	50	
Cost of goods sold	808	861	917	978	6.59
Dollar value of sales	1,027	1,099	1,176	1,258	7.00
Accounts receivable collected	(1,500)	(1,145)	(1,111)	(1,160)	(8.22)
Accounts receivable (net)	1,527	1,481	1,546	1,645	2.51
Reduction of accounts payable	840	336	987	395	(22.25)
Accounts payable	560	1,645	658	1,550	40.39
Production payroll	228	244	261	279	7.00
Production cost per unit ($/unit)	0.885	0.885	0.885	0.885	
Production volume (000 units)	(800)	(856)	(916)	(980)	7.00
Additions to inventory (000 lbs.)		2,368		2,144	
Raw material inventory (000 lbs.)	3,200	4,712	3,796	4,960	15.73

sorting, percent difference, lags and leads, maximum/minimum of a set of numbers, year-to-date, and rounding. The statistical features include a number of time series analyses and forecasting routines such as exponential smoothing, linear extrapolation, deseasonalization, multiple regression, cluster analysis, and factor analysis. EXPRESS contains the report generator and display features for the system. All the display capabilities are integrated with the system's data management, analysis, and modeling routine. The system has full graphic display capabilities.

Encore Plus

This package was developed by Ferox Microsystems. The analytical functions are similar to IFPS, but Encore has more model building capability. For

EXHIBIT 29-14 The Simulated SIMPLAN Result with Policy Assumption

	1994	1995	1996	1997	Average
Policy Assumptions					
Sales growth rate (%)	8.50	8.50	8.50	8.50	8.50
Selling price ($/unit)	1.20	1.20	1.20	1.20	1.20
Raw material price ($/unit)	0.60	0.60	0.60	0.60	0.60
Cost of labor ($/unit)	0.28	0.28	0.28	0.28	0.28
Inventory reorder point (000 lbs.)	3,000	3,000	3,000	3,000	3,000

	1994	1995	1996	1997	Percent Growth
Results (all in $000 unless otherwise noted)					
Cash	1,432	2,005	1,873	2,386	18.55
Accounts receivable (net)	1,542	1,516	1,605	1,732	3.95
Current value of inventory	1,920	2,842	2,277	3,026	16.38
Total current assets	4,894	6,362	5,755	7,144	13.44
Sales (000 units)	868	942	1,022	1,109	8.50
Variable costs	768	833	904	981	8.50
Fixed costs	50	50	50	50	
Cost of goods sold	818	883	954	1,031	8.02
Dollar value of sales	1,042	1,130	1,226	1,330	8.50
Accounts receivable collected	(1,500)	(1,156)	(1,137)	(1,204)	(7.07)
Accounts receivable (net)	1,542	1,516	1,605	1,732	3.95
Reduction of accounts payable	840	336	1,000	400	(21.91)
Accounts payable	560	1,666	667	1,629	42.76
Production payroll	228	247	268	291	8.50
Production cost per unit ($/unit)	0.885	0.885	0.885	0.885	
Production volume (000 units)	(800)	(868)	(942)	(1,022)	8.50
Additions to inventory (000 lbs.)		2,404		2,271	
Raw material inventory (000 lbs.)	3,200	4,736	3,794	5,044	16.38

example, it is stronger in its risk analysis than IFPS, and even includes a Monte Carlo Simulator. Since Encore Plus is more powerful at the application development level than, say, IFPS, it requires a higher level of programming ability.

CHECKLIST TO EVALUATE MODELING SOFTWARE

As was discussed, there is a number of software packages for financial and corporate modeling. Companies just entering the modeling arena must keep in mind that the differences that exist between the software packages available in the market can be substantial. A comparison should be made by examining the software in light of the planning system, the information system,

EXHIBIT 29-15 Checklist to Evaluate Modeling Software

- Main application area
  Corporate modeling
  Financial modeling
  Marketing modeling
  Production modeling
- Type of system
  Fixed structure
  Flexible, modular structure
- Mode of operation
  Batch
  Real time
  In-house
  Service bureau
- Costs of system
  Purchasing, leasing
  Consulting, training
  Storage
  Operation
- Type of language
  Free format–fixed format
  Compiler–interpreter
  Restrictions
  English-like or symbolic text
- Flexibility of input and output
  Choice and number of formats
  Sequence
  Graphics and histograms
- Type of data base
  File and data set structure
  Internal, external data base
  Connection and hierarchies of data
  bases and files
- Basic time intervals
  Maximum number
  Interval transformations
- Maximum size of model
  Statements
  Number and size of
  arrays, matrices and
  tables, and files and
  number of data
- Arithmetic
  Operators
  Column arithmetic
  Line arithmetic
  Table arithmetic
  Built-in functions
- Systems logic
  Linear sequential
  Logical branching

- Hardware requirements
  Main storage
  External storage
  Input–output facilities
- Software requirements
  Compilers and source languages
  Interfaces
  File organization, data access methods
  Index calculations
  IF, GOTO
  DO loop, END
  Forward, backward iterations
  Labels
  Subroutines
  Table access methods
- Handling of nonnumeric data
  Character string operations
  List and tree processing
  Set statements
- Macroinstructions
  Practitioner methods; e.g.,
  interpolation and extra-
  polation; financial indicators
  Short-term forecasting
  Trend forecasting
  Econometric methods
  Specification and verification
  testing
  Random numbers and
  stochastic simulation
  Matrix algebra and linear
  programming
  Nonlinear solution and
  optimization methods
  Experimental designs
  Graph analysis
- Security system
  Physical security of data base,
  model and CSPS
  Authorization codes and pass-
  words for data base, files,
  models—privacy
- Documentation and support
  User and system manuals
  Debugging and error tracing
  Menu programs, prompting,
  and "help" explanations
  Computer-aided instruction
  Consulting support

and the modeling activities. The companies also consider making effective use of in-house computer hardware (whether micro, mini, or mainframe) and data bases. An effective modeling system does not necessarily imply an outside time-sharing system or an external economic data base.

Below is a checklist for factors to consider in the evaluation of modeling software.

CONCLUSION

In recent years, computer-based models and spreadsheet software have been used for budgeting in an effort to facilitate the budgeting process and to allow budget analysts to investigate the effects of changes in budget assumptions. Financial models comprise a functional branch of a general corporate planning model. They are essentially used to generate pro-forma financial statements and financial ratios. These are the basic tools for budgeting and profit planning. Also, the financial model is a technique for risk analysis and "what-if" experiments. The financial model is also needed for day-to-day operational and tactical decisions for immediate planning problems.

Part 6

SERVICE AND
NOT-FOR-PROFIT ORGANIZATIONS

Chapter 30

Budgeting for Service Businesses*

A budget is important to meet goals and objectives. Most discussions of the budgetary process tend to focus on manufacturing firms. However, there are more businesses becoming engaged in nonmanufacturing activities today and such businesses can benefit greatly from a properly designed budgetary planning and control system. Budgeting may be used by a service business (which does not have merchandise inventory). For example, an airline may budget the average occupancy rate for seats and passenger miles. A hotel may budget the occupancy rate for rooms and the cost per room. For the most part, the budgeting methods and procedures described for manufacturing companies also apply to service businesses. There are two reasons why special attention should be devoted to budgetary planning and control techniques in the service industry.

First, planning and control are critical functions in all business, whether they produce and sell goods or provide services. Many service businesses have become more competitive in recent years. This increase in competition can be attributed to many things, such as the growth of the economy and the increase in demand for specialized services. When competition increases, planning and control become even more important.

Second, the practice of budgeting is probably not as well developed in service companies as it is in manufacturing firms. In manufacturing indus-

* We are indebted to our graduate students Charles Simons, Brion Tanous, and Scott Wherity of California State University at Long Beach for coauthoring this chapter.

tries, budgeting is forced upon the business by the need to keep sales and production coordinated. A manufacturing firm's investment in inventory forces the company to plan.

In service companies, however, the business activity largely requires human effort, and personal services are generally performed after the orders are received. The investment in inventory as we know it in manufacturing does not exist. There is no production activity. As a result, the management of a service company may not see the same need for planning and control.

Because budgeting is a planning and control system, the techniques applied to service companies will be very similar to those applied to manufacturing companies. The service company must not only develop an overall budget or profit plan for the year but also must establish good budgetary control that follows a well thought out plan of organization. The major difference in budgeting nonmanufacturing activities relates to the types of costs incurred and therefore to the control techniques applied. In most service industries, the major cost element is that of personnel, being reflected in salaries, wages, commissions, bonuses, and fringe benefits. Because of this fact, budgeting techniques are primarily concerned with planning the use of personnel and with controlling personnel effectiveness.

A professional service business sells the employees' expertise. Emphasis is given to labor productivity and controlling overhead costs. Pricing policies are budgeted based upon either a daily rate, hourly rate, fixed rate for the job, or a contingent fee based on, for example, the dollar value of property sold, a court settlement, or sales price.

Problems may occur if there are inadequate numbers of qualified workers or insufficient capital facilities to meet customer demand. It is important that employee time be used productivity. A productivity report should be prepared of sales dollars generated per professional and the associated direct costs. The format of the report is:

Revenue generated
Less: Direct costs
Residual profit
Less: Overhead
Profit

A service business relies heavily on its reputation for fast and quality service. Otherwise, customers will switch to competitors. Rendering poor quality for short-term opportunities has disasterous long-term effects. It is best to grow at a steady, quality rate.

A service company must place a premium on defining the operations required to produce a service profitably and on assigning responsibility for planning and controlling such operations efficiently. For example, whereas receivables and inventories are two current asset areas for planning and control emphasis in a manufacturing company, most service companies regard only receivables as an important current asset. So emphasis on points of cost control and specific balance sheet items may shift between the two types of business concerns. The underlying concept of budgeting, however, does not change.

For growing service companies, a common pattern is observed while implementing a budgetary system:

1. A profit or target for the company is established.
2. An annual plan is developed that indicates expected revenues and expenses by the organizational segments and in total, by month.
3. The cash budget is established.
4. A planned statement of financial position is developed and tested against selected standards.
5. Actual performance is measured against plan by specific levels of management position.
6. Corrective action is taken as deemed necessary.

Service companies typically have prepared budgets for departmental expenses and have tracked these expenses against plan. However, it can be seen that budgetary control should extend to profit centers, where accountability for revenues as well as costs can be placed. Keeping personnel costs well within the limits set for planned revenues, is critical in order to achieve net income objectives.

In a professional service firm, such as a CPA firm, law practice, consulting business, or advertising agency, revenue dollars may be specifically identified to specific individuals. The revenue and direct costs per individual may be determined. Indirect costs are budgeted separately and allocated based on revenue. These businesses are labor intensive and have high variable cost structures.

In service companies, investments in inventories, plant and equipment typically are relatively small, but the planning and control techniques should still extend to the statement of financial position so that acceptable financial ratios are maintained. However, it is difficult to control a business with high long-term capital investment, such as transportation companies, computer service business, and leasing companies.

Service businesses should make long-term commitments *only* for salaries and facilities if it is confident of future sales. Otherwise, if future sales fall off, the high fixed costs will hurt profits.

This chapter presents the budgeting aspects of certain service industries to aid the reader's comprehension of the subject. These include airlines, hotels, training centers, and television production.

AIRLINES

Airlines face a problem of perishable services. Airlines have systems known as yield management systems. These systems constantly adjust what fares are available and the number based on sales. For example, if an airline's LA to New York seats are selling very briskly, the system will severely limit or eliminate discounted seats. However, the inverse is also true, if a flight is slow selling, the amount of discounted fares available will increase to stimulate sales. The goal of the yield management system is to maximize revenue, taking into account that if the seat goes unsold, it is a lost revenue opportunity.

HOTELS

The calculation of sales volume and unit price is much more difficult for hotels than manufacturers. Hotels have a maximum capacity of rooms each night and annually, like a factory's production capacity. However, the demand for a hotel's rooms can vary greatly from day to day, month to month, and year to year.

For hotels, it is very difficult to predict sales and average unit selling price. Historical data can be of some help, but it does not take into account many environmental factors, such as the economy, new competitors, aging facilities, bad weather, unstable governments, fluctuating currencies, and current travel trends.

Reservations forecasting is much more art (and luck) than a science. Modern computer systems have done little to improve accuracy of hotel room sales. One problem is that a hotel room is a perishable commodity. If it is not sold one night, the potential value for that time is lost forever.

Hotels also try to maximize their revenues per room, but an airline system will not work. Airlines deal with one customer occupying one seat on a flight. Hotels however, have customers staying different lengths of time, staying longer than they have reserved, departing early; they also have no-shows. Hotels do not have fare products like airlines, they have market segments. The hotel's goal is to book as many of the next highest paying segments, and so on. The results of this can be a small number of rooms allocated to a low paying market group. A hotel's reservation system does not function like an airline's; the number of each market segment is not automatically adjusted for yield maximization. The rooms allocated to the various market segments must be done manually, for the reasons listed above.

Hotels, like airlines, can refuse potential business. If a hotel is projected to be full or near full, it will stop taking reservations or will stop selling highly discounted rates. If there are cancellations, these rooms now stand the chance of going unsold (not producing revenue). Hotels may also refuse potential discounted reservations because they think they can sell the remaining rooms to full-paying clients, taking a chance that these rooms will not sell at all. For these reasons, hotels as well as airlines overbook. They gamble that they will have a sufficient amount of no-shows and cancellations to accommodate everyone, which is not always the case. A projected sales budget for hotels is presented in Exhibit 30-1.

To estimate the gross sales, multiply the projected number of rooms in each category by the averaged rate paid by each market segment. A sample rate structure is presented in Exhibit 30-2.

Having estimated in the budget that Monday XX, 19XX, you will have projected room revenue of $29,125 on a projected occupancy of 81 percent.

Projected sales are done on a daily, monthly, and annual basis. The sales are very closely monitored because they are selling a perishable commodity. If a room is not sold one night, then its potential for revenue for that time is lost forever. If a slow period is projected from reports and bookings, management will really push to try to sell these rooms. They will often reduce rates (especially on weekends, when business travel is low) to try to stimulate sales. This hopefully will provide at least a minimal amount of revenue. The notion of reducing rates is somewhat tricky when dealing with image. Additionally, hotels that are located in areas of high competition (such as Anaheim, California), use rates as one of their competitive weapons.

From the sales budget you can now develop a projected cash collections schedule. For a hotel, this is not as straightforward as for a manufacturer. When a manufacturer sells its finished goods to a retailer or wholesaler, generally, they have terms such as net 30. It knows from past experience that it will collect X percent one month after the sale, Y percent in the second

EXHIBIT 30-1 Hotel Projected Sales Budget

	MON	TUES	WED	THUR	FRI	SAT	SUN
Leisure	50	60	60	70	100	100	40
Corporate	75	80	80	50	10	10	60
Government	100	90	90	50	10	10	50
Group	100	70	120	120	40	60	70
Total Rooms	325	300	350	290	160	180	220
(%)	81%	75%	88%	73%	40%	45%	55%

Average (%) for the week: 65% (based on a 400-room hotel)

EXHIBIT 30-2 Sample Hotel Rate Structure

Market Segment	Rates	Avg. Rate Paid
Leisure	$100–130	$120
Corporate	$ 80–115	$ 95
Government	$ 75–105	$ 90
Group	$ 60– 90	$ 70

Monday's revenues would look like this:

Leisure	(50) ($120) =	$ 6,000
Corporate	(75) ($ 95) =	$ 7,125
Government	(100) ($ 90) =	$ 9,000
Group	(100) ($ 70) =	$ 7,000
		$29,125

month, Z percent in the third, while leaving some percentage uncollected as bad debt.

Hotels have different cash collection patterns. Most individual customers pay for their charges with a credit card. After the charges have been processed, the hotel is electronically credited each individual amount. However, one does not know exactly what percentage of guests will charge their accounts or pay some other way, by check or cash.

Groups, corporate, and government accounts can all pay individually upon departure, or more likely, all charges will go to a master account. The master account can be processed and billed to the company upon the group's departure. This would occur when a group only has one function and does not have a running account. However, for most accounts of this type, there is a running total and the company is billed monthly for charges the group has incurred during the period. As everyone knows, some companies can be very slow in paying their bills, especially big corporations and the government. This fact must be taken into consideration when projecting your cash collections estimation. One last monkey wrench in this whole system is advance deposits. Many groups and individuals are required to leave advance deposits to guarantee space. This will make the estimation of cash collections even more difficult because you do not know where and when these deposits will occur.

The next step for a manufacturer would be to construct a production budget. However, for a service firm this would not be appropriate, they are not building anything, they are selling a service (e.g., lodging).

From the production budget a manufacturer would then develop a direct materials budget, direct labor budget, and overhead budget. However, a hotel would do this a little differently. It can construct a direct materials budget, but it is somewhat difficult to estimate. For a hotel, this would primarily be the food and beverage that it sells. The demand for the food and beverage is difficult to exactly estimate, but a ballpark figure can be calculated.

A direct labor budget is probably one of hotel's most critical budgets, along with the sales budget. Hotels, especially full-service luxury resorts, are very labor intensive. Based upon projected sales, hotels can budget their expected labor costs. When the actual budgeted period has begun, these figures are watched very closely for any variations. A target productivity is sought by each department. When a difference occurs between the budgeted figure and the actual numbers, this will cause an investigation.

Overhead for a hotel is like a factory. Any cost that is not direct labor or direct materials will be accounted for as overhead. For a hotel, its overhead can be broken down into two main categories:

1. rooms overhead and

2. food and beverage overhead.

These two areas are the main revenue centers for most hotels. There is a fine line in what costs could be direct labor or materials or overhead. It falls to management to classify each cost.

The next step for a manufacturer would be to develop a cost of goods sold budget. For a manufacturer this budget is helpful in setting prices and estimating gross income. For a hotel, this budget step would only yield minimal benefit. Hotels do not produce products, as we all know, they provide services. A cost of goods sold budget would provide a hotel with the cost of major departments such as rooms and food and beverage.

Now the selling and administrative (S&A) expense budget would be compiled. This budget is as helpful to a manufacturer as a hotel. All organizations need to know their selling expenses. The selling expenses are combined with general administrative costs. This budget combines both fixed and variable S & A costs such as insurance, rent, office salaries, sales salaries, and commissions.

Now you have reached the step in the budgeting process where different parts of the budget you have previously constructed are combined: the budgeted income statement. This statement summarizes the various component projections of revenue and expenses for the budget period. This is usually an annual budget, however, for better control, it may be done quarterly or even monthly. This budget subtracts variable expenses from sales to obtain a contribution margin. Then it subtracts fixed expenses to arrive at operating income, less interest expenses providing income before taxes (IBT). Income taxes are subtracted to produce your goal: net income.

A cash budget also needs to be prepared. This budget will signal when there will be cash surpluses or shortages. This budget is very important; remember, a company can go broke while making a profit. By having this budget available, one will know when funds are available for investment growth or expansion, or when funds are just needed to pay the bills.

EXHIBIT 30-3 Comparison Capital Budgets

	Service Firms	Hospitality Firms	Lodging Chains
	1984	1980	1990
IRR	82%	33%	74%
Payback	63%	71%	66%
NPV	67%	36%	55%

When all the budgets have been completed, a budgeted balance sheet can be compiled. The balance sheet is constructed by adjusting the balance sheet from the period that just ended. The budget balance sheet serves three primary purposes: it can disclose potentially unfavorable financial conditions; it allows management to perform a number of different ratio calculations; lastly, it highlights future resources and obligations.

One area in budgeting of major concern for hotels is capital expenditures. Hotels have begun to use more sophisticated ways of calculating the potential value of a capital expenditure.

What do hotels consider a "major" expenditure? A recent survey showed that 16 percent of lodging chains consider a major expense to be greater than $10,000. Forty-four percent of lodging chains feel that $50,000 or more is a major expense. While 12 percent do not feel that an expense is major unless it exceeds $1,000,000.

The use of different formulas to calculate a project's value has changed to include time value of money and project risk.

Exhibit 30-3 shows what formulas hotels use in relation to service firms in general for capital budgeting.

Exhibit 30-4 shows those formulas that hotels prefer to use for different investment decisions. *Note:* The charts were taken from Schmidgall and Damitio's article "Current capital budgeting practices of major lodging chains."

Here is one example of how the different formulas can provide different information on potential investments.

A hotel is considering purchasing a bus to transport its customers. The bus will cost $100,000 and provide a one or a two percent increase in room

EXHIBIT 30-4 Hotel Investment Formulas

Type of Investment	Payback		NPV		IRR	
	1980	1990	1980	1990	1980	1990
All Investments	19%	24%	12%	15%	7%	30%
Replacement	49%	46%	16%	19%	12%	35%
Renovation	42%	35%	17%	28%	14%	44%
Expansion	44%	39%	17%	37%	14%	57%
Acquisition	37%	37%	21%	46%	9%	57%
Never Use	27%	34%	71%	45%	77%	26%

EXHIBIT 30-5 NPV Sales Increases

NPV Based on 1 Percent Sales Increase	Outlay	2 Percent Increase
$100,000		$100,000
$ 60,000	1st year cash flow	$120,000
$ 60,000	2nd year cash flow	$120,000
$ 60,000	3rd year cash flow	$120,000
$ 20,000	Salvage value	$ 20,000
NPV +$ 58,345		NPV +$202,455

sales of $6,000,000 annually. The bus will provide these cash flows for three years and have a $20,000 salvage value, the cost of capital is 12 percent. Using NPV, IRR, and Payback, what would the hotel's decision be? See Exhibit 30-5 for NPV sales increases.

The hotel would buy the bus using any method as long as sales increased by at least 1 percent.

- IRR based on the same cash flows for a 1 percent sales increase equals 41.96 percent

- IRR based on the above cash flows for a 2 percent sales increase equals 109.3 percent

- Payback based on a 1 percent sales increase is 1.67 years

- Payback based on a 2 percent sales increase is .833 years

However, budgets do present problems for business. Budgets are said to to control the wrong things like head counts, and to miss important areas like quality of customer service and profits. Just because one does not go over budget, does not mean that the money has been spent well. Everyone has heard of the traditional autumn spending sprees. Executives sometimes feel that a penny saved is a penny lost from next year's budget. For budget effectiveness to increase, companies need to eliminate the "use it or lose it" attitude. Another problem with budgets is that they do not measure. Budgets can show what was spent on customer service, but they cannot tell what value customers put on it. Lastly, phrases such as "it's not in this year's budget" can kill potential opportunities. Budgets can stifle growth while retaining poor products.

TANOUS TRAINING AND CONSULTING SERVICES

Tanous Training & Consulting Services is a sole proprietorship which began actively marketing its services in October of 1992. The budgets developed in this chapter are actual budgets to be followed for the 1993 calendar year used by Tanous Training & Consulting Services. All costs are actual based either on historical data during development of the business or on current policies of the organization.

Tanous Training & Consulting Services offers custom training and consulting for manufacturing, processing, and assembly companies in the area of statistical process improvement. Statistical skills and process improvement methodology is applied to job-shops, continuous production environments, and every type of operation in-between. Tanous Training has available a variety of teaching environments to choose from for any particular company's needs.

Tanous Training provides manufacturing firms methodology to apply within their operations that will allow them to realize their process improvement objectives. Information is the core product that is being sold. This core product is translated into advice, help, direction, knowledge, and experience which aim to commence, reinforce, or accelerate efforts to improve and affect the bottom line.

Tanous Training conducts structured seminar training for engineers, supervision, and management. Depending upon the scope of the subject matter agreed upon by the client and Tanous Training, seminars can range from 8 hours to extensive 64 hour programs. Material for each seminar is provided in the form of a technical manual containing specific modules of methodology. Exercises to reinforce material covered and break out sessions are also included in the manual. This material is intended to be taken to the workplace and referenced frequently during implementation of the process improvement program.

Additionally, Tanous Training provides on-the-job training to production supervision and operators, focusing on previously established improvement objectives. This training can occur in one-on-one settings on the shop floor or in small groups in the workplace. The different team members can be addressed individually if desired, or the team can be addressed as a whole.

Consulting services are also available for the firms which have progressed beyond the introductory stages of implementing statistical process control. If particular personnel require additional skills or reinforcement of previously learned material, those individuals can receive additional attention to achieve the greatest effect on the program.

Tanous Training will promote 8 hour sessions on Saturdays by offering a 15 percent discount on the base contract fee (discount does not apply to the price of technical manuals). It is estimated that 50 percent of all contracted training hours will take place on Saturdays. Half day wrap-ups or review sessions can also be contracted. Consulting service hours will be considerably more flexible.

An integrated direct marketing strategy will be used to develop awareness among prospective clients. To introduce this new service category, an informative advertising strategy will be used to build primary demand. Direct mail advertising will attempt to reach an average of 200 target firms per month in each of the geographical areas served. The frequency of exposure to direct mail advertisements will average 90 days.

Sales will also be established through the use of sales representatives. All sales representatives will be paid a flat 20 percent commission based on the base service contract excluding revenue generated from the sale of technical manuals at the seminars. Tanous Training has estimated that 50 percent of all contracts will be established through sales representatives. The remaining 50 percent will be established through direct mail advertising.

All administrative work, training and consulting will be conducted by the sole proprietor. All compensation to the sole proprietor shall be in the form of business profits. As a result salaries, administration expenses, and benefits are not budgeted.

The Master Budget

The master budget represents the complete budget package for an organization. The budgetary process results in a comprehensive master budget. The master budget includes all of the individual budgets for each part of the organization, combined into one overall budget for the entire organization.

The components of the master budget form the firm's detailed operating plan for the coming year. The master budget is divided into the operating budget and the financial budget. The operating budget includes revenues, product or service costs, operating expenses, and other components of the income statement. The financial budget includes the budgeted balance sheet, cash budget, and other budgets used in financial management, such as the budgeted statement of cash flows. A large part of the financial budget is determined by the operating budget and the beginning balance sheet.

Operating Budget Components

The Sales Budget.   The sales budget, or revenue budget, begins the budgetary process. It is usually the most important budget because so many other budgets are dependent upon and are developed from the sales budget. Sales budgets are influenced by many factors, including general economic conditions, pricing decisions, competitor actions, industry conditions, and marketing programs.

A combination of estimating methods and the use of judgment are needed to develop a suitable sales plan. The methods used in forecasting sales include statistical methods (trend analysis and correlation analysis), judgmental methods (sales department estimate, customer surveys and executive opinion composite) and other methods (share of the market, product line analysis and end user analysis).

Tanous Training & Consulting Services has chosen to use sales department estimates based on predicted response rate from direct mail advertising for the start-up year. The consulting service industry dictates that a .5 percent response rate to direct mail advertising would be a conservative forecast for a start-up firm. This response rate is used as a basis for predicting monthly revenues of the firm. It is assumed that one potential client will respond from a direct mailing of 200 per month. See Exhibit 30-6.

Two client parties are forecasted for the third quarter of the year. A 15 percent discount will be given for 8 hour blocks contracted for Saturdays. It is expected that half of all training days will be conducted during this discount period. Furthermore, it is assumed that the average service contract will be 16 hours of training at the client's facility. It is expected that nine client employees will attend the training sessions on average.

In addition to the base service contract, the technical training manual will be a source of revenue. One manual per participant will be sold for each contracted client. While the base contract revenue represents pure service revenue, the technical manuals represent direct materials and are priced in accordance with standard mark-up above variable costs.

The schedule of cash receipts demonstrates the collection policy of Tanous Training & Consulting Services. The service contract states that 70 percent of full contract price will be collected two days prior to the first training session. The remaining 30 percent is due and will be collected within 30 days of the final training session. The accounts receivable for the beginning of the year are zero. January is the first month forecasting sales. See Exhibit 30-7.

The Direct Material Budget. Direct material, as traditionally defined, includes all material that is an integral part of the finished product and that can be traced to the cost of the finished article, such as raw materials and purchased parts. It does not include material not directly traceable to the finished article. Tanous Training & Consulting Services uses a direct material budget to supply the basic quantity data so that the materials cost element of the finished product (technical training manual) can be calculated and controlled. See Exhibit 30-8.

The purchasing function makes plans for obtaining and stocking the necessary items for production. These plans are summarized in a direct materials budget and related schedule of cash disbursements. Purchase plans are always expressed in both units required and associated costs. Purchase requirements equal sales requirements plus the planned ending inventory minus the beginning inventory. In the case of Tanous Training, each technical train-

EXHIBIT 30-6 Sales Forecast
Tanous Training & Consulting Services
For the Year ending December 31, 1993

	Jan	Feb	Mar	Apr	May	Jun	Jul	Aug	Sep	Oct	Nov	Dec	Year Total
SALES													
Service Revenue:													
Training Hours	8	8	16	16	16	16	32	32	32	16	16	16	224
Number of 8 hr. blocks	1	1	2	2	2	2	4	4	4	2	2	2	28
Number of client parties	1	1	1	1	1	1	2	2	2	1	1	1	15
Revenue @ $1,800 per 8 hour block	1,800	1,800	3,600	3,600	3,600	3,600	7,200	7,200	7,200	3,600	3,600	3,600	50,400
Less: Saturday discount @ 15%	135	135	270	270	270	270	540	540	540	270	270	270	3,780
Net Service Revenue	1,665	1,665	3,330	3,330	3,330	3,330	6,660	6,660	6,660	3,330	3,330	3,330	46,620
Manuals sold @ 1/participant/client	9	9	9	9	9	9	18	18	18	9	9	9	135
Revenue @ $16.50 per manual	149	149	149	149	149	149	297	297	297	149	149	149	2,228
TOTAL SALES	1,814	1,814	3,479	3,479	3,479	3,479	6,957	6,957	6,957	3,479	3,479	3,479	48,848

Half of contracted blocks forecasted as Saturday sessions at 15 percent discounted rate.

EXHIBIT 30-7 Schedule of Expected Cash Receipts
Tanous Training & Consulting Services
For the Year ending December 31, 1993

	Jan	Feb	Mar	Apr	May	Jun	Jul	Aug	Sep	Oct	Nov	Dec	Year Total
Accounts Receivables 12/31/92	0												
Sales:													
January Sales	1,269	544											
February Sales		1,269	544										
March Sales			2,435	1,044									
April Sales				2,435	1,044								
May Sales					2,435	1,044							
June Sales						2,435	1,044						
July Sales							4,870	2,087					
August Sales								4,870	2,087				
September Sales									4,870	2,087			
October Sales										2,435	1,044		
November Sales											2,435	1,044	
December Sales												2,435	
Total Cash Collections	1,269	1,814	2,979	3,479	3,479	3,479	5,913	6,957	6,957	4,522	3,479	3,479	47,804

70% of contract revenue collected 2 days prior to initial training block.

30% of contract revenue collected within 30 days of contract completion.

EXHIBIT 30-8 Direct Material Budget
Tanous Training & Consulting Services
For the Year ending December 31, 1993

	Jan	Feb	Mar	Apr	May	Jun	Jul	Aug	Sep	Oct	Nov	Dec	Year Total
Number of client parties	1	1	1	1	1	1	2	2	2	1	1	1	15
Manuals sold	9	9	9	9	9	9	18	18	18	9	9	9	135
Binders @ $2.65 ea. per manual	24	24	24	24	24	24	48	48	48	24	24	24	358
Copies @ $4.00 per manual	36	36	36	36	36	36	72	72	72	36	36	36	540
Dividers @ $1.29 per manual	12	12	12	12	12	12	23	23	23	12	12	12	174
Material Needs for Production	80	80	80	80	80	80	161	161	161	80	80	80	1,207
Desired ending inventory	0	0	0	0	0	0	0	0	0	0	0	0	0
Total Needs	80	80	80	80	80	80	161	161	161	80	80	80	1,207
Less: Beginning Inventory	0	0	0	0	0	0	0	0	0	0	0	0	0
Materials to Be Purchased	80	80	80	80	80	80	161	161	161	80	80	80	1,207
Total Purchase Cost	80	80	80	80	80	80	161	161	161	80	80	80	1,207

ing manual will be tailored for the specific needs of the client party. As a result, no inventory will be maintained. All manuals are created one week prior to training and distributed on the first day of the contract. Purchase of materials for the manuals will be made on credit. Payments shall be made 30 days after purchase. All purchased materials will be used up prior to the end of the month purchased. See Exhibit 30-9.

The Service Overhead Budget.

By definition, overhead expenses are those costs that cannot be charged to, or are not directly identifiable with, a specific product, process or job. Typical overhead expenses include indirect salaries, power, supplies, rent, depreciation and communications. The nature of overhead expenses has, for large firms, rendered the budgeting, or planning and control, of this element somewhat more difficult than the other production factors. There are several reasons for this. First, there are many items of cost, each often of small consequence at the point of application, each originating from different sources, and each requiring different methods and time of control.

Another reason is that the responsibility for control is widely distributed throughout the organization. The expenditures of direct material and labor are usually under immediate supervision, but the responsibility for overhead items is distributed among several individuals in the firm. Additionally, the individual items of cost comprising this composite called overhead behave in differing ways as the level of activity changes.

The variable overhead items for services provided by Tanous Training consist of the supplies needed at each training session while the fixed component of overhead includes phone services, mailbox services and depreciation. Fixed overhead items are expensed on a monthly basis and do not change throughout the calendar year. See Exhibit 30-10.

The Marketing Expense Budget.

Sales volume is determined, to some degree, by the marketing effort. Consequently, the marketing expense budget is prepared early in the budgeting process. As presented in this example, marketing expenses are broken into variable and fixed components. See Exhibit 30-11.

The variable portion of the marketing expense budget consists of selling expenses in the form of sales commissions. Sales commissions consist of 20 percent of the base client contract excluding revenue generated by the sale of technical manuals. The fixed component of marketing expense budget consists of costs incurred as a result of the direct mail advertising campaign.

Sales commission is paid upon full collection of the service contract, while expenditures on direct mail advertising are disbursed 30 days after purchase of material and printing services as detailed in the schedule of cash disbursements for marketing expenses. See Exhibit 30-12.

EXHIBIT 30-9 Schedule of Expected Cash Disbursements
Direct Materials
Tanous Training & Consulting Services
For the Year ending December 31, 1993

	Jan	Feb	Mar	Apr	May	Jun	Jul	Aug	Sep	Oct	Nov	Dec	Year Total
Accounts Payable 12/31/92	**0**												
January Purchases		80											
February Purchases			80										
March Purchases				80									
April Purchases					80								
May Purchases						80							
June Purchases							80						
July Purchases								161					
August Purchases									161				
September Purchases										161			
October Purchases											80		
November Purchases												80	
December Purchases													
Total Cash Disbursements	**0**	**80**	**80**	**80**	**80**	**80**	**80**	**161**	**161**	**161**	**80**	**80**	**1,126**

All direct material cash disbursements made 30 days after purchase.

EXHIBIT 30-10 Service Overhead Budget
Tanous Training & Consulting Services
For the Year ending December 31, 1993

	Jan	Feb	Mar	Apr	May	Jun	Jul	Aug	Sep	Oct	Nov	Dec	Year Total
Variable Overhead													
Number of 8 hr. blocks	1	2	2	2	2	2	4	4	4	2	2	2	28
Overheads @ $3.00 per 8 hr. block	3	6	6	6	6	6	12	12	12	6	6	6	84
Pads @ 4$4.50 per client	5	5	5	5	5	5	9	9	9	5	5	5	68
Pens and utensiles @ $2 per client	2	2	2	2	2	2	4	4	4	2	2	2	30
Total Variable Overhead	10	13	13	13	13	13	25	25	25	13	13	13	182
Fixed Overhead													
Phone	18	18	18	18	18	18	18	18	18	18	18	18	216
P.O. Box	12	12	12	12	12	12	12	12	12	12	12	12	144
Depreciation:													
Equipment & software	66	66	66	66	66	66	66	66	66	66	66	66	792
Total Depreciation	66	66	66	66	66	66	66	66	66	66	66	66	792
Total Fixed Overhead	96	96	96	96	96	96	96	96	96	96	96	96	1,152
TOTAL BUDGETED OVERHEAD	106	106	109	109	109	109	121	121	121	109	109	109	1,334
Less: Total depreciation	66	66	66	66	66	66	66	66	66	66	66	66	792
CASH DISBURSEMENTS FOR OVERHEAD	40	40	43	43	43	43	55	55	55	43	43	43	542

All cash disbursements for overhead expenses made during month incurred.

EXHIBIT 30-11 Marketing Expense Budget
Tanous Training & Consulting Services
For the Year ending December 31, 1993

	Jan	Feb	Mar	Apr	May	Jun	Jul	Aug	Sep	Oct	Nov	Dec	Year Total
Variable Marketing Expenses													
Sales Commissions @ 20% of Net													
Service Revenue on 50% of clients	167	167	333	333	333	333	666	666	666	333	333	333	4,662
Budgeted Variable Marketing Expenses	167	167	333	333	333	333	666	666	666	333	333	333	4,662
Fixed Marketing Expenses													
Direct Mailings	200	200	200	200	200	200	200	200	200	200	200	200	2,400
Brochure Printing (Every 6 mos.)	0	0	0	220	0	0	0	0	220	0	0	0	440
Business Card Printing (Every 6 mos.)	0	0	0	85	0	0	0	0	85	0	0	0	170
Envelopes @ $.01ea.	2	2	2	2	2	2	2	2	2	2	2	2	24
Clips @ $.03ea.	6	6	6	6	6	6	6	6	6	6	6	6	72
Letters @ $.05ea.	10	10	10	10	10	10	10	10	10	10	10	10	120
Stamps @ $.29 ea.	58	58	58	58	58	58	58	58	58	58	58	58	696
Budgeted Fixed Marketing Expenses	76	76	76	381	76	76	76	76	381	76	76	76	1,522
Total Marketing Expenses	243	243	409	714	409	409	742	742	1,047	409	409	409	6,184

EXHIBIT 30-12 Schedule of Expected Cash Disbursements
Marketing Expenses
Tanous Training & Consulting Services
For the Year ending December 31, 1993

	Jan	Feb	Mar	Apr	May	Jun	Jul	Aug	Sep	Oct	Nov	Dec	Year Total
Accounts Payable 12/31/92	0												
January Disbursements		243											
February Disbursements			243										
March Disbursements				409									
April Disbursements					714								
May Disbursements						409							
June Disbursements							409						
July Disbursements								742					
August Disbursements									742				
September Disbursements										1,047			
October Disbursements											409		
November Disbursements												409	
December Disbursements													
Total Cash Disbursements	0	243	243	409	714	409	409	742	742	1,047	409	409	5,775

Commission paid upon full collection of contract revenue.

Fixed expenses paid 30 days after purchase.

The Budgeted Income Statement.   The budgeted income statement is the combination of all preceding budgets. This budget shows the expected revenues and expenses from operations during the budget period. Budgeted income is a key figure in the firm's profit plan and reflects a majority of the firm's effort for the budgeting period.

A firm may have budgeted nonoperation items such as interest on investments or gains or losses on the sale of fixed assets. If nonoperating items are expected, they should be included in the budgeted income statement.

Income taxes are levied on actual, not budgeted, net income, but the budget plan should include expected taxes. Therefore, the last figure in the budgeted income statement is budgeted after-tax net income.

In the case of Tanous Training & Consulting Services, a contribution income statement has been developed. Variable expenses, which include direct materials, variable marketing expenses and variable overhead expenses are subtracted from total revenue to arrive at a contribution margin. Due to the structure of the firm and the nature of sole proprietorships, fixed expenses are a relatively small component of the firm's costs. For Tanous Training, this relationship allows for an extremely rapid break-even point.

A combined Federal and State income tax rate has been estimated at 32 percent for the 1993 calendar year. Income tax will be paid quarterly (during the month following the calendar quarter) as reflected in the cash budget. See Exhibit 30-13.

Financial Budget Components

The financial budget presents the plans for financing the operating activities of the firm. The financial budget is comprised of a number of different budgets, each providing essential financial information. Typically the financial budgeting process will include a capital expenditure budget. While this type of budget is required for most service organizations and all manufacturing organizations, Tanous Training does not plan for capital expansion in the 1993 calendar year. As a result, the capital expenditure budget has been omitted from this year's budget plans.

The Cash Budget.   Of all the components of the master budget, none is more important than the cash budget. Liquidity is of critical importance to a firm. Some companies may lose money for many years, but with adequate financing they are able to remain in business until they can become profitable. On the other hand, firms that cannot remain liquid are unable to pay their bills as they come due.

The cash budget is a very useful tool in cash management. The cash budget estimates all expected cash flows for the budget period. The typical

EXHIBIT 30-13 Budgeted Income Statement
Tanous Training & Consulting Services
For the Year ending December 31, 1993

	Jan	Feb	Mar	Apr	May	Jun	Jul	Aug	Sep	Oct	Nov	Dec	Year Total
Sales	1,814	1,814	3,479	3,479	3,479	3,479	6,957	6,957	6,957	3,479	3,479	3,479	48,848
Manuals sold	9	9	9	9	9	9	18	18	18	9	9	9	135
Less: Variable Expenses													
Direct Materials	80	80	80	80	80	80	161	161	161	80	80	80	1,207
Variable Marketing Expenses	167	167	333	333	333	333	666	666	666	333	333	333	4,662
Variable Overhead Expenses	10	10	13	13	13	13	25	25	25	13	13	13	182
Total Variable Expenses	256	256	426	426	426	426	852	852	852	426	426	426	6,050
Contribution Margin	1,557	1,557	3,053	3,053	3,053	3,053	6,105	6,105	6,105	3,053	3,053	3,053	42,797
Less: Fixed Expenses													
Fixed Marketing Expenses	76	76	76	381	76	76	76	76	381	76	76	76	1,522
Fixed Overhead Expenses	96	96	96	96	96	96	96	96	96	96	96	96	1,152
Total Fixed Expenses	172	172	172	477	172	172	172	172	477	172	172	172	2,674
Net Operating Income	1,385	1,385	2,881	2,576	2,881	2,881	5,933	5,933	5,628	2,881	2,881	2,881	40,123
Less: Interest Expense	0	0	0	0	0	0	0	0	0	0	0	0	0
Net Income Before Taxes	1,385	1,385	2,881	2,576	2,881	2,881	5,993	5,993	5,628	2,881	2,881	2,881	40,123
Less: Income Taxes @ 32%	443	443	922	824	922	922	1,899	1,899	1,801	922	922	922	12,839
Net Income	942	942	1,959	1,751	1,959	1,959	4,034	4,034	3,827	1,959	1,959	1,959	27,284

starting point is cash from operations, which is net income adjusted for non-cash items, such as depreciation. All nonoperating cash items are also included. The net income for an accounting period is usually very different from the cash flow for the period because of nonoperating cash flow items or changes in working capital.

Cash management is intended to optimize cash balances. This means having enough cash to meet liquidity needs, but not so much cash that profitability is sacrificed. Excess cash should be invested in earning assets rather than remain idle in the cash account. Cash budgeting is useful in dealing with both types of cash problems.

The preparation of a cash budget is a basic tool of forecasting cash. The cash budget establishes the sources, timing, and amounts of cash receipts and disbursements. Cash budgets can identify the high and low points in a company's cash cycle. Low points alert management not to schedule large discretionary payments during these periods. High points enable management to plan a short-term investment strategy to utilize profitably on excess of funds. See Exhibit 30-14.

The Budgeted Balance Sheet

The budgeted balance sheet is derived from the budgeted balance at the beginning of the budgeting period and the expected changes in the account balances, reflected in the operating budget and cash budget. See Exhibit 30-15. The budgeted balance sheet is more than a collection of residual balances resulting from other budget estimates. Undesirable projected balances and account relationships may cause management to change the operating plan.

Paid-in Capital for Tanous Training & Consulting Services consists of all personal investments made during development and start-up of the company. Retained earnings represent losses for the 1992 year during which time no revenue was generated. See Exhibit 30-16.

The Budgeted Statement of Cash Flows

The final element of the master budget package is the statement of cash flows. The increased emphasis by management in recent years on cash and the sources and uses of cash has made this an ever more useful management tool. This statement is usually prepared from data in the budgeted income statement and changes in the estimated balance sheet between the beginning and end of the budget period. In the case of Tanous Training, the statement of cash flows has been simplified by only including those changes in assets and liabilities which the firm experiences. See Exhibit 30-17.

EXHIBIT 30-14 Cash Budget
Tanous Training & Consulting Services
For the Year ending December 31, 1993

	Jan	Feb	Mar	Apr	May	Jun	Jul	Aug	Sep	Oct	Nov	Dec
Cash Balance, Beginning	2,200	3,340	4,881	7,495	8,633	11,274	14,221	16,922	22,921	28,920	26,594	29,540
Add: Receipts from Customers	1,269	1,814	2,979	3,479	3,479	3,479	5,913	6,957	6,957	4,522	3,479	3,479
Total Cash Available	3,469	5,243	7,860	10,973	12,111	14,753	20,134	23,879	29,878	33,442	30,072	33,019
Less: Disbursements												
Direct Materials	0	80	80	80	80	80	80	161	161	161	80	80
Marketing Expenses	0	243	243	409	714	409	409	742	742	1,047	409	409
Overhead Expenses	40	40	43	43	43	43	55	55	55	43	43	43
Income Tax (Paid Quarterly)	0	0	0	1,808	0	0	2,668	0	0	5,598	0	0
Total Disbursements	40	362	365	2,340	837	532	3,212	958	958	6,849	532	532
Cash Surplus (Deficit)	3,430	4,881	7,495	8,633	11,274	14,221	16,922	22,921	28,920	26,594	29,540	32,487
Financing:												
Borrowing	0	0	0	0	0	0	0	0	0	0	0	0
Repayment	0	0	0	0	0	0	0	0	0	0	0	0
Interest	0	0	0	0	0	0	0	0	0	0	0	0
Total Financing	0	0	0	0	0	0	0	0	0	0	0	0
Cash Balance, Ending	3,430	4,881	7,495	8,633	11,274	14,221	16,922	22,921	28,920	26,594	29,540	32,487

EXHIBIT 30-15 Budgeted Balance Sheet
Assets
Tanous Training & Consulting Services
For the Year ending December 31, 1993

	Jan	Feb	Mar	Apr	May	Jun	Jul	Aug	Sep	Oct	Nov	Dec
ASSETS												
Current Assets:												
Cash	3,430	4,881	7,495	8,633	11,274	14,221	16,922	22,921	28,920	26,594	29,540	32,487
Accounts Receivable	544	544	1,044	1,044	1,044	1,044	2,087	2,087	2,087	1,044	1,044	1,044
Total Current Assets	3,974	5,425	8,538	9,676	12,318	15,265	19,009	25,008	31,007	27,637	30,584	33,530
Fixed Assets:												
Furniture & Equipment	3,666	3,666	3,666	3,666	3,666	3,666	3,666	3,666	3,666	3,666	3,666	3,666
Software	294	294	294	294	294	294	294	294	294	294	294	294
Total Assets	3,960	3,960	3,960	3,960	3,960	3,960	3,960	3,960	3,960	3,960	3,960	3,960
Accumulated Depreciation	66	132	198	264	330	396	462	528	594	660	726	792
Net Fixed Assets	3,894	3,828	3,762	3,696	3,630	3,564	3,498	3,432	3,366	3,300	3,234	3,168
TOTAL ASSETS	7,868	9,253	12,300	13,372	15,948	18,829	22,507	28,440	34,373	30,937	33,818	36,698

EXHIBIT 30-16 Budgeted Balance Sheet
Liabilities & Owner Equity
Tanous Training & Consulting Services
For the Year ending December 31, 1993

LIABILITIES & EQUITY

Liabilities:

	Jan	Feb	Mar	Apr	May	Jun	Jul	Aug	Sep	Oct	Nov	Dec
Current Liabilities												
Accounts Payable	323	323	489	794	489	489	903	903	1,208	489	489	489
Income Tax Payable	443	886	1,808	824	1,746	2,668	1,899	3,797	5,598	922	1,844	2,765
Total Current Liabilities	766	1,209	2,298	1,619	2,235	3,157	2,802	4,700	6,806	1,411	2,333	3,255
Owner's Equity												
Paid-in Capital	7,378	7,378	7,378	7,378	7,378	7,378	7,378	7,378	7,378	7,378	7,378	7,378
Retained Earnings	(1,218)	(1,218)	(1,218)	(1,218)	(1,218)	(1,218)	(1,218)	(1,218)	(1,218)	(1,218)	(1,218)	(1,218)
Net Profit/(Loss) for Year	942	1,884	3,842	5,594	7,553	9,511	13,546	17,580	21,407	23,366	25,325	27,284
Total Equity	7,102	8,044	10,002	11,754	13,713	15,671	19,706	23,740	27,567	29,526	31,485	33,444
TOTAL LIABILITIES & EQUITY	7,868	9,253	12,300	13,372	15,948	18,829	22,507	28,440	34,373	30,937	33,818	36,698

EXHIBIT 30-17 Statement of Cash Flows
Tanous Training & Consulting Services
For the Year ending December 31, 1993

	Jan	Feb	Mar	Apr	May	Jun	Jul	Aug	Sep	Oct	Nov	Dec
Cash From Operations												
Net Income (Loss)	942	942	1,959	1,751	1,959	1,959	4,034	4,034	3,827	1,959	1,959	1,959
Add - Depreciation & Amortization	66	66	66	66	66	66	66	66	66	66	66	66
Net Cash From Operations	1,008	1,008	2,025	1,817	2,025	2,025	4,100	4,100	3,893	2,025	2,025	2,025
Add (Deduct)												
(Increase)/Decrease Net Accts Rec.	(544)	0	(500)	0	0	0	(1,044)	0	0	1,044	0	0
Net Change in Assets	(544)	0	(500)	0	0	0	(1,044)	0	0	1,044	0	0
Add (Deduct)												
Increases/(Decreases) in Accts Pay.	323	0	167	305	(305)	0	413	0	305	(718)	0	0
Increases/(Decrease) Income Tax Pay.	443	443	922	(984)	922	922	(769)	1,899	1,801	(4,676)	922	922
Net Change in Liabilities	766	443	1,088	(679)	617	922	(356)	1,899	2,106	(5,395)	922	922
Total Cash Available (Used)	1,230	1,451	2,614	1,138	2,642	2,947	2,701	5,999	5,999	(2,327)	2,947	2,947
Beginning Cash	2,200	3,430	4,881	7,495	8,633	11,274	14,221	16,922	22,921	28,920	26,594	29,540
Ending Cash	3,430	4,881	7,495	8,633	11,274	14,221	16,922	22,921	28,920	26,594	29,540	32,487

Conclusion: Tanous Training

Once the operating and financial budgets are prepared and approved, they become the major planning and control documents for the period. They reflect the company's plan of operations in financial terms. Comprehensive budgets are generally static budgets. They reflect the probable results of operations at the level of activity specified in the budget. If the scale of operations differs from the planned level, a static budget must be modified to correspond with the realized activity level. In this sense, all budgets become somewhat flexible.

One must keep in mind that budgets and plans are a series of estimates. Because the profit plan is based on estimates, there are bound to be differences between planned and actual performances. The estimates, however, should be based on available facts and the exercise of good judgment.

Budgeting tends to force management to base its actions on adequate consideration of study. The budgeting process further tends to instill the practice of careful study before decisions are made. Additionally, budgets assist in motivating management to meet the objectives of the business.

Budgeting enlists the aid of the entire organization in selecting the most profitable course of action. The interaction of the various groups during the budgeting process tends to result in a better profit plan than would be established by a budgeting process conducted by one individual.

The budgets established will be used as an operating plan for 1993 by Tanous Training & Consulting Services. As growth is experienced by the firm, additional budgets will be developed to incorporate the addition of salaried personnel to support business activities.

BUDGETING FOR A TELEVISION PRODUCTION COMPANY

A budget for a television production company follows many of the same principals as any other industry. You must understand that you are in a service oriented businesses, in which labor is your driving cost mechanism. Further, your talent, director and other staff personnel are your asset, and using them efficiently is as important to you, as it is for a car manufacturer to use steel and glass efficiently. This section will now review the budget process, and then review a case study of a small-sized television production company.

In order to design a competent budget for a TV production company, there are three basic areas that must be completely understood. First you must thoroughly understand the product or service you are providing, which in this case will be television production. Without a thorough understanding, you probably won't develop a budget which is geared to provide the information needed to make competent decisions and to isolate the areas where cost can be reduced. Further, the people administering the budget process are not going to be able to determine realistic cost standards, as well as tell when abusive requests are being made.

The second area of understanding is the marketing and sales philosophies of the company. It does not matter what industry you are in, there is always going to be a need to market your good(s) or service(s). Only by understanding the marketing and sales philosophies of the company will you be able to derive accurate sale and revenue estimates. Further, the budget must concentrate on the long-term philosophies of the company. Concentrating on the long-term philosophies will allow the budget to illustrate if the philosophies are working or if they need to be rethought.

Finally, money must be handled wisely. This means the money should be used efficiently so that it helps to generate revenues, while allowing sufficient cash flow for the business operations. Wise handling of the money also means that sufficient controls are placed on it to avoid fraud and embezzlement. Remember that without sufficient cash flow a business can go bankrupt while still making a profit. In a service oriented company, inventory levels will not be a major concern; however, accounts receivable must be thoroughly reviewed on a regular basis, as bad debts will be a major liability. In an entertainment based company you usually have supplied a service; so if you have a bad debt it is usually a complete loss, since the service has been used and there is nothing to repossess or liquidate.

In any service oriented business you must understand that your personnel is your main asset, as opposed to a capital intensive industry such as a car manufacturer or printer whose main assets will be factories and the equipment and material used to manufacture their product. A capital intensive industry budget is concerned with depreciation expense flow and how fixed assets are being used. Conversely, a service industry budget is concerned with its labor, since labor is the driving cost factor and asset of the company. By understanding the personnel, the jobs they perform and the amount of work which can realistically be produced by each person, you can evaluate how much an employee is worth, and how many of them will be needed in order to achieve your goals. In either case, you are concerned with the return on investment. A TV production company, for example, must understand the job of a stage manager and how that job applies to a particular production, so they may evaluate how many stage managers they will need. And although efficiency is important in any industry, it must be understood that using too few employees is just as bad as too many, since the product will suffer as will the morale of the employees. You should also notice how similar the concept of efficient use of personnel is to the concept of how fixed assets are being used.

The budgeting process for an entertainment company is comparable to that of most other industries; however, there are some differences that should be examined. A television production company is a service business as opposed to other companies which are considered manufacturing or capital intensive businesses. Service industries are those which provide an intangible product, and since a TV production does not provide a use other than to entertain or inform people, consider its value intangible. The first key difference is that service companies are generally not concerned with inventory, but must be very concerned with accounts receivable balances. Television production for the most part has no inventory items which are to be converted to a finished product. The finished product is the result of a labor intensive effort. The production's sets are the only tangible item of the project and they are manufactured by a contractor and generally have no salvage value.

When budgeting for a project in television production, it is likely that the revenue will dictate the cost of the project, because television revenue for a project is limited. Unlike a motion picture project, which if successful can stay in the movie theaters for an unlimited amount of time, a television project will usually have one major airing, which will produce most of the revenue attributable to the project. Although syndication is an important revenue source, the advertising time sold on a project's first run will generally be the main revenue source. Further, the increased viewing variety which cable has produced has greatly reduced ratings of all television shows, but cable has also made syndication more of a factor.

It is important that the syndication value of the show be determined accurately, because in many cases the syndication value will be a material source of revenue from the project, and in some cases it will determine if the project is profitable. Syndication has become a more material revenue source in recent years because of the growth in cable. The forty—plus channels offered by most cable companies today, compared to the ten or so channels offered fifteen years ago, means that there is an increased demand for shows to be aired. Because many of these channels that are providing air time for projects which will receive a Nielson rating of two or less, it is financially unrealistic for these channels to incur the cost of producing a show. Nielson ratings are a scientific estimate of the percentage of total U.S. televisions which are tuned to a particular show, and a Nielson share is the scientific estimate percentage of total televisions which are tuned in at a particular time period, which are watching the show in question. In television production, unlike film production, it is doubtful that the project will have any value on the video market.

Budgeting expenses for a TV production company can be broken into two separate parts: company overhead and events. Company overhead will generally consist of regular staff salaries, office supplies, office equipment costs, staff travel and entertainment, company marketing costs, etc. A basic rule of thumb is that any expenses not directly related to an event should be considered company overhead. This part of the budget is easier to administrate since it will generally cover more consistent items. Items such as staff salaries is basically a predetermined item, except for overtime, and because you have a track record of past overtime costs this figure should not be difficult to estimate, unless the company's organizational structure has gone through a material change.

Budgeting for the events is generally more difficult because they tend to be of a unique nature. Budgeting for an event that has occurred on a regular basis will generally have more changes in format than will company overhead. These changes can be traced to the creative element of the product, and a constant need to change. Otherwise, the consumer will tire of your product.

When budgeting for a recurring event, it is not necessary to use zero—based budgeting in all areas of the budget; however, any area which will be materially affected by a change in the show format should be subject to some form of zero—baded budgeting. The first step in this process is determining which costs are fixed and which are variable. Fixed costs are items such as union labor and benefits, contractual obligations for equipment or services, and depreciation. These are items you have no control over and they will be budgeted accordingly.

Variable costs are the areas where you will be able to review and control costs. These costs will consist of use of nonwage regulated labor, set costs, and travel costs. These are the areas which must be researched to determine the most cost effective way to meet the event's objectives.

When budgeting for a first time event you have the unenviable task of budgeting for the unknown. While you will have some concept of what will be required for the event to be a success, there will be a learning curve with respect to the event budget. This budget will be a zero—based budget because of its very nature. It is important to remember that for such budgets you should be somewhat conservative, but at the same time develop cost standards which you feel to be obtainable and reasonable. Without budgeting on this basis, the budget will be less effective as a tool to make the event more cost efficient. Management must take the learning curve into consideration when reviewing and rating the production department.

Whereas budgeting for a TV production company is similar to that of any other service business, it does have unique qualities, and these qualities must be understood in order for an effective budget to be devised. Further, the people compiling the budget must understand the show's concept and format, as well as the strategies of the company producing the event.

A CASE STUDY: STRONG MAN, INC.

Now that you have reviewed the budget process for a TV production company, now examine a hypothetical TV production company and how the budget and modeling for this company works. The case study will be Strongman,

Inc. ("SM"), which is a hypothetical TV production company in the business of producing and promoting live television specials: specifically bodybuilding.

Assume SM is a small TV production company which has been in business for many years and has a permanent staff of twenty people. SM was initially formed to help market clothing, both in the U.S.A. and around the world, through the Strongman Contests. In the early seventies the contests were placed on television and have held strong consistent ratings since.

SM produces the contests for its sponsor XYZ Company who pays SM a fee for producing the shows. The LMN Network airs the shows. The contests are also syndicated throughout the world.

The concept which keeps the broadcasts profitable is that the contests serve as a marketing tool for tourism and industry in the host community. SM provides the show host with approximately six minutes of direct television exposure and five minutes of indirect exposure over LMN and throughout the world. The direct exposure is provided through a mini-documentary and a fun segment which illustrates to the viewer what the community has to offer in terms of industry and tourism. The indirect exposure is accomplished through the prize and opening segments of the show.

In a barter transaction for this exposure, the host will provide SM with all or some of the following items: hotel rooms for the production staff, airfare for the staff, a theater, ground transportation, delegate meals, local stage labor, etc. The value of this barter will range from $300 thousand to $2.5 million, and the barter value will play a critical part in determining the profitability of the event. In addition to the barter, the host will supply SM with a location fee which ranges from $100 thousand to $1.5 million. Without the barter and site fee revenues, these productions would not be financially successful.

International sales revenue is comprised of syndication sales throughout the world. These sales are counted on an accrual basis, except for Latin American sales which are counted on a cash basis. The sales are done through DEF Pictures, which receives a 35 percent commission on the sales. A listing of the 1992 sales is in Exhibit 30-18 of this case study. Please keep in mind that the sales report and the actual sales recognized for the year will not match because of the cash basis the Latin sales are recognized on.

An additional revenue stream is television mentions. TV mentions is the revenue received from prize sponsors, less any cash prize given to the winner. This revenue is return for the air time the sponsors product receives during the prize segment and credits at the end of the show.

Personal appearance revenues come from appearances made by the various title holders during their reigns. The country of origin for a Mr. Strongman will have a material effect on the year's revenues in this area. A winner from Latin America or Asia will be far more marketable than a titleholder from Europe or Africa.

SM's budget process is a combination of top down and bottom up approaches. The financial planning department will meet with the President and V.P. of Production of the company at the beginning of the process, and will discuss their feelings regarding last year's contest and how the companies long—term strategies are progressing. A general growth goal and an expense increase goal are set in these meetings. Finally, the annual budget is updated quarterly.

The first step in the budget process is to budget for revenues. With respect to revenues, approximately 85 percent of the revenues are contractually locked—in prior to the budgeting process, so this part of the process is relatively simple. The areas which need to be planned are Personal Appearance, TV Mentions and International Sales. Personal Appearance, as stated earlier, is partially determined by the existing contracts and is further determined by origin of the winner during the year. Based on this scenario, it is best to be conservative when determining the revenue goal. This goal is proposed by the Personal Appearance department, but is subject to review by the President. TV Mentions is handled in a similar manner, in that Advertising Sales proposes a goal, which is then reviewed by the President. Finally, International Sales is given to SM by DEF Pictures, because its sales staff has the best knowledge on what next year will bring.

The next step in this process is for the financial planning department to meet with all department heads and to discuss how last year's budget is progressing, and what they would like to see their budget look like next year. During these meetings financial planning will advise the department heads of the company's general strategies and growth goals for the coming year. The result of these meetings will be a preliminary budget which will first be shown to the department head for his or her approval, and then this will be taken to the President for his comments.

When financial planning reviews the preliminary budgets with the President, they will provide the President with a written narrative explaining how the budget was derived. Over the course of the review certain proposed changes will be made and these proposed changes will then be sent to the respective department heads for comments. This process will continue for a couple of weeks until a final budget is signed by the President. Upon the President's approval this budget will be sent to corporate headquarters for final approval. Please keep in mind the same process may go on between SM and Corporate; however, because of the strong communications between SM and Corporate's financial planning departments as far as strategies and growth goals, SM's budgets tend to be left alone once they reach Corporate.

The contest budgets are compiled by the production department, as they have the best understanding of how the show operates. Once it proposes the show budgets, they are reviewed first by financial planning and then by the President, similar to the process which was discussed above.

Once the budget numbers are determined they are loaded into the financial model in the following Exhibits. The model provides moderate detail of each departments costs, as well as a monthly report. The monthly report will illustrate the monthly variances for each line, as well as a year-to-date total variance.

Although this case study is brief, it should provide you with an understanding of how the concepts which were described earlier will actually be applied.

EXHIBIT 30-18 Harris Corporation
1992 Business Plan 4
Entertainment Group
($ in thousands)

	Nov 1991	Dec 1991	Jan 1992	Feb 1992	Mar 1992	Apr 1992	May 1992	Jun 1992	Jul 1992	Aug 1992	Sep 1992	Oct 1992	1992 Actuals	1992 BP4	1992 BP1	1991 Actuals
REVENUE																
Television Fees	0	0	0	2,101	0	0	2,101	0	0	1,786	0	0	5,988	5,988	5,987	6,501
Location Fees	0	0	0	0	0	0	875	0	0	92	0	0	967	967	1,197	1,100
International Sale	0	0	144	0	0	52	0	0	250	0	0	178	623	521	494	489
Personal Appearance Fees	26	35	18	44	9	44	0	55	55	(6)	39	39	358	368	368	578
TV Mentions	0	0	0	166	0	0	162	0	0	262	(21)	(4)	565	544	599	516
Royalties	0	0	6	12	15	0	18	15	21	6	1	86	178	172	157	223
Barter	0	0	0	318	0	0	2,227	0	0	386	0	0	2,931	2,914	0	0
Other	0	0	0	0	0	0	0	0	0	0	0	0	0	0	92	5
Total Revenues	26	35	168	2,641	24	96	5,383	70	326	2,525	18	298	11,610	11,475	8,895	9,412
EXPENSES																
Division Office	22	21	23	20	21	26	19	19	18	25	32	31	277	303	318	461
Production	20	22	27	1,818	21	24	3,354	21	24	1,702	5	(1)	7,038	7,128	4,111	4,650
Sales & Promotion	40	46	64	73	68	75	48	76	72	57	77	85	781	799	938	1,052
Legal & Finance	106	109	124	90	95	65	49	55	68	112	65	66	1,003	943	929	974
General & Administrative	56	61	59	60	64	65	47	67	64	60	35	83	722	742	72	1,092
Total Expenses	244	259	297	2,060	270	256	3,517	237	246	1,956	215	264	9,821	9,915	6,969	8,240
NET TOTAL	(218)	(224)	(129)	581	(246)	(160)	1,866	(167)	80	568	(197)	35	$1,789	1,560	1,926	$1,172

EXHIBIT 30-19 Harris Corporation
1992 Business Plan 4
Entertainment Group
($ in thousands)

	Oct 1992	BP4 Oct 1992	Oct (Under) Over	YTD (Under) Over
Television Fees	0	0	0	0
Location Fees	0	0	0	0
International Sale	178	149	29	101
Personal Appearance Fees	39	45	(6)	(10)
TV Mentions	(4)	0	(4)	20
Royalties	86	20	65	6
Barter	0	0	0	18
Other	0	0	0	0
Total Revenue	298	215	84	135
Division Office	31	33	(2)	(27)
Production	(1)	33	(34)	(90)
Sales & Promotion	85	76	9	(17)
Legal & Finance	66	80	(14)	60
General & Administrative	83	64	19	(20)
Total Expenses	264	286	(23)	(95)
NET TOTAL	35	(72)	106	230

EXHIBIT 30-20

	Nov 1991	Dec 1991	Jan 1992	Feb 1992	Mar 1992	Apr 1992	May 1992	Jun 1992	Jul 1992	Aug 1992	Sep 1992	Oct 1992	1992 Actuals	1992 BP4	1992 BP1	1991 Actuals
General Salaries	18,628	17,829	20,507	17,476	17,347	22,141	16,125	17,347	24,755	22,436	20,620	23,461	238,672	234,893	236,735	374,480
Overtime	0	0	0	0	0	0	0	0	0	0	0	0	0	0	0	0
Payroll Taxes	338	271	2,346	1,406	1,504	319	197	383	1,055	539	412	333	9,102	11,975	12,896	11,387
Total Salaries	18,966	18,100	22,853	18,882	18,851	22,459	16,322	17,730	25,810	22,975	21,032	23,793	247,774	246,868	249,632	385,867
Travel & Entertainment	(82)	3,735	(42)	566	1,440	3,448	2,233	885	(8,921)	1,424	10,841	3,350	18,876	25,792	57,111	55,061
Dues & Subscriptions	172	286	0	0	0	0	0	22	0	85	313	412	1,301	921	921	928
Office Temporaries	0	0	0	0	0	0	0	0	0	0	0	1,990	1,990	921	1,842	5,849
Other	3,441	(1,497)	279	100	949	226	15	132	920	777	36	1,234	6,612	6,448	8,290	13,410
Total Operating Expenses	3,532	2,524	237	677	2,389	3,674	2,248	1,039	(8,001)	2,285	11,190	6,986	28,779	34,083	68,165	75,248
DEPARTMENT TOTAL	22,498	20,624	23,090	19,559	21,240	26,133	18,569	18,769	17,809	25,261	32,222	30,779	276,552	280,951	317,797	461,115

EXHIBIT 30-21

	Oct 1992	BP4 Oct 1992	Oct (Under) Over	YTD (Under) Over
General Salaries	23,461	27,634	(4,174)	3,779
Overtime	0	0	0	0
Payroll Taxes	333	1,842	(1,510)	(2,873)
Total Salaries	23,793	29,477	(5,683)	905
Travel & Entertainment	3,350	2,763	587	(6,916)
Dues & Subscriptions	412	0	412	380
Office Temporaries	1,990	0	1,990	1,069
Other	1,234	921	313	164
Total Operating Expenses	6,986	3,685	3,301	(5,304)
DEPARTMENT TOTAL	30,779	33,161	(2,382)	(4,398)

EXHIBIT 30-22 Production

	Nov 1991	Dec 1991	Jan 1992	Feb 1992	Mar 1992	Apr 1992	May 1992	Jun 1992	Jul 1992	Aug 1992	Sep 1992	Oct 1992	1992 Actuals	1992 BP4	1992 BP1	1991 Actuals
Production Services	20,216	22,216	26,750	21,237	21,011	24,221	28,709	20,562	24,340	28,450	19,166	27,465	284,343	297,531	303,058	313,225
Mr. Strongman	0	0	0	1,796,590	0	0	(18,423)	0	0	0	(13,817)	1,575	1,765,925	1,777,819	1,403,832	1,464,628
Senior Strongman	0	0	0	0	0	0	3,343,773	0	0	0	0	(4,610)	3,339,163	3,343,773	1,116,433	1,530,797
Junior Strongman	0	0	0	0	0	0	0	0	0	1,673,729	0	(25,653)	1,648,076	1,665,438	1,287,767	1,341,972
Total	20,216	22,216	26,750	1,817,827	21,011	24,221	3,354,059	20,562	24,340	1,702,179	5,349	(1,223)	7,037,506	7,084,562	4,111,091	4,650,622

EXHIBIT 30-23 Production

	Oct 1992	*BP4 Oct 1992*	*Oct (Under) Over*	*YTD (Under) Over*
Production Services	27,465	33,161	(5,696)	(13,188)
Mr. Strongman	1,575	0	1,575	(11,894)
Senior Strongman	(4,610)	0	(4,610)	(4,610)
Junior Strongman	(25,653)	0	(25,653)	(17,363)
Total	(1,223)	33,161	(34,385)	(47,055)

EXHIBIT 30-24 Production Services

	Nov 1991	Dec 1991	Jan 1992	Feb 1992	Mar 1992	Apr 1992	May 1992	Jun 1992	Jul 1992	Aug 1992	Sep 1992	Oct 1992	1992 Actuals	1992 BP4	1992 BP1	1991 Actuals
General Salaries	18,204	18,504	23,471	19,313	18,701	21,567	19,822	18,642	20,129	22,542	18,597	22,542	242,035	245,947	240,420	245,592
Overtime	0	0	0	0	0	0	0	0	0	0	0	0	0	0	0	2,075
Payroll Taxes	870	917	3,215	1,788	1,661	1,842	701	1,233	2,283	728	889	889	17,015	18,423	16,581	16,874
Total Salaries	19,074	19,421	25,686	21,101	20,362	23,409	20,523	19,876	22,412	23,270	19,486	23,431	259,050	264,370	257,001	264,541
Travel & Entertainment	1,126	2,377	35	122	216	404	(105)	437	1,471	1,160	3,296	2,681	13,219	21,186	33,161	35,992
Office Temporaries	0	0	0	0	0	0	0	0	0	0	0	0	0	921	1,842	0
Office Supplies	0	349	29	15	433	407	0	250	458	404	0	1,352	3,697	921	921	4,326
Telephone	0	0	0	0	0	0	0	0	0	0	0	0	0	0	1,842	276
Consultant Fees	0	0	0	0	0	0	9,211	0	0	3,616	(3,616)	0	9,211	8,290	8,290	7,178
Other	17	69	0	0	0	0	(921)	0	0	0	0	0	(835)	1,842	0	912
Total Operating Expenses	1,142	2,796	64	136	648	812	8,185	686	1,929	5,180	(320)	4,034	25,293	33,161	46,057	48,684
DEPARTMENT TOTAL	20,216	22,216	26,750	21,237	21,011	24,221	28,709	20,562	24,340	28,450	19,166	27,465	284,343	297,531	303,058	313,225

EXHIBIT 30-25 Production Services

	Oct 1992	BP4 Oct 1992	Oct (Under) Over	YTD (Under) Over
General Salaries	22,542	27,634	(5,092)	(3,912)
Overtime	0	0	0	0
Payroll Taxes	889	1,842	(953)	(1,408)
Total Salaries	23,431	29,477	(6,046)	(5,320)
Travel & Entertainment	2,681	3,685	(1,003)	(7,967)
Office Temporaries	0	0	0	(921)
Office Supplies	1,352	0	1,352	2,776
Telephone	0	0	0	0
Consultant Fees	0	0	0	921
Other	0	0	0	(2,678)
Total Operating Expenses	4,034	3,685	349	(7,868)
DEPARTMENT TOTAL	27,465	33,161	(5,696)	(13,188)

EXHIBIT 30-26 Mr. Strongman Contest

	Nov 1991	Dec 1991	Jan 1992	Feb 1992	Mar 1992	Apr 1992	May 1992	Jun 1992	Jul 1992	Aug 1992	Sep 1992	Oct 1992	1992 Actuals	1992 BP4	1992 BP1
Production Staff	0	0	0	197,071	0	0	0	0	0	0	0	0	197,071	197,126	201,732
Music	0	0	0	72,354	0	0	0	0	0	0	0	0	72,354	72,771	78,298
Talent	0	0	0	95,998	0	0	0	0	0	0	0	0	95,998	95,800	100,405
Costumes	0	0	0	22,353	0	0	0	0	0	0	0	0	22,353	22,108	24,871
Props	0	0	0	15,094	0	0	0	0	0	0	0	0	15,094	14,738	16,581
Technical	0	0	0	139,058	0	0	0	0	0	0	0	0	139,058	139,094	122,513
Edit Theater	0	0	0	44,197	0	0	0	0	0	0	0	0	44,197	44,215	46,057
Lighting	0	0	0	146,522	0	0	0	0	0	0	0	0	146,522	146,463	134,488
Scenic	0	0	0	239,515	0	0	0	0	0	0	0	0	239,515	239,499	237,657
Computer	0	0	0	14,228	0	0	0	0	0	0	0	0	14,228	13,817	6,448
Communications	0	0	0	26,203	0	0	0	0	0	0	0	0	26,203	26,713	25,792
Hair	0	0	0	1,105	0	0	0	0	0	0	0	0	1,105	921	1,842
Hotels & Maintenance	0	0	0	91,295	0	0	0	0	0	0	0	0	91,295	91,194	80,140
Survey Expense	0	0	0	920	0	0	0	0	0	0	0	0	920	921	11,054
Opening	0	0	0	7,579	0	0	0	0	0	0	0	0	7,579	7,369	6,448
Fun/Act	0	0	0	13,884	0	0	0	0	0	0	0	0	13,884	13,817	18,423
Prize/Minidoc	0	0	0	41,890	0	0	0	0	0	0	0	0	41,890	42,373	42,373
Employee Tax	0	0	0	31,565	0	0	0	0	0	0	0	0	31,565	31,319	29,477
Pension	0	0	0	13,567	0	0	0	0	0	0	0	0	13,567	13,817	13,817
Health & Welfare	0	0	0	13,192	0	0	(18,423)	0	0	0	0	0	13,192	12,896	11,975
Vacation	0	0	0	994	0	0	0	0	0	0	0	0	994	921	3,685
Per Diem	0	0	0	58,456	0	0	0	0	0	0	0	0	58,456	58,954	61,717
Contest	0	0	0	91,366	0	0	0	0	0	0	0	0	91,366	91,194	80,140
Administration	0	0	0	48,947	0	0	0	0	0	0	0	0	48,947	48,821	35,004
Marketing	0	0	0	23,514	0	0	0	0	0	0	0	0	23,514	23,950	12,896
Hotel Costs	0	0	0	189,129	0	0	0	0	0	0	0	0	189,129	188,836	0
Prize Package	0	0	0	156,595	0	0	0	0	0	0	0	0	156,595	156,595	0
Misc. Cost Adjustment	0	0	0	0	0	0	0	0	0	0	(13,817)	1,575	(30,665)	0	0
Total	0	0	0	1,796,590	0	0	(18,423)	0	0	0	(13,817)	1,575	1,765,925	1,796,242	1,403,832

503

EXHIBIT 30-27 Mr. Strongman Contest

	Oct 1992	BP4 Oct 1992	Oct (Under) Over	YTD (Under) Over
Production Staff	0	0	0	(55)
Music	0	0	0	(417)
Talent	0	0	0	198
Costumes	0	0	0	245
Props	0	0	0	356
Technical	0	0	0	(36)
Edit Theater	0	0	0	(18)
Lighting	0	0	0	59
Scenic	0	0	0	17
Computer	0	0	0	411
Communications	0	0	0	(510)
Hair	0	0	0	184
Hotels & Maintenance	0	0	0	101
Survey Expense	0	0	0	(1)
Opening	0	0	0	210
Fun/Act	0	0	0	66
Prize/Minidoc	0	0	0	(483)
Employee Tax	0	0	0	246
Pension	0	0	0	(251)
Health & Welfare	0	0	0	296
Vacation	0	0	0	73
Per Diem	0	0	0	(497)
Contest	0	0	0	172
Administration	0	0	0	126
Marketing	0	0	0	(436)
Hotel Costs	0	0	0	293
Prize Package	0	0	0	0
Misc. Cost Adjustment	1,575	0	1,575	(30,665)
Total	1,575	0	1,575	(30,317)

EXHIBIT 30-28 Mr. Strongman Contest

	Nov 1991	Dec 1991	Jan 1992	Feb 1992	Mar 1992	Apr 1992	May 1992	Jun 1992	Jul 1992	Aug 1992	Sep 1992	Oct 1992	1992 Actuals	1992 BP4	1992 BP1
Production Staff	0	0	0	0	0	0	233,051	0	0	0	0	0	233,051	229,366	229,366
Music	0	0	0	0	0	0	69,086	0	0	0	0	0	69,086	67,244	67,244
Talent	0	0	0	0	0	0	100,405	0	0	0	0	0	100,405	100,405	100,405
Costumes	0	0	0	0	0	0	16,581	0	0	0	0	0	16,581	14,738	14,738
Props	0	0	0	0	0	0	23,950	0	0	0	0	0	23,950	17,502	17,502
Technical	0	0	0	0	0	0	115,144	0	0	0	0	0	115,144	74,613	74,613
Edit Theater	0	0	0	0	0	0	15,936	0	0	0	0	0	15,936	13,817	13,817
Lighting	0	0	0	0	0	0	70,929	0	0	0	0	0	70,929	78,298	78,298
Scenic	0	0	0	0	0	0	58,954	0	0	0	0	0	58,954	58,954	58,954
Computer	0	0	0	0	0	0	17,962	0	0	0	0	0	17,952	10,133	10,133
Communications	0	0	0	0	0	0	51,584	0	0	0	0	0	51,584	32,240	32,240
Hair	0	0	0	0	0	0	1,290	0	0	0	0	0	1,290	1,842	1,842
Hotels & Maintenance	0	0	0	0	0	0	29,477	0	0	0	0	0	29,477	27,634	27,634
Survey Expense	0	0	0	0	0	0	14,001	0	0	0	0	0	14,001	11,975	11,975
Fun Act/Opening	0	0	0	0	0	0	1,382	0	0	0	0	0	1,382	19,344	19,344
Prize/Minidoc	0	0	0	0	0	0	18,423	0	0	0	0	0	18,423	45,136	45,136
Employee Tax	0	0	0	0	0	0	36,846	0	0	0	0	0	36,846	41,452	41,452
Pension	0	0	0	0	0	0	15,660	0	0	0	0	0	15,660	15,6 60	15,660
Health & Welfare	0	0	0	0	0	0	15,291	0	0	0	0	0	15,291	12,896	12,896
Vacation	0	0	0	0	0	0	1,382	0	0	0	0	0	1,382	3,685	3,685
Per Diem	0	0	0	0	0	0	55,269	0	0	0	0	0	55,269	81,061	81,061
Contest	0	0	0	0	0	0	88,430	0	0	0	0	0	88,430	106,853	106,853
Administration	0	0	0	0	0	0	42,373	0	0	0	0	0	42,373	38,688	38,688
Marketing	0	0	0	0	0	0	23,029	0	0	0	0	0	23,029	12,896	12,896
Barter	0	0	0	0	0	0	2,227,340	0	0	0	0	0	2,227,340	2,210,759	0
Misc. Cost Adjustment	0	0	0	0	0	0	0	0	0	0	0	(4,610)	(4,610)	46,057	0
Total	0	0	0	0	0	0	3,343,773	0	0	0	0	(4,610)	3,339,163	3,373,250	1,116,433

505

EXHIBIT 30-29 Mr. Strongman Contest

	Oct 1992	BP4 Oct 1992	Oct (Under) Over	YTD (Under) Over
Production Staff	0	0	0	3,685
Music	0	0	0	1,842
Talent	0	0	0	0
Costumes	0	0	0	1,842
Props	0	0	0	6,448
Technical	0	0	0	40,531
Edit Theater	0	0	0	2,119
Lighting	0	0	0	(7,369)
Scenic	0	0	0	0
Computer	0	0	0	7,830
Communications	0	0	0	19,344
Hair	0	0	0	(553)
Hotels & Maintenance	0	0	0	1,842
Survey Expense	0	0	0	2,027
Fun Act/Opening	0	0	0	(17,962)
Prize/Minidoc	0	0	0	(26,713)
Employee Tax	0	0	0	(4,606)
Pension	0	0	0	0
Health & Welfare	0	0	0	2,395
Vacation	0	0	0	(2,303)
Per Diem	0	0	0	(25,792)
Contest	0	0	0	(18,423)
Administration	0	0	0	3,685
Marketing	0	0	0	10,133
Barter	0	0	0	16,581
Misc. Cost Adjustment	(4,610)	0	(4,610)	(50,668)
Total	(4,610)	0	(4,610)	(34,087)

EXHIBIT 30-30 Junior Strongman Contest

	Nov 1991	Dec 1991	Jan 1992	Feb 1992	Mar 1992	Apr 1992	May 1992	Jun 1992	Jul 1992	Aug 1992	Sep 1992	Oct 1992	1992 Actuals	1992 BP4	1992 BP1
Production Staff	0	0	0	0	0	0	0	0	0	196,205	0	0	196,205	205,416	205,416
Music	0	0	0	0	0	0	0	0	0	70,929	0	0	70,929	71,850	71,850
Talent	0	0	0	0	0	0	0	0	0	94,878	0	0	84,878	98,563	98,563
Costumes	0	0	0	0	0	0	0	0	0	22,292	0	0	22,292	23,950	23,950
Props	0	0	0	0	0	0	0	0	0	15,660	0	0	15,660	15,660	15,660
Technical	0	0	0	0	0	0	0	0	0	189,757	0	0	189,757	134,488	134,488
Edit Theater	0	0	0	0	0	0	0	0	0	49,282	0	0	49,282	45,136	45,136
Lighting	0	0	0	0	0	0	0	0	0	134,488	0	0	134,488	129,882	129,882
Scenic	0	0	0	0	0	0	0	0	0	221,076	0	0	221,076	186,072	186,072
Computer	0	0	0	0	0	0	0	0	0	14,837	0	0	14,837	5,527	5,527
Communications	0	0	0	0	0	0	0	0	0	27,634	0	0	27,634	26,713	26,713
Hair	0	0	0	0	0	0	0	0	0	1,474	0	0	1,474	1,842	1,842
Hotels & Maintenance	0	0	0	0	0	0	0	0	0	164,886	0	0	164,886	78,298	78,298
Survey Expense	0	0	0	0	0	0	0	0	0	3,125	0	0	3,125	6,448	6,448
Opening	0	0	0	0	0	0	0	0	0	1,842	0	0	1,842	2,763	2,763
Fun/Act	0	0	0	0	0	0	0	0	0	13,817	0	0	13,817	9,211	9,211
Prize/Minidoc	0	0	0	0	0	0	0	0	0	38,596	0	0	38,596	38,688	38,688
Employee Tax	0	0	0	0	0	0	0	0	0	29,477	0	0	29,477	27,634	27,634
Pension	0	0	0	0	0	0	0	0	0	14,738	0	0	14,738	13,817	13,817
Health & Welfare	0	0	0	0	0	0	0	0	0	12,896	0	0	12,896	11,975	11,975
Vacation	0	0	0	0	0	0	0	0	0	3,685	0	0	3,685	2,763	2,763
Per Diem	0	0	0	0	0	0	0	0	0	77,377	0	0	77,377	48,821	48,821
Contest	0	0	0	0	0	0	0	0	0	73,692	0	0	73,692	64,480	64,480
Administration	0	0	0	0	0	0	0	0	0	34,083	0	0	34,083	32,240	32,240
Marketing	0	0	0	0	0	0	0	0	0	19,620	0	0	19,620	5,527	5,527
Hotel Costs	0	0	0	0	0	0	0	0	0	0	0	0	0	0	0
Barter	0	0	0	0	0	0	0	0	0	0	0	0	0	368,460	0
Misc. Cost Adjustment	0	0	0	0	0	0	0	0	0	0	0	(25,653)	(25,653)	9,211	0
Prize Package	0	0	0	0	0	0	0	0	0	147,384	0	0	147,384	9,211	0
Total	0	0	0	0	0	0	0	0	0	1,673,729	0	(25,653)	1,648,076	1,665,438	1,287,767

507

EXHIBIT 30-31 Junior Strongman Contest

	Oct 1992	BP4 Oct 1992	Oct (Under) Over	YTD (Under) Over
Production Staff	0	0	0	(9,211)
Music	0	0	0	(921)
Talent	0	0	0	(3,685)
Costumes	0	0	0	(1,658)
Props	0	0	0	0
Technical	0	0	0	55,269
Edit Theater	0	0	0	4,145
Lighting	0	0	0	4,606
Scenic	0	0	0	35,004
Computer	0	0	0	9,310
Communications	0	0	0	921
Hair	0	0	0	(368)
Hotels & Maintenance	0	0	0	86,588
Survey Expense	0	0	0	(3,323)
Opening	0	0	0	(921)
Fun/Act	0	0	0	4,606
Prize/Minidoc	0	0	0	(92)
Employee Tax	0	0	0	1,842
Pension	0	0	0	921
Health & Welfare	0	0	0	921
Vacation	0	0	0	921
Per Diem	0	0	0	28,556
Contest	0	0	0	9,211
Administration	0	0	0	1,842
Marketing	0	0	0	14,094
Hotel Costs	0	0	0	0
Barter	0	0	0	(368,460)
Misc. Cost Adjustment	(25,653)	0	(25,653)	(34,865)
Prize Package	0	0	0	147,384
Total	(25,653)	0	(25,653)	(17,363)

Exhibit 30-32 Sales & Promotion

	Nov 1991	Dec 1991	Jan 1992	Feb 1992	Mar 1992	Apr 1992	May 1992	Jun 1992	Jul 1992	Aug 1992	Sep 1992	Oct 1992	1992 Actuals	1992 BP4	1992 BPI	1991 Actuals
BPI Marketing Administration	5,625	2,675	3,027	4,080	2,323	2,578	2,153	1,224	99	0	0	0	23,784	33,161	141,187	153,160
Advertising & Promotion	185	421	77	10,133	2,105	(599)	0	833	2,393	6,955	1,290	(2,260)	21,533	20,265	39,609	103,895
Public Relations	9,659	17,404	27,649	19,768	20,643	24,208	10,615	29,680	23,939	11,940	27,135	24,893	247,534	252,395	239,499	233,444
Personal Appearances	15,612	17,688	20,041	29,907	32,954	34,890	30,011	35,824	30,324	29,070	40,864	51,676	368,861	355,564	389,646	462,232
Advertising Sales	8,683	7,830	13,645	8,838	10,057	13,830	5,683	8,182	15,406	9,269	8,104	10,205	119,733	123,434	128,040	109,524
Total	39,763	46,018	64,440	72,726	68,082	74,908	48,463	75,742	72,162	57,233	77,393	84,515	781,445	784,819	937,982	1,062,255

EXHIBIT 30-33 Sales & Promotion

	Oct 1992	BP4 Oct 1992	Oct (Under) Over	YTD (Under) Over
Marketing Administration	0	3,685	(3,685)	(117,403)
Advertising & Promotion	(2,260)	0	(2,260)	(18,077)
Public Relations	24,893	21,186	3,707	8,035
Personal Appearances	51,676	35,925	15,752	(20,785)
Advertising Sales	10,205	14,738	(4,533)	(8,307)
Total	84,515	75,534	8,981	(156,536)

EXHIBIT 30-34 Marketing Administration

	Nov 1991	Dec 1991	Jan 1992	Feb 1992	Mar 1992	Apr 1992	May 1992	Jun 1992	Jul 1992	Aug 1992	Sep 1992	Oct 1992	1992 Actuals	1992 BP4	1992 BP1	1991 Actuals
General Salaries	3,977	2,000	2,411	2,015	2,005	2,429	2,004	977	0	0	0	0	17,818	26,713	113,301	119,315
Overtime	232	333	0	1,001	148	0	0	0	0	0	0	0	1,714	1,842	0	5,445
Payroll Taxes	237	158	337	352	169	149	149	104	0	0	0	0	1,655	1,842	6,448	7,783
Total Salaries	4,445	2,490	2,748	3,369	2,323	2,578	2,153	1,081	0	0	0	0	21,187	30,398	119,749	132,543
Travel & Entertainment	709	185	0	711	0	0	0	143	0	0	0	0	1,748	1,842	18,423	18,622
Stationary & Supplies	0	0	0	0	0	0	0	0	99	0	0	0	0	921	0	(176)
Dues & Subscriptions	470	0	28	0	0	0	0	0	0	0	0	0	497	0	921	1,676
Administrative meetings	0	0	0	0	0	0	0	0	0	0	0	0	0	0	1,842	495
Agency fees	0	0	251	0	0	0	0	0	0	0	0	0	251	0	251	0
Total Operating Expenses	1,179	185	279	711	0	0	0	143	99	0	0	0	2,497	2,763	21,438	20,617
DEPARTMENT TOTAL	5,625	2,675	3,027	4,080	2,323	2,578	2,153	1,224	99	0	0	0	23,685	33,161	141,187	153,160

EXHIBIT 30-35 Marketing Administration

	Oct 1992	BP4 Oct 1992	Oct (Under) Over	YTD (Under) Over
General Salaries	0	2,763	(2,763)	(8,896)
Overtime	0	0	0	(128)
Payroll Taxes	0	921	(921)	(187)
Total Salaries	0	3,685	(3,685)	(9,211)
Travel & Entertainment	0	0	0	(94)
Stationary & Supplies	0	0	0	(921)
Dues & Subscriptions	0	0	0	497
Administrative meetings	0	0	0	0
Agency fees	0	0	0	251
Total Operating Expenses	0	0	0	(266)
DEPARTMENT TOTAL	0	3,685	(3,685)	(9,477)

EXHIBIT 30-36 Advertising Promotion

	Nov 1991	Dec 1991	Jan 1992	Feb 1992	Mar 1992	Apr 1992	May 1992	Jun 1992	Jul 1992	Aug 1992	Sep 1992	Oct 1992	1992 Actuals	1992 BP4	1992 BP1	1991 Actuals
Promotion Materials																
Video Presentation	185	0	0	1,842	2,105	(1,819)	0	0	0	0	0	196	2,509	0	1,842	5,516
Brochures	0	0	0	0	0	0	0	0	0	0	0	0	0	0	0	26,786
One Sheets/Folders	0	421	0	0	0	0	0	0	0	0	0	0	421	921	921	481
Logo Design	0	0	0	0	0	0	0	0	0	0	0	0	0	0	0	1,263
Research	0	0	77	0	0	1,221	0	0	0	0	1,290	0	0	0	0	0
Trade Advertising	0	0	0	0	0	0	0	833	2,393	872	0	46	6,732	9,211	9,211	25,204
Consumer Advertising	0	0	0	0	0	0	0	0	0	0	0	262	262	1,842	0	0
Finder Fee	0	0	0	8,290	0	0	0	0	0	0	0	0	0	0	0	4,325
Affiliate Promotions	0	0	0	0	0	0	0	0	0	6,082	0	(2,763)	11,609	8,290	27,634	33,320
Satalite Promotions	0	0	0	0	0	0	0	0	0	0	0	0	0	0	0	7,000
DEPARTMENT TOTAL	185	421	77	10,133	2,105	(599)	0	833	2,393	6,955	1,290	(2,260)	21,533	20,265	39,609	103,895

EXHIBIT 30-37 Advertising Promotion

	Oct 1992	BP4 Oct 1992	Oct (Under) Over	YTD (Under) Over
Promotion Materials				
Video Presentation	196	0	196	2,509
Brochures	0	0	0	0
One Sheets/Folders	0	0	0	(500)
Logo Design	0	0	0	0
Research	46	0	46	(2,480)
Trade Advertising	262	0	262	(1,581)
Consumer Advertising	0	0	0	0
Finders Fee	(2,763)	0	(2,763)	3,319
Affiliate Promotions	0	0	0	0
Satalite Promotions	0	0	0	0
DEPARTMENT TOTAL	(2,260)	0	(2,260)	1,268

EXHIBIT 30-38 Public Relations

	Nov 1991	Dec 1991	Jan 1992	Feb 1992	Mar 1992	Apr 1992	May 1992	Jun 1992	Jul 1992	Aug 1992	Sep 1992	Oct 1992	1992 Actuals	1992 BP4	1992 BP1	1991 Actuals
General Salaries	6,602	6,526	8,576	6,647	6,647	7,325	7,607	7,968	1,012	4,643	2,469	5,111	71,133	86,588	81,982	81,678
Overtime	0	0	0	0	0	0	0	0	0	1,292	0	0	1,292	0	0	2,585
Payroll Taxes	489	489	1,254	588	1,239	9	250	664	376	89	179	179	5,804	8,290	6,448	6,607
Total Salaries	7,091	7,015	9,830	7,235	7,886	7,334	7,856	8,632	1,388	6,024	2,647	5,290	78,230	94,878	88,430	90,870
Travel & Entertainment	184	669	5,308	433	1,793	4,582	0	(1,293)	13,277	333	742	6,491	32,518	20,265	18,423	22,046
Audio/Video Dubs	1,030	(3,324)	3,289	0	479	92	157	296	391	0	27	397	2,832	4,606	2,763	3,367
Press Kits	84	0	0	2,394	0	0	2,237	0	0	0	2,400	55	7,170	4,606	2,763	3,735
News Letter	806	2,377	0	0	0	0	0	0	0	0	0	0	3,183	4,606	12,896	6,901
Mailings	232	241	0	519	516	286	0	800	710	0	959	2,736	7,000	11,975	5,527	880
Clipping Services	0	0	0	0	0	0	0	488	0	0	228	472	1,188	2,763	2,763	17,461
Photographers	0	(8)	0	0	146	0	0	5,527	(62)	0	6,496	31	12,130	13,817	20,265	19,653
Photographs	0	917	837	322	999	447	365	3,992	2,225	56	3,668	4,767	18,598	14,738	13,817	61,413
PR Agency	0	9,497	4,606	8,908	4,580	11,069	0	9,420	6,008	5,527	5,441	1,995	67,051	65,402	59,875	0
Guide Books	0	0	0	0	0	0	0	0	0	0	0	0	0	0	0	0
Press Conferences	0	0	0	0	0	0	0	0	0	0	0	0	0	921	921	0
Gifts	112	19	5	(43)	176	0	0	50	0	0	0	259	578	3,685	2,763	1,722
Media Training	0	0	0	0	1,382	0	0	1,769	0	0	0	1,930	5,080	5,527	4,606	0
Other	120	0	3,776	0	2,686	397	0	0	0	0	4,527	470	11,976	4,606	2,763	3,896
Total Operating Expenses	2,568	10,389	17,820	12,533	12,757	16,874	2,759	21,048	22,551	5,916	24,488	19,603	169,305	157,517	151,069	142,574
DEPARTMENT TOTAL	9,659	17,404	27,649	19,768	20,643	24,208	10,615	29,680	23,939	11,940	27,135	24,893	247,534	252,395	239,499	233,444

EXHIBIT 30-39 Public Relations

	Oct 1992	BP4 Oct 1992	Oct (Under) Over	YTD (Under) Over
General Salaries	5,111	8,290	(3,179)	(15,455)
Overtime	0	0	0	1,292
Payroll Taxes	179	921	(742)	(2,486)
Total Salaries	5,290	9,211	(3,921)	(16,649)
Travel & Entertainment	6,491	1,842	4,649	12,253
Audio/Video Dubs	397	0	397	(1,774)
Press Kits	55	0	55	2,564
News Letter	0	0	0	(1,422)
Mailings	2,736	1,842	894	(4,975)
Clipping Services	472	921	(450)	(1,575)
Photographers	31	0	31	(1,688)
Photographs	4,767	1,842	2,925	3,860
PR Agency	1,995	4,606	(2,611)	1,650
Guide Books	0	0	0	0
Press Conferences	0	921	(921)	(921)
Gifts	259	0	259	(3,107)
Media Training	1,930	0	1,930	(447)
Other	470	0	470	7,370
Total Operating Expenses	19,603	11,975	7,628	11,788
DEPARTMENT TOTAL	24,893	21,186	3,707	(4,861)

EXHIBIT 30-40 Personal Appearance

	Nov 1991	Dec 1991	Jan 1992	Feb 1992	Mar 1992	Apr 1992	May 1992	Jun 1992	Jul 1992	Aug 1992	Sep 1992	Oct 1992	1992 Actuals	1992 BP4	1992 BP1	1991 Actuals
General Salaries	12,259	12,476	17,443	16,581	16,505	17,515	25,983	19,016	17,217	16,650	19,363	12,016	203,023	206,338	204,495	215,689
Overtime	0	0	0	0	0	0	0	0	0	0	0	0	0	0	0	10,741
Payroll Taxes	1,517	765	3,221	3,936	1,846	1,081	2,028	1,614	1,615	2,937	2,859	796	24,215	21,186	18,423	26,122
Total Salaries	13,776	13,242	20,664	20,517	18,351	18,595	28,011	20,630	18,832	19,586	22,222	12,812	227,238	227,524	222,918	252,552
Travel & Entertainment	(1,082)	(890)	(3,341)	1,188	2,266	6,378	(484)	5,038	364	2,706	13,902	8,137	34,182	25,792	55,269	74,348
Outside Services	713	636	1,261	924	1,488	809	63	2,290	1,391	1,222	1,209	1,403	13,407	19,344	4,606	15,612
Food & Beverage	700	605	737	870	1,069	875	0	1,397	818	729	602	857	9,259	7,369	7,369	8,231
Wardrobe	0	216	0	314	8,717	2,905	2,284	895	406	3,146	1,400	9,344	29,627	24,871	25,792	35,509
Cleaning	1,147	223	0	1,578	698	1,005	137	892	310	7	419	433	7,887	7,369	6,448	5,511
Gifts/Flowers	0	1,562	0	0	0	371	0	0	1,179	176	1,070	204	3,526	2,763	1,842	3,220
Photographs	90	60	95	14	52	33	0	0	0	9	0	150	503	921	1,842	520
Supplies	0	167	625	294	313	130	0	328	0	0	40	576	2,472	3,685	7,369	3,796
National Director Duty	0	0	0	0	0	0	0	0	0	0	0	0	0	0	11,054	11,012
Temporary Salaries	0	0	0	0	0	0	0	0	1,795	0	0	0	0	0	0	0
Royalty Expense	0	0	0	4,209	0	3,737	0	2,162	5,228	1,434	0	17,761	34,531	33,161	41,452	48,638
Furniture	0	0	0	0	0	0	0	0	0	0	0	0	0	1,842	0	1,786
Other	268	1,868	0	0	0	52	0	2,191	0	53	0	0	4,433	921	3,685	1,497
Total Operating Expenses	1,836	4,446	(623)	9,390	14,603	16,295	2,000	15,193	11,492	9,483	18,642	38,864	139,828	128,040	166,728	209,680
DEPARTMENT TOTAL	15,612	17,688	20,041	29,907	32,954	34,890	30,011	35,824	30,324	29,070	40,864	51,676	367,066	355,564	389,646	462,232

EXHIBIT 30-41 Personal Appearance

	Oct *1992*	*BP4* *Oct* *1992*	*Oct* *(Under)* *Over*	*YTD* *(Under)* *Over*
General Salaries	12,016	21,186	(9,170)	(3,314)
Overtime	0	0	0	0
Payroll Taxes	796	1,842	(1,046)	3,029
Total Salaries	12,812	23,029	(10,216)	(286)
Travel & Entertainment	8,137	4,606	3,531	8,390
Outside Services	1,403	921	482	(5,937)
Food & Beverage	857	0	857	1,890
Wardrobe	9,344	0	9,344	4,756
Cleaning	433	0	433	518
Gifts/Flowers	204	0	204	763
Photographs	150	921	(771)	(418)
Supplies	576	921	(345)	(1,212)
National Director Duty	0	0	0	0
Temporary Salaries	0	0	0	0
Royalty Expense	17,761	5,527	12,234	1,370
Furniture	0	0	0	(1,842)
Other	0	0	0	3,511
Total Operating Expenses	38,864	12,896	25,968	11,788
DEPARTMENT TOTAL	51,676	35,925	15,752	11,502

EXHIBIT 30-42 Advertising Sales

	Nov 1991	Dec 1991	Jan 1992	Feb 1992	Mar 1992	Apr 1992	May 1992	Jun 1992	Jul 1992	Aug 1992	Sep 1992	Oct 1992	1992 Actuals	1992 BP4	1992 BP1	1991 Actuals
General Salaries	7,726	6,412	10,642	7,571	7,543	11,345	5,403	7,493	9,928	7,207	7,493	9,096	97,858	99,484	97,642	94,579
Overtime	0	0	0	0	0	0	0	0	0	0	0	0	0	0	0	79
Payroll Taxes	249	248	1,300	660	1,408	0	281	560	1,349	91	560	283	6,990	7,369	6,448	6,812
Total Salaries	7,974	6,660	11,942	8,231	8,952	11,345	5,683	8,053	11,279	7,298	8,053	9,379	104,848	106,853	104,090	101,470
Travel & Entertainment	708	1,170	1,703	607	1,105	2,485	0	129	4,129	1,796	52	826	14,711	16,581	23,950	6,073
Office Supplies	0	0	0	0	0	0	0	0	0	174	0	0	0	0	0	1,981
Total Operating Expenses	708	1,170	1,703	607	1,105	2,485	0	129	4,129	1,970	52	826	14,711	16,581	23,950	8,054
DEPARTMENT TOTAL	8,683	7,830	13,645	8,838	10,057	13,830	5,683	8,182	15,406	9,269	8,104	10,205	119,559	123,434	128,040	109,524

EXHIBIT 30-43 Advertising Sales

	Oct 1992	BP4 Oct 1992	Oct (Under) Over	YTD (Under) Over
General Salaries	9,096	11,054	(1,957)	(1,626)
Overtime	0	0	0	0
Payroll Taxes	283	921	(638)	(380)
Total Salaries	9,379	11,975	(2,596)	(2,005)
Travel & Entertainment	826	2,763	(1,937)	(1,870)
Office Supplies	0	0	0	0
Total Operating Expenses	826	2,763	(1,937)	(1,870)
DEPARTMENT TOTAL	10,205	14,738	(4,533)	(3,875)

EXHIBIT 30-44 Legal & Finance

	Nov 1991	Dec 1991	Jan 1992	Feb 1992	Mar 1992	Apr 1992	May 1992	Jun 1992	Jul 1992	Aug 1992	Sep 1992	Oct 1992	1992 Actuals	1992 BP4	1992 BP1	1991 Actuals
Legal & Business Affairs	90,109	92,043	103,670	76,109	80,425	50,097	31,891	40,324	44,964	98,987	50,622	49,662	808,902	748,895	739,683	780,681
Finance & Planning	7,008	7,121	10,833	7,095	7,671	5,811	10,403	7,099	12,150	6,946	7,663	8,783	98,583	93,957	87,509	86,891
Contest Operations	8,669	9,946	9,182	6,770	7,191	8,947	6,209	7,724	10,760	5,799	6,327	7,925	95,449	101,326	102,248	106,545
Total	105,786	109,110	123,685	89,974	95,287	64,854	48,502	55,147	67,874	111,732	64,612	66,370	1,002,934	944,178	929,440	974,117

EXHIBIT 30-45 Legal & Finance

	Oct 1992	BP4 Oct 1992	Oct (Under) Over	YTD (Under) Over
Legal & Business Affairs	49,662	60,796	(11,134)	60,007
Finance & Planning	8,783	8,290	493	4,626
Contest Operations	7,925	11,054	(3,129)	(5,878)
Total	66,370	80,140	(13,770)	(1,252)

EXHIBIT 30-46 Legal & Business Affairs

	Nov 1991	Dec 1991	Jan 1992	Feb 1992	Mar 1992	Apr 1992	May 1992	Jun 1992	Jul 1992	Aug 1992	Sep 1992	Oct 1992	1992 Actuals	1992 BP4	1992 BP1	1991 Actuals
General Salaries	13,959	13,973	17,806	14,074	14,749	18,321	16,367	15,356	19,761	15,286	15,699	18,975	194,328	191,599	186,072	193,898
Overtime	0	0	0	0	0	0	0	0	0	0	0	0	0	0	0	0
Payroll Taxes	346	348	2,286	1,155	1,102	1,777	579	1,159	1,488	473	686	513	11,913	13,817	11,975	12,730
Total Salaries	14,305	14,321	20,094	15,229	15,850	20,098	16,946	16,514	21,249	15,760	16,385	19,488	206,241	205,416	198,047	206,628
Travel & Entertainment	2,019	2,445	99	404	871	350	1,140	1,340	73	408	0	455	9,606	16,581	28,556	28,674
Outside Services	0	0	0	0	0	0	0	0	0	0	0	0	0	0	0	0
Office Supplies	0	0	0	0	0	13	0	0	0	0	0	106	120	1,842	1,842	747
Meetings & Seminars	0	0	0	0	0	0	0	0	0	0	0	0	0	921	921	1,022
Printing	0	0	0	0	0	0	0	0	0	0	0	0	0	0	0	44
Memberships	0	440	0	276	92	0	0	0	0	107	0	0	915	1,842	1,842	688
Dues & Subscriptions	0	0	0	0	129	0	0	0	0	0	0	0	129	921	921	2,489
Professional Fees	73,784	74,837	83,476	60,199	63,482	29,636	13,804	22,470	23,642	82,712	34,236	29,613	591,892	521,371	507,553	540,284
Office Temporaries	0	0	0	0	0	0	0	0	0	0	0	0	0	0	0	105
Total Operating Expenses	75,803	77,722	83,576	60,880	64,574	29,999	14,945	23,810	23,715	83,227	34,236	30,174	602,661	543,478	541,636	574,053
DEPARTMENT TOTAL	90,109	92,043	103,670	76,109	80,425	50,097	31,891	40,324	44,964	98,987	50,622	49,662	808,902	748,895	739,683	780,681

EXHIBIT 30-47 Legal & Business Affairs

	Oct 1992	BP4 Oct 1992	Oct (Under) Over	YTD (Under) Over
General Salaries	18,975	21,186	(2,212)	2,728
Overtime	0	0	0	0
Payroll Taxes	513	1,842	(1,329)	(1,904)
Total Salaries	19,488	23,029	(3,541)	824
Travel & Entertainment	455	1,842	(1,387)	(6,975)
Outside Services	0	921	(921)	(1,842)
Office Supplies	0	0	0	120
Meetings & Seminars	0	0	0	0
Printing	0	921	(921)	(921)
Memberships	106	0	106	(928)
Dues & Subscriptions	0	0	0	(792)
Professional Fees	29,613	34,083	(4,469)	70,521
Office Temporaries	0	0	0	0
Total Operating Expenses	30,174	37,767	(7,593)	59,183
DEPARTMENT TOTAL	49,662	60,796	(11,134)	60,007

EXHIBIT 30-48 Financial Planning

	Nov 1991	Dec 1991	Jan 1992	Feb 1992	Mar 1992	Apr 1992	May 1992	Jun 1992	Jul 1992	Aug 1992	Sep 1992	Oct 1992	1992 Actuals	1992 BP4	1992 BP1	1991 Actuals
General Salaries	5,891	5,786	7,805	5,942	5,948	5,104	8,210	6,119	8,784	5,380	6,186	7,581	78,737	78,298	77,377	73,441
Overtime	639	729	1,723	308	745	308	1,828	489	1,024	1,383	925	489	10,590	6,448	0	4,724
Payroll Taxes	478	485	1,305	707	882	399	364	491	1,196	183	530	690	7,709	8,290	7,369	5,809
Total Salaries	7,006	7,000	10,833	6,957	7,575	5,811	10,403	7,099	11,004	6,945	7,641	8,760	97,036	93,036	84,746	83,974
Travel & Entertainment	0	0	0	138	97	0	0	0	1,146	0	22	23	1,426	921	2,763	2,063
Office Temporaries	0	0	0	0	0	0	0	0	0	0	0	0	0	0	0	0
Training	0	0	0	0	0	0	0	0	0	0	0	0	122	0	0	694
Other	0	122	0	0	0	0	0	0	0	0	0	0	0	0	0	160
Total Operating Expenses	0	122	0	138	97	0	0	0	1,146	0	22	23	1,548	921	2,763	2,917
DEPARTMENT TOTAL	7,008	7,121	10,833	7,095	7,671	5,811	10,403	7,099	12,150	6,946	7,663	8,783	98,583	93,957	87,509	86,891

EXHIBIT 30-49 Financial Planning

	Oct 1992	BP4 Oct 1992	Oct (Under) Over	YTD (Under) Over
General Salaries	7,581	7,369	212	439
Overtime	489	0	489	4,141
Payroll Taxes	690	921	(231)	(581)
Total Salaries	8,760	8,290	470	4,000
Travel & Entertainment	23	0	23	505
Office Temporaries	0	0	0	0
Training	0	0	0	0
Other	0	0	0	122
Total Operating Expenses	23	0	23	626
DEPARTMENT TOTAL	8,783	8,290	493	4,626

EXHIBIT 30-50 Pageant Operations

	Nov 1991	Dec 1991	Jan 1992	Feb 1992	Mar 1992	Apr 1992	May 1992	Jun 1992	Jul 1992	Aug 1992	Sep 1992	Oct 1992	1992 Actuals	1992 BP4	1992 BP1	1991 Actuals
General Salaries	5,580	6,459	7,634	5,931	5,931	7,054	6,095	5,931	8,002	5,524	5,887	7,147	77,178	78,298	75,534	83,201
Overtime	0	0	0	0	0	0	0	0	0	0	0	0	0	0	0	374
Payroll Taxes	415	485	1,097	574	1,112	0	220	440	1,051	88	440	440	6,362	6,448	6,448	8,628
Total Salaries	5,995	6,944	8,732	6,505	7,043	7,054	6,315	6,372	9,053	5,613	6,327	7,588	83,540	84,746	81,982	92,203
Travel & Entertainment	327	2,010	450	265	148	1,893	(107)	573	684	186	0	337	6,768	8,290	6,448	10,247
Printing	2,347	0	0	0	0	0	0	779	1,022	0	0	0	4,149	3,685	3,685	2,462
Photographs	0	0	0	0	0	0	0	0	0	0	0	0	0	0	0	28
Other	0	992	0	0	0	0	0	0	0	0	0	0	992	4,606	10,133	1,605
Total Operating Expenses	2,674	3,002	450	265	148	1,893	(107)	1,352	1,707	186	0	337	11,909	16,581	20,265	14,342
DEPARTMENT TOTAL	8,669	9,946	9,182	6,770	7,191	8,947	6,209	7,724	10,760	5,799	6,327	7,925	95,449	101,326	102,248	106,545

EXHIBIT 30-51 Pageant Operations

	Oct 1992	BP4 Oct 1992	Oct (Under) Over	YTD (Under) Over
General Salaries	7,147	9,211	(2,064)	(1,120)
Overtime	0	0	0	0
Payroll Taxes	440	921	(481)	(86)
Total Salaries	7,588	10,133	(2,545)	(1,206)
Travel & Entertainment	337	921	(584)	(1,523)
Printing	0	0	0	464
Photographs	0	0	0	0
Other	0	0	0	(3,614)
Total Operating Expenses	337	921	(584)	(4,672)
DEPARTMENT TOTAL	7,925	11,054	(3,129)	(5,878)

EXHIBIT 30-52 General & Administrative

	Nov 1991	Dec 1991	Jan 1992	Feb 1992	Mar 1992	Apr 1992	May 1992	Jun 1992	Jul 1992	Aug 1992	Sep 1992	Oct 1992	1992 Actuals	1992 BP4	1992 BP1	1991 Actuals
Rent	20,283	19,782	21,637	21,045	21,008	19,445	19,073	19,426	18,963	22,798	20,851	20,515	244,824	242,262	242,262	266,256
Stationary & Supplies	1,638	1,364	646	1,542	2,964	4,655	712	2,536	2,540	1,062	1,066	2,780	23,505	28,556	33,161	44,249
Telephone	1,257	3,841	4,334	3,525	5,815	5,940	2,005	12,613	11,926	3,336	(18,819)	26,151	61,926	65,402	60,796	59,227
Postage	1,353	1,474	0	1,474	737	737	34	1,474	921	0	917	0	9,120	17,502	11,975	55,098
Messengers	313	5,621	2,951	4,481	6,636	7,103	1,584	3,448	4,544	2,456	4,765	2,262	46,165	49,742	60,796	15,577
Benefits	23,950	23,950	18,423	22,108	22,108	22,108	22,108	22,108	22,108	22,108	22,108	22,108	265,291	270,818	287,399	277,935
Equipment Rental	548	1,038	1,137	1,223	1,555	1,047	0	2,580	0	1,680	1,110	2,087	14,006	16,581	16,581	17,398
Repairs & Maintenance	303	304	147	364	1,089	226	227	147	869	234	295	507	4,711	3,685	3,685	5,032
Travel & Entertainment	5,402	2,111	1,400	2,746	(291)	3,053	1,543	1,991	1,481	3,380	1,665	1,840	26,320	23,950	24,871	36,787
Dues &Subscriptions	0	24	12	12	0	129	0	24	12	24	12	0	249	0	921	1,195
Food & Beverage	410	371	483	353	754	580	0	356	442	216	428	247	4,640	3,685	5,527	5,020
Outside Services	193	325	367	239	473	453	96	458	323	132	249	157	3,464	1,842	1,842	5,566
Depreciation	0	0	0	0	0	0	0	0	0	0	0	3,912	3,912	2,763	5,527	1,325
Other	142	446	7,214	507	1,439	0	0	0	0	2,592	768	834	13,941	7,369	(82,903)	301,408
DEPARTMENT TOTAL	55,791	60,651	58,750	59,619	64,286	65,476	47,382	67,161	64,129	60,017	35,415	83,398	722,074	734,156	672,439	1,092,073

EXHIBIT 30-53 General & Administrative

	Oct 1992	BP4 Oct 1992	Oct (Under) Over	YTD (Under) Over
Rent	20,515	19,344	1,171	2,562
Stationary & Supplies	2,780	3,685	(905)	(5,051)
Telephone	26,151	6,448	19,702	(3,475)
Postage	0	1,842	(1,842)	(8,382)
Messengers	2,262	5,527	(3,265)	(3,577)
Benefits	22,108	22,108	0	(5,527)
Equipment Rental	2,087	1,842	245	(2,575)
Repairs & Maintenance	507	921	(415)	1,026
Travel & Entertainment	1,840	921	918	2,370
Dues & Subscriptions	0	0	0	249
Food & Beverage	247	921	(674)	955
Outside Services	157	0	157	1,622
Depreciation	3,912	921	2,991	1,149
Other	834	0	834	6,571
DEPARTMENT TOTAL	83,398	64,480	18,918	(12,082)

EXHIBIT 30-54 1992 Mr. Strongman, Inc. International Telecast Sales

Market	Mr. Strongman
ARGENTINA	3,500
ARUBA	0
AUSTRALIA	42,000
BAHAMAS	600
BARBADOS	0
BELGIUM (FLEMISH)	3,000
BELGIUM (FRENCH)	SEE LUXEMBOURG
BOLIVIA	SEE ARGENTINA
BRAZIL	48,400
CHILE	40,000
COLUMBIA	27,000
COSTA RICA	2,750
CYPRUS	600
CZECHOSLOVAKIA	1000
DENMARK	0
DOMINICAN REPUBLIC	2,800
ECUADOR	4,000
EGYPT	0
EL SALVADOR	3,250
FINLAND	4,000
FRANCE	
GERMANY	25,000
GREECE	7,000
GUATEMALA	0
HOLLAND	0

EXHIBIT 30-54 (cont.)

Market	Mr. Strongman
HONDURAS	1,600
HONG KONG	15,000
ICELAND	0
INDIA	0
INDONESA	1,800
IRELAND (EIRE)	0
ISRAEL	1,500
ITALY	0
JAMAICA	650
JAPAN	0
KOREA	0
LEBANON	880
LUXEMBOURG	0
MALAYSIA	5,000
MALTA	300
MAURITIUS	500
MEXICO	30,000
NAMIBIA CANNOT SELL SINCE EXCLUSIVE IN SO. AFRICA	
NETH ANTILLES (CURACA)	0
NEW ZEALAND	7,000
NICARAGUA	1,000
NORWAY (SEE COMMENT)	5,000
PANAMA	1,450
PARAGUAY	SEE ARGENTINA
PERU	6,300
PHILIPPINES	17,000
POLAND	0
PORTUGAL	0
PUERTO RICO	40,000
SINGAPORE	3,900
SOUTH AFRICA	50,000
SPAIN	35,000
SRI LANKA	SEE MALAYSIA
SWEDEN	6,000
TAIWAIN	0
*THAILAND	SEE BELOW
TURKEY	6,000
UNITED KINGDOM	40,000
URUGUAY	0
U.S. ARMED FORCES	2,820
VENEZUELA	120,000
TOTALS	$615,200

REFERENCES

Anderson, James, "Budgeting In A Service Company," *Handbook of Budgeting* (New York, 1988).

Jones, Reginald and Trentin, George, *Budgeting: Key to Planning and Control* (New York: American Management Association, 1971).

Koehler, Kenneth, "Budgeting Pays If You Do It Right," *CMA*, May-June 1986, p. 12.

Lewis, Daniel, *A Practical Guide to Budgetary and Management Control Systems* (Mass.: Lexington Books, 1979).

Mathews, Lawrence, *Practical Operating Budgeting* (New York: McGraw-Hill, 1977).

Pyhrr, Peter, *Zero-Base Budgeting* (New York: John Wiley, 1973).

Schmidgall, Raymond and Damitio, James, "Current Capital Budgeting Practices of Major Lodging Chains," *Real Estate Review,* Fall 1990., p. 40.

Wilson, James D., *Budgeting and Profit Planning Manual* (Boston, Massachusetts: Warren, Gorham & Lamont, 1983).

Woelfel, Charles J., *Accounting, Budgeting, and Finance* (New York: AMACOM, 1990).

Woelfel, Charles J., *Budgeting, Pricing & Cost Controls* (Chicago, Illinois: Probus Publishing Company, 1987).

Arvey, Richard, "Controlling Service Sector Costs," *Management Accounting,* July-August 1990, p. 26.

Chapter 31

Budgeting for Nonprofit Organizations

This chapter is an overview of the budgeting process with nonprofit organizations, intended to give a general picture. Nonprofit organizations ordinarily do not pay income, property, or sales taxes. Most nonprofit entities are service organizations. Planning is needed to accomplish goals in a productive, economical way.

Nonprofit organizations can be broken down into three major types. The first is comprised of voluntarily supported organizations, such as hospitals, churches, colleges, foundations, health and welfare agencies, and privately funded schools. The second type includes organizations supported through tax assessments, such as government units and state-supported schools. The third type operates primarily for the benefit of its supporters, such as cooperatives, country clubs, and other community-based organizations.

Budgets are widely employed by nonprofits. Budgets are usually required by regulatory authorities, e.g., legislatures, boards of trustees, and administrative agencies that monitor activities. Because nonprofits rarely produce products, they do not begin with a sales forecast. They provide services to their users and must prepare a forecast of the services to be rendered during a specific planning horizon (typically one year) to establish a starting point for the master budget.

In the not-for-profit organization, some form of planning tool is essential to ensure that the activities meet service objectives. The major planning tool is the budget. The budget is the formal statement of expected resources and proposed expenditures. In many government units, the budget is deemed so significant that it may be in legal form with limits placed on government expenditures. In many other not-for-profit organizations, the budget requires formal approval of a governing body such as the board of directors or trustees. The nonprofit budget process includes long-range planning, program planning, budget planning, budget development, and budget control.

The nonprofit organization must find an alternative method to quantify its success other than profit, to control its operations, to appraise performance, and to make resource allocation decisions. This increases the need for the nonprofit organization to formulate its priorities before budget development.

The objective of financial reporting is accountability to the public rather than to investors. There is no profit distribution. The accounting equation associated with fund accounting is: Assets = Restrictions on Assets. A nonprofit entity may have a surplus or deficit depending on whether revenues exceed expenditures.

Many accounting and budgeting techniques that were originally developed for business can be applied by nonprofits. These include:

1. responsibility center accounting,
2. flexible budgeting,
3. cost standards and performance,
4. work measurement techniques, and
5. time reporting.

Operating objectives and procedures must be set to accomplish goals. An evaluation is needed of tasks to be accomplished and costs to be expected. Funds are established to ensure accountability and expenditure for designated purposes. The adopted budget is the maximum amount the organization can spend. Many agencies are funded by federal, state, or local governments. Some nonprofit entities such as charities rely on contributions and dues. Revenues must be raised and expended in accordance with special regulations, restrictions, or limitations.

This chapter discusses planning, recordkeeping and reporting, budgeting and accounting bases, budget development and control, budgeting revenue and expenditures, effectiveness and control measures, organization structure, functional and program reporting, and budget adaptability. It presents an overview of the budgeting aspects for government, voluntary hospitals, colleges, and professional associations.

PLANNING

A long-term plan should be formulated based on short-term objectives. Programs should be evaluated to ascertain if they should be continued. New programs should be formulated. Capital expenditures should be made for long-term viability and growth. Alternative ways to accomplish objectives should be specified. The major activities in the planning stage are defining major objectives, specifying strategies for accomplishing objectives, and initiating the program planning process.

The long-term planning process begins with a mission statement that reflects the entity's purpose, specifies objectives to be reached, and identifies viable paths (or strategies) that may satisfy these objectives. The mission statement should be broad enough to be flexible and noncontroversial. It should require very few modifications over the years. The fiscal policies supporting that mission statement can be more specific and subject to revision as the situation changes.

If the organization does not have a statement of purpose, it should develop one. If there is an existing "outdated" statement of purpose, it should be modified. Once the statement of purpose is clearly established, more specific long-term objectives consistent with this purpose should be defined.

Next comes devising ways to accomplish objectives. There may be numerous such strategies, some more feasible than others. The purpose at this stage is to consider alternatives and not to assess them in depth. Detailed analysis comes in the program planning phase.

As objectives are being formulated and strategies for achieving them identified, the organization should initiate a program planning group including "key" policy makers such as the director, financial officers, and departmental supervisors. The group's role is to take the statements of purpose and objectives formulated in the long-range planning phase and translate these into programs.

FUNDS

Every nonprofit organization contains a fund through which its operations are handled. Among governmental and municipalities, this is referred to as the general fund. This fund consists of resources used to conduct general operations. The general fund shows the inflow of resources, typically in the form of taxes, licenses, fines and forfeits, governmental assessments, and miscellaneous revenue. The budget will also include cash outflows for such activities as general administration, sanitation, recreation, public safety, and education.

A fund is a fiscal and accounting entity with a self-balancing set of accounts which are segregated for the purpose of carrying on specific activities or attaining certain objectives in accordance with special regulations, restrictions, or limitations.

The following types of governmental funds exist:

General fund—used to account for all financial resources, except those required to be accounted for in another fund.

Special revenue fund—used to account for the proceeds of specific revenue sources that are legally restricted to expenditure for specified purposes. Examples of special revenue funds are those established for the purpose of financing schools, parks, and libraries.

Special assessment fund—services or capital improvements provided by local governments which are intended primarily to benefit a particular property owner or group of property owners rather than the general citizenry.

Capital projects fund—used to account for financial resources to be expended for the acquisition or construction of major capital facilities.

Debt service fund—used to account for the accumulation of resources for, and the payment of, general long-term debt principal and interest.

Enterprise fund—used to account for operations that are financed and conducted in a manner similar to private business enterprises such as utilities.

Internal service fund—used to account for goods and services performed by one department for another on a cost-reimbursement basis. Examples are data processing and maintenance.

Trust and agency fund—used to account for assets held by a government unit as trustee or agent.

RECORDKEEPING AND REPORTING

A budget should be prepared for each fund group and a total budget for all funds combined. Funds may be restricted or unrestricted. Restricted funds are restricted by outside agencies or persons. Unrestricted funds have no external restriction as to use or purpose.

Financial reports for nonprofit entities, except for hospitals and health and welfare agencies, typically reflect the sources of attained dollars and the methods in which those dollars have been used in reporting the results of their overall operations. Minimal attention is placed on measuring the benefits that these organizations have provided from their resources.

A host of differences in accounting methods in the nonprofit sector compared to those in the private sector may materially impact nonprofit budgeting procedures. Fund accounting is practiced in most areas of the government sector. An entity that employs fund accounting will report a balance sheet and statement of activity for each fund. Fund accounting requirements may make the budgeting process more difficult because a single transaction may need to be classified in more than one way including by source, by function or program, by responsibility unit, and by natural object of expenditure. The budget must be prepared along these same lines.

Many nonprofit entities use either the cash basis method to account for revenues and expenses or the modified accrual method. Under the latter, the cash basis books are converted to accrual at year's end. A cash-based accounting system records actual cash receipts and disbursements, but not payables or receivables. Thus, budget data may be inadequate. Budget reports will convey no knowledge of receivables due or commitments to pay for goods and services already received. Depending on the net effect of accrual adjustments, a cash basis statement could be substantially over or under budget when restated on the accrual basis.

Other accounting concerns include recording "expenditures," measuring goods and services acquired during an accounting period, and measuring goods or services used or consumed during an accounting period. Further, some nonprofit organizations, such as religious institutions and most government funds, do not depreciate their fixed assets. They keep track of expired capital costs through separate records that do not enter the financial statements. A final area of difference concerns donated goods and services, which are unique to the nonprofit arena. Most are valued and reported only if the following conditions exist:

1. the services performed are part of the organization's normal functions and would otherwise be conducted by paid personnel,
2. the organization has control over the services being rendered, and
3. the value of the services can be measured.

External funding sources influence the manner in which a nonprofit organization budgets and accounts for its costs. External parties establish reporting principles that the recipient nonprofit organization must fulfill as a precondition to obtaining funding, or being reimbursed for costs incurred.

A prime budget concern for the recipient organization is to be reimbursed for all of its grant or contract-related costs and not be required to meet any unexpected costs from general funds. It will be beneficial to do the following:

1. minimize grant-related costs that are not permitted for reimbursement under the funding party's guidelines,
2. account for and charge to the funding party as many indirect and administrative costs as can be appropriately attributed to the grant,
3. assure there are no cost overruns on grant projects, and
4. find ways to charge to the project the costs of scaling down a grant project after the cut-off date and by so doing absorbing the least amount with general funds.

Nonprofit entities are increasingly being requested to report their expenses on a functional, or program, basis. This requirement represents an improvement in reporting for two reasons. First, it focuses the nonprofit financial reports on what the end results are of an organization's use of its funds instead of monitoring the source of the funds. This facilitates determining how well the organization is accomplishing its objectives. Second, it makes the organization think through its programs, to collect cost information, and to start to manage itself along program lines.

GOVERNMENT BUDGETS AND ACCOUNTING BASES

Profit, if any, accrues to the benefit of the particular governmental or institutional unit only. Budgets are adopted and recorded in the accounts of the related fund. Encumbrances, which are contractual obligations, are given effect in some government funds.

Budgetary accountability differs from for-profit accounting in that budgetary amounts are actually recorded in the accounts of a fund. Recording the budgetary balances in the accounts has a dual effect. The control aspect of the budgetary function is stressed and recognition is given to the legal foundations of the budget.

The need for budgetary recording in the accounts is consistent with the responsibility focus of fund accounting. The concern is for performance in terms of authority to act. Recording of both the budget and actual transactions helps to allocate responsibility.

Government funds (except for proprietary funds and trust and agency funds) use the modified accrual accounting basis. Revenue is recognized when it becomes available and measurable. Expenditures are recognized in the period in which the liability is incurred *except for:*

- Inventories of materials and supplies, which may be considered expenditures either when purchased or used.
- Interest on general long-term debt, which is recognized when due.
- Use of encumbrances.

GOVERNMENT RECORDKEEPING FOR BUDGET ACCOUNTABILITY

The entry to record the adoption of a budget is:

Estimated revenues	70,000,000	
Fund balance	200,000	
Appropriations		70,200,000

Estimated Revenues is the authorization to raise funds while Appropriations is the authorization to spend funds. Fund Balance is similar to an equity account. In this case, there is authority to spend $70,200,000, of which $70,000,000 will come from various revenues and $200,000 will be applied from the preceding year's closing fund balance. Of course, the Estimated Revenues and Appropriations budget lines will each be broken down into an itemization of specific sources of revenue and expenditure categories.

The entry to record the closing of a budget is:

Revenues
Fund balance
   Estimated revenues
   Expenditures
   Encumbrances

Budgetary and actual accounts affect fund balance.

GOVERNMENT INTERFUND TRANSACTIONS

There may be interfund loans or advances which are temporary shifts of resources to be repaid. They are recorded in "due to" and "due from" accounts. Transactions which represent reimbursements from one fund to another are classified as expenditures in the responsible fund and as reductions of expenditures in the fund being reimbursed.

Quasi-external transactions would be treated as revenue, expenditures, or expenses if they involved organizations external to the government unit. Examples are electricity generated by a utility fund and for the general fund, or services performed by an internal service fund for another fund.

Interfund transactions which are not loans or advances, reimbursements, or quasi-external transactions are classified as "transfers." Examples of transfers are:

1. transfers of tax revenue from a special revenue fund to a debt service fund and
2. transfers from a general fund to a capital project fund.

CAPITAL AND OPERATING BUDGETS

Capital budgets apply to the purchase or sale of assets that have a useful life of more than one year. However, operating budgets are prepared annually showing expected revenues, support, and expenses. Nonprofit organizations that are on a cash basis with little capital plans will not need to separate capital from the operating budget, but nonprofits with large capital programs must separate these two. Failure to do so distorts the annual operating budget.

BUDGET DEVELOPMENT

Initially, the nonprofit organization must estimate revenues. This is typically achieved by the chief financial officers because many units do not fund themselves or do so only partly. Decisions must be made by upper management with regard to issues such as what service levels to provide, what to charge for services performed, how to obtain other funds required to support these services, and how to allocate these funds among programs or departments.

The organization should determine its revenues first on an overall basis, and then on individual revenues. This gives the units initial direction in budget preparation. The unit's budget report should identify revenue by type, expenses by category, output measures, and unit cost for the service. It is difficult to project revenues over the next year. The organization may estimate different revenue levels on a best-case, worst-case basis, and then have its program budget and make plans for activity at several different levels.

After the responsibility unit receives estimates of its activity level and its expected revenues, it then budgets its expenditures. Worksheets should be prepared to break expenditures into categories, including personnel compensation, supplies, capital expenditure items, and so on.

When preparing expense budgets, responsibility units need to evaluate how their costs change with the service level provided. Many costs will be fixed over a large range of activities, whereas, some costs will vary directly with the level of activity.

After the responsibility center reports are prepared, they should be combined into a consolidated budget for the organization. During the consolidation process, safeguards should assure that a proper balance between revenues and expenses is kept, the stated objectives and planned activities of the responsibility centers do not conflict, and the budget is in conformity with the organization's long-term strategic and financial objectives.

The operating budget may be prepared in several ways. One of the most common approaches is to take the previous year's budget and to make needed adjustments for the current environment, line by line for each item of revenue and expenditure for each activity detailed in the budget. These are then summed to arrive at budget totals. One of the major difficulties with this approach is that it often leads to arbitrary adjustments of revenue and expenditure items and it does not encourage alternative operating methods.

Another way to develop a budget is to determine overall revenues and/or allowable expenditures and then to apportion percentages to certain activities. This method, too, fails to encourage alternative operational plans. It also encourages spending "all of the allotted amounts for fear that budgeted amounts would be cut the following year."

When revenue is not related to costs, guidelines stated in nonmonetary, service-related terms may seem more useful in guiding budget preparation. In client-oriented entities, budget guidelines could be based on the number of clients served and the breakdown of type of service generally provided clients. Other organizations may formulate budgets on the number of hours of operations and estimated traffic during these hours. Nonmonetary guidelines are often difficult to develop for all areas, however; thus both monetary and nonmonetary guidelines may be combined where feasible in the budget guideline document providing the maximum amount of guidance.

In addition to guidelines for costs and/or operations, guidelines must also be issued on the format and timing of the budget. "Program directors" may be asked to prepare their budgets to satisfy program objectives, but they need some form of procedure to fulfill this. Costs should be collected in a manner consistent with those of previous years to aid comparison. Further, area costs should be broken down into unit costs where practical and some form of cost per unit of output should be developed; these steps facilitate not only analysis at the budget stage but also comparisons of actual versus planned performance.

The availability of resources for a particular area is often based on a judgement allocation. Therefore, whether these allocated figures are made available to lower-level managers must be an upper-management or budget-officer decision, since it is their responsibility to match revenues and costs while putting the entire budget together.

BUDGETING REVENUE

The estimated revenue for the not-for-profit firm differs from that of the profit-oriented firm in two ways. First, the revenues of many not-for-profit organizations have no direct relationship to the services provided. Second, since the firm is nonprofit, the excess of revenues over expenditures in any period should be available in the next period since the objective in any one period is to have an equality between revenues and expenditures. Finally, a difference arises in the budgeting process: rather than the estimation of revenues limiting expenditures, necessary program expenditures may be estimated first and revenues raised accordingly. For example, property taxes are often "levied" on this basis.

Most not-for-profit organizations have one or more revenue sources which provide the bulk of their resources. These are called primary sources, while smaller amounts from varied sources are called secondary sources. In estimating primary revenues, the actual sources are easily identified. A city's primary source will generally be the property taxes; a hospital's primary source is patient revenue from either the patients themselves or from "third-party reimbursements." A church's primary source is its weekly offerings from its members. A university may have several primary sources, such as tuition and room and board.

Nonprofit organizations often have difficulties in budgeting revenues because so many revenues do not result directly from the rendering of services to individuals. The annual income on investments of endowment funds may be recorded as part of operating revenue; however, there is controversy over just how to measure this income. Grants and contracts obtained from the federal government, foundations, or other third parties often pose questions for budgeters. Uncertainties exist whether or not they will come through, and if so, when and for how long a period of time. Fund raising or membership drives may boost revenues, but uncertainties exist about what new gains can be made and whether past fund-raising success can be maintained. The higher the proportion of soft revenue sources (resulting from one-time promotional efforts which may not be renewable) in an organization's budget, the greater the risks that it will not be accomplished.

Some nonprofit organizations obtain much of their financial resources from sales. This is the case with many community hospitals, private schools and colleges from student tuition, and research organizations whose resources come from contracts for specific projects. Other nonprofit entities receive substantial financial support from sources other than revenues from services rendered. These are referred to as "public-supported organizations." In these organizations, there is no direct connection between the services received and the resources provided. Individuals receive essentially the same services from a government unit regardless of the taxes paid.

When revenues fail to cover estimated costs, the first reaction is often to cut costs by cutting services so that they do not exceed estimated revenues. Another method of balancing the budget is to increase revenues by raising taxes or fees or having "special fund drives."

EXPENDITURES

The accurate forecasting of departmental expenditures is a difficult but necessary task. While revenue sources may be somewhat limited, the width of expenditures is usually broad. The estimation of expenses are usually more manageable than budgeting revenue; however, many times it is almost impossible to match expenses incurred in providing a program service, or in operating a department, to any specific revenue sources that support these services. It will be easier to prepare the budget if expenditures are grouped into separate categories: salaries, supplies, operating expenses, and capital equipment.

For many not-for-profit organizations, the personnel costs represent a major portion of current operating expenditures. Therefore, this area should be constantly monitored since it has a major impact on the total budget.

Operating expenditures are defined as expenditures other than those for personnel services, supplies, and capital outlays. They include gas and electric utility bills, telephone expenses, and reproduction costs.

ENCUMBRANCES

Encumbrances is an integral part of budget accountability. Encumbrances represent commitments related to unfilled contracts for goods and services (including purchase orders). The purpose of encumbrances is to prevent further expenditure of funds in light of commitments already made. At year-end, encumbrances still open are not accounted for as expenditures and liabilities but, rather, as reservations of fund balance.

The closing entry for a budget at the end of the year is:

Fund Balance
    Encumbrances

BUDGETARY CONTROL

Cost controls should be implemented to save on costs. This may allow for expanded services and increased user services. Many cost items are of a discretionary nature. Because there is no "bottom line" in nonprofit entities, identifying objectives are more difficult than in profit-making businesses. Therefore, control systems are not used as much in nonprofits for several reasons. First, organizational goals are less clear and are often multiple, necessitating trade-offs. Second, professionals (such as physicians, lawyers, and teachers) typically dominate nonprofit organizations and are less receptive to control systems and measures. Third, measurement is more difficult because there is no profit to determine; a heavy amount of discretionary fixed costs exist; and the relationship between inputs and outputs is difficult to specify. Thus, the budget process in the public sector is related to playing bargaining games with higher authorities to obtain the largest authorization of discretionary fixed costs.

When budgetary outlays for a unit are approved, they are appropriated for the individual items in the budget. Management can spend appropriable funds up to the amount provided in the budget for each item. Typically, any expenditure over the prescribed amount must receive authorization. The term appropriation control can be used to describe the mechanism used to regulate the amount of resources that can be expended for salaries, supplies, and other cash outflows.

Budgetary control reporting for nonprofit entities is similar to profit-oriented ones. Heads of responsibility units normally receive monthly reports showing actual performance to budget. Financial and nonfinancial statistics of the units' activities are provided.

Reports and variances should be reviewed and evaluated by the heads of responsibility centers, as well as by financial officers and administrators higher up in the organization. Variance reports should be broken down into two parts:

1. that part arising from offering more or less services than what was originally budgeted and
2. that part due to reasons of efficiency or unplanned changes in input prices.

Variance analysis may show that an organization or responsibility center needs to modify its original budget and to cut back or expand its previously planned activities.

Nonprofit budgets are often treated as inflexible once they are established. However, nonprofit organizations do have choices over what services to offer and where to target them. This is particularly true for nonprofit organizations that can vary client services somewhat and for which they get at least partial payment from the clients. The budget should not only be considered a planning device but also as a means of identifying needs for change and making those changes on a timely basis.

As an element of control, budgets in nonprofits should distinguish between restricted and unrestricted sources and uses of funds and should show any expected transfer from one to the other. This is important because the management of the nonprofit has no discretionary use over the restricted funds. These funds must be used for the purposes for which they were obtained. To use them otherwise is to violate the contract under which the funds were obtained. Therefore, it is important that if the amounts of restricted funds are shown as receipts in the budget, then it is similarly shown that they are restricted. Restricted funds do not always come from external sources. The board of directors may set aside a certain portion of the annual revenues for some special reason and restrict the management from using it for any other reason.

Guidelines must be developed because services provided and revenues raised are frequently unrelated. Therefore, guidelines often take a form which does not necessarily lead to efficient use of resources such as "costs should not exceed last year's by more than the rate of inflation." Other guidelines such as overall reductions in expenditures are more common. Areas with a high dependence on fuel and utility costs may need one specific set of guidelines, while the areas unaffected by these economic changes may apply a different set of guidelines.

VARIANCES

Revenue and costs should be accumulated. The variance between actual and budgeted revenue and costs should be computed. Problem areas should be identified so corrective action may be taken.

A flexible budget can be established based upon the level of expected services, taxes, and assessments. Then, variances can be evaluated against actual operating results and the budgeted amount for the actual level of service. A budgeted general fund balance sheet estimates resources available in the general fund at the end of the period. Typically, categories with unfavorable variances that are controllable by management will be evaluated for possible methods of improvement.

EFFECTIVENESS AND CONTROL MEASURES

Most nonprofit organizations provide services, not tangible products. Thus, the problem of developing measures of effectiveness in providing services is especially difficult. One principal operating problem is that a service must be provided at a particular time. This causes difficulties in short-term scheduling and longer-term capacity planning. Another problem is that most services are labor-intensive and the labor required may vary substantially from one time a service is performed to the next. This makes service work more difficult to schedule and control than machine operations. The measurement of services is perhaps an even more fundamental problem. Many services are difficult to quantify. Measuring and controlling the quality of services is also difficult particularly when professional effort is involved. Standards of quality simply do not exist. Efficiency measurements are similarly difficult to obtain.

ORGANIZATION STRUCTURE

The structure of a nonprofit entity may restrict its efforts to establish an effective budgeting system. One major reason may be the absence of a reliable responsibility structure. A responsibility system of budgeting divides the organization into work units, assigns individual responsibility for each activity of the unit, and classifies costs as controllable or noncontrollable by that unit. It is used as a tool for managers to control that area of the organization for which they are directly accountable. Many nonprofit entities have recognized that, although responsibility budgeting is a good tool for controlling expenditures, it does not provide sufficient control over services performed.

This recognition has brought to the surface the concept of program structure. The program structure aligns itself with either the types of services the organization renders or the classes of individuals who benefit from its services. Nonprofit entities have not often organized along program lines. Their accounting systems do not typically support program concepts. In consequence, program costs are difficult to quantify and record on a consistent yearly basis.

The program planners should start by turning each possible strategy defined in long-range planning into specific actions. The following questions should be raised: What organizational functions does it involve? What groups does it reach? What objectives does it satisfy?

Several alternative strategies will likely exist at this time to meet each objective. Program planners will need to evaluate individual strategies to determine which one meets the prescribed objective at minimum cost. Cost-benefit analysis may be helpful. However, since benefits will almost always be imprecisely estimated, organizations cannot decide solely on the basis of the analysis.

Cost-benefit analysis will reveal which strategies will meet the objective and at what cost. It will eliminate alternatives which are financially not justified. However, the program planners must ask several other questions before a final decision. First, they must determine whether the resources are available to undertake the suggested program. If not, the objective needs to be modified or an alternative strategy selected. They must also study the risk involved and whether there are any environmental constraints. Finally, planners should take into account whether a new program is a good fit.

Once the desired strategies are chosen, they need to be converted into specific program plans. Some areas a program plan should address are the objectives it will help to achieve, its benefits to the public, the costs of the program, funding, risks, personnel needed, and time to accomplish.

On-going programs should be reviewed frequently. Older programs may have outgrown their usefulness or lost the support of their constituency. The review should consider ways to restructure the program, to improve its efficiency, or to merge it with other programs.

Formal program planning leads to a program structure. Many nonprofit entities have formulated meaningful program structures, but fewer of them have actually translated them into budget terms. Program plans are devised with a longer time period in mind than the usual one-year budget. The plans include less detail about costs and revenues and do not provide an operating plan. This means that program plans require some translation into specific dollar terms to become useful inputs to annual budgets.

Secondly, the program structure, which is directed on outputs, often goes across traditional departmental responsibility lines. This causes the organization to emphasize the services it provides. Organizations such as hospitals, however, will not shift their organizational structure to match programs. The reason is that traditional departmental structure corresponds to the background and training of the organization's staff and to the way they divide the work. The daily activities follow departmental lines, and so must the budget if the organization is to control these activities.

If the program budgets are not formally used, the organization should monitor how well it is accomplishing its program objectives. Ways to do this include having a committee to track and report on program performance, reporting on program revenues and expenses, establishing performance measures, and reporting on the success in meeting program objectives.

The budget structure follows the daily operating structure. If the organization operates on a program basis, the budget will be a program budget. If the organization is departmental, so is the budget. If the organization is arranged departmentally, revenues and expenses will be tracked by natural objective of classification and department. This will give a department supervisor the data to control expenses and revenues. If the organization has completed program planning, it should also classify revenues and expenses by program. A computerized accounting system with a properly designed chart of accounts can provide program-based budget reports in any detail level of responsibility.

The development of measurement tools is the next step in budget planning. An accounting system must be supplemented by both financial and nonfinancial measures that show what the department or program is doing with its resources and what it is achieving. In nonprofit entities, efficiency measures are more common because they are easily generated from internal statistics and do not require the organization to measure its outputs.

In most cases, a program may rely more on effectiveness measures, while a department may rely more on efficiency measures. However, each program and department should have both effectiveness and efficiency in varying portions.

Budget guidelines should then be prepared. Directors should communicate general information that the department or program heads can follow.

FUNCTIONAL OR PROGRAM REPORTING

Certain not-for-profit organizations, such as voluntary health and welfare, report expenses by function (or program). There should also be supporting schedules providing details of the items included for each program. Under functional reporting, expenses (expenditures) are accumulated according to the program purpose for which costs were incurred rather than by object of expenditure (i.e., research program).

A preliminary budget for each program is needed so that the organization may compare benefits and costs before selecting among programs. Before the chosen programs can be implemented, a final budget must be formed so that the managers know the amount of resources that is planned for the programs, the sources of these dollars (from grants, fees, and so on), the way those dollars are expected to be allocated among competing uses within each program, and a schedule of expenditures and receipts over the life of the program.

BUDGET ADAPTABILITY

Nonprofit budgets are typically not easily adapted to changing circumstances. One reason is that many nonprofit entities do not undergo significant variations in the service levels they provide annually. Another reason is that their cost structure often contains many costs that are deemed fixed. Noticeably, this lack of adaptability arises from prevailing attitudes in nonprofit organizations. Most entities are simply not accustomed to the idea of modifying budget allocations once they are set and are not yet willing to adapt to flexible budgeting techniques.

BUDGET PARTICIPANTS

Preparation of the budget tends to involve just about anyone of importance who is associated with a nonprofit entity, including community representatives, funding sources, and regulatory agencies. These external parties have different backgrounds and often have different budget expectations. A nonprofit organization must respond directly to these external forces which often have conflicting objectives and can therefore make it difficult to manage and plan the organization's future. Internal budget participants may also have different goals. Professional concerns for the quality of service often tend to override issues of cost. Financial managers of nonprofit entities often have a different background from that of others in the organization and may set financial priorities that are at variance with the interests of the professionals. The budget often is a compromise between various conflicting internal parties.

VOLUNTARY HOSPITALS

Voluntary hospitals report:

- *Patient service revenues*—directly related to patient care.
- *Other operating revenue*—revenues indirectly related to providing patient services such as tuition from educational programs, cafeteria revenue, parking fees, gift shop revenues, and research grants.

- *Nonoperating gains and losses*—incidental transactions to operation from events beyond management's control. Examples are general contributions, income from investments, rents, unrestricted income from endowment funds.

Revenue is subdivided as to public support and revenue.

- Public support is the conveyance of property without consideration. Examples are contributions, gifts, grants, and bequests.
- Revenue such as membership dues and interest income.

The fund groups for voluntary hospitals are:

- *General (Unrestricted) funds* comprising of:
  —*Operating funds*—for routine hospital activities including plant assets and related long-term debt.
  —*Board-designated funds*—resources set aside for specific use.
- *Restricted funds* comprising of:
  —*Specific purpose*—resources restricted for specific operating purposes.
  —*Endowment*—principal remains intact. Earnings may or may not be available subject to donor restrictions.
  —*Plant replacement and expansion*—resources restricted for plant and equipment acquisition.

Hospital budgets must respond to the expected level of operations. Hence, a flexible budget should be established for each revenue-producing department. The departmental costs must be separated into their fixed and variable components. This budget allows management to forecast the cost of providing one unit of service at various levels of operations. Thus, management must estimate the probable level of activities for the period. Then, the operating plan, including cost goals and service billing prices can be formulated. The fundamental billing unit for most hospitals is a day of room occupancy. Consequently, the level of room operations is typically expressed in terms of the rate of room occupancy. In Exhibit 31-1, actual expenses incurred during the period are compared with the budgeted expenses and the reasons for the variances are given.

COLLEGES AND UNIVERSITIES

Nonprofit entities receive funds from several sources, each with its appropriate subgroups. Colleges and universities usually have more sources than hospitals and most governmental agencies.

The fund groups for colleges and universities follow:

EXHIBIT 31-1 J. K. Shim Hospital
Flexible Budget for Department 1

Level of operations	70 percent	80 percent	90 percent	100 percent
(Related to capacity)				
Direct expenses (variable)	$262,500	$300,000	$337,500	$375,000
Direct expenses (fixed)	100,000	100,000	100,000	100,000
Allocated general expenses (fixed)	80,000	80,000	80,000	80,000
Allocated service dept. expenses				
Dept. 5 (fixed)	100,000	100,000	100,000	100,000
Dept. 6 (fixed)	20,000	20,000	20,000	20,000
Dept. 7 (semifixed)	55,000	60,000	65,000	70,000
Total expenses	$617,500	$660,000	$702,500	$745,000
Billing units	57,750	66,000	74,250	82,500
Cost per unit of service	$10.69	$10.00	$9.46	$9.03

Flexible Budget Variance Analysis for Department 1

	Actual Expenses	Budgeted Allocation	Variances
	$320,000	$318,750	(1,250)—Unfavorable
Direct expenses (variable)	101000	100000	(1,000)—Unfavorable
Direct expenses (fixed)	78000	80000	2,000—Favorable
Allocated general expenses (fixed)			
Allocated service dept. expenses			
Dept. 5 (fixed)	20,500	20,000	(500)—Unfavorable
Dept. 6 (fixed)	65,000	62,500	(2,500)—Unfavorable
Dept. 7 (semifixed)	101,500	100,000	(1,500)—Unfavorable
TOTALS	$686,000	$681,250	$4,750—Unfavorable

Direct variable expense variance probably resulted in the department's lack of ability to control variable costs.

Direct fixed expense variance suggests that the departmental supervisor "overspent" his allocated fixed expenses.

Departments 5 and 6 variances probably caused by inadequate methods of cost control.

Department 7 variance could have been caused by having too many employees or the inability to control costs.

In all unfavorable cases, all individual expense items should be reviewed with departmental supervisors.

- *Current funds*—resources available to carry out the primary educational objectives of the institution. It may be restricted or unrestricted. University unrestricted current funds, obtained from tuition, student fees, and endowment revenue, can be transferred to various operating activities, unless otherwise specified by the governing board. On the other hand, the use of restricted current funds are specified by the donors or other outside agencies. These funds are usually obtained through endowments, gifts, contracts, grants and appropriations from private organizations and governments for research, public service, or other restrictive purposes.

EXHIBIT 31-2

Colleges and Universities	Voluntary Health and Welfare	Hospitals
Unrestricted	Unrestricted	Unrestricted
Restricted	Restricted	Specific purpose
Plant funds	Land, bldg. & equipment	Plant replacement
Endowment fund	Endowment fund	Endowment fund
Agency fund		Agency fund
Annuity and life Income funds		
Loan funds		Loan funds

- *Loan funds*—repayment of principal and interest are returned to the fund and made available for further loans to students and staff.
- *Endowment funds*—principal cannot be used but income earned may or may not be.
- *Annuity and life income funds*—these are restricted funds which provide for repayment to the donor of a portion of fund income.
- *Agency funds*—the resources are managed by the institution as an agent on behalf of others. These funds are restricted. Examples are when the university acts as an agent for student government or faculty organization.
- *Plant funds*—these funds include plant assets and related debt, and assets to be used for future acquisition.

Municipal accounting principles dictate that the accounting system used provide budgetary control of both revenues and expenditures. Although college and university financial statements do not require such control, a complete system is typically adopted by these institutions.

Although a large number of individual items associated with the budget of a college or university is appropriation controlled, several are formula controlled. This allows allocations to vary with changes in the level of operations. In this regard, the college or university budget is more flexible than that of governmental entities. Hence, budgetary data may be given less formal recognition in the accounts of colleges and universities.

A comparison of fund groups for colleges and universities, voluntary health and welfare entities, and hospitals is provided in Exhibit 31-2.

PROFESSIONAL ASSOCIATIONS

An illustrative budget for a nonprofit professional association follows in Exhibit 31-3.

EXHIBIT 31-3 Budgeted Revenue for a Nonprofit Professional Association

| | | | Quarters | | |
	1	2	3	4	Annual
Dues					
Magazine					
Conferences					
Continuing professional education					
Miscellaneous					

Budgeted Costs

| | | | Quarters | | |
	1	2	3	4	Annual
Administration					
Conferences					
Publications					
Committees					
Computer					
Other					

A variance analysis report may then be prepared comparing budget and actual figures, such as:

Variance Analysis Report

| | First Quarter | | | Annual | | |
	Budget	Actual	Variance Percent	Budget	Actual	Variance Percent
Revenue						
Dues						
Magazines						
Conferences						
CPE						
Miscellaneous						
Costs						
Administration						
Conferences						
Publications						
Committees						
Computer						
Other						

CONCLUSION

A nonprofit is defined as a legal entity which does not conduct substantial commercial activity or earn a profit as its primary purpose. The goal is typically to provide services. In nonprofit organizations, management decisions are intended to result in furnishing the best possible service given resource constraints; success is measured by how much service the organization provides and by how well these services are performed. Basically, the success of a nonprofit entity is measured by how much it contributes to the public well-being.

Nonprofit organizations include governmental and private nonprofit entities. Within the governmental category, there exists federal, state, and local. Within the private grouping, there is a key difference between charities, for which donor contributions are tax deductible, and commercial and membership organizations, whose donor contributions typically are not tax deductible. The former category includes health, educational, social service, religious, cultural, and scientific. The latter category includes social clubs, fraternal organizations, labor unions, chambers of commerce, trade associations, and business leagues.

REFERENCES

R. Anthony and D. Young, *Management Control in Nonprofit Organizations* (Illinois: Richard Irwin, 1988).

G. Dabbs, "Nonprofit Business in the 1990s: Models for Success," *Business Horizons,* Sept.-Oct. 1991.

P. Drucker, "What Business Can Learn from Nonprofits," *Harvard Business Review,* July-August 1989.

L. Haller, *Financial Resource Management for Nonprofit Organizations* (New Jersey: Prentice-Hall, 1982).

E. Henke, *Accounting for Nonprofit Organizations* (New York: Wadsworth, 1983).

H. Orlans, *Nonprofit Organizations: A Government Management Tool* (New York: Praeger, 1980).

J. Siegel and J. Shim, "Governmental and Nonprofit Accounting," *Barron's Accounting Handbook* (New York: Barron's Educational Series, chapter 12, 1990).

R. Vinter and R. Kish, *Budgeting for Not-for-Profit Organizations* (New York: Free Press, 1984).

B. Weisbrod, "Rewarding Performance that is Hard to Measure: The Private Nonprofit Sector," *Science,* May 5, 1991.

CONCLUSION

Chapter **32**

Conclusion

Budgets are prepared not only for the company in its entirety but also for each of its major segments including sales territories, divisions, departments, responsibility centers within departments, and products. Budgets may be prepared for manufacturing, service, and nonprofit activities. A budget is historical in nature.

Budgets must take into account many factors to assure reliability including competition, industry conditions, economic conditions, political aspects including regulatory environment, marketing, management, product trends, and risk.

A budget is an extremely important tool in managing corporate affairs. Budgets specify plans and strategies. A sound budget mechanism not only directly affects corporate profitability but may indeed be the difference between success or failure.

Budgeting is essential for proper planning to adequately carry out business activities. It is like a "road map" to follow. An improperly prepared budget may lead to wrong decisions.

In preparing a budget, management must know where it is headed and its goals and objectives. The budget shows what is expected in financial terms in the future. Budgets establish priorities to be accomplished within the firm.

Each company has its own procedures of preparing, reviewing, and approving budgets. Budgets can be used within all areas of the company including management, marketing, manufacturing, personnel, accounting, finance, and distribution.

The budgeting process involves formulating objectives, evaluating resources, coordinating budget components, and approval. Budgets assist in planning, coordinating, directing, analyzing, and controlling.

Budgets allow for prediction, channels of communication, authority, responsibility, reliable and timely information, compatibility, and organizational support.

A budget shows resources and how they are to be used. Budgets assist in the allocation of resources including money, personnel and equipment, as well as in scheduling production.

Some business goals include sales and profit growth, maximization of return on investment, cost control, improvement in quality, and efficient production.

Budgets help keep expenditures within fund limitations. The budget is a guideline to action. It may be expressed in dollars, volume, hours, manpower, etc. The budget must be carefully designed and implemented. Sound strategies and policies must be formulated to accomplish goals.

A budget may cover any period of time. However, the longer the period a budget covers the less reliable it is and the more general. A short-term budget is more accurate and is provided in more detail. Typically, budgets are prepared yearly, quarterly, and monthly. The budget period varies based on corporate goals and the use of the budget in planning. The budget period is partly based on corporate sales, stability, manufacturing activity, and risk.

Besides showing numbers, the budget should present major assumptions upon which the numbers are based. These assumptions and estimates must be reasonable. Budgeting is a "what-if" analysis tool.

Budgets may be prepared for products and projects examining anticipated revenue and expenses to ascertain feasibility.

Long-term plans are broad and typically broken down into short-term plans. Long-term and short-term goals and objectives must be met.

The budget is a control device by which actual performance can be measured against the budget. Hence, budgeted figures have to be realistic—not too loose or too tight. The budget should be organized, systematic, and comprehensive to achieve the best results. The budget communicates to all members of the company what is expected of them. The budget should include all inter-related departments.

A budget should be based on previous experience plus a change in light of the current environment. A budget should be prepared for any practical area within the business.

A budget can provide "red flags" of looming problems. At the beginning of the period, the budget is a plan. At the end of the period, it is a control measure to aid management in seeing whether the plans have been met or not and the reasons. Budget revisions will need to be made to take into account new developments and current conditions. A short-term budget is more suitable for a business that rapidly changes.

There is always room for "management by exception" in the budgetary process. All those affected by a budget should have input into its preparation to assure full support.

Budgets are required if the business is to operate efficiently and effectively. Poor budgeting practice, which means poor allocation of business resources, can hurt profitability and in extreme cases result in corporate failure.

BUDGETING ESSENTIALS

The sales budget considers sales volume and selling price. Sales may be forecasted through the use of moving averages, time series, and regression. Sales may be target income sales or even breakeven sales. Market share may be estimated via Markov analysis.

Resource requirements must be determined to see if they are sufficient for manufacturing. Production must be planned and scheduled. Inventory policies must have adequate inventory balances to meet demand. Inventory management tries to reach the correct mixture between carrying costs and ordering costs for optimal ordering. Materials requirements planning attempts to have enough material on hand for manufacturing operations at a reasonable cost.

Besides production quantities, consideration must be given to product quality. Inventory planning requires that the economic order quantity be such as to minimize total inventory costs. Economic order quantity is the point where total carrying cost equals total ordering cost. A reorder point has to be set at which a specified inventory level requires a reorder of merchandise. A safety stock prevents against stockouts when reorders are made.

Just-in-time inventory, which can be applied to many industries, is when inventory is ordered and received just when it is needed for production. This lowers carrying cost.

Direct labor budgeting estimates what the company's manpower needs are at different parts of the year and for which processes. Budgeted direct labor cost considers direct labor hours and wage rates. Direct labor costs must be controlled.

Factory overhead budgets estimate the factory costs other than direct material and direct labor to manufacture goods. They can be prepared using the variable-fixed breakdown.

Flexible budgeting is used to provide flexibility in revenue and cost estimation. Budgeted costs are examined at different capacity levels. At idle capacity, fixed cost remains constant but variable costs change. The segregation of a semi-variable cost (part fixed and part variable) into fixed and variable elements may be determined through such methods as the high-low method and least squares. Flexible budgeting also allows for contingencies.

Operating expenses must be budgeted. These include selling and general administrative expenses. Research and development must be planned. Research and development should be allocated by program. Research and development efforts must be appraised as to success.

In budgeting capital expenditures, estimates must be made of facility and capacity expansion needs. The company's cash position also must be taken into account to see if sufficient funds are available. Capital budgeting requires selection of the best long-term investment alternative. The attractiveness of a capital investment may be determined by its return on investment, payback period (the number of years it takes to get your money back), present value, and internal rate of return (the discount rate earned on the proposal). Proposals can be ranked in priority order by comparing the present value of cash inflows to the present value of cash outflows. The ranking (profitability) index is used to rank mutually exclusive proposals. Inflation should be taken into account in making capital budgeting decisions. There should be a post-audit project review to see how the capital project is doing. Is it living up to its expectations? Variances in capital expenditures between budget and actual should be investigated.

Cash must be forecasted since a company needs appropriate cash balances. Software programs may be used to predict cash. Expectations must be made for cash receipts and cash payments. Cash may be forecasted by taking a percentage of sales and/or statistically. There are ways to improve cash flow through sound cash management.

BUDGET CONSIDERATIONS

Budgets consider staff number and quality, manufacturing conditions, pricing, capacity, resources, product line, raw material availability and cost, technological conditions, inventory balances and status, inventory and accounts receivable turnover rates, product or service obsolescence, accuracy of input data, market stability, industry conditions, cyclicality, and financing requirements.

The budget should be allocated among divisions, departments, cost objectives and programs. Alternatives may have to be specified in the budget to allow for flexibility.

Budgets may be used to motivate employees. All people affected by the budget should participate in its preparation. There should be complete coordination and interchange of information within all departments. Management and employee responsibilities in the budget should be carefully specified. A budget should be comprehendable by those who will be using it so that it will have practical benefit. There should be budget education to overcome any unfounded complaints and resistance to the budget.

Budgeted costs should be adjusted to allow for changes in production volume.

The timetable for the budget must be adhered to so everything proceeds according to schedule.

Budget revisions may be necessary because of mistakes, new information, feedback, or changes in corporate planning. Revisions are more prevalent in unstable industries.

A budget should be flexible and innovative and accommodate unexpected conditions. A budget should be reviewed and revised to take into account new developments. For example, unexpected occurrences and technological advances have a direct effect on present operations.

An arbitrary across-the-board cut is not wise. Each program or activity must be considered on its own.

DEPARTMENTAL BUDGETS

Budgets are needed in each department. For example, the sales department forecasts sales volume by product or service, as well as by the selling price. It will most likely budget revenue by sales territory and customer. It also estimates costs such as salaries, travel, and promotion and entertainment. The production department estimates future costs to produce the product or service and the cost per unit. The production manager may need to budget work during the manufacturing process so everything flows smoothly. The purchasing department budgets units and dollar purchases. A breakdown by supplier may exist. The stores department budgets the costs for holding inventory. Products may be broken down by category. The finance department estimates how much money will be received and where it will be spent.

TYPES OF BUDGETS

Forecasting is predicting the outcome of future events while budgeting is planning for a result. A good budget should provide constant feedback on how things are doing.

A master budget consists of sub-budgets tied together to summarize the planned activities of the business. The size and nature of a budget depends on the characteristics of the particular company.

Incremental budgeting examines the increase in the budget in dollars or percentage terms without taking into account the whole accumulated body of the budget.

Budgets include those for revenue, cost, profit, cash flow, working capital, production, purchases, capital expenditures, balance sheet, income statement, direct materials, direct labor, overhead, programs, selling expenses, general and administrative expenses, and research.

After sales are estimated, manufacturing costs and operating expenses are predicted. Budgeted figures may be made at expected, optimistic, or pessimistic amounts to allow for flexibility.

An *add-on budget* occurs when the prior years' budgets are reviewed and modified for new information such as inflation and staff changes. Money is added to the budget to meet new requirements.

A *supplemental budget* provides additional funding for something which was not included in the regular budget.

A *bracket budget* is a contingency plan in which costs are estimated at higher and lower amounts than the base figure. Sales are then budgeted to meet these levels. This budget might be advisable when downside risks exist and a significant decline in revenue is expected.

A *stretch budget* is an optimistic budget. It is usually used for sales projected on the high side. Operating managers may not be held accountable for stretch figures.

A *strategic budget* combines strategic planning and budgeting control. It is used when uncertainty and instability exists.

Activity-based budgeting is expected costs for specific activities.

A *target budget* is a plan that categorizes major expenditures and matches them to corporate goals. Significant dollar expenditures and special projects must be specially approved.

The company may "roll a budget" which is recurring budgeting for an additional period at the end of the current period. The new period is added to the remaining periods to form the new budget.

FORECASTS AND PROJECT BUDGETS

A project budget provides budgeted time and costs by projects. A project must be planned to accomplish it in the best possible way. A time schedule has to be prepared to make sure it is proceeding as expected. Cost control measures are needed to assure project profitability.

Zero-base budgeting starts from "scratch" and everything above a zero funding level must be justified. There are decision packages for projects showing the recommended way of doing something in terms of dollar cost and time. Alternative ways are also specified if upper management wants to select another path such as one that is cheaper or takes less time. A priority ranking is given to decision packages to see which ones pass the minimum funding level.

PLANNING

Budgets are an important part of the strategic planning process. Planning examines what should be done, how it should be done, when it should be done, and who should do it. Segments of the business should interface to aid in communication and cooperation. Potential problems should be considered and rectified.

PROFIT PLANNING

Profit planning and control is essential to business success. A profit plan is to project an attainable profit. The budget should set limits on certain expenditures. Amounts over those limits should be justified. Managers should be given credit when their costs are under budget.

VARIANCE ANALYSIS

A comparison should be made between budgeted revenue and costs to actual revenue and costs. The variance indicates areas of efficiency and inefficiency. Unfavorable variances are investigated as to cause and corrective action taken. Sales variances may be broken down into sales volume and selling price. Cost variances apply to the manufacturing costs of direct material, direct labor, and factory overhead. Variances interrelate so one affects another. For example, a favorable material price variance because of lower prices may be due to cheaper quality material resulting in an unfavorable material quantity variance and unfavorable labor quantity variance. The profit variance is due to the components of sales and costs. Ways must be discovered to improve profitability. Performance reports should be prepared to spot problem areas and to track progress.

CONTROL AND EVALUATION

When reprojections are made to an initial budget estimate, the manager should provide a full explanation as to the reasons. An example is when a high-cost planned capital addition is scrapped because of a sudden cash flow crisis or a recessionary environment.

Supplementary information may be included in budgets such as break-even analysis by product and department.

Budget slack must be minimized. It refers to underestimating revenue and overestimating expenses. Ways to correct inefficiencies must be provided.

The budget is a control mechanism for revenue, costs, and operations. Budget control may be over financial and nonfinancial activities.

A budget audit looks at the accuracy of budgeted figures. Costs have to be properly appraised.

FINANCIAL MODELS AND SOFTWARE

Mathematical models and computerized software greatly aid budget preparation and analysis.

Financial models are useful in budget preparation and planning. Some quantitative techniques useful in budget formulation and analysis include linear programming, regression analysis, what-if analysis, and goal programming. Multiple goals must be solved by the computer simultaneously. What-if scenarios and optimization models provide the best solutions. Model specification must consider all important factors. Financial modeling languages exist such as IFPS and SIMPLAN. Assumptions must be clearly stated and tested. Models may be linked to aid in planning.

A management information system (MIS) obtains all relevant data which must be taken into account in making a forecast. Decision support systems and expert systems imitate the human mind in making decisions after it has been programmed with a knowledge base. Graphics depict the budgeted numbers in a clear manner.

Program Evaluation and Review Technique (PERT) is the series of steps necessary to complete a long-term project.

In addition to modeling software, spreadsheet software is widely used for budget preparation and analysis. An example is Lotus 1-2-3™ which allows for what-if analysis. As one variable changes, the related variables also change. For example, a change in selling price will result in a change in profit.

MANUALS AND FORMS

The budget process is facilitated by using manuals and standardized forms. Tables and charts may be used to explain difficult combinations of numbers.

The budget manual lists the procedures and guidelines formulating and analyzing a budget. It clearly sets forth who is to do what and when. A timetable is provided.

OTHER ORGANIZATIONS

Budgeting for service businesses involve determining expected service capability. An example is how many seats are expected to be filled on an airplane.

Nonprofit organizations need budgets to formulate planning and control of activities. Expected revenue must be matched with appropriations. Revenue must be spent in accordance with regulations and laws.

Present Value and Future Value Tables

TABLE 1 Future Value of $1

Interest Rate

Number of Years	1%	2%	3%	4%	5%	6%	7%	8%	9%	10%	12%	14%	15%	16%	18%	20%	24%	28%	32%	36%
1	1.0100	1.0200	1.0300	1.0400	1.0500	1.0600	1.0700	1.0800	1.0900	1.1000	1.1200	1.1400	1.1500	1.1600	1.1800	1.2000	1.2400	1.2800	1.3200	1.3600
2	1.0201	1.0404	1.0609	1.0816	1.1025	1.1236	1.1449	1.1664	1.1881	1.2100	1.2544	1.2996	1.3225	1.3456	1.3924	1.4400	1.5376	1.6384	1.7424	1.8496
3	1.0303	1.0612	1.0927	1.1249	1.1576	1.1910	1.2250	1.2597	1.2950	1.3310	1.4049	1.4815	1.5209	1.5609	1.6430	1.7280	1.9066	2.0972	2.3000	2.5155
4	1.0406	1.0824	1.1255	1.1699	1.2155	1.2625	1.3108	1.3605	1.4116	1.4641	1.5735	1.6890	1.7490	1.8106	1.9388	2.0736	2.3642	2.6844	3.0360	3.4210
5	1.0510	1.1041	1.1593	1.2167	1.2763	1.3382	1.4026	1.4693	1.5386	1.6105	1.7623	1.9254	2.0114	2.1003	2.2878	2.4883	2.9316	3.4360	4.0075	4.6526
6	1.0615	1.1262	1.1941	1.2653	1.3401	1.4185	1.5007	1.5869	1.6771	1.7716	1.9738	2.1950	2.3131	2.4364	2.6996	2.9860	3.6352	4.3980	5.2899	6.3275
7	1.0721	1.1487	1.2299	1.3159	1.4071	1.5036	1.6058	1.7138	1.8280	1.9487	2.2107	2.5023	2.6600	2.8262	3.1855	3.5832	4.5077	5.6295	6.9826	8.6054
8	1.0829	1.1717	1.2668	1.3686	1.4775	1.5938	1.7182	1.8509	1.9926	2.1436	2.4760	2.8526	3.0590	3.2784	3.7589	4.2998	5.5895	7.2058	9.2170	11.703
9	1.0937	1.1951	1.3048	1.4233	1.5513	1.6895	1.8385	1.9990	2.1719	2.3579	2.7731	3.2519	3.5179	3.8030	4.4355	5.1598	6.9310	9.2234	12.166	15.916
10	1.1046	1.2190	1.3439	1.4802	1.6289	1.7908	1.9672	2.1589	2.3674	2.5937	3.1058	3.7072	4.0456	4.4114	5.2338	6.1917	8.5944	11.805	16.059	21.646
11	1.1157	1.2434	1.3842	1.5395	1.7103	1.8983	2.1049	2.3316	2.5804	2.8531	3.4785	4.2262	4.6524	5.1173	6.1759	7.4301	10.657	15.111	21.198	29.439
12	1.1268	1.2682	1.4258	1.6010	1.7959	2.0122	2.2522	2.5182	2.8127	3.1384	3.8960	4.8179	5.3502	5.9360	7.2876	8.9161	13.214	19.342	27.982	40.037
13	1.1381	1.2936	1.4685	1.6651	1.8856	2.1329	2.4098	2.7196	3.0658	3.4523	4.3635	5.4924	6.1528	6.8858	8.5994	10.699	16.386	24.748	36.937	54.451
14	1.1495	1.3195	1.5126	1.7317	1.9799	2.2609	2.5785	2.9372	3.3417	3.7975	4.8871	6.2613	7.0757	7.9875	10.147	12.839	20.319	31.691	48.756	74.053
15	1.1610	1.3459	1.5580	1.8009	2.0789	2.3966	2.7590	3.1722	3.6425	4.1772	5.4736	7.1379	8.1371	9.2655	11.973	15.407	25.195	40.564	64.359	100.71
16	1.1726	1.3728	1.6047	1.8730	2.1829	2.5404	2.9522	3.4259	3.9703	4.5950	6.1304	8.1372	9.3576	10.748	14.129	18.488	31.242	51.923	84.953	136.96
17	1.1834	1.4002	1.6528	1.9479	2.2920	2.6928	3.1588	3.7000	4.3276	5.0545	6.8660	9.2765	10.761	12.467	16.672	22.186	38.740	66.461	112.13	186.27
18	1.1961	1.4282	1.7024	2.0258	2.4066	2.8543	3.3799	3.9960	4.7171	5.5599	7.6900	10.575	12.375	14.462	19.673	26.623	48.038	85.070	148.02	253.33
19	1.2081	1.4568	1.7535	2.1068	2.5270	3.0256	3.6165	4.3157	5.1417	6.1159	8.6129	12.055	14.231	16.776	23.214	31.948	59.567	108.89	195.39	344.53
20	1.2202	1.4859	1.8061	2.1911	2.6533	3.2071	3.8697	4.6610	5.6044	6.7275	9.6463	13.743	16.366	19.460	27.393	38.337	73.864	139.37	257.91	468.57
21	1.2324	1.5157	1.8603	2.2788	2.7860	3.3996	4.1406	5.0338	6.1088	7.4002	10.803	15.667	18.821	22.574	32.323	46.005	91.591	178.40	340.44	637.26
22	1.2447	1.5460	1.9161	2.3699	2.9253	3.6035	4.4304	5.4365	6.6586	8.1403	12.100	17.861	21.644	26.186	38.142	55.206	113.57	228.35	449.39	866.67
23	1.2572	1.5769	1.9736	2.4647	3.0715	3.8197	4.7405	5.8715	7.2579	8.9543	13.552	20.361	24.891	30.376	45.007	66.247	140.83	292.30	593.19	1178.6
24	1.2697	1.6084	2.0328	2.5633	3.2251	4.0489	5.0724	6.3412	7.9111	9.8497	15.178	23.212	29.625	35.236	53.108	79.496	174.63	394.14	783.02	1602.9
25	1.2824	1.6406	2.0938	2.6658	3.3864	4.2919	5.2474	6.8485	8.6231	10.834	17.000	26.461	32.918	40.874	62.668	95.396	216.54	478.90	1033.5	2180.0
26	1.2953	1.6734	2.1566	2.7725	3.5557	4.5497	5.8074	7.3964	9.3992	11.918	19.040	30.166	37.856	47.414	73.948	114.47	268.51	612.99	1364.3	2964.9
27	1.3082	1.7069	2.2213	2.8834	3.7335	4.8223	6.2139	7.9881	10.245	13.110	21.324	34.389	43.535	55.000	87.259	137.37	332.95	784.63	1800.9	4032.2
28	1.3213	1.7410	2.2879	2.99897	3.9201	5.1117	6.6488	8.6271	11.167	14.421	23.883	39.204	50.065	63.800	102.96	164.84	412.86	1004.3	2377.2	5483.8
29	1.3345	1.7758	2.3566	3.1187	4.1161	5.4184	7.1143	9.3173	12.172	15.863	26.749	44.693	57.575	74.008	121.50	197.81	511.95	1285.5	3137.9	7458.0
30	1.3478	1.8114	2.4273	3.2434	4.3219	5.7435	7.6123	10.062	13.267	17.449	29.959	50.950	66.211	85.849	143.37	237.37	634.81	1645.5	4142.0	10143.
40	1.4889	2.2080	3.2620	4.8010	7.0400	10.285	14.974	21.724	31.409	45.259	93.050	188.88	267.86	378.72	750.37	1469.7	5455.9	19426.	66520	•
50	1.6446	2.6916	4.3839	7.1067	11.467	18.420	29.457	46.901	74.357	117.39	289.00	700.23	1083.6	1670.7	3927.3	9100.4	46890.	•	•	•
60	1.8167	3.2810	5.8916	10.519	18.679	32.987	57.946	101.25	176.03	304.48	897.59	2595.9	4383.9	7370.1	20555	56347	•	•	•	•

TABLE 2 Future Value of an Annuity of $1

Interest Rate

Number of Years	1%	2%	3%	4%	5%	6%	7%	8%	9%	10%	12%	14%	15%	16%	18%	20%	24%	28%	32%	36%
1	1.0000	1.0000	1.0000	1.0000	1.0000	1.0000	1.0000	1.0000	1.0000	1.0000	1.0000	1.0000	1.0000	1.0000	1.0000	1.0000	1.0000	1.0000	1.0000	1.0000
2	2.0100	2.0200	2.0300	2.0400	2.0500	2.0600	2.0700	2.0800	2.0900	2.1000	2.1200	2.1400	2.1500	2.1600	2.1800	2.2000	2.2400	2.2800	2.3200	2.3600
3	3.0301	3.0604	3.0909	3.1216	3.1525	3.1836	3.2149	3.2464	3.2781	3.3100	3.3744	3.4396	3.4725	3.5056	3.5724	3.6400	3.7776	3.9184	4.0624	4.2096
4	4.0604	4.1216	4.1836	4.2465	4.3101	4.3746	4.4399	4.5061	4.5731	4.6410	4.7793	4.9211	4.9934	5.0665	5.2154	5.3680	5.6842	6.0156	6.3624	6.7251
5	5.1010	5.2040	5.3091	5.4163	5.5256	5.6371	5.7507	5.8666	5.9847	6.1051	6.3528	6.6101	6.7424	6.8771	7.1542	7.4416	8.0484	8.6999	9.3983	10.146
6	6.1520	6.3081	6.4684	6.6330	6.8019	6.9753	7.1533	7.3359	7.5233	7.7156	8.1152	8.5355	8.7537	8.9775	9.4420	9.9299	10.980	12.135	13.405	14.798
7	7.2135	7.4343	7.6625	7.8983	8.1420	8.3938	8.6540	8.9228	9.2004	9.4872	10.089	10.730	11.066	11.413	12.141	12.915	14.615	16.533	18.695	21.126
8	8.2857	8.5830	8.8923	9.2142	9.5491	9.8975	10.259	10.636	11.028	11.435	12.299	13.232	13.726	14.240	15.327	16.499	19.122	22.163	25.678	29.731
9	9.3685	9.7546	10.159	10.582	11.026	11.491	11.978	12.487	13.021	13.579	14.775	16.085	16.785	17.518	19.085	20.798	24.712	29.369	34.895	41.435
10	10.462	10.949	11.463	12.006	12.577	13.180	13.816	14.486	15.192	15.937	17.548	19.337	20.303	21.321	23.521	25.958	31.643	38.592	47.061	57.351
11	11.566	12.168	12.807	13.486	14.206	14.971	15.783	16.645	17.560	18.531	20.654	23.044	24.349	25.732	28.755	32.150	40.237	50.398	63.121	78.998
12	12.682	13.412	14.192	15.025	15.917	16.869	17.888	18.977	20.140	21.384	24.133	27.270	29.001	30.850	34.931	39.580	50.894	65.510	84.320	108.43
13	13.809	14.680	15.617	16.626	17.713	18.882	20.140	21.495	22.953	24.522	28.029	32.088	34.351	36.786	42.218	48.496	64.109	84.852	112.30	148.47
14	14.947	15.973	17.086	18.291	19.598	21.015	22.550	24.214	26.019	27.975	32.392	37.581	40.504	43.672	50.818	59.195	80.496	109.61	149.23	202.92
15	16.096	17.293	18.598	20.023	21.578	23.276	25.129	27.152	29.360	31.772	37.279	43.842	47.580	51.659	60.965	72.035	100.81	141.30	197.99	276.97
16	17.257	18.639	20.156	21.824	23.657	25.672	27.888	30.324	33.003	35.949	42.753	50.980	55.717	60.925	72.939	87.442	126.01	181.86	262.35	377.69
17	18.430	20.012	21.761	23.697	25.840	28.212	30.840	33.750	36.973	40.544	48.883	59.117	65.075	71.673	87.068	105.93	157.25	233.79	347.30	514.66
18	19.614	21.412	23.414	25.645	28.132	30.905	33.99	37.450	41.301	45.599	55.749	68.394	75.836	84.140	103.74	128.11	195.99	300.25	459.44	700.93
19	20.810	22.840	25.116	27.671	30.539	33.760	37.379	41.446	46.018	51.159	63.439	78.969	88.211	98.603	123.41	154.74	244.03	385.32	607.47	954.27
20	22.019	24.297	26.870	29.778	33.066	36.785	40.995	45.762	51.160	57.275	72.052	91.024	102.44	115.37	146.62	186.68	303.60	494.21	802.86	1298.8
21	23.239	25.783	28.676	31.969	35.719	39.992	44.865	50.442	56.764	64.002	81.698	104.76	118.81	134.84	174.02	225.02	377.46	633.59	1060.7	1767.3
22	24.471	27.299	30.536	34.248	38.505	43.392	49.005	55.456	62.873	71.402	92.502	120.43	137.63	157.41	206.34	271.03	469.05	811.99	1401.2	2404.6
23	25.716	28.845	32.452	36.617	41.430	46.995	53.436	60.893	69.531	79.543	104.60	138.29	159.27	183.60	244.48	326.23	582.62	1040.3	1850.6	3271.3
24	26.973	30.421	34.426	39.082	44.502	50.815	58.176	66.764	76.789	88.497	118.15	158.65	184.16	213.97	289.49	392.48	723.46	1332.6	2443.8	4449.9
25	28.243	32.030	36.459	41.645	47.727	54.864	63.249	73.105	84.700	98.347	133.33	181.87	212.79	249.21	342.60	471.98	898.09	1706.8	3226.8	6052.9
26	29.525	33.670	38.553	44.311	51.113	59.156	68.676	79.954	93.323	109.18	150.33	208.33	245.71	290.08	405.27	567.37	1114.6	2185.7	4260.4	8233.0
27	30.820	35.344	40.709	47.084	54.669	63.705	74.483	87.350	102.72	121.09	169.37	238.49	283.56	337.50	479.22	681.85	1383.1	2798.7	5624.7	11197.9
28	32.129	37.051	42.930	49.967	58.402	68.528	80.697	95.338	112.96	134.20	190.69	272.88	327.10	392.50	566.48	819.22	1716.0	3583.3	7425.6	15230.2
29	32.450	38.792	45.218	52.966	62.322	73.689	87.346	103.96	124.13	148.63	214.58	312.09	377.16	456.30	669.44	984.06	2128.9	4587.6	9802.9	20714.1
30	34.784	40.568	47.576	56.084	66.438	79.058	94.460	113.28	136.30	164.49	241.33	356.78	434.74	530.31	790.94	1181.8	2640.9	5873.2	12940	28172.2
40	48.886	60.402	75.401	95.025	120.79	154.76	199.63	259.05	337.88	442.59	767.09	1342.0	1779.0	2360.7	4163.2	7343.8	22728	63977	•	•
50	64.473	84.579	112.79	152.66	209.34	290.33	406.52	573.76	815.08	1163.9	2400.0	4994.5	7217.7	10435	21813	45497	•	•	•	•
60	81.669	114.05	163.05	237.90	353.58	533.12	813.52	1253.2	1944.7	3034.8	7471.6	18535	29219	46057	•	•	•	•	•	•

TABLE 3 Present Value of $1

										Interest Rate										
Number of Years	1%	2%	3%	4%	5%	6%	7%	8%	9%	10%	12%	14%	15%	16%	18%	20%	24%	28%	32%	36%
1	0.9901	0.9804	0.9709	0.9615	0.9524	0.9434	0.9346	0.9259	0.9174	0.9091	0.8929	0.8772	0.8696	0.8621	0.8475	0.8333	0.8065	0.7813	0.7576	0.7353
2	0.9803	0.9612	0.9426	0.9246	0.9070	0.8900	0.8734	0.8573	0.8417	0.8264	0.7972	0.7695	0.7561	0.7432	0.7182	0.6944	0.6504	0.6104	0.5739	0.5407
3	0.9706	0.9423	0.9151	0.8890	0.8638	0.8396	0.8163	0.7938	0.7722	0.7513	0.7118	0.6750	0.6575	0.6407	0.6086	0.5787	0.5245	0.4768	0.4348	0.3975
4	0.9610	0.9238	0.8885	0.8548	0.8227	0.7921	0.7629	0.7350	0.7084	0.6830	0.6355	0.5921	0.5718	0.5523	0.5158	0.4823	0.4230	0.3725	0.3294	0.2923
5	0.9515	0.9057	0.8626	0.8219	0.7835	0.7473	0.7130	0.6806	0.6499	0.6209	0.5674	0.5194	0.4972	0.4761	0.4371	0.4019	0.3411	0.2910	0.2495	0.2149
6	0.9420	0.8880	0.8375	0.7903	0.7462	0.7050	0.6663	0.6302	0.5963	0.5645	0.5066	0.4556	0.4323	0.4104	0.3704	0.3349	0.2751	0.2274	0.1890	0.1580
7	0.9327	0.8706	0.8131	0.7599	0.7107	0.6651	0.6227	0.5835	0.5470	0.5132	0.4523	0.3996	0.3759	0.3538	0.3139	0.2791	0.2218	0.1776	0.1432	0.1162
8	0.9235	0.8535	0.7894	0.7307	0.6768	0.6274	0.5820	0.5403	0.5019	0.4665	0.4039	0.3506	0.3269	0.3050	0.2660	0.2326	0.1789	0.1388	0.1085	0.0854
9	0.9143	0.8368	0.7664	0.7026	0.6446	0.5919	0.5439	0.5002	0.4604	0.4241	0.3606	0.3075	0.2843	0.2630	0.2255	0.1938	0.1443	0.1084	0.0822	0.0628
10	0.9053	0.8203	0.7441	0.6756	0.6139	0.5584	0.5083	0.4632	0.4224	0.3855	0.3220	0.2697	0.2472	0.2267	0.1911	0.1615	0.1164	0.0847	0.0623	0.0462
11	0.8963	0.8043	0.7224	0.6496	0.5847	0.5268	0.4751	0.4289	0.3875	0.3505	0.2875	0.2366	0.2149	0.1954	0.1619	0.1346	0.0938	0.0662	0.0472	0.0340
12	0.8874	0.7885	0.7014	0.6246	0.5568	0.4970	0.4440	0.3971	0.3555	0.3186	0.2567	0.2076	0.1869	0.1685	0.1372	0.1122	0.0757	0.0517	0.0357	0.0250
13	0.8787	0.7730	0.6810	0.6006	0.5303	0.4688	0.4150	0.3677	0.3262	0.2897	0.2292	0.1821	0.1625	0.1452	0.1163	0.0935	0.0610	0.0404	0.0271	0.0184
14	0.8700	0.7579	0.6611	0.5775	0.5051	0.4423	0.3878	0.3405	0.2992	0.2633	0.2046	0.1597	0.1413	0.1252	0.0985	0.0779	0.0492	0.0316	0.0205	0.0135
15	0.8613	0.7430	0.6419	0.5553	0.4810	0.4173	0.3624	0.3152	0.2745	0.2394	0.1827	0.1401	0.1229	0.1079	0.0835	0.0649	0.0397	0.0247	0.0155	0.0099
16	0.8528	0.7284	0.6232	0.5339	0.4581	0.3936	0.3387	0.2919	0.2519	0.2176	0.1631	0.1229	0.1069	0.0930	0.0708	0.0541	0.0320	0.0193	0.0118	0.0073
17	0.8444	0.7142	0.6050	0.5134	0.4363	0.3714	0.3166	0.2703	0.2311	0.1978	0.1456	0.1078	0.0929	0.0802	0.0600	0.0451	0.0258	0.0150	0.0089	0.0054
18	0.8360	0.7002	0.5874	0.4936	0.4155	0.3503	0.2959	0.2502	0.2120	0.1799	0.1300	0.0946	0.0808	0.0691	0.0508	0.0376	0.0208	0.0118	0.0068	0.0038
19	0.8277	0.6864	0.5703	0.4746	0.3957	0.3305	0.2765	0.2317	0.1945	0.1635	0.1161	0.0829	0.0703	0.0596	0.0431	0.0313	0.0168	0.0092	0.0051	0.0029
20	0.8195	0.6730	0.5537	0.4564	0.3769	0.3118	0.2584	0.2145	0.1784	0.1486	0.1037	0.0728	0.0611	0.0514	0.0365	0.0261	0.0135	0.0072	0.0039	0.0021
25	0.7798	0.6095	0.4776	0.3751	0.2953	0.2330	0.1842	0.1460	0.1160	0.0923	0.0588	0.0378	0.0304	0.0245	0.0160	0.0105	0.0046	0.0021	0.0010	0.0005
30	0.7419	0.5521	0.4120	0.3083	0.2314	0.1741	0.1314	0.0994	0.0754	0.0573	0.0334	0.0196	0.0151	0.0116	0.0070	0.0042	0.0016	0.0006	0.0002	0.0001
40	0.6717	0.4529	0.3066	0.2083	0.1420	0.0972	0.0668	0.0460	0.0318	0.0221	0.0107	0.0053	0.0037	0.0026	0.0013	0.0007	0.0002	0.0001	·	·
50	0.6080	0.3715	0.2281	0.1407	0.0872	0.0543	0.0339	0.0213	0.0132	0.0085	0.0035	0.0014	0.0009	0.0006	0.0003	0.0001	·	·	·	·
60	0.5504	0.3048	0.1697	0.0951	0.0535	0.0303	0.0173	0.0099	0.0057	0.0033	0.0011	0.0004	0.0002	0.0001	·	·	·	·	·	·

TABLE 4 Present Value of an Annuity of $1

| | | | | | | | | | | | | Interest Rate | | | | | | | | |
Number of Years	1%	2%	3%	4%	5%	6%	7%	8%	9%	10%	12%	14%	15%	16%	18%	20%	24%	28%	32%
1	0.9901	0.9804	0.9709	0.9615	0.9524	0.9434	0.9346	0.9259	0.9174	0.9091	0.8929	0.8772	0.8696	0.8621	0.8475	0.8333	0.8065	0.7813	0.7576
2	1.9704	1.9415	1.9135	1.8861	1.8594	1.8334	1.8080	1.7833	1.7591	1.7355	1.6901	1.6467	1.6257	1.6052	1.5656	1.5278	1.4568	1.3916	1.3315
3	2.9410	2.8839	2.8286	2.7751	2.7232	2.6730	2.6243	2.5771	2.5313	2.4869	2.4018	2.3216	2.2832	2.2459	2.1743	2.1065	1.9813	1.8684	1.7663
4	3.9020	3.8077	3.7171	3.6299	3.5460	3.4651	3.3872	3.3121	3.2397	3.1699	3.0373	2.9137	2.8550	2.7982	2.6901	2.5887	2.4043	2.2410	2.0957
5	4.8534	4.7135	4.5797	4.4518	4.3295	4.2124	4.1002	3.9927	3.8897	3.7908	3.6048	3.4331	3.3522	3.2743	3.1272	2.9906	2.7454	2.5320	2.3452
6	5.7955	5.6014	5.4172	5.2421	5.0757	4.9173	4.7665	4.6229	4.4859	4.3553	4.1114	3.8887	3.7845	3.6847	3.4976	3.3255	3.0205	2.7594	2.5342
7	6.7282	6.4720	6.2303	6.0021	5.7864	5.5824	5.3893	5.2064	5.0330	4.8684	4.5638	4.2883	4.1604	4.0386	3.8115	3.6046	3.2423	2.9370	2.6775
8	7.6517	7.3255	7.0197	6.7327	6.4632	6.2098	5.9713	5.7466	5.5348	5.3349	4.9676	4.6389	4.4873	4.3436	4.0776	3.8372	3.4212	3.0758	2.7860
9	8.5660	8.1622	7.7861	7.4353	7.1078	6.8017	6.5152	6.2469	5.9952	5.7590	5.3282	4.9464	4.7716	4.6065	4.3030	4.0310	3.5655	3.1842	2.8681
10	9.4713	8.9826	8.5302	8.1109	7.7217	7.3601	7.0236	6.7101	6.4177	6.1446	5.6502	5.2161	5.0188	4.8332	4.4941	4.1925	3.6819	3.2689	2.9304
11	10.3676	9.7858	9.2526	8.7605	8.3064	7.8869	7.4987	7.1390	6.8052	6.4951	5.9377	5.4527	5.2337	5.0286	4.6560	4.3271	3.7757	3.3351	2.9776
12	11.2551	10.5753	9.9540	9.3851	8.8633	8.3838	7.9427	7.5361	7.1607	6.8137	6.1944	5.6603	5.4206	5.1971	4.7932	4.4392	3.8514	3.3868	3.0133
13	12.1337	11.3484	10.6350	9.9856	9.3936	8.8527	8.3577	7.9038	7.4889	7.1034	6.4235	5.8424	5.5831	5.3423	4.9095	4.5327	3.9124	3.4272	3.0404
14	13.0037	12.1062	11.2961	10.5631	9.8986	9.2950	8.7455	8.2442	7.7862	7.3667	6.6282	6.0021	5.7245	5.4675	5.0081	4.6106	3.9616	3.4587	3.0609
15	13.8651	12.8493	11.9379	11.1184	10.3797	9.7122	9.1079	8.5595	8.0607	7.6061	6.8109	6.1422	5.8474	5.5755	5.0916	4.6755	4.0013	3.4834	3.0764
16	14.7179	13.5777	12.5611	11.6523	10.8378	10.1059	9.4466	8.8514	8.3126	7.8237	6.9740	6.2651	5.9542	5.6685	5.1724	4.7296	4.0333	3.5026	3.0882
17	15.5623	14.2919	13.1661	12.1657	11.2741	10.4773	9.7632	9.1216	8.5436	8.0216	7.1196	6.3729	6.0472	5.7487	5.2223	4.7746	4.0591	3.5177	3.0971
18	16.3983	14.9920	13.7535	12.6593	11.6896	10.8276	10.0591	9.3719	8.7556	8.2014	7.2497	6.4674	6.1280	5.8178	5.2732	4.8122	4.0799	3.5294	3.1039
19	17.2260	15.6785	14.3238	13.1339	12.0853	11.1581	10.3356	9.6036	8.9501	8.3649	7.3658	6.5504	6.1982	5.8775	5.3162	4.8435	4.0967	3.5386	3.1090
20	18.0456	16.3514	14.8775	13.5903	12.4622	11.4699	10.5940	9.8181	9.1285	8.5436	7.4694	6.6231	6.2593	5.9288	5.3527	4.8696	4.1103	3.5458	3.1129
25	22.0232	19.5235	17.4131	15.6221	14.0939	12.7834	11.6536	10.6748	9.8226	9.0770	7.8431	6.8729	6.4641	6.0971	5.4669	4.9476	4.1474	3.5640	3.1220
30	25.8077	22.3965	19.6004	17.2920	15.3725	13.7648	12.4090	11.2578	10.2737	9.4269	8.0552	7.0072	6.5660	6.1772	5.5168	4.9789	4.1601	3.5693	3.1242
40	32.8347	27.3555	23.1148	19.7928	17.1591	15.0463	13.3317	11.9246	10.7574	9.7791	8.2438	7.1050	6.6418	6.2335	5.5482	4.9966	4.1659	3.5712	3.1250
50	39.1961	31.4236	25.7298	21.4822	18.2559	15.7619	13.8007	12.2335	10.9617	9.9148	8.3045	7.1327	6.6605	6.2463	5.5541	4.9995	4.1666	3.5714	3.1250
60	44.9550	34.7609	27.8656	22.6235	18.9293	16.1614	14.0392	12.3766	11.0480	9.9672	8.3240	7.1401	6.6651	6.2492	5.5553	4.9999	4.1667	3.5714	3.1250

Statistical Tables

TABLE 1 Standard Normal Distribution Table

Areas Under the Normal Curve

Z	0	1	2	3	4	5	6	7	8	9
.0	.5000	.5040	.5080	.5120	.5160	.5199	.5239	.5279	.5319	.5359
.1	.5398	.5438	.5478	.5517	.5557	.5596	.5636	.5675	.5714	.5753
.2	.5793	.5832	.5871	.5910	.5948	.5987	.6026	.6064	.6103	.6141
.3	.6179	.6217	.6255	.6293	.6331	.6368	.6406	.6443	.6480	.6517
.4	.6554	.6591	.6628	.6664	.6700	.6736	.6772	.6808	.6844	.6879
.5	.6915	.6950	.6985	.7019	.7054	.7088	.7123	.7157	.7190	.7224
.6	.7257	.7291	.7324	.7357	.7389	.7422	.7454	.7486	.7517	.7549
.7	.7580	.7611	.7642	.7673	.7703	.7734	.7764	.7794	.7823	.7852
.8	.7881	.7910	.7939	.7967	.7995	.8023	.8051	.8078	.8106	.8133
.9	.8159	.8186	.8212	.8238	.8264	.8289	.8315	.8340	.8365	.8389
1.0	.8413	.8438	.8461	.8485	.8508	.8531	.8554	.8577	.8599	.8621
1.1	.8643	.8665	.8686	.8708	.8729	.8749	.8770	.8790	.8810	.8830
1.2	.8849	.8869	.8888	.8907	.8925	.8944	.8962	.8980	.8997	.9015
1.3	.9032	.9049	.9066	.9082	.9099	.9115	.9131	.9147	.9162	.9177
1.4	.9192	.9207	.9222	.9236	.9251	.9265	.9278	.9292	.9306	.9319
1.5	.9332	.9345	.9357	.9370	.9382	.9394	.9406	.9418	.9430	.9441
1.6	.9452	.9463	.9474	.9484	.9495	.9505	.9515	.9525	.9535	.9545
1.7	.9554	.9564	.9573	.9582	.9591	.9599	.9608	.9616	.9625	.9633
1.8	.9641	.9648	.9656	.9664	.9671	.9678	.9686	.9693	.9700	.9706
1.9	.9713	.9719	.9726	.9732	.9738	.9744	.9750	.9756	.9762	.9767
2.0	.9772	.9778	.9783	.9788	.9793	.9798	.9803	.9808	.9812	.9817
2.1	.9821	.9826	.9830	.9834	.9838	.9842	.9846	.9850	.9854	.9857
2.2	.9861	.9864	.9868	.9871	.9874	.9878	.9881	.9884	.9887	.9890
2.3	.9893	.9896	.9898	.9901	.9904	.9906	.9909	.9911	.9913	.9916
2.4	.9918	.9920	.9922	.9925	.9927	.9929	.9931	.9932	.9934	.9936
2.5	.9938	.9940	.9941	.9943	.9945	.9946	.9948	.9949	.9951	.9952
2.6	.9953	.9955	.9956	.9957	.9959	.9960	.9961	.9962	.9963	.9964
2.7	.9965	.9966	.9967	.9968	.9969	.9970	.9971	.9972	.9973	.9974
2.8	.9974	.9975	.9976	.9977	.9977	.9978	.9979	.9979	.9980	.9981
2.9	.9981	.9982	.9982	.9983	.9984	.9984	.9985	.9985	.9986	.9986
3.	.9987	.9990	.9993	.9995	.9997	.9998	.9998	.9999	.9999	1.0000

TABLE 2 Distribution Table
Values of t

d.f.	t0.100	t0.050	t0.025	t0.010	t0.005	d.f.
1	3.078	6.314	12.706	31.821	63.657	1
2	1.886	2.920	4.303	6.965	9.925	2
3	1.638	2.353	3.182	4.541	5.841	3
4	1.533	2.132	2.776	3.747	4.604	4
5	1.476	2.015	2.571	3.365	4.032	5
6	1.440	1.943	2.447	3.143	3.707	6
7	1.415	1.895	2.365	2.998	3.499	7
8	1.397	1.860	2.306	2.896	3.355	8
9	1.383	1.833	2.262	2.821	3.250	9
10	1.372	1.812	2.228	2.764	3.169	10
11	1.363	1.796	2.201	2.718	3.106	11
12	1.356	1.782	2.179	2.681	3.055	12
13	1.350	1.771	2.160	2.650	3.012	13
14	1.345	1.761	2.145	2.624	2.977	14
15	1.341	1.753	2.131	2.602	2.947	15
16	1.337	1.746	2.120	2.583	2.921	16
17	1.333	1.740	2.110	2.567	2.898	17
18	1.330	1.734	2.101	2.552	2.878	18
19	1.328	1.729	2.093	2.539	2.861	19
20	1.325	1.725	2.086	2.528	2.845	20
21	1.323	1.721	2.080	2.518	2.831	21
22	1.321	1.717	2.074	2.508	2.819	22
23	1.319	1.714	2.069	2.500	2.807	23
24	1.318	1.711	2.064	2.492	2.797	24
25	1.316	1.708	2.060	2.485	2.787	25
26	1.315	1.706	2.056	2.479	2.779	26
27	1.314	1.703	2.052	2.473	2.771	27
28	1.313	1.701	2.048	2.467	2.763	28
29	1.311	1.699	2.045	2.462	2.756	29
Inf.	1.282	1.645	1.960	2.326	2.576	Inf.

The t-value describes the sampling distribution of a deviation from a population value divided by the standard error.

Degrees of freedom (d.f.) are in the first column. The probabilities indicated as subvalues of t in the heading refer to the sum of a one-tailed area under the curve that lies outside the point t.

For example, in the distribution of the means of samples of size $n = 10$, d.f. $= n - 2 = 8$; then 0.025 of the area under the curve falls in one tail outside the interval $t \pm 2.306$.

Number of	K = 1	K = 2	K = 3	K = 4	K = 5

EXHIBIT 3 Values for *F* for *F* Distributions with 0.05 of the Area in the Right Tail

Example: For a test at a significance level of 0.05 where there are 15 degrees of freedom for the numerator and 6 degrees of freedom for the denominator, the appropriate *F* value is found by looking under the 15 degrees of freedom column and proceeding down to the 6 degrees of freedom row; there one finds the appropriate *F* value to be 3.94.

0.05 of area

3.94

Degrees of Freedom for Numerator

d.f. for denom- inator	1	2	3	4	5	6	7	8	9	10	12	15	20	24	30	40	60	120	=
1	161	200	216	225	230	234	237	239	241	242	244	246	248	249	250	251	252	253	254
2	18.5	19.0	19.2	19.2	19.3	19.3	19.4	19.4	19.4	19.4	19.4	19.4	19.4	19.5	19.5	19.5	19.5	19.5	19.5
3	10.1	9.55	9.28	9.12	9.01	8.94	8.89	8.85	8.81	8.79	8.74	8.70	8.66	8.64	8.62	8.59	8.57	8.55	8.53
4	7.71	6.94	6.59	6.39	6.26	6.16	6.09	6.04	6.00	5.96	5.91	5.86	5.80	5.77	5.75	5.72	5.69	5.66	5.63
5	6.61	5.79	5.41	5.19	5.05	4.95	4.88	4.82	4.77	4.74	4.68	4.62	4.56	4.53	4.50	4.46	4.43	4.40	4.37
6	5.99	5.14	4.76	4.53	4.39	4.28	4.21	4.15	4.10	4.06	4.00	3.94	3.87	3.84	3.81	3.77	3.74	3.70	3.67
7	5.59	4.74	4.35	4.12	3.97	3.87	3.79	3.73	3.68	3.64	3.57	3.51	3.44	3.41	3.38	3.34	3.30	3.27	3.23
8	5.32	4.46	4.07	3.84	3.69	3.58	3.50	3.44	3.39	3.35	3.28	3.22	3.15	3.12	3.08	3.04	3.01	2.97	2.93
9	5.12	4.26	3.86	3.63	3.48	3.37	3.29	3.23	3.18	3.14	3.07	3.01	2.94	2.90	2.86	2.83	2.79	2.75	2.71
10	4.96	4.10	3.71	3.48	3.33	3.22	3.14	3.07	3.02	2.98	2.91	2.85	2.77	2.74	2.70	2.66	2.62	2.58	2.54
11	4.84	3.98	3.59	3.36	3.20	3.09	3.01	2.95	2.90	2.85	2.79	2.72	2.65	2.61	2.57	2.53	2.49	2.45	2.40
12	4.75	3.89	3.49	3.26	3.11	3.00	2.91	2.85	2.80	2.75	2.69	2.62	2.54	2.51	2.47	2.43	2.38	2.34	2.30
13	4.67	3.81	3.41	3.18	3.03	2.92	2.83	2.77	2.71	2.67	2.60	2.53	2.46	2.42	2.38	2.34	2.30	2.25	2.21
14	4.60	3.74	3.34	3.11	2.96	2.85	2.76	2.70	2.65	2.60	2.53	2.46	2.39	2.35	2.31	2.27	2.22	2.18	2.13
15	4.54	3.68	3.29	3.06	2.90	2.79	2.71	2.64	2.59	2.54	2.48	2.40	2.33	2.29	2.25	2.20	2.16	2.11	2.07
16	4.49	3.63	3.24	3.01	2.85	2.74	2.66	2.59	2.54	2.49	2.42	2.35	2.28	2.24	2.19	2.15	2.11	2.06	2.01
17	4.45	3.59	3.20	2.96	2.81	2.70	2.61	2.55	2.49	2.45	2.38	2.31	2.23	2.19	2.15	2.10	2.06	2.01	1.96
18	4.41	3.55	3.16	2.93	2.77	2.66	2.58	2.51	2.46	2.41	2.34	2.27	2.19	2.15	2.11	2.06	2.02	1.97	1.92
19	4.38	3.52	3.13	2.90	2.74	2.63	2.54	2.48	2.42	2.38	2.31	2.23	2.16	2.11	2.07	2.03	1.98	1.93	1.88
20	4.35	3.49	3.10	2.87	2.71	2.60	2.51	2.45	2.39	2.35	2.28	2.20	2.12	2.08	2.04	1.99	1.95	1.90	1.84
21	4.32	3.47	3.07	2.84	2.68	2.57	2.49	2.42	2.37	2.32	2.25	2.18	2.10	2.05	2.01	1.96	1.92	1.87	1.81
22	4.30	3.44	3.05	2.82	2.66	2.55	2.46	2.40	2.34	2.30	2.23	2.15	2.07	2.03	1.98	1.94	1.89	1.84	1.78
23	4.28	3.42	3.03	2.80	2.64	2.53	2.44	2.37	2.32	2.27	2.20	2.13	2.05	2.01	1.96	1.91	1.86	1.81	1.76
24	4.26	3.40	3.01	2.78	2.62	2.51	2.42	2.36	2.30	2.25	2.18	2.11	2.03	1.98	1.94	1.89	1.84	1.79	1.73
25	4.24	3.39	2.99	2.76	2.60	2.49	2.40	2.34	2.28	2.24	2.16	2.09	2.01	1.96	1.92	1.87	1.82	1.77	1.71
30	4.17	3.32	2.92	2.69	2.53	2.42	2.33	2.27	2.21	2.16	2.09	2.01	1.93	1.89	1.84	1.79	1.74	1.68	1.62
40	4.08	3.23	2.84	2.61	2.45	2.34	2.25	2.18	2.12	2.08	2.00	1.92	1.84	1.79	1.74	1.69	1.64	1.58	1.51
60	4.00	3.15	2.76	2.53	2.37	2.25	2.17	2.10	2.04	1.99	1.92	1.84	1.75	1.70	1.65	1.59	1.53	1.47	1.39
120	3.92	3.07	2.68	2.45	2.29	2.18	2.09	2.02	1.96	1.91	1.83	1.75	1.66	1.61	1.55	1.50	1.43	1.35	1.25
=	3.84	3.00	2.60	2.37	2.21	2.10	2.01	1.94	1.88	1.83	1.75	1.67	1.57	1.52	1.46	1.39	1.32	1.22	1.00

EXHIBIT 3 (Continued) Values of F for F Distributions with 0.01 of the Area in the Right Tail

Example: For a test at a significance level of 0.01 where there are 7 degrees of freedom for the numerator and 5 degrees of freedom for the denominator, the appropriate F value is found by looking under the 7 degrees of freedom column and proceeding down to the 5 degrees of freedom row; there one finds the appropriate F value to be 10.5.

0.01 of area — 10.5

d.f. for denom-inator	|					Degrees of Freedom for Numerator												
	1	2	3	4	5	6	7	8	9	10	12	15	20	24	30	40	60	120	=
1	4,052	5,000	5,403	5,625	5,764	5,859	5,928	7,982	6,023	6,056	6,106	6,157	6,209	6,235	6,261	6,287	6,313	6,339	6,366
2	98.5	99.0	99.2	99.2	99.3	99.3	99.4	99.4	99.4	99.4	99.4	99.4	99.4	99.5	99.5	99.5	99.5	99.5	99.5
3	34.1	30.8	29.5	28.7	28.2	27.9	27.7	27.5	27.3	27.2	27.1	26.9	26.7	26.6	26.5	26.4	26.3	26.2	26.1
4	21.2	18.0	16.7	16.0	15.5	15.2	15.0	14.8	14.7	14.5	14.4	14.2	14.0	13.9	13.8	13.7	13.7	13.6	13.5
5	16.3	13.3	12.1	11.4	11.0	10.7	10.5	10.3	10.2	10.1	9.89	9.72	9.55	9.47	9.38	9.29	9.20	9.11	9.02
6	13.7	10.9	9.78	9.15	8.75	8.47	8.26	8.10	7.98	7.87	7.72	7.56	7.40	7.31	7.23	7.14	7.06	6.97	6.88
7	12.2	9.55	8.45	7.85	7.46	7.19	6.99	6.84	6.72	6.62	6.47	6.31	6.16	6.07	5.99	5.91	5.82	5.74	5.65
8	11.3	8.65	7.59	7.01	6.63	6.37	6.18	6.03	5.91	5.81	5.67	5.52	5.36	5.28	5.20	5.12	5.03	4.95	4.86
9	10.6	8.02	6.99	6.42	6.06	5.80	5.61	5.47	5.35	5.26	5.11	4.96	4.81	4.73	4.65	4.57	4.48	4.40	4.31
10	10.0	7.56	6.55	5.99	5.64	5.39	5.20	5.06	4.94	4.85	4.71	4.56	4.41	4.33	4.25	4.17	4.08	4.00	3.91
11	9.65	7.21	6.22	5.67	5.32	5.07	4.89	4.74	4.63	4.54	4.40	4.25	4.10	4.02	3.94	3.86	3.78	3.69	3.60
12	9.33	6.93	5.95	5.41	5.06	4.82	4.64	4.50	4.39	4.30	4.16	4.01	3.86	3.78	3.70	3.62	3.54	3.45	3.36
13	9.07	6.70	5.74	5.21	4.86	4.62	4.44	4.30	4.19	4.10	3.96	3.82	3.66	3.59	3.51	3.43	3.34	3.25	3.17
14	8.86	6.51	5.56	5.04	4.70	4.46	4.28	4.14	4.03	3.94	3.80	3.66	3.51	3.43	3.35	3.27	3.18	3.09	3.00
15	8.68	6.36	5.42	4.89	4.56	4.32	4.14	4.00	3.89	3.80	3.67	3.52	3.37	3.29	3.21	3.13	3.05	2.96	2.87
16	8.53	6.23	5.29	4.77	4.44	4.20	4.03	3.89	3.78	3.69	3.55	3.41	3.26	3.18	3.10	3.02	2.93	2.84	2.75
17	8.40	6.11	5.19	4.67	4.34	4.10	3.93	3.79	3.68	3.59	3.46	3.31	3.16	3.08	3.00	2.92	2.83	2.75	2.65
18	8.29	6.01	5.09	4.58	4.25	4.01	3.84	3.71	3.60	3.51	3.37	3.23	3.08	3.00	2.92	2.84	2.75	2.66	2.57
19	8.19	5.93	5.01	4.50	4.17	3.94	3.77	3.63	3.52	3.43	3.30	3.15	3.00	2.92	2.84	2.76	2.67	2.58	2.49
20	8.10	5.85	4.94	4.43	4.10	3.87	3.70	3.56	3.46	3.37	3.23	3.09	2.94	2.86	2.78	2.69	2.61	2.52	2.42
21	8.02	5.78	4.87	4.37	4.04	3.81	3.64	3.51	3.40	3.31	3.17	3.03	2.88	2.80	2.72	2.64	2.55	2.46	2.36
22	7.95	5.72	4.82	4.31	3.99	3.76	3.59	3.45	3.35	3.26	3.12	2.98	2.83	2.75	2.67	2.58	2.50	2.40	2.31
23	7.88	5.66	4.76	4.26	3.94	3.71	3.54	3.41	3.30	3.21	3.07	2.93	2.78	2.70	2.62	2.54	2.45	2.35	2.26
24	7.82	5.61	4.72	4.22	3.90	3.67	3.50	3.36	3.26	3.17	3.03	2.89	2.74	2.66	2.58	2.49	2.40	2.31	2.21
25	7.77	5.57	4.68	4.18	3.86	3.63	3.46	3.32	3.22	3.13	2.99	2.85	2.70	2.62	2.53	2.45	2.36	2.27	2.17
30	7.56	5.39	4.51	4.02	3.70	3.47	3.30	3.17	3.07	2.98	2.84	2.70	2.55	2.47	2.39	2.30	2.21	2.11	2.01
40	7.31	5.18	4.31	3.83	3.51	3.29	3.12	2.99	2.89	2.80	2.66	2.52	2.37	2.29	2.20	2.11	2.02	1.92	1.80
60	7.08	4.98	4.13	3.65	3.34	3.12	2.95	2.82	2.72	2.63	2.50	2.35	2.20	2.12	2.03	1.94	1.84	1.73	1.60
120	6.85	4.79	3.95	3.48	3.17	2.96	2.79	2.66	2.56	2.47	2.34	2.19	2.03	1.95	1.86	1.76	1.66	1.53	1.38
=	6.63	4.61	3.78	3.32	3.02	2.80	2.64	2.51	2.41	2.32	2.18	2.04	1.88	1.79	1.70	1.59	1.47	1.32	1.00

EXHBIT 4 Values of the Durbin-Watson *d* for Specified Sample Sizes (*T*) and Explanatory Variables (*K'* = *K* – 1)

This table gives the significance points for d_L and d_U for tests on the autocorrelation of residuals (when no explanatory variable is a lagged endogenous variable) using the Durbin-Watson test statistic at the 0.05 significance level. The number of explanatory variables, *K'*, *excludes* the constant term. The next page of the table gives corresponding values for the 0.01 significance level.

Significance level = 0.01

Number of residuals	*K = 1*		*K = 2*		*K = 3*		*K = 4*		*K = 5*	
T	d_L	d_U	d_L	d_U	d_L	d_U	d_L	d_U	d_L	d_U
15	1.08	1.36	0.95	1.54	0.82	1.75	0.69	1.97	0.56	2.21
16	1.10	1.37	0.98	1.54	0.86	1.73	0.74	1.93	0.62	2.15
17	1.13	1.38	1.02	1.54	0.90	1.71	0.78	1.90	0.67	2.10
18	1.16	1.39	1.05	1.53	0.93	1.69	0.82	1.87	0.71	2.06
19	1.18	1.40	1.08	1.53	0.97	1.68	0.86	1.85	0.75	2.02
20	1.20	1.41	1.10	1.54	1.00	1.68	0.90	1.83	0.79	1.99
21	1.22	1.42	1.13	1.54	1.03	1.67	0.93	1.81	0.83	1.96
22	1.24	1.43	1.15	1.54	1.05	1.66	0.96	1.80	0.86	1.94
23	1.26	1.44	1.17	1.54	1.08	1.66	0.99	1.79	0.90	1.92
24	1.27	1.45	1.19	1.55	1.10	1.66	1.01	1.78	0.93	1.90
25	1.29	1.45	1.21	1.55	1.12	1.66	1.04	1.77	0.95	1.89
26	1.30	1.46	1.22	1.55	1.14	1.65	1.06	1.76	0.98	1.88
27	1.32	1.47	1.24	1.56	1.16	1.65	1.08	1.76	1.01	1.86
28	1.33	1.48	1.26	1.56	1.18	1.65	1.10	1.75	1.03	1.85
29	1.34	1.48	1.27	1.56	1.20	1.65	1.12	1.74	1.05	1.84
30	1.35	1.49	1.28	1.57	1.21	1.65	1.14	1.74	1.07	1.83
31	1.36	1.50	1.30	1.57	1.23	1.65	1.16	1.74	1.09	1.83
32	1.37	1.50	1.31	1.57	1.24	1.65	1.18	1.73	1.11	1.82
33	1.38	1.51	1.32	1.58	1.26	1.65	1.19	1.73	1.13	1.81
34	1.39	1.51	1.33	1.58	1.27	1.65	1.21	1.73	1.15	1.81
35	1.40	1.52	1.34	1.58	1.28	1.65	1.22	1.73	1.16	1.80
36	1.41	1.52	1.35	1.59	1.29	1.65	1.24	1.73	1.18	1.80
37	1.42	1.53	1.36	1.59	1.31	1.66	1.25	1.72	1.19	1.80
38	1.43	1.54	1.37	1.59	1.32	1.66	1.26	1.72	1.21	1.79
39	1.43	1.54	1.38	1.60	1.33	1.66	1.27	1.72	1.22	1.79
40	1.44	1.54	1.39	1.60	1.34	1.66	1.29	1.72	1.23	1.79
45	1.48	1.57	1.43	1.62	1.38	1.67	1.34	1.72	1.29	1.78
50	1.50	1.59	1.46	1.63	1.42	1.67	1.38	1.72	1.34	1.77
55	1.53	1.60	1.49	1.64	1.45	1.68	1.41	1.72	1.38	1.77
60	1.55	1.62	1.51	1.65	1.48	1.69	1.44	1.73	1.41	1.77
65	1.57	1.63	1.54	1.66	1.50	1.70	1.47	1.73	1.44	1.77
70	1.58	1.64	1.55	1.67	1.52	1.70	1.49	1.74	1.46	1.77
75	1.60	1.65	1.57	1.68	1.54	1.71	1.51	1.74	1.49	1.77
80	1.61	1.66	1.59	1.69	1.56	1.72	1.53	1.74	1.51	1.77
85	1.62	1.67	1.60	1.70	1.57	1.72	1.55	1.75	1.52	1.77
90	1.63	1.68	1.61	1.70	1.59	1.73	1.57	1.75	1.54	1.78
95	1.64	1.69	1.62	1.71	1.60	1.73	1.58	1.75	1.56	1.78
100	1.65	1.69	1.63	1.72	1.61	1.74	1.59	1.76	1.57-	1.78

Number of residuals	K = 1		K = 2		K = 3		K = 4		K = 5	
T	d_L	d_U	d_L	d_U	d_L	d_U	d_L	d_U	d_L	d_U
15	0.81	1.07	0.70	1.25	0.59	1.46	0.49	1.70	0.39	1.96
16	0.84	1.09	0.74	1.25	0.63	1.44	0.53	1.66	0.44	1.90
17	0.87	1.10	0.77	1.25	0.67	1.43	0.57	1.63	0.48	1.85
18	0.90	1.12	0.80	1.26	0.71	1.42	0.61	1.60	0.52	1.80
19	0.93	1.13	0.83	1.26	0.74	1.41	0.65	1.58	0.56	1.77
20	0.95	1.15	0.86	1.27	0.77	1.41	0.68	1.57	0.60	1.74
21	0.97	1.16	0.89	1.27	0.80	1.41	0.72	1.55	0.63	1.71
22	1.00	1.17	0.91	1.28	0.83	1.40	0.75	1.54	0.66	1.69
23	1.02	1.19	0.94	1.29	0.86	1.40	0.77	1.53	0.70	1.67
24	1.04	1.20	0.96	1.30	0.88	1.41	0.80	1.53	0.72	1.66
25	1.05	1.21	0.98	1.30	0.90	1.41	0.83	1.52	0.75	1.65
26	1.07	1.22	1.00	1.31	0.93	1.41	0.85	1.52	0.78	1.64
27	1.09	1.23	1.02	1.32	0.95	1.41	0.88	1.51	0.81	1.63
28	1.10	1.24	1.04	1.32	0.97	1.41	0.90	1.51	0.83	1.62
29	1.12	1.25	1.05	1.33	0.99	1.42	0.92	1.51	0.85	1.61
30	1.13	1.26	1.07	1.34	1.01	1.42	0.94	1.51	0.88	1.61
31	1.15	1.27	1.08	1.34	1.02	1.42	0.96	1.51	0.90	1.60
32	1.16	1.28	1.10	1.35	1.04	1.43	0.98	1.51	0.92	1.60
33	1.17	1.29	1.11	1.36	1.05	1.43	1.00	1.51	0.94	1.59
34	1.18	1.30	1.13	1.36	1.07	1.43	1.01	1.51	0.95	1.59
35	1.19	1.31	1.14	1.37	1.08	1.44	1.03	1.51	0.97	1.59
36	1.21	1.32	1.15	1.38	1.10	1.44	1.04	1.51	0.99	1.59
37	1.22	1.32	1.16	1.38	1.11	1.45	1.06	1.51	1.00	1.59
38	1.23	1.33	1.18	1.39	1.12	1.45	1.07	1.52	1.02	1.58
39	1.24	1.34	1.19	1.39	1.14	1.45	1.09	1.52	1.03	1.58
40	1.25	1.34	1.20	1.40	1.15	1.46	1.10	1.52	1.05	1.58
45	1.29	1.38	1.24	1.42	1.20	1.48	1.16	1.53	1.11	1.58
50	1.32	1.40	1.28	1.45	1.24	1.49	1.20	1.54	1.16	1.59
55	1.36	1.43	1.32	1.47	1.28	1.51	1.25	1.55	1.21	1.59
60	1.38	1.45	1.35	1.48	1.32	1.52	1.28	1.56	1.25	1.60
65	1.41	1.47	1.38	1.50	1.35	1.53	1.31	1.57	1.28	1.61
70	1.43	1.49	1.40	1.52	1.37	1.55	1.34	1.58	1.31	1.61
70	1.43	1.49	1.40	1.52	1.37	1.55	1.34	1.58	1.31	1.61
75	1.45	1.50	1.42	1.53	1.39	1.56	1.37	1.59	1.34	1.62
80	1.47	1.52	1.44	1.54	1.42	1.57	1.39	1.60	1.36	1.62
85	1.48	1.53	1.46	1.55	1.43	1.58	1.41	1.60	1.39	1.63
90	1.50	1.54	1.47	1.56	1.45	1.59	1.43	1.61	1.41	1.64
95	1.51	1.55	1.49	1.57	1.47	1.60	1.45	1.62	1.42	1.64
100	1.52	1.56	1.50	1.58	1.48	1.60	1.46	1.63	1.44	1.65

Note: K = number of explanatory variables excluding the constant term.

Appendix C

A List of Popular Budgeting Software

In addition to specialized budgeting and financial modeling software, there are a variety of computer software designed specifically for budgeting. Some are stand-alone packages, others are templates, and still others are spreadsheet add-ins. They are described below.

1. BUDGET EXPRESS (ADD-IN)

Budget Express "understands" the structure of financial worksheets and concepts such as months, quarters, years, totals, and subtotals, speeding budget and forecast preparation. The program creates column headers for months, automatically totals columns and rows, and calculates quarterly and yearly summaries. And for sophisticated what-if analyses, just specify your goal and Budget Express displays your current and target values as you make changes.

2. PROPLANS (TEMPLATE)

It creates your financial plan automatically and accurately—slicing months from your annual planning and reporting process. Simply enter your forecast data and assumptions into easy-to-follow, comprehensive data-entry screens, and ProPlans automatically creates the detailed financials you need to operate your business for the next year: income statement, balance sheet, cash flow statement, receipts and disbursements cash flow statements, and ratio reports.

3. PROFIT PLANNER (TEMPLATE)

It provides titles and amounts for revenues, cost of sales, expenses, assets, liabilities, and equity in a ready-to-use 1-2-3 template. Financial tables are automatically generated on screen. It presents results in 13 different table formats, including a pro forma earnings statement, balance sheet, and cash flow. Profit Planner even compares your earnings statement, balance sheet, and ratios against industry averages, so you are not working in a vacuum.

4. UP YOUR CASH FLOW (STAND-ALONE)

This program generates cash flow and profit and loss forecasts; detailed sales by product/product line and payroll by employee forecasts; monthly balance sheets; bar graphs; ratio and break-even analyses, and more.

5. CASH COLLECTOR (STAND-ALONE)

It assists in reviewing and aging receivables. You always know who owes what; nothing "falls through the cracks." What happens when collection action is required? Simply click through menu-driven screens to automatically generate letters and other professionally written collection documents (all included) that are proven to pull in the payments.

6. INVENTORY ANALYST (TEMPLATE)

Inventory Analyst calculates precisely how much inventory to order and when to order it. Choose from four carefully-explained ordering methods: economic order quantity (EOQ), fixed order quantity, fixed months requirements, and level load by work days. Inventory Analyst ensures that you will always have sufficient stock for your ordering period.

Simply load up to 48 months of inventory history, and Inventory Analyst makes the forecast based on one of three forecasting methods: time series, exponential smoothing, or moving averages. It explains which method is best for you. Inventory Analyst will adjust your forecast for seasonality, too.

7. CAPPLANS (TEMPLATE)

It evaluates profitability based on Net Present Value (NPV), Internal Rate of Return (IRR), and payout period. Choose among five depreciation methods, including MACRS. Run up to four sensitivity analyses. And project profitability over a 15-year horizon. In addition to a complete report of your analysis, CapPLANS generates a concise, 4-page executive summary—great for expediting approval. Add ready-made graphs to illustrate profitability clearly at a glance.

8. PROJECT EVALUATION TOOLKIT (TEMPLATE)

It calculates the dollar value of your project based on six valuation methods, including discounted cash flow and impact on the corporate balance sheet. Assess intangibles such as impact on corporate strategy, investors, or labor relations. Use scenario planning to demonstrate the effects of changing start dates, sales forecasts, and other critical variables.

9. @RISK (ADD-IN)

How will a new competitor affect your market share? @RISK calculates the likelihood of changes and events that affect your bottom line. First use @Risk's familiar @ functions to define the risk in your worksheet. Then let @Risk run thousands of what-if tests using one of two proven statistical sampling techniques: Monte Carlo or Latin Hypercube. You get a clear, colorful graph that shows you the likelihood of every possible bottom-line value. At a glance you will know if your risk is acceptable, or if you need to make a contingency plan.

10. WHAT'S BEST! (STAND-ALONE)

If you have limited resources—for example, people, inventory, materials, time, or cash—then *What's Best!* can determine how to allocate these resources in order to maximize or minimize a given objective, such as profit or cost. *What's Best!* uses a proven method—linear programming—to help you achieve your goals. This product can solve a variety of business problems that cut across every industry at every level of decision-making.

11. CFO SPREADSHEET APPLICATIONS (TEMPLATE)

These ready-to-use spreadsheet templates offer easy ways to make many financial decisions. They are divided into four modules: cash management, tax strategies, capital budgeting, and advanced topics.

Glossary

Accuracy. Criterion for evaluating the performance of alternative forecasting methods and models. It refers to the correctness of the forecast as measured against actual events. Accuracy can be measured using such statistics as mean squared error (MSE) and mean absolute percentage error (MAPE).

Activity Base. Applies to manufacturing activity used to relate factory overhead to production (e.g., units produced, direct labor costs, direct labor hours, machine hours). The activity base chosen should be the one that most realistically measures the overall activity of the responsibility center (See RESPONSIBILITY CENTER.) There are several criteria for selecting an activity base that should be considered:

1. it should measure fluctuations in the output that cause the expenses to vary,
2. it should be affected as little as possible by factors other than output,
3. it should be understood easily, and
4. it should be cost-effective and reliably measurable.

Actual Cost. Expenditure made to purchase an asset, manufacture a product, or render a service. The actual cost to produce an item consists of direct material, direct labor, and factory overhead. Actual costs are entered into work-in-process. (See also STANDARD COST and NORMAL COSTING SYSTEM.)

Administrative Budget. A financial plan by which management may direct daily operations and functions. An administrative budget may best handle functions that are not influenced by the day-to-day sales level where manhours and output are not always the same.

Allocate. Assignment of revenue or cost to two or more business segments (e.g., square footage, sales, number of employees). Costs may also be allocated to products and territories. For example, the allocation of budgeted service department costs to producing departments involves the assignment of direct and indirect manufacturing costs to various categories. A cost may be reallocated several times within a production cycle.

Allotment. A part of an appropriation which may be encumbered or expended during an allotment period, which is usually a period of time less than one fiscal year. Bi-monthly and quarterly allotment periods are most common.

Analysis of Variances. Analysis and investigation of causes for variances between standard costs and actual costs; also called variance analysis. A variance is considered favorable if actual costs are less than standard costs; it is unfavorable if actual costs exceed standard costs. Unfavorable variances are those that need further investigation for their causes. Analysis of variances reveals the causes of these deviations. This feedback aids in planning future goals, controlling costs, evaluating performance, and taking corrective action. Management by exception is based on the analysis of variances and attention is given to only the variances that require remedial actions.

Annual Budget. A budget prepared yearly on a calender or fiscal year basis. In an annual budget, both operating and nonoperating areas are covered which makes it easier to survey and review other budget segments as they relate to the budget.

Annualize. Extending an item to an annual basis. An amount applicable to part of a year is multiplied by 12 and divided by the number of months involved. For example, if income for 4 months is $80,000, it will be annualized as follows:

$$\$80,000 \times 12/4 = \$240,000$$

Appropriation. Authorization to spend money within a specified time period for a designated amount to accomplish a desired objective. The expenditure must be approved in advance. Also, if it is an appropriation budget (which is common in governmental budgeting but has restricted usage in business), the authorization is formalized by the board of directors, which is usually used in connection with advertising expenses, charitable contributions, or research and development expenses.

Artificial Intelligence (AI). Attempt to build machines that think, that is the study of mental faculties through the use of computational models. Artificial intelligence performs complicated strategies that compute the best or worst way to achieve a task or avoid an undesirable result. An example of an application is in tax planning involving tax shelter options given the client's financial position. See also EXPERT SYSTEMS.

Autocorrelation. Extent to which a time series variable, lagged one or more time periods, is correlated with itself.

Balanced Budget. A budget in which total revenue equals total expenses. There is a budget deficit if expenditures exceed revenues. A budget surplus exists if revenues exceed expenditures.

Base Period. A designated time period that acts as a basis for a comparison (standard) to facilitate financial analysis. The base period should be the one that is the most representative (typical) for the business.

Break-even. The level of sales where total costs equal total revenue resulting in a zero profit. The break-even equation is:

$$\text{Units} \times \text{Selling Price} = \text{Variable Cost Per Unit} \times \text{Units} + \text{Fixed Cost}$$

The one problem with this term is that the relationships are used mostly to determine the profit impact of decisions and not usually used to calculate the break-even point of a business or a business segment.

Break-even Chart. Chart where sales revenue, variable costs, and fixed costs are plotted on the vertical axis while volume, x, is plotted on the horizontal axis. The break-even point is the point at which the total sales revenue line intersects the total cost line.

Break-even Sales. Sales which result in there being no profit or loss, also called break-even point. It is the sales volume, in units or in dollars, where total sales revenue equals total costs. Thus, zero profit results. See also BREAK-EVEN.

Budget. Quantitative plan of activities and programs expressed in terms of assets, liabilities, equities, revenue, and expenses. It relates to executing the plan, or in other quantitative terms such as units of product or service. The budget states the company's goals in terms of specific financial and operating objectives. More specifically, a budget helps in developing a company's long-term plans, goals, long-term profit plans, short-term profit plans, system of evaluating employee performance, and follow-up procedures. Advantages of budget preparation are planning, communicating company-wide goals to subunits, fostering cooperation between departments, control by evaluating actual figures to budget figures, and revealing the interrelationship of one function to another. See also MASTER BUDGET.

Budget Control. Budgetary actions performed in accordance with the budget plan. The budget is the standard expected to be accomplished. Actual performance is then compared to budgeted performance to determine how effectively plans were carried out. Those responsible for good performance should be rewarded. Those responsible for undesirable performance should be identified so corrective action may be taken. Corrective action may be necessary to ensure that the company's objectives, goals, policies, and standards are met effectively. Budgets may be modified based on new information. Budget control is exercised by using personal evaluation, periodic performance reports, and special reports.

Budget Cost. The expected cost at the beginning of a period of manufacturing a product, performing a service, or buying an asset. It is a projection on past experience taking into account the current environment.

Budget Manual. A manual describing the company's budgeting procedures, job descriptions, and time schedule. It is normally used to improve communication, to directly explain procedures, and to demonstrate that the operation of the system is reasonably stable.

Budget Variance. The difference between a budgeted amount and an actual amount. When the variance is large enough, management should find a remedy for the difference by using the appropriate corrective action.

Budgeting Software. Programs that aid in financial forecasting such as spreadsheets which perform "what-if" analysis.

Budgeted Balance Sheet. Schedule of expected assets, liabilities, and stockholders' equity. It forecasts a company's financial position at the end of the reporting period. A budgeted balance sheet is prepared for the following reasons: It

1. discloses unfavorable financial conditions that management wants to avoid,

2. acts as a check on the computational accuracy of other budgets, and

3. identifies future resources and obligations.

Budgeted Income Statement. Summarizes the component projections of revenues and expenses for the budgeting period. The result is the expected net income. In order to prepare the planned income statement, the director of planning needs copies of the sales, factory cost and expense budgets. Income taxes will be estimated to complete the budgeted income statement.

Budgeting Fund. Annual budgets of estimated revenues and estimated expenditures prepared for most governmental funds. The approved budgets of such funds are recorded in "budgetary accounts" in the accounting system to provide control over governmental revenues and expenditures.

Budgeting Models. Mathematical models used in the budgetary and planning processes. The models aid in answering "what-if" questions. The resultant computations provide a basis for choice among alternatives under conditions of uncertainty. The models are typically quantitative and computer-based. Although these computerized models replaced manual procedures, some decision-making and judgments made by the manager cannot be substituted. There are primarily two approaches to modeling in the corporate budgeting process: simulation and optimization. See also FINANCIAL MODELS: SIMULATION MODELS.

Capacity. Ability to produce or service during a designated time period. There is an upper limit restricted by space, capital, machinery, labor or other constraining factors. Idle capacity means facilities are available to take on additional production or work. Full capacity has not been reached. At idle capacity, additional volume does not increase fixed costs which by definition are constant. Break-even capacity is reached when the sales value of the goods produced is equal to the cost of producing and selling those goods. Capacity may be stated in terms of size, dollars, hours, or units.

Capital Budget. A plan of proposed acquisitions and replacements of fixed assets and their financing. A capital budget decision involves the long-term commitment of a firm's resources, such as cash. The three stages of the capital budget process are:

1. to define the project and to estimate the cash flow,

2. to evaluate the project and to select it and

3. to review the performance of the project.

Capital Budgeting. Process of making long-term planning decisions for capital investments. There are usually two kinds of investment decisions:

1. selecting new facilities or expanding existing ones and

2. replacing existing facilities with new ones.

Examples of (1) include: (a) investments in long-term assets such as property, plant, and equipment, and (b) resource commitments in the form of new product development, market research, refunding of long-term debt, introduction of a computer, etc. Examples of (2) include replacing a manual bookkeeping system with a computerized system and replacing an inefficient lathe with one that is numerically controlled. The manager must choose the alternative investment opportunity which is most attractive. The techniques to appraise investment proposals include payback, accounting rate of return, internal rate of return, and net present value. The payback technique measures the length of time required to recover the initial net cash outlay. The accounting rate of return is computed by dividing the average net income after taxes by the initial net cash outlay. The internal rate of return method computes the yield that is expected to be earned on an investment. The internal rate of return for an investment is the discount rate that will make the present value of the cash flow from operations equal to the initial net cash outlay. And the net present value (NPV) and the internal rate of return are discounted cash flow techniques which take into consideration the time value of money. The NPV is a measure of the dollar profit of a project in present value terms.

Capital Expenditure Budget. A plan developed for individual capital expenditure projects. The time frame for this budget depends upon the project. Capital expenditures include acquisitions, replacement, or construction, and they involve a company's operating assets, such as land, equipment, and cash. The capital expenditure budget is very important because the projects it influences involve a large amount of time and money.

Capital Rationing. Selecting the mix of acceptable projects that generate the highest overall net present value when there is a capital budget limitation. The profitability index equals the present value of cash inflows divided by the present value of cash outflows. It is used widely in ranking projects competing for limited funds. A budget limitation may occur for two reasons:

1. the amount of funds the firm can raise may be restricted due to problems in the capital market and

2. an internal limitation imposed by management on the amount of funds that can be used for capital expenditures.

Cash Budget. A budget for cash planning and control that shows expected cash receipts and cash payments for a specified time period. It helps to keep cash balances in reasonable relationship to its needs. It assists in avoiding idle cash and cash shortages. The form of the budget is beginning cash balance, cash collections, cash disbursements, and ending cash balance. If cash is inadequate, additional financing may occur or expenditures will have to be controlled.

Cash Flow.

1. Cash receipts less cash disbursements for a stated time period,
2. Cash basis net income equal to cash revenue less cash expenses.

Another way to calculate cash flow from operations is net income plus noncash expenses less noncash revenue. The control of cash flows is important to most enterprises, and cash budgeting is an effective way to control them. For example, in large businesses, before being granted large loans, they're asked to present cash flow projections.

Cash Flow Forecasting. Forecasts of cash flow including cash collections from customers, investment income, and cash disbursements.

Causal Forecasting Model. A forecasting model which relates the variable to be forecast to a number of other variables that can be observed.

Classical Decomposition Method. Approach to forecasting that seeks to decompose the underlying pattern of a time series into cyclical, seasonal, trend, and random subpatterns. These subpatterns are then analyzed individually, extrapolated into the future, and recombined to obtain forecasts of the original series.

Coefficient of Determination. Statistical measure of how good the estimated regression equation is, designated as R^2 (read as R-squared). Simply put, it is a measure of "goodness of fit" in the regression. Therefore, the higher the R-squared, the more confidence you can have in the equation.

Comprehensive Budget. See MASTER BUDGET.

Constant Variance. See HOMOSCEDASTICITY.

Continuous Budget. A budget that rolls over each period irrespective of the fiscal year so that a 12-month or other periodic forecast is available. This type of budget enhances control when decisions must be made in advance to be most effective when dealing with cash position.

Contribution Margin (CM). Difference between sales and the variable costs of the product or service, also called marginal income. It is the amount of money available to cover fixed costs and generate profits. Total contribution margin will change if any one of the following changes:

1. volume (units sold),
2. sales price, or
3. variable cost ratio.

Contribution (Margin) Income Statement. Income statement that organizes the cost by behavior. It shows the relationship of variable costs and fixed costs, regardless of the functions a given cost item is associated with.

Contribution Margin (CM) Variance. Difference between actual contribution margin per unit and the budgeted contribution margin per unit, multiplied by the actual number of units sold. If the actual CM is greater than the budgeted CM per unit, a variance is favorable; otherwise, it is unfavorable. CM variance = (actual CM per unit − budgeted CM per unit) × actual sales

Contribution Margin (CM) Ratio. Contribution margin (CM) as a percentage of sales.

Control Concept. Concept that ensures that actions are implemented according to a plan or goal.

Controller. Chief accounting officer. His or her duties typically include planning, control, financial reporting and analysis, tax preparation and planning, and internal audits. The controller may also be responsible for designing an effective system of cost control.

Corporate Planning Model. Integrated business planning model in which marketing and production models are linked to the financial model. More specifically, it is a description, explanation, and interrelation of the functional areas of a firm (accounting, finance, marketing, production, and others), expressed in terms of a set of mathematical and logical equations to produce a variety of reports including pro forma financial statements. Corporate planning models are the basic tools for risk analysis and "what-if" experiments.

Correlation Coefficient (r). Measure of the degree of correlation between two variables. The range of values it takes is between -1 and $+1$. A negative value of r indicates an inverse relationship; a positive value of r indicates a direct relationship; a zero value of r indicates that the two variables are independent of each other; the closer r is to $+$ and -1, the stronger the relationship between the two variables.

Correlation. Degree of relationshp between business and economic variables such as cost and volume. Correlation analysis evaluates cause/effect relationships. It looks consistently at how the value of one variable changes when the value of the other is changed. A prediction can be made based upon the relationship uncovered. An example is the effect of advertising on sales. A degree of correlation is measured statistically by the coefficient of determination (R-squared).

Cost Behavior Patterns. Tracks the way a cost will react or respond to changes in the level of activity. Costs may be viewed as variable, fixed, or mixed (semivariable). A mixed cost is one that contains both variable and fixed elements. For planning, control, and decision purposes, mixed costs need to be separated into their variable and fixed components, using such methods as the high-low method and the least-squares method. An application of the variable-fixed breakdown is a break-even and cost-volume-profit (CVP) analysis.

Cost-Benefit Analysis. Analysis to determine whether the favorable results of an alternative are sufficient to justify the cost of taking that alternative. This analysis is widely used in connection with capital expenditure projects.

Cost Control. Steps taken by management to assure that the cost objectives established in the planning stage are attained, and to assure that all segments of the organization function in a manner consistent with its policies. For effective cost control, most organizations use standard cost systems, in which the actual costs are compared against standard costs for performance evaluation and the deviations are investigated for remedial actions. Cost control is also concerned with feedback that might change any or all of the future plans, the production method, or both.

Cost Effective. Among decision alternatives, the one whose cost is lower than its benefit. The most cost effective program would be the one whose cost-benefit ratio is the lowest among various programs competing for a given amount of funds. See also COST-BENEFIT ANALYSIS.

Cost-Volume Formula. A cost function in the form of

where: Y = the semivariable (or mixed) costs to be broken up
X = any given measure of activity such as volume and labor hours
a = the fixed cost component
b = the variable rate per unit of X

Accountants use the formula for cost prediction and flexible budgeting purposes.

Cost-Volume-Profit (CVP) Analysis. Analysis that deals with how profits and costs change with a change in volume. More specifically, it looks at the effects on profits of changes in such factors as variables costs, fixed costs, selling prices, volume, and mix of products sold. By studying the relationships of costs, sales and net income, management is better able to cope with many planning decisions.

Decision Model. Conceptualization of the relationship of variables that are relevant in planning.

Decision Support System (DSS). Branch of the broadly defined Management Information System (MIS). It is an information system that provides answers to problems and that integrates the decision-maker into the system as a component. The system utilizes such quantitative techniques as regression and financial planning modeling. DSS software furnishes support to the accountant in the decision-making process.

Delphi Method. Qualitative forecasting method that seeks to use the judgement of experts systematically in arriving at a forecast of what future events will be or when they may occur. It brings together a group of experts who have access to each other's opinions in an environment where no majority opinion is disclosed.

Dependent Variable. Variable whose value depends upon the values of other variables and constants in some relationship. For example, in the relationship $Y = f$ (X), Y is the dependent variable. For example, market price of stock is a dependent variable influenced by various independent variables, such as earnings per share, debt-equity ratio, and beta. See also INDEPENDENT VARIABLE.

Deseasonalized Data. Removal of the seasonal pattern in a data series. Deseasonalizing facilitates the comparison of month-to-month changes.

Direct Allocation Method. Method to allocate costs of each service department directly to production departments. This is the most common method used because it is mathematically simple and it is easy to apply. It is also appropriate in allocating the service department costs if no reciprocal services exist.

Direct Labor. Work directly involved in producing a product. An example is the wages of factory workers who directly work on producing automobiles.

Direct Labor Budget. Schedule for expected labor cost. Expected labor cost depends upon expected production volume. Labor requirements are based on production volume multiplied by direct labor hours per unit. Direct labor hours needed for production are then multiplied by direct labor cost per hour to obtain budgeted direct labor costs. This budget will be translated by the personnel department to determine how many workers are needed. If more workers are needed, they will provide a training program to train new workers. And if they have too many workers, they will provide a list of workers to be laid off.

Direct Material. All the material that becomes an integral part of the finished product, and also represents a major material cost of producing that product. An example is the steel used to make a truck.

Direct Material Budget. Schedule showing how much material will be needed for production and how much material must be purchased to satisfy production requirements. The purchase depends on both anticipated usage of material and inventory levels.

Discounted Cash Flow (DCF) Techniques. Methods of selecting and ranking investment proposals such as the net present value (NPV) and internal rate of return (IRR) methods where time value of money is taken into account.

Discounted Payback Period. Length of time needed to recoup the initial cash outflow from the discounted future cash inflows. The problem with using the discounted payback technique is that, although it takes into consideration the time value of money, it still does not consider cash flows beyond the discounted payback period and therefore the profitability of the project.

DSS. See DECISION SUPPORT SYSTEM.

Durbin-Watson Statistic. Summary measure of the amount of autocorrelation in the error terms of the regression. By comparing the computed value of the Durbin-Watson test with the appropriate values from the table of values of the D-W statistic, the significance can be determined. See also AUTOCORRELATION.

Earnings Forecast. Projection of earnings or earnings per share (EPS) frequently made by management and independent security analysts. Examples of forecast sources include:

1. Lynch, Jones and Ryan's Institutional Brokers Estimate System (IBES),

2. Standard & Poor's The Earnings Forecaster, and

3. Zacks Investment Research's Icarus Service.

Economic Order Quantity (EOQ). Order size that minimizes the sum of carrying and ordering costs. At the EOQ amount, total ordering cost equals total carrying cost.

Efficiency Variance. Difference between inputs (materials and labor) that were actually used (i.e., actual quantity of inputs used) and inputs that should have been used (i.e., standard quantity of inputs allowed for actual production), multiplied by the standard price per unit. See also MATERIAL QUANTITY VARIANCE and LABOR EFFICIENCY VARIANCE.

Expected Volume. Estimated volume of activity for a future period based on budgeted sales of product or service, adjusted for planned changes in inventory levels.

Expert Systems. Computer software involving stored reasoning schemes and containing the knowledge of experts in an area. This is the area of Artificial Intelligence (AI) that has received great attention from business decision makers. There are recent advances in this area of software systems which are designed to mimic the way human experts make decisions. Currently available expert systems applied to accounting include Auditor, CORP-TAX, Financial Advisor, CASH VALUE, and Capacity Planner.

Exponential Smoothing. Forecasting technique that uses a weighted moving average of past data as the basis for a forecast. The procedure gives heaviest weight to more recent information and smaller weights to observations in the more distant past. The method is effective when there is random demand and no seasonal fluctuations in the data. The method is a popular technique for short-run forecasting by business forecasters.

F-Test. In statistics the ratio of two mean squares (variances) can often be used to test the significance of some item of interest. For example, in regression the ratio of (mean square due to the regression) to (mean square due to error) can be used to test the overall significance of the regression model. By studying F-tables, the degree of significance of the computed F-value can be determined.

Factory Overhead. Total of all manufacturing costs except direct material and direct labor. These costs are included in factory overhead because they cannot be directly identified with specific products. Examples are factory rent, factory insurance, and factory property taxes.

Factory Overhead Budget. Schedule of expected production costs excluding direct material and direct labor. Factory overhead items include indirect material, indirect labor, factory rent, and factory insurance. Factory overhead may be fixed, variable, or a combination. (These are defined later in the Glossary.)

Favorable Variance. Excess of standard (or budgeted) costs over actual costs. See also STANDARD COST SYSTEM; VARIANCE.

Financial Budget. One embracing the effects of the financial decisions of the company. It includes a budgeted balance sheet which shows expected assets, liabilities, and stockholders' equity. It also presents a cash budget showing cash inflows and cash outflows. A cash budget indicates whether sufficient funds are available at the right time. The availability of these funds is most often used in long-term cash planning.

Financial Model. Functional branch of a general corporate planning model. It is essentially used to generate pro forma financial statements and financial ratios. A financial model is a mathematical model describing the interrelationships among financial variables of the firm. It is the basic tool for budgeting and budget planning. Also, it is used for risk analysis and "what-if" experiments. Many financial models of today are built using special modeling languages such as IFPS or spreadsheet programs such as Lotus 1-2-3™. See CORPORATE PLANNING MODEL.

Financial Projection. An element of planning used in budgeting activities and estimating future financing requirements. Financial projections (forecasts) start with estimating sales and their related expenses. The basic steps in financial forecasting are:

1. estimating sales,
2. projecting expenses,
3. estimating the investment needed in assets to support the projected sales, and
4. determining financial needs.

Financial forecasting may be performed using various methods including percent-of-sales method, regression analysis, and financial modeling. They are also conditional, where they normally must be prepared before managements decisions or plans in areas such as plant expansion, price changes, promotional programs, production scheduling, expansion or contraction of marketing activities, and other commitments.

Fixed Budget. See STATIC BUDGET.

Fixed Costs. Expenses that remain the same in total irrespective of changes in volume. Examples are rent, insurance, and property taxes. Fixed cost per unit fluctuates with any changes in activity.

Fixed Overhead. The part of the total overhead that remains constant over a stated time period irrespective of changes in volume. Examples are factory rent and factory insurance.

Fixed Overhead Variance. Difference between actual fixed overhead incurred and fixed overhead applied to production.

Flash Report. Report that provides the highlights of key information promptly to the financial manager. An example is an exception report, such as performance reports, that highlight favorable or unfavorable variances. A flash report allows managers to take a corrective action for an unfavorable variance.

Flexible Budget. One based on varying capacity levels. It is useful for comparing actual costs to the costs allowable for the activity level achieved. It is dynamic in nature rather than static. This type of budget is better than a static budget because it shows anticipated costs at different activity levels, where static budgets only show anticipated costs at one level of activity, making the assumption that production will not deviate much from the level selected. Flexible budgets are a more realistic form of budgeting.

Flexible Budget Formula. See COST-VOLUME FORMULA.

Flexible Budget Variance. See BUDGET VARIANCE.

Flexible Budgeting. See FLEXIBLE BUDGET.

Forecast. Projection or estimate of future sales, costs, profits, assets, liabilities, and so on. The estimate is based on past experience plus a change in light of the current environment. Also, a forecast is not a plan because it is conditional, and therefore management may accept, modify, or reject it.

General and Administrative Expense. Expense incurred to perform general and administrative activities. It is one type of operating expenses for the period. Examples include accounting fees and executive salaries. Although most of these expenses are fixed, some companies find it helpful to apply the fixed-variable expense concept to administrative expenses. This helped to show that when sales dropped, then some of these expenses should drop also, or else profit could be lowered.

Goal Seeking. Situation where a manager wishes to determine what change must take place in the value of a specified variable in a specified time period to achieve a specified value for another variable.

Goodness-of-Fit. Degree to which a model fits the observed data. In a regression analysis, the goodness-of-fit is measured by the coefficient of determination (R-squared).

Homoscedasticity. One of the assumptions required in a regression in order to make valid statistical inferences about population relationships, also known as constant variance. Homoscedasticity requires that the standard deviation and variance of the error terms is constant for all X, and that the error terms are drawn from the same population. This indicates that there is a uniform scatter or dispersion of data points about the regression line. If the assumption does not hold, the accuracy of the b coefficient is open to question.

Incremental (Marginal) Cost. Difference in costs between two or more alternatives. This is when the cost is increasing from one alternative to another. However, if the cost is decreasing from one alternative to another, it is called a decremental cost.

Incremental (Marginal) Revenue. Change in revenue from one or more alternatives to another.

Independent Variable. Variable which may take on any value in a relationship. For example, in a relationship $Y = f(X)$, X is the independent variable. For example, independent variables that influence sales are advertising and price. See also DEPENDENT VARIABLE.

Internal Rate of Return (IRR). Rate earned on a proposal. It is the internal rate that equates the initial investment (I) with the present value of future cash flows. A project is accepted if the IRR exceeds the cost of capital. An advantage of the IRR method is that it takes into consideration the time value of money. One disadvantage is that the IRR is effected by the size of the investment. A second disadvantage is that the IRR calculation assumes that the cash flows can be reinvested at the IRR. A last disadvantage is that an investment project may not have an IRR or may have many rates of return.

Investment Center. Responsibility center within an organization that has control over revenue, cost and investment funds. It is a profit center whose performance is evaluated on the basis of the return earned on invested capital.

Judgmental (Qualitative) Forecast. Forecasting method that brings together in an organized way personal judgements about the process being analyzed.

Labor Efficiency Variance. Difference between the amount of labor time that should have been used and the labor that was actually used, multiplied by the standard rate.

Labor Rate (Price) Variance. Any deviation from standard in the average hourly rate paid to workers.

Labor Variance. Difference between the actual costs of direct labor and the standard costs of direct labor. Labor variance is divided into two specific variances: labor rate variance and labor efficiency variance.

Least Squares Method. Statistical technique for fitting a straight line through a set of points in such a way that the sum of the squared distances from the data points to the line is minimized.

Line Item Budget. A budget in which budgeted financial statement elements are grouped by object. The budgeted groups are typically shown incrementally relative to a prior period.

Linear Programming (LP). Problem of allocating limited resources among competing activities in an optimal manner. Specifically, it is a mathematical technique used to maximize revenue, contribution margin (CM), or profit function, or to minimize a cost function, subject to constraints.

Linear Regression. Regression that deals with a straight line relationship between variables. It is in the form of $Y = a + bX$, whereas nonlinear regression involves curvilinear relationships such as exponential and quadratic functions. See also REGRESSION ANALYSIS.

Long-Range Budget. Projections that cover more than one fiscal year; also called strategic budgeting. The five-year budget plan is the most commonly used in practice. See also ANNUAL BUDGET.

LP. See LINEAR PROGRAMMING.

Management by Exception. Management concept or policy by which management devotes its time to investigating only those situations in which actual results differ significantly from planned results. The idea is that management should spend its valuable time concentrating on the more important items (such as the shaping of the company's future strategic course).

Management by Objective (MBO). System of performance appraisal having the following characteristics:

1. It is a formal system in that each manager is required to take certain prescribed actions and to complete certain written documents; and

2. the manager and subordinates discuss the subordinate's job description, agree to short-term performance targets, discuss the progress made towards meeting these targets, and periodically evaluate the performance and provide the feedback.

Management Control System. System under which managers assure that resources are obtained and used effectively and efficiently in the accomplishment of the organization's goals.

Management Information System (MIS). Computer-based or manual system which transforms data into information useful in the support of decision-making.

Markov Analysis. Method of analyzing the current behavior of some variable to predict the future behavior of that variable.

Master (Comprehensive) Budget. Plan of activities expressed in monetary terms of the assets, equities, revenues, and costs which will be involved in implementing the plans. Simply put, a master budget is a set of projected or planned financial statements. It is the summary of the objectives of all the functions of an organization. It is based on the prior periods master budget plus expectations for the upcoming period. Items that are included for the first time in the master budget require approval from upper-level management.

Material Requirement Planning (MRP). Computer-based information system designed to handle ordering and scheduling of dependent-demand inventories (such as raw materials, component parts, and subassemblies, which will be used in the production of a finished product).

Materials Price Variance. Difference between what is paid for a given quantity of materials and what should have been paid, multiplied by actual quantity of materials used.

Materials Purchase Price Variance. See MATERIALS PRICE VARIANCE.

Materials Quantity (Usage) Variance. Difference between the actual quantity of materials used in production and the standard quantity of materials allowed for actual production, multiplied by the standard price per unit.

Materials Variance. Difference between the actual costs of materials and the standard costs of materials. Material variance is divided into two specific variances: materials price variance and materials quantity variance.

Mean Absolute Deviation (MAD). Mean or average of the sum of all the forecast errors with regard to sign.

Mean Absolute Percentage Error (MAPE). Mean or average of the sum of all the percrntage errors for a given data set taken without regard to sign. (That is, their absolute values are summed and the average computed.) It is one measure of accuracy commonly used in quantitative methods of forecasting.

Mean Squared Error (MSE). Measure of accuracy computed by squaring the individual error for each item in a data set and then finding the average or mean value of the sum of those squares. The mean squared error gives greater weight to large errors than to small errors because the errors are squared before being summed.

Mixed Costs. Contain both fixed and variable characteristics. There are two types: semivariable cost and step cost. Semivariable costs have both fixed and variable characteristics. The fixed portion is usually a minimum fee. The variable portion is the cost for actually using the service. Step costs are costs that change abruptly at various activity levels because they are acquired in indivisible portions.

Model. Abstraction of a real-life system used to enhance understanding and to assist in decision-making.

Modeling Languages. Usually English-like programming languages that are used to solve a specific task and to generate various reports based on the solution and analysis. For example, financial planning modeling languages such as IFPS (Integrated Financial Planning System) are computer software packages that help financial planners develop a financial model in English terms (not requiring any computer programming knowledge on his part), perform various analyses such as "what-if" analysis, and further generate pro forma financial reports.

Moving Average. For a time series an average that is updated as new information is received. With the moving average, the analyst employs the most recent observations to calculate an average, which is used as the forecast for the next period.

Multicollinearity. Condition that exists when the independent variables are highly correlated with each other. In the presence of multicollinearity, the estimated regression coefficients may be unreliable. The presence of multicollinearity can be tested by investigating the correlation between the independent variables.

Multiple Regression Analysis. Statistical procedure that attempts to assess the relationship between the dependent variable and two or more independent variables. For example, sales of Coca Cola is a function of various factors such as its price, advertising, taste, and the prices of its major competitors. For forecasting purposes a multiple regression equation falls into the category of a casual forecasting model. See also REGRESSION ANALYSIS.

Naive Forecast. Forecasts obtained with a minimal amount of effort and data manipulation and based solely on the most recent information available are frequently referred to as naive forecasts. One such naive method would be to use the most recent datum available as the future forecast.

Net Present Value (NPV). Difference between the present value (PV) of cash inflows generated by the project and the amount of the initial investment (I).

Net Present Value Method. Calculates the current worth of future sums of money to determine the financial attractiveness of alternative long-term investment opportunities. The present value of all cash inflows from a project is compared to the initial investment. If the difference between the initial investment and the present value of net cash inflows is favorable to the net cash inflows, the project will earn more than the target rate of return. If the difference is not favorable to the net cash inflows, then the project will earn the target rate of return.

Normal Costing System. Is where the actual costs of direct materials and direct labor are entered into work-in-process, but overhead is entered into work-in-process at a predetermined rate.

Office of Management and Budget (OMB). An agency within the Executive Office of the President. The OMB has broad financial management power as well as the responsibility of preparing the executive budget.

Participative Budgeting. A budgetary process in which managers of a department and key employees provide input. Those affected by the budget contribute to its formulation. Participation budgeting is good for motivational purposes because participants internalize the goals of the budget as their own. It results in greater cooperation.

Payback Period. The number of years it takes to recover the initial amount of a capital investment. The payback period equals the initial investment divided by the annual cash flows.

Percent-of-Sales Method. An item is predicted based on its relationship to sales. For example, production might be projected as 85% of sales volume. Selling expenses might be estimated based on 10% of sales dollars.

Performance Budget. Intermediate to short-term budget, highlighting the performance of individuals or departments within the organization.

Planning. Selection of short- and long-term objectives and the formulation of tactical and strategic plans to accomplish desired goals. The planning process includes enumerating the steps needed to accomplish an end-result. After strategies have been formulated, specific plans are drawn up, such as locations, methods of financing, and hours of operation, that are then communicated throughout the company. The implementation of the plans involves coordination of all segments of the business so that each segment is moving in the right direction.

Pro Forma Balance Sheet. See BUDGETED BALANCE SHEET.

Pro Forma Income Statement. See BUDGETED INCOME STATEMENT.

Price Variance. Difference between actual price and standard price multiplied by actual quantity of input used. An unfavorable variance is when actual price is more than standard price.

Product Life Cycle. Concept that is particularly useful in forecasting and analyzing historical data of new products. It presumes that demand for a product follows an S-shaped curve growing slowly in the early stages, achieving rapid and sustained growth in the middle stages, and slowing again in the mature stage.

Product Mix. See SALES MIX.

Production Budget. Schedule of expected units to be manufactured. It specifies the units expected to be produced to meet budgeted sales and inventory needs. Expected production volume is determined by adding desired ending inventory to planned sales and then subtracting beginning inventory. A production budget should be developed in terms of quantities of physical units of finished goods and is simplified if it is possible to plan sales volume by units and also by dollar amounts.

Production Mix Variances. Cost variances arising from a deviation between actual product mix and budgeted mix. Mix variances explain the portion of the quantity variance caused by using inputs (direct material and direct labor) in ratios different from standard proportions, thus helping to determine the efficiency of mixing operations. A mix variance has no meaning if the products are NOT substitutes for each other. In order to have a favorable mixed variance a company must have:

1. sold less units of the less profitable product or
2. sold more units of the more profitable product.

Production Yield Variances. Difference between actual yield and standard yield. Yield is a measure of productivity. It is a measure of output from a given amount of input. An unfavorable yield variance occurs if actual yield is less than expected yield.

Profit Center. Unit in an organization that is responsible for revenues earned and costs incurred. A manager of a profit center has control over both revenues and costs and attempts to maximize profit.

Profit Planning. Formulation of a profit plan outlining planned sales and expenses and the profit for a time period. Profit planning requires a master budget and analyses taking into account risk and "what-if" scenarios. Some of the features found in a profit plan are:

1. estimates that are real and based on all available facts,
2. a plan that is always adapting to fit changing circumstances,
3. the exertion by management of a serious and aggressive effort towards accomplishing the plan goal, and
4. it is only used as an aid for management, not as a substitute for management. Tools for profit planning include the cost-volume-profit (CVP) analysis and budgeting.

Profit Variance. Difference between actual profit and budgeted profit. Profit is affected by selling price, sales volume, costs, and product mix. If actual profit is less than budgeted profit, the variance is unfavorable.

Profit-Volume Chart. A chart that determines how profits vary with changes in volume. Profits are plotted on the vertical axis while units of output are shown on the horizontal axis.

Profitability Index. Ratio of the total present value (PV) of future cash inflows to the initial investment (I).

Program Evaluation and Review Technique (PERT). Useful management tool for planning, coordinating, and controlling large complex projects such as formulation of a master budget, construction of buildings, installation of computers, and scheduling the closing of books.

Programming-Planning-Budgeting System (PPBS). An approach to formulating a program budget. A program budget is one in which expenditures are based primarily on programs of work and secondarily on character and object. The budget helps in making policy decisions that lead to specific, detailed budgets. PPBS focuses on the output of the organization. It concentrates on allocating the company's limited resources to the activities that promise the greatest return.

Projected (Budgeted) Balance Sheet. Schedule for expected assets, liabilities, and stockholders' equity. It projects a company's financial position as of the end of the budgeting year. Reasons for preparing a budgeted balance sheet follow:

1. discloses unfavorable financial condition that management may want to avoid,
2. serves as a final check on the mathematical accuracy of all other budgets, and
3. highlights future resources and obligations.

Projected (Budgeted) Income Statement. Summary of various component projections of revenues and expenses for the budget period. It indicates the expected net income for the period.

Program-Planning-Budgeting System (PPBS). Planning-oriented approach to developing a program budget. A program budget is a budget wherein expenditures are based primarily on programs of work and secondarily on character and object. It is a transitional budget between the traditional character and object budget, on the one hand, and the performance budget on the other. The major contribution of PPBS lies in the planning process, i.e., the process of making program policy decisions that lead to a specific budget and specific multi-year plans.

Quantitative Forecasting. Technique that can be applied when information about the past is available, if that information can be quantified and if the pattern included in past information can be assumed to continue into the future.

Quantitative Methods (Models). Collection of mathematical and statistical methods used to solve managerial problems. A first type of method is Management Science, which is often used in business administration to analyze and solve managerial problems. Other models used are optimization models. These are:

1. Network Models, which are useful in solving problems for planning and controlling long-term, nonrepetitive projects;

2. Inventory Models, which aid management in finding the proper inventory policy as far as keeping total carrying costs and total ordering costs to a minimum; and

3. Mathematical Programming Models, which are used to solve problems that involve the allocation of resources in such a way as to optimize a quantifiable goal. There are also other types of quantitative models that help the decision maker realize the impact of alternative choices which are known as Descriptive Models.

Quantity Variance. Difference between actual quantity and standard quantity multiplied by selling price. A favorable variance is when actual quantity is less than standard quantity because less quantity is required than expected to make the same number of goods.

R-Squared. R^2 adjusted for the degrees of freedom. See also **COEFFICIENT OF DETERMINATION.**

Ranking (Profitability) Index. Ratio of total present value of future cash inflows to the initial investment. The index is used to rank projects in descending order of financial benefit. It is only profitable to accept a project if the index is 1 or better.

Reciprocal Allocation Method. Method of allocating service department costs to production departments, where reciprocal services are allowed between service departments.

Regression Analysis. Statistical procedure for estimating mathematically the average relationship between the dependent variable (sales, for example) and one or more independent variables (price and advertising, for example).

Regression Coefficients. When a dependent measure Y is regressed against a set of independent measures X_1 through X_k, the analyst wishes to estimate the values of the unknown coefficients by least squares procedures. For example, in a linear regression equation $Y = a + bX$, a and b are regression coefficients. Specifically, a is called y-intercept or constant, while b is called a slope. The properties of these regression coefficients can be used to understand the importance of each independent variable (as it relates to Y) and the interrelatedness among the independent variables (as they relate to Y).

Regression Equation (Model). Forecasting model which relates the dependent variable (sales, for example) to one or more independent variables (advertising and income, for example).

Reorder Point. Inventory level at which it is appropriate to replenish stock.

Residual. A synonym for error. It is calculated by subtracting the forecast value from the actual value to give a "residual" or error value for each forecast period.

Responsibility Accounting. Collection, summarization, and reporting of financial information about various decision centers (responsibility centers) throughout an organization.

Responsibility Center. Unit in the organization which has control over costs, revenues, or investment funds. For accounting purposes, responsibility centers are classified as cost centers, revenue centers, profit centers, and investment centers, depending upon the responsibilities of each center.

Risk Analysis. Process of measuring and analyzing the risks associated with financial and investment decisions. Risk refers to the variability of expected returns (earnings or cash flows).

Root Mean Squared Error (RMSE). Square root of the mean squared error (MSE).

S-Curve. Most frequently used form to represent the product life cycle. Several different mathematical forms, such as the logistics curve, can be used to fit an S-curve to actual observed data.

Sales Budget. An operating plan specified in sales volume and selling prices for each type of product or service. The preparation of a sales budget is the beginning point in budgeting because sales volume affects almost all other items in the budget. A sales budget is the starting point in developing the master budget, which is based on product, territory, and customer. All other operating and financial budgets depend upon the sales budget.

Sales Forecast. Projection or prediction of future sales. It is the basis for the quantification of the entire business plan and a master budget. It is the foundation for budgeting, production and inventory planning, manpower planning, purchasing planning, and capacity planning. There are two major ways of sales forecasting: qualitative and quantitative. Qualitative approaches include polling salespeople and customers. Quantitative approaches include regression analysis, trend analysis, exponential smoothing, and moving average. A sales forecast is converted to a sales plan when management is ready to: make judgments, apply well-planned strategies, use resources, and take aggressive actions to reach sales goals.

Sales Mix. Relative proportions of the product sold. Also, the relative profitability of each product must be evaluated. The profitability of the product must be analysed along with the identification of the fixed and variable costs.

Sales Plan. Is decided by management based on the sales forecast and management judgments concerning things such as sales volume, prices, sales efforts, production, and financing.

Sales Price Variance. Difference between actual selling price per unit and the budgeted selling price per unit, multiplied by the actual number of units sold.

Sales Variance. The difference between actual sales and budgeted sales due to the changes in price and quantity. Once the sales variance is known, management must discover what caused the variance.

Sales Volume Variance. Difference between that actual number of units sold and the budgeted number, multiplied by the budgeted selling price per unit; also called sales quantity variance.

Selling Expense. Cost incurred to sell (e.g., advertising, salesperson commissions) or distribute (e.g., freight out) merchandise. It is one of the types of operating expenses for the period. The expenses incurred to sell are usually variable expenses, and the expenses incurred to distribute are usually fixed expenses.

Semivariable Cost. Expense that varies with changes in volume but does not vary in direct proportion. It is part fixed and part variable. An example is a telephone bill that has a fixed charge plus a variable charge depending upon the number of calls made. (Also defined further under MIXED COSTS.)

Sensitivity Analysis. Form of simulation that enables decision-makers to experiment with decision alternatives using a "what-if" approach. The manager might wish to evaluate alternative policies and assumptions about the external environment by asking a series of "what-if" questions. See also "WHAT-IF" ANALYSIS.

Serial Correlation. See AUTOCORRELATION.

Simple Regression. Regression analysis which involves one independent variable. For example, the demand for automobiles is a function of its price only. See also MULTIPLE REGRESSION ANALYSIS; REGRESSION ANALYSIS.

Simulation. Approach to represent a real-life system with a model to ascertain how a change in one or more variables impacts the rest of the items. It is a technique of "what-if" scenarios. It compares the effects of alternative approaches. Simulation provides management with information about problems so they can assess the risks of a particular course of action. A very popular type of simulation is the Monte Carlo Simulation, which is used when probability distributions are assigned to each random variable.

Simulation Models. "What-if" models that attempt to simulate the effects of alternative management policies and assumptions about the firm's external environment. They are basically a tool for management's laboratory.

Slope. Steepness and direction of the line. More specifically, the slope is the change in Y for every unit change in X.

Software (Program). A collection of computer instructions to perform a function or activity. A collection of programs to carry out a specific task is referred to as a package. Software packages are available to perform budgeting.

Spreadsheet. Table of numbers in rows and columns. Spreadsheets facilitate the budgeting process because they provide for instantaneous changes in numbers as a variable changes. These programs are excellent tools for a variety of "what-if" experiments and financial projections. Spreadsheets are also valuable because they provide managers who do not possess a great amount of computer knowledge with the capability of easily performing significant quantitative analyses.

Standard. Quantitative expression of a performance objective, such as standard hours of labor allowed for actual production or a standard purchase price of materials per unit. Sometimes the terms standard and budget are used interchangeably.

Standard Cost. A predetermined cost of making a product or rendering a service. It is a target cost that should be attained. In a standard costing system you would enter a standard or predetermined cost to work in process.

Standard Cost System. System by which production activities are recorded at standard costs and variances from actual costs are isolated.

Standard Error of the Regression Coefficient. Measure of the amount of sampling error in a regression coefficient.

Standard Error of the Estimate. Standard deviation of the regression. The statistic can be used to gain some idea of the accuracy of your predictions.

Standard Hours Allowed. Standard time that should have been used to manufacture actual units of output during a period. It is obtained by multiplying actual units of production by the standard labor time.

Standard Labor Rate. Standard rate for direct labor that would include not only base wages earned but also an allowance for fringe benefits and other labor-related costs.

Standard Materials Price. Standard price per unit for direct materials. It reflects the final, delivered cost of the materials, net of any discounts taken.

Standard Quantity Allowed. Standard amount of materials that should have been used to manufacture units of output during a period. It is obtained by multiplying actual units of production by the standard material quantity per unit.

Static (Fixed) Budget. One geared for only one activity level (e.g., one particular volume of sales or production). Actual costs are compared against budgeted costs only at the original budget activity level. See also FLEXIBLE BUDGET.

Strategic Budgeting. A long-term budget in which projections cover more than one year. A commonly used period is 5 years.

Strategic Planning. Implementation of a company's objectives. A decision is made on which products to produce or services to perform. A manufacturing strategy is decided upon to result in the best possible product consistent with cost level which is decided upon by management. Strategic planning is of a long-term horizon and considers the long-term objectives of the business. On the other hand, operational planning involves the daily decisions.

t-**Statistic.** See *t*-VALUE.

t-**Test.** In regression analysis, a test of the statistical significance of a regression coefficient. It involves basically two steps:

1. compute the *t*-value of the regression coefficient as follows: *t*-value = coefficient/standard error of the coefficient;

2. compare the value with the t table value. High *t*-values enhance confidence in the value of the coefficient as a predictor. Low values (as a rule of thumb, under 2.0) are indications of low reliability of the coefficient as a predictor. See also *t*-VALUE.

t-**Value.** Measure of the statistical significance of an independent variable *b* in explaining the dependent variable *Y*. It is determined by dividing the estimated regression coefficient *b* by its standard error.

Tactical Planning. Is developed along with the strategic long-term plan. These plans are usually developed by upper-level management, which, unfortunately can deny total involvement by middle management. This can be a problem because it can cause unfavorable behavioral effects.

Template. Worksheet or computer program that includes the relevant formulas for a particular application but not the data. It is a blank worksheet that you save and fill in the data as needed for a future forecasting and budgeting application.

Theil *U* Statistic. Measure of the predictive ability of a model which is based upon a comparison of the predicted change with the observed change. The smaller the value of *U*, the more accurate are the forecasts. If *U* is greater than or equal to 1, the predictive ability of the model is lower than a naive no-change extrapolation.

Time Series. A multiple regression analysis that determines the correlation between independent (explanatory) variables and a dependent variable over a specified time period. An example is the effect upon sales volume of advertising and pricing. It is a chronologically arranged sequence of values of a particular variable.

Time-Series Model. Function that relates the value of a time series to previous values of that time series, its errors, or other related time series.

Time Value of Money. Concept that a dollar today is worth more than a dollar tomorrow. The reason is that today's dollars can earn interest through investment. And in determining how much money must be received at an earlier date to be equivalent to money to be received in the future is known as DISCOUNTING. Also, COMPOUNDING INTEREST is a situation where interest is earned not only on the principal invested but also on the previous interest earned.

Tracking Signals. One way of monitoring how well a forecast is predicting actual values. The running sum of forecast error is divided by the mean absolute deviation (MAD). When the signal goes beyond a set range, corrective action may be required.

Treasurer. Executive who deals with financial and money matters and who is often faced with resolving financial problems. His or her job responsibilities usually include obtaining financing, using the funds in the business, managing working capital, investment selection and management, establishing credit policy, collection matters, and banking and custody.

Trend Analysis. A forecasting technique that relies principally on historical time series data to predict the future. The analysis involves selecting the appropriate trend equation that describes the trend of the data series. It may be a linear or nonlinear trend.

Trend Equation. Special case of simple regression, where the X variable is a time variable. This equation is used to determine the trend in the variable Y, which can be used for forecasting.

Turning Point Error (also known as "error in the direction of prediction.") Represents the failure to forecast reversals of trends.

Variable Cost. Expense that varies in total in direct proportion to changes in activities such as machine hours and labor hours. Examples are direct material and direct labor. Variable cost per unit is constant. As far as planning and control by management of variable costs, with all other factors held constant, each desired per unit expansion of productive activity leads to an incremental change in total variable costs equal to a constant amount per unit. As long as the selling price per unit exceeds the variable cost per unit, productive activity should be expanded.

Variable Overhead. The portion of total overhead that changes over a specified time period with changes in volume. Examples are indirect material, indirect labor, and supplies.

Variable Overhead Efficiency Variance. Difference in actual and budgeted variable overhead costs that are incurred due to inefficient use of indirect materials and indirect labor.

Variable Overhead Spending Variance. Difference in actual and budgeted variable overhead costs that result from price changes in indirect materials and indirect labor and insufficient control of costs of specific overhead items.

Variance. Difference of revenues, costs, and profit from the planned amounts. One of the most important phases of responsibility accounting is establishing standards in costs, revenues, and profit and establishing performance by comparing actual amounts with the standard amounts. The differences (variances) are calculated for each responsibility center, analyzed, and unfavorable variances are investigated for possible remedial action. See also VARIANCE ANALYSIS.

Variance Analysis. Is the technique that is used by management to measure performance, correct inefficiencies, and to deal with the accountability function.

"What-If" Analysis. See SIMULATION.

Z Score. Score produced by Altman's bankruptcy prediction model, is known to be about 90 percent accurate in forecasting business failure one year in the future and about 80 percent accurate in forecasting it two years in the future.

Zero-Base Budgeting. Planning and budgeting tool that uses cost/benefit analysis of projects, programs, and functions to improve resource allocation in an organization. Traditional budgeting tends to concentrate on the incremental change from the previous year. It assumes that the previous year's activities and programs are essential and must be continued. Under zero-base budgeting, however, cost and benefit estimates are built up from scratch, from the zero level, and must be justified. Proposals are ranked in priority order considering budgetary constraints. The ranking should be based on the goals and objectives of decision packages relative to the goals and the objectives of the organization.

Index

USER'S GUIDE

to accompany

THE COMPLETE BUDGETING WORKBOOK AND GUIDE

DR. JAE K. SHIM
California State University Long Beach
DR. JOEL G. SIEGEL
California State University Long Beach

BY:

RENE' RAMELOW—PORTER

California State University Long Beach

TABLE OF CONTENTS

The supplemental User Guide and Diskette contain 11 printed templates, suggested user information and what–if solutions for selected problems, models, and concepts from The Complete Budgeting Workbook and Guide text. The User Guide and diskette are provided to assist the reader in applying the basic concepts presented in the text.

Examples presented in text Chapters 6, 20 and 29 are duplicated in User Guide sections M0601, T2001, T2901, T2902 and M2903, respectively. The remaining templates expand on the concepts presented in their corresponding chapters (i.e., T0401 and T0402 – Chapter 4, T0501 and T0502 – Chapter 5, and T0602– Chapter 6). These templates do not necessarily use the same company names or layout(s) as presented in the text.

NAMING THE TEMPLATES

The following codes have been adopted to identify the templates on the diskette.
It works as follows:

Position	Meaning
1	Identifies the file as a template (T) or model (M).
2,3	Identifies the chapter, e.g., 04 is Chapter 4 and 29 is Chapter 29
4,5	Identifies the template/model number within the Chapter.

For example, T0401 is Template 1 for Chapter 4. M0601 would be the Model Template 1 for Chapter 6. Also, LOTUS automatically includes the extension .WK1 for a worksheet e.g., the template for Chapter 4, Template 1 would actually be T0401.WK1.

USER GUIDE DISKETTE

The User Guide diskette contains completed LOTUS spreadsheet templates. The user DOES NOT need to design new spreadsheet layouts to benefit from the templates. All formulas and data pertaining to each template are pre–designed. The user, however, is encouraged to change the data to conduct What–if analysis or to reflect his or her own individual needs. Please see Introduction – Section "Approach Used."

Viewing The Formulas

In cases where formulas have been entered, you can see the formulas in either of two ways:

1. Move the cursor to the cell whose formula you want to see and observe the formula in the upper left corner of the screen; or

2. Use the / Range Format Text command sequence to display formulas instead of numbers in those cells which contain formulas. You can print this out if you wish using the regular print commands.

NOTE: To display cell values again, you must either reformat the spreadsheet (or cells) using the / Range Format command sequence (i.e., comma) or use the <Alt><M> "RESTORE FILES TO ORIGINAL" function under the startup menu.

OPERATING WITHIN THE TEMPLATE

When first entering the template, HIT ESCAPE to immediately receive access. Otherwise, select a MENU option. Within each template there is a standard set of operating instructions located at "Cell A1". They are listed below:

Accessing The Worksheet:

Press <ALT> and <M> simultaneously to invoke submenu (i.e., pressing the M key while holding down the ALT key).

Press <ALT> and <R> simultaneously to select specific area of worksheet

> Example:
>
> Press <ALT><R> then type "RANGES"
> The "RANGE TABLE" identifies all sections of the current worksheet accessible by the user.

Press F5 and enter range name (if range name already known eg. "ranges")

In addition, the following helpful hints are provided:

> 1. Once the file is retrieved, you can either use the sub−menu options (<ALT><M>) for printing or restoring the selected problem, or use the "ESC" key (exits user from sub−menu) to begin working in the file.
>
> 2. <ALT> <M> invokes the sub−menu. This sub−menu was designed to simplify printing and restoring options for the user and LOTUS beginner. The sub−menus are standard throughout the templates with a selection of either:
>
>> a. Printing the Template (Identified by Document Title); and,
>> b. Restoring the Template To Its Original Form

PRINTING

To print the template (original data and/or solutions) OR after the user has completed the input of their own data, the <Alt><M> function should be used to print the results.

ALL templates have PRE−SET print settings acceptable to HEWLETT PACKARD (HP) laser series printers. If you do not have access to these models, please refer to your printer's user manual for the appropriate "setup string". Also, the Z−Model template is setup to include a graph. If the user does not have LOTUS 1−2−3 WYSIWIG files, they must exit the spreadsheet and access the "PGRAPH" utility to print it.

THE APPROACH USED

In general, the concepts, examples, and models are taken directly from The Complete Budgeting Workbook and Guide text. Each template is based on the concept of an "input/solution" file. DATA INPUT is typically requested in the first section of the template. Where this approach differs it is so indicated (i.e., Z−Model). The balance of the template provides solutions and conclusions based on the DATA INPUT.

ALL templates provided on the diskette DO NOT require initial DATA INPUT by the user. All layouts, formulas and printing requirements are pre−designed. Once the user is familar with the template and its associated data, the user can then try inputing their own information. Or, the user can change the data to conduct "What−if" scenarios. What−if scenarios are very helpful when first working within the template and visualizing what changes occur when certain data change.

IT IS HIGHLY RECOMMENDED THAT THE USER USE THE "INPUT" SECTION SINCE ALL SUBSEQUENT SOLUTIONS AND CONCLUSIONS ARE FORMULATED FROM THAT DATA.

Helpful Hints:

1. If changes to data are made and the user does not wish to save them, exit the file without saving the changes.

2. If changes to the layout, formulas and/or data are made AND saved, the template can still be restored to its original format by using the following submenu command:

   <Alt><M> "RESTORE TO ORIGINAL"

The User's Guide is divided into four parts.   Each section directly corresponds to a specific
section of the text. Please refer to the text Table of Contents.

o PART II   —   FINANCIAL ANALYSIS

o PART III   —   PREPARATION AND ANALYSIS OF BUDGETS

o PART IV   —   FINANCIAL FORECASTING AND QUANTATATIVE METHODS

o PART V   —   FINANCIAL MODELS

REQUIRED LOTUS KNOWLEDGE

The purpose of the user guide is not to teach LOTUS. However, most users will find the
introduction contains sufficient information for them to complete and process the templates.
If the user has not been exposed to spreadsheets at all, it may be helpful to spend a short time
reviewing the LOTUS tutorial or LOTUS user's guide.

T0401   MIXED COSTS – HIGH/LOW AND SIMPLE REGRESSION METHODS

Lotus is particularly helpful when a simple regression analysis is needed for calculating the values of mixed costs given a specific set of data. LOTUS provides an "output" section which identifies the relevant values for thet Cost–Volume Formula. They include: the constant (or fixed cost), the X Coefficient (or b) of the variable costs, and various regression statistics that test the accuracy and reliability of the regression results. Please refer to text CHAPTERS 4 and 24 for a detailed explanation of regression statistics.

Flexible Manufacturing Company decided to relate total factory overhead costs to direct labor hour (DLH) to develop a Cost–Volume Formula in the form "y = a + bx". Twelve monthly observations were collected and are provided below:

	A	B	C	D	E	F	G	H	I
27				DIRECT LABOR		FACTORY			
28		MONTH		HOURS (x)		OVERHEAD (y)			
29									
30		January		9	Hours	$15			
31		February		19		20		(DATA INPUT)	
32		March		11		14			
33		April		14		16			
34		May		23		25			
35		June		12		20			
36		July		12		20			
37		August		22		23			
38		September		7		14			
39		October		13		22			
40		November		15		18			
41		December		17		18			
43				174	Hours	$225			

PROBLEM:

(A) Determine the cost–volume formula using LOTUS Least Squares Regression function.
(B) Determine the cost–volume formula using the high–low method.

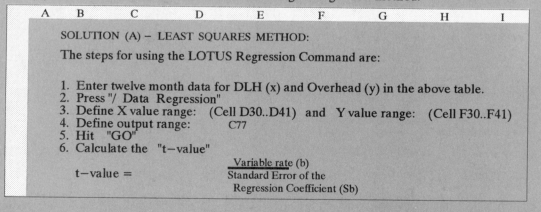

SOLUTION (A) – LEAST SQUARES METHOD:

The steps for using the LOTUS Regression Command are:

1. Enter twelve month data for DLH (x) and Overhead (y) in the above table.
2. Press "/ Data Regression"
3. Define X value range: (Cell D30..D41) and Y value range: (Cell F30..F41)
4. Define output range: C77
5. Hit   "GO"
6. Calculate the "t–value"

$$\text{t–value} = \frac{\text{Variable rate (b)}}{\text{Standard Error of the Regression Coefficient (Sb)}}$$

T0401   MIXED COSTS – HIGH/LOW AND SIMPLE REGRESSION METHODS

The LOTUS regression output is shown below:

	A	B	C	D	E	F	G	H	I
75			REGRESSION OUTPUT						
76									
77			Constant			10.58364312			
78			Std Err of Y Est			2.343622208			
79			R Squared			0.608373258			
80			No. of Observations			12			
81			Degrees of Freedom			10			
82									
83			X Coefficient(s)			0.5631970			
84			Std Err of Coef.			0.1428931			
85									
86			t–value			3.94138526			
87			(Calculated Independently)						
88									
89		The results show:							
90									
91			y' =	10.583643	+	0.563197 x			
92									
93		With:							
94									
95			(1) r–squared =		0.6083732 =		60.84%		
96			(2) Standard Error of the Estimate =				2.3436222		
97			(3) Standard Error of the Coefficient =				0.1428931		
98			(4) t–value =				3.9413852		

ANALYSIS

1. R–Squared tells us how good the estimated regression equation is. The results show
    that about 60.84% of the total variation in Factory Overhead is explained by Direct
    Labor Hours. The remaining 39.16% is still unexplained.

2. Since t = 3.94, we conclude that the "b" co–efficient (.5632) is statistically significant in
    in explaining the dependent variable y.

3. In summary, the "b" co–efficient is significant in explaining the relationship of
    Direct Labor Hours to Factory Overhead. But, there is room for improvement in
    the regression equation. Machine Hours or a combination of Direct Labor Hours
    and Machine Hours might improve the R–Squared.

4. The LOTUS regression commands can also be used for multiple regression analysis.
    Please reference CHAPTER 29 for more details on multiple regression.

T0401   MIXED COSTS – HIGH/LOW AND SIMPLE REGRESSION METHODS

	A	B	C	D	E	F	G	H	I

SOLUTION (B) – HIGH/LOW METHOD

The high–low points selected from the monthly observations are:

		X	Y	
112				
113				
114	HIGH	23 Hours	$25	May Pair
115	LOW	7	14	September Pair
116				
117	DIFFERENCE	16 Hours	11	
118				

122	VARIABLE RATE b	$=$	Difference in Y
123			Difference in X
124			
125			$11
126		$=$	$16 Hours
127			
129		$=$	$0.6875 Per DLH

133   FIXED COST PORTION =

		HIGH	LOW
136	Factory Overhead (y)	$25	$14
138	Variable Expense	(15.8125)	(4.8125)
139	($0.6875 per DLH)		
140		$9.1875	$9.1875

144   The cost–volume formula for Factory Overhead using the High/Low Method is:

147		$9.1875	fixed plus	$0.6875 per DLH
148				
149			OR	
150				
151	y' =	$9.1875	+	$0.6875 x
152				
153				

T0402   FLEXIBLE BUDGETS & PERFORMANCE REPORTING

A flexible budget is an extremely useful tool for cost control. It is geared toward a range of activity rather than a single level of activity. Using the cost–volume formula (Reference T0401), a series of budgets can easily be developed for various levels of activity. The primary use of the flexible budget is to accurately measure performance by comparing actual costs for the same level of output. T0402 presents Ina Machine Company's flexible budget and a performance report for the actual production of 6,200 units.

A	B	C	D	E	F	G	H	I
	INA MACHINE COMPANY – FLEXIBLE BUDGET						(DATA INPUT)	
29	CONVERSION		COST–VOL	NUMBER OF UNITS				
30	COST		FORMULA	5,000	6,000	7,000		
32	Direct Labor		$7.00	$35,000	$42,000	$49,000		
33	Variable Overhead:							
34	Supplies		0.90	4,500	5,400	6,300		
35	Utilities		0.15	750	900	1,050		
36	Maintenance		1.25	6,250	7,500	8,750		
38			$9.30	$46,500	$55,800	$65,100		
40	September Production Budget:			6,000 Units				
41	September Actual Production:			6,200 Units				
43	Actual Converion Costs Incurred:							
44	Direct Labor			$44,300				
45	Supplies			6,120				
46	Utilities			965				
47	Maintenance			7,920				

PROBLEM:

(A) Prepare a performance report for September. Indicate whether variances are favorable (F) or unfavorable (U).

A	B	C	D	E	F	G	H	I
	SOLUTION (A) – PERFORMANCE REPORT							
68	Budgeted Production:			6,000 Units				
69	Actual Production:			6,200 Units				
71	Conversion		COST–VOL	Budget @	Actual			
72	Costs		FORMULA	6,200 Units	Costs	Variance	(F) / (U)	
74	Direct Labor		$7.00	$43,400	$44,300	$900	(U)	
75	Variable Overhead:							
76	Supplies		0.90	5,580	6,120	540	(U)	
77	Utilities		0.15	930	965	35	(U)	
78	Maintenance		1.25	7,750	7,920	170	(U)	
80			$9.30	$57,660	$59,305	$1,645	(U)	
81				(1)	(2)			

(1)   The flexible budget formula (i.e., Cost–Volume Formula) can be determined using the least–squares or high–low methods.   Reference Template T0401 for calculating the mixed costs values.

(2)   When analyzing the variance between budgeted costs versus actual costs, the budget used for comparison is based on "actual" costs. The comparison costs are then developed using the cost–volume formula used for the original budget estimates

T0501   COST−VOLUME−PROFIT (CVP) ~ BREAK−EVEN ANALYSIS

The break−even point represents the level of sales revenue that equals the total of the variable and fixed costs for a given volume of output at a particular capacity use rate. For example, you might want to ask the Break−Even occupancy rate (or vacancy rate) for a hotel or the Break−Even load rate for an airliner. Generally, the lower the Break−Even point, the higher higher the profit and the less the operating risk, other things being equal. The Break−Even point also provides managerial accountants with insights into profit planning.

For accurate CVP analysis, a distinction must be made between costs as being either variable or fixed. Mixed (or Semi−Variable) costs must be separated into their variable and fixed components (See T0502). Once mixed costs are determined, the following concepts can be used to compute the Break−Even point and completing various CVP analyses.

1.	Unit Contribution Margin (Unit CM) =	Price (p) − Variable Unit Cost (v)
2.	Contribution Margin Ratio (CM Ratio) =	Unit Contribution Margin (Unit CM) / Price (p)
		OR
3.	Break−Even Point in Units =	Fixed Costs / Unit CM
4.	Break−Even Point in Dollars =	Fixed Costs / CM Ratio
5a.	Target Income Sales in Units =	Fixed Cost + Desired Net Income / Unit CM
5b.	Target Income Sales in Units =	Fixed Cost / Unit CM − (Desired % of Sales x Unit Price)

Template T0501 provides a complete CVP analysis using the Break−Even concept. The following information is given for Eagle−Kamp Inc.:

A	B	C	D	E	F	G	H	I
20						(DATA INPUT)		
21								
22	UNIT SALES PRICE:				$10		y = a + bx	
23	VARIABLE COST PER UNIT:				$6	(b)	(Reference T0401)	
24	TOTAL FIXED COSTS:				$50,000	(a)		
25	DESIRED NET INCOME IN DOLLARS:				$4,000			
26	DESIRED INCOME AS % OF SALES:				15.0%			

Using the information provided for Eagle−Kamp Inc., determine the following:

(A)   Contribution Margin Per Unit

(B)   Contribution Margin Ratio

(C)   Break−Even Sales In Units

(D)   Break−Even Sales In Dollars

(E)   Sales In Units Required to Achieve a Net Income of $4,000

(F)   Sales Units Required to Achieve a Net Income of 15% of Sales

T0501   COST—VOLUME—PROFIT (CVP) ~ BREAK—EVEN ANALYSIS

Using the Contribution Margin and Break—Even formulas (concepts) Items A — F
can be determined:

A	B	C	D	E	F	G	H	I
58								
59	SOLUTIONS:							
60								
61	(A) Contribution Margin Per Unit							
62								
63	Unit Contribution Margin (Unit CM) =							
64	Price (p) — Variable Unit Cost (v) =			$4				
65								
66								
67	(B) Contribution Margin Ratio							
68								
69	Contribution Margin Ratio (CM Ratio) =							
70	Unit CM / Unit Price (p) =			40%				
71								
72								
73	(C) Break—Even Sales In Units							
74								
75	Break—Even Point in Units =							
76	Fixed Costs / Unit CM =			12,500 Units				
77								
78								
79	(D) Break—Even Sales In Dollars							
80								
81	Break—Even Point in Dollars =							
82	Break—Even Units x Unit Price =			$125,000				
83	(12,500 x $10)							
84								
85	Or, Alternatively,							
86								
87	Fixed Costs / CM Ratio =			$125,000				
88	($50,000/0.4)							
89								
90	(E) Sales In Units Required to Achieve a Net Income of $4,000							
91								
92	Target Income Sales in Units =							
93	Fixed Cost + Desired Net Income / Unit CM =			13,500 Units				
94								
95	(F) Sales Units Required to Achieve a Net Income of 15% of Sales							
96								
97	Target Income Sales in Units =							
98	Fixed Cost / Unit CM — (Desired % of Sales x Unit Price) =					$20,000		
99								
100								

T0502   CVP ~ BREAK–EVEN ANALYSIS – SALES MIX

CVP ~ Break–Even Analysis requires additional computations and assumptions when a company produces and sells more than one product. In multi–product firms, SALES MIX is an important factor in calculating an overall company break–even point.

Different selling prices and different variable costs result in different Unit CM and CM Ratios. As a result, the Break–Even points and CVP relationships vary with the relative proportions of the products sold, called the SALES MIX. Template T0502 demonstrates how the Break–Even point is impacted given the Andrew Company's projected SALES MIX.

<u>NOTE:</u>   Changes to the DATA INPUT will cause ALL formulas in Items A — F to automatically recalculate.

A.   Andrew manufactures two products: (1) Baubles and (2) Trinkets. The following data are PROJECTED for the coming year:

A	B	C	D	E	F	G	H
23	ANDREW MANUFACTURING, INC.:				(DATA INPUT)		
24							
25		BAUBLES		TRINKETS	TOTAL		
26							
27	SALES UNITS	10,000		8,000	18,000		
28	SALES DOLLARS	$10,000		$10,000	$20,000		
29	FIXED COST	$2,000		$5,600	$7,600		
30	VARIABLE COST	$6,000		$3,000	$9,000		
31	TOTAL COST	$8,000		$8,600	$16,600		
32	SALES MIX	60.0%		40.0%			
33							

Using the above information determine the following:

(A)   Determine the break–even sales in units for Baubles assuming that the facilities are not jointly used.

(B)   Determine the break–even sales in dollars for Trinkets, assuming that the facilities are not jointly used.

(C)   Calculate the composite "unit" contribution margin, assuming that consumers purchase composit units of six (6) Baubles and four (4) Trinkets.

(D)   Determine the break–even units for both products, assuming that consumers purchase composit units of six (6) Baubles four (4) Trinkets.

(E)   Calculate the composite contribution margin ratio, assuming that a composite unit is defined as one (1) Bauble and one (1) Trinket.

(F)   Determine the break–even sales in dollars, assuming that Baubles and Trinkets become 1–to–1 complements and that there is no change in the company's costs.

T0502   CVP ~ BREAK–EVEN ANALYSIS – SALES MIX

A. – F. Preliminary information and calculations are presented below:

A	B	C	D	E	F	G	H

PRELIMINARY INFORMATION:

80 To determine the values for Items A – F, certain single product "PRELIMINARY"
81 calculations must be completed. These include:

82
83
84   PRODUCT Unit Cost   PRODUCT Unit CM
85   PRODUCT Variable Cost   PRODUCT CM Ratio
86
87 Also, the original projected data available did not include "VARIABLE UNIT
88 COSTS" so this was derived using the formula "Total Cost – Fixed Cost". This is
89 a quick, convienient way to determine projected variable costs, since fixed costs
90 and total costs are usually easier to obtain than specific variable costs.
91
92
93   **PRELIMINARY CALCULATIONS:**
94
95   Product Unit Cost – BAUBLES   = $1.00
96   Product Unit Cost – TRINKETS   = $1.25
97   Variable Unit Cost – BAUBLES   = $0.600
98   Variable Unit Cost – TRINKETS   = $0.375
99
100   Unit Contribution Margin –   BAUBLES
101   Price (p) – Variable Unit Cost (v) = $0.400
102
103   Unit Contribution Margin –   TRINKETS
104   Price (p) – Variable Unit Cost (v) = $0.875
105
106   Contribution Margin Ratio –   BAUBLES
107   Unit CM / Unit Price (p) =   40%
108
109   Contribution Margin Ratio –   TRINKETS
110   Unit CM / Unit Price (p) =   70%

In CVP and Break–Even analysis, it is necessary to predetermine the SALES MIX and then
compute a weighted average Unit CM. It is also necessary to assume that the sales mix does
not change for a specified period. The Break–Even formula for the company as a WHOLE is:

$$\text{Break–Even Sales in Units (or Dollars)} = \frac{\text{Fixed Costs}}{\text{Weighted Average Unit CM (or CM Ratio)}}$$

T0502   CVP ~ BREAK−EVEN ANALYSIS − SALES MIX

A. − F. Given the preliminary calculations, the solutions for Items A − F are as follows:

A	B	C	D	E	F	G	H
	SOLUTIONS BASED ON THE "DATA INPUT"						

114
115 116 (A) Determine the break−even sales in UNITS for: BAUBLES
assuming that the facilities are not jointly used.

118   Fixed Costs / Unit CM =   5,000 Units

120 121 (B) Determine the break−even sales in DOLLARS for: TRINKETS
122   assuming that the facilities are not jointly used.

123   Fixed Costs / CM Ratio = $8,000
124   ($5,600/0.7)
125

126 127 128 (C) Calculate the COMPOSITE "UNIT" contribution margin, assuming that consumers
purchase composit units of six (6) Baubles and four (4) Trinkets.

130   Sales Mix: BAUBLES   =   60.0%
131   TRINKETS   =   40.0%
132

133 134   Composite Unit CM (or weighted average) = $0.59

135 136 137   (Baubles Unit CM x Baubles Sales Mix %) +
(Trinkets Unit CM x Trinkets Sales Mix %)

139 140 141 (D) Determine the break−even units for both products, assuming that consumers
purchase composit units of six (6) Baubles four (4) Trinkets.

143 144   Break−Even For Both Products =   12,881 Units
TOTAL Fixed Costs / COMPOSITE Unit CM

146   OR, INDIVIDUALLY

148 149 BAUBLES =   60.0%   x   12,881   =   7,729
TRINKETS =   40.0%   x $12,881   =   5,153

150

153 154 (E) Calculate the composite contribution margin ratio, assuming that a composite unit is
defined as one (1) Bauble and one (1) Trinket.

157 158   Composite (or weighted average) CM Ratio =   57%
TOTAL Unit CM / TOTAL Sales Price
159   ($1.275 / $2.250)   =   0.57 %

162 163 (F) Determine the break−even sales in dollars, assuming that Baubles and Trinkets
become one−to−one complements and that there is no change in the company's costs.

166 167 168   Product Mix Break−Even Point in Dollars = $13,333.33
TOTAL Fixed Costs / COMPOSITE CM Ratio
($7,600 / 0.57)

M0601 NORTON COMPANY – BUDGET PLANNING MODEL

The Norton Company model is a "comprehensive" model. Any changes to data should be input in the "DATA INPUT" area. All formulas within each section of the model are linked to the "DATA INPUT" information. The Norton model contains 11 examples, from Sales Budget to Balance Sheet, and any change in the data will automatically change all examples. Each example is presented in detail within CHAPTER 6 of the text. Budget planning information was collected for Norton Company and is presented below:

A B	C	D	E F	G	H	I J	K	L
	BUDGET PLANNING INFORMATION:					(DATA INPUT)		
19								
20 Company Name:			NORTON COMPANY					
21 Period:			For the Year Ending December 31, 19B					
23				Quarter				
24								
25			1	2	3	4	1	
26								
27 SALES:								
28 Expected sales (units)			800	700	900	800	1,000	Estimate
29 Unit Price			$80	$80	$80	$80	$80	
30 A/R Begin Balance:			$9,500					
31 A/R Collection:			70.0%	28.0%				
32	(Qtr of Sale)			(Qtr following sale)				
33								
34 PRODUCTION:								
35 Desired ending inventory (%):				10.0%	Of next quarters sales			
36 Beginning inventory:				80				
37								
38 DIRECT MATERIAL:								
39 Material needs/unit (lbs):				3				
40 Material unit price:				$2				
41 Desired ending inventory (%):			10.0%					
42 Beginning inventory:				237				
43 Cash disbursement (%)/Qtr			50.0%					
44 Desired end inventory 4th Quarter:				250	Estimate			
45 Accounts Payable (12/31/19A)			$2,200					
46								
47 DIRECT LABOR:								
48 Direct labor hours/unit:				5	Hours			
49 Direct labor cost/hour:				$5				
50								
51 FACTORY OVERHEAD:								
52 Variable overhead rate:				$2				
53 Fixed overhead:				$6,000	Per quarter			
54 Depreciation expenses:				$3,250	Per quarter			

M0601 BUDGETING FOR PROFIT PLANNING — THE NORTON COMPANY MODEL

A	B	C	D	E	F	G	H	I	J	K	L
56	SELLING & ADMINISTRATIVE:							(DATA INPUT)			
57	Variable S & A Expense			$4.00	Per Unit						
	Advertising			$1,100	Fixed/Qtr		Taxes	$1,200			
	Insurance			$2,800	Fixed/Qtr						
	Office Salaries			$8,500	Fixed/Qtr						
	Rent			$350	Fixed/Qtr						
59	CASH INFORMATION:										
60	Cash (Beginning Balance)			$10,000	Fixed Assets:						
61	Income Tax Quarter 1			$4,000	Land			$50,000			
62	Stockholders' Equity:				Build and Eqpt			$100,000			
63	Common Stk, No−Par(19xA)			$70,000	Accumtd Depr			($60,000)			
64	Retain Earnings (19xA)			$37,054	Machine Purchase			$24,300	2nd Quarter		
65	Income Tax Rate			20%							

NOTE:

It is recommended that the user reference this User Guide section when viewing the NORTON model template on the computer. The NORTON model is the largest of all templates provided for this text. To assist the user in moving around the template and locating specific "Examples", RANGE NAMES were created. FOR EXAMPLE:

Press <Alt> <R> and type "EXAMPLE_1" or "EXAMPLE_5", etc.

The examples in linked within this model are:

EXAMPLE 1 — SALES BUDGET
EXAMPLE 2 — PRODUCTION
EXAMPLE 3 — DIRECT MATERIAL
EXAMPLE 4 — DIRECT LABOR
EXAMPLE 5 — FACTORY OVERHEAD
EXAMPLE 6 — ENDING INVENTORY
EXAMPLE 7 — SELLING & ADMINISTRATIVE
EXAMPLE 8 — CASH BUDGET
EXAMPLE 9 — BUDGETED INCOME STATEMENT
EXAMPLE 10 — BALANCE SHEET
EXAMPLE 11 — BUDGETED BALANCE SHEET

EXAMPLE 1 — SALES BUDGET

The sales budget is the starting point in preparing the master budget, since estimated sales volume influences nearly all other items appearing throughout the master budget. The volume (units) should be determined first. Volume is then multiplied by the sales price. Also, the sales budget usually includes a table for computing expected cash collections from credit sales. Cash collections information is used in the cash budget. The Data Input section requests the expected sales and unit price per quarter.

EXAMPLE 1 –   SALES BUDGET

A	B	C	D	E	F	G	H	I	J	K	L

NORTON COMPANY

Sales Budget
For the Year Ending December 31, 19B

Quarter

	1	2	3	4	Total
Expected sales (units)	800	700	900	800	3,200
Unit sales price	$80	$80	$80	$80	$80
Total sales	$64,000	$56,000	$72,000	$64,000	$256,000

SCHEDULE OF EXPECTED CASH COLLECTIONS

		1	2	3	4	Total
Acct. Rec. 12/31/19A		$9,500 *				$9,500
1st Qtr Sales	$64,000	44,800 +	$17,920 ++			62,720
2nd Qtr Sales	$56,000		39,200	$15,680		54,880
3rd Qtr Sales	$72,000			50,400	$20,160	70,560
4th Qtr Sales	$64,000				44,800	44,800
Total cash collections		$54,300	$57,120	$66,080	$64,960	$242,460

*	All accounts recievable balance is assumed to be collectible in the first quarter.
+	70.0% percent of a quarter's sales are collected in the quarter of sale
++	28.0% percent of a quarter's sales are collected in the quarter following and the remaining 2 percent are uncollectible.

EXAMPLE 2 –   PRODUCTION

The expected volume of production is determined by subtracting the estimated inventory at the beginning of the period from the sum of the units expected to be sold and the desired inventory at the end of the period. The production for each quarter is: (Planned Sales Units + Desired Ending Inventory) – Beginning Inventory.   The Data Input requests the following information: Desired ending inventory as a percentage of the next quarters sales and the beginning inventory for the budget period.

EXAMPLE 3 –   DIRECT MATERIAL

Once the level of production has been computed, a direct material budget should be constructed. It will show total MATERIAL REQUIRED for production and HOW MUCH MATERIAL MUST BE PURCHASED to meet production requirements. Purchases will depend on both expected usage of materials asnd inventory levels.   The Direct Material Budget is usually accompanied by a computation of expected cash payments for materials.

The largest amount of information requested under the "Data Input" section is in this area and includes: Materials needed per unit, material costs, beginning inventory, beginning balance on accounts receivable, and cash disbursements rate.

NORTON COMPANY
Direct Material Budget
For the Year Ending December 31, 19B

A B C D E F	G	H	I J	K L
		Quarter		
	1	2	3	4	Total

	1	2	3	4	Total
Units to be produced	790 *	720	890	820	3,220
Material needs/unit (lbs)	3	3	3	3	3
Material needs for production	2,370	2,160	2,670	2,460	9,660
Desired end inventory of materials	216 +	267	246	250 #	250
Total needs	2,586	2,427	2,916	2,710	9,910
Less: Begin inventory of materials **	237	216	267	246	237
Materials to be purchased	2,349	2,211	2,649	2,464	9,673
Material unit price	$2	$2	$2	$2	$2
Materials purchase cost	$4,698	$4,422	$5,298	$4,928	$19,346

SCHEDULE OF EXPECTED CASH DISBURSEMENTS

		1	2	3	4	Total
Acct.Pay. 12/31/19A		$2,200				2,200
1st Qtr Pur.	$4,698	2,349	$2,349 ++			4,698
2nd Qtr Pur.	$4,422		2,211	$2,211		4,422
3rd Qtr Pur.	$5,298			2,649	$2,649	5,298
4th Qtr Pur.	$4,928				2,464	2,464
Total disbursements		$4,549	$4,560	$4,860	$5,113	$19,082

EXAMPLE 4 –   DIRECT LABOR

The production requirements, as set forth in the production budget, also provides the starting point for preparation of the direct labor budget. To compute direct labor requirements, expected production volume for each period is multiplied by the number of direct labor hours required to produce a single unit. The direct labor hours to meet production requirements are then multiplied by the direct labor cost per hour to obtain budgeted total direct labor costs.

Requested data for calculating Direct Labor costs include: Direct Labor Hours/unit and Direct Labor cost/hour.

EXAMPLE 5 –   FACTORY OVERHEAD

The Factory Overhead budget should provide a schedule of all manufacturing costs other than direct materials and direct labor. Using the contribution approach to budgeting requires the development of a predetermined overhead rate for the variable portion of the factory overhead.

In developing the cash budget, you must remember that depreciation does not entail a cash outlay and therefore must be deducted from the total factory overhead in computing cash disbursement for factory overhead. Data required for this section includes: Variable Overhead rate, fixed overhead, and depreciation expenses.

NORTON COMPANY

Factory Overhead Budget
For the Year Ending December 31, 19B

	Quarter				
	1	2	3	4	Total
Budgeted Direct Labor Hrs	3,950 *	3,600	4,450	4,100	16,100
Var. Overhead rate	$2	$2	$2	$2	$2
Var. OHd budgeted	$7,900	$7,200	$8,900	$8,200	$32,200
Fixed overhead budgeted	6,000	6,000	6,000	6,000	24,000
Total budgeted overhead	$13,900	$13,200	$14,900	$14,200	$56,200
Less: Depreciation	3,250	3,250	3,250	3,250	13,000
Cash disbursement for overhead	$10,650	$9,950	$11,650	$10,950	$43,200

*   From Example 4

EXAMPLE 6 –   ENDING INVENTORY

The desired ending inventory budget provides us with the information required for the construction of "budgeted" financial statements. It will help in computing the cost of goods sold (budgeted income statement) and it will give the dollar value of the ending materials and finished goods inventory (budgeted balance sheet).

A	B	C	D	E	F	G	H	I	J	K	L
				NORTON COMPANY							
				Ending Inventory Budget							
				For the Year Ending December 31, 19B							
264						Unit					
265				Units		Cost	Total				
266											
267	Direct materials			250		$2	$500				
268				(Example 3)							
269	Finished goods			100		$41	$4,100				
270				(Example 2)							
271											
272											
273	* The unit variable cost of $41 is computed as follows:										
274											
275				Unit Cost		Units	Total				
276	Direct materials			$2		3	$6				
277	Direct labor			$5		5	$25				
278	Variable overhead			$2		5	$10				
279											
280	Total variable overhead						$41				
281											

EXAMPLE 7 –   SELLING & ADMINISTRATIVE EXPENSE

The Selling & Administrative (S&A) budget lists the operating expenses involved in selling the products and in managing the business.   In order to complete the budgeted income statement, in contribution format, variable selling and administrative expene per unit must be computed. The S&A budget includes variable cost considerations such as agents' comissions, shipping, ans supplies.

EXAMPLE 8 –   CASH BUDGET

The cash budget is prepared for the purpose of cash planning and control. It presents cash inflows and outflows for a designated period. It aides in avoiding unecessary idle cash and possible cash shortages. there are four major section in the Cash Budget: receipts, disbursements, cash surplus/deficit, and financing. The Data Input section also requests information pertaining to fixed assets, retained earnings, income tax rate, etc.

NOTE: The financing section under this Example must be computed separately and input directly into Example 8.

EXAMPLE 8 –   CASH BUDGET

NORTON COMPANY

Cash Budget
For the Year Ending December 31, 19B

		Quarter				
		1	2	3	4	Total
Cash Balance (beginning)	Given	$10,000	$9,401	$5,461	$9,106	$10,000
Add: Receipts						
Collection from customers	1	$54,300	$57,120	$66,080	$64,960	$242,460
Total cash available		$64,300	$66,521	$71,541	$74,066	$252,460
Less: Disbursements:						
Direct materials	3	$4,549	$4,560	$4,860	$5,113	$19,082
Direct Labor	4	$19,750	$18,000	$22,250	$20,500	$80,500
Factory overhead	5	$10,650	$9,950	$11,650	$10,950	$43,200
Selling and Admin.	6	$15,950	$12,750	$14,750	$13,150	$56,600
Machinery purchase	Given	$0	$24,300	$0	$0	$24,300
Income Tax	Given	$4,000	$0	$0	$0	$4,000
Total disbursements		$54,899	$69,560	$53,510	$49,713	$227,682
Cash surplus (deficit)		$9,401	($3,039)	$18,031	$24,353	$24,778
Financing:						
Borrowing		0	$8,500	0	– – –	$8,500
Repayment		0	0	($8,500)	– – –	($8,500)
Interest		– – –	$0	($425)	$0	($425)
Total financing		$0	$8,500	($8,925)	$0	($425)
Cash balance, ending		$9,401	$5,461	$9,106	$24,353	$24,353

EXAMPLE 9 –   BUDGETED INCOME STATEMENT

The budgeted income statement summarizes the various component projections of revenue and expenses for the budgeting period. However, for control purposes, the budget can be divided into quarters or even months depending on the need. Example 9 – identifies each section of this template that information has been taken from. For example, Sales is from Example 1 and S&A is from Example 7.

EXAMPLE 9 –   BUDGETED INCOME STATEMENT

A	B	C	D	E	F	G	H	I	J	K	L

NORTON COMPANY

Budgeted Income Statement
For the Year Ending December 31, 19B

			From Example			
377						
378						
379	Sales		1			$256,000
380	3,200 units @	$80				
381	Less: Variable expenses					
382	Variable cost of goods sold					
383	3,200 units @	$41	6	$131,200		
384	Variable selling and admin		7	$12,800		$144,000
385						
386	Contribution margin					$112,000
387	Less: Fixed expenses					
388	Factory overhead		5	$24,000		
389	Selling and Admin		7	$43,800		$67,800
390						
391	Net operating income					$44,200
392						
393	Less: Interest expense		8			$425
394						
395	Net Income before taxes					$43,775
396	Less: Income taxes		20%			$8,755
397						
398	Net income					$35,020
399						
400						

EXAMPLE 10 –   BALANCE SHEET

EXAMPLE 11 –   BUDGETED BALANCE SHEET

Both the Balance Sheet and the Budgeted Balance Sheet are calculated directly from the original Data Input. These two section are recommended for viewing after data has been changed to identify the impact of certain changes.

T0602   BUDGETING FOR PROFIT PLANNING – A SELLING & ADMINISTRATIVE BUDGET

A. Foster Company has gathered the following information for the month of July, 19x1:

A	B	C	D	E	F	G	H	I
					(DATA INPUT)			
22								
23								
24								
25	Sales:				$200,000			
26	Sales commission:				10%	of sales		
27	Advertising expenses:				$5,000	+ 2% of sale	2%	
28	Miscellaneous selling expense:				$1,000	+ 1% of sale	1%	
29	Office salaries:				$7,000			
30	Office supplies:				0.50%	of sales		
31	Travel & entertainment:				$4,000			
32	Misc. administrative expense:				$1,750			

PROBLEM:

(A) Prepare a selling and administrative budget.

A	B	C	D	E	F	G	H	I
			FOSTER COMPANY					
			Selling and Administrative Expense Budget For the Month of July, 19A					
48	Selling Expenses:							
49	Sales commissions					$20,000		
50	Advertising expense					9,000		
51	Miscellaneous selling expense					3,000		
52								
46	Total					$32,000		
54								
54	Administrative Expenses:							
54	Office salaries					$7,000		
57	Office supplies					1,000		
58	Miscellaneous expense					1,750		
59	Travel & entertainment					4,000		
60								
61	Total					$13,750		
62								
63	Total Selling & Administrative Expense					$45,750		

T0602   BUDGETING FOR PROFIT PLANNING – A SELLING & ADMINISTRATIVE
BUDGET

B. WHAT–IF?

What would the Selling and Administrative budget look like if sales commissions were
increased from 10% to 15%?

A	B	C	D	E	F	G	H	I
			FOSTER COMPANY					
			Selling and Administrative Expense Budget For the Month of July, 19A					
48		Selling Expenses:						
49		Sales commissions				$30,000		
50		Advertising expense				9,000		
51		Miscellaneous selling expense				3,000		
52								
46		Total				$42,000		
54								
54		Administrative Expenses:						
54		Office salaries				$7,000		
57		Office supplies				1,000		
58		Miscellaneous expense				1,750		
59		Travel & entertainment				4,000		
60								
61		Total				$13,750		
62								
63		Total Selling & Administrative Expense				$55,750	**	

**   The 5% increase in sales commisions, increased the total Selling & Administrative
budget by $10,000.

T1601   STANDARD COSTS & VARIANCE ANALYSIS

A. – F. The following information applies to Wallace Shirt company:

A	B	C	D	E	F	G	H	I
18								
19								
20								
21					(DATA INPUT)			
22	STANDARD DATA:							
23					Per Unit			
24	Material:		3 pieces @	$2.00	$6			
25	Labor:		2 hours @	$3.00	$6			
26	Overhead:							
27	Fixed		2 hours @	$2.50	$5	($50,000/10,000 units)		
28	Variable		2 hours @	$4.00	$8	($80,000/10,000 units)		
29								
30	ACTUAL DATA:							
31								
32	Material:		25,000	$2.10	24,000	(Actually Used)		
33	Labor:		17,000	$2.50				
34	Overhead:							
35	Fixed		$43,000					
36	Variable		$69,000	$7.67				
37								
38	Actual Units Produced:			9,000	27,000	(Actually Produced)		
39								

COMPUTE THE FOLLOWING:

(A) Materials purchase price variance
(B) Materials quantity (usage) variance
(C) Labor rate variance
(D) Labor efficiency variance
(E) Variable overhead spending variance
(F) Variable overhead efficiency variance

When calculating the above values, the following formulas will help:

> Price Variance =
>
> Actual Quantity x (Actual Price – Standard Price)
>
> Quantity Variance =
>
> (Actual Quantity – Standard Quantity) x Standard Price

Solutions for Items A. thru F. are as follows:

T1601   STANDARD COSTS & VARIANCE ANALYSIS

A. – D. The variance analysis, computed from the standard cost information for Wallace
         Shirt Company, is itemized below:

A	B	C	D	E	F	G	H	I

SOLUTIONS

62

63   (A) Materials purchase price variance

64

65   =   25,000   x ($2.10   – $2.00)

66

67   Price Variance: $2,500 (U)

68

69   (B) Materials quantity (usage) variance

70

71   AQ of Inputs @ SP   SQ allowed for Output @ SP

72

73   AQ x SP   SQ x SP

74

75 $48,000 $54,000

76

77   Quantity Variance: $6,000   (F)

78

80   (C) Labor rate variance

81

82   AH of Inputs @ AR   AH of Inputs @ SR

83

84   AH x AR   AH x SR

85

86 $42,500 $51,000

87

88   Rate Variance: $8,500   (F)

89

90

91   (D) Labor efficiency variance

92

93   AH of Inputs @ SR   SH allowed for Output @ SR

94

95   AH x SR   SH x SR

96

97 $51,000 $54,000

98

99   Efficiency Variance: $3,000   (F)

101   TOTAL VARIANCE: $11,500

T1601   STANDARD COSTS & VARIANCE ANALYSIS

E. & F. The variance analysis, computed from the standard cost information for Wallace Shirt Company, is itemized below:

A	B	C	D	E	F	G	H	I
104								
105	(E)	Variable overhead spending variance						
106								
107		AH of Inputs @ AR			AH of Inputs @ SR			
108								
109		AH x AR			AH x SR			
110								
111		$69,000			$68,000			
112								
113		Spending Variance:		($1,000) (U)				
114								
115								
116	(F)	Variable overhead efficiency variance						
117								
118		AH of Inputs @ SR			SH allowed for Output @ SR			
119								
120		AH x SR			SH x SR			
121								
122		$68,000			$72,000			
123								
124		Efficiency Variance:		$4,000 (F)				
125								
126		TOTAL VARIANCE:		$3,000 (F)				
127								

T2001   FORECASTING FINANCIAL STATEMENTS – PERCENT–OF–SALES METHOD

Percentage of sales is the most widely used method for projecting the company's financing needs. This method involves estimating the various expenses, assets, and liablities for a future period as a percent of the sales forecast and then using these percentages, together with the projected sales, to construct pro forma balance sheets.

Basically, forecasts of future sales and their related expenses provide the firm with the information needed to project its future needs for financing. The basic steps in projecting financing needs are:

STEP 1   Project the firm's sales. The sales forecast is the initial most important step. Most other forecasts (budgets) follow the sales forecast.

STEP 2   Project additional variables such as expenses.

STEP 3   Estimate the level of investment in current and fixed assets required to support the projected sales.

STEP 4   Calculate the firm's financing needs.

The following example illustrates how to develop a pro forma balance sheet and determine the amount of external financing needed using the step by step method (Discussed in detail later). It assumes that sales for 19x1 = $20, projected sales for 19x2 = $24, net income = 5% of sales, and the dividend payout ratio = 40%. All dollar amounts are in millions.

A	B	C	D	E	F	G	H	I
21	PRO FORMA BALANCE SHEET:							
22								
23				(in millions)		(DATA INPUT)		
24	19X1 SALES:			20				
25	19X2 SALES:			24				
26	19X1 CURRENT ASSETS:			2				
27	19X1 FIXED ASSETS:			4				
28	19X1 CURRENT LIABILITIES			2				
29	19X1 LONG–TERM DEBT			2.5				
30	NET INCOME AS % OF SALES:			5.0%				
31	DIVENDEND PAYOUT RATIO:			40%				
32	19X1 COMMON STOCK:			0.1				
33	19X1 CAPITAL EARNINGS			0.2				
34	19X1 RETAINED EARININGS:			1.2				
35								
36								

T2001   FORECASTING FINANCIAL STATEMENTS – PERCENT–OF–SALES METHOD

The output section of the financial forecasting model (Pro Forma Balance Sheet) is illustrated below:

	A	B	C	D	E	F	G	H	I

Pro Forma Balance Sheet
(in Millions of Dollars)

	Present (19x1)	% of Sales (19x1 Sales=$20)	Projected (19x2 Sales=$24)
ASSETS			
Current assets	2	10%	2.4
Fixed assets	4	20%	4.8
Total assets	6		7.2
LIABILITIES AND STOCKHOLDERS' EQUITY			
Current liabilities	2	10%	2.4
Long–term debt	2.5	N.A.	2.5
Total liabilities	4.5		4.9
Common stock	0.1	N.A.	0.1
Capital surplus	0.2	N.A.	0.2
Retained earnings	1.2		1.92 (1)
Total equity	1.5		2.22
Total liabilities & stockholders' equity	6		7.12 Total financing provided
External Financing Needed			0.08 (2)
Total			7.2

(1) 19x2 Retained Earnings =
    19x1 retained earnings + projected net income – cash dividends

$$= \$1.2 + 5\%(\$24) - 40\%[5\%(\$24)]$$

$$= \$1.2 + \$1.2 - \$0.48 = \$2.4 - \$0.48 = \$1.92$$

(2) External Financing Needed =
    Projected Total Assets   –   (Projected Total Liabilities + Projected Equity)

$$= \$7.2 - (\$4.9 + \$2.22) = \$7.2 - \$7.12 = \$0.08$$

T2001   FINANCIAL FORECASTING – PERCENT–OF–SALES METHOD

The steps for the computations are outlined as follows:

Step 1.   Express those balance sheet items that vary directly with sales as a percentage of sales. Any item such as long–term debt that does not vary directly with sales is designated "n.a.", or "not applicable".

Step 2.   Multiply these percentages by the 19x2 projected sales (= $24) to obtain the projected amounts as shown in the last column.

Step 3.   Simply insert figures for long–term debt, common stock and paid–in–capital from the 19x1 balance sheet.

Step 4.   Compute 19x2 retained earnings as shoen in (b).

Step 5.   Sum the asset accounts, obtaining a total projected assets of $7.2, and also add the projected liabilities and equity to obtain $7.12, the total financing provided. Since liabilities and equity must total $7.2, but only $7.12 is projected, we have a shortfall of $0.08 "external financing needed".

Although the forecast of additional funds required can be made by setting up proforma balance sheets as described above, it is often easier to use the following formula:

External Funds Needed (EFN) = Required Increase in Assets – Spontaneous Increase in Liabilities – Increase in Retained Earnings

$$EFN = (A/S)\,\hat{e}S \; - \; (L/S)\,\hat{e}S \; - (PM)(PS)(1-d)$$

Where:
- A/S = Assets that increase spontaneously with sales as a percentage of sales.
- L/S = Liabilities that increase spontaneously with sales as a percentage of sales.
- $\hat{e}S$ = Change in sales.
- PM = Profit margin on sales.
- PS = Projected sales.

T2901   FINANCIAL MODELS – PROJECTING A CONTRIBUTION INCOME STATEMENT

Templates T2901 and T2902, show how to develop projected income statements using the "contribution" and the "traditional" method, respectivley. These are different income statement approaches for two hypothetical firms.

A. The "Input" section and predetermined rates for the Contribution Income Statement (T2901) is shown below.

A	B	C	D	E	F	G	H	I
18						(DATA INPUT)		
19	NAVISTAR INCOME DATA INPUT:							
20	MONTH 1 SALES:				$60,000			
21	SALES FORECAST (%):				5.00%			
22	COST OF SALES RATE:				42.00%	(% OF SALES)		
23	OPERATING EXPENSE RATE:				5.00%	(% OF SALES)		
24	TOTAL FIXED COSTS:				$120,000			
25	TAX RATE:				46.00%			

B. Based on this information, the contribution income statement spreadsheet is created. The projections are provided for the next 12 months and the total for the year.

A	B	C	D	E	F	G	H	I
	Firm Name:		Navistar International					
35			1	2	3	4		
36								
37	Sales		$60,000	$63,000	$66,150	$69,458		
38	Less: Variable Costs							
39	Cost of sales		$25,200	$26,460	$27,783	$29,172		
40	Operating expense		$3,000	$3,150	$3,308	$3,473		
41								
42	Contribution Margin		$31,800	$36,540	$38,367	$40,285		
43	Less: Fixed Costs							
44	Operating expenses		$10,000	$10,000	$10,000	$10,000		
45								
46	Net income		$21,800	$26,540	$28,367	$30,285		
47	Less: Tax		$10,028	$12,208	$13,049	$13,931		
48								
49	Net Income after tax		$11,772	$14,332	$15,318	$16,354		
50								

T2901   FINANCIAL MODELS – PROJECTING A CONTRIBUTION INCOME STATEMENT

A	B	C	D	E	F	G	H	I
52								
53	Firm Name:		Navistar International					
54								
55			5	6	7	8	9	
56								
57	Sales		$72,930	$76,577	$80,406	$84,426	$88,647	
58	Less: Variable Costs							
59	Cost of sales		$30,631	$32,162	$33,770	$35,459	$37,232	
60	Operating expense		$3,647	$3,829	$4,020	$4,221	$4,432	
61								
62	Contribution Margin		$42,300	$44,415	$46,635	$48,967	$51,415	
63	Less: Fixed Costs							
64	Operating expenses		$10,000	$10,000	$10,000	$10,000	$10,000	
65								
66	Net income		$32,300	$34,415	$36,635	$38,967	$41,415	
67	Less: Tax		$14,858	$15,831	$16,852	$17,925	$19,051	
68								
69	Net Income after tax		$17,442	$18,584	$19,783	$21,042	$22,364	

A	B	C	D	E	F	G	H	I
75			10	11	12	TOTAL	PERCENT	
76								
77	Sales		$93,080	$97,734	$102,620	$955,028	100%	
78	Less: Variable Costs							
79	Cost of sales		$39,093	$41,048	$43,101	$401,112	42%	
80	Operating expense		$4,654	$4,887	$5,131	$47,751	5%	
81								
82	Contribution Margin		$53,986	$56,686	$59,520	$550,916	58%	
83	Less: Fixed Costs							
84	Operating expenses		$10,000	$10,000	$10,000	$120,000	13%	
85								
86	Net income		$43,986	$46,686	$49,520	$430,916	45%	
87	Less: Tax		$20,234	$21,475	$22,779	$198,221	21%	
88								
89	Net Income After Tax		$23,753	$25,210	$26,741	$232,695	24%	

C. What–If ?:

If the input section were changed to reflect a 10% increase in the First Month's Sales and the Cost of Sales Rate was decreased (5%) to 37%, the Net Income After Tax would increase by $58,113 to $290,808 (or a 4% increase). In this What–If, the (5%) decrease in the Cost of Sales Rate, directly increased the available contribution margin by the same 5%. The What–If Data Input and total projection section is shown on the next page.

T2901   FINANCIAL MODELS – PROJECTING A CONTRIBUTION INCOME STATEMENT

A	B	C	D	E	F	G	H	I
20	NAVISTAR – WHAT–IF INCOME DATA INPUT:							
21								
22	MONTH 1 SALES:		$66,000					
23	SALES FORECAST (%):		5.00%					
24	COST OF SALES RATE:		37.00%	(% OF SALES)				
25	OPERATING EXPENSE RATE:		5.00%	(% OF SALES)				
26	TOTAL FIXED COSTS:		$120,000					
	TAX RATE:		46.00%					

A	B	C	D	E	F	G	H	I
75			10	11	12	TOTAL	PERCENT	
76								
77	Sales		$102,388	$107,507	$112,882	$1,050,530	100%	
78	Less: Variable Costs							
79	Cost of sales		$37,883	$39,778	$41,766	$388,696	37%	
80	Operating expense		$5,119	$5,375	$5,644	$52,527	5%	
81								
82	Contribution Margin		$64,504	$67,729	$71,116	$658,534	63%	
83	Less: Fixed Costs							
84	Operating expenses		$10,000	$10,000	$10,000	$120,000	11%	
85								
86	Net income		$54,504	$57,729	$61,116	$538,534	51%	
87	Less: Tax		$25,072	$26,556	$28,113	$247,726	24%	
88								
89	Net Income After Tax		$29,432	$31,174	$33,003	$290,808	28%	

T2902   FINANCIAL MODELS – PROJECTING A TRADITIONAL INCOME STATEMENT

A. SIGMA Company wishes to prepare a three–year projection of net income using the following information:

A	B	C	D	E	F	G	H	I
	SIGMA INCOME DATA INPUT:							
21	PROJECTION PERIOD:			1994–1996				
22	BASE YEAR:			1993				
23	BASE SALES:			$4,500,000				
24	BASE COST OF SALES:			$2,900,000				
25	BASE SALES & ADMIN:			$800,000				
28	PROJECTION ASSUMPTIONS:							
29						YEAR		
30	SALES RATE Y1:			6.00%		1994		
31	SALES RATE Y2:			7.00%		1995		
32	SALES RATE Y3:			8.00%		1996		
33	TAX RATE:			46.00%				
34	COST OF SALES RATE:			5.00%	(EACH YEAR)			
35	SALES & ADMIN RATE:			1.00%	(1994 ONLY)			

B. SIGMA Comany's three year income projection is presented below:

A	B	C	D	E	F	G	H	I
37								
41				SIGMA Company				
42			Three–Year Income Projections					
43			1994–1996					
44								
45								
46			1993	1994	1995	1996		
47								
48	Sales		4,500,000	4,770,000	5,103,900	5,512,212		
48	Cost of Sales		2,900,000	3,045,000	3,197,250	3,357,113		
50								
51	Gross Profit		1,600,000	1,725,000	1,906,650	2,155,100		
52	S & A		800,000	808,000	808,000	808,000		
53								
54	NI Before Tax		800,000	917,000	1,098,650	1,347,100		
56	Tax		368,000	421,820	505,379	619,666		
57								
58	NI After Tax		$432,000	$495,180	$593,271	$727,434		

M2903   FORECASTING BANKRUPTCY WITH THE "Z−MODEL"

If you want to do bankruptcy forecasting yourself you can use the template provided with this
User Guide. The user guide includes a template with data for Navistar International. There is
also a blank template with formulas but no data. Either of the templates can be used for
calculating a "Z−Score" and identifying possiblities of bankruptcy. Here is the
step−by−step procedure:

Step 1.   Within LOTUS 1−2−3, retrieve the file called MO110.WK1 or
             "Z−SHIM.WK1".

Step 2.   Enter the following requested data:

FINANCIAL DATA	RANGE
Current Assets	B15 − B26
Total Assets	C15 − C26
Current Liabilities	D15 − D26
Total Liabilities	E15 − E26
Retained Earnings	F15 − F26
Sales	H15 − H26
EBIT	I15 − I26
(Earnings Before Interest & Taxes)	
Equity	J15 − J26
(Net Worth for Privately−held Firms)	

As you enter the data, the words "0" and "ERR", will disappear and "Z" scores will be
automatically computed. The spreadsheet created from your input will look like the one
for Navistar International provided in the tect. The data of Navistar International (formerl
International Harvester) was obtained from Moody's and Standard & Poor's for the
period 1979 through 1990.

The template can accomodate forecasting data from 1 to 11 years

Step 3.
If you wish to see the Z−score chart (graph), as shown for the Navistar International,
press F10. In the graph, two horizontal lines are drawn, top gray line and
bottom gray line. The top gray line is drawn at the "Z" score of 2.9 and bottom one at the
"Z" score of 1.81. The "Z" score falling between these two lines (that is 1.81 and 2.99)
represents the "uncertain zone", where determination of whether a firm will go bankrupt is
unclear.

The financial data and Navistar International's "Z−Score" are shown on the following
tables:

FORECASTING CORPORATE BANKRUPTCY

Date: 05/26/93

TABLE 1 - Z-SCORE OF NAVISTAR INTERNATIONAL

| | Balance Sheet | | | | | Income Statement | | | Stock Data | Calculations | | | | | | Misc Graph Values | |
| | Current Assets | Total Assets | Current Liability | Total Liability | Retained Earnings | Working Capital | SALES | EBIT | Mkt Value/ Net Worth | WC/ TA | RE/ TA | EBIT/ TA | MKT-NW/ TL | SALES/ TA | Z Score | TOP GRAY | BOTTOM GRAY |
Year	CA	TA	CL	TL	RE	WC	SALES	EBIT	MKT-NW	X1	X2	X3	X4	X5	A	B	C
1979	3266	5247	1873	3048	1505	1393	8426	719	1122	0.2655	0.2868	0.1370	0.3681	1.6059	3.00	2.99	1.81
1980	3427	5843	2433	3947	1024	994	6000	-402	1147	0.1701	0.1753	-0.0688	0.2906	1.0269	1.42	2.99	1.81
1981	2672	5346	1808	3864	600	864	7018	-16	376	0.1616	0.1122	-0.0030	0.0973	1.3128	1.71	2.99	1.81
1982	1656	3699	1135	3665	-1078	521	4322	-1274	151	0.1408	-0.2914	-0.3444	0.0412	1.1684	-0.18	2.99	1.81
1983	1388	3362	1367	3119	-1487	21	3600	-231	835	0.0062	-0.4423	-0.0687	0.2677	1.0708	0.39	2.99	1.81
1984	1412	3249	1257	2947	-1537	155	4861	120	575	0.0477	-0.4731	0.0369	0.1951	1.4962	1.13	2.99	1.81
1985	1101	2406	988	2364	-1894	113	3508	247	570	0.0470	-0.7872	0.1027	0.2411	1.4580	0.89	2.99	1.81
1986	698	1925	797	1809	-1889	-99	3357	163	441	-0.0514	-0.9813	0.0847	0.2438	1.7439	0.73	2.99	1.81
1987	785	1902	836	1259	-1743	-51	3530	219	1011	-0.0268	-0.9164	0.1151	0.8030	1.8559	1.40	2.99	1.81
1988	1280	4037	1126	1580	150	154	4082	451	1016	0.0381	0.0372	0.1117	0.6430	1.0111	1.86	2.99	1.81
1989	986	3609	761	1257	175	225	4241	303	1269	0.0623	0.0485	0.0840	1.0095	1.1751	2.20	2.99	1.81
1990	2663	3795	1579	2980	81	1084	3854	111	563	0.2856	0.0213	0.0292	0.1889	1.0155	1.60	2.99	1.81

Note: (1) To calculate " Z " score for private firms, enter Net Worth in the MKT-NW column. (For public-held companies, enter Markey Value of Equity).
(2) EBIT = Earnings Before Interest and Taxes

PRINTING INSTRUCTIONS:

The PRINT string is setup for an HP LaserJet printer. The printer, however, needs to be set to "LANDSCAPE" manually.
To print the GRAPH, exit LOTUS 1-2-3 and enter PGRAPH.
 - Change the hardware setting to your source drive (i.e., a:\)
 - Change the character print to "BLOCK1.FNT"
 - Select the "Z-SHIM.PIC" graph file to print.

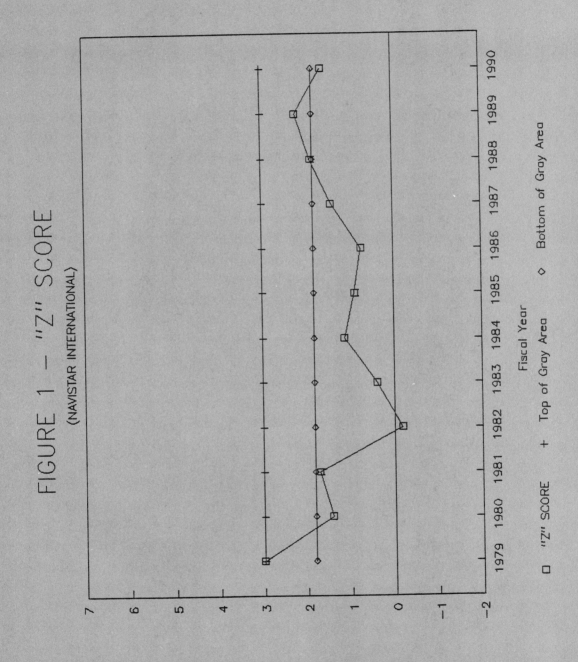

FIGURE 1 – "Z" SCORE
(NAVISTAR INTERNATIONAL)

"Z" SCORE

Fiscal Year

□ "Z" SCORE   + Top of Gray Area   ◇ Bottom of Gray Area